An engaging, well-organized, and comprehensive treatment of the core issues in environmental sociology. Carolan's conversational style and pragmatic focus will help students connect with the subject rather than become depressed.

Richard York, University of Oregon

I think this book is unique in its foregrounding of pragmatism. Even though both Bell and this book are positive, I think the manuscript in progress is more hopeful and accessible than Bell's book. The special strength that would appeal to my students is its interdisciplinarity, its accessibility, and its *lack* of social scientific jargon.

Shaunna Scott, University of Kentucky

Carolan masterfully presents complex environmental problems (and their solutions) in a concise and lucid manner that will hold students' attention. The standard framework for considering issues, the inclusion of exceptional case studies and ethical questions that will create a point of departure for many good class discussions, and the consideration of applied and practical efforts to protect the environment and manage resources all contribute to making this an excellent text and the backbone for any course in environmental sociology. Hats off to the author!

Stephanie McSpirit, Eastern Kentucky University

Society and the Environment

Without focusing entirely on what is wrong with the world around us, the third edition of *Society and the Environment* centers its discussion on realistic solutions to the problems that persist and examines current controversies within a socio-organizational context. After introducing "pragmatic environmentalism," Carolan discusses the complex pressures and variables that exist where ecology and society collide, such as population growth and the concurrent increase in demands for food and energy, and transportation and its out-sized influence on urban and community patterns. With further attention given to the social phenomena and structural dynamics driving today's environmental problems, the book concludes with an important reflection on truly sustainable solutions and what constitutes meaningful social change.

Each chapter in this interdisciplinary text follows a three-part structure beginning with an overview of what is wrong and why. This leads into a discussion on each issue's wide-ranging implications and, finally, a balanced consideration of realistic solutions. Featuring updated and expanded examples, discussion points, and coverage of recent developments including the US withdrawing from the Paris Agreement, "booming" national economies and wealth distribution, growing global interest in environmental justice—with particular focus on the links between injustice and race and inequality—climate change, and renewable energy, this new edition remains an essential companion for courses on environmental sociology and sustainability.

Michael Carolan is Professor of Sociology and Associate Dean for Research and Graduate Affairs at Colorado State University, where he teaches courses in environmental sociology and the sociology of food and agriculture. His books include *The Real Cost of Cheap Food* (Earthscan), *No One Eats Alone: Food as a Social Enterprise* (Island Press), and *The Food Sharing Revolution: How Start-Ups, Pop-Ups, and Co-Ops Are Changing the Way We Eat* (Island Press). He also mentors and supervises students in sustainability-related research around the world, including Australia, Brazil, Canada, Columbia, New Zealand, Switzerland, and the United Kingdom.

Society and the Environment

Pragmatic Solutions to Ecological Issues

THIRD EDITION

Michael Carolan

Colorado State University

Routledge
Taylor & Francis Group

NEW YORK AND LONDON

Third edition published 2020
by Routledge
52 Vanderbilt Avenue, New York, NY 10017

and by Routledge
2 Park Square, Milton Park, Abingdon, Oxon, OX14 4RN

Routledge is an imprint of the Taylor & Francis Group, an informa business

First edition published by Westview 2013
Second edition published by Westview 2016

Library of Congress Cataloging-in-Publication Data
A catalog record has been requested for this book

ISBN: 978-0-367-43144-0 (hbk)
ISBN: 978-0-367-42774-0 (pbk)
ISBN: 978-1-003-00491-2 (ebk)

Typeset in Caslon
by Wearset Ltd, Boldon, Tyne and Wear

Brief Table of Contents

Preface to the Third Edition xix
Acknowledgments xxiiii

1. Introduction: Individuals, Societies, and Pragmatic Environmentalism 1

Part I: Living in a Material World

2. Greenhouse Gases: Warmer Isn't Better 17
3. Waste: Our Sinks Are Almost Sunk 44
4. Biodiversity: Society Wouldn't Exist Without It 68
5. Water: There's No Substitute 89

Part II: At the Intersection of Ecology and Society

6. Population: A Problem of Quantity or Quality? 115
7. Transportation: Beyond Air Pollution 138
8. Food: From Farm to Fork 162
9. Energy Production: Our Sun-ny Prospects 187

Part III: Organizing a Sustainable Society

10. Political Economy: Making Markets Fair and Sustainable 209
11. Governance: Biases and Blind Spots 232
12. Inequality and Growth: Prosperity for All 251

Part IV: Shifting the Focus to Results

13. From Our Beliefs to Our Behaviors: Pragmatic Environmentalism in Action 281

Glossary 308
References 313
Index 344

Expanded Table of Contents

Preface to the Third Edition xix
Acknowledgments xxiii

Chapter 1. Introduction: Individuals, Societies, and Pragmatic Environmentalism 1
　　Individualism: Too Much and Not Enough 2
　　The Contribution of the Social Sciences 4
　　Material Things Have Momentum 7
　　The Messy Relationship between Behaviors and Attitudes 10
　　The Journey Ahead 12
　　Important Concepts 13
　　Discussion Questions 14
　　Suggested Additional Readings 14
　　Relevant Internet Links 14
　　Suggested Videos 14

　　　　ECONNECTION 1.1. Some of Those Deep Sociological Drivers 9

Part I: Living in a Material World

Chapter 2. Greenhouse Gases: Warmer Isn't Better 17
　　Fast Facts 18
　　Implications 19
　　　　Urban Areas 20
　　　　Food Security 24
　　　　Children, Women, and the Elderly 25
　　　　Climate Change Refugees 28
　　Solutions 31
　　　　Environmental Movements Matter 31

   Stabilization Triangle and Wedges 33

   Behavioral Change 35

   Green Building 35

   Geoengineering 38

   Carbon Markets and Offsets 39

  Important Concepts 42

  Discussion Questions 42

  Suggested Additional Readings 42

  Relevant Internet Links 42

  Suggested Videos 42

    ECONNECTION 2.1. The US Public's Knowledge of Climate Change 19

    ETHICAL QUESTION 2.1. The Most Threatened Are the Least Responsible 21

    CASE STUDY 2.1 African Americans Are Disproportionately Exposed to Extreme Heat 22

    CASE STUDY 2.2. Climate Change and the Wine Industry 25

    ECONNECTION 2.2. Climate Change Linked to Food-Related Vulnerabilities for Certain Populations 26

    ECONNECTION 2.3. Notes from a Filmmaker's Diary 28

    CASE STUDY 2.3. Climate Refugees from Indonesia and Bangladesh 29

    MOVEMENT MATTERS 2.1. Beyond Coal and Its Unusual Bedfellows 32

    ECONNECTION 2.4. Examples of Geoengineering, Mitigation, and Adaptation 38

    ECONNECTION 2.5. Biochar 41

Chapter 3. Waste: Our Sinks Are Almost Sunk 44

  Fast Facts 45

  Implications 47

   Energy Waste and the Life-Cycle Analysis 49

   Recycling 51

   Food Waste 53

   Waste and Public Health 59

   E-Waste 61

  Solutions 63

   MSW Management Alternatives from around the World 63

   Extended Producer Responsibility 64

  Important Concepts 66

  Discussion Questions 66

  Suggested Additional Readings 67

  Relevant Internet Links 67

  Suggested Videos 67

CASE STUDY 3.1. The Great Pacific Garbage Patch 48

ETHICAL QUESTION 3.1. What Ought to Be Most Valued? 51

CASE STUDY 3.2. The Close Loop Fund and Recent Recycling Trends 53

ECONNECTION 3.1. The Recycling Loophole 54

ETHICAL QUESTION 3.2. Public Health and Value Judgments 61

ECONNECTION 3.2. E-Waste and Public Health 62

MOVEMENT MATTERS 3.1. The Fight against Packaging 64

ECONNECTION 3.3. Closed Loop Fund and the Amazon Effect 66

Chapter 4. Biodiversity: Society Wouldn't Exist Without It 68

Fast Facts 69

Implications 70

Changing Definitions of Biodiversity 70

Biodiversity: The Fuel Driving Ecosystem Services 75

Biocultural Diversity 77

Biopiracy 78

Solutions 80

Community Conservation 80

Agrobiodiversity Conservation 84

Important Concepts 87

Discussion Questions 87

Suggested Additional Readings 88

Relevant Internet Links 88

Suggested Videos 88

ECONNECTION 4.1. Thinking about Ecosystem Services Conceptually 72

ETHICAL QUESTION 4.1. Sophie's Choice: What If We Can't Save Them All? 73

ECONNECTION 4.2. The Tragedy of the Commodity 73

ETHICAL QUESTION 4.2. The Power of Conservation Maps 75

ECONNECTION 4.3. The Irreplaceable Bee 76

ETHICAL QUESTION 4.3. Sustainability: For Whom and toward What End? 81

ECONNECTION 4.4. Socioecological Benefits Known to Arise from Community Conservation 83

CASE STUDY 4.1. Participatory Forest Management in Kenya 84

MOVEMENT MATTERS 4.1. Open Source Seed 85

CASE STUDY 4.2. The Seed Bank That Makes Memories 86

ECONNECTION 4.5. Moral Framing on Conservation Behaviors 87

Chapter 5. Water: There's No Substitute 89

    Fast Facts 89

    Implications 94

        Bottled Water 95

        Privatizing Water 96

        Agriculture 99

        Climate Change 103

    Solutions 104

        Water as a Human Right at the Right Value 104

        Water Governance 109

    Important Concepts 110

    Discussion Questions 111

    Suggested Additional Readings 111

    Relevant Internet Links 111

    Suggested Videos 111

> **CASE STUDY 5.1.** China's Water Woes 94
>
> **ECONNECTION 5.1.** The IMF and the World Bank 97
>
> **ECONNECTION 5.2.** US Bureau of Reclamation 99
>
> **CASE STUDY 5.2.** Neoliberalism and Water Privatization: The Case of India 100
>
> **CASE STUDY 5.3.** Desalinization in California 105
>
> **MOVEMENT MATTERS 5.1.** Grassroots Organizations Take On Nestlé in North America 108
>
> **CASE STUDY 5.4.** Micro-Watershed Councils in Mexico and Guatemala 109

Part II: At the Intersection of Ecology and Society

Chapter 6. Population: A Problem of Quantity or Quality? 115

    Fast Facts 116

    Implications 117

        Greenhouse Gases 117

        Urban Sprawl 117

        Food 121

        Feeding a Growing Nonhuman Animal Population 123

        Feeding a Growing Automobile Population 124

    Solutions 125

        Socioeconomic Development 127

        The Future Role of Cities 131

        The Case for a Population Explosion 133

        "Up Rather Than Out": If It Works for Cities, Can It Work for Farms? 134

    Important Concepts 136

    Discussion Questions 136

Suggested Additional Readings 136
Relevant Internet Links 136
Suggested Videos 137

> **ECONNECTION 6.1.** From IPAT to STIRPAT 118
>
> **ETHICAL QUESTION 6.1.** Do Countries Have a Right to Their Fair Share of CO_2 Emissions? 122
>
> **CASE STUDY 6.1.** Japan: A Rapidly Shrinking Country 126
>
> **CASE STUDY 6.2.** Socioeconomic Development in Kerala, India 129
>
> **ETHICAL QUESTION 6.2.** Whose Behaviors Should Change? 130
>
> **CASE STUDY 6.3.** Family Planning in Ethiopia 130
>
> **CASE STUDY 6.4.** Contextualizing Urban Density 133

Chapter 7. Transportation: Beyond Air Pollution 138

Fast Facts 140
Implications 141
    Pollution and Public Health 141
    Habitat and Biodiversity 145
    Community 147
Solutions 148
    Dense, Livable, Intermodal Cities 149
    From Street Hierarchy to Interconnectivity 154
    Disincentivizing the Car 156
Important Concepts 160
Discussion Questions 160
Suggested Additional Readings 161
Relevant Internet Links 161
Suggested Videos 161

> **ECONNECTION 7.1.** Effective Speed 143
>
> **ECONNECTION 7.2.** Social Capital 147
>
> **ECONNECTION 7.3.** Community Severance 148
>
> **CASE STUDY 7.1.** The Rise of Bike-Share Programs 151
>
> **ETHICAL QUESTION 7.1.** Value Judgments Embedded in Transportation Policy 153
>
> **ECONNECTION 7.4.** High-Occupancy Vehicle Lanes 153
>
> **CASE STUDY 7.2.** "Daylighting" the Cheonggyecheon Stream in South Korea 155
>
> **CASE STUDY 7.3.** Buses and Trains Are Not Useful to Most People 156
>
> **ECONNECTION 7.5.** Have Cars Reached Their Peak? 158
>
> **MOVEMENT MATTERS 7.1.** The Rise of Public- and Micro- Transit Movements 159
>
> **CASE STUDY 7.4.** The London Congestion Charge 160

Chapter 8. Food: From Farm to Fork 162

>   Fast Facts 163
>
>   Implications 167
>
>>   Environmental Impacts 167
>>
>>   Community Impacts 170
>>
>>   Malnutrition and the Green Revolution 171
>>
>>   The "Treadmills" of Agriculture 175
>
>   Solutions 177
>
>>   Agroecology 177
>>
>>   La Via Campesina and Other Peasant-Based Movements 179
>>
>>   Urban Gardens 183
>
>   Important Concepts 184
>
>   Discussion Questions 185
>
>   Suggested Additional Readings 185
>
>   Relevant Internet Links 185
>
>   Suggested Videos 186

>>   **CASE STUDY 8.1.** Mobile Bay Jubilee 169
>>
>>   **ECONNECTION 8.1.** Fish In Fish Out (FIFO) Ratio 169
>>
>>   **ECONNECTION 8.2.** Negative Impacts of Industrialized Farms 171
>>
>>   **ECONNECTION 8.3.** Yes! We Have No Bananas 176
>>
>>   **ECONNECTION 8.4.** Agroecology: Growing More Than Food and Fiber 178
>>
>>   **CASE STUDY 8.2.** Landless Workers' Movement (MST) 180
>>
>>   **MOVEMENT MATTERS 8.1.** Food Sovereignty Movement Scores Victory in Ecuador, and Beyond 181

Chapter 9. Energy Production: Our Sun-ny Prospects 187

>   Fast Facts 188
>
>   Implications 189
>
>>   "Clean" Coal 190
>>
>>   Hydraulic Fracturing (aka Fracking) 191
>>
>>   Nuclear Power 195
>
>   Solutions 198
>
>>   Efficiency and Curtailment 199
>>
>>   Renewables 202
>>
>>   Incentivizing Renewables and Household Efficiency 203
>
>   Important Concepts 205
>
>   Discussion Questions 205
>
>   Suggested Additional Readings 205
>
>   Relevant Internet Links 206
>
>   Suggested Videos 206

CASE STUDY 9.1. Three Gorges Dam 188

CASE STUDY 9.2. Incentivizing Carbon Capture 191

ECONNECTION 9.1. Mountaintop Removal Mining 192

ECONNECTION 9.2. Floating on a Cloud ... of Fossil Fuel Emissions 193

ECONNECTION 9.3. More Cheap Fracking Plastic 194

MOVEMENT MATTERS 9.1. The Fight over Local Control 197

CASE STUDY 9.3. Fukushima Nuclear Disaster as "Normal Accident" 198

ECONNECTION 9.4. Social Sciences and Energy Transitions 202

ECONNECTION 9.5. Social Norms and Behavior 204

Part III: Organizing a Sustainable Society

Chapter 10. Political Economy: Making Markets Fair and Sustainable 209

Fast Facts 212

Implications 213

The Growth Imperative 214

The Treadmill of Production 215

Internal Contradictions 216

Metabolic Rift 216

Another Contradiction of Capitalism 218

Globalization of Environmental Goods and Bads 219

Critiquing the Environmental Kuznets Curve 220

World-Systems Framework 222

Solutions 222

Total Cost Accounting 224

Fair versus Free Trade 226

Important Concepts 230

Discussion Questions 230

Suggested Additional Readings 230

Relevant Internet Links 231

Suggested Videos 231

CASE STUDY 10.1. Macroeconomic Rebound Effect 210

ECONNECTION 10.1. Treadmill/Metabolic Rift: Declining Global Fish Stocks 219

ECONNECTION 10.2. Capital Shaping Humans in Its Image: A Third Contradiction? 221

ECONNECTION 10.3. Forest Transition Theory 223

ECONNECTION 10.4. "Apolitical Ecologies" and Foucauldian Governance 227

ECONNECTION 10.5. Fair Trade 228

MOVEMENT MATTERS 10.1. Italy's Gruppi di Aquisto Soledale (GAS): Solidarity Purchasing Groups 229

Chapter 11. Governance: Biases and Blind Spots 232

    Fast Facts 232

    Implications 233

        Welfare Economics and Cost–Benefit Analyses 233

        Tyranny of the Present: Discounting 236

        The Self-Interested Straw Person 238

    Solutions 240

        From Tragedy to Drama 241

        Absolute Sustainability 243

        The Precautionary Principle 246

    Important Concepts 249

    Discussion Questions 249

    Suggested Additional Readings 249

    Relevant Internet Links 249

    Suggested Videos 250

> **ETHICAL QUESTION 11.1.** Unpacking "Science" 235
>
> **ECONNECTION 11.1.** Discounting and Forest Management 237
>
> **MOVEMENT MATTERS 11.1.** Dams: Making Changes to How Things Are Counted 239
>
> **CASE STUDY 11.1.** Grassland Management in Inner Mongolia 241
>
> **CASE STUDY 11.2.** Reducing Emissions from Deforestation and Forest Degradation 244

Chapter 12. Inequality and Growth: Prosperity for All 251

    Fast Facts 252

    Implications 252

        Rethinking Growth 253

    The Sociology of Consumption 259

        Social Comparison 260

        Creation of Self-identity 260

        Specialization 260

        Sociotechnical Systems 260

        Planned Obsolescence 261

        Environmental Justice 262

    Solutions 264

        A Postgrowth Society 264

        Development as Freedom, Justice, and Empowerment 273

    Important Concepts 276

    Discussion Questions 276

    Suggested Additional Readings 276

    Relevant Internet Links 276

    Suggested Videos 277

ECONNECTION 12.1. Freedom Isn't Free, and Apparently Best in Moderation 257

ECONNECTION 12.2. The Plight of Native Americans 265

CASE STUDY 12.1. Links between Commercial Shrimp Farms and Slavery 266

ETHICAL QUESTION 12.1. Is There a Right Level of Inequality? 267

ECONNECTION 12.3. Consume Less, Yes … But What About That Next Day Shipping? 268

CASE STUDY 12.2. Kellogg's Six-Hour Day 269

ECONNECTION 12.4. Community Capitals Framework 274

MOVEMENT MATTERS 12.1. Fighting for Environmental Justice in China 275

Part IV: Shifting the Focus to Results

Chapter 13. From Our Beliefs to Our Behaviors: Pragmatic Environmentalism in Action 281

Fast Facts 281

Implications 284

Knowledge and Worldviews 284

Denial and Countermovements 288

Consumerism, Advertising, and Marketization 288

Solutions 290

Advertisements, Freedom, and the Public Good 290

Collaborative Consumption 293

Globalization of Environmental Concern 296

Pro-Environmental Behavior 301

Social Movements 302

Pragmatic Environmentalism 304

Important Concepts 305

Discussion Questions 306

Suggested Additional Readings 306

Relevant Internet Links 306

Suggested Videos 307

ECONNECTION 13.1. Living Worlds Apart 282

ETHICAL QUESTION 13.1. Is Pollution Natural? 285

ECONNECTION 13.2. The "Money Makes You a Jerk" Thesis 291

ECONNECTION 13.3. Every Cloud Has a Silver Lining: From "Waste" to "Untapped Idling Capacity" 294

ECONNECTION 13.4. Not All Sharing is the Same: When "Collaborative Consumption" Harms Social Relations 297

CASE STUDY 13.1. Buycott 298

ECONNECTION 13.5. The New Environmental Paradigm (NEP) 298

Glossary 308

References 313

Index 344

Preface to the Third Edition

Society and the Environment: Pragmatic Solutions to Ecological Issues was born of my personal frustration as an educator. In my department at Colorado State University, we have an undergraduate specialization environmental sociology. I was the first to teach the introductory-level course in that specialization, called Global Environmental Issues. Every semester in the class, I engaged with roughly 130 students about the environmental state of affairs, while also going to great lengths to explain how sociology can inform our understanding of how we've arrived at this state. It's an incredibly fun class to teach, not only because it deals with subject matter that's close to my heart, but because the students tend to be really interested in the material as well. But when I first taught the class, over the course of the term my students' early excitement changed to something cooler. They were becoming, to put it in one word, depressed.

Sociology students talk frequently about their desire to make the world a better place. Yet in our environment classes, day after day, we focused on all that was wrong with the world. I was feeding my students a steady diet of pessimism—about how they can't *really* make it better—yet still asking them to take individual responsibility for our environmental future. No wonder they were getting indigestion. When I realized this—when the CFL bulb went on over my head—I began to make *solutions* a central component of my class. My students still occasionally feel disheartened or upset, but these days I rarely see a true cloud of depression settle over them.

I talk about solutions in two ways. Think of the first like a steady drumbeat: problem/solutions, problems/solutions.... Each chapter, following this arrangement, begins by stating environmental issues and their implications for society. At each chapter's midpoint, the discussion becomes solution oriented, tackling the possible solutions to the problem immediately at hand. Yet in the end, solutions—*real* solutions—to our environmental ills come not from fiddling around at the margins but from deep systemic change; we need to also come up with solutions that take us *in other directions*. The second way I therefore talk about solutions takes the form of an argumentative arch that builds throughout the entire book. Think of it as a complementary drumbeat that slowly crescendos until the cymbals crash in Parts III and IV, where attention centers on collectively reorganizing a sustainable society.

I have found this two-part technique for talking about solutions to be particularly useful in the classroom. Sociologists have long been suspect of bolt-on solutions; after all, we are trained to see the root causes of problems—sometimes to a fault. But I would argue that small changes to behavior (such as turning down the temperature on one's hot water heater) and technological fixes (like compact fluorescent bulbs) have their place as long as they are met with an equal zest to create deeper structural change. At the same time, I realize such short-term fixes risk creating apathy, which can derail attempts to solve today's environmental problems at their root. To those reading and assigning this book, I recommend a critical reflection on the solutions proposed in each of the following chapters. Ask yourself: What do they fix and what do they miss?

Much of the material that populates the book comes from my Global Environmental Issues class, so you could say it has, from a student's perspective, been truly *peer* reviewed. It is loaded with figures, tables, and images as well as a variety of text boxes: the Case Study, to briefly highlight case studies; the Ethical Question, to highlight the value disputes that underlie environmental conflicts; the ECOnnection, which allows me to interject additional information into a subject; and the Movement Matters, new in this edition, which offer vignettes on grassroots movements that have affected legislation. I also include at the end of every chapter, which I again draw right from class material, suggested additional readings, discussion questions, relevant online sources, and suggested videos. Finally, I take time at the end of every chapter to highlight particularly important concepts. Definitions of these terms and of all the terms appearing in boldface are then provided in the glossary located near the end of the book.

Talking, thinking, and learning about environmental issues in a pragmatic way may also require going beyond the pages of the book in your hands. It will link you to the social web by way of video clips, podcasts, and interesting, informative blogs and websites. Slides of the figures, tables, and images as well as a variety of slides expanding on issues raised in the text boxes are available to help bring the subject matter to life during lectures. Sample quiz questions are available for use as a study guide to give to students or as a starting place for crafting your own exams. Additionally, the website provides a selection of exercises, scenarios, and games, all of which are designed specifically to promote active learning in the classroom. If you have suggestions for additional resources, please feel free to share them with me via the website.

Before you dig into the book, I want to say a few words about my intentional use of the term *pragmatic* in the book's subtitle (indeed, originally the plan was to call this book *Pragmatic Environmentalism*). As with solutions, my understanding of *pragmatic* operates at two levels. At one level, the term is meant to evoke a very commonsense understanding, relating to practical matters of fact where results are of greater importance than philosophical debates. Yet as is also made clear in the chapters that follow, the world is not that black and white. Matters of fact, particularly when dealing with environmental issues, are rarely self-evident. Philosophical and ethical questions are often embedded within debates around what ought to constitute a fact. I would therefore caution anyone from operating solely according to this understanding of the term as they search for answers to the environmental problems that plague us. Yet you could say this book is *pragmatic* insofar as short-term solutions go.

This brings me to the second interpretation of *pragmatic*: as *pragmatism*. For those unfamiliar with this term, it references a distinct philosophical tradition, whose relevance for environmental sociology I delve into in Chapter 13. At the moment, I will say only that I appreciate the pragmatist approach, for it offers an alternative to overt structuralism, on the one hand, and methodological individualism, on the other. The way it does this, I should also add, makes it inherently *hopeful*, as the changes it seeks are deep and therefore lasting. But you'll have to read the rest of the book to find out how this optimistic story ends.

Finally, a few words about the revisions and changes made, as this book represents a third generation: *Society and the Environment 3.0.* I am often disheartened to see new editions of texts come out with only cosmetic changes—updated citations and statistics but little else. Don't get me wrong; any good text needs to be current. But I also believe authors have a responsibility to update text in additional ways. Fields change, or at least they'd better—you shouldn't be taking a class on a subject if it doesn't! And authors don't always get everything right the first time. I certainly didn't. After the release of the first edition, I realized there were areas of literature that deserved greater attention. The second edition represented a major overhaul. That edition certainly didn't get everything right but it represented an honest attempt to improve on the range of literature offered in the first edition. With the third edition, based on what I had been hearing and reading from those using the book, I focused more on the details—discussing more timely case studies and social movements, trying to make the chapters even more accessible, updating data whenever possible, adding images to help convey points, etc.

Having surveyed current instructors who have adopted my book, the consensus was *not* to add additional chapters. Rather, they were of the opinion that my energies would be better spent adding material within the existing chapter format. That is what I have done. Some of those substantive additions include the following (in no particular order):

- expanded the international flavour—discussing even more case studies from around the world
- expanded discussion on how worldviews shape interrelationships between people and between people and the planet
- expanded discussion on climate change
- more visual elements—photos, figures, and tables
- expanded ancillaries, offered on the instructor website
- expanded discussion on social movements.

Acknowledgments

How does one begin to acknowledge people when one's career is filled with supportive relationships and enlightening encounters? From my graduate student days, when I was lucky enough to have Michael Bell as my PhD adviser, to today, when I have the good fortune of being chair of a sociology department full of faculty and students interested in issues related to environment sustainability and justice, my experience with scholarship has been inherently collective, and this book is a reflection of this. So: I'll focus on naming those with a presence more directly felt. First, Evan Carver, the original acquisitions editor at Westview Press who talked me into taking this project on. Without you there would be no book. Period. I also owe a debt of gratitude to the various editors and assistants who have helped immensely over the years—Brooke Maddaford, Leanne Silverman, Krista Anderson, James Sherman, Grace Fujimoto, and, most recently, Tyler Bay and Erik Zimmerman.

I leaned on a number of colleagues for images and articles and in a couple of cases used some as sounding boards for ideas and arguments. Those colleagues include Shannon Bell, Brett Clark, Maurie Cohen, Jennifer Cross, Riley Dunlap, Cornelia Flora, Jan Flora, Jason Hickel, Lori Hunter, Colin Khoury, Jack Kloppenburg, Luis Lassaletta, Aaron McCright, Kari Norgaard, Thomas Rudel, and Richard York. A heartfelt note of thanks must also be extended to these scholars who provided constructive comments and criticisms of the book in preparation for the second edition: Dr. Shaunna L. Scott (University of Kentucky), Dr. Krista E. Paulsen (University of North Florida), Dr. Manuel Vallee (University of Auckland), Dr. Kooros Mohit Mahmoudi (University of Northern Arizona), Dr. Jesse T. Weiss (University of the Ozarks), Dr. Susan G. Clark (Yale University), and Dr. Christopher Oliver (University of Kentucky). Another half dozen reviewers gave direction when revising for the third edition, though your identities are anonymous to me. Let me reciprocate by saying, very non-anonymously, "Thanks!"

I am also grateful to all those students whom I have had the good fortune of learning from each semester in my Global Environmental Issues class (the introductory class for our environmental sociology specialization at Colorado State University). This book is the culmination of a lot of trial and error in that class as I sought to make the material interesting, relevant, and, importantly, hopeful in tone. This work was supported in part by the following grant: Social Science Korea (SSK), National Research Foundation of Korea (grant number NRF-2013S1A3A2055243).

Finally: to Nora. Thanks to you I am assured that my days will be full of nonmaterial contentment, while in our children, Elena and Joey, I find hope that the future will be in good hands.

Introduction: Individuals, Societies, and Pragmatic Environmentalism

Why must books on the environment be so gloomy? Chapter after chapter detail what's wrong, followed, if you're lucky, by a chapter or two on what could be done to turn things around. No wonder my students express bewilderment and, in a few cases, something akin to borderline clinical depression when, during the first week of my Global Environmental Issues class, I ask about their thoughts on the ecological state of the world. A quick query using Google Books yields more than 4.4 million books when the term "environmental problems" is typed into the search bar. A search of the term "environmental solutions", conversely, brought up 44,800 books. Sex, apparently, isn't the only thing that sells books. We can add apocalyptic ecological predictions to that list.

I understand why, historically, all this attention has been paid to environmental problems. People are not much interested in reading about solutions until they've been convinced that there's a problem in need of solving. Almost sixty years have passed since the publication of Rachel Carson's *Silent Spring*. Since then we have been exposed to a steady diet of problem talk, with measurable effect. A 2018 Ipsos poll across twenty-eight countries found that 87 percent of the world agrees that the world climate is changing, while 80 percent reported being concerned about the environmental impact of product waste (Ipsos 2018). In 2017, over half of the adult population in the Netherlands were surveyed, replicating a similar survey five years earlier. Fifty-five percent of respondents indicated that air, soil, and water are severely polluted, compared to 40 percent in 2012. Seventy-five percent reported that nature had been damaged seriously, versus 59 percent in 2012. Such awareness, coupled with a degree of environmental anxiety, no doubt helps explain why, in 2017, 34 percent of respondents in the Netherlands said they would be willing to pay higher taxes for the sake of a better environment, against 24 percent in 2012 (Central Bureau of Statistics 2017). As for Americans: more than half (55 percent) ranked the environment a top policy issue that President Trump and Congress ought to tackle, according to a 2017 survey, just behind poverty (56 percent), race relations (56 percent), and reducing crime (56 percent) (Pew Research Center 2017). (Respondents were asked to list several priorities, which explains why percentages do not add up to 100.) Even friends of mine who would rather lose a limb than be called *environmentalists* acknowledge the problematic ecological conditions that surround us. (Granted, they might still be in denial about climate change, but not much else.) Who is left to convince? Isn't it time to turn the corner and talk about—and even celebrate—instances of positive socioecological change?

This book is a bit of both: a bit about problems, a little bit more about solutions. By focusing on ecological solutions—rather than entirely on problems—I am striving to make this book hopeful, recognizing that if we can't at least think and talk about and point to sustainable alternatives, we really are in trouble. But I am a realistic dreamer, as indicated by my evoking the term *pragmatic* in the book's subtitle. Although it never hurts to be imaginative about what could be, we must be realistic about the possibilities. Too often we confuse criticism, to the point of focusing only on what is bad and wrong, with gritty realism. That kind of negative approach is not realism but pessimism.

Pragmatism decries grand narratives—those totalizing theoretical views of the world that claim to explain human mind, body, and society since the beginning of time. As someone who finds social theory interesting, I admit that it is fun to try to "scoop up" the world in one all-encompassing conceptual framework. Grand narratives are like flying at 30,000 feet: they are great for discussing the big picture—things like global capitalism and world political and economic systems. When the time comes to roll up one's sleeves and talk about practical policy solutions, however, I find these approaches less helpful, especially when issues revolve around sustainability. (I realize grand narratives have their solutions too, but they are often unrealistic, nebulous, and even polemical. In a word, they're not pragmatic.) Theoretical grand narratives aside, the nontheoretical sustainability literature is equally rife with overly simplistic, one-size-fits-all solutions. Single-handed praise for such phenomena as rooftop urban agriculture (Orsini et al. 2017), climate engineering (National Research Council 2015), bioenergy and biofuels (Konur 2018), and edible insects (as "the last great hope to save the planet," Martin 2014) generates considerable interest in and excitement around a topic. As a professional sociologist, however, I cannot help but cringe when the pilots of these tomes spend the majority of their time at cruising altitude. Fine-grain details matter; often they determine whether a solution will work in a particular space. A pragmatic environmentalist enjoys big pictures like anyone else. But he or she also realizes that there is no substitute for having one's feet planted firmly on the ground for establishing what works—and what's sustainable—for any given situation.

Individualism: Too Much and Not Enough

The pragmatic value of many environmental books is further limited by the problem of individualism. That is, they place either too much or not enough emphasis on individual action. In the former case we're reduced to selfish, autonomous actors—for instance, sovereign consumers—while in the latter case human behavior isn't even factored into the equation. Both of these extremes miss the *collective* nature of social life. As for ascribing too much weight to individual action, the standard argument goes something like this: saving the environment starts with each of us "doing our part"—so go plant a tree, buy organic food, ride a bike, install solar panels on your house, recycle, and so on. You don't have to be a sociologist to know that our actions, every one of them, are shaped by a whole host of factors. Evidence of this is all around. Most people, for example, already have a good basic understanding of how they can reduce their ecological footprint—who hasn't heard of the "three Rs" of reduce, reuse, recycle, for example? Yet people's actions seemingly belie this knowledge. I see this all the time in my students: they recognize the negative ecological impacts of many of their actions yet still do them. (I am certainly just as guilty of this.) While we act in ways that reflect our wants and interests, those very wants and interests are heavily shaped by existing structures—cultural, technological, infrastructural, political, organizational, legal, and so forth. It is not that individual action has no value when it comes to creating meaningful socioecological change. But individual action devoid of collective mobilization—think shopping—will never produce the same level of change as, for example, a well-organized social movement.

Too much focus on the individual can also create dangerous blind spots that risk making circumstances worse for some people. We see this occasionally in the "sacrifice talk" that abounds in the environmental literature—downshift, buy less, give up your car, stop shopping, and so forth. For one thing, I have found this sacrifice talk to be somewhat demoralizing among people genuinely concerned about the environment. Focusing on what one can't do, rather than on what one can, contributes to the malaise described by many of my students. Moreover, not everyone can afford to sacrifice. To give up something requires you to have something to give up. But not everyone wants to sacrifice, or they are willing to sacrifice only so much for the environment. And in some cases, even wanting to sacrifice may still not be enough to elicit a particular behavior—I know someone, for example, who despises driving his car, yet when the temperature drops below freezing, he makes the choice to drive his child to day care to avoid exposure to the elements. This is why environmental education, as a strategy to change behaviors, can take us only so far: because behaviors do not occur in a vacuum. In order for people to make a "greener" choice, they must have viable greener choices to choose from. And to have those choices often requires collective (not just individual) action.

I think I can speak for all sociologists when I encourage readers to resist the temptation to inject individualist thinking into causal explanations of inequality. To put things plainly, don't blame individuals for a systemic problem. As you'll soon see, rising rates of inequality cannot be chalked up to the failings of specific individuals. Inequality is a *sociological* phenomenon. You will also be hard-pressed to find a greater risk factor for suffering from environmental problems than being poor, which is why issues of global environmental justice are increasingly being discussed in classrooms, courtrooms, and political arenas the world over. Poor people are the least responsible for our environmental ills and yet most affected by them. How is that fair? If we hope to ever make things right, we have to grasp the roots of poverty, which means we have to get over blaming poor people for their lot in life and begin thinking sociologically about how and why we have organized society in such a way that allocates "goods" and "bads" so inefficiently and unjustly. And then we must ask how we can do better, while being clear about what "better" means. The pages that follow are intended to spur on that conversation.

Then there's the other extreme: the world-without-people perspective. I encounter this often in material written by specialists who obviously know a lot more about technoscientific matters than they do about human behavior and social change. These are the books, essays, and research papers that tout impressive technological solutions to a variety of our social and ecological ills, like the one declaring the need for a "rooftop revolution" and promising to explain to readers "how solar power can save our economy—and our planet—from dirty energy," to quote directly from the book's subtitle (Kennedy 2012). Don't misunderstand my critique; I enjoy reading these materials. Moreover, they contain just the type of outside-the-box thinking that we need. Nor do I doubt the technological feasibility of many of the solutions proposed; indeed, the authors usually go to great lengths to convince us of their long-term practicality. Yet just because something is technologically *possible* does not automatically mean it is socially, economically, politically, and organizationally *probable*. Too often the two are conflated, leaving the reader guessing as to how to take something that works in a lab or on paper and scale it up to the level of city, state, nation, or entire world.

The Contribution of the Social Sciences

One explanation for why books with an environmental focus tend to concentrate on problems, and superficially on what ought to be done to change things, is the nature of how expertise has historically been attached to the subject. They are called *environmental* problems, after all. The discussion is therefore dominated by natural or environmental scientists and engineers. All are very competent to tell us *what* the state of things is (though even so-called objective facts, as is made clear in later chapters, are mediated and conditioned by social variables and are often premised on the making of subtle value judgments). Yet by nature of their training, they lack a strong grasp of *why* we got ourselves into this mess and *how* we might be able to get ourselves out of it. These "why" and "how" questions inevitably require a firm working knowledge of social, political, economic, and cultural variables, which makes these questions better suited for social scientists. Feelings of doom and gloom arise when too much focus is placed on the "what" and not enough on the "why" and "how." To be fair, the social sciences share some blame in this. They spent a good part of the twentieth century turning away from the material world, preferring instead to focus almost exclusively on phenomena such as language, nonmaterial culture, and, later, **social constructivism**, an approach that focuses entirely on the sociologically dependent knowledge of a phenomenon rather than on any inherent qualities that the thing possesses (Carolan 2005a, 2005b; Catton and Dunlap 1978). For much of the last century the "worlds" studied by the social and natural sciences had been distinct—indeed, to some degree, even mutually exclusive.

Of my various professional identities, one is "environmental sociologist." Although I am proud to identify myself with this subfield of sociology, I admit to being tired of answering the question, "What does sociology have to do with the environment?" Much of this, I realize, stems from a general misunderstanding of how the so-called social and natural worlds interact. The very fact that we separate the social from the natural sciences at universities underscores the pervasiveness of this misunderstanding. Yet the longer I study the world, the blurrier this division becomes for me. What does sociology have to do with the environment? More than most realize.

Sociology has a long history of sidestepping environmental variables, phenomena historically understood as under the purview of the natural sciences. It is important to remember that early social thought was developed, at least in part, as a reaction to social

Darwinism, which sought to explain much of social life by way of biology. To avoid a repeat of this dark chapter in sociology's history, social thinkers found safer territory studying phenomena they took to be largely decoupled from the natural world. The problem with environmental issues, however, is that they make a terrible mess of this historically rooted division of labor between the "social" and the "natural" sciences. I do not want to say much more about this now, as the remainder of the book details ways that the social sciences can contribute to discussions about today's most pressing environmental issues. I will, however, add this: I cannot think of a single environmental problem today that does not touch, in some way, human society. All environmental controversies are the result of social action, and none can be resolved without social action.

Figure 1.1 shows us a way to visualize this interrelationship while marking the terrain that is comfortably within the realm of what social scientists study. As the figure illustrates, environmental sociologists are *equally* interested in material (or ecological) and social variables. Although acknowledging the fallibility of all knowledge claims, the "emphasis [among environmental sociologists] tends to be on analyzing linkages between the symbolic, social-structural and material realms" (Dunlap 2010, 23).

One could argue that the **sociological imagination**—a way of thinking that involves making connections over time and across scales between the particular and the general—knows no limits, as evidenced by the fact that sociologists have studied such seemingly "natural" phenomena as quarks (Pickering 1999), genes (Carolan 2010), and carbon (Stuart et al. 2019). I will leave it to someone else to determine exactly where the boundaries of the

FIGURE 1.1 Operational Space for the Social Sciences

Social World

Material World

⬭ = Operational space for the social sciences

↕ = Operational space investigated in this book

Source: Author.

sociological imagination lie. That said, for students wondering if something falls within what the figure refers to as the "operational space for the social sciences," they need only ask themselves: Has human society ever been of consequence to the phenomenon's existence?

Let's take, for example, the sun. Whereas our *understanding* of the sun is an entirely relevant subject for sociological analysis, I would argue that the sun *itself* is not (since the existence of human society has been of no consequence to the sun's life cycle). While we are shaped by the sun daily, there is no evidence that the relationship is symmetrical. So-called natural ecological processes and phenomena, on the other hand, are very much shaped by our presence as we are by them, making them prime candidates for a thorough sociological treatment. Thus, as Richard York (2006) has astutely noted, sociologists who, for example, study environmental controversies or the framing or discursive construction of environmental problems—rather than the interactions between the social and material worlds—might best be described as practicing "sociology of environmental issues."

The double-headed arrows in Figure 1.1 are a key component of the diagram. Although on paper they may appear insignificant, they represent the figure's conceptual heart. If you want to understand—*really* understand—environmental problems, with the hope of devising practical solutions, then you have to understand how these two realms interact with each other. And I am not just talking about understanding how society affects ecological conditions (which implies a unidirectional arrow). We are shaped as much by the material world as the material world is shaped by us. Shying away from this basic fact will only distract us from what's really going on.

Along with my colleague Diana Stuart, I have, more recently, elaborated upon this figure (Carolan and Stuart 2016). Today, a growing number of social scientists are openly talking and writing as if nature, from an analytical, conceptual, and causal standpoint, matters. And yet, while the social sciences seem to be coming around to the fact that the biophysical matters, we still have some way to go in forcefully articulating how sociological variables equally matter—that they too can have force much like so-called laws of ecology and therefore constitute "real" events in the causally efficacious sense. I hear this critique all too often about the social sciences: that the phenomena we interrogate and the processes we hold up as being consequential are not really real—not, that is, like the phenomena the natural sciences encounter.

The specifics of this argument get fairly theoretical, bordering on the metatheoretical. This is not the place to delve into such a discussion. Cutting right to the chase: Stuart and I overlaid my original figure with a three-part framework that allows us to talk about deep sociological drivers in realist terms, as illustrated in Figure 1.2. The importance of this framework lies in how it further legitimizes the social sciences—and social theory—by pointing to the unique insights these disciplines provide into *all* of the issues that grip us today, from climate change to consumerism, inequality, and hunger and malnutrition. The revised figure now points to three levels: empirical, actual, and real. We use the example of climate change to flesh these levels out. Generally speaking, most of the social scientific literature on the subject can be located within at least one of these analytic boxes: the empirical, those looking at attitudes and knowledge claims toward climate change; the actual, those looking at surface-level drivers contributing to it (for example, food waste, population, transportation, over-consumption); and the real, those looking at deep drivers, where the root causes of it lie (this is where social theory comes into play). Social theories, especially those we take as espousing grand narratives, are trying to point

FIGURE 1.2 Socioecological Operational Space for the Social Sciences

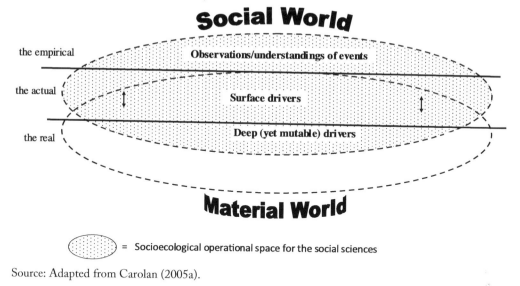

Source: Adapted from Carolan (2005a).

to real things that cannot be easily pointed to. (You cannot point to, for example, the treadmill of production the way you can point to a polluted river; see ECOnnection 1.1.) I try to convey in this book, especially in the later chapters, the nature of those deep drivers: the sociological forces underlying today's environmental ills—drivers that also must be addressed as we envision more sustainable, just futures. As the book progresses, I drill further down in an attempt to better grasp the really real—the phenomena driving these debates.

Material Things Have Momentum

Environmental controversies are never just about any one thing. The above discussion ought to have made this clear. Context matters.

It is important to remember, however, that this context also changes over time, a point that is particularly salient when discussion turns to behavioral, and ultimately socioecological, change. Structures—social, economic, political, legal, and even technological—can gather what could be thought of as *sociological momentum* over time. I am drawing here on the term *technological momentum*, which was coined and developed by the famed historian of technology, Thomas Hughes (1969).

According to Hughes, society has the greatest control over a technology when it is first introduced. As a technology matures, however, and becomes embedded within society—and society becomes further intertwined with the technology—it becomes increasingly difficult to change paths. Today's gas-powered automobile, for example, would be of considerably less effect were it not for oil, roads, automotive engineers, gas stations, car companies, government taxes on fuel, pro-automobile cultural imperatives, and the like. The now classic movie *Back to the Future, Part III* (1990) illustrates this perfectly. Marty McFly (played by Michael J. Fox) finds himself in 1885 with a gasoline-powered DeLorean, and his "futuristic" vehicle is worthless: cars are nothing more than processed raw materials when abstracted from the system out of which they emerged. Even under-standings of *fuel* are conditioned by these contextual conditions. Nothing is inherently fuel. *Fuel* is simply a term for a carrier of energy. A system must be in place that utilizes a particular carrier of energy if said carrier is to be called fuel. Even oil. Before society organized around it, thereby giving it the designation of *fuel*, oil was once viewed "with indifference or annoyance" (Bolles 1878, 772).

When thought of in abstract isolation, technological artifacts—indeed, all "things"—appear innocuous and open to change. In reality, however, as contexts change, and as society organizes itself around particular ways of doing things, these artifacts can gather momentum. What I like about the metaphor *momentum* is that it keeps us from reducing these discussions to a focus on unembedded things.

I frequently come across comparisons between the truly impressive public transporta-tion systems in Western Europe and Japan and the truly abysmal system found in the United States. Pointing to the widespread use of mass and individual (e.g., biking) transit in parts of Europe, a number of people have told me, "There's no reason we can't dupli-cate that system here." True enough; there is no reason we can't duplicate that system in the United States. But there are a lot of reasons we have not.

Before World War II, US cities arguably had the best public transportation systems in the world. Following the war, the nation found itself at a crossroads: should those systems be rebuilt and updated (as was being done throughout Europe), or should another trans-portation model be adopted, namely, the car? We all know the outcome of that decision. And since then, over the course of more than a half century, the country as a whole has slowly organized itself around the automobile. In doing this, the United States has sunk literally trillions of dollars of capital into this transportation model, virtually guaranteeing that the car will remain a central fixture in our lives for decades to come. Here are some examples of how we have stacked the deck in favor of the "choice" to drive a car over other methods of transportation: building parking lots and making space for cars to park on taxpayer-funded streets; government funding of an extensive infrastructure of roads and bridges that in many cases can be used only by automobiles; restaurants like Star-bucks and McDonald's incorporating the automobile into their architectural plans by offering drive-through lanes; and the proliferation of urban sprawl, which simultaneously was made possible because of the car while further making ownership of one a necessity. This level of organization—this *momentum*—makes using the car quite attractive. On the other hand, policy decisions make public transportation, the bike, and walking less con-venient and therefore less attractive. This is especially apparent when comparing the United States to other countries, where the decision was made long ago to structurally organize around multiple modes of transportation. This explains why in the Netherlands 27 percent of all trips are by bike (and where the average resident owns 1.3 bikes), versus less than 1 percent in the United States (and where each resident owns 0.3 bikes) (Bicycle Dutch 2018).

Sociological structures, however, refer to more than bricks, concrete, and rails. Another reason why the Dutch use their bikes more than Americans is because the former are less pressed for time. A study out of University of California, Los Angeles, highlights three important differences between the two countries that produce these asymmetries in avail-able time (Smart et al. 2014). First, family-friendly labor policies like flex time and pater-nity leave allow Dutch families to divide childcare responsibilities more evenly than

Some of Those Deep Sociological Drivers

The literature is full of frameworks designed to help us grasp why institutions, groups, and cultures treat the environment in the manner they do. Three such approaches, among many, include the treadmill of production, metabolic rift, and the privileging worldview.

TREADMILL OF PRODUCTION (SEE ALSO CHAPTER 10):

Modern capitalistic societies are driven by a never-ending commitment to growth—a treadmill. With the support of government and a complicit public, industrial production is allowed to expand, and this in turn places still further demands on nature while creating growing amounts of waste (which in turn overload waste sinks, like the Earth's ability to absorb carbon dioxide). The process contains the following paradox: economic growth is privileged, yet the environmental destruction that follows disrupts and severely threatens the system's ability to ensure long-term economic expansion (Schnaiberg 1980).

METABOLIC RIFT (SEE ALSO CHAPTER 10):

A metabolic rift exists in the exchange between social systems and natural systems, which is hypothesized to lead to ecological crisis (Foster 1999). The origins of the concept lie in the writings of Karl Marx, and referred to the crisis in soil fertility generated by urbanization—nutrients from the soil were exported to cities in the form of agricultural products but not returned to the land, causing a disruption in the aforementioned exchange. Over time the process created an ecological crisis, namely, in the case of London, a human waste filled River Thames and depleted soil in the countryside. Similar rifts have been shown to exist in the Earth's carbon cycle (Foster et al. 2010) and the oceans' fisheries (Longo and Clark 2016).

PRIVILEGING WORLDVIEW (SEE ALSO CHAPTER 13):

This is an especially diverse literature, encompassing how philosophers since the time of Plato separated nature from society (and mind from body) as well as the historical tendency to feminize nature and the hypermasculine language tied to civilization's need to dominate and tame "her." One especially influential tradition has its roots in a 1967 article by Lynn White Jr. published in the magazine *Science*. The essay, "The Historical Roots of Our Ecologic Crisis," argues that in order to understand environmental problems we must first examine and critique our attitudes toward nature. According to White, prevailing attitudes toward nature are rooted in religious beliefs. As White wrote, "What people do about their ecology depends on what they think about themselves in relation to things around them. Human ecology is deeply conditioned by beliefs about our nature and destiny—that is, by religion" (White 1967, 1206). White focused his analysis on Western Christianity (both Protestantism and Roman Catholicism). He asserted that Western Christianity is "the most anthropocentric religion the world has seen" (White 1967, 1205) and that it encourages and legitimizes a dangerous indifference to the integrity of ecological systems. White argued that within Christian theology, "nature has no reason for existence save to serve" (1967, 1207) humanity and thus "bears a huge burden of guilt" (1967, 1206) for the environmental mess we are in.

IMAGE 1.1 Human-Power Mobility on Display in the Netherlands

Source: "Bikes, Amsterdam," by jadcab (flickr.com/photos/jadecab) is licensed copyright © 2015 under CC BY-ND 2.0.

American families. Second, workweeks in the Netherlands are shorter. Lastly, Dutch parents do less chauffeuring of children than American parents. Walkable neighborhoods and a high-quality bike infrastructure in the Netherlands make it easy and safe for children to walk or bike to school (see Image 1.1).

In short, the automobile, as the dominant mode of transportation in the United States, has a significant amount of momentum behind it. This is not to suggest that our hands are tied, that we cannot move away from the car and replicate a transportation system more like what's found in, say, the Netherlands. Rather, it is an acknowledgment that change of such magnitude comes with significant transaction costs. The question is: Are we willing to pay them? And a related question: Should all members of society pay these costs equally?

The Messy Relationship between Behaviors and Attitudes

In the small rural Iowa town where I grew up, my parents carefully separate their recyclables from the other rubbish that ends up in the garbage truck. They also have to dutifully study every plastic container and verify its number (only certain numbers, and very few numbers at that, can be recycled). Finally, they have to haul their recycle bins to the nearest pickup site, which, fortunately for them because they live in town, is only about three-quarters of a mile away. It would be so much easier if my parents just threw everything away. But they don't. They put up with the "cost" of recycling. I know many in my hometown, and especially those living in the surrounding countryside, however, who do not. For them, all household waste ends up in either the landfill or the burn pile.

Once, one of my more ecologically passionate friends, after hearing this story, looked at me with disbelief, unable to accept that people choose not to recycle. He asked me,

"Why do they do this? Don't they care about the environment?" I think his questions missed the mark. These divergent behaviors seem not to reflect vast differences in attitudes. For example, one individual from my hometown who does not recycle, a lifelong friend, has been a card-carrying member of the Sierra Club for as long as I can remember. He has a hard time walking, lives far from town, and prefers not to drive, which makes the practice of recycling very difficult. Similarly, I know some people in the town where I now live, Fort Collins, Colorado, who admit to having very little interest in reducing their impact on the environment but still diligently recycle.

Fort Collins has a mixed recycling program. In other words, if it is recyclable—and, unlike in my parents' town, every piece of plastic is recyclable—it goes into a massive blue bin that is wheeled out with the trash to be picked up. That's it. Easy. Moreover, unlike my parents, whose garbage fee allows them to set out as many trash bags as they wish, there is an economic incentive in Fort Collins to divert waste into the recycle stream; namely, you pay more for larger trash cans. To put it in cost-and-benefit terms: whereas it costs my parents to recycle—in terms of time, hassle, and braving the elements (Iowa winters can be brutal)—it costs residents of Fort Collins *not* to.

This goes back to a point I made earlier about the need to contextualize social behavior. I supervised a visiting student from Russia for six months who wanted to learn more about the field of environmental sociology. One of the things that interested her was how attitudes toward the environment in the United States differed from those in Russia. Coming across a statistic about the amount of solid waste that Colorado State University—my employer—recycles (something like 56 percent at the time), she assumed this behavior was evidence of deep attitudinal affinities toward the environment. After noting how comparatively little her Russian university recycles, she asked, "What do they do here to develop these green attitudes?" Holding up a ubiquitous recycle bin and pointing to the words *mixed recycling*, I proceeded to tell her about how socio-organizational changes now make recycling as easy as throwing things away (if not easier, as rubbish bins are notoriously difficult to find in certain university buildings).

The moral of these two stories: structural changes go a long way toward changing behavior. And many times, these changes go further than attitudinal changes alone. As my nonrecycling but otherwise environmentally minded friend from my hometown reminds us, having the "right" attitudes does not do anyone (or the environment) any good if society fails to provide cost-effective ways to act on those beliefs.

I realize that the idea of changing behaviors *prior to* attitudes is somewhat counterintuitive. Yet, for some people at least, perhaps that is what we ought to be shooting for. Just to be clear: I am not talking about making people do something that they don't want to do. In fact, I am saying just the opposite. Recognizing that sacrifice is not for everyone, we should strive to reorganize society in such a way that individuals choose a more sustainable path—like those I know who recoil at the thought of being labeled an "environmentalist" but still diligently recycle. Sacrifice is a rather uninspired solution, and my experience has been that the message tends to turn people off, especially those with exceedingly large ecological footprints. How can we have people want to *act* like an environmentalist even if they don't want to be called it?

I lay no claim to having the answers about what ought to be done. That is a question best left for us all, collectively, to decide. But I do know we will never be able to answer it comprehensively until we have a grasp of the level of complexity involved. The road ahead is not going to be easy, but, as the following chapters explain, there are viable ways forward.

The Journey Ahead

Some readers (and colleagues) might wonder why, as a professionally trained environmental sociologist, I did not include the term *environmental sociology* in the book's title. You might say it was a pragmatic move to select a title that does not tie me to any one particular disciplinary narrative. Citing my own earlier plea (see Carolan 2005b) to social scientists to expand their sociological imaginations and see the explanatory power of nontraditional sociological variables, Riley Dunlap calls for the "*pragmatic* employment of environmental indicators in empirical research investigating linkages between social and biophysical phenomena" (2010, 23; emphasis added). This book takes this pragmatic call to heart. The conceptual and analytic approaches discussed in the forthcoming chapters come from many disciplines: sociology, to be sure, but also anthropology, geography, political science, science and technology studies, and economics, among others. As I tell my students, there are many ways to make sense of today's ecological state. Undoubtedly, there will be those who find fault with how I go about discussing a particular environmental issue, thinking I should have used "theory X" or "analytic device Y." I accept such criticism. I make no claims that the analyses that follow are the only ways—or even the best ways—to make sense of the environmental issues discussed. Space constraints limit the amount of detail that can be conveyed about any particular topic. But that's okay. The chapters are meant to *start* discussions, not stifle them by claiming to be the last word on any given subject. I urge you to critique, elaborate, and refine the theories and arguments in this book.

The following chapters are problem *and* solution focused. In addition to describing what is wrong (and why), they also discuss alternative institutional, cultural, technological, ethical, and political forms that seek to facilitate more sustainable outcomes. Each chapter follows a similar organizational structure: a brief overview on the current state of the issue, an overview of some of the ways social scientists have explored it, followed by a sociological (and thus still critical) discussion of solutions.

Although each chapter is written to stand alone, the full pragmatic force of the text is best felt when it is read cover to cover. The reason for this is simple: the most sustainable solutions (in other words, the *real* solutions) rarely apply to just one problem. In fact, if we dug deep enough, we would discover that many of today's environmental problems have related causes. Having already cautioned readers to thinking only in terms of grand narratives, it should not come as a surprise that I reject the view that environmental problems are the result of any one thing. Yet I do not symmetrically assign fault, either. The problems we face may not be entirely the product of any one thing, but some things certainly deserve their fair share of the blame. Thus, as the book progresses from "Living in a Material World" (Part I) to "At the Intersection of Ecology and Society" (Part II) to "Organizing a Sustainable Society" (Part III) and, finally, to "Shifting the Focus to Results" (Part IV), critiques sharpen, and proposed solutions become more complete, as the discussion moves closer to those notably culpable sociological artifacts, which I zero in on in the later chapters. As noted earlier, with each section I attempt to drill further down to uncover the really real social dynamics on which considerable blame can be laid and which, once changed, point to opportunities for true sustainability.

Thus, if the solutions proposed early in the text seem shallow, they are. This does not lessen their importance: when you're sick, you need to treat the symptoms as much as the cause. Yet the pragmatist in me wants more; after all, pragmatic solutions need to not only be realistic but also to resolve that which ails us.

The first part focuses on issues related to certain environmental phenomena. Specifically, time is taken in this part of the book to examine problems and solutions linked to greenhouse gases (Chapter 2), waste (Chapter 3), biodiversity (Chapter 4), and water (Chapter 5). One of the themes of Part I is that the social sciences have plenty to say about artifacts often assumed to be within the exclusive purview of natural scientists and engineers. Part II adjusts its investigation slightly to discuss phenomena that explicitly weave the "social" and "natural" realms together in complex and fascinating ways. The problems and solutions discussed here revolve around issues relating to population (Chapter 6), transportation (Chapter 7), food (Chapter 8), and energy production (Chapter 9). Part III offers the most pointed response to the question, "What does sociology have to do with today's environmental problems?" To put it plainly: everything. By highlighting the phenomena driving today's environmental problems—those phenomena located in the realm of "the real" in Figure 1.2—my wish is to approach the closing chapter on a sincerely hopeful note. Only by naming the root dynamics of today's environmental ills—from the political economy (Chapter 10) to issues of governance (Chapter 11) and inequality and growth (Chapter 12)—can we expect to have a real chance of naming truly sustainable solutions. Part IV concludes our journey. Whereas a considerable amount of attention is given throughout the book to structural phenomena (like the aforementioned sociological momentum), the book concludes by elaborating on how social change ultimately hinges on people behaving and thinking in particular ways (Chapter 13). Change must start with us. Lest we forget, although social forces act on us as if independent from us, they are products of our making. This fact is perhaps the most hopeful message of all.

The reader will also find a number of features provided in the forthcoming chapters. In addition to many figures, tables, and images, a variety of text boxes are interspersed throughout to add either further detail or an illustrative case study to bolster a point, concept, or theme in the main text. These take four forms: Case Studies, which briefly highlight case studies relevant to points made throughout the text; Ethical Questions, to highlight the value judgments that lurk everywhere when talking about environmental phenomena; ECOnnections, which I use to interject additional information into the text with minimal disruption to the flow of the main narrative; and Movement Matters, which offer vignettes on grassroots movements that have affected legislation. Finally, suggestions for additional readings are provided at the end of every chapter, as are questions to help spur further thought and discussion on the subject matter. Also at the end of each chapter are Important Concepts, Relevant Internet Links, and Suggested Videos (many of the videos are available for free online).

IMPORTANT CONCEPTS
- ecological complexity
- environmental sociology
- sociological drivers

- sociological imagination
- sociological momentum
- technologically possible versus sociologically probable

DISCUSSION QUESTIONS

1. How can sociology inform our understanding of environmental problems and solutions?
2. In your experience do people, books, and professors and instructors seem more interested in talking about environmental problems than solutions? If so, why do you think this is?
3. Do old distinctions between the social and natural sciences still hold when facing today's environmental problems? What about disciplines? Do we still need them? Why or why not?
4. What actions of yours clearly cost the environment? Why do you still do them? What would it take for those behaviors to change?

SUGGESTED ADDITIONAL READINGS

Bohr, J., and R. Dunlap. 2018. "Key Topics in Environmental Sociology, 1990–2014: Results from a Computational Text Analysis." *Environmental Sociology*, 4(2): 181–195.

Schor, J. 2018. "Consumption and Social Inequality." In *Core Concepts in Sociology*, edited by J.M. Ryan, pp. 46–49. New York: Wiley.

Zinda, J., Y. Li, and J. Liu. 2018. "China's Summons for Environmental Sociology." *Current Sociology*, 66(6): 867–885.

RELEVANT INTERNET LINKS

- http://envirosoc.org. The Environment Sociology subsection of the American Sociological Association. This is an excellent resource for anyone interested in environmental sociology.

SUGGESTED VIDEOS

- *Disruption* (2014). Shot during the 100 days prior to the People's Climate March held on September 21, 2014 in New York City, the film serves as a cautionary countdown intended to motivate viewers to take action on the issue of climate change.
- *Earth on Fire* (2014). A one-hour, Australian special that focuses on mega fires and fires in general as they relate to forests and the ecosystem.
- *Living the Change* (2018). New Zealand filmmakers explore solutions to the global crisis.
- *Racing Extinction* (2015). Scientists, activists, and others draw attention to humankind's role in the potential loss of at least half of the world's species.
- *Tomorrow* (2015). This two-hour award winning French documentary (English subtitles) takes you around the world to investigate concrete solutions to environmental and social challenges.

Part I

LIVING IN A MATERIAL WORLD

2

Greenhouse Gases: Warmer Isn't Better

A friend once told me that you know when a person, catchphrase, or subject has become part of our collective consciousness when it has been immortalized on a bumper sticker. Well, I once saw a bumper sticker that read, "**Greenhouse gases**: proof that you can have too much of a good thing." (Greenhouse gases are any gases in the atmosphere that absorb and emit radiation within the thermal infrared range.) True to my friend's words, the topic of human-induced **climate change**—a change in climate patterns that results from human activity like burning fossil fuels—has become unavoidable. (The terms *climate change* and *global warming* are used interchangeably throughout the book.)

Contrary to what certain politicians and media personalities might be saying, scientific debate around climate change is ending. To be sure, there is still a climate change debate within the peer-reviewed literature. Yet that debate is ultimately around questions such as "What are we to do about climate change?" and "Do we all bear equal responsibility for it, or do some individuals and nations deserve a greater share of the blame?" rather than "Is climate change happening?" Interestingly, whereas the peer-reviewed scientific literature is nearly unanimous in its support of the thesis that climate change is occurring and that it is *anthropogenic* (aka human induced) (Cook et al. 2016), the general public holds a greater diversity of views (see ECOnnection 2.1).

It is not enough to chalk these divergent positions up to the belief that some just have more, and better, knowledge on the subject. I say this knowing the overwhelming empirical evidence concerning how cultural and political beliefs filter the facts we choose to see and acknowledge (Howe 2018). One study analyzed survey data of the US public, scientists who were actively publishing on energy technologies, and congressional policy advisors. The surveys gauged attitudes toward climate change. The authors' findings are stunning, uncovering "evidence that the ideological divide about global warming gets significantly larger according to respondents' knowledge about politics, energy, and science" (Bolsen et al. 2015, 271). To put an even sharper point on the study's conclusion: more knowledge was shown to *increase* the divide between climate change skeptics and those believing it to be real and human induced.

So: we are left with sociological questions. Some of these include, for example, "What might account for the aforementioned discrepancy between the views held among climate scientists and the general public?" "How did we get ourselves into this mess?" and "Why is it proving so hard to change course?" A thorough treatment of these questions will have to wait until later chapters, when we talk about pressures and drivers. In this chapter I address various societal impacts that we can expect from climate change—there are, unfortunately, many—and suggest potential solutions.

Fast Facts

- A portion of the sun's short-wave radiation that enters the atmosphere is absorbed by the Earth's surfaces, where it is then transferred into long-wave radiation (namely, heat) and reradiated back into space. Some of this energy, however, is absorbed by the planet's atmosphere, thanks to greenhouse gases like carbon dioxide (CO_2), a process known as the **greenhouse effect**. (Other major greenhouse gases are methane and nitrous oxide.)
- Not only are atmospheric levels of greenhouse gases rising, but the *rate of increase is growing*. Total CO_2 emissions rose by 1.6 percent in 2017 to 36.2 gigatons. (A gigaton is equal to 1 billion metric tons.) The data look even worse for 2018, as the number has climbed to a record 37.1 gigatons of CO_2. That is equal to an annual growth rate of 2.7 percent between 2017 and 2018 (Levin and Murakami 2019).
- While humans were in some way responsible for emitting 37.1 billion tons of CO_2 into the atmosphere in 2018, natural emissions (coming from plants breathing out CO_2 and outgassing from the ocean) equal about 776 billion tons of CO_2 per year (Olivier et al. 2014). Natural sources, however, absorb *more* than they emit—roughly 788 billion tons annually. Yet this difference is not enough to compensate for all that humans pump into the atmosphere.
- A comparison between satellite data from 1970 to 1996 found a steady decline in the amount of energy escaping to space at the wavelengths that greenhouse gases absorb. Since there was no indication that there was less solar energy coming in, this is *direct experimental evidence* for a significant increase in the Earth's greenhouse effect (Harries et al. 2001). This evidence has since been independently corroborated by other studies (e.g., Chen et al. 2007; Ohring et al. 2014).
- More than 80 percent of the trapped energy that is the result of the increased greenhouse effect goes into warming the oceans (which isn't terribly surprising, given that oceans cover 71 percent of the Earth's surface). The world's oceans, like its land and atmosphere, have been steadily warming over the past half century. For an example of this differential heating of oceans and land, recall the last time you walked on a dry beach on a sunny day. The sand gets warmer faster than the ocean. That is because water is a slow conductor of heat and thus needs to absorb more energy than the sand (or land) for its temperature to increase. Similarly, once warmed, water takes longer to lose its heat than sand (or land).
- Three billion years ago, the Earth's atmosphere contained very low levels of oxygen but a great deal of CO_2. At the time, the world was teeming with bacteria, many of which survived by breaking down sugars and chemicals present in their environment—a process known as fermentation. These fermenting bacteria produced methane and CO_2—two greenhouse gases—as waste products. Over time these bacteria evolved to use sunlight to

ECOnnection 2.1
The US Public's Knowledge of Climate Change

The Yale Project on Climate Change Communication (with funding from the National Science Foundation) released the findings of a national survey on the public's understanding of climate change in December, 2018 (Leiserowitz et al. 2018). The survey sought to measure general public understanding in the United States about how the climate system works and the causes and impacts of, and potential solutions to, global warming. Below are some of the findings contained in this extensive report.

- Seventy-three percent of Americans think global warming is happening, an increase of 10 percentage points since March 2015, while only 14 percent think global warming is not happening.
- Americans are also increasingly sure about global warming's presence—51% are "extremely" or "very" sure it is happening, an increase of 14 percentage points since March 2015, matching the highest level since 2008. By contrast, far fewer—7%—are "extremely" or "very sure" global warming is not happening.
- Approximately six in ten Americans (62%) understand that global warming is mostly human-caused. By contrast, about one in four (23%) attribute it largely to natural changes in the environment.
- While more than half of Americans (57%) understand that scientific consensus exists about global warming, only one in five (20%) understand how strong that level of consensus is (i.e., that more than 90% of climate scientists have concluded that human-caused global warming is happening).
- Forty-six percent of Americans say they have personally experienced the effects of global warming—an increase of 15 percentage points since March 2015.

The full report can be accessed at https://tinyurl.com/tcv2vnm.

split the strong bonds of hydrogen and oxygen found in water. The waste produced was oxygen, which over many millions of years began accumulating and changed the composition of the Earth's atmosphere (which today contains roughly 78 percent nitrogen, 20 percent oxygen, 1 percent argon, around 1 percent water vapor, and 0.039 percent CO_2). This atmosphere killed off many species ill adapted to an oxygen-rich environment. But it also led to the emergence of new life forms, such as, eventually, humans. In sum, the history of life *itself* is an intricate story of the coevolution between life, the Earth, and the atmosphere.

Implications

While changing ecological conditions affect all life, some species are clearly more threatened than others. We are still learning how climate change affects human societies. Yet although the image emerging lacks high resolution, it is clear that climate change is going to be of major sociological consequence. The forthcoming discussion is organized around the following themes to speak of some of these consequences: urban areas; food security; children, women, and the elderly; and climate change refugees.

Urban Areas

As the number of people living in cities continues to grow—more than half of the world's population now resides in an urban area—so too will the number of urban residents vulnerable to climate change (see Ethical Question 2.1). Climate change related risks affecting those residing in urban centers are a function not only of actual events but also of the capacity (or lack thereof) of organizations, social networks, and governments (local and national) to respond to and withstand environmental threats. For example, the quality of housing and infrastructure-based services (like water and sewage), which are typically taken for granted in affluent nations, will considerably shape a society's ability to withstand certain hazards.

Within **informal settlements** (unplanned housing constructed on land illegally or not in compliance with current building regulations, or both), residential structures rarely comply with official safety standards and are often crowded and poorly maintained, making for a deadly witch's brew of sorts in a future where drastic weather swings become increasingly the norm. There is also very little planning between neighbors when building these structures and altering the landscape, which increases the entire neighborhood's vulnerability to climate change. Homes in the low-lying outskirts of many cities in lower-income countries are thus frequently built in an uncoordinated fashion, as many of these neighborhoods are made up of newly arrived residents who have yet to develop a sense of community among themselves. Some of these homes are elevated. And throughout the settlement, soil has been moved without any thought given to drainage. When it rains, some homes are hit particularly hard either because they are low-lying or as a result of landscape alterations that place them in the path of most of the runoff (Williams et al. 2019).

The vast majority of the world's poor also live without air-conditioning or adequate insulation, making heat waves lethal to the very young, the elderly, and those who are sick (Di Ruocco et al. 2015). Exacerbating matters further is the fact that in many cities in low-income countries, a sizable proportion of the poor live in tenements and central districts with excessively high densities, precisely where the urban **heat island effect** is most pronounced. This effect describes the well-documented phenomenon of how built-up areas are warmer than nearby rural areas. Because concrete, tarmac, and other common construction materials absorb heat readily, the annual average air temperature of a city with at least one million people is between 1.8° and 5.4° Fahrenheit (1–3° Celsius) warmer than the area outside of the city. In the evening, as this solar energy is released back into the atmosphere, the difference in temperature between city and countryside can be as high as 22° Fahrenheit (12° Celsius) (see Image 2.1). (My 98-year-old grandmother has told me stories of going to bed as a child in the winter with a heated brick under the covers. It's the same principle.) Heat islands increase summertime peak energy demands, air-conditioning costs, greenhouse gas emissions, and heat-related illness and mortality. And as the mean atmospheric temperature continues to rise, the effect will become only more pronounced in the years ahead (see Case Study 2.1).

Countries with adequate resources and institutions, infrastructure, services, as well as regulations to protect public health will be able to adapt rapidly to a changing climate. Many measures have been implemented in affluent nations that—often unknowingly—enhance a city's adaptive capabilities to climate change: integrated health-care services

The Most Threatened Are the Least Responsible

Many of the urban centers that face the largest increases in threats from climate change—and with the least capacity to deal with these threats—are in nations least responsible for global warming, as their national greenhouse gas emissions per capita are among the lowest in the world. As illustrated in Figure 2.1, whereas countries in Western Europe, North America, the United Kingdom, and the Mediterranean, along with Australia, Japan, and New Zealand, account for only 19.7 percent of the world's population, they are far and away the leading contributors of total global greenhouse gas emissions, with a national average of 16.1 tons of CO_2 equivalent per capita. The term *CO_2 equivalent* is used to reduce different greenhouse gases to a common unit. For any quantity and type of greenhouse gas, this signifies the amount of CO_2 that would have the equivalent global warming impact.

The rest of the world, meanwhile, as a result of being less affluent, has less capacity to adequately respond to the hazards of climate change. Is this fair? Since they bear a significant share of blame, do affluent nations have a responsibility to help the rest of the world adapt to climate change?

FIGURE 2.1 Regional per Capita Greenhouse Gas Emissions Relative to Population

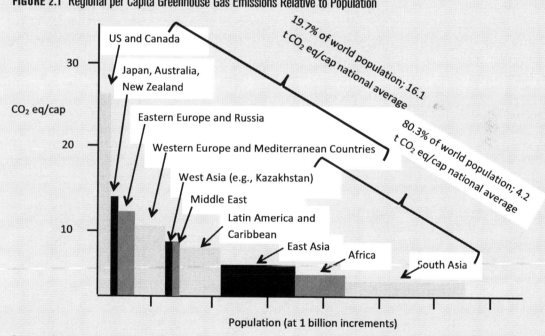

Source: Adapted from IPCC (2014).

IMAGE 2.1 Urban Heat Island Effect

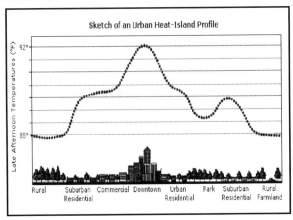

Source: NASA.

Note:
The dotted line represents the mean late-afternoon summer temperatures for the average city (with at least one million inhabitants) and surrounding landscapes. Research indicates that cities are between 1.8° and 5.4° Fahrenheit (1–3° Celsius) warmer than the countryside immediately surrounding them, while temperature increases recorded in suburban residential districts show a slightly less pronounced heat island effect.

CASE STUDY 2.1

African Americans are Disproportionately Exposed to Extreme Heat

Researchers recently examined the average number of days with a heat index above 105° Fahrenheit in countries where African Americans make up 25 percent or more of the population versus those countries that are less than 25 percent African American. What did they find? Countries with large African American populations are exposed to extreme temperatures 2–3 more days per year than those countries with smaller African American populations. And, by mid-century, the expectation is that those same countries would experience about twenty more extreme heat days per year based on climate models—that's about three additional weeks of extreme heat compared to countries with a lower (less than 25 percent) ratio of African Americans.

Adapted from Hollis (2019).

with emergency services; sufficient sewer and drainage capacity to serve not only daily requirements but also less frequent (yet high-capacity) storm events; structures that conform to building codes and health and safety regulations and that are serviced by piped water, sewers, all-weather roads, and electricity twenty-four hours a day; and institutions that can respond rapidly to high-impact weather events, from utility companies to repair downed power lines to the National Guard (as in the United States) for more severe events. A summary of some urban and associated health impacts linked to climate change confronting populations within low-income nations can be found in Table 2.1.

A growing proportion of the world's population is also residing in what are known as **low-elevation coastal zones** (LECZ), a trend occurring most rapidly in least-developed countries. This refers to areas within 10 meters of mean sea level—about 2 percent of the

TABLE 2.1 Urban and Health Impacts of Climate Change

CHANGE	URBAN IMPACTS	HEALTH IMPACTS
Temperature	Increased energy demand for heating /cooling; worsening of air quality	Increased vulnerability to respiratory diseases; young and elderly particularly at risk
Precipitation	Increased risk of flooding; increased risk of landslides; distress migration	Increase in water-borne and water-washed diseases; food shortages and malnutrition
Sea level rise	Coastal flooding; salinization of water sources	Loss of land and property; health problems from salinated water (especially children)
Extreme rainfall/tropical cyclones	More intense flooding; higher risk of landslides; disruption to livelihoods and city economies	Higher levels of mortality and morbidity; loss of income and assets
Drought	Water shortages; higher food prices; disruption of hydro-electricity	Higher prevalence of waterborne and water-washed diseases; food shortages
Heat or cold waves	Short-term changes in energy demand	Mortality from extreme heat or cold
Abrupt climate change	Rapid and extreme sea level rise; rapid and extreme temperature change	Significant effects on morbidity and mortality (especially in most vulnerable groups)
Population movements	Movements from stressed rural habitats	Increased population; increased stress on infrastructure and resources
Biological changes	Extended vector habitats	Increased risk of diseases such as malaria and dengue

Source: Adapted from Kjellstrom et al. (2016) and Watts et al. (2017).

world's land mass. The coastal cities most at risk are in low-income countries, as fifteen of them contain over 90 percent of the world's LECZ rural poor (Barbier 2015). The Caribbean Sea islands look to be especially vulnerable to sea rise. The Bahamas' highest point is a mere 63 meters above sea level, for example. This explains why 88.4 percent of the island's population lies in a LECZ (Wheeler 2011). The Caribbean is also home to biodiversity hotspots that are uniquely threatened by sea rise. A one meter sea level increase is expected to submerge 9 percent of the islands (i.e., sixty-three islands among the 723 identified as biodiversity hotspots by Bellard et al. 2014), while a six meter increase would eliminate half of the islands (Becker et al. 2019).

Some of the fastest urban expansion in low-income nations is also taking place in floodplains, along mountain slopes, and in other zones prone to flooding, sea surges, or other weather-related hazards. Typically, individuals living in these risky sites are poor, as those with means can afford to live someplace safer. Consequently, not only are the sites themselves not well suited for settlement, but the houses are also often structurally deficient and thus do not provide adequate protection from more intense and frequent weather-related threats.

Food Security

According to the Food and Agriculture Organization of the United Nations (FAO), the world's poor will likely be (if not already) the first affected by global warming, as they are food insecure to begin with. Future climate changes will only exacerbate this vulnerability through an increased risk of crop failure, new patterns of pests and diseases, lack of appropriate seeds and planting material for the changing micro and macro climates, and the loss of livestock (FAO 2015). It is worth noting, so it can be immediately set aside, the claim that CO_2 emissions are good for humanity because they will turn the world into a lush oasis—CO_2, after all, is "plant food." Let's remember that plants rely on more than just CO_2 to survive. Any so-called CO_2 fertilizer effect will therefore be limited, as ecosystems become increasingly overwhelmed by the negative effects of heat damage and drought. To put it simply: plants can't metabolize CO_2 when stressed by a lack of water and excessive heat. Or to put it more simply still: they can't grow when they're dying (see Case Study 2.2).

With models informed by the *Fifth Assessment Report* by the **Intergovernmental Panel on Climate Change** (IPCC), Dawson et al. (2016) calculate global mean caloric consumption, on a per-capita basis, under different climate change and social-economic scenarios for 2050, 2085, and 2100. Under a no-climate change scenario, based upon projected changes in population and agricultural land use only, findings show that 31 percent (2.5 billion people by 2050) of the global population is at risk of undernourishment if no adaptations are made. An additional 1.7 billion people are at risk of undernourishment by 2050 when climate change is taken into consideration. "However," the authors point out, "the model does not account for future trends in technology, improved crop varieties or agricultural trade interventions" that "will need to be embraced on a global scale if society is to ensure adequate food supplies for a projected global population of greater than 9 billion people" (Dawson et al. 2016, 429).

Yet putting all of our eggs in the "technological innovation" basket is itself problematic. For instance, what foods do you think we will be eating thanks to these innovations?

CASE STUDY 2.2
Climate Change and the Wine Industry

Few crops are as vulnerable to temperature and extreme weather events as wine grapes. And with the prime agroecological conditions go the spoils: for example, there was a fifteen-fold price difference in 2006 between cabernet sauvignon grapes grown in Napa Valley, California ($4,100 per ton) and those raised in California's warmer Central Valley ($260 per ton). The difference in average temperature between the regions: 5° Fahrenheit (or roughly 2.8° Celsius) (Hertsgaard 2010).

In France there is worry that the famed Champagne region will become too hot to produce premium-quality champagne. In another prime wine-growing area in southeastern France, the prized white soil, once cherished for its ability to hold heat, may become the region's downfall. Rising temperatures have caused some of Europe's biggest producers to buy land in places like the Pyrenees foothills, northern China, and southern England, which are said to have climates that resemble the French Champagne region of the 1970s (Pitrelli 2018).

Thanks to climate change, the premium wine grape production area in the United States could shrink by as much as 81 percent by this century's end. In California, warming temperatures coupled with the state's water crisis have many worried that this could result in an enormous loss of land suitable for premium grape production, especially in Napa and Santa Barbara Counties, where land loss could be near 50 percent of present levels (Mozell and Thach 2014).

Answer: those that are most amenable to technological innovation—in other words, foods that are *already* being exposed to capital investments (Carolan 2018a). We are not solving anything if it means eating more ultra-processed foods. The average person faces a 14 percent higher risk of early death with each 10 percent increase in the amount of ultra-processed foods they eat (Adams and White 2015).

Assuming there are gains to be had, such as through **precision agriculture** techniques, not all farmers will have equal access to these innovations. While affluent farmers will have the resources to adopt new technologies and techniques suited for future agroecological conditions, those living at a subsistence level (and especially those living in **abject poverty**—a severe state of poverty) will not. The biggest losers from climate change could well be those who depend most on agriculture, aquaculture, and pastoral animal husbandry and who have the least alternative sources of income—the poor (see ECOnnection 2.2).

Children, Women, and the Elderly

The roles of women in less developed countries are as diverse as they are important. A classic piece from 1991 on women's work in tribal India highlights the following major areas of work in poor rural areas that are overwhelmingly performed by women: food procurement, such as food gathering and production; the protection of life and property, including the procurement of water, energy (e.g., firewood, charcoal), and fodder; and

ECOnnection 2.2

Climate Change Linked to Food-Related Vulnerabilities for Certain Populations

The FAO has highlighted certain populations that warrant special attention because of their heightened food-related vulnerabilities attributable to climate change. These populations include:

- low-income groups in drought- and flood-prone areas with poor food-distribution infrastructure and limited access to emergency response
- low- to middle-income groups in flood-prone areas that may lose homes, stored food, personal possessions, and means of obtaining an income
- farmers whose land risks becoming submerged or damaged due to sea-level rise or saltwater intrusions
- farmers who lack capital to adjust to changing temperature and rainfall conditions
- farmers at risk from high winds
- low-income livestock keepers in drylands

where changes in rainfall patterns will affect forage availability and quality
- low-income livestock keepers who, because of heat waves, will lose animals from excessive heat
- fishers whose infrastructure for fishing activities (e.g., port, landing, and storage facilities; fishponds; and processing areas) becomes submerged or damaged by sea-level rise, flooding, or other extreme weather events
- fishing communities whose livelihoods depend on the presence of healthy coral reefs for food and protection from natural disasters
- fishers and aqua farmers whose catch suffers from shifts in fish distribution and the productivity of aquatic ecosystems as a result of changes in ocean currents and temperatures, increased discharge of freshwater into oceans, or both.

Adapted from FAO (2015).

childbearing and rearing, including the maintenance of health standards for the household, like securing clean water and collecting medicinal plants (Menon 1991). Note how climate change has the ability to touch on all these areas. Floods, droughts, wildfires, and higher or colder than average temperatures all affect the lives of those responsible for the well-being of the household, which, especially in less affluent nations, continues to be women (see Figure 2.2). It is another case of climate change having a disproportional impact on a population that is neither to blame for its existence nor capable of responding to its effects because of a lack of resources (see ECOnnection 2.3).

During extreme events in poor countries, like flooding, high winds, landslides, and tsunamis (i.e., hurricanes), the loss of life is disproportionately higher among children, women, and the elderly (Zhou et al. 2014). Patriarchal norms might limit the health care available to women and girls, especially in those societies that place greater value in having

FIGURE 2.2 Women and Their Vulnerability to Climate Change

Source: Adapted from Flatø et al. (2017) and Sapkota et al. (2016).

a male heir. Gendered norms may also directly impact a female's ability to respond to a weather event. They might not, for example, be taught to swim or climb trees, skills vital to surviving a flood or tsunami. We also know that gendered norms mean women are less willing to save themselves. They might be constrained by societal expectations that discourage them from leaving the home without male permission or because care of children and the elderly, while the able-bodied males are away, slow their escape (Bradshaw and Fordham 2015). Rising temperatures are also expanding the range of tropical diseases, with children the most susceptible to these illnesses (Blum and Hotez 2018).

Climate change is ultimately about greater fluctuations in weather extremes, which include both very hot and very cold temperatures. Hence the U-shaped relationship between temperature and mortality: deaths occur when temperatures spike and when they drop. A study examining the temperature–mortality relationship in four subtropical Chinese cities shows that in those areas accustomed to hot temperatures "the cold effect was more durable and pronounced than the hot effect" among elderly populations (Wu et al. 2013, 355). The authors of the study speculate that while these areas have adapted to hotter temperatures, they are woefully maladapted to low temperature extremes, thus making the effects all the more dangerous.

ECOnnection 2.3
Notes from a
Filmmaker's Diary

Kisilu: The Climate Diaries was filmed over four years and offers a portrait of a Kenyan family—Kisilu and Christina (husband and wife, respectively) and their seven young children—on the front line of climate change. Below are reflections of the experience from the perspective of the filmmaker, Julia Dahr.

The month we stayed with Kisilu to film was supposed to be the wettest time of the year. Instead, we experienced a rainy season with almost no rain. […] Kisilu's unceasing optimism was stretched to the limits as he had to worry constantly about having enough food and money to send the children to school. However, Kisilu never gave up his fighting spirit, and in incredible ways he always found motivation to keep up the hard work towards long term change and impact.
[…]
However, though Kisilu looked calm and talked only positive and visionary words, when I got to know him better he revealed that there is a real storm inside him. He feels that he has to look calm to keep the spirit of the family and the community up, but on the inside he is worried about today and the future. One evening he told me how much it hurts when his children are sent home from school, as he knows education is one of their main chances of having a different life than him—a life where they do not need to rely solely on farming because farming is becoming too unreliable. He feels as if he is stuck in the poverty trap. He struggles to pay his children's school fees, but he knows that education is the way out for his children.

As we stayed with Kisilu and the family the drought got worse and worse. Then one afternoon suddenly, on the horizon, we could see rain clouds approaching. Kisilu was extremely happy to see rain in sight. Ten minutes later, the children were dancing and celebrating in the rain. Unfortunately, the happiness was soon replaced by distress; the rain brought with it a strong wind that carried the entire roof of the family's house away. I can still remember today how it felt to be inside the house when the roof was torn off, and how we barely escaped the iron sheets and the falling bricks as the house started collapsing around us. In the end no one got hurt, but the family tragically lost their house in that storm.

Quoted in Dahr (2015).

Climate Change Refugees

Climate change will fundamentally alter the lives of millions who will eventually be forced in the years ahead to leave their villages and cities in search of refuge, fresh water, food, employment, and the like. The **climate change refugees** crisis is expected to surpass all known refugee crises in terms of the number of people affected. (The term *climate change refugees* refers to populations that have been displaced as a result of climate change.) The problem will likely be most pronounced in poorer countries, where the adaptive capacity of people, cities, and nations to the effects of climate change is low (see Case Study 2.3). In more affluent countries, a refugee crisis may be largely avoided through successful steps at adapting to climate change, such as fortified coastal protections or changes in agricultural production and water-supply management (and by having the capability to tightly patrol and effectively close one's borders). The term **adaptation** is useful here, as it refers to actions taken to adjust socioecological systems in response to existing or predicted climatic effects in order to reduce harmful effects. It is worth wondering, however, how many of these displaced people in the future will be seeking refuge in countries like the United States and whether they will be granted access.

At present, the developing world hosts the vast majority of the world's refugees. According to the United Nations (2014), at the beginning of 2014 an estimated 51.2 million people worldwide had been forcibly displaced as a result of persecution, conflict, generalized violence, or human rights violations, the majority of them concentrated in climate change hotspots (places particularly vulnerable to its effects) around the world. As for climate change refugee estimates, the United Nations notes in some of its publications that up to 250 million people could be displaced by climate change by the year 2050 (United Nations 2014). Within the three most vulnerable regions—Sub-Saharan Africa, South Asia, and Latin America—143 million people could be displaced by these impacts by 2050 (World Bank 2018). And this does not even account for "internal migrants". It adds that such movements could accelerate after 2050.

In addition to having few financial resources, refugees are also usually poorly integrated into the community and lack connections to influential people, institutions, and

CASE STUDY 2.3
Climate Refugees from Indonesia and Bangladesh

Two countries viewed as prime candidates for climate change induced migration are Indonesia and Bangladesh.

- *Indonesia*: Roughly 85 percent of this island nation of about 300 million people live within just a few miles of the coast. The steep inland terrain makes much of the noncoastal parts of the country poorly suited for large-scale resettlements. Some of the population could move inland temporarily to escape tidal surges and tropical storms. The more likely scenario, however, has a sizable population leaving the island entirely as sea levels rise.
- *Bangladesh*: This is a country of 160 million people living essentially at sea level. It has already been hit by serious storms (see Image 2.3). Hurricane Sidr (Category 4), for example, devastated the nation in 2007, killing, officially, 3,447 people, though some estimates place the death toll closer to 10,000. (The weaker Aila—Category 1—that hit two years later displaced two million residents, showing that there is no such thing as a "little" typhoon.) These storms are expected to increase in both intensity and frequency in the future. This development, coupled with even a modest sea level rise, risks making much of the country potentially uninhabitable. From Bangladesh alone, the world could see an additional 100 million refugees.

Based on Nash (2010) and Islam and Hasan (2016).

IMAGE 2.3 Hurricanes Surround Hawaii

Source: National Oceanic and Atmospheric Administration (image taken August 31, 2015).

Note
Hurricane Kilo is located approximately 1,220 miles west of Honolulu, Hurricane Ignacio is located around 315 miles east of Hilo, and Hurricane Jimena is located around 1,425 miles east of Hilo. Climate modelers predict greater atmospheric activity—phenomena that can include tropical storms—as a result of climate change (see, e.g., Sarthi et al. 2015).

organizations, having left behind all their social networks when they moved (Parsons 2018). In most cases, it takes years for refugees to embed themselves into local social networks, at which point they may begin to participate in community organizations and local government (Elliott and Yusuf 2014).

Population displacement resulting from climate change has been linked to conflict (Gemenne et al. 2014). Some contributing factors to climate change induced conflict include the following:

- Competition: The arrival of climate change refugees in an area can increase the competition over already scarce resources, especially in nations where property rights are underdeveloped.
- Ethnic tension: When climate migrants and residents belong to different ethnic groups, climate-induced migration may promote tension. This will be a particular problem in regions and countries with long-standing ethnic disputes between migrants and residents.
- Fault lines: Conflict may also follow previously established socioeconomic fault lines, such as between migrant pastoralists and resident farmers competing over land or migrants and residents competing over jobs.
- Weak states: Political instability and civil strife in receiving countries will also increase the likelihood of conflict, as weak states are less capable of keeping the peace if tensions arise between migrants and residents for any of the above reasons.

Solutions

Let's say we lived on a planet whose sun was expanding and consequently warming at an alarming rate. If nothing were done, future generations would experience wildly different climate patterns. Under this scenario I am willing to bet—just as if an asteroid were on a collision course with the Earth—there would be considerable social and political will to take action. That action would likely include not only adapting to post-tipping point climate patterns but also **mitigation** strategies—that is, lessening our greenhouse gas footprint—knowing the role emissions play in contributing to the greenhouse effect. (As opposed to adaptation, mitigation refers to making reductions in the concentration of greenhouse gases by reducing their sources, increasing absorption capacity, or both.) My point is that we know the Earth's atmospheric temperature is rising, and we know these warming trends are going to have devastating social effects. Does it really matter who—or what—we assign blame to for all of this? With that in mind, let's turn to some solutions to the problems of greenhouse gas emissions and climate change more generally.

Environmental Movements Matter

A 2015 study examined the extent to which politics and collective action mitigate the effects of economic and demographic factors on environmental outcomes (Dietz et al. 2015). Examining variations in CO_2 emissions across and within US states, the team found that the impacts of well-known drivers of anthropocentric climate change—namely, growth in both an economic and a demographic sense—can in part be offset by a local and regional political climate supportive of the environment. Thus, while the authors warn that a do-nothing attitude toward climate change will "substantially increase anthropogenic environmental stress," they add that "the effect of environmentalism is a potentially powerful mediating factor" (Dietz et al. 2015, 4). As they explain,

> even as efforts to establish a national policy to limit emissions have yet to be implemented, at the state level, it appears that a strong and broadly accepted environmental movement does produce a mix of shifts in policy, consumption patterns, and production practices that slows emissions.
>
> (Dietz et al. 2015, 4)

It is important to qualify these findings by noting how trade can greatly obscure what's really going on at local and state levels. That is to say, effective social movements do occasionally merely move environmental pressures into someone else's backyard, improving conditions in one spot but doing little to reduce overall impacts. While this pattern can be difficult to track, there is compelling research documenting how international trade allows affluent countries to export a good chunk of their ecological footprint to lower-income nations, resulting in the latter's incurring the ecological costs of the former's affluence by having goods and food produced in their backyards. There is considerable research documenting, for instance, how by exporting jobs to China the United States is also exporting negative health impacts to that country in terms of air and water pollution—recognizing that those industries have their own ecological footprints (Wiedmann and Lenzen 2018). Fortunately, there are plenty of examples supporting the conclusions of

MOVEMENT MATTERS 2.1

Beyond Coal and Its Unusual Bedfellows

King Coal might soon be demoted to a prince, or perhaps even to a baron. While coal today generates close to 30 percent of US power, that's down from the more than 50 percent figure I would have cited a dozen years ago (EIA 2018a). More stunning still, practically every watt of new generating capacity is not coming from coal but from natural gas, wind, or solar. The solar industry now puts more than twice the number of people to work in the United States than coal—the very industry coal proponents laughed at for decades as being just another fad (Eckhouse 2018). (Natural gas employs almost 8 percent more people than solar, though more than 80 percent of those jobs are related to producing the fuel rather than using it to generate electricity.)

The Sierra Club's Beyond Coal campaign, which has brought together grassroots activists, lawyers, manufacturers, and other business interests, has been responsible, to a large extent, for coal's fall from grace (see Image 2.2). There were 523 coal-fired power plants in the United States when Beyond Coal began targeting them a little more than a decade ago. Early in 2015, the campaign celebrated its 190th "retirement" (another way of saying "coal plant closing"). By early 2018, that number was just shy of 270 (Merchant 2018). Coal had produced cheap electricity—not anymore. Now that it has to internalize some of the costs it used to externalize, the electricity it produces is becoming more expensive, and the costs of gas, wind, and solar are dropping. That's why businesses are lining up alongside environmentalists, because coal is bad for their bottom line: it means higher electricity bills. An analysis found that at least 40 percent of recent coal retirements in the United States could not have happened without Beyond Coal's advocacy (Grunwald 2015). It's an example of how collective action can often result in strange bedfellows—unconventional alignments that may be necessary to create sufficient leverage to overpower even the most powerful actors.

IMAGE 2.2 Beyond Coal and Gas Jamboree 2018, Australia

Source: "Beyond Coal and Gas Jamboree 2018" by Karl Goodsell (flickr.com/photos/beyondcoalandgas/) is licensed copyright © 2018 under CC BY 2.0.

Note
The 2018 Beyond Coal and Gas Jamboree brought together more than 340 people from communities across Australia as part of a movement to take the country beyond fossil fuels into a future that puts people and the planet first (https://beyondcoalandgas.org/).

the study by Dietz and colleagues, where the environmental movement played a clear role in reducing the overall impacts of known greenhouse gas contributors (see Movement Matters 2.1).

Stabilization Triangle and Wedges

Carbon emissions from the burning of fossil fuels are projected to double in the next fifty years. This business-as-usual scenario will lead to a tripling of atmospheric CO_2 from pre-industrial levels. But let's say we wanted to keep emissions essentially flat over the next fifty years, followed by a decrease in CO_2 emissions as technologies improve and become cheaper (see Figure 2.3). In the United States, such a strategy would require cutting the projected carbon output by some nine billion tons per year by 2060; globally, 225 billion tons might need to be cut annually. The amount that would need to be cut to level off CO_2 emissions has been called the "stabilization triangle" (Pacala and Socolow 2004). The triangle is made up of large units of CO_2 emissions that would no longer be produced if the right policies and incentives were used; these units are referred to as *wedges*. Let's say, then, that a unit of one billion tons of CO_2 avoided is represented by one wedge. (At the global level, each wedge represents 25 billion tons, as the entire stabilization triangle involves cutting CO_2 output by some 225 billion tons per year by 2060.) Nine wedges like this in the United States would stabilize CO_2 output, and nine at twenty-five billion tons

FIGURE 2.3 Stabilization Triangle

Source: Remik Ziemlinski, The Carbon Mitigation Initiative, Princeton University.

Note
The stabilization triangle refers to the total carbon savings that must be achieved to hold CO2 emissions at a constant level and avoid the predicted tripling of output by 2060.

a piece would stabilize levels worldwide. The question then is: Can we do it? It looks as if we can.

Wedges can take different forms, involving technologies like wind and solar power. Still other wedges might come from building carbon-storage capacity or **sinks**: natural or artificial reservoirs—like a forest—that hold and store greenhouse gases for an indefinite period, thus preventing their accumulation in the atmosphere. There may also be a wedge by moving toward carbon capture and storage coal plants, though this technology, as discussed further in Chapter 9, is still in its infancy (Simon 2018). One thing is certain: we cannot afford to wait. Robert Socolow, Princeton University professor and codirector of the Carbon Mitigation Initiative, noted that in 2011 nine wedges were required to fill the stabilization triangle (Socolow 2011). Yet only *seven* would have been needed if we had acted when the stabilization triangle was first introduced back in 2004 (see Figure 2.4). Our collective unwillingness to take climate change seriously also means we could expect an extra half degree Celsius rise in the average surface temperature of the planet even if we were to come up with all nine wedges today because the atmosphere has stabilized at a higher total emissions level (indicated in Figure 2.4 by "Additional" to the right of the wedges). And if we wait still longer to act, even more wedges will be required, which means an even higher average surface temperature after stabilization.

FIGURE 2.4 Stabilization Triangle, Now versus Then

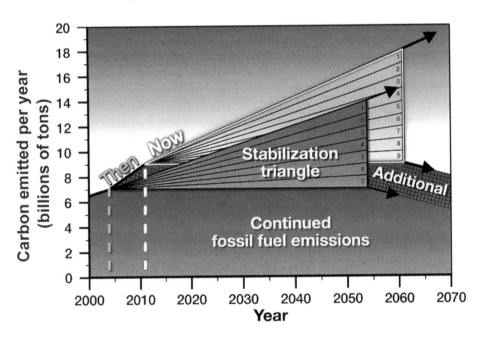

Source: Remik Ziemlinski, the Carbon Mitigation Initiative, Princeton University.

Note
If we had acted in 2004, when the stabilization triangle was first introduced, we would have only needed seven wedges. But in 2011, nine wedges were required to fill the stabilization triangle. The effect is compounding.

Behavioral Change

One critique of the stabilization triangle and its wedges is its focus on technical innovation and its utter lack of attention to questions surrounding human behavior, collective mobilization, and technology adoption. This is where social scientists come into the picture.

Not all strategies to combat climate change are equal, obviously. We know this is true in terms of their emissions impact—a bike, full-sized sedan, and RV (recreational vehicle) are all transportation options with very different carbon footprints. But strategies are also not equal in terms of their likelihood of being adopted.

A group of researchers first developed this idea back in 2009 (Dietz et al. 2009; see also Stern 2017), where they estimated what they call plasticity into their study. This, according to the authors, "introduces a behavioral realism" (Dietz et al. 2009, 18453) into how we think about and compare household strategies to combat climate change. This plasticity represents an assessment of the percentage of current nonadapters who could be enticed to make the behavioral change.

The authors analyzed seventeen types of household activities that rely upon existing technology, are low in cost or bring attractive returns on investment, and do not require appreciable changes to one's lifestyle. They then estimated the potential emissions reduction (PER) in terms of CO_2 after ten years from each action—in other words, the total reduction that would be achieved if every household in the United States adopted it. Table 2.2 shows the seventeen behavioral changes along with their associated PER, behavioral plasticity, adjusted PER after accounting for behavioral plasticity (aka "reasonably achievable emissions reduction," or RAER), and RAER as a percentage of total US household-sector emissions. As illustrated in the table, the four lowest-hanging fruits are (1) the adoption of fuel-efficient vehicles, (2) weatherization, (3) the adoption of high-efficiency appliances, and (4) the use of more efficient home heating and cooling systems. Combined, these four steps are estimated to result in a 12 percent reduction in CO_2 emissions in the United States. The takeaway point: when talking about solutions it does not hurt to be also thinking about ordering them, starting with those most likely to have the biggest impact.

Green Building

In 2017, close to 40 percent of total US energy consumption was consumed by residential and commercial buildings (EIA 2018b). Globally, the building and building construction sectors combined are responsible for 36 percent of energy consumption and nearly 40 percent of total direct and indirect CO_2 emissions (IEA 2019). In light of these figures, any serious attempt to reduce greenhouse gas emissions must include changes to the building sector. Yet buildings are not as flexible as, say, behaviors. Whereas I could conceivably be enticed to drastically change my ways in an attempt to radically reduce my CO_2 footprint, it is often not as easy (or cost-effective in the short term) to turn an old, poorly insulated, leaky building into a paragon of ecoefficiency. Yet, when constructing new build, there is now little excuse not to go green. According to analyses by the Morgan Stanley Institute for Sustainable Investing, the return on investment in energy-efficient features is substantial, lowing the cost of ownership by up to 50 percent (Forbes 2017).

TABLE 2.2 Achievable Carbon Emission Reductions Resulting from Household Actions

BEHAVIORAL CHANGE	PER (MTC)	BEHAVIORAL PLASTICITY (%)	RAER (MTC)	RAER AS PERCENTAGE OF TOTAL US HOUSEHOLD SECTOR EMISSIONS
Weatherization	25.2	90	21.2	3.39
HVAC (central heating, ventilation and air-conditioning systems) and equipment	12.2	80	10.7	1.72
Low-flow showerheads	1.4	80	1.1	0.18
Efficient water heater	6.7	80	5.4	0.86
Appliances	14.7	80	11.7	1.87
Low rolling resistance tires	7.4	80	6.5	1.05
Fuel-efficient vehicle	56.3	50	31.4	5.02
Laundry temperature	0.5	35	0.2	0.04
Water heater temperature	2.9	35	1.0	0.17
Standby electricity	9.2	35	3.2	0.52
Thermostat setbacks	10.1	35	4.5	0.71
Line drying	6.0	35	2.2	0.35
Change HVAC air filers	8.7	30	3.7	0.59
Tune up AC (air conditioner)	3.0	30	1.4	0.22
Routine auto maintenance	8.6	30	4.1	0.66
Driving behavior	24.1	25	7.7	1.23
Carpooling	36.1	15	6.4	1.02
Totals	233	–	123	20

Source: Adapted from Dietz et al. (2009).

Note: PER: potential emissions reduction; RAER: reasonably achievable emissions reduction; MTC: million tonnes of carbon.

Investment managers further estimate that applying existing technology could generate annual savings in office buildings ranging from $32 million in Philadelphia to $239 million in New York City, thus creating $489 million and $4.8 billion of asset value, respectively (Morgan Stanley 2016).

There are still other ways it pays to go green when it comes to our buildings, beyond the obvious saving in energy costs. Green building, to put it bluntly, also makes people happy. In buildings that optimize the use of daylight, students perform better (Earthman 2014), while employees express greater satisfaction and display greater productivity (Leder et al. 2016). As employers, on average, pay 100 times more for people as they do for energy, a "mere" 1 percent increase in productivity would go a long way toward offsetting the costs of green building (Lovins and Cohen 2011, 100).

Our minds tend immediately to go to the ecological benefits of green building—as they should; I'm not suggesting otherwise. But if you are trying to sell the idea to someone who has a habit of only thinking in terms of the bottom-line, as many business people do, then another approach might be in order. After all, increased workforce productivity holds the greatest potential financial benefit of green design—far greater than energy or water savings. To quote David Pogue, Global Director of Corporate Responsibility at CBRE (US Commercial Real Estate Services),

> Generally, utility costs are approximately $2.50 a square foot, and if we reduce energy use by 20%, we've saved 50 cents a foot. A tenant's average rent is around $25 [per sq. ft]. But a tenant can spend as much as $250 a foot for employee costs. If you get a 10% increase in productivity, you have saved their rent.
>
> (quoted in Lockwood 2019, 49)

Taking a step back, let's talk briefly about the urban built environment. Cities are now home to more than half of the world's population. Cities consume about 75 percent of the world's energy and emit between 50 and 60 percent of its total greenhouse gases, though this figure rises to roughly 80 percent when the indirect emissions generated by urban inhabitants are included (United Nations 2015a). If New York worked to reduce its carbon emissions by 30 percent over the next twenty years, the city would see substantial savings from this effort in terms of energy consumed and emissions released into the atmosphere. Perhaps less recognized, however, are benefits to the labor market that would follow as tens of thousands of new jobs would be created to retrofit, caulk, seal, and insulate the city's buildings.

The CDP (formerly Carbon Disclosure Project), in operation since 2000, is a UK-based not-for-profit. CDP's mission, according to its website, is to operate a "global disclosure system for investors, companies, cities, states and regions to manage their environmental impacts" (www.cdp.net/en). Disclosing environmental data through CDP allows these entities to partner with this not-for-profit, receiving in return an evaluation of policy responses, benchmarking of performances against peers, and the highlighting of opportunities for the organization or city. CDP also has a Matchmaker Program, which pairs up cities with investors, enabling ambitious green projects designed to boost resilience in cities around the world. At the time of writing, there are more than 1,000 projects listed by CDP seeking public–private partnerships. Between 2012 and 2018, there was a twenty-fold increase in the number of climate actions from disclosing cities.

Geoengineering

Geoengineering (also known as climate engineering) is a term often used "to describe activities specifically and deliberately designed to effect a change in the global climate with the aim of minimizing or reversing anthropogenic climate change" (House of Commons 2010, 11). In discussions about societal responses to global warming, geoengineering increasingly accompanies mitigation (strategies seeking to reduce our collective greenhouse gas footprint) and adaptation (strategies seeking to make communities, regions, and nations more resilient to the effects of climate change). Methods typically involve either CO_2 removal from the atmosphere or solar-radiation management, whereby the amount of solar energy that penetrates the Earth's atmosphere is reduced (see ECOnnection 2.4). The idea of literally engineering the climate is nothing new, as scientists have been seriously discussing the possibility for well over a decade. What has changed in recent years, however, is that it is no

ECOnnection 2.4

Examples of Geoengineering, Mitigation, and Adaptation

CO₂ REMOVAL (GEOENGINEERING)

Ocean fertilization: Iron filings would be dumped into the ocean to spur phytoplankton blooms that draw CO_2 from the atmosphere, a saltwater version of forestation. Some downsides: we do not know what this would do to ocean life (it could likely have a negative effect), and blooms could release methane—another greenhouse gas.

SOLAR-RADIATION MANAGEMENT (GEOENGINEERING)

Space mirrors: Hundreds of thousands of thin reflective disks fired into low earth orbit could lower the amount of solar energy that enters the Earth's atmosphere. Some downsides: cost aside, the rocket fuel burned to place these little mirrors in orbit would inject massive quantities of black soot into the atmosphere, which would absorb sunlight, trap heat, and thus exacerbate global warming.

MITIGATION

Carbon tax: Impose a tax on carbon emissions, and therefore reward green behavior at both industry and household levels. Some downsides: energy-efficient technologies—from hybrid cars to high-efficiency furnaces—are more likely to be adopted by high-income households, meaning such a tax could fall disproportionately on those least able to afford it.

ADAPTATION

Genetically engineered (GE) food: Crops are currently being engineered to withstand changes to climate (e.g., drought tolerance). Some downsides: the seeds would likely be patented, meaning those most vulnerable—the poor—would likely not have access to these technologies; these plants may require additional inputs like fertilizer, which has its own significant CO_2 footprint that could push the cost of production even higher; and there is always the risk that the crops will cross-breed with conventional or traditional (non-GE) plant varieties.

longer just scientists who are talking about it. A watershed moment occurred in 2006 with an editorial essay by Nobel Prize winning atmospheric scientist Paul Crutzen (2006). In this essay, Crutzen calls for serious consideration of geoengineering. With the idea now out in the open—as evidenced by the very fact that I am mentioning it here—talk of climate engineering has expanded beyond the scientific community, becoming a popular focal point of discussion and sometimes heated debate.

Late in 2010, during its meeting of the **Convention on Biological Diversity** (CBD) in Nagoya, Japan, the United Nations voted to impose a moratorium on geoengineering projects and experiments. (The CBD—an international legally binding treaty that entered into force in 1993—has three main goals: conservation of biological diversity, sustainable use of biological resources, and fair and equitable sharing of the benefits arising from genetic resources.) The moratorium means all signatories to the CBD—a group of nations that, it is worth noting, does not include the United States—must ensure that climate engineering projects do not take place until risks to the environment as well as social, cultural, and economic impacts have been properly assessed. This builds on a United Nations moratorium on ocean fertilization adopted in 2008. As noted, the United States is not a signatory, which was why many were concerned when the prestigious National Academy of Sciences released two studies in February 2015 that assessed the potential impacts, benefits, and costs of two different proposed classes of climate intervention: (1) CO_2 removal and (2) albedo modification (reflecting sunlight). In the words of one such critic, "the report is balanced in its assessment of the science. Yet by bringing geoengineering from the fringes of the climate debate into the mainstream, it legitimizes a dangerous approach" (Hamilton 2015). When it gathered at its Thirteenth Conference of the Parties in Mexico in 2016, the CBD voted to reaffirm the moratorium.

The question arises, then: Does geoengineering really *solve* anything, or do these "solutions" better represent temporary technological Band-Aids? By totally ignoring the root cause(s) of climate change, what's to stop unrestrained emissions from rearing their ugly head again sometime in the future when we can no longer engineer away the warming effects of an atmosphere dense with greenhouse gases? I also worry that these strategies will make us complacent about the impact our actions have on the environment. Geoengineering, it could be argued, merely reinforces the unfounded belief that technology will always ride in at the eleventh hour and save us.

Carbon Markets and Offsets

Cap and trade programs seek to halt (the "cap"), and eventually reduce, greenhouse gas emissions that result from human activity. Cap and trade systems are regulatory programs that cap harmful greenhouse gas emissions by limiting them through a permitting system and distributing the allotted emissions (what are known as allowances, permits, or credits) to different participants, who then trade them. The goal of the "cap" is to prevent further increases in net emissions. Cap and trade systems in principle, therefore, seek absolute rather than just relative emissions efficiency. Those businesses that find it most economical to reduce emissions can do so. The resulting **carbon credits** can then be sold to those who cannot yet modify operations to achieve emission reductions. Being market based, cap and trade schemes have found a receptive global audience, especially in comparison to more top-down approaches that spell out specifically what businesses can and cannot emit. Under cap and trade, companies still have a choice to pollute at higher levels. But to do so they will need to purchase allowances. Polluters therefore have an incentive to eventually clean up their acts.

Let's say, for example, that for a given year Company X has ten carbon allowances, representing 1,000 metric tons of greenhouse gas. Yet, thanks to recently adopting certain greener technologies, they are able to reduce their annual greenhouse gas emissions to 700 metric tons. This company will therefore have three emissions allowances, representing 300 metric tons of greenhouse gas, which it can sell on the market.

The **Kyoto Protocol**—a UN treaty signed in 1997 that requires its signatories to reduce greenhouse gas emissions—is perhaps the most famous cap and trade scheme. But it's not the only one. Although refusing to sign up to Kyoto, the United States does house examples of successful cap and trade programs, as individuals, companies, and states are voluntarily making agreements to reduce emissions or purchase credits (or both) from others who have done so successfully. One example is the Regional Greenhouse Gas Initiative (RGGI). According to RGGI's website, this initiative "is a cooperative effort among the states of Connecticut, Delaware, Maine, Maryland, Massachusetts, New Hampshire, New York, Rhode Island, and Vermont to cap and reduce CO_2 emissions from the power sector" (www.rggi.org). But like all cap and trade schemes, RGGI's journey has not been free of controversy. Take the 2011 announcement, by then governor Chris Christie, that New Jersey will be leaving the RGGI. According to Governor Christie, "RGGI does nothing more than tax electricity, tax our citizens, tax our businesses—with no discernible or measurable impact on our environment" (quoted in Newman 2011). For others, cap and trade programs like the RGGI don't go far enough. The argument goes something like this: we can't fix a problem using the same business-as-usual, market-driven mentality that caused global warming in the first place.

Something must be working, given that the RGGI states agreed in August 2017 to a new round of carbon pollution cuts through 2030. Moreover, New Jersey and Virginia are in the process of joining the RGGI market. In 2012–2013, its pollution cap was 165 million allowances per year. In 2017, that cap was 84,344,203 (1 allowance equals 1 short ton of CO_2). The cap is slated to be reduced even more by 2020—78,175,215 units. Other benefits include new jobs. RGGI has created more than 45,000 jobs since its launch and added $4.3 billion in economic value to the region. Meanwhile, energy efficiency measures and cost-saving renewable energy projects saved consumers roughly $800 million (eventually saving $6.98 billion over the lifetime of these measures) (Hibbard et al. 2018). During RGGI's first eight years, electricity prices in the region fell by 6.4 percent as prices rose by an average of 6.2 percent in other states (Stutt et al. 2017).

Different from cap and trade, though still a market approach to climate change mitigation, **carbon offsets** are also gaining in popularity. Carbon offsetting is just as it sounds: individuals and organizations buy carbon credits to offset some of their own carbon footprint (see ECOnnection 2.5). One popular offset organization is Carbonfund, a not-for-profit organization based in Silver Spring, Maryland, that provides carbon offsetting options to individuals, businesses, and organizations. Clicking on the "carbon calculator" on its website, I find that I can offset the one-year carbon footprint of my four-person household by paying Carbonfund $214.33. (Interestingly, four years earlier, when writing the second edition of this book, the total was $222.16. The cost of offsetting has gone *down*.) Carbonfund claims to allow consumers to live a "carbon-neutral" lifestyle, or even a carbon-*negative* lifestyle if one purchased sufficient offsets.

ECOnnection 2.5
Biochar

The standard approach to removing carbon from the atmosphere is to grow plants (typically trees) that sequester CO_2 in their biomass or in soil. **Sequestering CO_2**—the act of removing CO_2 from the atmosphere and holding it in a sink—through reforestation is in fact one of the more popular ways to offset carbon emissions. This sequestration can be taken a step further by heating the plant biomass without oxygen, producing biomass derived charcoal, or **biochar**. Biochar is another name for charcoal derived from a thermochemical decomposition of organic material at heightened temperatures in the absence of oxygen. In some places, it has long been used to improve soil fertility and sequester carbon. Biochar oil and gas by-products can also be used as biofuels.

Fossil fuels are known as carbon positive, which is to say they add more carbon to the atmosphere. Sequestering carbon through typical biomass systems is, over the long term, largely carbon neutral, as much of the carbon captured will eventually be returned to the atmosphere when plants are burned for energy or through the inevitable process of decomposition. Biochar systems, however, can be carbon *negative* because they retain a substantial portion of the carbon fixed by plants. The precise length of time that the carbon remains locked up in biochar is still under debate, with claims ranging from millennia to "only" centuries. Calculations indicate that emissions reductions can be greater than 90 percent if biochar is put back into the soil instead of being burned to offset fossil fuel use; burning, of course, would release some of the sequestered carbon into the atmosphere (Verheijen et al. 2013). Mixing it into the soil also reduces the need for fertilizer, leading to reduced emissions from fertilizer production, while increasing soil microbial life, which in turn leads to still greater carbon storage capacity in the soil.

Carbon offsets have also had a mixed reception. On its face, sequestering (also referred to as *retiring*) carbon from the carbon cycle—that is, fixing it out of the atmosphere and storing it for long periods of time—seems an admirable goal. Yet rarely do carbon offsets challenge the underlying factors responsible for climate change. In fact, many contend they have just the opposite effect, by providing "moral cover" for consumers of fossil fuels (Bachram 2004). Irrespective of their claims of actually retiring carbon, carbon offsets also raise serious social justice issues. For example, corporations from industrialized countries are enclosing land areas in less developed nations and forcibly evicting local residents. The Oakland Institute (2017) has released a report titled "Carbon Colonialism" that details injustices against a region in Uganda by Norwegian plantation forestry and carbon offset company, Green Resources. Given residents' high reliance upon land for subsistence food production and grazing—the loss of access to firewood is also important as wood is the major energy source for these communities—the loss of land due to the forestry project presents acute challenges for local communities. Unfortunately, residents of African nations have faced injustices like this more than once (see, for example, Leach and Scoones 2015).

IMPORTANT CONCEPTS

- adaptation and mitigation
- climate change refugees
- costs of action versus inaction
- human-induced climate change
- stabilization triangle
- vulnerable populations

DISCUSSION QUESTIONS

1. Why do some Americans continue to deny the existence of anthropogenic climate change? (This question is investigated further in Chapter 13.)
2. What are your thoughts on geoengineering? Can we effectively engineer ourselves out of this mess and thus avoid making any substantial changes to the status quo?
3. How is climate change a social justice issue?
4. What are some of the more pronounced impacts of climate change for those in low-income countries? And for those residing in high-income countries?

SUGGESTED ADDITIONAL READINGS

Brulle, R.J. 2018. "The Climate Lobby: A Sectoral Analysis of Lobbying Spending on Climate Change in the USA, 2000 to 2016." *Climatic Change*, 149(3–4): 289–303.

Norgaard, K. 2018. "The Sociological Imagination in a Time of Climate Change." *Global and Planetary Change*, 163: 171–176.

Tagg, N., and T. Jafry. 2018. "Engaging Young Children with Climate Change and Climate Justice." *Research for All*, 2(1): 34–42.

RELEVANT INTERNET LINKS

- www.noaa.gov/education/resource-collections/climate-education-resources. Resource on climate change provide by the National Oceanic and Atmospheric Administration (NOAA). Be sure to check out the tabs on the left side of the screen.
- http://climate.nasa.gov/resources/education. Listings of student and educator resources related to global climate change, including NASA products.
- www.nature.org/greenliving/carboncalculator/index.htm. Calculate your carbon footprint.
- www.skepticalscience.com. Excellent resource for debunking climate change skeptics.
- www.skepticalscience.com/. A great resource for rebutting climate science misinformation.

SUGGESTED VIDEOS

- *Before the Flood* (2016). Arguably the highest-profile environmental film since Al Gore's *An Inconvenient Truth*, the film provides a straightforward survey of the science on climate change along with constructive suggestions on how to reduce the impacts.

- *Climate Refugees* (2010). Investigates the global mass migrations caused by climate change. An older documentary but still timely.
- *Meet the Climate Sceptics* (2011). A journey into the heart of climate skepticism to examine the key arguments against human-made global warming and to try to understand the people who are making them.
- *Our Rising Oceans* (2015). Investigates the science behind climate change and the doubters that remain, even when faced with seemingly indisputable evidence.
- *Sun Come Up* (2011). Academy Award nominated film that follows the relocation of the Carteret Islanders, who live on a remote island chain in the South Pacific Ocean—some of the world's first climate change refugees.
- *This Changes Everything* (2015). A look at seven communities around the world that are trying to change our economic system into something better.
- *True North* (2018). Travel alongside scientists, cartographers, and others in the remote Arctic and learn how climate change is affecting local populations and ecosystems.
- *Years of Living Dangerously* (2014). A nine-part documentary concentrating on climate alteration. James Cameron, Jerry Weintraub, and Arnold Schwarzenegger are executive producers. The episodes promote celebrity "detectives" who travel to regions around the world hit by global warming to consult professionals and ordinary people about the effects of climate change.

Waste: Our Sinks Are Almost Sunk

The trash can is a remarkable artifact, sociologically speaking. To begin with, it's the "rabbit hole"—to draw momentarily on one of my daughter's favorite stories (*Alice in Wonderland*)—into the postconsumer world we all know exists but that few from the middle class and above have actually experienced. Whether the rubbish cans in your

IMAGE 3.1 Garbage Burning at East Broadway and Gouverneur Street, New York City, 1907

Source: Library of Congress.

classroom, the Dumpster next to your friend's apartment complex, or the sixty-gallon waste bin in the alley behind your parents' house: stuff goes in, and … that's just it; it goes in and then "poof"—gone!

We moderns really want our waste to just disappear. The trash can, toilet, and kitchen sink are all designed to get our waste out of sight almost as quickly as we're able to generate it. Of course, it wasn't always this way. For our ancestors, there was no hidden world when it came to waste. As recently as a century ago, waste for many of the world's urban dwellers was largely a household issue. As evidenced in Image 3.1, which shows a New York sanitation worker in 1907 disposing of municipal waste by burning it right on the street, it wasn't until well into the twentieth century that the **municipal solid waste** (MSW) rabbit hole as we know it today started to take shape. (MSW, generally speaking, refers to all solid waste originating from homes, industries, businesses, demolition, land clearing, and construction.)

Yet the rabbit hole is filling up (see Case Study 3.1). This is a problem. And like all environmental problems, there are multiple entry points into the subject. Importantly, I do not see waste as just a problem of *management*. If "merely" a management issue, the problem of waste would disappear once we figured out how to utilize resources more efficiently during the production process and improve our disposal techniques. I don't buy that it's just a management issue, for reasons discussed shortly.

Fast Facts

- MSW consists of items like product packaging, grass clippings, furniture, clothing, bottles, food scraps, newspapers, appliances, and batteries. Not included in this category are materials that may also end up in **landfills**, such as construction and demolition materials, municipal wastewater treatment sludge, and nonhazardous industrial wastes. In 2018, the world generated 242 million tons of plastic waste—12 percent of all municipal solid waste. Meanwhile, an estimated 1.6 billion tons of CO_2-equivalent greenhouse gas emissions were generated from solid waste management, which represented about 5 percent of global emissions (World Bank Group 2018; see Table 3.1).
- Controlled landfills, serviced by a waste infrastructure (e.g., garbage trucks), are almost exclusively the domain of high- and upper-middle-income countries. Lower-income countries generally rely on open dumping—just as it sounds, waste is dumped wherever. Upper-middle-income countries generally have the highest percentage of waste in landfills. As countries become more affluent, more investments are made to divert waste for recycling and compost (World Bank Group 2018).
- MSW management varies widely by country. Germany, for instance, imposed a ban on traditional landfills in 2005. This country of eighty-three million inhabitants operates with fewer than 300 landfills, and the only thing they accept is waste after recycling and incinerating. (By comparison, Canada has a population of thirty-four million and more than 10,000 landfills.) In 2001, Germany recycled about 48 percent of its municipal waste, approximately 25 percent was landfilled, and 22 percent was incinerated. In 2010, the level of recycling had increased to 62 percent, landfilling was practically 0 percent, and incineration had increased to 37 percent (EEA 2013). By 2016, Germany was recycling 65 percent, the highest rate of any country. South Korea came in second, at 59 percent. The United States recycled 35 percent, which was only slightly above the average for a

developed country. At the other extreme is Turkey, which landfills 99 percent of its MSW (Eddy 2016).

- The average nuclear power plant generates approximately twenty metric tons of used nuclear fuel annually. Worldwide, the nuclear industry produces a total of about 8,800 metric tons of used fuel per year. If all the world's used fuel assemblies were stacked end to end and side by side, they would cover a football field roughly a yard deep. (Depending on reactor type, a fuel assembly may contain up to 264 fuel rods and have dimensions of five to nine inches square by about twelve feet long.)

- An analysis published in 2018 reports that US consumers wasted 422 grams (0.93 pounds) of food per person daily. Higher quality diets were associated with greater amounts of food waste and greater amounts of wasted irrigation water and pesticides. This was due to the more perishable nature of fruits and vegetables, which are health-promoting and require small amounts of cropland yet also require substantial amounts of agricultural inputs (Conrad et al. 2018). On the whole, Americans consume about 54 percent of the foods produced by our food system (Heller and Keoleian 2015; see Figure 3.1).

- In 2018, the world's internet users surpassed the four billion mark, considering also that many of those users access the internet via multiple electronic devices—in my house alone we have three smart phones, two iPads, and four computers! In short, there are a lot of mobile devices, tablets, and computers currently in use around the world. Yet as the average life expectancy of a computer is between three and four years, and even less for a mobile phone, we are talking about possibly billions of gadgets annually destined for the landfill.

- Waste has multiple links to climate change. First, everything we discard is **embodied energy** and thus contains already-emitted greenhouse gases. (Embodied energy refers to the sum total of the energy utilized throughout an entire product life cycle.) When we discard, say, a chair or an uneaten apple, we are therefore wasting more than just a chair or an apple but everything that went into making and transporting that object. Landfilling,

FIGURE 3.1 Food and Food Loss Flows in the United States

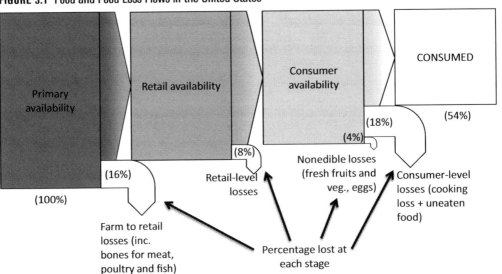

Source: Adapted from Heller and Keoleian (2015).

the most common waste-management practice, also contributes to climate change. The trucks used to haul waste to landfills emit greenhouse gases (though the same can be said for vehicles that haul material for recycling). Landfills also release significant quantities of methane (CH_4) into the atmosphere from the **anaerobic decomposition** (the breaking down of biodegradable material by microorganisms in an oxygen-free environment) of organic materials—a process known as fermentation. (And CH_4 is twenty-one times more potent at trapping heat in the atmosphere than CO_2.) Landfills are the third-largest human source of CH_4 emissions in the United States. Encouragingly, this "landfill methane" is beginning to be harnessed in some countries for energy generation—what's known as biogas production. Landfills also act as carbon sinks. Lacking oxygen, organisms that feed on waste and respire CO_2 are not present a few meters below a landfill's surface. Items such as grass clippings, then, which drew in carbon from the atmosphere to grow, will have their carbon sequestered when buried in a landfill. The carbon sequestering potential of landfills, however, does not offset its methane emissions (EPA 2019).

Implications

The very concept of waste is a social construction. There is no waste in the so-called natural world; everything released, emitted, secreted, and discarded is *food* for something else. *Waste* refers to what we (read: humans) have no use for. In his book *Rubbish Theory*, Thompson (1979) points out the fluidity of the term *rubbish*. Even something once deemed "waste" can regain societal value. Take *scrap*, a term that reclassifies objects of

TABLE 3.1 Solid Waste Generation (in Metric Tons) by Region and Globally, Selected Years

REGION	1972	1980	1990	2009	2018
East Asia	25	45	100	170	368
Europe	150	125	170	202	392
Latin America	35	50	72	110	231
Middle East	5	25	45	75	90
North Africa	2	5	20	25	31
North America	110	125	165	243	289
Pacific Rim	40	50	52	74	100
Sub-Sahara	5	10	20	50	174
Southeast Asia	10	17	28	52	334
World	400	500	660	1,001	2,009

Source: Adapted from Defra (2011), EEA (2013), and World Bank Group (2018).

CASE STUDY 3.1
The Great Pacific Garbage Patch

"It's a giant trash island, as big as Texas!": I frequently hear this about the massive floating field of waste trapped by the North Pacific Gyre. (The North Pacific Gyre, located in the northern Pacific Ocean, is one of five major oceanic gyres, which are large systems of rotating ocean currents caused by the Coriolis Effect.) This is where a lot of the renegade plastic goes after having escaped the municipal waste stream. When people hear that plastic hangs around for hundreds of years, they assume that means in its present form. After all, plastic is not biodegradable. But plastic does break down—which is part of the problem. Rather than being consumed by microorganisms and transformed into compounds found in nature, plastic is broken down into ever smaller pieces as sunlight photodegrades the bonds in its polymers. Plastic never goes away. The pieces just break down and thus multiply in number, making it easier for plastic to find a pathway into organisms and the food chain. And that is precisely what is happening. Plastic pieces now outweigh surface zooplankton in the Great Pacific Garbage Patch by a factor of six to one.

Further compounding matters is the fact that plastics take even longer to break down in seawater than on land, as cool sea-water and ultraviolet-ray-blocking seaweed act as preservatives. Thus, except for what is picked up manually during sea-cleaning expeditions, every piece of plastic to find its way into the ocean over the last half century is still there. And it's not confined to the North Pacific Gyre. According to recent estimates, there are 5.25 trillion pieces of plastic debris in the world's oceans. Approximately one-quarter of a million tons float on the surface, leaving some four billion pieces per square kilometer littering the deep sea (Parker 2015).

waste as having real economic (and thus societal) value. *Collector's item* is another term that varies considerably over time and can rescue an object from being identified as trash.

Pollution is another interesting term, referring to a specific type of waste. Pollution is, quite simply, matter that is out of place. Or, to be still more specific, it refers to waste that is out of place. A while back, I examined societal understandings of odor pollution as they related to large-scale hog farms in Iowa (Carolan 2008c). To do this, I interviewed people working in and living near hog confined animal-feeding operations. One thing I found was that the odors emanating from these facilities were not in and of themselves defined as "pollution" by those I spoke to. Only when "out of place" were the odors classified as such. Thus, for example, no one said the inside of the highly odorous hog facilities was "polluted," as everyone expected the place to smell terrible. There the odors were "in place." Conversely, when *those same odors* were detected in a neighbor's kitchen while eating breakfast, they were classified as pollution, where they were viewed as clearly out of place. Extending this thinking, we tend not to see a landfill as polluted, as the space by definition is meant to be filled with trash. The same holds for, say, sewage treatment plants, even though they are spaces where human excrement concentrates. Yet take those same artifacts—trash and human fecal matter—and put them where they are out of place, and presto: pollution! There are, in short, many ways to talk about waste sociologically. Rather than aim to be comprehensive, the goal of this section is to give the reader a sense of this diversity.

Energy Waste and the Life-Cycle Analysis

Traditional approaches to environmental impacts have tended to focus on a single business or link in the **commodity chain** (a term that refers to the collective networks encompassing the beginning and end of a product's life cycle) and on one or two pollutants. Doing this, however, can lead to **footprint shifting**, where ecological efficiencies might be achieved at one stage of a product's life cycle only to increase environmental impacts in another. Examining the entire life cycle of a product also allows hotspots—links where impacts are high and where reductions can be achieved at minimal cost and effort—to be identified. The life-cycle analysis (LCA) is a useful tool when attempting to assess overall ecological footprints of practices, like landfilling and recycling, and competing commodities, such as disposable versus reusable coffee cups. By doing this, though, much to the chagrin of my students, we frequently learn that what's best from the perspective of environmental sustainability is rarely black and white.

Take the disposable-paper versus reusable-ceramic versus disposable-foam coffee cup debate. The winner is obvious: the reusable ceramic coffee cup, right? It depends. In fact, under certain circumstances, either disposable cup may well be the "greener" choice (at least in terms of energy consumption) over the ceramic mug. Confused? Let me explain.

Everything, obviously, takes energy and resources to be made. Reusable cups, as they have to be made to be reusable (and thus withstand the abuses of dishwashing, drying, and so on), consume more energy than disposable varieties when being produced—quite a bit more, in fact. The average ceramic mug requires, at least according to one often-cited LCA (Institute for Lifecycle Energy Analysis 2002), 25.5 times more energy to make than the average paper cup—14 megajoules (MJ) versus 0.55 MJ per cup. The embedded energy disparity is even greater with foam cups, 14 MJ compared to 0.20 MJ per cup—a difference of 700 percent. Does that therefore mean it takes roughly twenty-six use cycles for the ceramic mug to reach its break-even point with the paper cup and 700 use cycles before it matches the embedded energy of a foam mug? Not quite. Remember, those reusable ceramic mugs need to be washed.

This is where the calculations get a little more uncertain, as washing techniques and frequencies vary considerably from case to case. Dishwashers generally require less energy than hand washing, as the newest models are made to make particularly efficient use of hot water, and hot water usage is the most energy-intensive part of washing dishes. Moreover, not all households run their dishwasher using the "hot water" or "high temperature" setting. The same, however, cannot be said of commercial settings. Industrial-grade dishwashers (like those found at Starbucks) always use hot water to guarantee their dishes and mugs are fully sanitized. Factoring in for dishwashing after each ceramic mug use, its actual break-even point was calculated at thirty-nine uses when compared to the paper cup and 1,006 uses when compared to the foam cup (see Figure 3.2).

There are a couple of take-home points to be derived from such analyses. First, if we choose to go with a reusable mug, we had better make sure we are going to reuse it. I know someone, for example, who buys a new ceramic mug monthly. From an energy conservation standpoint, that's a bad move. Similarly, we need to ask whether the setting will allow a reusable ceramic mug to survive for a couple dozen (or 1,006!) uses. Friends who work in coffee shops have confirmed my suspicions: ceramic mugs do not stand up nearly

FIGURE 3.2 Uses of Ceramic Cup to Reach Energy Breakeven Point Relative to Alternatives

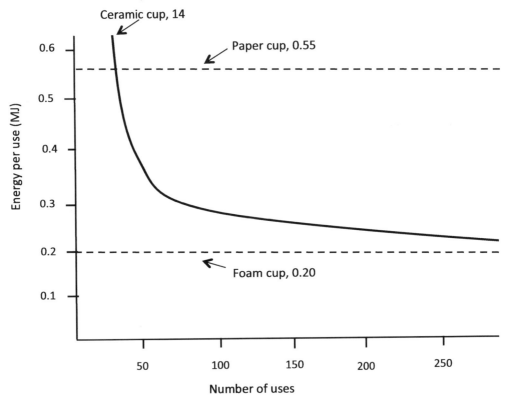

Source: Adapted from Institute for Lifecycle Energy Analysis (2002).

Note
Ceramic cups require on average 14 megajoules (MJ) to produce (and additional energy to clean after every use). For paper and foam cups those figures are 0.55 and 0.20 MJ, respectively. Recognizing this, it is important to maximize reuse of a ceramic cup before disposing it for a new one. Those prone to losing or breaking reusable mugs might want to rethink how they transport coffee.

as well in commercial applications as they do at home, where they tend to be better cared for. If a ceramic mug at your local coffee shop survives, say, only twenty use cycles, you might be better off, from an energy-saving perspective, never using them. There are also clear energy (not to mention water) savings if we can avoid washing our reusable mugs after each use. Or, if you really want to cut energy waste, try reusing disposable paper cups.

That's just energy use. Air pollution and landfill impacts tell a somewhat different story. Clearly, while 1,006 foam coffee cups might be "equal," in terms of energy consumed, to 1,006 ceramic-mug use cycles, those foam cups will have a significantly greater landfill footprint than a single ceramic mug used 1,006 times. That's what I meant earlier when I said LCAs rarely cast the world in black-and-white terms. We have to ultimately choose for ourselves what to value (see Ethical Question 3.1). What's worse: landfill impacts, air pollution, water consumption, energy use …?

ETHICAL QUESTION 3.1

What Ought to Be Most Valued?

LCAs show that being an informed, green consumer is less about being able to choose between "good" and "evil" products than it is about choosing between, say, the lesser of two (or three, four, or more) evils. All products come with some environmental footprint. And if it comes down to deciding between affecting, for instance, water, air, soil, or energy resources, the consumer must somehow rank these resources when deciding which product ought to be purchased. Then there are all the other *social* variables missed in LCAs, which insert into the equation an even more diverse array of ethical questions. For example, when striving for both social justice and ecological sustainability, should we select bananas grown by smaller farmers in cooperatives in the Caribbean or those grown on plantations in Central America but by unionized and politically empowered workers? Should we place ecological concerns above social ones when forced to privilege one set of concerns over others, which is something we often have to do as consumers? If you're having a problem answering these questions, you should. That's my point.

Recycling

Judging by increasing recycling rates around the world, the practice of recycling appears to be catching on. Nevertheless, these rates continue to vary tremendously across regions as well as within countries. And, interestingly, a nation's level of affluence seems at best marginally correlated with recycling levels. San Francisco and Adelaide, Australia, for example, each report recycling rates of around 80 percent. The average for Dutch cities is 50 percent, whereas in Houston only 6 percent of the city's MSW is recycled (the recycling rate in Texas is only 22 percent, well below the 34 percent national average).

LCAs have been very helpful in providing empirical support to what most environmentalists have been saying for decades: that recycling, to put it plainly, is good for the environment. These LCAs calculate the energy consumed from the moment the recycling trucks stop at your place of residence until this "waste" is processed into brand-new products. This figure is then compared with the amount of energy required to send the same goods to landfills or incinerators and to make new consumer goods from scratch. We find, for example, that aluminium requires 96 percent less energy when made from recycled cans than when processed using bauxite. Recycled plastic bottles use 76 percent less energy, newsprint about 45 percent less, and recycled glass about 21 percent less than when processed from raw (unrecycled) materials. Across the board, recycled goods come out on top, as the energy used to extract and process raw materials is an order of magnitude higher than what is used to recover the same material through recycling (Brogaard et al. 2014; Corcelli et al. 2018).

An additional point to bear in mind when assessing the economics of recycling: the revenue generated from recycling need not actually surpass its costs to be a good investment for a city. This might at first sound counterintuitive—after all, how could a money-losing venture be a good investment? You must keep in mind that landfilling costs money too. Let's say it costs $175 a ton to collect and process mixed recyclables—a figure not too far off from what a lot of US cities pay. Let's further suppose that those recyclables can be sold on the open market for $120 a ton, which represents still another sensible assumption. This does not necessarily mean, however, that recycling is a money loser. What matters is the cost of taking that material to a landfill. If it is more than $50 a ton, then a recycling program is still a good investment. Looking toward the future, the price of mixed recyclables is expected to climb. This will be due, in large part, to the rising cost of energy, which is increasing the price of raw materials, and recognizing that the extraction and processing of these materials is energy intensive. Another variable driving up the price of recyclables is the growing demand for consumer goods in places like China, though the recent economic slump in that country has dampened this a bit. Nevertheless, more municipalities ought to find value in recycling (see Case Study 3.2).

Yet at what—or more specifically, *whose*—expense? That is a question asked by those not yet ready to embrace recycling unconditionally. A body of compelling evidence indicates that, in some instances at least, the ecological gains of recycling may come at the expense of social justice (Amuzu 2018). To enhance efficiencies, a number of cities mix rubbish with recyclables during pickup. The rationale: to cut expenses by eliminating what are perceived as unnecessary redundancies—like two trucks making separate trips to each house—when handling MSW. The contents of each garbage and recycling truck are then sorted. This is bringing workers—those responsible for manually sorting through everything set out for residential pickup—into closer contact with environmental hazards, such as **biohazards** (environmental threats resulting from biological agents or conditions, like used needles) and other toxic substances (United Nations 2010; Yuwono and Ersa 2018).

Once separated, recycled waste itself can be hazardous. Plastic waste, for instance, often contains residues from its original contents, like toxic cleaners, pesticides, and herbicides. And in recycling operations in less affluent nations especially, workers may not be given protective clothing to safeguard against exposure to these potentially toxic chemicals. Yet the problems are not limited to the developing world. Tens of millions of pounds of electronic waste (televisions, computers, and the like) in the United States get funneled annually into its prison system for recycling. The prisoners break the components down (which, according to some reports, involves smashing with hammers) and then pack them up for shipment to processors (Conrad 2011). The organization responsible for overseeing this program, Federal Prison Industries (a government-owned corporation created in 1934 that produces goods and services from the labor of inmates), was the focus of a four-year US Justice Department investigation for exposing prisoners to unnecessary health risks. The findings of that investigation were released in 2010, noting that inmates and employees at ten federal prisons were exposed to toxic metals and other hazardous substances while processing electronic waste for recycling (Kauman 2010). Environmental justice scholars have, in recent years, noted how the prison and jail systems in countries such as the United States produce and exacerbate public and environmental health risks for inmates and communities surrounding prisons (e.g., Pellow 2017), for reasons exemplified by the above Justice Department investigation.

CASE STUDY 3.2
The Close Loop Fund and Recent Recycling Trends

Consumers and stockholders are asking companies to do more to reduce waste, and those businesses, in turn, are responding by promising to use more recycled materials in their products. But there's a problem: not enough high-grade recycled material exists to meet their needs. Coca-Cola, for example, pledged to use at least 25 percent recycled plastic in its containers by 2015 but has since revised that percentage downward because of a lack of supply. Walmart is also having a hard time sourcing sufficient material to meet its goal to use three billion pounds of recycled plastic in its packaging and products by 2020 (E.B. 2015). As a result, companies—including Walmart, Coca-Cola, Kuerig, Johnson & Johnson, PepsiCo, and Goldman Sachs—have aligned with the Close Loop Fund, a multi-stakeholder program that looks to invest $100 million in recycling programs. The fund offers zero-interest loans to municipalities so that they can develop new recycling programs. It will also provide below-market loans to private companies so they can develop new local recycling infrastructures (Kaye 2015).

Let's leave aside the fact that analysts estimate that $1.25 billion is needed to fully modernize America's recycling infrastructure (E.B. 2015). As the old saying goes, "junk in, junk out." When municipalities, in an attempt to make recycling easier, began moving toward single-stream (also known as "fully commingled") recycling, they began seeing their streams contaminated with residue at greater rates. The problem has only increased since cities began increasing the size of their bins, assuming bigger was better for keeping material from landfills. Consumers have been using those bigger bins, but often in ways that *increase* the waste going to landfills thanks to that aforementioned contamination. *What* we consume has also changed since recycling plants were built ten to fifteen years ago. Back then, newspaper, thick plastic bottles, and aluminium were king. Now newspapers have all but disappeared, plastic bottles have gotten thinner to cut down on transportation costs, and aluminium cans have been replaced with vacuum-packed plastic with little recycling value (Davis 2015).

Let's go back for a moment to the ecological gains associated with recycling. While proponents of recycling proudly tout the practice as green, the more critically minded should be asking in response, "Relative to what?" The empirical evidence is indisputable: recycling is clearly a win for the environment relative to landfilling (at least when recycling streams are not contaminated and the materials actually get recycled). But what if we were comparing recycling to the act of not consuming the item in the first place? Recycling is a big ecological loser in this head-to-head comparison. Remember the so-called "three Rs" of environmentalism: reduce, reuse, and recycle. Recycling is last in this hierarchy for good reason (see ECOnnection 3.1).

Food Waste

A study by the FAO reports that 33 percent of all food produced for human consumption is lost or wasted globally. That constitutes roughly 1.2 billion metric tons of food annually (Gustavsson et al. 2011). A 2013 study by the Institution of Mechanical Engineers paints

ECOnnection 3.1

The Recycling Loophole

Technically speaking, the recycling symbol (and accompanying number) only identifies the plastic resin used in making the article in question, never mind that the chasing arrows that prominently envelope the resin code are the internationally recognized symbol used to designate recyclable materials. The recycling rates of each resin code vary greatly from one recycling facility to another (see Table 3.2). And even when a facility is capable of recycling a particular resin, a whole host of other variables enter into the picture that could cause it to still be landfilled.

The following recycling rates represent averages for the United States as a whole:

- number 1 plastic, also known as polyethylene terephthalate (PET or PETE), the resin most likely to be recycled—recycling rate 13 percent
- number 2, high density polyethylene (HDPE)—recycling rate 8 percent
- number 3, polyvinyl chloride (PVC)—recycling rate less than 1 percent
- number 4, low density polyethylene (LDPE)—recycling rate 6 percent
- number 5, polypropylene (PP)—recycling rate less than 1 percent

- number 6, polystyrene (PS)—recycling rate less than 1 percent
- number 7, the enigmatic category simply called "other"—US average recycling rate of 7.5 percent.

Recycling facilities are also in the business—lest we forget they are businesses too—of making money. And they are paid by the quality of the bales they produce. Not surprisingly, the less contaminated bales are typically worth more. Recycling facilities therefore tend to focus on those plastics sure to capture a price premium: namely, clear narrow-neck (e.g., soda and water) bottles made with PET/PETE (aka number 1 plastic). Since it is relatively easy to spot bales composed of alternative-shaped plastic objects, many facilities ignore those containers entirely so as not to risk obtaining a lower market price, even those made with PET/PETE. The risk for buyers is twofold: odd-shaped containers have a higher likelihood of not only being made of an alternative resin, which cannot be easily recycled, but also of being contaminated. Ever wonder how that empty laundry detergent container gets clean enough to have its resin reclaimed? The answer is simple: it doesn't.

an even more depressing picture, estimating that as much as two billion metric tons of food are wasted annually (Fox 2013). The House of Lords in the United Kingdom conducted a study looking at the cost of food waste across the European Union. It concluded that an estimated eighty-nine metric tons of food are wasted every year in the European Union and projected that figure to rise to around 126 metric tons by 2020 if no action is taken (House of Lords 2014). In light of these trends, in 2015 France's parliament announced measures to reduce food waste: it passed legislation banning supermarkets from landfilling unsold food and requiring them to pass the food on to charities or put it to other uses, such as using it for animal feed (Chrisafis 2015). But according to the House of Lords (2014) study, the future of food waste lies in the hands of households, as its report estimates that 42 percent of all food wasted (by weight) occurs in the home

TABLE 3.2 Plastic Packaging Resins

RESIN CODES	DESCRIPTION	PRODUCT APPLICATIONS	PRODUCTS THAT COULD BE MADE WITH RECYCLED CONTENT
1	Polyethylene Terephthalate (PET/PETE)	Plastic bottles for soft drinks, water, juice, sports drinks, beer, mouthwash, catsup, and salad dressing. Food jars for peanut butter, jelly, jam, and pickles. Microwavable food trays.	Fiber for carpet, fleece jackets, comforter fill, and tote bags. Containers for food, beverages (bottles), and non-food items.
2	High Density Polyethylene (HDPE)	Bottles for milk, water, juice, cosmetics, shampoo, dish and laundry detergents, and household cleaners. Bags for groceries and retail purchases. Cereal box liners.	Bottles for non-food items, such as shampoo, conditioner, liquid laundry detergent, household cleaners, motor oil and antifreeze. Plastic lumber for outdoor decking, fencing and picnic tables. Pipe, floor tiles, buckets, crates, flower pots, garden edging, film and sheet, and recycling bins.
3	Polyvinyl Chloride (PVC)	Rigid packaging applications include blister packs and clamshells. Rigid applications such as pipe, siding, window frames, fencing, decking and railing. Flexible applications include medical products such as blood bags and medical tubing, wire and cable insulation, carpet backing, and flooring.	Pipe, decking, fencing, paneling, gutters, carpet backing, floor tiles and mats, resilient flooring, mud flaps, cassette trays, electrical boxes, cables, traffic cones, garden hose, and mobile home skirting. Packaging, film and sheet, and loose-leaf binders.
4	Low Density Polyethylene (LDPE)	Bags for dry cleaning, newspapers, bread, frozen foods, fresh produce, and household garbage. Shrink wrap and stretch film. Coatings for paper milk cartons and hot and cold beverage cups. Container lids. Toys. Squeezable bottles (e.g., honey and mustard).	Shipping envelopes, garbage can liners, floor tiles, paneling, furniture, film and sheet, compost bins, trash cans, landscape timber, and outdoor lumber.

continued

RESIN CODES	DESCRIPTION	PRODUCT APPLICATIONS	PRODUCTS THAT COULD BE MADE WITH RECYCLED CONTENT
5	Polypropylene (PP)	Containers for yogurt, margarine, takeout meals, and deli foods. Medicine bottles. Bottles for catsup and syrup.	Automobile applications, such as battery cases, signal lights, battery cables, brooms and brushes, ice scrapers, oil funnels, and bicycle racks. Garden rakes, storage bins, shipping pallets, sheeting, trays.
6	Polystyrene (PS)	Food service items such as cups, plates, bowls, cutlery, hinged takeout containers (clamshells), meat and poultry trays, and rigid food containers (e.g., yogurt). Protective foam packaging for furniture, electronics and other delicate items. Compact disc cases and aspirin bottles.	Thermal insulation, thermometers, light switch plates, vents, desk trays, rulers, and license plate frames. Cameras or video cassette casings.
7	Other	3 and 5 gallon reusable water bottles, citrus juice and catsup bottles. Oven-baking bags, barrier layers, and custom packaging.	Containers and plastic lumber.

Source: Adapted from the American Chemistry Council (http://plastics.americanchemistry.com/Plastic-Resin-Codes-PDF).

(while 39 percent is in food/drink manufacturing, 14 percent food in service/hospitality, and 5 percent in retail/wholesale). As a percentage of their total food, lower-income countries do not fare much better in terms of wasting food. What varies is *where* in the food system losses occur. As illustrated in Figure 3.3, whereas high-income regions incur considerable losses at the consumer end, most of the food lost in lower-income regions occurs prior to its arrival in people's homes.

One way to think about food waste sociologically is through the concept of **waste regimes**, developed by environmental sociologist Zsuzsa Gille (2007). Gille points out that institutions, regulations, policy initiatives, and social conventions determine not only what is considered waste but also how waste is valued. In other words, a number of factors are responsible for all this food waste. Some might be classified as cultural. The Chinese have a long-held practice of providing more than their guests can eat, as hosts seek to "gain face" (Smil 2004, 107). Rising costs for waste disposal caused one Shanghai branch of the roast-duck restaurant Quanjude to offer its customers a 10 percent discount if they would finish their food, as many of its customers were eating less than half of what they ordered (Smil 2004). Another variable is aesthetics, or what could be referred to as the

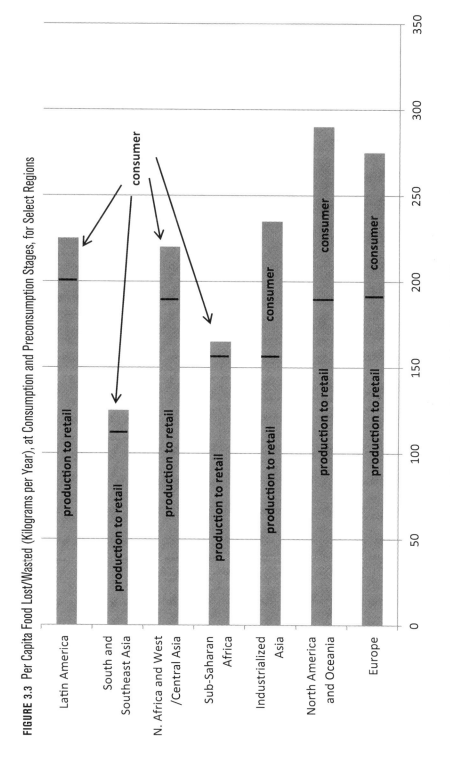

FIGURE 3.3 Per Capita Food Lost/Wasted (Kilograms per Year), at Consumption and Preconsumption Stages, for Select Regions

Source: Gustavsson et al. (2011).

cultural expectations about how we think particular foods ought to look. The state of Queensland, Australia, disposes of more than a 100,000 tons of bananas annually because the fruits fail to meet national cosmetic retail standards (Hurst 2010).

Tristram Stuart (2009, 103–111) tells the story of a large British carrot farmer who supplies the supermarket chain Asda. Annually, 25 to 30 percent of his crop fails to meet the chain's aesthetic standards. "Asda insists," the farmer explains, "that all carrots should be straight so the consumer can peel the full length in one easy stroke" (Stuart 2009, 104). Any—and only—oversized carrots go to food processors, which account for about a third of those unwanted by Asda. Small carrots require too much labor to handle, so food processors usually avoid using them. What's left, the remaining two-thirds of that originally rejected by Asda, is fed to livestock (see Image 3.2).

IMAGE 3.2 From What Was Then Called the US Food Administration (1917)

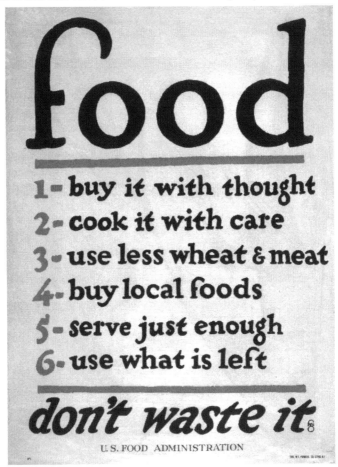

Source: Library of Congress, LC-USZC4–9739.

Note
Can you imagine the US government encouraging the American public to do some of these things today? Granted, it could happen. But not without incredibly forceful pushback from certain powerful food players.

The power wielded by food processors and supermarkets through **market concentration** (the dominance of a particular market by a few large corporations) in these sectors also encourages food waste. Supermarkets in particular have considerable leverage over those operating earlier in the food chain. This leverage comes from **buyer power**—an effect that results when a market has numerous sellers but only one or a few buyers. Buyer power means that whereas supermarkets or processors can select from a range of farmers to work with, the inverse is less often the case, giving the former tremendous leverage over the latter when it comes to setting the terms of the contract. In some cases, farmers supply only one processor, which effectively allows the buyer (the processor) to write the terms of the contract. This allows companies like Birds Eye, for example, to contractually forbid their growers from selling their peas to anyone else, even those rejected by the company for not meeting certain standards. In such a scenario, growers are left with no choice but to either feed their surplus to livestock or recycle the vegetables back into the soil (Stuart 2009, 117). In this case, the cost of waste is pushed onto farmers.

As already noted, consumers waste a lot of food. Yet in some instances, it's not entirely their fault, thanks to a nifty little marketing strategy by supermarkets called the buy-one-get-one (BOGO) free promotion. Grocers often reserve these campaigns for items on the brink of expiring, items that they would lose money on if they held onto them just a day or two longer. These schemes might be a great deal if you actually use the "free" one. The research indicates, however, that most do not (Gooch et al. 2010). In Britain, in light of the aforementioned House of Lords (2014) study, the government is now urging supermarkets to end BOGO offers in an effort to stem the amount of food being wasted by customers (Cox 2014). In the United States, conversely, BOGO schemes remain very popular. It is also worth noting that "sell by," "best by," and "use by" dates go largely unregulated around the world. In the case of the United States, for instance, the federal government regulates such statements only when they apply to infant formula. That means companies decide on these dates. Yet they have an incentive to make those freshness windows unduly short, which further encourages food waste.

Waste and Public Health

All waste represents a potential health hazard (see ECOnnection 3.2). Those of us living in affluent countries often do not think about waste in the context of public health. Although all societies put their waste somewhere, the characteristics of this location can vary considerably from nation to nation. In countries such as Australia, Japan, and the United States, "somewhere" is often a combination of landfills, incinerators, and recycling facilities. In less affluent nations with poor waste management practices it's usually a lot closer, like in nearby rivers, lakes, or parks; along public roadways; or in huge heaps in the middle of the street, creating a toxic playground of sorts for neighborhood children (World Bank 2012). **Collective coverage**, as it's called in the waste management community, is the proportion of an area serviced by the municipal waste stream, and it varies widely not only between developing nations but also within nations. This is particularly noticeable when "slum" and "nonslum" households are separated. As Table 3.3 details, some nations (like Colombia) have quite high coverage rates for all of their inhabitants. Many, however, have a long way to go.

TABLE 3.3 Collective Coverage for Nonslum and Slum Households for Select Countries in Africa and the Middle East; and Latin America and the Caribbean

COUNTRY	PERCENTAGE OF HOUSEHOLDS WITH A COLLECTION SERVICE	
	Nonslum/incorporated	Slum/unincorporated
Region: Africa and the Middle East		
Benin	50	11
Egypt	90	65
Ethiopia	61	32
Ghana	46	46
Kenya	46	46
Senegal	75	50
Region: Latin America and the Caribbean		
Bolivia	93	93
Colombia	100	91
Dominica	84	66
Guatemala	75	19
Nicaragua	89	48
Peru	92	54

Source: Adapted from World Bank (2012).

Note: Collective coverage among select low-and middle-income countries varies considerably. Some countries (such as Columbia) have been quite successful at providing collection services for all strata of society, while others (like Kenya and Ghana) have had considerably less success.

Uncollected waste is a scourge for everyone involved. It clogs drains and sewers, causing flooding and thus the spread of infectious disease. Stagnant water—from, for example, backed-up storm drains—offers a prime breeding habitat for mosquitoes and rodents, which can also lead to the spread of disease. Uncollected waste can make it more difficult to attract businesses and tourists. It can also disrupt a country's ability to provide basic utilities. In Costa Rica, for example, an electric utility company has problems maintaining power to their grid from a hydroelectric plant because plastic litter repeatedly clogs its turbines (United Nations 2010).

Even after it is collected, waste represents a potential public health hazard. One review looked at the health risks associated with domestic waste composting facilities and their

ETHICAL QUESTION 3.2
Public Health and Value Judgments

As members of a social network—with its own norms, identity structures, and social conventions—epidemiologists' understanding of "evidence" often differs from that of those embedded within different social networks (e.g., community activists). Among professional epidemiologists, social norms strongly discourage the making of false positives—that is, concluding that there is a causal link between contaminant X and a cancer cluster when there isn't one (also known as a **Type I error**). This explains why higher confidence limits—of typically 90 percent or higher—are usually the norm within this professional field. Scientists have a reputation to uphold as a result of their membership in a larger professional community, which could be severely undermined if they were to proclaim a causal link when none exists. Such Type I errors could not only be embarrassing but potentially damaging to one's membership within the community and the resources therein embedded (e.g., access to grants). If such errors occurred with great frequency, it could in fact undermine the legitimacy of the entire profession.

On the other hand, community activists, as a result of their different network connections and interests, have equally compelling reasons to avoid false negatives (known as **Type II errors**). For them, erring on the side of caution, if it means saving their lives and the lives of loved ones, it is well worth making a false negative occasionally. This in part explains why proponents of what has been called **popular epidemiology** (a type of citizen science that involves laypeople) prefer a much lower confidence limit when examining causal relationships between pollutants and cancer clusters.

---

product (Domingo and Nadal 2009). Since MSW contains a number of chemical and biological agents, compost was found to be a potential biohazard. The contaminants were cited as creating varying levels of risk to plant workers at composting facilities as well as to the consumers of vegetable products grown in soils treated with the adulterated compost. Other studies point to the public health risk of living next to waste management facilities and solid waste incinerators (e.g., Domingo et al. 2015). There is also tentative evidence linking certain negative health effects to living near landfill sites, such as low birth weight, birth defects, and certain types of cancers (Ashworth et al. 2014; see also Ethical Question 3.2).

E-Waste

Those of us in affluent nations throw away an awful lot of electronic waste, or what is becoming commonly known as e-waste. How often do you get a new cell phone? Every year? Perhaps every two? My service provider currently incentivizes getting a new phone every year, offering a hefty new phone credit after owning the device for only twelve months. And what about your computer? How often do you replace it?

This e-waste—discarded computers, printers, mobile phones, pagers, digital photo and music devices, refrigerators, toys, and televisions—is expected to rise sharply in the

ECOnnection 3.2
E-Waste and Public Health

A systematic review of five electronic databases (PubMed, Embase, Web of Science, PsycNET, and CINAHL) summarized what the peer-reviewed literature has to say about e-waste's impact on public health (Grant et al. 2013). Some of the findings highlighted include the following:

- Outcomes associated with exposure to e-waste include changes in thyroid function, changes in cellular expression and function, adverse neonatal outcomes, changes in temperament and behavior, and decreased lung function.
- Children living in e-waste recycling towns had a lower forced vital capacity than those living in a control town. (A forced vital capacity is the volume change of the lung between a full inspiration to total lung capacity and a maximal expiration to residual volume.)
- Findings from most studies showed increases in spontaneous abortions, stillbirths, and premature births, and reduced birth weights and birth lengths associated with exposure to e-waste.
- People living or working in e-waste recycling towns had evidence of greater DNA damage than those living in control towns.
- One study related exposure to e-waste and waste electrical and electronic equipment to lower educational outcomes.

decades ahead. A United Nations-backed study, global e-waste—defined as anything with a plug or a battery—grew by a record forty-five million tons in 2016 (Baldé et al. 2017). The study also found that raw materials thrown out as e-waste—metals such as gold, silver, copper, platinum, and palladium—were worth $64.61 billion in 2016. But despite this economic incentive, only 8.9 million tons of e-waste were recovered. The report also explains that while countries vary widely in recycling capacity, not one comes close to recycling even half of its e-waste. Europe, at 35 percent, has the highest collection rate. Meanwhile, Australia and New Zealand—the two nations that produce the highest e-waste per person at thirty-eight pounds—collect and recycle only 6 percent of their electronics (Baldé et al. 2017).

The majority of e-waste in developed countries is exported to less affluent nations to be recycled. China currently receives the largest share of the world's e-waste: roughly 70 percent of the world's discarded gadgets—a strange twist given that most were also manufactured there (Watson 2013). Recycling in China takes many hazardous forms, such as incinerating materials over an open flame in order to recover valuable metals like gold. These practices release toxic gases while yielding very low metal recovery rates, especially compared to modern industrial facilities. Some of the toxic materials found in e-waste include barium, cadmium, lead, lithium, mercury, nickel, palladium, rhodium, and silver. Exposure to these materials has been linked, among other things, to birth defects and organ, nervous system, and skeletal system damage (e.g., Feldt et al. 2014).

Solutions

I have noticed when discussing the subject of waste in the classroom that the conversation inevitably turns to individuals. "We need to stop wasting so much!," a student told me when asked how we solve the problem of waste. Yes, we do waste too much. But why do we? Are we the only ones to blame for this? Solutions to waste must reflect the multifaceted nature of the problem, or, as I told my student, "Working only to change what we as consumers do to produce waste will not effectively solve much" (See Movement Matters 3.1).

MSW Management Alternatives from around the World

There is a tendency to think that what works in affluent countries when it comes to MSW management will work equally well for less affluent countries. Unfortunately, to quote from a United Nations document on the subject, "Nothing could be further from the truth" (United Nations 2010, 93). The average inhabitant of a developing nation generates a fraction of what their counterpart in an affluent nation generates. Thus, the twenty-five-ton garbage trucks that seem so necessary to MSW planners in countries like the United States are a needless expense in countries that do not generate sufficient waste; these vehicles can cost more than $130,000 new. And let's not forget: many roads and bridges in low-income nations just can't handle trucks of that size.

A popular trend, which started in China and has since spread outside of Asia to the Middle East, Africa, and Latin America, is a hybrid approach to waste transfer. This system involves setting up small, local transfer stations around the city to which people bring their trash. As labor costs in low- and middle-income countries are relatively low, this can be accomplished far more cost effectively using handcarts and the like than with expensive trucks. The transfer stations also facilitate small-scale entrepreneurialism, as people are employed to collect and deposit trash from the neighborhood at these sites for those who choose not or are unable to do it themselves. Once at the transfer station, the city takes over and hauls the waste away. Once concentrated at one site, capital-intensive technologies like large trucks become more cost effective. In countries using this system, the waste is collected daily and the transfer stations washed down to minimize odor and prevent rodent problems (Pariatamby and Tanaka 2014).

And what about all the food waste? Some commentators have argued that if food were more expensive—if its retail price more accurately reflected the actual costs that went into producing, processing, and transporting it—we would likely not waste so much of it. Perhaps. Yet there are other ways to disincentivize the act of wasting food, such as by charging people who do it. That's exactly what South Korea does. In 2005 they made it illegal to send food to the landfill; you won't actually go to jail for breaking this law, but you will be fined. South Koreans now must separate all food waste and place it in a special 100 percent compostable bag. The policy has been incredibly successful. The country has managed to remove more than 98 percent of food waste from its MSW stream, just the opposite of the United States, where just 2.6 percent of food waste is composted (Thyberg et al. 2015).

Food waste can also be fed to livestock. Poultry and pigs thrive on organic waste. Under European laws, however, feeding food waste to pigs is banned. Conversely, in

MOVEMENT MATTERS 3.1
The Fight against Packaging

McDonald's styrofoam clamshells, which it had used to package the Big Mac and other sandwiches, had become the target of an aggressive campaign by environmental activists in the 1980s. Children, at the time, had picketed McDonald's dressed as "Ronald McToxic." A former McDonald's vice president, Bob Langert, explained the pressure against the clamshells this way: "McDonald's image suddenly warped from a symbol of happiness and fun to an icon of waste amid a disposable society. In 1990, McDonald's announced that it would phase out its clamshell and replace it with paper packaging."

Today, activists want to see that fate befall the single-use cup. But there's one problem: from an engineering perspective, today's disposable cups—like those Starbucks uses—are close to perfect. They do not leak, break, or melt, do not change the way beverages taste, they are light and stackable, and are incredibly cheap to make. Those are a lot of boxes to tick for anyone searching for a greener alternative. An eco-friendly cup has to do *all that* AND then break down easily.

One advocacy group, Stand.Earth, has gone after Starbucks specifically for their proliferation of single-use cups, organizing multiple protests outside its headquarters, its stores and company events. The group built a wall made of paper cups and installed a twelve-foot cup monster, with bloodshot eyes and raised arms, made of 1,000 paper cups. Not far away, kids sang a version of "Jingle Bells" with these lyrics:

dashing through the cups,
which used to be the woods,
but you chopped them all down,
so you could sell your goods.

Adapted from Wiener-Bronner (2019).

Japan, South Korea, and Taiwan, a percentage of the nation's food waste must be diverted to livestock, which makes sense when you consider that of the 28 million tons of food wasted annually in Japan, at least 6.5 million is still suitable for *human* consumption (Japan Times 2019).

Extended Producer Responsibility

"Waste isn't the fault of consumers—it's a design flaw," I once had a friend tell me. Although she was perhaps overstating matters a bit—clearly, as consumers we can do better when it comes to reducing our waste—I appreciate her point. As long as consumers continue to need (or think they need) the things supplied by the market, they have little choice but to waste. I realize that many consumers confuse "wants" for "needs," so the problem of waste must also be addressed from the angle of consumption (which is discussed in Part III of this book). But sometimes these needs are legitimate; for example, when someone's job requires the purchase of a computer and a printer. And even when those needs are not legitimate, the pragmatist in me realizes that people are going to continue to buy stuff, at least for the foreseeable future. So why not buy stuff that can be recycled and reused?

That's what my friend meant when she said waste is a design flaw. We're currently not making things that can easily be reused and recycled. This is where the concept of **extended producer responsibility** (EPR) comes in. Under EPR, manufacturers are held responsible for a product beyond the time of sale, thereby relieving consumers, governments, future generations, and the environment from the costs associated with landfilling and recycling hazardous materials. EPR is an attempt to internalize some of the costs of a product that have previously been externalized (not included in the retail price) onto society, taxpayers, the environment, and future generations. This cost externalization model is not only terribly unfair—by forcing people to pay for the consequences of actions not of their own doing—but also creates completely unsustainable actions and business models. Think about it in the context of waste. When, for example, companies manufacture computers, most are currently responsible for the product only from the moment it was manufactured through the life of its warranty. And not surprisingly, their design reflects these parameters. Consequently, they have no interest in designing products that can either be disposed of safely (e.g., that are not full of hazardous materials) or recycled and reused. Computer manufacturers currently don't care what the consumer does with their product when it reaches the end of its life. And why should they? Similarly, when the consumer disposes of their computer (and it is sent off to the landfill or to be recycled), they may pay a nominal disposal fee, but it is society, taxpayers, future generations, and the environment that are paying the real costs of this action. How is that fair?

EPR extends the producer's responsibility for a product throughout its life cycle, from cradle to grave. The concept was first used and defined in a report by Thomas Lindhqvist for the Swedish Ministry of the Environmental and Natural Resources in 1990 (see Lindhqvist and Lidgren 1990). EPR seeks to prioritize preventative measures (by asking questions like "How do we make things better so they don't become waste?") over end-of-pipe approaches (which involve questions such as "What should we do with the waste?"). EPR makes producers the primary actors responsible for the entire life cycle of their products. The logic behind this is simple: making producers responsible for having to recycle and reuse what they manufacture will lead them to redesign products for this end. When products are not designed to be recycled, they often are not. We often mistake **downcycling** (converting waste into new materials or products of lesser quality and decreased functionality) for recycling. Carpet, for instance, not designed to be recycled is typically down-cycled to, for example, carpet padding.

Maine was the first state in the United States to pass an EPR e-waste law in 2004, requiring manufacturers to be financially responsible for recycling specific electronics. Under this law, while cities still ensure that collection sites are available and consumers must bring their e-waste to these sites, the manufacturers pay for all recycling costs. Since 2004 twenty-four states have enacted similar legislation. EPR has an even longer track record in Europe, where the problem of landfill shortage is particularly acute.

We also need to create incentives that entice businesses—and electronics companies in particular in light of what was just said about e-waste—to make products that can be repaired. It's often cheaper to buy a new appliance or piece of electronic equipment than it is to get that old one repaired because it's not designed with that aim in mind, making repair expensive. I find it curious how much we as a society focus on the recycling aspect of the equation—on, in other words, the *end* of the life cycle. We talk about expanding recycling markets and improving recycling technology, which we hope will bring down its

ECOnnection 3.3

Closed Loop Fund and the Amazon Effect

The "Amazon Effect": the burden placed on municipalities and waste collection services that need to dispose of packaging from Amazon and other e-commerce stores—a strain that has led to a decline in cardboard recycling rates in the United States as the system becomes swamped by an unrelenting stream of this packaging (Bershidsky 2018). According to the American Forestry and Packaging Association, the recycling rate for cardboard fell to 88.8 percent in 2017 from 92.9 percent in 1999 (Shu 2018).

In light of all this, Amazon announced, in October 2018, that it had invested $10 million in the Closed Loop Fund. The Closed Loop Fund finances the creation of recycling infrastructure and services in US cities. Amazon claimed when announcing this investment that it will result in one million tons of recyclable material being kept out of landfills and "eliminate the equivalent of two million metric tons of CO_2 by 2028, equivalent to shutting down a coal-fired power plant for six months" (cited in Shu 2018).

costs and help keep countries like the United States from shipping its e-waste overseas, where labor is cheap and where environmental and labor laws are weak. But if goods are not designed and manufactured to be recycled, what good does any of this do? And lest we forget: designing products that could actually be repaired or upgraded would effectively render this entire discussion about recycling moot. If we could just focus a fraction of those moneys and political energies on encouraging and regulating businesses to make electronic products that can be refurbished, recycled, reused, and easily repaired, just think how far that would go toward reducing e-waste and stopping the types of recycling practices currently used in developing countries that are placing the health of individuals and the environment at risk (see ECOnnection 3.3).

IMPORTANT CONCEPTS

- e-waste
- extended producer responsibility (EPR)
- food waste
- life-cycle analysis (LCA)
- "three Rs" of environmentalism
- waste and public health

DISCUSSION QUESTIONS

1. It is often said that we've become a throwaway society. Why do you think this is?
2. When something of yours breaks, rips, or simply stops working, how often do you first try to get it repaired? What are some of the barriers to repair and reuse?

3. Do corporations bear any responsibility for waste, or is it a problem best addressed among consumers and through better municipal waste management practices?

4. Is necessity the mother of invention, to repeat an old and familiar saying, or is invention the mother of necessity?

SUGGESTED ADDITIONAL READINGS

Amuzu, D. 2018. "Environmental Injustice of Informal E-Waste Recycling in Agbogbloshie-Accra: Urban Political Ecology Perspective." *Local Environment*, 23(6): 603–618.

Baldé, C.P., V. Forti, V. Gray, R. Kuehr, and P. Stegmann. "The Global E-waste Monitor—2017." United Nations. https://drive.google.com/file/d/11DCXXZM-bflxHxk92gOXbweIceb40brP/view.

Hannibal, B., and A. Vedlitz. 2018. "Throwing It out: Introducing a Nexus Perspective in Examining Citizen Perceptions of Organizational Food Waste in the US." *Environmental Science & Policy*, 88: 63–71.

RELEVANT INTERNET LINKS

- www.footprintnetwork.org/en/index.php/GFN/page/calculators. An ecological footprint calculator. Find out how large your footprint is.
- www.lovefoodhatewaste.com. A useful resource for learning more about food waste and how you can cut down on the amount you produce.
- www.nationalgeographic.com/environment/urban-expeditions/austin/take-this-food-waste-quiz-show-off-your-knowledge/. Take this quiz, and learn your food waste IQ.
- www.youtube.com/watch?v=IKG8xRTFktg. An instructional video on how to practice backyard composting.

SUGGESTED VIDEOS

- *Bag It!* (2011). A film that examines our love affair with plastic.
- *Inside the Garbage of the World* (2014). A look at how we're trashing our world and what we can do to turn things around.
- *Plasticized* (2012). A journey through the center of the South Atlantic Ocean aboard the *Sea Dragon* with the 5 Gyres Institute on the very first scientific expedition focused on plastic waste.
- *The Plastic Cow* (2012). An examination of the impact of our almost complete dependence on plastic bags, which we use and discard carelessly every day, often to dispose of our garbage and kitchen waste.
- *Unwasted: The Future of Business on Earth* (2011). There is no waste in nature; humans are in fact the only animals on the planet to create waste that nature cannot process. Can we create an economy that uses waste rather than makes it?
- *Waste Wars* (2011). http://vimeo.com/32400188. Documents a battle over access to and control over garbage, as waste pickers and recyclers in Delhi fight attempts to privatize trash collection.
- *Wasted! The Story of Food Waste* (2017). A documentary on, you guessed it, food waste.
- *Wasted Waste* (2018). Full documentary: https://vimeo.com/237492712. Documentary about Freegan lifestyles, based on the rejection of any form of human or animal exploitation.

Biodiversity: Society Wouldn't Exist Without It

It has been my experience that while everyone seems to believe biodiversity ought to be preserved, few can articulate the reasons we value it to the level we do. I discuss the subject every semester in my Global Environmental Issues class. And every semester, when I ask why we ought to preserve biodiversity, I receive in return … silence. Sure, after an awkward stillness I hear from a few in the audience, but the silence always quickly reappears. It then becomes my turn to speak. I usually begin by making some grand statement pertaining to the value of biodiversity to society, talking about its links to quality of life, therapeutic applications, ability to limit infectious disease, and its role in maintaining "services." In short, biodiversity supports a number of things that lead to happier and healthier humans. Human *health*, as the term is defined here, and as the World Health Organization (WHO) has defined it since 1948, is "a state of complete physical, mental, and social well-being and not merely the absence of disease or infirmity" (WHO 2012). I will touch briefly on each of the four benefits mentioned above.

Quality of life can be enhanced innumerably by biodiversity, as it boosts mental and spiritual health, provides opportunities for recreation, and enriches human knowledge.

Biodiversity is also responsible for supplying *therapeutic applications*, thanks to medicinal and genetic resources coming from plants and other organisms. The United Nations, for example, recently valued anticancer agents from marine organisms at roughly $1 billion a year, while the global value of herbal medicine has been estimated to be worth more than $80 billion annually (Booker et al. 2015).

Biodiversity places *limits on infectious disease* through biological controls that rein in **disease vectors** (an organism, such as a mosquito or tick, that carries disease-causing microorganisms from one host to another). For instance, when an ecosystem is biologically diverse, predation throughout the food chain is likely to keep populations of all species under control, including those linked to the spread of infectious disease.

The benefits of biodiversity-dependent *services* are incalculable, as many of these values cannot (and should not) be reduced to a monetary figure. This is not to say some haven't tried. Take the concept of **ecosystem services**: the processes by which the environment produces resources that we often take for granted but need for our survival, such as clean air and water, timber, habitat for fisheries, and pollination of native and agricultural plants. A 1997 article published in *Nature* placed the value of seventeen ecosystem services at approximately $33 trillion per year, compared to a gross world product at the time of around $18 trillion (Costanza et al. 1997). More recently, a revised estimate based on updated data was published in 2011 and valued global ecosystem services at between $125 trillion and $145 trillion per year, compared to a gross world product at the time of around $72 trillion (Costanza et al. 2014). From this estimated range, the study's authors calculate the loss of eco services from 1997 to 2011 as a result of land use change at between $4.3 trillion and $20.2 trillion annually. You can also find estimates broken down by biome or land type. For instance, a 2018 analysis places global forest ecosystem services annual loss at $716 billion between 2000 and 2012 (Song 2018). Land use changes include anything from, for example, decreases in coral reef area to deforestation and the draining of wetlands. Yet we can't—nor would we want to—put a price tag on everything that's provided by ecosystems. Right? (See ECOnnection 4.1.)

Fast Facts

- Approximately 1.5 million species (excluding bacteria) have already been cataloged—just a fraction of the 1–6 billion species estimated to exist (Larsen et al. 2017).
- We are losing species at an alarming rate, many before even being discovered. Famed biologist Edward O. Wilson ([1992] 1999) has estimated the current rate of species extinction at roughly 27,000 annually, or 74 per day (see Ethical Question 4.1). A study published in *Science* estimates that current extinction rates are up to a thousand times higher than they would be if we humans were not around (Pimm et al. 2014; see Image 4.1).

IMAGE 4.1 Photograph from the Mid-1870s of a Pile of American Buffalo Skulls Waiting to Be Ground for Fertilizer.

Source: Courtesy of the Burton Historical Collection, Detroit Public Library.

- An analysis of ninety-four studies comparing biodiversity under organic and conventional farming methods found that, on average, organic agriculture *increased* species richness by about 30 percent relative to biodiversity levels on conventionally farmed land (Tuck et al. 2014).
- Although we have been talking about needing to protect rainforests for as long as I can remember, we are still losing rainforests at astounding rates. Brazil is the deforestation leader with 11.1 million acres (4.5 million hectares) lost in 2017, followed by the Democratic Republic of Congo in a distant second place with 3.7 million acres (1.5 million hectares) (Taylor and Streck 2018).

Implications

As detailed in Table 4.1, a great number of events and activities (most of which are human induced) threaten biodiversity. And these threats will only grow in the decades ahead, especially as the world becomes warmer (thanks to climate change), more crowded (as a result of population growth and urbanization trends), and more affluent (particularly in Southeast Asia). Complicating matters further are the ways in which pressures upon biodiversity can act at different temporal and spatial scales. For instance, sediments from deforestation in the headwaters of the Orinoco River along the Venezuelan/Brazilian border negatively affect marine life in the Caribbean more than 1,000 miles away by altering the nutrient availability and clarity of the waters (Ríos-Touma and Ramírez 2019).

The reasons for biodiversity decline will come up again later, as many of the pressures and drivers discussed in Table 4.1 are subjects of later chapters. What I am most interested in detailing at the moment are impacts. (Even so, those "deep" sociological drivers discussed in Chapter 1 should never be far from our minds; see ECOnnection 4.2.) Yet before we look at impacts, there is one small conceptual problem that requires our attention: What precisely does *biodiversity* even mean? Only after working our way through this question can we begin having a conversation about the various consequences associated with biodiversity loss.

Changing Definitions of Biodiversity

Early definitions of biodiversity tended to focus almost entirely on species diversity, in which case biodiversity was simply another way of saying "species richness" (see, for example, Lovejoy 1980). Later, the definition of the term expanded to include, along with species richness, genetic diversity (within and across species) and ecological diversity (which includes ecosystem services and habitat) (see, for example, Hunter and Gibbs 2007). Yet the problem doesn't lie just in deciding which criteria to include in our definition. It also stems from the inherent ambiguity of the criteria themselves. Take the concept—or, I should say, *concepts*—of species.

A review of the modern biological literature roughly two decades ago found at least twenty-four different species concepts (Mayden 1997), a figure that has no doubt increased in recent years, given the expanding literature on the subject. The **species problem**, as it has come to be known, refers to the inherent ambiguity surrounding the use and definition of the species concept. The three more widely utilized contemporary species concepts include the biological species concept (centering on the property of

TABLE 4.1 Threats to Biodiversity

Residential and Commercial Development • Housing and urban areas • Commercial and industrial areas • Tourism and recreation areas	**Agriculture and Aquaculture** • Annual and perennial non-timber crops • Wood and pulp plantations • Livestock farming and ranching • Marine and freshwater aquaculture
Energy Production and Mining • Oil and gas drilling • Mining and quarrying • Renewable energy	**Transportation and Service Corridors** • Roads and railroads • Utility and service lines • Shipping lanes • Flight paths • Air and space transport
Biological Resource Use • Hunting and collecting terrestrial animals • Gathering terrestrial plants • Logging and wood harvesting • Fishing and harvesting aquatic resources	**Human Intrusions and Disturbance** • Recreational activities • War, civil unrest, and military exercises • Work and other activities
Natural System Modifications • Fire and fire suppression • Dams and water management/use • Other ecosystem modifications	**Invasive and Problematic Species and Genes** • Invasive non-native/alien species • Problematic native species • Introduced genetic material
Pollution • Household sewage and urban waste water • Industrial and military effluents • Agricultural and forestry effluents • Garbage and solid waste • Airborne pollutants • Excess heat, sound, or light that disturbs wildlife and/or ecosystems	**Geological Events** • Volcanoes • Earthquakes/tsunamis • Avalanches/landslides
Climate Change and Severe Weather • Habitat shifting and alteration • Droughts • Temperature extremes • Storms and flooding	

Source: Adapted from Conservation Measures Partnership (2012).

reproductive isolation), the ecological species concept (emphasizing speciation through ecological selection), and the phylogenetic species concept (focusing on the property of common descent). This all matters tremendously from a conservation standpoint, for ultimately which species concept we adopt affects the number of species we find.

It has been argued, for instance, that the biological species concept tends to overemphasize gene flow between populations and thus aggregates species together, while the phylogenetic species concept often splits such populations into distinct and thus potentially new species (Meijaard and Nijman 2003). This inflation and deflation of biodiversity levels based on which species concept is ultimately employed has been well documented.

ECOnnection 4.1
Thinking about Ecosystem Services Conceptually

Ecosystems cannot provide any benefits to humanity without the presence of skilled people (human capital), their communities and social networks (social capital), and their built environment (built capital). This interaction, articulated by Costanza et al. (2014), is illustrated in Figure 4.1. (Seven types of capital are highlighted in Chapter 12, which go well beyond the four presented here.) The challenge for policies aimed at sustainable development involves understanding how this interaction plays out in enhancing well-being and then taking steps to appropriately enhance all capitals to maximize outcomes.

One thing I appreciate about this figure is that it contextualizes value. Values are not plucked out of thin air. What we value and the degree to which something is valued cannot be abstracted from social context. This is plainly evident in debates over the value of ecosystem services. The $125 trillion to $145 trillion range calculated by Costanza et al. (2014) is a lot—an order of magnitude larger than what the global economy produces in a year. And yet our actions indicate that we don't actually value global ecosystem services that much, or anywhere even close to that much (otherwise we wouldn't be trashing them). Why is that? What is it about our political systems, cultures, markets, and social norms and routines that cause us to undervalue ecosystem services to the degree we do?

FIGURE 4.1

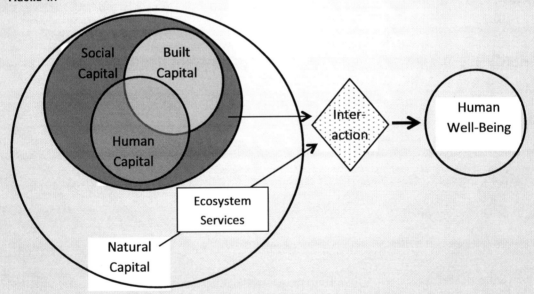

Source: Adapted from Costanza et al. (2014).

Sophie's Choice: What If We Can't Save Them All?

According to a recent United Nations report, approximately one *million* species are at risk of extinction (Leahy 2019). If we had endless resources to commit to saving them all, we wouldn't have to choose which to save. But that's not reality. Ecologists have long argued that how we choose which species live or die is often unscientific, skewed heavily toward preserving cute and fuzzy animals even if those species do little to keep the planet humming by contributing to ecosystem functions (and those ever important services). For example, ants play a foundational role in most ecosystems: distributing seeds, aerating soils, eating other insects, and providing food for other species. And yet, for every child with a poster of ants in their bedroom there are tens of thousands with posters of pandas, elephants, and polar bears. In the words of Marc Bekoff, an ethologist at the University of Colorado, Boulder, "if we're going to save pandas rather than ants, we need a good reason, and being cute is not a good reason" (Dell'Amore 2013). What about those species that we're *trying* to make extinct—for instance, dozens of weeds are on the verge of being wiped from the Earth in Australia (Csurhes 2018). How do we decide which species to eradicate and which to save?

Something else to think about: cost. Should the cost of conservation play into our calculations? If so, those charismatic megafaunas come with a pretty hefty price tag—managing the world's tiger reserves costs more than $82 million annually (N. L. 2010). Then again, how can you place a price tag on the existence of a species, when once it is gone, it is gone for good? But if we do not take into consideration the annual cost of saving each individual animal of a given species—what some conservationists call ROI (return on investment)—what variables *should* we use?

The Tragedy of the Commodity

In Chapter 11 you will learn about the theory of the tragedy of the commons—the belief that species extinction (and environmental ruin more generally) is exacerbated in those instances where natural capital has yet to be privatized. Rebecca Clausen and Stefano Longo (along with, more recently, Brett Clark) turn this thinking on its head, arguing for what they call the **tragedy of the commodity** thesis (e.g., Clausen and Longo 2012; Longo et al. 2015). Accordingly, rather than being our ecological savior, "commodification is a primary *contributor* to decline as well as an underlying *cause* for the failure of environmental policy prescriptions" to protect biodiversity (Clausen and Longo 2012, 231; emphasis in original). As the authors explain, "once the precedent has been set to view the value of a resource through the lens of a commodity, government regulations to help 'solve' the ecological problem will prioritize market-based solutions that accommodate capitalist needs for growth and accumulation" (Clausen and Longo 2012, 232). As evidence for their thesis, they point to the AquAdvantage Salmon—selected by *Time* magazine as one of "The Best Inventions in 2010" (Clausen and Longo 2012). Here's a "solution" of salmon recovery and conservation that allows the status quo to continue, a technological fix that at least in the short term allows the treadmill of production to not miss a beat. In the long run, however, it is allowing biologically diverse natural salmon stocks to literally be gobbled up, along with their habitat.

A team of researchers reanalyzed organisms, which had earlier been classified according to other species definitions, utilizing a phylogenetic species concept (Agapow et al. 2004). The reanalysis yielded a species *increase* of 121 percent. Focusing on avian endemism in Mexico (birds that are found only in Mexico), another team applied two alternative species concepts: the phylogenetic species concept and the biological species concept (Peterson and Navarro-Siguenza 1999). Their findings indicate not only divergent levels of biodiversity based on which species concept was used but also divergent **biodiversity hotspots** (a biogeographic region with a significant reservoir of biodiversity that is under threat from humans), signifying where endemism is particularly concentrated. When the biological species concept was used, 101 bird species were found to be endemic to Mexico, with populations concentrated in the mountains of the western and southern portions of the country. Using the phylogenetic species concept, the endemic species total rose to 249, with population concentrations in the mountains and lowlands of western Mexico.

Equally problematic is the concept of "ecosystem"—a phenomenon, as mentioned previously, recently folded into biodiversity definitions. Maps of biologically diverse hotspots typically include tropical rain forests, for reasons related not only to species richness but also to the important ecosystem services, such as climate regulation and nutrient cycling, they provide. Wetlands and marshes, however, are typically ignored in these maps, even though they provide equally essential ecosystem services, such as nutrient cycling, erosion control, water purification, and storm protection. (See Ethical Question 4.2.)

And what about humans? Are we not a species that creates and alters ecosystems? Shouldn't *we* factor into measures of biodiversity, other than being viewed as yet another thing that negatively affects it?

The Bombay Natural History Society noticed in the late 1970s that bird populations were on the decline in the Bharatpur Bird Sanctuary (what is today known as Keoladeo National Park) in Rajasthan, India. An accusatory finger was eventually pointed at cattle and buffalo, which were entering the reserve in sufficient quantities and disrupting what was believed to be an otherwise balanced ecosystem. In an attempt to correct the problem of decreasing bird populations, Bharatpur was declared a national park in 1981. This act was quickly followed by a ban on all grazing activities within the park. (Nine people were killed in the resulting riots that ensued as the park was cleared of its earlier human inhabitants.)

By the mid-1980s, something was amiss. Studies were beginning to indicate the seemingly impossible: bird diversity within the park had *declined further* since the ban on grazing (Vijayan 1987). By the early 1990s, it was irrefutable: biodiversity had not only declined since the grazing ban but was diving downward at an alarming rate. The absence of grazing animals, it turns out, had a disastrous effect on the ecology of the park. Weed species were taking over wetlands and choking canals, thereby reducing fish populations. As the open wetland habitat—a habitat that once attracted a tremendous mix of birds—was being overrun by a handful of fast-growing opportunistic plant species, avian species went elsewhere in search of more suitable places to nest. In 1991, in a stunning course reversal, the Bombay Natural History Society—originally the most vocal opponent of grazing in the park—concluded that, to avoid further weed takeover, grazing animals needed to be brought back. A report announcing this policy reversal admitted the shortsightedness of conservation policies that place humans apart from—rather than as a part of—biologically diverse ecosystems: "In the case of most wetlands in this country, [human] interaction with them has become almost inseparable and hence, [humans have] to actively manage them" (Vijayan 1991, 1).

The Power of Conservation Maps

A wealth of literature has emerged in the past thirty years examining the power embedded within maps (e.g., Edney 1997; Harley 1989; Wood 1993). For example, modern maps embody the commercial and political interests of Western European and North American nation-states. Most world maps place north at the top, have zero degrees longitude running through Greenwich, England, and are centered on either Western Europe, North America, or the North Atlantic. Maps can also reflect societal preferences for certain landscapes and ecosystems. For example, forests are far more frequently mapped than grasslands (Hazen and Anthamatten 2004). Yet even what's defined as *forest* is hotly contested. A mapped, legally defined *forest* may not in fact contain a single tree (Vandergeest 1996).

Similar to how world maps give readers the sense that political boundaries are natural and objectively given, conservation maps also tend to naturalize a static view of ecological and social systems. In other words, while the socioecological space being represented in conservation images is inherently fluid, once mapped these spaces take on a near timeless, permanent quality. Maps also tend to minimize differences across geophysical space. Harris and Hazen (2006), for instance, examined a widely distributed map created by the United Nations Environment Programme that visually depicts the spatial distribution of internationally recognized "protected" areas. Such global perspectives, however, risk endorsing the view that conservation spaces are comparable across what are in reality widely divergent areas. They point out how places of conservation in the United States and the United Kingdom are often appreciably different. For example, as a result of divergent historical trajectories, national parks in the United States reflect the wilderness ideal (an image of nature devoid of human presence), while in the United Kingdom they are often populated agricultural landscapes. Although such spaces are radically different on the ground, these differences are washed away when viewed at the level of a global map. As argued in an article on the power of ecosystem service maps, "designing maps is thus a means of exercising power" (Hauck et al. 2013, 28). The authors go on to note that "the designer makes decisions on what to include and which scales are to be chosen" (Ibid.). One strategy then to avoid these pitfalls is to incorporate "a high degree of transparency with regard to the specific reasons for mapping" (Ibid.).

Biodiversity: The Fuel Driving Ecosystem Services

Biodiversity loss is our loss. Biodiversity may not make the world go around, but it certainly makes the planet inhabitable. Here I speak in a little more detail about some of the services provided by biodiversity.

AGRICULTURE

No amount of technology and innovation could substitute for the ecosystem services provided by biodiversity in the production of food and fiber (see ECOnnection 4.3). Biodiversity makes soil habitable for plant growth, as it is central to the breakdown and

ECOnnection 4.3
The Irreplaceable Bee

Pollinators—honey and native bees in addition to certain birds, bats, and butterflies—not only provide a critical ecosystem service but are also an essential component of food security. Honey bees alone enable the production of at least ninety commercially grown crops in North America. Pollinators are responsible for between $235 and $577 billion worth of annual global food production (Modern Agriculture 2018). The number of managed bee colonies in the United States has dropped over the past sixty years, from six million colonies in 1947 to just 2.5 million today. Crops like almonds are almost exclusively pollinated by honey bees. California's almond industry, which supplies 80 percent of the world's almonds, requires the pollination services of roughly 1.4 million beehives annually—that's 60 percent of all beehives in the United States (White House 2014). Unable to discern insect friend from insect foe, pesticides have had a major impact on all insect pollinators and are suspected of playing a significant role in what is known as colony collapse disorder (Chensheng et al. 2014; Doublet et al. 2015).

recycling of nutrients within this life-giving medium. Biodiversity also makes pollination possible and is essential for pest control, without which productivity losses would be even greater. Biodiversity may well also hold the key to future food security in light of climate change, as plant breeders will have to look increasingly into the gene pool to come up with varieties suitable to withstand and ideally thrive under a variety of agroecological conditions.

FORESTS

As with agriculture, commercial forestry depends on biodiversity for nutrient recycling and pest control. Some forests also generate revenue from hunting, the collection of wild food (e.g., berries and fungi), the collection of firewood, and bird watchers and nature photographers. Forests also offer spaces for recreation, itself a major revenue-generating activity. Finally, there is an incalculable intrinsic value associated with these spaces, as they not only serve as sources of creativity and inspiration but also hold religious and cultural significance for populations around the world.

FISHERIES

Waterways provide a provisioning ecosystem service in the form of fish catch. The fish catch, however, is heavily dependent on a functioning biologically diverse ecosystem that supplies nutrients, prey species, habitats, and a desirable water quality. There is also an intensely cultural component to fishing, as many societies have deep historical roots in this practice.

WATER

Biodiversity performs an irreplaceable service in terms of both recycling nutrients and ensuring desirable water quality for agricultural use, fisheries, and human consumption. A significant amount of research has emerged in recent years documenting that species-rich aquatic ecosystems are more efficient at removing excess nutrients and even some pollutants from water than those with fewer species (Carnicer et al. 2015).

ATMOSPHERIC REGULATION

Forests and other vegetation—and to a lesser extent all organisms—modify climate (though humans look to be the most influential organism). Plants and trees affect solar reflection, water vapor release, wind patterns, and moisture loss. Forests help maintain a humid environment, as evidenced by the fact that half of all rainfall in the Amazon basin is produced locally by the forest–atmosphere cycle (Kozloff 2010).

Biocultural Diversity

As acknowledged by the United Nations Environment Programme, "biodiversity also incorporates human cultural diversity, which can be affected by the same drivers as biodiversity, and which has impacts on the diversity of genes, other species, and ecosystems" (UNEP 2007, 160). The term **biocultural diversity** speaks to an unmistakable and increasingly well-documented empirical fact: that cultural diversity does not merely parallel biological diversity but is profoundly interrelated with it (Sobo 2017).

There is a subtle but noticeable disdain toward humans in many environmental texts in their noting only the ways in which humans threaten biodiversity. It is unquestionably true that we are the greatest threat to the Earth's biodiversity. But this shouldn't lead to the conclusion that humans somehow represent an *inherent* risk to biological diversity. Granted, it's far easier to see the various ways in which we are mucking things up, as we read routinely about the latest species threatened or lost entirely at our own hands. Yet growing evidence points to how humans are also positively contributing to ecosystems and biodiversity levels.

There are two general approaches to biological conservation: *ex situ* and *in situ*. *Ex situ* conservation involves the sampling, transferring, and storage of a species in a place other than the original location in which it was found, like a zoo or seed bank. The other option is *in situ* conservation, which involves the management of a species at the location of discovery. The *ex situ* model is often what comes to mind (at least for most in the developed world) when people think of biodiversity conservation, which is understandable in light of the more than 1,400 seed and gene banks and over 1,000 zoos worldwide.

The popularity of the *in situ* model, however, has grown considerably among conservationists in recent decades. Proponents of the *in situ* approach argue that it provides a more complete form of conservation, in that it makes room, unlike *ex situ* approaches, for socioecological dynamics. It is no coincidence that most of the world's biologically diverse hotspots are also its **cultural hotspots**—biogeographic regions with a significant reservoir of cultural diversity that are under threat of extinction (Lieskovský and Bürgi 2018; Stepp et al. 2004). Research looking at indigenous populations in North America consistently notes a correlation between measures of biodiversity within a given region and its levels of cultural and linguistic diversity (Smith 2001; Stephenson et al. 2014).

Virginia Nazarea has extensively studied sweet potato farmers in the Philippines. At one site they were beginning the processes of commercializing production, while at another they remained firmly at the level of subsistence agriculture. She had hypothesized that commercialization causes a narrowing of genetic and cultural diversity among sweet potatoes raised. Her hypothesis was confirmed. Yet she also observed something unexpected. There was a large disparity between the two sites in terms of the number of varieties known or remembered, compared to the biodiversity that actually existed. At the commercial site, farmers had knowledge about a far lower percentage of sweet potato varieties than at the other site, having forgotten many that still existed and were being planted elsewhere in the country. This suggests a faster erosion of cultural knowledge than genetic diversity itself. Reflecting on this research, Nazarea (2005, 62) writes how this finding signified that "in the context of agricultural development and market integration, knowledge may actually be the first to go."

Sociologists MacKenzie and Spinardi (1995) argued a while back that nuclear weapons are becoming "uninvented" as a result of global nuclear disarmament trends and nuclear test-ban treaties. It is their contention that "if design ceases, and if there is no new generation of designers to whom that tacit knowledge can be passed, then in an important (though qualified) sense nuclear weapons will have been uninvented" (MacKenzie and Spinardi 1995, 44). They are pointing, to put it simply, to the importance of putting knowledge to work. A lot of knowledge has to be acted out—literally *practiced*—for it to exist and be passed along to others. Try, for example, teaching someone to ride a bike with words alone—it just doesn't work. The same principle applies to our knowledge of biodiversity. This is why the term *biocultural diversity* is so apt, because the cultural knowledge tied to traditional crops is very much rooted in practice. Many traditional cultures are oral, meaning that much of this folk knowledge is not physically recorded (written down) anywhere. Once lost, there is a good chance this knowledge—and with it a piece of biocultural diversity—is gone forever.

Biopiracy

Although we often think about biological loss in the context of, say, extinction, this is not the only way it is experienced. In some cases, while the object of concern still exists (perhaps even thrives), the loss felt is the result of the misappropriation of biocultural knowledge. Enter **biopiracy**: essentially the loss of biocultural diversity through legal and sometimes illegal means.

It is estimated that developing nations would be owed $5 billion per year if they received royalties of 2 percent for their contributions to pharmaceutical research and another $302 million annually for royalties from agricultural products (see, e.g., Ramon 2011). Biopiracy—or what's called *bioprospecting* by those doing it—occurs when folk knowledge and biological artifacts are conjointly exploited for commercial gain without just compensation to those responsible for discovering or originating it. Although it's easy to chalk biopiracy up to the greedy actions of powerful multinational corporations seeking to exploit the knowledge and resources of indigenous populations, it is important to understand certain sociolegal realities that make such activities possible in the first place.

To begin with, patent law makes it exceedingly difficult for indigenous populations to call biocultural knowledge their own. According to patent law, no patent can be issued where prior art exists because of the statutory requirement that patents are to be granted only for new inventions on the basis of novelty and nonobviousness. An invention is generally not regarded as new if it was patented or described in a printed publication. **Indigenous knowledge**—or local knowledge, which is knowledge unique to a given community, culture, or society—however, has tended to be an oral and embodied effect, acquired through years of literally *doing* and applying that knowledge. As such, it is rarely ever written down. Its transmission occurs through storytelling, not book reading. The knowledge of these indigenous societies can thus often be freely plundered for private gain, as evidenced by corporations patenting and claiming as their own knowledge that had for centuries been part of the (indigenous) public domain.

One way indigenous groups are responding to this legal reality is by publishing their biocultural knowledge in large digital libraries—what are commonly known as Traditional Knowledge Data Libraries (TKDLs). Transforming this age-old embodied and oral knowledge into a written form turns it into something that patent law recognizes and that therefore constitutes prior art. Many countries—such as South Korea, Thailand, Mongolia, Cambodia, South Africa, Nigeria, Pakistan, Nepal, Sri Lanka, and Bangladesh—are following in the footsteps of India, which developed one of the first TKDLs in the late 1990s.

To what extent is biopiracy occurring? That's not easy to say, as a number of national laws, international agreements, and legally binding treaties make biopiracy illegal. So whatever is occurring is taking place under the radar. The most consequential legal structure to emerge to reduce biopiracy is the Convention of Biological Diversity (CBD), which was adopted at the Earth Summit in Rio de Janeiro in 1992. Its objectives are threefold: the conservation of biodiversity, the sustainable use of biodiversity, and the equitable sharing of benefits arising from the use of genetic resources.

Agreements reached through the CBD, however, do not apply to materials collected before 1992. Thus, any material in a gene or seed bank before 1992 can still be exploited for commercial ends without any money going back to the source country as compensation. Take the case involving a disease-resistant peanut from Brazil. The peanut was first picked in 1952 by Alan Beetle. It was not until 1987, however, that Beetle's sample would be used for commercial ends. In 1987 the tomato spotted wilt virus (TSWV) was first detected in US peanuts. This virus severely injures or kills any peanut plant that it infects. It quickly spread throughout Georgia, Florida, Alabama, and South Carolina, seriously threatening the US peanut industry. Beetle's sample peanut was known to be resistant to TSWV and was quickly sought out for this trait by breeders. A number of peanut varieties have since been bred to be resistant to TSWV using this nut from Brazil. In fact, the germplasm from this nut was estimated roughly a decade ago to add at least $200 million annually to the US economy (Edmonds Institute 2006). Brazil, conversely, receives nothing. Nevertheless, as a recent report on the subject adds, "no laws were transgressed." Rather, this example speaks to a perfectly legal case of "preCBD biopiracy" (Ibid., 3).

Even with CBD, however, biopiracy remains a problem. Let's look briefly at two recent well-publicized cases of biopiracy, involving Bt brinjal from India and herbal teas from South Africa.

Bt brinjal is a genetically modified strain of brinjal (eggplant) created by India's largest seed company, Mahyco, which also happens to be a subsidiary of the multinational company Monsanto. Bt brinjal has been engineered to be resistant to lepidopteran insects, particularly the brinjal fruit and shoot borer. According to the National Biodiversity Authority (NBA) of India, the development of Bt brinjal is a case of biopiracy, which means Monsanto and Mahyco could face criminal proceedings. The NBA charges these alleged biopirates with accessing nine Indian varieties of brinjal to develop their genetically modified eggplant without prior permission from the NBA or relevant national and local boards. This is a violation of the country's 2002 Biological Diversity Act, which provides for the conservation of biological diversity and calls for fair and equitable sharing of the benefits that arise from the use of biocultural resources. (It is also illegal under the CBD.) By using the local brinjal varieties without permission, Monsanto and Mahyco weakened India's sovereign control over its resources while denying economic and social benefits to local communities under the benefit-sharing requirements of the Biological Diversity Act (Jebaraj 2011).

Example two: biopirated tea. Global food giant Nestlé is facing allegations of biopiracy after applying for patents based on two South African plants used in the making of herbal teas without first receiving permission from the South African government. This puts Nestlé in direct violation of South African law as well as the CBD. The controversy centers on two South African plants, rooibos and honeybush, commonly used to make herbal teas with well-known—and long-known—medicinal benefits. A Nestlé subsidiary has filed five international patent applications seeking to claim ownership over some of those medicinal benefits, such as using the plants to treat hair and skin conditions and for anti-inflammatory treatments. At issue is benefit sharing: namely, Nestlé believes it does not need to share any future profits that might be derived from these patents. Yet, according to the 2004 South African Biodiversity Act, businesses must obtain a permit from the government if they intend to use the country's genetic resources for research or patenting. And these permits can be obtained *only* in exchange for a benefit-sharing agreement (ICTSD 2010).

Solutions

As biodiversity is threatened by multiple practices, pressures, and events, solutions directed at the problem of biodiversity loss must be equally multiple and diverse. I offer here two strategies that have had some success at enhancing biodiversity levels. In the space that remains, I discuss the practice of community conservation and agrobiodiversity conservation. These are not our only two solutions. Later chapters examine many of the other drivers of biodiversity loss and their potential solutions.

Community Conservation

The modern conservation movement emerged in Europe in the nineteenth century. The wilderness model, around which so many of the world's national parks are built, came shortly thereafter out of the United States. Although these top-down—which is to say they are typically implemented and overseen by the state—conservation methods have had their successes, they are not without their problems.

For one thing, conservation has historically been viewed as separate from economic development and "progress." Indeed, in some camps they are antithetical to each other. The social costs of these conventional models of conservation have been great. Removing,

ETHICAL QUESTION 4.3
Sustainability: For Whom and toward What End?

The term *sustainability* reminds me a lot of the term *nature*: we seem to talk endlessly about both but struggle when forced to offer a clear definition of either. *Social sustainability, environmental sustainability*, and *economic sustainability* are hotly contested terms. What they mean depends on whom you ask. For example, when we talk about social sustainability, do we mean improving social justice or reducing inequality or something else entirely? Or environmental sustainability: Do we mean zeroing out all ecological impact or just minimizing impact? If it is the latter, is everyone expected to reduce equally, or might those with the largest ecological footprints be asked to reduce more? Or economic sustainability: Does this mean simply that households and businesses need to be profitable, or does it also suggest a desire to reduce, for example, economic inequality?

What do you think about when you hear the term *sustainability*? If you're anything like my students, ecological sustainability likely comes to mind before social sustainability (and this is even among sociology students). Can you think of instances where an ecologically sustainable practice might not be socially sustainable?

sometimes forcibly, indigenous populations—like Native Americans in the United States and Parakuyo and Massai pastoralists in Tanzania—from lands they have lived on for centuries for purposes of "saving nature" is morally repugnant. But also, looking beyond the morality of these acts, the science refutes the ecological soundness of such policies. As the earlier case involving the Bharatpur Bird Sanctuary in India shows us, there may be better ways of conserving biodiversity than by removing people from the equation.

A paradigm shift of sorts is taking place in conservation and developmental circles. On the one hand, it is becoming clear that developmental policies that overlook conservation are unsustainable in the long run and ultimately offer no relief from threats to biodiversity. On the other hand, conservationists are beginning to understand that they can no longer afford to ignore the impoverishment they may be causing when they exclude human populations from habitats they are seeking to conserve. In fact, what we've learned is that those indigenous populations that conservationists have been so busy evicting over the past century may hold the key to truly sustainable development (see, e.g., Magni 2017; see also Ethical Question 4.3).

This is where community conservation comes into the picture (see ECOnnection 4.4). As generally practiced, community conservation is place-based and highly participatory. There are different "flavors" of community conservation, just as there are many different ways to define community involvement when it comes to conservation. This variability is captured in Table 4.2. As illustrated in the table, levels of community involvement can run the spectrum: from low, where an agency is in charge, to high, where independent community-centered groups develop their own initiatives as a result of a crisis or problem.

Arguably the most publicized community conservation success story comes out of Tanzania. It involves two woodland reserves, both of which were being poorly conserved under previous management regimes. In 1994 and 1995, communities located near the

TABLE 4.2 Citizen Involvement in Conservation Decision Making

	LOW (FULL CONTROL BY AGENCY IN CHARGE)		HIGH (FULL CONTROL BY STAKEHOLDERS)	
Process	**Information Sharing**: Builds awareness by telling people what is planned	**Consultation**: Identifies problems, offers solutions, and obtains feedback to broaden knowledge base allowing for better top-down decisions	**Co-directed**: Involves and actively engages stakeholders to contribute ideas and opinions when deciding best way to move forward	**Independent Community Initiatives**: Groups are enabled to act, in terms of process as well as outcome
Activity of Citizen Group	**Passive**: Receptors of information	**Marginally Engaged**: Predetermined phase is devoted to seeking public input	**Equal Players**: Involvement throughout entire processes	**Directing**: Groups set agenda and determine direction and outcome of project
Outcome	Information dissemination	Weak participation	Strong participation	Determination

Source: Adapted from Forgie et al. (2001) and Magni 2017.

Note: Citizen involvement can take many different forms. Some options offer little more than a façade of "involvement," while others put communities firmly in the driver's seat.

edge of the forests secured the return of control over woodlands they had previously informally managed for generations.

As one of the few remaining tracts of the Miombo woodlands in the Babati District, the Duru-Haitemba woodlands were targeted to be turned into a forest reserve as early as 1985. (The Miombo woodlands stretch in a broad belt across south-central Africa, extending from Angola to Tanzania.) The intention was to protect the forest against further deforestation by deploying government forest guards to prevent expanding human settlements. By taking control, local governments were promised a steady source of revenue through the issuing of licenses for timber and pole-wood extraction, which would be granted to people living adjacent to the forest (Wily 1999).

The plan met significant opposition among local people whose livelihoods were dependent on that tract of forest. There were also concerns about the plan's feasibility. As experience has shown, it is unrealistic to expect low-paid forest guards (many of whom are recruited from the same rural areas they are expected to police) to monitor the forest's border from villagers in need of forest products for basic subsistence. By the early 1990s, an agreement was reached to find a more acceptable management strategy. The solution ultimately involved allowing and assisting each of the eight villages that border the woodlands to take full rights and responsibility for their conservation.

ECOnnection 4.4

Socioecological Benefits Known to Arise from Community Conservation

FIRST BENEFIT: STRENGTHENS COMMUNITIES

- builds local skills, interests, and capacities
- builds a sense of stewardship and community capacity for environmental problem solving that will remain with the community
- builds community cohesion
- increases the likelihood that the community will be able to solve future problems on their own.

SECOND BENEFIT: APPROACHES ARE TAILORED TO LOCAL NEEDS

- As opposed to top-down approaches, which tend to serve nonlocal interests, community conservation can be highly responsive to unique community and environmental needs by incorporating local knowledge; and strategies and solutions will likely be well suited to local socioecological dynamics.

THIRD BENEFIT: POSITIVE OUTCOMES FOR INDIVIDUALS

- Knowledge of and relationship with surrounding ecosystems are enhanced.

- Working with others can have therapeutic benefits.
- Building social ties with others enhances individual well-being.

FOURTH BENEFIT: INCREASED LIKELIHOOD OF LOCAL ACCEPTANCE AND SUSTAINABLE OUTCOMES

- There is an increased likelihood of successful implementation when actions and decisions are viewed by those involved as responsible and appropriate.
- As local populations rely on having a healthy surrounding ecosystem, they have an incentive to be sure they get conservation strategies right.

FIFTH BENEFIT: EFFICIENT USE OF RESOURCES

- Enforcement and monitoring are often done cost-effectively, as informal social norms, trust, and a shared commitment to success are linked positively to compliance.

Adapted from Galvin et al. (2018).

The results have been unmistakable. The forests show visible signs of gain, as most of the earlier unregulated in-forest settlement, charcoal burning, and illicit timber harvesting have ceased. The size of the woodland has actually increased. In the Duru-Haitemba Forest, which had previously suffered the most damage, the return of understory shrubbery, grasses, and bees points to improved forest health. In other parts of the forest, increases in wildlife biodiversity are being recorded. Hundreds of young village men have volunteered to patrol the protected areas, at zero cost to the government, out of a vested interest in the health of the forest (see, e.g., Lupala et al. 2015; see also Case Study 4.1).

Agrobiodiversity Conservation

Agrobiodiversity—all forms of life directly relevant to agriculture, including crops and livestock but also many other organisms, such as soil fauna, weeds, pests, and predators— is the result of natural and human selection processes, involving farmers, herders, and fishers over millennia. The future of food security, it is widely believed (Duncan et al. 2020), hinges on agrobiodiversity, which gives us options when responding to whatever threats to food production we can expect to face in the future. Phenomena that can fall under the category of agrobiodiversity include harvested crop varieties, livestock breeds, fish species, and nondomesticated (wild) animals used for food; nonharvested species in production ecosystems that support food provision (like soil microbiota, pollinators, and other organisms such as earthworms); and nonharvested species in the wider environment that support food production ecosystems (such as species in a waterway that encourage the process of water purification).

Agrobiodiversity is not only viewed as representing one of the keys to future food security but also widely seen as central to any sustainable model of food production. There is compelling evidence that, through the implementation of agroecology farming techniques, an approach relying heavily on ecological principles rather than commercial inputs (see Chapter 8), agrobiodiversity can help increase crop productivity—potentially even outproducing conventional agriculture. Agrobiodiversity is also a key ingredient to the

---

CASE STUDY 4.1

Participatory Forest Management in Kenya

Kenya has widely embraced participatory forest management, a variation of community conservation. Because of its track record, it is believed that this approach not only effectively achieves sustainable forest management goals but also simultaneously involves stakeholders whose livelihoods depend on the forest (Mbuvi et al. 2015). Participatory forest management is supported under the Forest Act of 2005. This act provides for the establishment, development, and sustainable management of forest resources for the socioeconomic development of the country. The avenues through which Kenyans in general, and Kenyan forest communities in particular, can directly or indirectly participate in the management and monitoring of their forests include the following: as members of community forest associations, as representatives appointed to the forest conservation committees, as representatives appointed to the Board of the Kenya Forest Service, and as individuals.

The Forest Act of 2005 also allows forest communities to constitute up to 50 percent of the representation on the forest conservation committee that oversees the management of a recognized forest. The law further provides for community representation on the board of the Kenya Forest Service.

MOVEMENT MATTERS 4.1
Open Source Seed

On April 17, 2014, on the campus of the University of Wisconsin, Madison, the Open Source Seed Initiative (OSSI) released twenty-nine seed varieties under an open source pledge printed on all OSSI-distributed seed packets. It reads as follows:

> This Open Source Seed Pledge is intended to ensure your freedom to use the seed contained herein in any way you choose, and to make sure those freedoms are enjoyed by all subsequent users. By opening this packet, you pledge that you will not restrict others' use of these seeds and their derivatives by patents, licenses, or any other means. You pledge that if you transfer these seeds or their derivatives you will acknowledge the source of these seeds and accompany your transfer with this pledge.
>
> (quoted in Kloppenburg 2014)

In other words, any future plant that's derived from these **open source seeds** must be freely available. They cannot be patented, licensed, or commodified in any way, even in those instances where they have been bred or genetically modified into something new.

Irwin Goldman, professor of horticulture at the University of Wisconsin, Madison, was one of the organizers of the event. For him, OSSI is about restoring the practice of sharing that was once the rule among plant breeders around the world. In his words, "If other breeders asked for our materials, we would send them a packet of seed, and they would do the same for us." Regrettably, he further notes that because of intellectual property rights "that way of working is no longer with us" (quoted in Charles 2014).

For other members of the movement, the rationale of open source goes even deeper. For Jack Kloppenburg, professor of sociology at the University of Wisconsin, Madison, open source is a way to reshape our very food system: "The problem is concentration, and the narrow set of uses to which the technology and the breeding are being put" (quoted in Charles 2014). Within the first month after its launch, OSSI had received over 200 orders from eight countries (Shemkus 2014). In June 2015, after a three-day meeting near Hyderabad, India, saw the birth of Apna Beej (Hindi for "Our Seeds"): OSSI now has a sister organization, Open Source Seed System India (OSSSI). (See Image 4.2.)

IMAGE 4.2

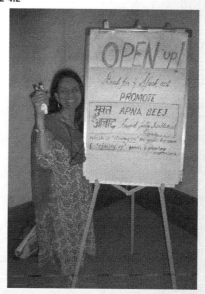

Pictured above is Indian attorney and prominent intellectual property rights activist Shahlini Butani. Six months prior to this picture being taken in June 2015, she was skeptical of open source seeds. She is now a vocal advocate, believing open source seeds encourage innovation and enhance biodiversity while respecting farmer livelihoods.

Source: Jack Kloppenburg and Shahlini Butani.

CASE STUDY 4.2

The Seed Bank That Makes Memories

The Seed Savers Exchange (SSE) is a United States based heritage seed bank in northeastern Iowa (see www.seedsavers.org). Founded in 1975, the SSE is a nonprofit organization that both saves and sells heirloom fruit, vegetable, and flower seeds. On this 890-acre farm, called the Heritage Farm, there are 24,000 rare vegetable varieties, including about 4,000 traditional varieties from eastern Europe and Russia; approximately 700 pre-1900 varieties of apples, which represent nearly every remaining pre-1900 variety left in existence out of the 8,000 that once existed; and a herd of the rare Ancient White Park cattle, which currently have an estimated global population below 2,000.

Although in part a gene and seed bank, the SSE is much more than that. Visitors can learn about the seeds being saved, including their history and how to cultivate the seeds and cook and prepare their harvest. If it's the right time of year, they can even experience how the fruits and vegetables taste. Indeed, calling SSE a memory bank doesn't go far enough, as many visitors find the organization also responsible for memory *making*. An example of this occurs at their heirloom tomato tasting workshop. During this event, participants get to not only taste more than forty different kinds of tomatoes but actively learn how to save the seeds of their favorite varieties for future planting (Carolan 2011, 2017).

effective control of disease and pest outbreaks without the use of harmful chemical inputs (Gliessman 2015).

The promotion of agrobiodiversity can take many forms. Simply allowing farmers to save seed from one year to be planted the next is a good place to start, particularly since patents and other controls like so-called **terminator technology** (genetically engineered seeds that produce sterile plants) are making this increasingly difficult (see Movement Matters 4.1). **Memory banks**, spaces that preserve not only genetic material but the skills to grow and save seeds and prepare the fruits of those labors, also help promote agrobiodiversity by ensuring that future generations have a working knowledge of this species diversity (see Case Study 4.2).

Agrobiodiversity (or more specifically agrobiocultural diversity) can also be promoted and enhanced through activities related to urban agriculture, whether those gardens are located in, for example, Denver (Carolan and Hale 2016); Chicago (Taylor and Lovell 2015); Moshi, Tanzania (Schlesinger et al. 2015); or Rio Negro, Brazil (Emperaire and Eloy 2015). One study examining urban agriculture in migrant neighborhoods in Chicago found their gardens to be quite diverse, though the level of biodiversity varied by ethnicity group. African-American gardens demonstrated the highest food plant richness (with an average of 16.3 food crops per garden), followed by Chinese-origin gardens (14.4) and Mexican-origin gardens (8.6) (Taylor and Lovell 2015). Cultural tastes and household-specific ethnic cuisine preferences also often compel urban gardeners to grow and thus preserve certain species not easily acquired at grocery stores and food markets (Carolan and Hale 2016). More than just a source of affordable food, these gardens also supply

ECOnnection 4.5
Moral Framing on Conservation Behaviors

Conservatives and liberals might not be as far apart on these issues (e.g., conservation, recycling, sustainability) as we tend to think, as long as appeals are made to relevant moral frames. Studies found that framing a pro-environmental message as patriotic—activities that will protect and preserve the American way of life—increased conservatives' likelihood of engaging in conservation behaviors, willingness to recycle, and to sign a pro-environmental petition (see, e.g., Feinberg and Willer 2013; Wolsko et al. 2016).

Think about how the media and activists talk about environmental issues. No wonder those messages do not tend to resonate with those on the Right.

households with ingredients necessary for the making of certain cultural dishes, thus helping ensure both plant species and cultural survival.

Although humans pose the gravest threat to biodiversity, at the moment we are also its greatest potential ally. Once we accept our rightful identity as being part of nature, rather than seeing ourselves independent of it, new possibilities open up (see ECOnnection 4.5). These links are particularly conspicuous between agricultural systems and ecological ones, given the former's grounding (pun intended) in the latter. Agriculture, when done ecologically—*agroecology*—can go a long way toward preserving the ecological integrity of systems while helping to safeguard biological as well as cultural diversity and enhancing long-term food security.

IMPORTANT CONCEPTS

- agrobiodiversity
- biocultural diversity
- biopiracy
- community conservation
- *ex situ* and *in situ* conservation
- memory banking
- open source seeds
- participatory forest management
- tragedy of the commodity

DISCUSSION QUESTIONS

1. What are the links between cultural and biological diversity?
2. Conventional agriculture has become a monoculture within a monoculture, where fields are populated not just by one crop but one variety of a single crop. What are some of the forces driving this specialization?

3. Can we rely entirely on zoos and gene banks when it comes to preserving our biological heritage?
4. Why isn't community conservation more popular in a country like the United States?

SUGGESTED ADDITIONAL READINGS

Besek, J.F., and R. York. 2018. "Toward a Sociology of Biodiversity Loss." *Social Currents*, 6(3): 239–254. https://doi.org/10.1177%2F2329496518815867.

Galvin, K., T. Beeton, and M. Luizza, 2018. "African Community-Based Conservation: A Systematic Review of Social and Ecological Outcomes." *Ecology and Society*, 23(3): 39. https://doi.org/10.5751/ES-10217-230339.

Vucetich, J.A., D. Burnham, E.A. Macdonald, J.T. Bruskotter, S. Marchini, A. Zimmermann, and D.W. Macdonald. 2018. "Just Conservation: What Is It and Should We Pursue It?" *Biological Conservation*, 221: 23–33.

RELEVANT INTERNET LINKS

- www.conservation.org/how/pages/hotspots.aspx. Excellent resource to learn more about biodiversity hotspots.
- www.gaiafoundation.org. The Gaia Foundation is committed to regenerating cultural and biocultural diversity and their website is rich in resources for those interested in the subject.
- www.madfeed.co/video/the-importance-of-a-rose-biocultural-diversity/. Video of Andrea Pieroni, professor of food botany, ethnobotany, and ethnobiology at the University of Gastronomic Sciences in Pollenzo, Italy. He calls upon scientists and chefs "to come down from their towers" and exchange ideas.
- https://foodtank.com/news/2015/01/fifteen-seed-saving-initiatives-protecting-biodiversity-for-future-generati/. Inspiring seed saving initiatives from around the world.

SUGGESTED VIDEOS

- *Drop in the Ocean?* (2015). In less than fifty years, ocean life as we know it could be completely done for. This not only means dead oceans, but a dead ecosystem, and the mass death of all who depend on it.
- *Rachel Carson's "Silent Spring"* (1993). Though more than twenty-five years old, this production from the PBS series *The American Experience* offers an excellent historical lesson for anyone not familiar with this landmark book and its pioneering author.
- *Salmon Confidential* (2013). What's killing British Columbia's wild salmon? Watch this video and find out.
- *The Fight for Amazonia* (2012). From the heart of the Amazon jungle comes a three-part series examining the strides being made to save the world's most endangered rain forest.
- *The Guide* (2014), a short documentary. Raised near Gorongosa National Park (a war-torn national park in Mozambique), young Tonga Torcida dreams of becoming a tour guide. But when he meets famed biologist E.O. Wilson, his new view of the world around him—and his future—places him at a crossroads. Should Tonga become a guide, or take on a bigger role in trying to keep the park alive?

Water: There's No Substitute

Until recently, economists were fond of discussing what's known as the "water and dia-monds paradox." The paradox, as summarized in an economics textbook from the 1990s, goes something like this: Why is it that "water, which has so much value in use, has no value in exchange, while diamonds, which have practically no value in use, are exchanged at high prices" (Ekelund and Hébert 1997, 294)? This is clearly less the case today, as in some instances people are willing to pay more for a liter of bottled water than they are for a comparable amount of gasoline. Indeed, the paradox now is, why are some willing to pay so much for this commodity when they can just as easily get it for free? The reason water seems to defy economic reasoning is that its value cannot be expressed in exclusively monetary terms. In this chapter, I explore some of the consequences associated with humanity's growing need for this life-giving resource and, later, articulate some potential responses to ensure that this need never exceeds supply.

Fast Facts

- The water cycle does not favor continents equally. Six countries—Brazil, Canada, China, Colombia, Indonesia, and Russia—account for half of the world's renewable freshwater.
- Approximately 70 percent of all the freshwater used by humans goes to agriculture, indus-try uses 22 percent, and the remaining 8 percent is used by municipalities and households (World Bank 2017).
- A per capita freshwater supply of below 1,700 cubic meters places countries in the category of being "water stressed." When annual water supplies drop below 1,000 cubic meters per person, the population faces "water scarcity." And when below 500 cubic meters, it is facing "absolute scarcity." As documented in Table 5.1, a number of countries currently fall well within, or dangerously close to, this category. One word describes the situation for many countries: *thirsty* (see Case Study 5.1).
- The **water footprint** of countries, as illustrated in Table 5.2, varies wildly. (A water foot-print is an indicator of freshwater use that looks at both direct and indirect water use by a consumer or producer.) The annual water footprint per capita in the United States, for

example, is 7,800 liters per day, compared to, say, China, which is 2,900 liters daily. China's population, however, is more than four times that of the United States, making its total water footprint much larger, despite its lower per capita use.

- **Virtual water** refers to water used during the growing, making, or manufacturing of a given commodity. Commodity water footprints are increasingly broken down into the green, blue, and grey water that go into their making. The *green water footprint* refers to the use of water resources (such as rainwater that does not become runoff) for growing crops. A *blue water footprint* denotes the use of water resources—surface and groundwater—along the supply chain of a product. And the *grey water footprint* represents the volume of freshwater required to assimilate and adequately dilute the load of pollutants that results from the production and processing of commodities. As shown in Table 5.3, a lot of (virtual) water goes into the making of common commodities.

- Dams, as solutions to water-starved areas, are not without their problems. In addition to changing the ecology of a watershed and potentially negatively affecting human communities (when they are displaced to make space for a reservoir), dams are often responsible for losing the very thing they are charged with storing: water. They can lose multiple meters of depth per year as a result of evaporation, especially in hot, dry climates (see, e.g., Vervoort 2014). The Aswan Dam on the Nile River, for instance, loses between 6–7 millimetres *daily* (Hassan et al. 2017). It might not sound like a lot, until you calculate losses in years. That's more than two meters annually lost to evaporation. Or take Lake Mead, roughly 30 miles southeast of Las Vegas, Nevada, which formed behind Hoover Dam and is the largest reservoir in the United States. According to the US Bureau of Reclamation (2015), this body of water is at 37 percent capacity and dropping rapidly.

- As of 2015, some 3,700 large hydroelectric dams were either being built or on the verge of being built around the world, most located in South America, Southeast Asia, and Africa. The number of free-flowing river systems worldwide will decrease by 21 percent if all these structures are built (Zarfl et al. 2015). This brings up a good question: What are we to make of the costs of these projects? A 2014 study examining the costs and benefits of 245 large dams built between 1934 and 2007 found that construction costs alone were on average nearly double their projections and that construction took 44 percent longer than originally promised (Ansar et al. 2014). The authors go on to warn, "Forecasts of costs of large dams today are likely to be as wrong as they were between 1934 and 2007," and conclude that "the actual construction costs of large dams are too high to yield a positive return" (Ansar et al. 2014, 44).

- Climate change is expected to drastically alter the water cycle. As mean atmospheric temperature rises, the water-holding capacity of the air increases exponentially. In the future we can therefore expect an atmosphere saturated with moisture, which will only serve to intensify storms and other weather events. A higher atmospheric temperature also means more energy to drive intense weather events. More water, falling at greater rates of intensity, means more floods and soil erosion for some regions. Elsewhere, rain will become an increasingly rare event, which, coupled with increased temperatures, will hasten the drying up of rivers, lakes, and reservoirs.

- According to a paper published by the World Health Organization (WHO) (Subbaraman and Murthy 2015) examining water use in Mumbai, India, the median price paid for water by residents of slum areas who lack access to municipal water was 135 Indian rupees (US$2.07) per 1,000 liters of water. This was more than thirty times the charge paid by other city residents whose communities were connected to city water infrastructure. Not surprisingly, then,

TABLE 5.1 Renewable Water Resources (RWR) per Capita for Select Countries, 2017

COUNTRY	2017 (M³/YR)
Kuwait	0
Bahrain	2
United Arab Emirates	16
Egypt	18
Bahamas	51
Saudi Arabia	84
Yemen	86
Israel	89
Jordan	100
Singapore	121
Libya	123
Niger	203
Algeria	247
Pakistan	289
Oman	380
Kenya	470
Somalia	600
Hungary	606
Rwanda	822
South Africa	893
Morocco	900
Lebanon	1,104
Ethiopia	1,196
Poland	1,369

Source: Adapted from World Bank (2019).

TABLE 5.2 Composition of Water Footprint (WF) for Select Countries

COUNTRY	POPULATION	WF, TOTAL (BILLION M³ PER YEAR)	WF, PER CAPITA (LITERS PER CAPITA PER YEAR)
Australia	24,000,000	156	6,500
Bangladesh	165,000,000	396	2,400
Brazil	209,000,000	1,170	5,600
Canada	37,000,000	237	6,400
China	1,400,000,000	4,340	3,100
Egypt	98,000,000	372	3,800
France	67,000,000	328	4,900
Germany	83,000,000	332	4,000
India	1,340,000,000	4,154	3,100
Indonesia	264,000,000	844	3,200
Italy	61,000,000	384	6,300
Japan	126,000,000	491	3,900
Jordan	10,000,000	46	4,600
Mexico	129,000,000	709	5,500
Netherlands	17,000,000	68	4,000
Pakistan	197,000,000	729	3,700
Russia	144,000,000	748	5,200
South Africa	57,000,000	200	3,500
Sudan	41,000,000	61	4,800
United Kingdom	66,000,000	251	3,800
USA	327,000,000	2,616	8,000
Zambia	17,000,000	46	2,700

Source: Adapted from Hoekstra and Mekonnen (2012) and Mubako (2018).

TABLE 5.3 Global per Unit Average of Virtual Water Content for Select Commodities

COMMODITY	VIRTUAL WATER (LITERS/KG)	GREEN (%)	BLUE (%)	GREY (%)
One sheet standard printer paper	10	3	3	3
Chocolate	1,7195	98	1	1
One tomato (70 g)	300	50	30	20
One potato (100 g)	287	66	11	22
Margarita pizza	1,259	76	14	10
Powdered milk	5,145	85	8	7
One orange (100 g)	560	72	20	9
One apple (100 g)	822	68	16	15
Leather (bovine)	17,093	93	4	3
Dates	2,277	41	55	4
Cotton	2,495	54	33	13

Source: Based on Fan et al. (2019) and Mekonnen and Hoekstra (2011).

these communities used less than 20 liters of water per person per day, which is well below the minimum consumption level recommended by WHO for ensuring basic hygiene.

- As watersheds are developed and become blanketed with impervious surfaces (streets, parking lots, tennis courts, rooftops, and so on), they lose their ability to absorb rainwater, resulting in more being lost to runoff. With increased runoff comes a heightened chance of flooding, soil erosion, and the overall disruption of a watershed's water cycle (see Table 5.4).

TABLE 5.4 Runoff versus Soil Infiltration for Every Three Inches of Rainfall on Select Surface Types

SURFACE TYPE	RUNOFF (INCHES)	INFILTRATION (INCHES)
Forest	0.6	2.4
Meadow	0.6	2.4
Cultivated agricultural field	1.0	2.0
Residental lawn	1.6	1.4
Parking lot, street, sidewalk	3.0	0.0

Source: Adapted from Marinelli (2011).

CASE STUDY 5.1
China's Water Woes

China has more than 20 percent of the world's population but only 7 percent of its fresh water, and most of that is polluted. According to one report, 80 percent of China's tested groundwater is affected by pollution (Yu 2018).

In 2011, residents of Hualiba Village in central China's Henan Province were relocated ten kilometers away (roughly six miles). Between their new homes and where they used to live and the fields they cultivated is a massive new concrete water canal. The canal started moving water from China's water-rich south to its water-poor north in 2014—the biggest water diversion project in the world. (The north of China holds a fifth of the country's freshwater while possessing two-thirds of its farmland.) Eleven of China's thirty-one provinces fall below the World Bank's definition of "water scarce," with less than 1,000 cubic meters of freshwater per person per year (Xichuan 2014).

The transfer is expected to ease the water stress experienced by Beijing (also located in the north), supplying the city with about a third of its annual demand. And of course it will help nourish farmland in the north. There is concern, however, that this project will actually make China's water situation worse in the long run. By reducing water stress in the short term, it incentivizes water-intensive practices—urbanization, conventional agriculture, and so forth—that will likely speed the country toward the peak water cliff. Huge social disruptions have also been caused by this project. Some estimates place the number of people displaced at more than half a million. Then there are the potential public health costs, like those associated with the spread of disease common in the south—such as schistosomiasis, a devastating snail-borne disease.

Implications

It is a bit surprising that sociologists have not been more interested in water. So much of our lives is touched, in some way, by this precious compound. Cities, nations, and entire civilizations all need water to survive, though not too much, either—I am reminded of a small town in Iowa near where I grew up that was relocated after the so-called Great Flood of 1993. (Sadly, there have been two other "Great Floods" in the state since then.) Water also resonates with us culturally. Take the case of the Klamath people in Northern California and southern Oregon, who were deemed, in the landmark legal decision *United States of America and the Klamath Indian Tribe* v. *Ben Adair* (1983), to have rights to water on reservation lands dating back to "time immemorial" (the distant past beyond memory) to protect culturally essential activities like hunting and fishing.

This chapter aims to give the reader a taste of how water affects our world. It has repeatedly been said that water promises to be to the twenty-first century what oil was to the twentieth century. If so, sociologists (and the social sciences more generally) ought to play as central a role in its study in this century as petroleum geologists did for oil in the last.

Bottled Water

Have you had bottled water in the past twelve months? Chances are good you have. The global bottled water market was valued at $113.14 billion in 2016. That figure is expected to reach $215.12 billion by 2025 (Grand View Research 2018). While campaigns against bottled water continue to affect the industry, they have not drastically damaged sales. In the United States, for instance, where bottled water bans have been adopted in some cities, national parks, and college campuses, sales continue to increase; sales in the so-called functional water market—water formulated with micronutrients—are increasing rapidly. Mexico has the world's highest per capita consumption rate of bottled water among countries, as noted in Table 5.5, though perhaps for not long (Statista 2015). China might appear conspicuously absent from the table. Remember, however, that this is a per capita breakdown. With a population of 1.4 billion, it would take *a lot* of sales for China to make the list. In terms of volume, however, it dominates. China has 7 percent of the world's freshwater supplies but 20 percent of its population, and its intake of bottled water doubled from 2010 to 2015, from nineteen billion to thirty-seven billion liters. In 2013, China overtook the United States as the biggest market for bottled water by volume (*The Economist* 2015).

WHO released a report in 2018 announcing the potential risks of plastic in drinking water. Its concern stems from an analysis of some of the world's most popular bottled water brands, where it found more than 90 percent contained tiny pieces of plastic. The analysis of 259 bottles from nineteen locations in nine countries across eleven different brands found an average of 325 plastic particles for every liter of water sold. One bottle of Nestlé Pure Life had concentrations equal to 10,000 plastic pieces per liter. Of those 259 bottles, only seventeen were free of plastics. The most common type of plastic found was

TABLE 5.5 Top Global Consumers of Bottled Water, 2009 and 2017 (Gallons per Capita)

COUNTRY	2009 CONSUMPTION	2017 CONSUMPTION
Mexico	59.2	67.2
Thailand	26.3	57.5
Italy	49	48.2
United States	27.6	42.1
Germany	34.7	37.9
France	34.4	36.4
Belgium/Luxemburg	35.5	35.1
United Arab Emirates	25	33.9
Spain	27.7	32.6

Source: Adapted from Statista (2015, 2019).

polypropylene—used to make bottle caps. The bottles analyzed were purchased in the United States, China, Brazil, India, Indonesia, Mexico, Lebanon, Kenya, and Thailand (Mason et al. 2018).

Bottled water also risks contributing to political apathy, as Andrew Szasz argues in his important book *Shopping Our Way to Safety* (2007). Szasz develops a term for the type of individualized consumer "solutions" that things like bottled water are meant to represent. He argues these consumer-focused solutions create an "inverted quarantine." Similar to a conventional quarantine, the inverted quarantine seeks to provide protection from a threat. Unlike a traditional quarantine, which works by isolating threats to a particular area, the inverted quarantine works by isolating the consumer in "a personal commodity bubble" (Szasz 2007, 97) from the threats, which are ubiquitous. As the title of the book aptly proclaims, we try to shop our way to safety by, among other things, purchasing organic food, bottled water, and air purifiers for our homes.

But there are problems with this strategy. First, all consumer-based solutions are biased toward those who can afford them. From the perspective of the working poor, this strategy might better be called "shopping *their* way to safety." In addition, in buying safety for themselves and their loved ones, the middle- and upper-class risk becoming politically indifferent to attempts at larger social change that could solve the problem for *all* segments of society. If, for example, bottled water was not available and the world's middle class and above had to drink from their tap, I wonder if greater willingness would be expressed for public investment in clean and affordable water.

Privatizing Water

Another way society is affected by water is through recent attempts to privatize public water utilities under the guise of **neoliberalism**. According to David Harvey (2005, 2),

> neoliberalism is in the first instance a theory of political economic practices that proposes that human well-being can best be advanced by liberating individual entrepreneurial freedoms and skills within an institutional framework characterized by strong private property rights, free markets, and free trade.

(Neoliberalism is discussed further in Chapter 10). As opposed to liberalism, which prioritizes individual liberties, neoliberalism elevates free enterprise above all else, even if that means grossly impinging on those allegedly sacred individual liberties. Neoliberalism is also said to transform the state. The neoliberalization of the state results in an erosion of government commitment in areas such as education and health while the power of private sector actors increases. The rise of neoliberalism on the world economic stage can be seen in recent decades with the rapid push to hollow out the state by eliminating regulations and privatizing anything and everything, even water.

There is also an environmental argument, some contend, for privatizing water. **Market environmentalism**—emphasizing markets as a solution to environmental problems—is a way of packaging neoliberalism in green wrapping. The thinking goes something like this: by strengthening and expanding private property rights to resources like water and relying more on markets for the allocation of resources, environmental goods will be more efficiently used, leading ultimately to less environmental degradation and a more sustainable use of resources.

Two influential international bodies that have heavily pushed for **water privatization** are the World Bank and the International Monetary Fund (IMF) (see ECOnnection 5.1). Put simply, water privatization means treating water like any other commodity and leaving questions of access and sanitation to market mechanisms. Yet this risks creating two water worlds: affluent nations that still overwhelmingly rely on publicly-funded water services (and that would never dream of handing control of them over to profit-seeking corporations) and the rest of the world, which may have no choice but to get its water from a private water company. Beyond obvious access questions—for example, what about slums and other areas where a profit could not be made by supplying its people with water?—the two-world scenario advantages affluent nations. We can see this occurring, for example, in the farming sector. The amount of money recovered by the US Bureau of Reclamation from irrigation projects averages at around 10 to 20 percent; the remaining 80 to 90 percent comes out of taxpayers' pockets (Peterson 2009; see ECOnnection 5.2). US farmers, under the above scenario, would benefit tremendously if many of their global competitors had to get their water from a corporation seeking full-cost recovery plus a little more (the profit). It would give them a significant market advantage if they could obtain this valuable input for a fraction of the price it costs their competitors overseas.

In 1990 approximately fifty million people globally received their water from private water companies. In 2013, that number surpassed one billion for the first time (see Case Study 5.2). To ensure this shift toward water privatization, developing countries are now

ECOnnection 5.1

The IMF and the World Bank

The World Bank and the IMF are known collectively as the Bretton Woods Institutions, after the small community in rural New Hampshire where they were founded in July 1944. Each is charged, in different ways, with directing and supporting the structure of the world's economic and financial order. The World Bank's first loans were granted following World War II to help finance the reconstruction of Western Europe. As these nations recovered, the bank turned increasingly to the world's poorer countries, in part to help them "develop" by folding them into the world economy and thus lure them away from communism; this was at the height of the Cold War. The World Bank's stated mission is to promote economic growth and social progress in developing countries—though the bank believes the latter comes only *after* the former.

Whereas the World Bank is primarily a lending institution, the IMF's main role is to keep the international monetary system running smoothly. It does this by monitoring the world's currencies, making sure the unpredictable variations that helped to trigger (and unduly extended) the Great Depression in the 1930s do not happen again. Thus, although the IMF does provide loans, it is more than just a bank. Both institutions wield considerable power over international affairs, as their loans come with substantial conditions. Some of the strings attached to the loans have required countries to privatize their municipal water systems.

unable to borrow from the World Bank or IMF without having in place a domestic water privatization policy. It's fair to say that the majority of public utility privatization deals that have occurred in the past decade in lower-income countries are the result of the direct participation of these global monetary institutions.

Unfortunately, the societal cost of privatization has been great. No profit-seeking company can expect to expand their services to populations that cannot pay. So: the water situation for the poor remains deplorable in many countries that were promised they would be saved by these privatization schemes. It is estimated that 75 percent of the costs of running a water utility are for infrastructure alone (Lappé 2014). Corporations are interested in cutting costs in order to maximize profits, which is precisely what you see happening among private water entities—cuts to spending on infrastructure. While the World Bank continues to promote water privatization, its own data reveal deep problems with the approach. According to its Private Participation in Infrastructure Database, there was a 34 percent failure rate for all private water and sewerage contracts entered into between 2000 and 2010, compared to a failure rate of 7 percent for transportation, 6 percent for energy, and 3 percent for telecommunications during the same period.

This might explain why attitudes toward water privatization are changing. Many cities—approaching 200 in thirty-five countries—that initially rushed to sign agreements with private water companies have chosen to terminate those agreements and return urban water provision to public control.

> Direct experience with common problems of private water management—from lack of infrastructure investments, to tariff hikes to environmental hazards—has persuaded communities and policymakers that the public sector is better placed to provide quality services to citizens and promote the human right to water.
>
> (Satoko Kishimoto, water coordinator with the
> Transnational Institute in Brussels, quoted in Vidal 2015)

In fairness to advocates of privatization, whatever we did in the twentieth century to deliver clean water to the world's poor didn't work either, or at least didn't work as well as many had hoped. Clearly, a new approach is needed, as we know for a fact that improving access to clean water can help eradicate extreme hunger and poverty. Among other things, access to water has direct positive effects on education and gender equity. Severe and repeated cases of diarrhea, often the result of water-related diseases, contribute to malnutrition by reducing the body's ability to retain essential micro- and macronutrients, which impairs short- and long-term cognitive and physical development among children. Moreover, sick kids are more likely to miss school, thus further reducing their ability to take advantage of opportunities that could improve their lives. Because water is so difficult to access in some parts of the world—most notably, many nations in Africa—millions of women and children must walk long distances daily just to obtain this necessary resource for their families. There are countless reports of women and children in some African nations spending hours every day fetching water (see http://thewaterproject.org). All this time walking for water is time that could be spent, for example, in school.

ECOnnection 5.2
US Bureau of Reclamation

The US Bureau of Reclamation, the largest public purveyor of irrigation water in the American West, develops projects and delivers water to locally organized irrigation districts that provide water service to farmers. Congress directed the bureau to allow repayment without interest and to determine repayment schedules based on farmers' ability to pay and other special circumstances. The law that created the bureau allows farmers to receive three types of water subsidies:

1 interest-free repayment of a project's construction costs
2 reduced repayments based on ability to pay
3 reduced repayments under special circumstances (The federal government can cancel some or all of farmers' repayment obligation in the case of special circumstances, such as economic hardship, settlement of Native American water rights claims, unproductive lands, or drought.).

The cumulative values of such subsidies can be substantial. An example is the Tualatin irrigation project in Oregon. Its total construction costs were $58.7 million. Yet when water became available to farmers in 1976, the government determined that they could not repay the full amount. Instead, they repaid roughly 3 percent of total construction costs, shifting the remaining balance to other beneficiaries, namely, commercial users of electricity generated by the project (Wichelns 2010).

Agriculture

For a variety of reasons, it does not make sense to import large quantities of water for purposes of raising water-intensive agricultural commodities, especially given that the commodities themselves can be imported. A sizable portion of a country's virtual water footprint (or embedded water) thus comes in the form of the agricultural commodities it imports. The United States is the largest virtual water exporter, followed by China, India, and Brazil. You might be surprised to learn that the United States is also the largest virtual water importer, though this only offsets 75 percent of exports leaving the country with one of the largest virtual water trade deficits. Other major net exporters include Canada, Australia, India, Argentina, and Brazil. The world's largest net importers are North African, Middle Eastern, and European countries, in addition to Mexico, Japan, and, as mentioned, the United States (Hoekstra and Mekonnen 2012).

India, for instance, exports roughly 37.2 tonnes of basmati, raised using around ten trillion liters of water (Chandrasekhar and Ghosh 2019). To put it another way, India virtually exported ten trillion liters of water. In contrast, China has maintained mostly an import-intensive virtual water trade since 1960, meaning it has intentionally shifted to *importing* water intensive crops. Thus, while India receives about 50 percent more annual rainfall than China, the total water available for India is only about 67 percent of that of China (Goswami and Nishad 2015).

CASE STUDY 5.2

Neoliberalism and Water Privatization: The Case of India

While the Indian government once viewed water as a social good that ought to be left to local communities to use, value, and regulate, it now increasingly grasps water as a commodity whose value ought to be determined by the market. For example, the government's Eighth Plan explains,

> Water has to be managed as a commodity in exactly the same way as any other resource; supply of water to consumers should normally be based on the principle of effective demand which should broadly correspond to the standard of service, that the users are willing to maintain, operate and finance.
>
> (Eighth Plan, Five-Year Plan of India, 1951–Present, 14.12.2)

In its Ninth Plan, it is noted that water "should be managed as an economic asset" (Ninth Plan, Five-Year Plan of India, 1951–Present, 3.7.38). As Subramaniam (2014, 401) argues,

> the increased use of economic terms in the Plans, such as 'supply and demand,' 'scarcity,' 'consumers,' and the aforementioned 'stake-holders,' serves as evidence of a major shift in the understanding of water and water relations, distinct from

the ways in which local communities perceive this resource.

This movement toward privatized water occurred in India in two interrelated ways: contracting water harvesting and delivery to private enterprises and enticing private companies via tax breaks, lax environmental regulations, and so forth to take over water provisioning under the guise of economic development. The 2002 National Water Policy clearly articulates how the private sector should be involved in water delivery:

> Private sector participation should be encouraged in planning, development and management of water resources projects for diverse uses, wherever feasible. Private sector participation may help in introducing innovative ideas, generating financial resources and introducing corporate management and improving service efficiency and accountability to users. Depending upon the specific situations, various combinations of private sector participation, in building, operating, leasing, and transferring of water resources facilities, may be considered.
>
> (quoted in Subramaniam 2014, 401)

One thing that is as surprising and counterintuitive as it is disturbing is that a country's virtual water trade is not necessarily determined by its water situation. Virtual water can flow out of water-poor, land-rich countries into land-poor, water-rich countries. The evidence suggests that many countries import food not because they lack water but because they lack sufficient arable land that can be put to cultivation. In other words, water is not the limiting agricultural factor; fertile land is.

It would be careless of me to talk about water in the context of agriculture and not at least mention how agricultural practices can negatively affect water quality and human health. Take the case of pesticides. (More agriculture-related impacts on water supplies are discussed in Chapter 8.) One analysis places the cost of pesticides in the United States, after factoring in issues related to public and environmental health, at $9.645 billion dollars annually (Pimentel and Burgess 2014; see Table 5.6). Research shows that tobacco farmers in Brazil have high rates of cellular damage at the genetic level from the pesticides they regularly use and come into contact with (Kahl et al. 2016). Among agricultural workers in Sri Lanka, Costa Rica, and Nicaragua, 7.5 percent, 4.5 percent, and 6.3 percent, respectively, experience occupation pesticide poisoning annually (Garming and Waibel 2009; van der Hoek et al. 1998; Wesseling et al. 1993). And global pesticide use is increasing (Zhang and Liu 2017). A Chinese government report in 2016 stated that agricultural pesticide use in China has reached three times the global average (Zhang 2018). Another report notes that 70 percent of the pesticides used in China are not absorbed by plants, but instead seep into the soil and groundwater (Fan 2018).

Whereas agriculture continues to be a major water stakeholder—after all, approximately 70 percent of all the water used by humans globally goes to agriculture (Sterling and Vintinner 2012)—it is not the only one. As the demands from other interests increase, like the growing thirst of cities, water conflicts will arise and will not always be solved to the satisfaction of all stakeholders.

As revealed in Table 5.7, not all foods are equal when assessed according to their respective water footprints. The relative thirstiness of ground beef ("bovine meat" in the

TABLE 5.6 Total Estimated Environmental and Social Costs from Pesticides in the United States

IMPACT	COSTS (IN MILLIONS OF US DOLLARS)
Public health impacts	1,140
Domestic animal deaths and contaminations	30
Loss of natural enemies	520
Cost of pesticide resistance	1,500
Honey bee and pollination losses	334
Crop losses	1,391
Fishery losses	100
Bird losses	2,160
Groundwater contamination	2,000
Government regulations to prevent damage	470
Total	9,645

Source: Adapted from Pimentel and Burgess (2014).

TABLE 5.7 Global Average Water Footprint of Crop and Animal Products in Relation to Their Nutritional Value

FOOD ITEM	WATER FOOTPRINT PER UNIT OF WEIGHT (L/KG)				NUTRITIONAL CONTENT			WATER FOOTPRINT PER UNIT OF NUTRITIONAL VALUE		
	GREEN	BLUE	GREY	TOTAL	CALORIE (KCAL/KG)	PROTEIN (G/KG)	FAT (G/KG)	CALORIE (L/KCAL)	PROTEIN (L/G PROTEIN)	FAT (L/G FAT)
Sugar crops	130	52	15	197	285	0	0	0.69	0	0
Vegetables	194	43	85	322	240	12	2.1	1.34	26	154
Starchy roots	327	16	43	387	827	13	1.7	0.47	31	226
Fruits	726	147	89	962	460	5.3	2.8	2.09	180	348
Cereals	1,232	228	184	1,644	3,208	80	15	0.51	21	112
Oil crops	2,023	220	121	2,364	2,908	149	209	0.81	16	11
Pulses	3,180	141	734	4,055	3,412	215	23	1.19	19	180
Nuts	7,016	1,367	680	9,063	2,500	65	193	3.63	139	47
Milk	863	86	72	1,020	560	33	31	1.82	31	33
Eggs	2,592	244	429	3,265	1,425	111	100	2.29	29	33
Chicken meat	3,545	313	467	4,325	1,440	127	100	3	34	43
Butter	4,695	465	393	5,553	7,692	0	872	0.72	0	6.4
Pig meat	4,907	459	622	5,988	2,786	105	259	2.15	57	23
Sheep/goat meat	8,253	457	53	8,763	2,059	139	163	4.25	63	54
Bovine meat	14,414	550	451	15,415	1,513	138	101	10.19	112	153

Source: Hoekstra (2015).

table) is due in large part to the beef cow's consumption of grains. Even after factoring in for nutritional value, the global average confined beef cow requires 10.16 liters of water for every kilocalorie produced. As a protein source, it fares better than only nuts and fruits on a liter per gram of protein basis (Hoekstra 2015). Nuts also require copious amounts of water. Compared to other products listed in the table, they are especially large users of blue water.

More than 75 percent of the populations of developed countries reside in urban areas. This percentage is expected to increase to well over 80 percent by 2030. In less affluent nations, roughly 50 percent of the population lives in urban areas. Of this, more than 70 percent—or approximately one billion people—reside in slum-like conditions. By 2030 the urban population of poorer nations is expected to increase to just below 60 percent as a proportion of their total population. Meanwhile, the number of **megacities**, that is, cities with more than ten million residents, is expected to rise globally from forty-six to sixty-one between 2015 and 2030. The majority of these new megacities will be located in and around the Asian continent. Balancing the competing water demands of the city and the countryside, along with those of industry and wildlife—and let's not forget that all these people have to eat—promises to be a truly monumental task of the twenty-first century.

Climate Change

Freshwater systems are repeatedly cited as among the most vulnerable sectors to climate change. I will now briefly review, drawing from multiple sources (Heinke et al. 2019; Koutroulis et al. 2018; Martin-Ortega et al. 2015), the impact of climate change on important components of the Earth's freshwater systems. Even though our future water woes are not insurmountable, aggressively pursuing policies to combat climate change would go a long way toward making those woes a little less daunting.

SURFACE WATER

There is a remarkable similarity among climate models when it comes to predicting greater runoff in the tropics and higher latitudes and reduced runoff in many already dry, midlatitude regions such as the Mediterranean, South Africa, the southwestern United States and northwestern Mexico. In regions with significant snowmelt, we can expect changes to the timing of runoff and the rapidity of spring melt. In regard to the latter, this could lead to an increased risk of floods as that water overloads the capacity of the land to absorb it.

GROUNDWATER

Demand for groundwater is expected to increase to offset reduced surface flows in some regions. Some sites will also see reductions in the rate at which they recharge, while others will experience increases in recharge rates. Warmer temperatures will also result in higher evaporation rates, which could lead to increasing rates of groundwater **salinization** (the buildup of salt in soil and groundwater). Sea-level rise will also increase the risk of saltwater intrusion in coastal aquifers.

HYDROLOGIC EXTREMES

The frequency of intense flooding and drought conditions is expected to increase. Mid-continental regions, for example, are expected to be unusually dry during the summer. In all areas, climate models predict that when it does rain, the chances of an intense event will increase.

WATER QUALITY

Warmer atmospheric temperatures are expected to result in increases in the temperature of lakes, reservoirs, and rivers, which will in turn increase algal and bacterial blooms and cause dissolved oxygen concentrations in those bodies of water to decrease. More intense weather events could also increase soil erosion rates and negatively affect water quality. Similarly, significant flooding could increase the amount of pollutants and toxins that get washed into waterways.

WATER DEMAND

There are a lot of unknowns that make it difficult to speak definitively on the subject of future water demand. Water demand could increase dramatically in the agricultural sector, though if drought-tolerant crops are grown and improvements in irrigation efficiencies achieved, these demands could be tempered. Similarly, demand in urban areas might increase radically as, say, warmer temperatures further stress lawns, gardens, and parks, thus increasing irrigation rates in metropolitan areas. However, if drought-tolerant grasses, bushes, and trees are planted or xeriscape lawns become more culturally accepted, these demands too could be reduced dramatically.

Solutions

There are so many problems, tensions, and conflicts involving water that I couldn't begin to adequately summarize solutions to every single one. Consequently, to make this discussion manageable, this section will be broken up into two subsections. In the first, I talk about changing how we think about water. Technological solutions will get us only so far. It is also important to keep in mind that not everyone can afford them. Technological fixes also involve trade-offs—**desalinization** (the removal of salt and other minerals from saline water), for example, is immensely energy intensive (see Case Study 5.3). This is why we need to revisit how we think about water. Specifically, it is worth discussing first whether water is something to which we all have a fundamental human right. I conclude the chapter by discussing citizen engagement around water, also known as water governance.

Water as a Human Right at the Right Value

There are only two international conventions that explicitly recognize the right to water: the UN Convention on the Rights of the Child of 1989 (Article 24) and the UN Convention on the Elimination of All Forms of Discrimination Against Women of 1979

CASE STUDY 5.3
Desalinization in California

California is in trouble (see Image 5.1). The state needs water, or needs to use less of it—it all depends on how you look at the problem. One idea gaining favor is desalinization: converting seawater into drinking water. Desalinization plants are expensive to build and run. (One plant in Santa Barbara has been idle since the 1990s because of the costs.) Three main environmental considerations represent additional challenges to desalinization proponents: how seawater is brought in, how the drinkable water is separated out, and what happens to the salt afterward.

You can't just suck water in through a pipe, as that would risk trapping and killing sea life. Grates at the end of such a pipe still would allow in larvae and fish eggs. So the goal is to perfect a subsurface intake method: run a pipe hundreds of feet out and hundreds of feet beneath the dunes (whereby the sand acts as a natural filter). But that requires a large amount of energy to pump so much water so far. Once the seawater gets to the plant, it must be pushed through tiny membranes to filter out the salt. This requires immense pressure and thus immense amounts of energy. Finally, only half of the saltwater piped into a desalinization plant is made drinkable. The rest ends up as part of a thick salty soup that has to be disposed of. It can't just be dumped back into the sea—its density would cause the concoction to sink and kill anything in its path. It can't be dumped on land either: terrestrial life likes salt even less than marine life. One suggestion: blending the byproduct back into the ocean with sprayers that run thousands of feet out to sea (with small holes spaced roughly ten feet apart). This act too would require considerable energy (Potter 2015).

As of summer 2019, California has eleven desalination plants in operation. Under review are another eight new projects, or existing ones seeking expanded permits under new 2015 regulations included in the state Water Quality Control Plan for Ocean Waters of California. No permits under those regulations have yet been issued. And given the contentious environmental politics in California, many openly question if any ever will (Dooley 2019).

IMAGE 5.1

Photo taken in downtown Sacramento, CA, in August 2014.

(Article 14). Prior to 1979, one must go back to the Geneva Convention of 1949 (Article 26) to find any international legal document recognizing a human's right to water, though in this text that right extends only to prisoners of war. In 2002, General Comment Number 15 to the International Covenant on Economic, Social, and Cultural Rights, a major human rights treaty, was signed by 153 countries and recognizes that "the human right to water is indispensable for leading a life in human dignity" and "is a prerequisite for the realization of other human rights" (United Nations 2002, 1). The treaty also notes the importance of sanitation in the fulfillment of these rights.

According to this document, the human right to water entitles everyone to "sufficient," "safe," "acceptable," "physically accessible," and "affordable" water for personal and domestic uses. Of course, the precise meaning of these terms is up for debate. As a limited resource, we cannot treat the right to clean water the same as, say, the right to clean air. Indeed, precisely so we can ensure access to everyone, we will likely need to impose a *limit* to the right to water, a practice not all that unusual, as we impose limits on rights all the time. Those living in the United States, for example, are protected by strong free speech rights. Yet they still can't say anything they wish—like *bomb* in a crowded airplane. The scope of humans' right to water is normally limited, as it tends to refer to the fulfillment of basic needs, like those related to drinking, cooking, and other vital domestic needs (such as washing). It has proven very difficult, however, to translate this to a specific volume. Although it is generally agreed that an amount of three to five liters per day of clean water is the absolute minimum to allow for human survival, most understand that we can do better than just provide enough for mere survival. Research suggests that well-being improves significantly when these values increase to around twenty liters per day per person. That added water improves sanitary conditions considerably. For this reason, a number of international organizations, including the United Nations (see http://un.org/en/globalissues/water), proclaim humans have a right to between fifty and 100 liters per day per person, which, as noted earlier, must be safe, affordable (water costs should not exceed 3 percent of household income), and physically accessible (the water source has to be within 1,000 meters of the home and collection time should not exceed thirty minutes).

To say water is a human right does not mean, however, that it must be delivered for free. When many argue humans have a right to food, they are not arguing that it ought to be provided at no cost. To accept the principle of a human right to water does, however, require that we treat water as a *social* as well as an economic good. This is where that aforementioned change in how we think about water comes into play (see Image 5.2).

No discussion of rights is complete without talk of related responsibilities. Take property rights: if your bull gets out and destroys your neighbor's property and impregnates her cow, you are responsible for the damages incurred, and your neighbor owns the offspring of that encounter. In other words, your right to that bull also implies responsibility, namely, keeping the animal on your property. This legal principle dates back centuries and forms the backbone of common property law as we know it today (Carolan 2010). So: when corporations look to claim property rights over water, they need to be held to the responsibilities that ought to go along with owning that water (see Movement Matters 5.1).

Water doesn't fit into the "economic good" box as easily as other things. For one, the so-called law of supply and demand doesn't exist when talking about water. You can't

IMAGE 5.2 Everyone Needs Water

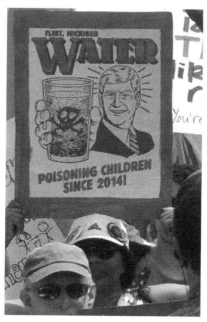

Source: "Climate March 1085" by Edward Kimmel (flickr.com/photos/22620970@N04/34368550705), April 29, 2017, is licensed copyright © 2017 under CC BY-SA 2.0.

choose what company's water you want piped into your house. That choice is made for you. Moreover, the price is based on a lot more than just market mechanisms. There are also social and political factors that shape the cost of tap water, most notably subsidies—either for the water itself or for, say, the electricity that pumps the water.

There are two main competing visions about how to think about water as an economic good. The first, supported by traditional economic approaches, explains that water should be priced at whatever the market will bear. The second vision believes value, especially when it comes to water, cannot and should not be left entirely to the free market to determine.

The first approach is problematic because it could—and likely would—disproportionately negatively affect rural populations and the urban poor who cannot "pay to play" in the life-sustaining game of water access. Water does seem to deserve the designation of a special economic good. It must be priced, but when going about establishing that price, we would do well to not let just the market determine it. Others have laid out five characteristics of water that they believe justify pricing it with a little more care than other economic goods (see, e.g., Cunha 2009; Staddon 2016):

1 Water is essential: there is no life, economic production, or environment without it.
2 Water is nonsubstitutable: there is no alternative.
3 Water is finite: the water that currently circulates through the hydrological cycle is all there is.
4 Water is a system: water is part of a complex system and helps make possible innumerable ecosystem services.
5 Water is bulky: water's physical properties make long-distance transportation difficult.

MOVEMENT MATTERS 5.1
Grassroots Organizations Take On Nestlé in North America

Wellington Water Watchers, a citizens' group in Wellington County, Ontario, along with Ecojustice and the Council of Canadians, played a key role in getting Nestlé Waters Canada to drop its quest to have drought restrictions removed from one of its water takings in Ontario, Canada. Nestlé is allowed to pump and package 1.13 million liters of groundwater per day in the town of Hillsburgh, approximately eighty kilometers north of Toronto. The company pays only CA$3.71 for every million liters of water it draws (Kerr 2013). A severe drought in the area, however, led the Ministry of the Environment to place restrictions on how much it could draw. Nestlé shortly thereafter announced it had persuaded the ministry to remove the mandatory reductions. The aforementioned community groups then successfully challenged the agreement through the Environmental Review Tribunal of Ontario. The tribunal ruled that the settlement agreement between Nestlé and the ministry was not in the public interest and that the original appeal should proceed to a full hearing, at which point Nestlé dropped their bid for special treatment.

Meanwhile, directly east in Michigan, across the border in the United States, Nestlé is facing resistance in the rural Osceola Township (population 900). Nestlé pays just $200 a year to the state to pump more than 130 million gallons of water annually (Agence France-Presse 2018). The community is fighting the company's plans to build a pumping booster station, which would allow Nestlé to pump 400 gallons of water per minute from an area wellhead, up from the 250 per minute currently. Some in the community praise the company for keeping the price of water low for residents, noting the extreme poverty in the area. Zackary Szakacs, city manager in a nearby community, is on record for making this point: "Thank God we have two of those wells in the city of Evart because I would have to lay people off" (cited in Agence France-Presse 2018). Others, however, do not trust the company to act in the community's best interests. To quote Peggy Case, president of the Michigan Citizens for Water Conservation,

> Nestle has a reputation worldwide of going to poor rural communities, offering all kinds of economic benefits to the community that never really materialize, and taking as much water as they can get and when the stream runs dry they leave.
> (quoted in Agence France-Presse 2018)

Town officials voted in early 2018 to appeal a county court's ruling in favor of Nestle's permit. The battle is now being fought in the courts.

Would the mere recognition of the human right to water actually improve conditions worldwide? Likely not. My point in talking about expanding our understanding of water as an economic good is a pragmatic realization that the imperatives to meet basic human water needs are more than just moral. They are also rooted in law and markets. We can change how people think about water all we want, but unless we likewise alter the social, economic, and political structures presently standing in the way of universal water access, millions will continue to go to bed at night in an unsanitary environment and thirsty.

Water Governance

Water resource management underwent a bit of a paradigm shift in the 1990s. Previously, the command-and-control—top-down, government-driven—model had proven modestly successful at regulating **point-source pollution** (pollution with an identifiable source). As recently as the 1970s, rivers were literally catching fire in affluent nations as a result of major pollution releases by industry. With the success of point-source pollution control measures, attention slowly turned to the impact of more diffuse pollution, called **nonpoint-source pollution**. From a governing standpoint, however, this shift complicates things for all but the most Orwellian of societies. The effective monitoring of pollution from nonpoint sources would require a level of government intrusion that most would be uncomfortable with. A new form of water governance has thus emerged: a broad social system of governance that operates at different levels of society while including, but not limiting itself to, the narrower perspective of government as the main decision-making political entity. A number of attributes of effective water governance have been identified (Norman et al. 2015):

- Participation: all water users should have a voice in the decision-making process.
- Transparency: the decision-making process should be transparent and open for scrutiny.
- Equity: all stakeholders should have opportunities to meaningfully participate in the process.
- Accountability: governments, the private sector, and civil society organizations should all be accountable to the public.
- Responsiveness: institutions and processes should serve stakeholders and respond properly to their interests (e.g., if a water source becomes contaminated, steps are immediately taken to address the problem).
- Ethics: effective water governance should be grounded in society's ethical principles (such as the belief that water is a fundamental human right).

CASE STUDY 5.4
Micro-Watershed Councils in Mexico and Guatemala

Deforestation and climate change are increasing the risk of flash flooding in communities located in the high-altitude watersheds near the Tacana volcano in Mexico and Guatemala. The water cycle has become particularly unpredictable in recent years, as an increase in frequency of flash floods has further eroded the formerly deep soils, which previously had tremendous capacity for water retention, thus further heightening the risk of flash flooding. With support from governmental and nongovernmental organizations, local communities are being empowered to form micro-watershed councils. These councils are leading watershed restoration projects. The projects are designed and implemented by the local councils. In addition to helping provide employment opportunities for community members, and thus also facilitating the meeting of development priorities, the micro-watershed councils are making local watersheds more secure and surrounding communities less vulnerable (Welling 2019).

These new participatory models are appealing to governments and **nongovernmental organizations** (NGOs) on a number of levels. (An NGO refers to any legally constituted organization that operates independently from any government.) Many governments, especially those in less affluent nations, express a desire for decentralized forms of governance, as they are already overstretched in attempting to deliver and maintain rural services. As for NGOs, many operate by constructing a number of water systems as part of a project but then leave the project area after several months or years to start new projects. Community-rooted governance projects have in some instances become a convenient method for shifting responsibility from the state and corporations to end users. And in light of future threats related to climate change, these locally-based models can help bolster watershed resilience, at least at the micro level, given the level of local expertise involved (see Case Study 5.4).

Most problems with such open models of water governance do not occur immediately. Problems, when they do occur, often appear later, after the initial excitement fades. A review of the literature came up with the following commonly cited reasons for the breakdown of community management systems (Cunha 2009; Norman et al. 2015):

- Participation often relies on voluntary inputs from community members that can erode over time, as there are often no long-term incentives to keep the activity going.
- Key individuals leave the community or die and are not easily replaced.
- The community organization charged with managing the water supply loses the trust and respect of the general community, perhaps from a lack of transparency and accountability.
- When some community members fail to contribute maintenance fees—whether they are free riders or because they cannot afford to—others become disillusioned.
- If government steps entirely away from the project, community members may feel they have been abandoned and become unmotivated.
- Communities are too poor to replace major capital items when they break down, which can be particularly problematic when or if government abdicates its responsibilities.

Too often public participation is viewed as something just needing to be checked off on a list of steps that are supposed to lead to successful environmental management. Nevertheless, when engaged meaningfully, public participation can produce long-term and sustainable results (OECD 2015b). It takes a lot of work to make community-level governance projects work. Yet, given the scope and severity of the problems at hand and the general excitement people tend to display when empowered to be involved in solution-oriented activities (Taylor et al. 2012), I have no doubt we can muster the energy and resources toward this end.

IMPORTANT CONCEPTS

- inverted quarantine
- neoliberalism
- virtual water
- water as a right
- water governance
- water privatization

DISCUSSION QUESTIONS

1. Do you drink bottled water? If so, why? Other than an outright ban, what policies would need to be implemented for you to stop your bottled-water consumption?
2. Do you believe humans have a fundamental right to water? If so, what's the best way to go about ensuring that right is fulfilled: the market, government, community-based governance, or perhaps something else?
3. What are some of the downsides of letting markets allocate water? And some benefits?
4. If you were made more aware of your water footprint, would your consumption patterns change? Why or why not? What are some of the barriers to change, and how could those barriers be overcome?

SUGGESTED ADDITIONAL READINGS

Barbier, E. 2019. *The Water Paradox: Overcoming the Global Crisis in Water.* New Haven, CT: Yale University Press.

Hammer, P.J. 2019. "The Flint Water Crisis, the Karegnondi Water Authority and Strategic–Structural Racism." *Critical Sociology*, 45(1): 103–119.

Markle, G. 2019. "Understanding Pro-Environmental Behavior in the US: Insights from Grid-Group Cultural Theory and Cognitive Sociology." *Sustainability*, 11(2). www.mdpi.com/2071-1050/11/2/532/pdf.

Middleton, C., and D. Gyawali. 2019. *The Water–Food–Energy Nexus: Power, Politics, and Justice.* New York: Routledge.

RELEVANT INTERNET LINKS

- www.watercalculator.org/. A water-footprint calculator.
- http://waterfootprint.org/en. A comprehensive resource for anything and everything having to do with water footprints.
- http://waterdata.usgs.gov/nwis. Real-time data from selected surface-water, groundwater, and water-quality sites from around the United States, among other things.
- www.wateruseitwisely.com/kids. A website full of useful information (and even some games) directed at water conservation.

SUGGESTED VIDEOS

- *Bottled Life: Nestlé's Business with Water* (2012; English version released in 2013). Swiss journalist Res Gehringer investigates the Nestlé water bottling company.
- *Chasing Coral* (2017). Coral reefs around the world are disappearing. This documentary discusses why that is, while documenting in vivid detail the beauty of these living structures.
- *DamNation* (2014). Film about changing attitudes in the United States concerning dams and a critical look at the role they should play in the future.
- *Damocracy* (2013). Debunks the myth of large-scale dams as clean energy and a solution to climate change.
- *Last Call at the Oasis* (2011). Illuminates the essential role water plays in our lives, exposes the defects in the current system, and shows communities already struggling under the

status quo. The film features activist Erin Brockovich; water experts Peter Gleick, Jay Famiglietti, and Robert Glennon; and a variety of social entrepreneurs in search of revolutionary solutions.

- *The Fight for Water* (2011). On February 28, 2009, near the tiny village of Santa Rosa, Ecuador, an oil pipeline broke inside the Amazon rain forest. An estimated 14,000 barrels of crude oil spilled into the Napo and Coca Rivers, both of which are tributaries of the Amazon River. This film tells what happened next.
- *Water & Power: A California Heist* (2017). California's water system is hotly contested and at times seems as though it favors the rich and power—aka the water barons. This film explores how small farmers and everyday citizens struggle for this basic resource in such a political environment.

Part II

AT THE INTERSECTION OF ECOLOGY AND SOCIETY

Population: A Problem of Quantity or Quality?

If I had written this book in the 1970s, I might have focused entirely on the subject of population growth. This was a period when people spoke of "the population bomb" and "a population explosion," when we were told that Earth was like a spaceship with a near maxed-out seating capacity. It was also around this time when a group of scientists commissioned by the Club of Rome—a global think tank founded in 1968 with a history of examining a variety of international issues—looked at **exponential growth** in resource use, population, and economic activity and announced that we should see significant resource scarcities before the new millennium.

Although perhaps this anxiety was a bit misplaced—after all, the global population growth rate has considerably lowered since that time—I understand why the subject grabbed the attention it did. We have to remember that some forty-plus years ago, world population was growing at an unprecedented (and since unprecedented) level. It was, quite frankly, a scary rate of growth, which explains the alarming talk of "bombs" and "explosions" when discussing world population levels.

In the previous century, countries could be fairly easily classified into one of two categories: affluent/developed or less affluent/developing. The former had low population growth rates, the latter high rates of population growth. With **birth rates** (or the ratio of live births per 1,000 people per year) now declining in the latter category, including much of Asia, Latin America, and the Middle East, the high population growth rates prevalent forty years ago are today restricted to the countries in Sub-Saharan Africa plus a few others (such as Liberia, Afghanistan, and the Palestinian territories). A number of less affluent countries in fact have birth rates that, a couple of decades ago, would have been found only in high-income countries. China has infamously slashed its birth rates, thanks in part to its **one-child policy**, by penalizing families that have more than one child. But strides toward lowering birth rates have also been made because of recent socioeconomic attainments. To quote Nobel economist Amartya Sen (1994, 22), "While China gets too much credit for its authoritarian measures, it gets far too little credit for other supportive policies it has followed that have helped to cut down the birth rate." Some countries that would certainly not be considered affluent yet have fertility rates below that found in the

United States (with a rate of 1.87) include Vietnam (1.81), Uzbekistan (1.76), Brazil (1.75), Slovenia (1.36), and Taiwan (1.13) (CIA 2017).

How environmental sociologists talk about population growth, however, tends to be different from how others—such as, say, Paul Ehrlich, author of *The Population Bomb* (1968)—have grappled with the subject. For environmental sociologists, it is not population growth per se that is the central focus of concern but rather the *relationships* between population and resource consumption, use, and waste, recognizing too that these relationships are fundamentally mediated by social structures. Focusing too much on population growth itself also risks sidetracking us from understanding the reasons behind those growth rates. From a pragmatic environmentalist standpoint, what good does it do to bemoan excessive population growth if it means being distracted from uncovering its underlying drivers?

This is not to suggest that population growth itself is not worth talking about. It is important, however, not to rest too much of the blame at the feet of those parts of the world with higher than average fertility rates. Lest we forget, the average US citizen's ecological footprint is 8.1 global hectares, whereas often demonized China (with its massive population of some 1.45 billion inhabitants) has a per capita ecological footprint of 3.6 global hectares (National Footprint Accounts 2019). When we talk about population, we need also to have an honest discussion about *which* populations are having the biggest ecological impact, as not all people are equal in this regard. Nevertheless, current growth rates, while down from just a couple of decades ago, are not making things any easier. The stark reality is that the more people there are on Earth, the more competition there will be for its already scarce resources, which only complicates matters as we strive to find ways to improve the livelihood of the world's poorest billion, a population who, quite frankly, are *not consuming enough*, as they live at subsistence levels—and some not even at those.

Fast Facts

- The world's population is about 7.6 billion (for the latest figure, see www.census.gov/popclock). We are all but certain to see a world population of at least nine billion people by 2050.
- The ecological footprint per capita of high-income countries is approximately five times greater than that of low-income countries. Uganda's population, for example, increased by roughly 400 percent between 1969 and 2015, and yet its per capita footprint remained essentially unchanged. If everyone in the world lived like the average person in the United Arab Emirates (the country with the world's highest per capita footprint), we would need the equivalent of six planets to regenerate resources and absorb CO_2 emissions. If everyone lived like the average resident of the United States, we would need the resources and waste sinks of more than 4.5 planets (National Footprint Accounts 2019).
- The United Nations median projection for global population growth from 2010 to 2050 estimates the addition of more than 2.5 billion people to our planet. While much of this growth will occur in lower-income countries, where some are arguably not presently consuming enough (which is to say they are living at absolute poverty levels), this is still the carbon equivalent of adding two United States to the planet (IPCC 2018).

- Exceedingly high national fertility rates are now almost exclusively concentrated in a single part of the world: Sub-Saharan Africa. All but one (Afghanistan) of the fourteen countries with estimated total fertility rates at five or higher can be found there. The same can be said for nearly all of the fifty-five countries with fertility rates of four or greater (CIA 2017).
- Although fertility rates in Sub-Saharan Africa tend to be high, the countries of this region also have very high child mortality rates. On the bright side, child mortality in this part of the world has been continuously falling for the last fifty years—one in four children died in the early 1960s, whereas today that figure is less than one in ten. On the not so bright side: that means nearly one child in ten still fails to see adulthood (Roser 2015). Conflict, AIDS/HIV, malaria, and extreme poverty have combined to drastically reduce life expectancy in this part of the world, in some cases close to forty years of age (Shapiro and Hinde 2017).

Implications

I understand the appeal of placing the responsibility for our ecological ills at the feet of population growth. Reducing environmental problems to demographics—thinking fewer people equals fewer environmental problems—is much easier than trying to deal with the root causes of global environmental impacts. And it's an attractive argument, especially for those living in affluent nations who can employ it to elude any moral responsibility for reducing their ecological footprints. To paraphrase sentiments I hear from those looking to make ecological scapegoats out of rapidly growing lower-income countries: "We can just keep doing what we're doing—no reason to change our actions. *They* are the ones—those in poor countries with the high fertility rates—who need to change!" Yet this argument fails to hold up to empirical scrutiny. In discussing the impacts of population, this section looks at whether today's environmental ills are primarily the result of population growth per se or a product of a process that's a bit more complex (see ECOnnection 6.1).

Greenhouse Gases

Table 6.1 compares different regions and countries with regard to their share of world population growth and CO_2 emissions growth between 1970 and 2017. It is clear from this table that population growth alone cannot account for rising CO_2 emissions. We see, for example, that Sub-Saharan Africa accounted for very little of the growth in CO_2 emissions between 1970 and 2010, while accounting for 19 percent of global population growth during this period. At the other extreme, while accounting for 3.4 percent of population growth, the United States is responsible for 13.6 percent of the growth of CO_2 emissions in the same time period. In light of these facts, we need to realize that the actual impact of future fertility rate reductions on greenhouse gas emissions will likely not be proportional, especially if those declines are occurring in countries in Sub-Saharan Africa (see Ethical Question 6.1).

Urban Sprawl

Urban sprawl—the spreading of urban development into areas adjoining cities—can occur with or without population growth. The causes of urbanization are multiple (Image 6.1).

TABLE 6.1 Share of Population and CO_2 Emissions Growth for Select Regions/Countries, 1970–2017

REGION/NATION	SHARE OF POPULATION GROWTH (%)	SHARE OF EMISSIONS GROWTH (%)
Northern Africa	2.5	2.5
Sub-Saharan Africa	21	2.3
China	16.5	44.5
India	22.5	10.8
United States	3.4	15.3
South Korea	0.4	3.9
Japan	0.4	3.7

Source: Adapted from IPPC (2018).

ECOnnection 6.1
From IPAT to STIRPAT

A widely applied accounting model to examine the relationship between human activities and the environment is the IPAT. First proposed in the early 1970s (see, for example, Ehrlich and Holden 1971), the IPAT model specifies that environmental *i*mpacts are the product of *p*opulation size, *a*ffluence (in terms of per capita consumption or production), and *t*echnology (defined as impact per unit of consumption or production). Each variable is assumed to have proportional effects on the environment. When calculating environmental impacts, in other words, IPAT reminds us that we cannot divorce talk about population from variables pertaining to levels of affluence and technology impacts.

Although a valuable accounting equation, the IPAT model remains a relatively crude instrument for social scientists, as it does not allow for the testing of hypotheses (York et al. 2003). To overcome this limitation, Dietz and Rosa (1994) advanced a new model that allows for the calculation of probabilities and hence an evaluation of competing hypotheses and theories. This alternative model is called STIRPAT: *s*tochastic *i*mpacts by *r*egression on *p*opulation, *a*ffluence, and *t*echnology (Rosa and Dietz 1998). One of the most notable contributions of the STIRPAT program has been its ability to show that basic material conditions such as demographic and economic factors shape the size of national-level ecological footprints to a significant degree. In practical policy terms, STIRPAT tells us that there is no "magic bullet" that will solve environmental problems and that we must deal with deeper driving forces, which include population but also things like economic growth. (Thanks to Richard York for helping me distill an otherwise extensive literature into a couple of sentences.)

IMAGE 6.1 Cityscape of Athens

Source: "Cityscape Athens 5 of 4" by Martin Lopatka (flickr.com/photos/apothecary), March 6, 2017, is licensed copyright © 2017 under CC BY-SA 2.0.

People may migrate from rural to urban areas for employment opportunities or for something as fundamental as food.

More than half of the world's expected nine billion people will live in large urban expanses by 2030; cities and their outskirts will cover an additional 1.2 million square kilometers—a tripling in size from today. For a point of comparison, urban areas increased by just 58,000 square kilometers between 1970 and 2000 (Seto et al. 2012). It has been estimated that the total population of cities in developing countries will double between 2000 and 2030, yet their built-up areas will triple. This calculation is not surprising, as cities in low-income countries are currently more than four times as densely populated as cities in affluent countries.

According to United Nations estimates, the 55 percent figure signifying the world's urban population today is expected to increase to 68 percent by 2050. The world's rural population is growing more slowly and is expected to reach its peak in a few years. The global rural population is now close to 3.4 billion and is expected to rise slightly before declining to 3.1 billion by 2050. In 2018, Africa and Asia held almost 90 percent of the world's rural population, with India (893 million) and China (578 million) holding the largest share (United Nations 2018).

Just how big are cities getting? There is a reason the adjective *mega* is used to describe today's largest urban centers. In 1950 there were two cities with ten million or more inhabitants. By 2005 that number had increased to twenty. In 2015, there were thirty-four cities with ten million or more residents, with three more being home to between nine and ten million individuals (Demographia 2019). While Tokyo, Japan, has been the world's largest city for a while (see Table 6.2), demographers expect Delhi, India, to become the most populous city in the world by 2028 when it surpasses forty million inhabitants (Tanzi and Lu 2018).

TABLE 6.2 Cities with Ten Million Inhabitants or More, 1950, 2000, and 2018 (in Millions)

1950		2000		2018	
CITY	POPULATION	CITY	POPULATION	CITY	POPULATION
New York-Newark	12.3	Tokyo	34.4	Tokyo-Yokohama	37.050
Tokyo	11.3	Mexico City	18.1	Jakarta	32.275
		New York-Newark	17.8	Delhi	27.280
		São Paulo	17.1	Manila	24.650
		Mumbai	16.1	Seoul-Incheon	24.210
		Shanghai	13.2	Shanghai	24.115
		Calcutta	13.1	Mumbai	23.265
		Delhi	12.4	New York-Newark	21.575
		Buenos Aires	11.8	Beijing	21.275
		Los Angeles-Long Beach-Santa Ana	11.8	Sao Paulo	21.100
		Osaka-Kobe	11.2	Mexico City	20.565
		Jakarta	11.1	Guangzhou	19.965
		Rio de Janeiro	10.8	Thirty additional cities with populations between ten and twenty million	

Source: GeoDataSource. "World Cities Database 2019." www.geodatasource.com/.

Just as there is growth that can be labelled as "smart," there are also forms that seem not so smart, like, for example, urban sprawl. There is now over a decade's worth of research showing that, after controlling for things like age, education, fruit and vegetable consumption, income, race/ethnicity, and smoking status, residents of more compact counties have lower BMIs (body mass indexes) and lower probabilities of obesity and chronic diseases (Ewing et al. 2003, 2006, 2014). (One possible reason for this: compact urban spaces encourage "active travel" as opposed to using one's car for every trip.) Ecological impacts also vary widely depending on which path of urban development is followed. Studies have shown that metropolitan regions ranking high on a quantitative index of sprawl experience a greater number of ozone exceedances (concentrations that exceed what is allowed by the federal government) than more spatially compact metropolitan regions. Importantly, this relationship held even after controlling for population size, average ozone seasonal temperatures, and regional emissions of nitrogen oxides and **volatile organic compounds** (compounds that evaporate from housekeeping, maintenance, and building products made with organic chemicals) (Hamidi et al. 2018; Kashem et al. 2014). In fact, most of the negative environmental indicators often attributed to urbanization are actually the result of urban sprawl.

Food

Many have a difficult time divorcing population growth from the subject of food security. It's a fair link to make. Each additional mouth that needs to be fed means additional competition for food. Fortunately, the links between population growth and food security are mediated by a number of social variables, which is cause for hope. But first, let's start with the bad news.

According to the United Nations, global agricultural production will need to be at least 60 percent higher in 2050 than 2007 levels (FAO 2019). This is a smaller output increase than the agriculture sector has achieved over the past half century. But before we let out a collective sigh of relief, it is questionable whether these increases can be achieved, let alone achieved sustainably. A 2013 study examined yields of four key staple crops: maize, rice, wheat, and soybeans (Ray et al. 2013). The findings are not encouraging, as the research notes that yields are increasing by only about 0.9 percent to 1.6 percent a year. That would lead to an overall yield increase of somewhere between 38 percent (low-end estimate) and 67 percent (high-end estimate) by 2050. In other words, it is actually plausible that there will not be enough food to go around by 2050. Next throw into the equation climate change, which could be a game changer as far as agriculture output is concerned (and not in a good way), plus rising demand for biofuels and certain animal proteins, and we have serious cause for concern.

If we cannot increase yields sufficiently to satisfy future demand—and there's plenty of research out there suggesting we can't (Ray et al. 2013; Willett et al. 2019)—perhaps we can increase the amount of land under cultivation. To make up for the yield shortfall, we'll need roughly 750 million additional hectares of land by 2050 (Schade and Pimentel 2010). There is an emerging consensus that there are roughly 1.4 billion hectares around the world that could be brought under cultivation (Alexandratos and Bruinsma 2012). Yet we must realize that a lot needs to be accomplished before land can be brought into production: land rights have to be settled, credit must be available to farmers so they can

ETHICAL QUESTION 6.1

Do Countries Have a Right to Their Fair Share of CO$_2$ Emissions?

A sizable proportion of future growth in the world's population will undoubtedly come from low-income people residing in low-income nations, who, unfortunately, will likely remain in a state of poverty for the foreseeable future. For these very poor nations, there will continue to be little connection between future population growth and greenhouse gas emissions. Yet some countries—most notably India and China—will undoubtedly see their standard of living and populations (and thus their CO$_2$ footprint) increase between now and 2050. India's population is expected to surpass China's, currently the most populous country in the world, by 2030, when it becomes home to some 1.53 billion people. For these countries, we can expect to see a positive correlation between population, affluence, and greenhouse gas emissions. Yet this situation raises an ethical question: Are countries entitled to a certain fair share of greenhouse gas emissions? And, if so, what should that level be? More to the point: If an impoverished country's per capita greenhouse gas emissions levels are drastically less than, say, those of the United States, do they have a right to *increase* those emissions up to a point? Or should we treat emission increases in the developing world the same as we would treat increases occurring in wealthy nations?

buy necessary inputs (like seed), and an infrastructure and market must be in place. These constraints explain why **arable land** (land that can be cultivated to grow crops) worldwide has grown by a net average of five million hectares per year over the past two decades, the result of deforestation and in some cases with the help of infrastructural investments (e.g., irrigation systems) (Han et al. 2019). As the easiest land to convert has already been plowed under, we can expect a slowdown in the annual growth of arable land, recognizing that what remains is increasingly marginal, which means it will require even more fertilizer and other inputs to be productive. Specifically, the annual growth of arable land is expected to slow from 0.30 percent between 1961 and 2005 to 0.10 percent between 2005 and 2050. This calculates out to an average annual net increase of arable area of 2.75 million hectares per year between 2005 and 2050, or a total of 120 million additional hectares (Rabobank Group 2010, 14). This figure is well below the most optimistic estimates that claim we need 200 million additional hectares by mid-century to satisfy global food demand. Furthermore, the estimate ignores the fact that arable land in developed and transitional countries is *declining* (thanks most notably to urban sprawl). For instance, there was an 8 percent drop in the number of acres cultivated in the United States from 1990 to 2012 (EPA 2013).

Another option is to "grab" arable land in another country. This is part of a practice known as the **global land grab**, which speaks to international land deals whereby corporations, investment firms, and/or state-owned enterprises lease or purchase large tracts of land in other countries for the production of food that is then exported to the country that is "home" to said investment. Although it has the largest population in the world,

China has only one-third of global average arable land area per capita. To ensure future food security, China's government set a "red line" in the Eleventh Five-Year Plan to ensure that the country's total arable land area never shrinks to less than 120 mega hectares (hectare x 10^6). It includes in this calculation land grabbed in other countries, which explains the country's investments in nations around the world, with a particular interest in the African continent (Han and Chen 2018).

In 1798 Thomas Malthus published his immensely influential *Essay on Population*. His argument, greatly oversimplified, was that growth in population will always outpace our ability to feed, shelter, and clothe people and that without some controls on population growth, it would ultimately be humanity's undoing. The future, in the eyes of Malthus, was bleak, especially for the poorest class. His view is held to this day by so-called **neo-Malthusians**, who advocate for the control of population growth. Before we declare the statistics cited above a testament to Malthus's foresight, let's look more closely at why there is food scarcity in the world today.

According to the Nobel Prize winning economist Amartya Sen (1981), modern food crises are less related to the absence of food as to the inability to buy it. Examining the 1943 Bengal famine, which at its peak claimed the lives of more than 50,000 Bengalese weekly (Fisher 1943), Sen describes how there was actually plenty of food to go around; he also looked at the 1974 Bangladesh famine and drew similar conclusions. The problem, in other words, was not a lack of food but a lack of *available* food, as those with the means to acquire it were engaging in acts of hoarding, knowing that its price would only go up. Whereas natural disasters may have been the main culprits in the past, extreme food insecurity today is more often than not the result of markets, governments, and civil society failing those at the margins of society.

This brings us to the subject of democracy. Sen argues that democracy creates an important political, social, and civil environment where famine is unlikely. Indeed, as Sen (1981, 16) famously wrote, "No famine has ever taken place in the history of the world in a functioning democracy." Famines tend to affect only the poorest segment of a country's population. In nondemocratic states, those most likely to experience famine are likewise the least likely to have political access. Their famine-related suffering is therefore allowable to elites, as it does little to threaten their grip on power. What democracy provides is a voice to those living on the margins of society who would otherwise lack access to any levers of political influence. In nondemocratic states, famines can also go on without most of the public even being aware of the suffering. A cornerstone of democracy is accountability, which is in part made possible through a free press. Without a free press, citizens have a very difficult time holding politicians accountable for, among other things, failing to act expeditiously when the first signs of calamity arise. As we saw throughout the twentieth century, whether the massive Soviet and Chinese famines of mid-century or the Ethiopian famine of the mid-1980s, food can all too easily be grossly misallocated when governments are not held accountable (Carolan 2018a).

Feeding a Growing Nonhuman Animal Population

When discussing the relationship between population growth and food security, it is also important to be clear about what exactly we mean by the term *population*. When talking about the "mouths" that our food systems feed, we need to be clear that we are not just talking about those of the human variety. We feed a lot more than just humans with the food we produce. If we fed only humans, the task at hand would be considerably easier. According to the Food and Agriculture Organization of the United Nations, world agriculture produces enough food to provide every woman, man, and child with some 2,700 calories a day. But we don't just feed humans. We also feed livestock, in the form of animal feed, and increasingly cars, in the form of biofuels.

If current trends continue, we are going to have to produce twice as much animal protein by 2050 just to keep up with demand. This means that by 2050, livestock will be consuming enough food to feed four billion people (the world's population in the early 1970s). In other words, if the world continues to eat meat at the rates that we are expecting—and since most of the animals that provide that meat are going to have to eat an enormous amount of grain—the world's effective population in 2050 will be 13.5 billion (9.5 billion, the projected human population, plus four billion, as that is how many people could be fed with the grain that is expected to be diverted to livestock) (Carolan 2018a). Why these trends matter from a food security perspective is because collectively, cattle, pigs, and poultry in high-income countries already consume around 70 percent of the available grains within those nations. Globally, livestock consume, at a minimum, one-third of the world's cereals, with 40 percent of such feed going to ruminants, chiefly cattle (Eisler at al. 2014). In case you're wondering: if the whole world were to consume meat at the same per capita rate as the average American, total grain output could sustain a global population of roughly only 2.6 billion people (Carolan 2018a).

Feeding a Growing Automobile Population

World ethanol production has increased from roughly 5.5 billion gallons (seventeen billion liters) in 2000 to 23.5 billion gallons (eighty-nine billion liters) in 2013 and 27.1 billion gallons (102.6 billion liters) in 2017 (US Department of Energy 2018). The production of biodiesel, which is still only a fraction of the world's biofuels, has also grown in the last decade, from less than two million metric tons in 2000 to approximately sixty-four million metric tons in 2012 and eighty-three million metric tons in 2018 (International Energy Agency 2019). To meet all the targets set throughout the world, biofuel production is going to have to increase considerably. Mandates for blending biofuels into vehicle fuels have been legislated in at least forty-one states and provinces and twenty-four countries; the laws require blending 10 to 15 percent ethanol with gasoline or 2 to 5 percent biodiesel with diesel fuel. For example, Brazil, Indonesia, and the European Union expect to meet 10 percent of their energy demands by 2020 with biofuels. China hopes to meet 5 percent of its energy demands by 2020 with biofuels. Meanwhile, the United States has its own biofuel aspirations, namely, to produce thirty-six billion gallons by 2022 (with at least sixteen billion gallons from cellulosic biofuels and a cap of fifteen billion gallons for cornstarch ethanol).

Of course, we can't separate automobile populations from human ones. After all, someone has to drive all those biofuel automobiles. And while car ownership is down in certain high-income countries (I'll get to why later in the book), it is increasing exponentially in other countries. There were, for instance, eighteen passenger cars per thousand Chinese in 2006 and sixty cars per thousand in 2015. In Jordan, during that same period, those figures increased from eighty-seven to 144 cars; in Syria, from eighteen to forty-two; in Bulgaria, from 230 to 362; and in Poland, from 351 to 470 (World Bank 2015a).

Solutions

It would be wrong to attribute all the world's ecological problems to population growth. Yet, as far as long-term sustainability is concerned, it is hard to deny the virtues of a less populated planet, as long as those growth rates are brought down in an ethical, just, and equitable manner. With that, I offer the following piece of encouraging news: there is evidence that population growth rates will come down in countries as their levels of prosperity grow—which is known as the **demographic transition model**.

The demographic transition model illustrates the move from a state of high birth rates and death rates to low birth rates and death rates, the time between representing a period of rapid population growth (see Figure 6.1). A brief summary of the model is in order. Preindustrial (stage 1) countries have high birth rates and death rates and consequentially fairly stable populations. In the earliest stage of industrialization (stage 2), death rates fall with improvements in food supply, sanitation, and health, while birth rates remain high because of lagging **pronatal social norms** (which refer to individual attitudes and societal expectations that promote high fertility rates). In late industrialization (stage 3), death rates continue to fall, while birth rates also begin to drop. Once a certain level of affluence is achieved (stage 4), however, birth rates begin flattening out to match death rates, causing the country's population to stabilize. Children in highly urbanized affluent countries are also more likely to be viewed as a "cost" to families much earlier than they are in rural, low-income nations, where they can help tend livestock and work the fields at a

FIGURE 6.1 Demographic Transition Model

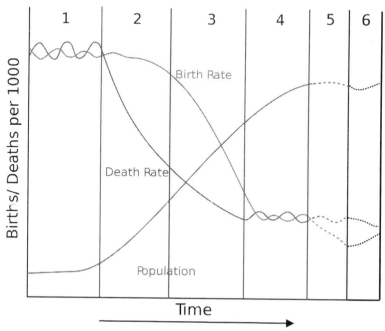

Source: Author.

Note
The dashed lines signify recently hypothesized stages.

relatively young age. More recently, adding to the original four stages, there is growing discussion about a fifth stage to represent countries that have below-replacement fertility rates (below 2.1 children per woman). As their resident population ages, some European and Asian countries, such as Germany and Japan, actually have higher death rates than birth rates (see Case Study 6.1). More recent still is the addition of a possible sixth stage. First suggested in a 1999 issue of the journal *Nature* (Myrskyla et al. 2009), this stage shows that high levels of economic and social development promote (in some countries at least) a rebound in fertility, notable exceptions being Germany and Japan. There is still considerable debate around the existence of this newly suggested stage.

The demographic transition model does not attempt to forecast what will happen. It's simply a statistical representation of what has occurred for countries that have already undergone the transition—countries like the United States, Japan, and those in Western Europe. It is therefore entirely fair to ask, "What makes us so sure those countries in stages 2 and 3 will move to stage 4 (or beyond) anytime in the foreseeable future?" If

CASE STUDY 6.1
Japan: A Rapidly Shrinking Country

Japan's population began falling in 2004 and is now aging faster than any other country on Earth. Roughly a quarter of the entire population is aged sixty-five or older (in the United States that figure is about 15 percent). The Ministry of Health, Labor and Welfare calculates that 921,000 babies were born in 2018—25,000 fewer than in the previous year (Ingber 2018). While roughly 127 million people live in the country today, that figure could drop below the 100 million mark by 2049 according to one government estimate (Ibid.). An earlier government report was even more dire: without policy changes, the number of Japanese could fall by 2110 to 42.9 million—a third of its current population (D.M. 2014).

In response, the government is seriously contemplating a solution that thirty years ago would have been ridiculed by all: mass migration. The figure being discussed is 200,000 new foreigners a year to help stabilize the population. (A United Nations estimate places that figure at closer to 650,000 new immigrants every year.) This is a remarkable suggestion when you consider that Japan remains, at least relative to many Western countries, a fairly homogeneous nation. But that wouldn't entirely keep the country from shrinking. The government would also need to raise the fertility rate from its current 1.40 (one of the world's lowest) to 2.07. But to elicit such a change—after all, you can't (or at least shouldn't) force people to procreate—would require radical changes, such as family-friendly labor laws like flex time, longer maternal and paternal leave, and subsidized childcare.

The population crisis has so alarmed the government that it created a ministerial post in 2005 charged specifically with raising fertility rates. The angst is understandable when you consider that the government has record-breaking budgets every year to pay for the health care and pensions of all its late-in-life residents and fewer and fewer working residents to pay for these benefits. From a sustainability perspective that might sound appealing. But from a political perspective it is an unacceptable outcome for many Japanese, especially considering its proximity to China, as it also means a drastically diminished economic, political, and military role not only in the world but in Asian matters too (D.M. 2014).

history is any guide, this demographic transition is anything but guaranteed; after all, many nations on the UN list of least-developed countries (LDCs) have essentially been stuck at their present level of development for decades. (The LDCs constitute about 12 percent of the world population but account for less than 2 percent of the world's gross domestic product and about 1 percent of global trade in goods.)

Another variable that is different today from a century ago is population mobility. This is not to suggest that people didn't move around the world in earlier decades. (I wouldn't be here if that were true, as all my ancestors emigrated from somewhere in Europe in the late 1800s.) There are, however, far more modes available today to travel great distances than generations ago. Moreover, there are powerful "push" variables at work, essentially forcing people to relocate: climate change, religious persecution, war, and so on. An irony in a post-9/11 age is that as police and various other security forces battle to keep immigrants at bay in countries across North America and Europe, another (non-terrorist-related) crisis is unfolding in those countries, one that is demographic in nature. With their low birth rates these countries desperately need more young people to pay taxes, work in their health care sectors, populate their rural areas, and look after their elderly before it's too late. Take Portugal. Unless steps are taken to radically increase birth rates (something very hard to do) or to entice a flood of immigrants over its borders, its population could drop from roughly 10.4 million to 6.3 million by 2060 (Kassam et al. 2015).

Socioeconomic Development

Although economic development helps reduce fertility rates, it is not the panacea it was once thought to be. A popular development slogan in the 1970s, which has since been debunked, was "economic development is the best contraceptive." The problem with putting all our eggs in the "economic development" basket is that it misses the fact that population growth, at least in some countries, is so great that it actually *hinders* the very thing so many are hoping will forestall it: economic growth. That fact alone should be taken as evidence that we cannot rely on pro-growth strategies alone in many of the world's fastest-growing countries to bring down fertility rates. Moreover, while gross domestic product (GDP) per capita is negatively correlated with a country's fertility rate (as the former goes up, the latter goes down), the correlation is not perfect. Quite a few countries, in fact, manage to maintain low fertility rates with GDP per capita levels well below that of, for example, the highly affluent United States, with its 2.01 fertility rate. Some of those countries include Costa Rica (1.91), Vietnam (1.85), Uruguay (1.84), Romania (1.32), and Lithuania (1.29).

While declines in fertility have been facilitated by **family planning** programs—most infamously in China with its one-child policy but also in places like Indonesia and Malaysia—these reductions were equally facilitated by social and economic transformations (see Image 6.2). Family planning refers to educational, social, and medical services that empower individuals to make choices around reproduction. In Brazil, sharp declines in fertility rates have been attributed mainly to wider socioeconomic transformations—including urbanization—that have encouraged people to limit family size. The old paradigm—out of which came the slogan "economic development is the best contraceptive"—was not necessarily wrong, just shortsighted.

What really matters is the *type* of development. A country can have an impressive GDP per capita, but if all that wealth is concentrated in the hands of a few, the average

IMAGE 6.2 Poster from 1986 Promoting China's One-Child Policy

Source: "Carry Out Family Planning, Implement the Basic National Policy," Zhou Yuwei, 1986. Image courtesy of the Lansberger Collection, International Institute of Social History (flickr.com/iisg), licensed copyright © 1986 under CC BY 2.0.

Note
The child in the image appears to be male. Coincidence?

citizen is essentially no better off than if he or she lived in any of the least developed countries (LDCs). What is required is *socio*economic development. This means improvements in literacy and rates of school enrollment, gender equity and women's empowerment, heath care, and social institutions (e.g., education) while also meeting the needs of individuals in terms of sexual and reproductive health. Economic development alone—a point discussed in greater detail in Chapter 12—is insufficient on many levels (see Case Study 6.2).

When talking about "development," the following fact should never be far from our minds: although socioeconomic enhancements tend to motivate people to reduce their fertility rates, they also tend to increase consumption levels. One solution, then, for reducing consumption and emissions in the short term would be to further reduce fertility rates in affluent countries to compensate for the increased consumption and emissions in other countries as they climb out of poverty. Reducing fertility rates among those whose offspring would have a sizable ecological footprint would clearly go a long way toward reducing the stress that ecosystems are currently being placed under. Yet I also realize this is not a terribly realistic suggestion, as many affluent countries have actually started taking steps to *increase* their birth rates. These pro-fertility policies are grounded in national interests triggered by demographic concerns about shrinking military and consumer might. It is therefore highly unlikely that a groundswell of popular support could be generated for fertility reduction campaigns in these countries (see Ethical Question 6.2).

We also need to realize that even immediate reductions in fertility in less affluent nations will not rapidly stabilize the world's population. This is where the term **demographic inertia**

CASE STUDY 6.2

Socioeconomic Development in Kerala, India

Kerala, an Indian state located on the southwest coast of the country, has made remarkable socioeconomic strides over the past couple of decades. Kerala's fertility rate is actually lower than China's, even with the latter's coercive one-child policy. The reason, undoubtedly, is tied to Kerala's impressive progress in areas relating to basic education, health care, and gender equality (see Table 6.3). And it has done this with a mediocre—by global standards—GDP per capita. If it were a country, its GDP per capita would be lower than that of, for instance, Peru, South Africa, and Turkey. When it comes to reducing fertility rates, Kerala's developmental trajectory disputes the need for oppressive population control policies like forced sterilization or the criminalization of families with multiple children. It should also serve as a reminder of the shortsightedness of approaches that place too much emphasis on economic development to the detriment of social improvements and overall welfare enhancement.

TABLE 6.3 Well-Being Indicators for Indian State of Kerala Compared to Entire Country of India

WELL-BEING INDICATORS	KERALA	INDIA
Birth rate (per 1,000)	13.9	22.2
Death rate (per 1,000)	6.2	7.1
Infant mortality rate (per 1,000)	11	50
Child mortality rate, 0–4 years (per 1,000)	3	17
Total fertility rate (children per woman)	1.7	2.5
Life expectancy at birth (age at death)		
a) male	71.7	67
b) female	77	68.7
c) total	74.3	66.9
Literacy rate		
a) male	95.2%	83.02%
b) female	88.16%	66.71%
c) total	91.91%	75.11%

Source: Adapted from Ministry of Home Affairs (2018).

ETHICAL QUESTION 6.2
Whose Behaviors Should Change?

Are we asking those in the developing world to change their behaviors so those of us in rich nations do not have to change ours? If consumption were not occurring in affluent countries at the rates they are, we likely would not be having this conversation about population growth. Residents of less affluent countries have told me how the finger wagging of countries like the United States toward poor regions of the world with higher fertility rates seems insincere. Rich countries are far from ecological sainthood, given their rampant consumerism and fertility rates that have actually risen slightly since the 1970s. Is it fair—or even empirically justified—to continue framing the population problem as a developing country problem?

CASE STUDY 6.3
Family Planning in Ethiopia

For every 100,000 live births in Ethiopia in 2015, 353 women died from pregnancy-related problems (UNICEF 2018). This figure is known as the **maternal mortality ratio**: the number of women who die from pregnancy-related causes while pregnant or within forty-two days of pregnancy termination per 100,000 live births. (For comparison, in the United States that figure was twenty-eight; in Italy, it was four; and in Israel, two.) As the country is predominantly rural, about 90 percent of women deliver at home. In light of these abysmal figures, the Ethiopian government has restructured its health care system. Particular attention has been given to the problems faced by rural women, as some 80 percent of the population resides outside of cities. The government now trains and has on its payroll approximately 30,000 health-extension workers, whose job it is to cover the countryside providing health services.

Access to affordable contraception has also become a top priority. In 2005 less than 15 percent of women had access to contraception. Since then, the Ethiopian government has implemented a plan for providing free birth control pills or a contraceptive injection with effects that last for three months. Yet these "short-term" birth control methods are still problematic, given that for some women, the nearest health center may be an eight-hour walk from where they live. In light of such barriers to access, there is a move to make widely and freely available an implant that protects women from pregnancy for three years. While the aforementioned figures are without question unacceptable, they are at least moving in the right direction. Just five years earlier—in 2010—the country's maternal mortality ratio was 500.

comes into the picture. This is a term from demography based on the fact that a time lag is to be expected before the full effects of changes to a fertility rate are seen—until the youngest cohort just prior to fertility rates dropping essentially becomes too old to have children. Take China. Although it reached a below-replacement level of fertility in the early 1990s, the nation will grow by an additional 320 million bodies before its population finally stabilizes and starts to decrease after 2035. In fact, the majority of population growth today is due less to present fertility patterns than to past fertility and mortality patterns. Nevertheless, some things can slow demographic inertia, such as if the age at marriage or age at conception of first child were delayed a year or two (see Case Study 6.3).

Figure 6.2 is based on demographic modeling by the United Nations (2015b), which attempts to estimate future world population to 2100 by offering a range within which future populations will most likely fall (at a 95 percent confidence level). Making such calculations is tricky given the uncertainties involved, as assumptions have to be made not only about fertility rates but also, for instance, infant survivability rates and life expectancies, both of which are predicated on future technological, food production, and sanitation improvements. According to the figure, we can say with a 95 percent degree of confidence that global population will be between 8.8 and 9.3 billion in 2040 and between 9.6 and 13.1 billion in 2100. In other words, global population is all but certain to rise in the short- to medium-term future. Later in the century, global population is still likely to continue to increase, though there is an approximately 23 percent chance that it could stabilize or begin to fall before 2100.

The Future Role of Cities

If you are like some of my students, you might be thinking, "Cities as a *solution* to our environmental ills? You can't be serious! Didn't we just get done discussing the problems

FIGURE 6.2 High and Low Future World Population Estimates (95 Percent Confidence Level)

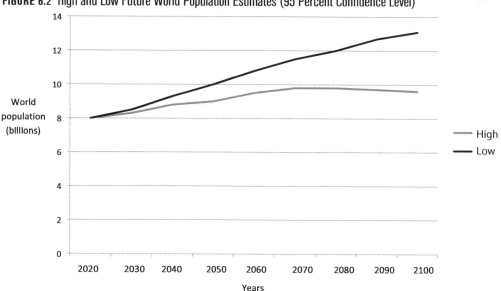

Source: Adapted from United Nations (2019).

associated with urban sprawl?" For reasons that are largely justified, cities have generally been viewed in a noticeably *un*ecological light. Otherwise well-intentioned approaches, like ecological footprint analyses, have further reinforced the idea that cities are fundamentally unsustainable, as they have a tendency to conflate sustainability with self-sufficiency. To be sure, urban areas concentrate people, cars, industries, and the like, which naturally means they concentrate emissions, pollution, noise, and consumption. And historically, this concentration made cities—and continues to make many cities around the world—hazardous places to live. Yet those very things that have often caused people to look on urban areas as a "brown" blight on the landscape also give them distinct green ecological advantages.

Urban residents, for example, tend to possess substantially smaller carbon footprints than residents elsewhere in the same country. Per capita greenhouse gas emissions in New York City are less than 30 percent of those for the United States as a whole, those for London roughly half of the British average. The average resident of Rio de Janeiro has a greenhouse gas footprint that's less than a third the size of the average Brazilian's, while the per capita greenhouse gas emissions in Barcelona is 33.9 percent of that for Spain as a whole (see, e.g., Chester et al. 2014). There are many reasons for this phenomenon. The concentration of services and industries lessens the need to travel long distances. Dense cities generally have better public transportation services, in part because the concentration makes building an efficient transportation system more cost-effective. Residents of dense cites also generally live in smaller residential dwellings because of the scarcity and high cost of land.

That said, not all cities possess this ecological profile. Many newly formed megacities in Asia suffer from overcrowding, in which case *reducing* urban density might help meet a number of social, environmental, and developmental needs (Hasan 2014). For example, while the average urban density for cities in the United States, New Zealand, and Australia is estimated to be roughly fifteen persons per hectare, the average density for certain Asian cities is in some cases in excess of 1,000 persons per hectare (see Case Study 6.4). Then there is the problem with suburbs. According to a study by University of California Berkeley researchers (Jones and Kammen 2014), while population-dense US cities contribute less greenhouse gas emissions per person than other areas of the country, their extensive suburbs typically wipe out these carbon benefits. Thanks primarily to emissions from cars, trucks, and other forms of transportation, suburbs account for roughly 50 percent of all household emissions in the United States. (The researchers have made interactive carbon footprint maps available for more than 31,000 US zip codes in all fifty states at coolclimate.berkeley.edu/maps.) While the average carbon footprint of households living in the center of large, population-dense urban cities is about 50 percent below the US average, the footprint of households in suburbs can be up to twice the average. The research also points to the fact that increasing population density cannot be the sole solution for reducing emissions. A tenfold increase in population density in central cities corresponds to only 25 percent lower greenhouse gas emissions. Increasing population density in suburbs is even more problematic, as population-dense suburbs have significantly higher carbon footprints than less dense suburbs, largely as a result of residents' higher incomes and greater levels of consumption.

Evidence suggests that the number of households in a country has a more direct environmental impact than its population per se (Liu et al. 2003; Marcotullio et al. 2014).

Contextualizing Urban Density

Population density, according to the Merriam-Webster dictionary, speaks to "the number of people living in each unit of area (such as a square mile)" (www.merriam-webster.com). But is it really that simple a calculation? How can population densities be based on residents alone given that the numbers of people in any neighborhood, at any a given time, is in constant flux—people who are working, playing, visiting, or even incarcerated (how do you count prison residents?). An increasing number of neighborhoods are mixed-use, meaning this fluidity presents a huge problem to these conventional definitions of the term. Or in areas that are not mixed-use: the same urban precinct could be densely populated during work hours and empty in the evenings and on weekends. We also need to separate *building* density from *street-life* density. You can have an urban core that is densely packed with people but that has little street-life vitality: outdoor vendors, cafes, parks and greenspaces, bike paths, walkers—that urban "buzz" that most of us find attractive. You know what I'm talking about. Think of those car-dominated high-rise neighborhoods that have desolate sidewalks and public spaces (Dovey and Pafka 2016).

Yet the number of households in a country and its population do not grow together. Globally, household formation exceeded population growth from 2007 to 2016. Household numbers increased by 10 percent to 2.5 billion—growth driven largely by China, India, and the United States, with 520 million, 288 million, and 140 million households, respectively, in 2016. In emerging markets, multigenerational households, which were once the norm, are becoming less common as living standards rise and young people sever ties with families to move to cities in search of work (Seales 2017). Meanwhile, countries such as the United States are seeing a return to multigenerational living. Roughly 20 percent of the country resides in multigenerational households, up from the 1980 low point when the rate was 12 percent. In 1950, the rate was 21 percent (Sisson 2017).

The Case for a Population Explosion

Although empirically unsubstantiated, there is an argument out there that the best solution to the problems associated with population growth is … *more* population growth. Let me start by offering a more moderate position: that given by Ester Boserup.

Boserup (1965) famously turned Thomas Malthus on his head. Malthus's argument was essentially that agricultural methods (and, more specifically, the available food supply) determine population size. Boserup, instead, argued that population determines agricultural methods and in turn food supply, suggesting that population pressures will sufficiently incentivize ways to feed those additional mouths. To put it simply: given the essential nature of food, people will always find ways to increase agricultural production by increasing their labor (or workforce), machinery, fertilizer applications, and other technologies.

Yet the Boserup effect, as it has come to be known, is also sensitive to certain realities that can dampen the otherwise optimistic scenario painted by its namesake. Having written extensively on the relationship between gender and development (giving us some of the earliest scholarship on the subject), she was well aware of how inequality can limit the impact of the Boserup effect. Making the necessary investments to one's operation to keep agricultural output ahead of population takes money and credit—two things, unfortunately, that are not always available to the millions of small farmers in less developed countries (Carolan 2018a). Boserup was also well aware that the sheer level of population growth that some countries were experiencing—especially in the 1960s, when she was formulating this argument—outstripped the capacity of their governments, economies, and agricultural sectors to keep ahead of growing needs. In sum: a Boserup effect might be discernible in some countries but certainly not all.

I would classify Boserup as a pragmatic optimist; her optimism, after all, was tempered by empirical reality. Another person rather famously takes technological optimism to the extreme. For Julian Simon (1981), people represent, as the title of the book detailing his position states, *The Ultimate Resource*. Hence, the greater the population, the greater the collective brainpower and the faster we'll find answers to all the problems that currently trouble us. An increase of 100 million, one billion, ten billion … the more, the better. Each birth, Simon reasons, increases our chances of yielding another Einstein or Mozart (he fails to acknowledge that by this reasoning it increases our chances of more Hitlers and Bin Ladens too). Simon's position epitomizes what is known as **cornucopian**. Based on the Greek myth of a horn from a goat that suckled Zeus and became filled with fruit, a cornucopian is someone who believes unending progress, economic growth, and material abundance can be had with advancements in technology.

Yet there is an enormous gap in this reasoning. Had Einstein been born to a poor family in, say, Calcutta, the capital of India during the British Raj until 1911, I doubt we would be speaking of him today. My point is that we already have billions of these underused "resources" available to us today: minds and bodies that, if just given a chance, could do great things. If we only spent more time concentrating on educating, feeding, and generally improving the lives of the more than one billion people living in poverty around the world (Banerjee and Duflo 2011), we would all be better off.

Simon also assumes that our resources are infinitely substitutable, that when we get low on one resource, we'll find, through technology, brainpower, and hard work, something else to use in its stead. That's an awfully big assumption to make, given the stakes involved. If anything shows the folly of this assumption, it is climate change. Simon died in 1998, well before the definitive evidence came out about climate change. It's hard enough to even think about what a substitute for things like clean water and clean air might look like. But with global climate change, how can we substitute an entire planet?

"Up Rather Than Out": If It Works for Cities, Can It Work for Farms?

I've already discussed some of the possible ecological benefits that urban density has over urban sprawl. Of course, to make something like this work will take an immense amount of coordination. Urban density is not going to solve anything without a sustainable supporting structure in place, like agriculture. The issue of food production takes center stage in Chapter 8, so I will limit my comments here. But the following question bears asking:

How are we going to feed tomorrow's megacities in a way that's ecologically sound? One possibility is to turn agriculture, literally, on its head: **vertical farming**—the practice of farming "up," rather than "out."

Other than the footprint of the facility itself, vertical farms require no land. Contrary to what we think we know about plant physiology, plants do not require soil to survive. Hydroponics—from the Greek words *hydro* (water) and *ponos* (labor)—involves growing plants using mineral nutrient solutions in water, without soil. The practice has been around since the 1930s and is used in nurseries around the world for seed germination. More recent still is what is known as aeroponics, essentially an ultra-efficient version of hydroponics in which tiny nozzles spray a nutrient-rich mist onto the plant's roots.

Another misconception about plant physiology: plants also do not need all the energy in sunlight to grow to maximum yield. Light-emitting diodes (LEDs) have recently been engineered just for plants, giving them only the parts of the spectrum of light that they need. On the horizon are light-emitting diodes (OLEDs) that promise to offer an even narrower spectrum of light, thus further reducing the energy demands of vertical farms (Cox 2009; Despommier 2010). Of course, in those regions of the world where sunlight is plentiful, vertical farms could take advantage of this free and abundant resource. Similarly, buildings could be powered using wind turbines and photovoltaic panels.

In his book *The Vertical Farm*, Despommier (2010) tells the story of a strawberry farmer who replaced his thirty-acre farm after it was destroyed by a hurricane with a one-acre vertical farm utilizing hydro-stackers (a hydroponic vertical gardening system). That single acre now yields as many strawberries as the thirty acres did prior to the hurricane. The farmer also reports that the remaining twenty-nine acres, those not replanted with strawberries, have returned to a more biologically diverse—or "wild"—state.

A recently published study attempts to "assess global aggregate ecosystem services from existing vegetation in cities and an intensive UA [urban agriculture] adoption scenario based on data-driven estimates of urban morphology and vacant land" (Clinton et al. 2018, 40). (Granted, enclosed vertical farming systems are different in certain ways from open-air urban agriculture [Carolan 2019].) The estimates the authors arrive at paint a beneficial picture of UA: ecosystem services provided by existing vegetation, US$33 billion annually; potential annual food production of 100–180 million tonnes; energy savings, of fourteen to fifteen billion kilowatt hours; nitrogen sequestration of between 100,000 and 170,000 tonnes; and avoided storm water runoff of between forty-five and fifty-seven billion cubic meters annually. The study also cites benefits due to pollination, climate regulation, soil formation and biological control of pests, which cumulatively "could be worth as much as $80–160 billion annually" (Clinton et al. 2018, 40).

It is not my suggestion that vertical farms could entirely support tomorrow's megacities. Yet we've got to ask how tomorrow's megacities are going to be fed, particularly in light of the growing interest in concepts like regional food security and resilience and rising energy prices. The world's largest megacities in 2030 are projected to have populations approaching forty million—not far away from the same population that lived on the *entire planet* in the year 1000 BCE (roughly fifty million people). To feed them all will require some outside-the-box—perhaps even some vertical—thinking.

IMPORTANT CONCEPTS

- Amartya Sen on famines
- Boserup effect
- demographic transition model
- global land grab
- IPAT
- Julian Simon's ultimate resource
- maternal mortality ratio
- socioeconomic development
- STIRPAT
- Thomas Malthus on population growth

DISCUSSION QUESTIONS

1. Is it fair to continue framing the population problem as a low-income country problem when the average US citizen's ecological footprint is thirty times greater than that of the average Indian and 100 times greater than that of the average person in the world's poorest countries?
2. Having large families in low-income nations is perfectly rational for many living in those environments. What are some of the sociological forces underlying high fertility rates in developing countries?
3. Does a person have a fundamental human right to have as many children as he or she chooses?
4. What is the Earth's carrying capacity (how many people can it hold)? What factors play into such a calculation?

SUGGESTED ADDITIONAL READINGS

Creamer, E., S. Allen, and C. Haggett. 2018. "'Incomers' Leading 'Community-Led' Sustainability Initiatives: A Contradiction in Terms?" *Environment and Planning C: Politics and Space*, 37(5): 946–964. https://doi.org/10.1177/0263774X18802476.

Flörke, M., C. Schneider, and R.I. McDonald. 2018. "Water Competition between Cities and Agriculture Driven by Climate Change and Urban Growth." *Nature Sustainability*, 1(1): 51–58.

Hartmann, B., A. Hendrixson, and J. Sasser. 2016. "Population, Sustainable Development, and Gender Equality." In *Gender Equality and Sustainable Development*, edited by M. Leach, pp. 56–81. New York: Earthscan/Routledge.

Toth, G., and C. Szigeti. 2016. "The Historical Ecological Footprint: From Over-Population to Over-Consumption." *Ecological Indicators*, 60: 283–291.

RELEVANT INTERNET LINKS

- www.census.gov/popclock. US and world population clocks, maintained by the US Census Bureau.

- http://populationpyramid.net. Population pyramids of the world and for every nation, based on United Nations data.
- www.prb.org/distilled-demographics-population-data/. Link to the Population Reference Bureau's (PRB) *Distilled Demographics* video series. In *Deciphering Population Pyramids* (www.prb.org/distilleddemographics1/), the PRB's senior demographer shows how population pyramids give us a snapshot of a country's demographic profile.
- http://rumkin.com/tools/population. Population statistics for every country.

SUGGESTED VIDEOS

- *Don't Panic: The Truth About Population* (2013). BBC documentary about human overpopulation.
- *Earth Days* (2009). Approaching "classic" status, this documentary is about the rise of the environmental movement in the United States and the first Earth Day in 1970. It also chronicles the late 1960s and 1970s, when talk of a "population bomb" was at its peak.
- *How Many People Can Live on Planet Earth?* (2011). http://documentaryvideos.org/bbc–documentary-about-earths-population. A BBC produced six-part series on the Earth's population.
- *Mother: Caring for 7 Billion* (2011). An award-winning film about the controversies surrounding our world of seven billion, and one woman's journey to make sense of it.
- *The Dirtiest Place on the Planet* (2012). Linfen, China: a day breathing its air is like smoking three packs of cigarettes. The scary part is that there are a lot of cities in China like this.
- *The Future of Cities* (2017). https://vimeo.com/195304295. An eighteen-minute mini-documentary that explores how citizens are mobilizing to address issues ranging from overcrowding to pollution, housing shortages, and aging infrastructure.

Transportation: Beyond Air Pollution

It is understandable why discussions on transportation in my classes repeatedly veer to pollution, since roughly 28 percent of US greenhouse gas emissions are transportation related (EPA 2016). The good news, as the EPA (n.d.) notes on a webpage titled, "What if we kept our cars parked for trips less than one mile?", is that car trips less than a mile account for ten billion miles of automobile travel per year. Using our legs instead of cars to make these trips, assuming an average fuel economy of twenty-two miles per gallon and an average fuel price of $2.50/gallon, would save us $575 million in fuel costs and two million metric tons of CO_2 emissions annually.

Yet it is more than just its links to pollution that make transportation a fascinating subject for sociologists. We often think about transportation as a response to changes in how society is organized. In this scenario, we drive because our urban environments require us to. Yet the data tell precisely the opposite story. Urban and community patterns, in other words, have taken the shape they have in part because of available transportation systems. The car, for example, made certain patterns of urbanization possible—patterns that, not surprisingly, are found today to be difficult to service under alternative transportation forms. Thus, although many urban environments leave us with little choice but to drive, those very environments place this demand on us only because the car makes their existence possible. Although we often like to think of the car's rise as the outcome of consumer democracy—where you vote with your wallet—a careful analysis reveals the votes have been rigged in its favor. After all, wouldn't you expect the automobile to win when the question is, "What mode of transportation would you choose in a society that's specifically designed for the automobile?"

Figure 7.1 offers idealized conceptual diagrams of three urban types that are meant to illustrate how the shape and character of cities have changed with available transportation systems. Cities prior to 1850 were highly dense and mixed-use—residential and commercial were mixed together. They reflected the fact that people got around either with their feet or by horse. As rail was established, suburbs began to form along the rail line. The city itself, however, while slowly beginning to grow outward, remained moderately to highly dense, as transportation within the city was limited. The car changed everything,

FIGURE 7.1 Idealized and Conceptual Diagrams of Traditional, Commuter, and Automobile Cities

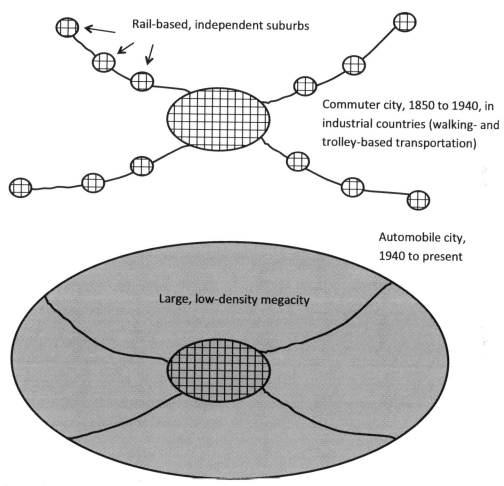

Traditional city, e.g., prior to 1850, in Europe (horse-carriage- and walking-based transportation)

Rail-based, independent suburbs

Commuter city, 1850 to 1940, in industrial countries (walking- and trolley-based transportation)

Automobile city, 1940 to present

Large, low-density megacity

Source: Adapted from Schiller and Kenworthy (2017).

ushering in an almost anything-goes model of urban sprawl. Those previously independent suburbs have since spread out, as has the inner city, making for all intents and purposes one large megacity. And without well thought out alternative transportation systems (like those discussed in the Solutions section of this chapter), many urban dwellers today have little choice but to take the car, even perhaps when going just a couple of blocks. I have a friend, for example, who must cross an eight-lane intersection when she wishes to walk to a local grocery store that's less than a mile away. How can we expect people to abandon their cars if doing so comes at great risk to life and limb?

Fast Facts

- We surpassed one billion vehicles on the road back in 2010 (Voelcker 2014). A 2018 estimate put the figure at over 1.4 billion, which is a long way away from the 670 million figure in 1996 and the 342 million figure in 1976 (Chesterton 2018).
- Household income has a curious relationship to annual miles travelled by car, as noted in Table 7.1 for American drivers.
- Approximately 1.24 million people die each year as a result of road traffic crashes. Road traffic injuries are the leading cause of death among young people aged fifteen to twenty-nine. Ninety-one percent of the world's traffic fatalities occur in low-income and middle-income countries, even though these countries only have approximately half of the world's vehicles. Without action, road traffic crashes are predicted to result in the deaths of around 1.9 million people annually by 2020. Only twenty-eight countries, representing 416 million people—7 percent of the world's population—have adequate laws that address all five major risk factors attributed to automobile injuries and deaths: speed, drunk driving, and the lack of helmets (in the case of motorcycles), seat belts, and child restraints (WHO 2018b).
- The American Automobile Association estimates the average annual cost of owning and operating a car in the United States based on driving 15,000 miles per year: for a small sedan, $7,606, or 38.0 cents per mile; for a medium sedan, $9,790, or 49.0 cents per mile; for a minivan, $10,571, or 52.9 cents per mile; for a large sedan, $11,906, or 59.5 cents per mile; and for a sport utility vehicle (SUV), $11,931, or 59.7 cents per mile (AAA 2015).

TABLE 7.1 Average Annual Miles per Driver by Household Income (United States)

HOUSEHOLD INCOME	MILLIONS OF MILES	PERCENTAGE OF TOTAL
Less than $10,000	7,506	3.5
$10,000–$14,999	7,528	3.5
$15,000–$24,999	15,521	7.2
$25,000–$34,999	18,890	8.8
$35,000–$49,999	27,100	12.6
$50,000–$74,999	38,000	17.6
$75,000–$99,999	30,807	14.3
$100,000–$124,999	25,441	11.8
$125,000–$149,999	14,855	6.9
$150,000–$199,999	14,480	6.7
$200,000 or more	15,275	7.1

Source: Adapted from US Federal Highway Administration (2018).

But wait! Americans own an average of 2.28 vehicles per household, and more than 35 percent of households own three or more cars. So the average household—assuming there are two cars in its garage—spends roughly $20,000 a year on its vehicles, more if it owns SUVs, a little less if the cars are small or medium sedans. And 35 percent spend at least $30,000 annually so they can have the "freedom" that a car allows.

- The Texas Transportation Institute at Texas A&M University released a report that measures the difference in travel time between congested and free-flowing conditions (Lomax et al. 2011). Commuters in Chicago and Washington, DC, see on average seventy hours of their lives eaten up by rush-hour traffic every year, followed by those in Los Angeles (sixty-three hours) and Houston (fifty-eight hours). That's not how much time they spend in a car but the *additional time* spent in a car because of congestion. Nearly three billion gallons of fuel were wasted in 2012 in the United States from traffic congestion (Texas A&M Transportation Institute 2013; see ECOnnection 7.1).

- Greenhouse gas emissions from transport represent approximately 14 percent of global emissions and 23 percent of CO_2 emissions from global fossil fuel combustion. Transport is the sector with the fastest growing consumption of fossil fuels and is also the fastest growing source of CO_2 emissions globally. Road transport is responsible for more than 70 percent of CO_2 emissions from the transport sector. At current rates, CO_2 emissions from transport are on track to double by 2050 (OECD 2015a).

Implications

This section focuses on the automobile because of its ubiquity and oversized ecological footprint. The following represents a brief overview of some of the socioecological impacts associated primarily with this mode of transportation. Our understanding of *transportation* broadens considerably when solutions are discussed.

Pollution and Public Health

It's ironic that the very technology to win praise a century ago from street cleaners, public health officials, and politicians because it delivered urban dwellers from a major environmental ill at the time—namely, horse manure that blanketed urban streets—would someday be responsible for far more severe public health threats. Although it is difficult to attach a specific amount in dollars to transportation-related health outcomes (some have tried; see Table 7.2), the car's deleterious effects to public health are obvious.

If we accept the argument that cars helped create urban conditions that eventually made them a necessity, which by definition discourages human-powered forms of transportation, then it is entirely fair to associate the cost of things like obesity to the automobile, as obesity has been closely linked to automobile-centered urban design (Chiu et al. 2015; Frederick et al. 2018). The data on this relationship are quite compelling.

Walk Score® (www.walkscore.com/) is a webtool that assigns a score to an address based on the proximity of local destinations and street connectivity around that location. A sizable body of research has emerged linking higher scores to the availability of public transportation, bike lanes, and the like (Cole et al. 2015; Hirsch et al. 2014), greater rates of walking for leisure (Hirsch et al. 2013), and lower levels of chronic diseases that have been connected to physical inactivity (Koohsari et al. 2018). In one study, researchers in

TABLE 7.2 Annual Cost of Transportation-Related Health Outcomes in the United States

HEALTH OUTCOME	COST (IN US$ BILLIONS)	ESTIMATE INCLUDES
Obesity and overweight	150–200	• Health-care costs • Lost wages due to illness and disability • Future earnings lost because of premature death
Air pollution from traffic	50–80	• Health-care costs • Future earnings lost because of premature death
Traffic crashes	175–235	• Health-care costs • Lost wages due to injuries • Property damage • Travel delay • Legal/administrative costs • Pain and suffering • Loss of quality of life

Source: Cole et al. (2019).

the United States examined the links between average life expectancy and five possible mediators: (1) annual vehicle miles traveled per household; (2) average body mass index; (3) crime rate; (3) air quality index; (4) percentage of smokers; and (5) socioeconomic status (Hamidi et al. 2018). The study found life expectancy to be "significantly" higher in compact counties than in those that were sprawling. The authors, however, were cautious when drawing causal arrows between sprawl and mortality. In their words, "the causal mechanism is unclear," and they added,

> For example, it may be that sprawling areas have higher traffic speeds and longer emergency response times, lower quality and less accessible health care facilities, or less availability of healthy foods. Compactness affects mortality indirectly through vehicle miles traveled, which is a contributor to traffic fatalities, and through body mass index, which is a contributor to many chronic diseases.
>
> Hamidi et al. (2018, 1)

Globally, approximately twenty-four million people die each year on roads, while another twenty to fifty million suffer nonfatal injuries. The overall global road traffic fatality rate is eighteen per 100,000 residents. Middle-income countries have the highest annual road traffic fatality rates, at 20.1 per 100,000, followed by low-income countries with a rate of 18.3, while the rate in high-income countries is 8.7 per 100,000. The risk of dying as a result of a road traffic injury is highest in the African Region (24.1 per 100,000 population), followed by the Eastern Mediterranean Region (21.3 per 100,000), Western Pacific Region (18.5 per 100,000), Southeast Asian Region (18.5 per 100,000), Regions of the Americas (16.1 per 100,000), and European Region (10.3 per 100,000) (WHO 2018b). As Table 7.3 illustrates, road traffic injuries are the leading cause of death for

ECOnnection 7.1

Effective Speed

Effective speed is, in some respects, calculated conventionally: speed equals distance divided by time. The novelty of the concept lies in its aim to consider *all* time costs when comparing transportation forms. For car drivers, a significant—though typically invisible—time cost is the time spent at work to earn the money to pay for all the expenses associated with this costly mode of transportation. Key variables needed to calculate effective speeds for any mode of transportation are: average trip speed; the direct and indirect costs of the mode of transportation; the average income of the population, which determines how much time is devoted to earning the money to pay the costs; and any other time devoted to the mode of transportation besides travel, such as time spent filling a vehicle with fuel.

Research has looked at effective speeds of cyclists in different cities, calculating how slow cyclists could travel and still be effectively faster than a car. If only out-of-pocket costs are considered, then the fastest that a cyclist would need to travel, among the cities studied, would be 13.3 miles per hour in Canberra, Australia; the slowest, 1.9 miles per hour, in Nairobi, Kenya. (The car's near-standstill effective speed in Kenya is largely a product of the country's abysmally low average income that makes car ownership a very time-consuming activity.) If external costs are also considered, cyclists in Canberra would need to average only 11.3 miles per hour to be faster than a car driver. In New York, Los Angeles, Tokyo, and Hamburg cyclists would not need to travel faster than eight miles per hour to outrun an automobile (Crozet 2017; Tranter 2012).

The idea of effective speed points to a speed paradox of sorts when it comes to the motor vehicle: the faster one tries to go with this mode of transportation, the slower it becomes. Increasing trip speeds has little impact on effective speed because the main time cost is not driving but the time spent earning money to pay for the costs of driving. Indeed, driving faster could further reduce effective speed by causing those costs to go up, such as by reducing gas mileage, increasing the rate of tire wear, and perhaps even resulting in a costly accident. There is also little that governments can do to reduce the car's effective speed. The costs of building wider roads, for instance, more than offset any reductions in travel time.

According to the INRIX 2018 Global Traffic Scorecard (http://inrix.com/scorecard/), which gives an analysis of congestion and mobility trends in more than 200 cities, across 38 countries, traffic congestion is not just an annoyance for the people who are trapped, but is a major problem for a city's economy. Los Angeles ranked number 1 internationally, with drivers spending an average of 102 hours in traffic jams annually, followed by Moscow and New York City, both with ninety-one lost hours (followed by Sao Paulo, Brazil, at eighty-six hours and San Francisco with seventy-nine). The firm also calculated the total cost to the cities based on these congestion figures. While Los Angeles loses $19.2 billion annually thanks to congestion, New York City's economy takes the biggest hit, losing $33.7 billion every year—or an average of $2,982 per driver. These figures are based on things like losses in productivity due to workers being stuck in their cars, higher road transportation costs, and fuel burned running idle for extended periods of time. Not taken into consideration in these figures include costs, for example, to public health (pollution, the sedentary nature of sitting in a car for so many hours a day, and so forth) and the environment (greenhouse gas emissions, habitat fragmentation, etc.).

TABLE 7.3 Leading Causes of Death, by Age, Worldwide

RANK	0–4 YEARS	5–14 YEARS	15–29 YEARS	30–44 YEARS	45–69 YEARS	70 AND ABOVE	AGGREGATE AVERAGE
1	Perinatal causes	Road traffic injuries	Road traffic injuries	HIV/AIDS	Ischemic heart disease	Ischemic heart disease	Ischemic heart disease
2	Lower respiratory infections	Lower respiratory infections	HIV/AIDS	Tuberculosis	Cerebro-vascular disease	Cerebro-vascular disease	Cerebro-vascular disease
3	Diarrhea	Malaria	Tuberculosis	Road traffic injuries	HIV/AIDS	Chronic pulmonary disease	Lower respiratory infections
4	Malaria	Drowning	Violence	Ischemic heart disease	Tuberculosis	Lower respiratory infections	Perinatal causes
5	Malaria	Meningitis	Self-inflicted injuries	Self-inflicted injuries	Chronic pulmonary disease	Trachea, bronchus, lung cancers	Chronic pulmonary disease
6	Congenital anomalies	Diarrhea	Lower respiratory infections	Violence	Trachea, bronchus, lung cancers	Diabetes	Diarrhea
7	HIV/AIDS	HIV/AIDS	Drowning	Lower respiratory infections	Cirrhosis of the liver	Heart disease	HIV/AIDS
8	Whooping cough	Tuberculosis	Fire	Cerebro-vascular disease	Road traffic injuries	Stomach cancer	Tuberculosis
9	Meningitis	Protein-energy malnutrition	War and conflict	Cirrhosis of the liver	Lower respiratory infections	Colon and rectum cancers	Trachea, bronchus, lung cancers
10	Tetanus	Fire	Maternal hemorrhage	Poisoning	Diabetes	Nephritis and dementias	Road traffic injuries
11	Protein-energy malnutrition	Measles	Ischemic heart disease	Maternal hemorrhage	Self-inflicted injuries	Alzheimer's and other dementias	Diabetes
12	Syphilis	Leukemia	Poisoning	Fire	Stomach cancer	Tuberculosis	Malaria
13	Road traffic injuries	Congenital anomalies	Abortion	Nephritis and dementias	Liver cancer	Liver cancer	Heart disease
14	Drowning	Trypanosomiasis	Leukemia	Drowning	Breast cancer	Esophagus cancer	Self-inflicted injuries
15	Fire	Falls	Cerebro-vascular disease	Breast cancer	Heart disease	Cirrhosis of the liver	Stomach cancer
...	••••	••••	••••	••••	••••	••••	••••
20	Epilepsy	Poisoning	Malaria	Trachea, bronchus, lung cancers	Mouth and oropharynx cancers	Road traffic injuries	Violence

Source: Adapted from WHO (2018a).

people aged five to twenty-nine, and is a major cause of death for most other age groups. While road traffic injuries are currently the tenth leading cause of death worldwide, the World Health Organization (WHO) estimates that by 2030, that ranking will be fifth (WHO 2018b).

Who are these people dying and getting injured on the world's roads? That again depends on whether the accidents are occurring in high-income or lower-income countries. In the United States and Canada, for instance, 65 percent of reported road deaths involve vehicle occupants. Conversely, in low-income and middle-income countries of the Western Pacific Region, 70 percent of reported road fatalities are among what are known as **vulnerable road users**. According to the WHO, this population includes pedestrians, cyclists, and users of motorized two-wheel vehicles (WHO 2018a).

There is also growing evidence pointing to a positive association between exposure to road traffic and aircraft noise and hypertension (high blood pressure) and ischemic heart disease (reduced blood supply to the heart) (WHO 2018a). Road traffic noise is known to increase the risk of ischemic heart disease, including myocardial infarction (heart attacks). A WHO report calculated **disability-adjusted life-years** (DALYs) resulting from noise pollution for all of Europe, recognizing that the majority of the noise comes from road traffic and airplanes. The WHO defines DALYs as "the sum of years of potential life lost due to premature mortality and the years of productive life lost due to disability" (WHO n.d.). It was estimated that DALYs lost in Europe from environmental noise equated to 61,000 years for ischemic heart disease, 45,000 years for cognitive impairment of children, 903,000 years for sleep disturbance, 22,000 years for tinnitus, and 654,000 years for annoyance. In short, more than one million healthy life years are lost annually in Europe as a result of automobile and airplane noise (WHO 2011). A study in Sweden, meanwhile, calculated the number of DALY attributed to traffic noise in Sweden to be 41,033 years (36,711—90 percent—related to road traffic and 4,322—10 percent—related to railway traffic), due principally to sleep disturbances (at 22,218 DALY) (Eriksson et al. 2017).

Habitat and Biodiversity

Habitat fragmentation—the emergence of discontinuities (or fragmentation) in an organism's preferred environment (or habitat)—is also a concern when looking at impacts associated primarily with the automobile. One of the more well-known examples involves the pygmy possum. The habitat of this threatened marsupial had become highly fragmented thanks to roads and other land-use changes. By constructing tunnels—or what are known in Australia as *talus tunnels* (tunnels of love) as they increase the rate of breeding in an area—to run under roadways, natural movements were restored (other times, they run *over* roadways, see Image 7.1). In the Netherlands, road mortality in the 1980s accounted for between 20 and 25 percent of total annual badger deaths. The installation of tunnels beneath many of the country's roadways caused national badger populations to increase some 65 percent while simultaneously reducing the animal's road mortality rates to 10 percent. A similar story, but involving panthers, comes from Florida. Roughly half of all panther deaths occurred on roads prior to the 1990s, as a result of collisions. The state has since built a number of underpasses that give animals (panthers included) safe passage beneath the busy four-lane divided interstate highway I-75.

IMAGE 7.1 Brisbane City Council Wildlife Corridor Connecting Areas of Natural Habitat to Karawatha Forest Park

Source: "Wildlife Corridor" by Brisbane City Council (flickr.com/photos/brisbanecitycouncil), March 12, 2012, is licensed copyright © 2012 under CC BY 2.0.

Habitat fragmentation has received a lot of attention over the past two decades. In the early 1990s, a five-year-old alpha female wolf, wearing a radio collar containing a satellite transmitter, began a remarkable two-year journey. She was tracked making an unexpectedly large circle, beginning far north, near Banff National Park in Alberta, Canada, then south into Montana, turning west through Idaho into Washington State, before heading north into British Columbia, finally ending up again near Banff. In other words, this wolf's habitat was literally thousands of times the size of Yellowstone National Park (Fraser 2009).

The term **islandization** is often used to talk about the disastrous effects that transportation systems like multilane roads can have on wildlife. It refers to the "chunking up" of habitats without **wildlife corridors** like underpasses and tunnels between roadways to connect them. Without this connectivity, the isolated plants and wildlife within an "island" risk going extinct. Island populations (an ecological term used to refer to largely isolated populations of species) are also susceptible to disease, overhunting, and major events like floods or fires. With climate change, the issue of connectivity becomes even more significant. As the ecological conditions of habitats change, wildlife will need to migrate in order to remain in optimal environments. Without wildlife corridors to facilitate this movement, the future of many species is at risk.

How to connect these islands depends on the situation and the species in question. Some animals, like badgers and possum, are more comfortable using tunnels under roadways. Other animals, such as deer, cross at higher rates when given the opportunity to go over the road, in which case a wildlife overpass may be the preferred option. To enhance their effectiveness, vegetation has proven to be an important component to overpasses, as it reduces noise and creates a visual wall between the animals and traffic.

Community

There is also compelling evidence pointing to the car's adverse impact on communities. Robert Putnam's (2001) famous book *Bowling Alone* is often cited as single-handedly bringing this link into popular light, through the conceptual lens of "social capital" (see ECOnnection 7.2). Putnam's extensive research led him to conclude that "the car and the

ECOnnection 7.2
Social Capital

Social capital formalizes what we all know intuitively: that who we know matters as much as what we know. A growing literature over the past two decades shows that social capital—social networks and the norms of trust and reciprocity that come with frequent social interaction—is central to community well-being. Norms of trust and reciprocity enhance social interaction much the same way cash enhances trade, namely, by allowing action to be taken without having to separately negotiate the terms of every exchange. But how? "Dense" social networks make it easier for individuals and the community as a whole to discover who should not be trusted. They also create a significant incentive to live up to people's trust expectations, as failing to do so will result in an immediate loss of reputation across the community as a whole. More generally, social capital makes working with others easier, enhances information flow across the community, encourages cooperative behavior, and reduces the likelihood of unproductive "defensive" behaviors, like locking doors, avoiding going out for walks at night, and so forth. Yet social capital can also have a dark side, as it can result in community exclusion, group think, and a general distrust of outsiders if levels of **"bridging" social capital** (networks between groups or weak ties) are not present at concentrations comparable to

"bonding" social capital forms (networks within groups or strong ties).

In light of these findings, some scholars have gone so far as to argue that "there is good reason, from a civic point of view, to encourage forms of community design that reduce commuting time and to encourage the preservation and increased livability of both our older neighborhoods and our central cities," adding, "the biggest payoff, at least from a political participation point of view, appears to be in getting Americans out of their cars" (Williamson 2002, 243).

Precisely *how* we do this, however, he does not say. What we do know is that many current urban planning practices tend to reduce community interaction by favoring vehicular mobility over alternative modes such as walking, cycling, and public transit. Traffic engineers generally evaluate transportation systems based on things like vehicle traffic speeds and road capacity, even if this practice degrades the pedestrian environment and reduces community cohesion (see ECOnnection 7.3).

The data suggest that this is not just an American issue. Countries around the world—from Brazil (Cafruni et al. 2019) to China (Wang et al. 2018)—have been shown to be socially, civically, and politically harmed by automobile dependency.

ECOnnection 7.3

Community Severance

Community severance is an important social impact associated with transportation. It can be defined as a real or perceived barrier to people's movement through an area that is created by the transportation infrastructure (like roads or rails) or traffic. Whereas physical severance is the most obvious type, there are also psychological and social forms. An example of the former might be having a fear of crossing busy roads, whereas an example of the latter could be when one's friendships do not go beyond the barrier in question, thus creating less of a social need to traverse any particular physical structure. Groups most adversely affected by severance include those without cars, those with restricted mobility—most notably, disabled and elderly people—and schoolchildren (Anciaes et al. 2016).

commute … are demonstrably bad for community life" (Putnam 2001, 213). He notes that "each additional ten minutes in daily commuting time cuts involvement in community affairs by 10 percent—fewer public meetings attended, fewer committees chaired, fewer petitions signed, fewer church services attended, less volunteering, and so on" (Ibid.). In sum, though not quite as powerful an influence on civic involvement as education, commuting time "is more important than almost any other demographic factor" (Ibid.).

Research generally supports Putnam's conclusions. For example, studies have shown that high dependence on the automobile and sprawling built environments are positively associated with weakened neighborhood social ties (Mazumdar et al. 2018), whether that community is located in the United States (Roe and Knöll 2018), South Korea (Seo and Chiu 2014), Colombia (Torres et al. 2013), or China (Dong and Qin 2017). Other studies suggest that the emotional and intellectual development of children is enhanced in more walkable, mixed-use communities, most likely from a combination of increased opportunities for physical activity, independence, and community cohesion (Møllegaard and Jæger 2015; Oliver et al. 2017). Automobile reliance is found to have a strong negative impact on whether an individual visits friends or participates in out-of-home sports, cultural activities, and civic events, and a positive effect on in-home and potentially asocial amusements such as watching television (Cafruni et al. 2019; Sallis et al. 2018).

Solutions

There is no going back. Having organized society over the past century around the automobile, we cannot pretend that those structures—whether made of concrete and reinforcing steel bars or of long-held habits and routines—are of no sociological consequence. There are, however, a number of ways forward that reduce the impacts addressed in the previous section, as I'll now explain.

Dense, Livable, Intermodal Cities

I've already talked a little about the potential ecological benefits associated with the high-density city, particularly in affluent nations, where the financial resources are available to maximize those benefits. We already know that population density is negatively associated with transportation-related energy consumption at the per capita level (see Figure 7.2). Dense cities come with reduced travel distances for the average inhabitant to things like work and social visits. Urban density also reduces the transaction costs for building a viable public transportation system, as the network can service more people per unit of track than is possible in sprawled-out cities.

One of the ecological benefits associated with mass public transit lies in its vehicle per passenger fuel efficiencies, especially when maxed to capacity. Table 7.4 documents the energy efficiency of various passenger modes, in terms of miles per gallon (mpg) and per passenger mpg (for average and maximum capacity). The Toyota Prius's respectable

FIGURE 7.2 Urban Density and Transport-Related Energy Consumption, Select Cities

Urban density (inhabitants per hectare)

Source: Twidell and Weir (2015).

Note: The dotted line represents the regression line when all cities are plotted. (A regression line comes as close to all points as possible through a scatterplot of two variables.) With over 7 million inhabitants packed onto an island of roughly 426 square miles, residents of Hong Kong never have to travel very far to get anywhere—a reality that also makes public transportation highly attractive from an urban planning standpoint. The city of Houston, conversely, spreads 2.1 million inhabitants over 656 square miles. This lower density means not only that Houstonians have to travel, on average, further than residents of Hong Kong, but that they do so in most instances using an inefficient mode of transportation: the automobile. This level of urban sprawl makes the car virtually the only option for many of the inhabitants of this iconic Texas city.

TABLE 7.4 Energy Efficiency of Various Passenger Modes (Land, Air, and Water)

MODE (EXAMPLE)	MPG	AVERAGE NO. PASSENGERS (MPG PER PERSON)	MAXIMUM NO. PASSENGERS (MPG PER PERSON)
Scooter (50cc engine)	75	1 (75)	2 (150)
Medium motorcycle (Suzuki GS500)	60	1 (60)	2 (120)
Hybrid auto (Toyota Prius)	47.6	1.5 (72)	5 (238)
Very small auto, highway (Smart Car)	41	1.5 (62)	2 (82)
Very small auto, city (Smart Car)	33	1.2 (40)	2 (66)
SUV, highway (Fort Explorer, V8)	21.6	2 (43)	7 (151)
SUV, city (Fort Explorer, V8)	14.1	1.2 (17)	7 (98)
40-foot diesel transit bus	3.1	25 (78)	90 (279)
40-foot trolley bus	9.77	30 (293)	77 (752)
Light rail	13.6	65 (887)	180 (2,460)
London Underground	7.4	19 (141)	152 (1,125)
Intercity rail (Swedish Railways Regina)	3.35	34 (114)	167 (560)
High speed rail (LGV Atlantique; runs from Paris to western France)	1.58	291 (460)	485 (767)
Private small airplane (Cessna 172)	12.6	1 (12.6)	4 (50.4)
Regional turboprop (DHC 8-300)	1.19	35 (41.7)	137 (58.9)
Short/medium range airliner (Boeing 737; average flight, 607 miles)	0.43	96 (41.3)	137 (58.9)
Medium/long range airliner (Airbus 320, average flight, 1,358 miles)	0.447	109 (48.7)	156 (69.7)
Very long distance airliner (Boeing 777-200ER, average flight, 6,818 miles)	0.252	211 (53.1)	301 (75.8)
Passenger-only ferry (Vancouver SeaBus)	0.25	140 (35)	400 (100)
Passenger and car ferry (BC Ferries Spirit Class)	0.0246	1,000 (24.6)	2,100 (51.7)
Transoceanic luxury ship (Queen Mary 2, 25 knots)	0.00753	2,000 (15)	3,090 (23.2)

Source: Adapted from Schiller et al. (2017).

Note: Vehicles are typically designed to carry more than just one passenger. Indeed, some—such as transoceanic luxury ships—can accommodate thousands. It is therefore inaccurate (and unfair) to compare modes of transportation by their miles per gallon without also factoring in for the number of people each can accommodate at any given time (or on average). The table shows the miles per gallon if only one person rode each mode of transportation, in addition to the miles per gallon per person according to both average capacity and maximum capacity per mode.

238 mpg per passenger (when fully loaded up with five occupants) pales in comparison to intercity rail, high-speed rail, the London Underground, or light rail, which, when fully loaded with passengers, register 560 mpg per passenger, 767 mpg per passenger, 1,125 mpg per passenger, and 2,460 mpg per passenger, respectively.

There are also social benefits that come when one abandons the solo commute for something less isolating. Recent research indicates that public transportation, for instance, can increase social capital for individuals and neighborhoods as a whole (Mattisson et al. 2015). And among those unable to drive, such as elderly and disabled people, having alternatives to the car is crucial to improving their integration within a community as well as to providing access to such life-sustaining resources as food and health care (Levasseur et al. 2015).

Yet just having alternatives to the automobile is rarely enough to make people choose to leave their cars in the garage. Multimodality gives individuals choices, but without intermodality—the ability to make efficient connections between modes—those alternative choices are rarely as attractive as the car. For example, if you still have to walk ten blocks after getting off the nearest light-rail stop to get to your friend's house, you'll likely choose to take the automobile more often than not (see Case Study 7.1). Just what those connections will involve will vary from community to community, depending on what those communities value (see Ethical Question 7.1). The overarching goal, however, is the same: to make alternative modes as attractive as—or ideally, more attractive than—the car.

We are presently doing a lot to incentivize driving. For example, many federal, state, and local government tax policies prioritize motor vehicle use. Fuel is exempt from

CASE STUDY 7.1
The Rise of Bike-Share Programs

Elliot Fishman (2015), director of the Institute for Sensible Transport, examined data and studies on large bike-sharing systems worldwide and found convenience to be a universal driving factor in whether people use them. For instance, Washington, DC's Capital Bikeshare surveyed more than 11,100 members and found that 69 percent of respondents said getting where they need to go fast was "very important" in encouraging them to use the program (Stein 2015). The distance between a rider's home and the nearest docking station also proved to be a central motivational variable in determining whether a person would pay for a membership. For example, residents of Montreal, Canada, living within three-tenths of a mile of a docking station were about three times more likely than the average resident to have used that city's bike-share program.

In general, those using bike-share programs are more likely to be affluent and better educated than the general population (Fishman 2015). However, this appears to be changing, as these sharing systems are extending into lower-income neighborhoods. (Sadly, stereotypes still dog some programs as organizers worry about bike theft in lower-income neighborhoods.) In London, the majority of early bike-share users were affluent. Yet the percentage of low-income residents using the system doubled from 6 to 12 percent between 2010 and 2013 (Stein 2015).

general taxes in many jurisdictions. Land devoted to public roads and parking facilities is exempt from rent and taxes. And oil companies are given significant tax exemptions and subsidies. Large taxpayer-funded roads represent a significant portion of land that cannot be taxed, while being of benefit primarily to private motorists. Similarly, private lands are typically taxed at a lower rate when paved over to make a parking lot.

Let's talk more about free parking. If it were not in such abundance (especially in the United States), do you think we would have as much of an incentive to drive? And who pays for that "free" parking? We all do, as taxpayers, regardless of whether we use it. Many current zoning codes also favor automobile-oriented land-use patterns, which include things like density restrictions, single-use zoning, and, yes, minimum parking requirements. An ambitious calculation was attempted by Mark Delucchi while employed by the Institute of Transportation Studies at University of California, Davis. (Unfortunately, given its ambitious nature, studies like this are not done routinely.) Using an extensive data set from the early 1990s, Delucchi calculated that the total cost of the automobile for Americans at the time was as high as $3.3 trillion—the equivalent of roughly $5.1 trillion in today's dollars, or one-third of the country's entire GDP (Delucchi 2004). There were only 188 million registered vehicles on the road in the United States in 1991. Today, the figure approaches 300 million, which means that the $5.1 trillion figure is undoubtedly too low to accurately reflect present costs. Just to show that this number is not an outlier in the literature: Todd Litman, founder and executive director of the Victoria Transport Policy Institute, places the cost of "free" parking at $3.4 trillion annually (Litman 2011) (see ECOnnection 7.4).

In a later publication, Litman (2016) offers the following recommendations when thinking about urban development policies:

- Unbundle parking, so parking spaces are rented separately from building space—e.g., rather than paying $1,000 per month for an apartment with two parking spaces renters pay $800 per month for the apartment and $100 per month for each parking space. This typically reduces parking requirements by 20 percent.
- Encourage businesses to implement commute trip reduction programs for employees, including cashing out free parking—e.g., employees are offered $50 per month if not using a parking space. This typically reduces automobile commuting by 20 percent.
- Include four carshare vehicles in the building. This typically substitutes for five personal vehicles.
- Incorporate improved walking facilities to allow convenient access to nearby destinations and public transportation.
- Incorporate bicycle parking and changing and showering facilities into the building.
- Provide information to residents, employees, and visitors about transit, rideshare and taxi services, bicycling facilities, and overflow parking options.

We also know, following the "fundamental law of highway congestion" first articulated back in the early 1960s (Downs 1962), that something different *must* be done. More roads, in the long term, only make traffic congestion worse (see Case Study 7.2). The fundamental law of highway congestion is this: any increase in road capacity will be met with a proportional (or greater) increase in traffic volume. In one study, a 10 percent increase in the interstate network within a typical urban county was met with a 10.3

ETHICAL QUESTION 7.1
Value Judgments Embedded in Transportation Policy

Value judgments are unavoidable in transportation policy. You can't value all transportation forms equally. If we decide we want dense, walkable cities, for example, we will need to stop giving priority to the automobile, recognizing that it creates an urban scale much too expansive (e.g., sprawl) for our feet. Below are some of the thorny questions embedded in any comprehensive transportation policy:

- Whose trips do we prioritize—individual citizens or freight interests?
- Which trips do we prioritize—work commutes, long-distance freight, local goods distribution, or leisure?

- Which transportation services—whether entire modes (e.g., light rail) or components of specific modes (e.g., free parking)—should be supported with public funding, and which should be left to individuals and private-sector interests?
- Should mobility be thought of as a right, recognizing that those unable to drive—most notably elderly and disabled people—can be dangerously isolated in communities where the car is the only transportation option?

Source: Adapted from Schiller and Kenworthy (2017).

ECOnnection 7.4
High-Occupancy Vehicle Lanes

High-occupancy vehicle (HOV) lanes are for automobiles, at least in the United States, carrying two or more passengers. (It says something about our transportation values when a car with two people is considered "high occupancy.") The goal of HOV lanes is to encourage ride sharing and thus reduce the total automobile volume on roads. There are a couple of inherent problems with ride sharing, however, that disincentivize its use. For one, the total commute time must be significant to overcome the time lost while waiting for the carpool to arrive and during travel when picking up and dropping off fellow carpoolers. In many cases, these additional costs more than offset the savings from traveling in the HOV lane. There are also what might be called inconveniences—different schedules, the need to run errands during the trip, and so on—that further make ride sharing unattractive to commuters.

So, do they work? Between 50 to 80 percent of HOV lanes are used by members of the same households. Other significant users are friends on an outing or a date. In other words, HOV lanes are overwhelmingly used by people who would have carpooled anyway.

Source: Schiller and Kenworthy (2017).

percent increase in vehicle distance traveled on those roads (Duranton and Turner 2009). An almost identical conclusion was arrived at in a more recent study looking at road expansion in China, where "newly-built urban roads lead to a more than proportional increase in traffic" (Chen and Klaiber 2017, 1). Elsewhere, in a study looking at road use patterns in the United States, the author concludes that "congestion relief from capacity expansion vanishes within five years of capacity expansion" (Hymel 2019, 57).

From Street Hierarchy to Interconnectivity

Urban planners have also been incentivizing the car—and disincentivizing alternatives— in how they have gone about laying out streets. Prior to the automobile, street systems maximized connectivity, as evidenced by the relatively high number of street intersections per square mile in older communities. Think about pre-automobile city centers—as found in any European city—and note the narrowness of streets and the diverse ways they interconnect. Connectivity in these spaces exists because these street systems provide multiple paths to reach surrounding major streets.

In the twentieth century, a concept known as **street hierarchy** came to dominate urban planning. Street hierarchy seeks to eliminate connections, funneling traffic up the hierarchy. Cul-de-sac streets are at the lowest level of the hierarchy, followed by primary or secondary collector streets. At this point, traffic is fed onto arterial streets (also occasionally called a boulevard), eventually ending up on intercity highways, which rest atop the hierarchy. This system has become a ubiquitous feature of the landscape in most modern cities (see Case Study 7.3).

A more interconnected street model is often criticized for the fact that it actually seeks to slow traffic down (a tough selling point in countries like the United States). Yet we must keep in mind that by resisting congestion, these systems also *save* us a tremendous amount of time that is otherwise lost in bumper-to-bumper traffic. Moreover, we are learning that as speeds slow down in a transportation system, the *scale* of the urban landscape is reduced too, thus making speed less important. In other words, communities that have slowed down no longer need the range and speed provided by the automobile—a truly remarkable discovery.

An excellent example of this comes to us from Home Depot. Store location and size formula for this company depend heavily on two factors: the income range of families living in the service area and the number of trips per day through the nearest intersection to the proposed site. (*Service area* is an estimation of a reasonable distance people would drive to get to the store.) Thus, the more taxpayers spend on hierarchical car-oriented infrastructure, the larger the service area—and thus the store and parking lot—will be. Yet, given the aforementioned fundamental law of congestion, forces are exerting themselves on today's automobile-oriented system in a way that is making congestion inevitable. In response, Home Depot has recently altered the formula used to calculate store location and size, leading the company to build smaller stores more frequently spaced across the urban landscape. The company realizes that traffic congestion is essentially *shrinking* the distance consumers are willing to cover in their cars. This is an interesting development. A major concern has been finding alternatives to the automobile that mimic its speed and range. Yet the Home Depot example contradicts this assumption, indicating that cities may actually scale down as we slow down. Quite a counterintuitive finding:

CASE STUDY 7.2
"Daylighting" the Cheonggyecheon Stream in South Korea

For more than fifty years, concrete (in the form of a major freeway) entombed a three-mile stretch of the Cheonggyecheon Stream that ran through the heart of Seoul, South Korea. It was finally liberated in 2001, when the former chief executive officer of Hyundai Engineering and Construction, Lee Myungbak, was elected mayor of Seoul. One campaign promise was to remove the freeway and restore the Cheonggyecheon Stream. This practice of uncovering previously concealed natural amenities like streams is known as **daylighting** within the urban planning community. Four years and $384 million later, the Cheonggyecheon was flowing freely through the heart of downtown Seoul (see Image 7.2).

The project has enhanced the quality of life, public health, and social interaction of those living downtown, though it has increased property values near the stream, pushing some poorer families out. Roughly 90,000 pedestrians visit the stream banks on an average day. Biodiversity along the Cheonggyecheon has increased, with the number of fish, bird, and insect species expanding from four to twenty-five, six to thirty-six, and fifteen to 192, respectively. Air pollution along the corridor has decreased, now that the tens of thousands of cars are gone. Small-particle air pollution along the corridor dropped from seventy-four to forty-eight micrograms per cubic meter. Moreover, summer temperatures are now routinely five degrees Fahrenheit cooler near the stream than in nearby areas because of a reduced heat-island effect. Finally, even with the loss of a major freeway, traffic speeds in the areas have actually *increased* thanks to transportation changes such as expanded bus services, restrictions on cars, and higher parking fees.

IMAGE 7.2

Source: Ken Smith Landscape Architect, © 2010.

Source: Lonsdorf (2011); Revkin (2009).

CASE STUDY 7.3
Buses and Trains Are Not Useful to Most People

The book, *Trains, Buses, People: An Opinionated Atlas of US Transit* (Spieler 2018) looks at public transportation systems across America. The book provides rich examples from across the United States of how, and why, public transportation systems are poorly laid out and thus under-utilized. For example, when asked why planners and politicians just don't do a better job locating train and light rail lines, Spieler explains,

> When you put transit into the middle of things, it has impacts. There may be fewer places to turn left. There is going to be construction when it gets built. Those businesses, those residents are going to be concerned. What you see often is the decision makers [saying to themselves], "You know this is too hard. We're just going to go for the easy path that doesn't have resistance." If you are building a transit line and nobody is against it, it's probably a bad project. Because it means you're not going where it actually affects anybody. You're going where nobody wants to go.
>
> (quoted in Bosselman 2019)

On the subject of so-called choice riders versus dependent rides:

> There are a lot of cities that frame their transit discussion around the idea of choice riders versus dependent riders. You essentially say, "we operate our bus network because there are these transit-dependent riders that we need to serve. And now we're going to build a rail line for the choice riders who we are trying to get out of their cars." In calling somebody a transit-dependent rider, you're essentially dismissing them. You're essentially thinking of them as somebody who has no choice but to ride our system, which means there's no argument for making the system any better for them.
>
> (quoted in Bosselman 2019)

that one strategy for decreasing the time we spend going from point A to point B is *to slow down*.

Then there is the issue of public safety, such as in regard to fire equipment access. Even here, the data do not support the need for either wide roads or the street-hierarchy model. No difference was detected in fire-related fatalities or response times between communities with narrow streets and those with wider ones (Swift et al. 2006). Any costs that come with narrower streets are more than offset by increased housing density, which reduces overall travel distance, and the benefit of having multiple routes to choose from (Condon 2010).

Disincentivizing the Car

How might we go about making the car a less attractive form of transportation? I have already discussed the importance of making the alternatives more attractive; after all, we can't expect people to choose to leave their cars at home if the alternatives take appreciably more time, cost more money, and might even be dangerous. What has not been discussed, however, are ways to make the car costlier to drive, a move that would effectively make alternatives immediately more attractive. Before criticizing such a scheme, remember all the money we already spend to incentivize the car (which makes any such criticism seem more than a bit insincere and hollow). In light of all these incentivizing structures, I am not a bit surprised that the vast majority of individuals in affluent nations "choose" to drive (though this might be changing; see ECOnnection 7.5). Who wouldn't choose an activity when they're paying for only a fraction of its real costs?

One widely discussed policy mechanism is a gas tax (or a further increase in existing gas taxes). The economic models are pretty clear as to their efficacy: such a tax would encourage consumers to drive less, switch from two vehicles to one, or buy more fuel-efficient vehicles (Eric et al. 2015). In addition to encouraging motorists to drive less, such taxes would signal to manufacturers the need to incorporate fuel-saving technologies in new vehicles, in response to consumers' choosing smaller, fuel-efficient vehicles. If implemented, however, we would need to make sure this tax wasn't regressive and therefore not unduly burdensome to those already socially and economically vulnerable (see Movement Matters 7.1). The other population such a tax would immediately affect is commuters. Of course, the goal of such a tax would be to discourage precisely this type of behavior. We must remember, however, that while people commute for a variety of reasons, one of these is because they cannot afford to live near where they work. I see this variable at play in Fort Collins, Colorado, where my employer (Colorado State University) is located. I know that a number of the janitorial and office staff, who make appreciably less than tenure-track professors, reside in surrounding communities because of the lower housing prices. The fact that I do not commute—I can actually walk to work—is a luxury not everyone can afford.

An even more promising policy is **pay-as-you-drive auto insurance**, where one's insurance rate (but not coverage) is contingent on, among other things, the number of miles driven. Nobel Prize winning economist William Vickrey (1968, 464) once quipped, "The manner in which [auto insurance] premiums are computed and paid fails miserably to bring home to the automobile user the costs he [or she] imposes in a manner that will appropriately influence his [or her] decisions." Little has changed in the fifty or so years since Vickrey made these comments. The current lump-sum pricing of auto insurance remains inefficient and inequitable (Nichols and Kockelman 2014). It is widely recognized that, just as an all-you-can-eat restaurant encourages more eating, all-you-can-drive insurance pricing encourages more driving, which also means more accidents, congestion, and greenhouse gas emissions. It is also terribly inequitable, in that miles driven is positively correlated with income. Low-mileage (and low-income) drivers therefore subsidize insurance costs for high-mileage (high-income) drivers.

The results of a recent study indicate that the average American will drive 2.7 percent less (237 fewer miles per year) if auto insurance is pay-as-you-drive (Nichols and Kockelman 2014). Another study, by the Brookings Institution, goes even further, calculating that if all motorists in the United States paid for auto insurance on a per-mile basis rather than as a lump sum, driving would decline by 8 percent nationwide, saving society the equivalent of about $50 billion to $60 billion a year through reduced driving-related harms (Bordoff and Noel 2008). The study further estimates that this reduction in driving would translate into a 2 percent decrease in CO_2 emissions and would reduce oil

ECOnnection 7.5
Have Cars Reached Their Peak?

Mobility services are expanding rapidly, from electric scooters to robo-taxis and Uber. Infrastructure investments are being made around the world—public transportation, bike lanes, walkable communities, and the like. Major urban centers such as London, Madrid, and Mexico City are restricting cars' access. Meanwhile, new cars are increasingly expensive, while only used for just a few hours a day. (A 2019 report by the Federal Reserve of New York notes that more than seven million Americans are at least ninety days behind on their auto loans—that's higher than the one-time peak in 2010 when the country was reeling from the global financial crisis [Cox, J. 2019].) Such realities are making automobile makers nervous. Talk of the possibility that the world is approaching "peak car" is on the lips of many.

Ten years ago, the automobile industry estimated annual global vehicle sales would surpass 100 million by now. Instead, sales have stalled, falling to 94.2 million in 2018, down one million from 2017. It looks likes the 100 million vehicle milestone will be hit sometime in the early 2020s, but only thanks to growth in China, India, and other emerging markets (Naughton and Welsh 2019). Yet "longer term," to quote Henner Lehne, vice president for forecasting with the London-based think tank IHS Markit, "we will see a flattening of private-car purchases" (cited in Naughton and Welsh 2019).

consumption by about 4 percent. The authors note that it would take a $1 per gallon increase in the gas tax to achieve the same reduction in driving. Yet unlike the gas tax, which would increase the cost of driving for everyone, roughly two-thirds of all US households would end up actually paying *less* for auto insurance; the average saving is estimated at $270 per car.

Other strategies to make driving less attractive could include doing away with ubiquitous free parking, which, as already mentioned, is a significant taxpayer-funded subsidy to motorists. We might also think about eliminating minimum parking requirements that are embedded in city planning codes around the world. Another option would be to increase the cost of registering vehicles, which could be placed on a sliding scale so as to not unfairly affect low-income households. There is also the strategy of charging people to access a given area with their car (see Case Study 7.4). Or we could base urban design more around interconnectivity, to reference a point made earlier, and thus allow narrower streets, more intersections, and slower average car speeds to take precedence over the street-hierarchy logic.

There are numerous empirical reasons for criticizing the automobile, from, for example, its negative impacts on the environment, public health, and community cohesion, to its links to climate change and air and noise pollution more generally. The good news is that there is nothing about the automobile that makes it an inherently superior form of transportation. Millions around the world choose this form of mobility over others not because of some quality inherent to the automobile but because societies have made such a good job of organizing around the car. Organize societies around the alternatives, and consumer choice will happily follow, with no sacrifice required.

MOVEMENT MATTERS 7.1
The Rise of Public- and Micro- Transit Movements

The public transit movement is an example of grassroots activism rooted in the belief that affordable and convenient public transit ought to be available to all. By organizing this previously invisible constituency—namely, lower-income riders that depend on public transit for their livelihoods—transit riders unions have emerged as an unlikely source of political power. The transit movement rose to prominence in Los Angeles in the 1990s, when bus riders, most of them black and Latino, came together to protest what was believed to be an unjust transit system that penalized riders from low-income neighborhoods. A success story occurred on March 1, 2015, in King County, Washington, when the county introduced a reduced fare for low-income people—a major win for Seattle's Transit Riders Union. On the same day, San Francisco's transit riders convinced the city's Municipal Transportation Association (MUNI) to make transit free for disabled people and low-income seniors.

A primary aim of these movements is to reduce the "affordability gap"—what workers are paid and what it costs to get to work. In the mid-1970s, a minimum-wage employee had to work for roughly ten minutes to pay for their bus fare to and from work. Today, that same employee must work more than half an hour (Roe 2015). As the US economy emerges out of the Great Recession, it is adding jobs. However, job proximity—the number of jobs near where a person lives—is declining, a trend especially pronounced for low-income households and people of color, making affordable public transportation all the more important for these groups (Kneebone and Holmes 2015).

The micro transit movement comes into play to address what is known as the "first-mile, last-mile" problem—that gap at the start and end of every trip that's difficult for traditional transit operators to serve in a cost-effective way. Perhaps the most well-known example of this is New York's unofficial shuttles, called "dollar vans" in some neighborhoods, offering a widely used transportation system that operates where the subway and buses do not (Reiss 2019).

CASE STUDY 7.4

The London Congestion Charge

By the late 1990s, more than one million people were entering into central London on any given workday. A study from 1998 concluded that the average driver spent almost 30 percent of his or her time stationary during peak traffic periods. In response, a "congestion charge" was proposed in 2000. In 2003, the City of London, which is a small area within Greater London that refers to its historic core, began charging motorists for driving or parking within Central London between 7a.m. and 6.30p.m. on weekdays. The standard charge is £10 (approximately $16) per day.

The number of private vehicles coming into the zone has declined by almost a third. But some are wondering if it isn't time to revisit the policy. Back in 2010, the reduction of private vehicles in this space translated into more access via bus, taxi, and bicycle. The average traffic speed within the zone, meanwhile, had increased by almost 17 percent (Skousen 2011). Yet since then there has been a substantial increase in the number of private for hire vehicles—e.g., Uber. Trips by taxi and private for hire vehicle as the main mode of the journey increased by 9.8 per cent between 2015 and 2016 alone, and by roughly 30 percent since 2000. This has reduced the speed of traffic through the city centre, which has affected the bus network. And as those buses slow down people are less likely to use them. The City of London has concluded that traffic congestion, including congestion in the city centre, is the primary reason why bus usage is down in London (Badstuber 2018).

IMPORTANT CONCEPTS

- costs of transportation to public and environmental health and community cohesion
- effective speed
- free parking
- fundamental law of highway congestion
- habitat fragmentation
- peak car
- street hierarchy versus interconnectivity

DISCUSSION QUESTIONS

1. How has the automobile altered how we plan and organize communities?
2. In what ways does society incentivize trips with the automobile and disincentivize alternative forms of transportation?
3. Some argue people want to continue this love affair with the automobile, as evidenced by the fact of just how many people *choose* to drive: "Shame on environmentalists for wanting to go against what people clearly want!" How would you rebut this argument?
4. What barriers keep you from choosing to leave your car at home and opting for alternative modes of transportation?

SUGGESTED ADDITIONAL READINGS

Bliss, L. 2018. "Uber Pivots to On-Demand Everything." *City Labs*, April 11. www.citylab.com/transportation/2018/04/uber-pivots-to-on-demand-everything/557528/.

Camarero, L., F. Cruz, and J. Oliva. 2016. "Rural Sustainability, Inter-Generational Support and Mobility." *European Urban and Regional Studies*, 23(4): 734–749.

Schiller, P.L., and J.R. Kenworthy. 2017. *An Introduction to Sustainable Transportation: Policy, Planning and Implementation*. London: Routledge.

RELEVANT INTERNET LINKS

- www.nativeenergy.com/travel.html. Calculate your transportation footprint.
- www.nature.org/greenliving/carboncalculator/index.htm. Calculate your carbon footprint.
- www.youtube.com/watch?v=NJkZYCiXRAw. Short video of the "daylighted" Cheong-gyecheon River in Seoul, South Korea (mentioned in Case Study 7.2).

SUGGESTED VIDEOS

- *Into the Future: Transport* (2015). Outlines the tremendous challenges associated with producing low-emission electric-powered vehicles, and convincing the public of their appeal as a viable, preferable option to traditional gas guzzlers.
- *Losing Ground* (2019). The agriculture industry has struggled against urban sprawl. The American Angus Association presents a film to expose the impact of urban sprawl on American agriculture.
- *Revenge of the Electric Car* (2011). Four different automobile visionaries race to capture the electric car market.
- *Taken for a Ride* (1996). www.youtube.com/watch?v=rAc4w11Yzys. An older but superb documentary about how American public mass transit was undermined and systematically destroyed during the first half of the twentieth century by General Motors and other corporations.
- *Urbanized* (2011). Architects, city planners, politicians, and others try to bring a fresh approach to dealing with the advantages and disadvantages of urban living.
- *Who Killed the Electric Car?* (2006). Details General Motors' efforts to hinder their own electric car research and development.

Food: From Farm to Fork

Few things are as obviously social *and* ecological as food and agriculture. Clearly, we need food to survive. As for *what* constitutes "food"—that too is a social act. Take bugs: an example of how one culture's pest is another's delicacy. As for agriculture, its links to the environment are obvious even to the uninitiated. *How* we produce food is also sociologically relevant, affecting society at all scales, from rural communities to entire nations. And how we've gone about feeding ourselves has changed drastically over the years.

One of the more consequential innovations in agriculture over the past 200 years has been the substitution of capital for labor—known widely as the **mechanical revolution**. Examples vary widely: from the cotton gin in 1793, which separated the cotton lint from the seed (and initially increased the demand for slave labor in Southern slave states), to the threshing machine in 1816, which separated grain from the stalk; to Cyrus McCormick's reaper in 1834, which cut grain; and to the John Deere steel plow in 1837, which turned the soil cleanly, thereby minimizing the drag that had bogged down earlier plows. Later in the nineteenth century came the tractor, which, unlike the horses it replaced, did not require food, water, or sleep and allowed the land used previously to raise hay and oats to feed one's horses to instead be put toward the production of commodities for sale.

This capital intensification (and energy intensification) had clear impacts on the **structure of agriculture**, at least in countries where this transition was well under way. (The term *structure of agriculture* is shorthand to describe how farms, rural populations, and agribusiness corporations are arranged to produce and distribute food and fiber.) Take, for example, the United States, where the requisite human hours to farm an acre of corn dropped rapidly throughout the first half of the twentieth century in no small part as a result of mechanization: from thirty-eight hours per acre in 1900 to thirty-three in 1920–1924, twenty-eight in 1930–1934, and twenty-five in 1940–1944. By 1955–1959, the figure had dropped to only ten hours of labor per acre. A study conducted by Iowa State College (now Iowa State University) in the 1930s concluded that a hired husker left between three and five bushels of corn per acre when the harvest occurred by hand. By comparison, a mechanical corn picker left two to three bushels. In addition, hired huskers charged on average $2 per acre, whereas custom mechanical pickers charged roughly

$1.25 to $1.50 per acre. It is not surprising, then, that by 1938, between 33 and 50 percent of the laborers previously hired to handpick corn were replaced by mechanical pickers (Colbert 2000). The mechanical revolution was favored early on in the rapidly expanding agricultural sector in the United States, especially in the Midwest and Great Plains, where land was plentiful but labor scarce (Pfeffer 1983).

Mechanization, in turn, also encourages specialization and scale increases at the farm level. Although not the only force driving the specialization trends illustrated in Table 8.1, the mechanization of agriculture undoubtedly contributed to the state's shrinking commodity basket. Iowa, depicted in the table, is representative of the commodity erosion occurring throughout much of the world where grains and livestock are raised for export and agroindustrial purposes (e.g., feed for livestock, biofuels, high fructose corn syrup, Chicken McNuggets, and so on). Why is mechanization at least partially responsible for this? It makes economic sense to spread the cost of these expensive capital investments over as much land as possible, which, from a labor standpoint, is relatively easy to do, as mechanization allows one or two individuals to work large tracts of land in a short amount of time.

This represents the barest of introductions into the incredibly nuanced and increasingly complex subject of food production (for more detail, see, for example, Carolan 2016, 2018a). Food systems are not static; they're continually changing, as are their impacts. Although the impacts about to be discussed are significant, it is heartening to know it doesn't have to be this way. These systems did not just appear. As products of our (society's) own creation, we hold the collective capacity to recreate them.

Fast Facts

- Industrial livestock farms—also known as CAFOs (Concentrated Animal Feeding Operations)—can produce more waste than many US cities. For example, a feeding operation with 800,000 pigs can produce over 1.6 million tons of waste a year, an amount that is one and a half times more than the annual sanitary waste produced by the city of Philadelphia. A lactating dairy cow can produce 150 pounds of manure every day. The mass of animal waste is forecast to increase by 40 percent from 2003–2030, hitting 4 billion tons (Cox, D. 2019).
- The global food system, from fertilizer manufacture to food storage and packaging, is responsible for up to one-third of all human-generated greenhouse gas emissions (Carrington 2018). An analysis of greenhouse gas data by the Food and Agriculture Organization of the United Nations (FAO) shows that global emissions from agriculture, forestry, and fisheries have nearly doubled over the past fifty years and are poised to increase an additional 30 percent by 2050 if steps are not immediately taken to reduce them (FAO 2017). Digging further down into the data, we see that global emissions from energy use in the agricultural sector have increased a whopping 75 percent since 1990.
- Since 2008, however, the top ten farm subsidy recipients each received an average of $1.8 million annually (or $150,000 per month). In 2017 alone, 389 entities, including farmers, corporations, and agri-businesses, were paid between $1 million and $9.9 million in federal agriculture subsidies (Andrezejewski and Smith 2018; see Figure 8.1).
- A wave of scholarship examining farmer perceptions concerning climate change and its accompanying risks has been published in recent years (e.g., Grimberg et al. 2018; Nguyen

TABLE 8.1 Number of Commodities Produced for Sale in at Least 1 Percent of All Iowa farms for Various Years from 1920 to 2017

1920	(%)	1935	(%)	1945	(%)	1954	(%)	1964	(%)	1978	(%)	1987	(%)	1997	(%)	2002	(%)	2017	(%)
Horses	(95)	Cattle	(94)	Cattle	(92)	Corn	(91)	Corn	(87)	Corn	(90)	Corn	(79)	Corn	(68)	Corn	(58)	Corn	(51)
Cattle	(95)	Horse	(93)	Chicken	(91)	Cattle	(89)	Cattle	(81)	Soybeans	(68)	Soybeans	(65)	Soybeans	(62)	Soybeans	(54)	Soybeans	(47)
Chicken	(95)	Chicken	(93)	Corn	(91)	Oats	(83)	Hogs	(69)	Cattle	(60)	Cattle	(47)	Hay	(42)	Hay	(37)	Hay	(31)
Corn	(94)	Corn	(90)	Horses	(90)	Chicken	(82)	Hay	(62)	Hay	(56)	Hay	(46)	Cattle	(42)	Cattle	(35)	Cattle	(29)
Hogs	(89)	Hogs	(83)	Hogs	(84)	Hogs	(79)	Soybeans	(57)	Hogs	(50)	Hogs	(35)	Hogs	(19)	Horses	(13)	Hogs	(07)
Apples	(84)	Hay	(82)	Hay	(81)	Hay	(72)	Oats	(57)	Oats	(34)	Oats	(25)	Oats	(12)	Hogs	(11)	Sheep	(03)
Hay	(82)	Potatoes	(64)	Oats	(80)	Horses	(42)	Chicken	(48)	Horses	(13)	Horses	(10)	Horses	(11)	Oats	(08)	Goats	(03)
Oats	(81)	Apples	(56)	Apples	(74)	Soybeans	(37)	Horses	(26)	Chicken	(09)	Sheep	(08)	Sheep	(04)	Sheep	(04)	Horses	(02)
Potatoes	(62)	Oats	(52)	Soybeans	(41)	Potatoes	(18)	Sheep	(17)	Sheep	(08)	Chicken	(05)	Chicken	(02)	Chicken	(02)	Oats	(02)
Cherries	(57)	Cherries	(34)	Potatoes	(40)	Sheep	(16)	Potatoes	(06)	Wheat	(01)	Ducks	(01)	Goats	(01)	Goats	(01)	Chicken	(01)
Wheat	(36)	Grapes	(28)	Grapes	(23)	Ducks	(05)	Wheat	(03)	Goats	(01)	Goats	(01)						
Plums	(29)	Plums	(28)	Cherries	(23)	Apples	(05)	Sorghum	(02)	Ducks	(01)	Wheat	(01)						
Grapes	(28)	Sheep	(21)	Peaches	(20)	Cherries	(04)	Red clover	(02)										
Ducks	(18)	Peaches	(16)	Pears	(16)	Peaches	(04)	Apples	(02)										
Geese	(18)	Pears	(16)	Sheep	(16)	Goats	(04)	Ducks	(02)										
Strawberry	(17)	Mules	(13)	Plums	(15)	Grapes	(03)	Goats	(02)										
Pears	(17)	Ducks	(12)	Red clover	(13)	Pears	(03)	Geese	(01)										
Mules	(14)	Wheat	(12)	Mules	(10)	Plums	(03)												
Sheep	(14)	Geese	(11)	Strawberry	(06)	Wheat	(03)												
Timothy	(10)	Sorghum	(10)	Ducks	(06)	Red clover	(03)												
Peaches	(09)	Barley	(09)	Wheat	(06)	Geese	(03)												
Bees	(09)	Red clover	(09)	Timothy	(04)	Popcorn	(02)												
Barley	(09)	Strawberry	(08)	Geese	(04)	Timothy	(02)												
Raspberry	(07)	Soybeans	(07)	Rye	(03)	Sweet potato	(02)												
Turkeys	(07)	Raspberry	(06)	Popcorn	(02)	Sweetcorn	(01)												

n = 34	n = 33	n = 29	n = 26	n = 17	n = 12	n = 12	n = 10	n = 10	n = 10
Water melon (06)	Bees (05)	Sweetcorn (02)	Turkeys (01)						
Sorghum (06)	Timothy (05)	Raspberry (02)							
Gooseberry (03)	Turkeys (04)	**Bees** (02)							
Sweetcorn (02)	Rye (02)	Sorghum (01)							
Apricots (02)	Popcorn (02)								
Tomatoes (02)	Sweetcorn (02)								
Cabbage (01)	Sweet clover (01)								
Popcorn (01)	Goats (01)								
Currants (01)									

Source: Based on data from the US Census of Agriculture, 1920–2017.

Note: Items in bold are grown on more than 50 percent of farms.

FIGURE 8.1 Asymmetries in USDA Farm Payments, 1995–2017

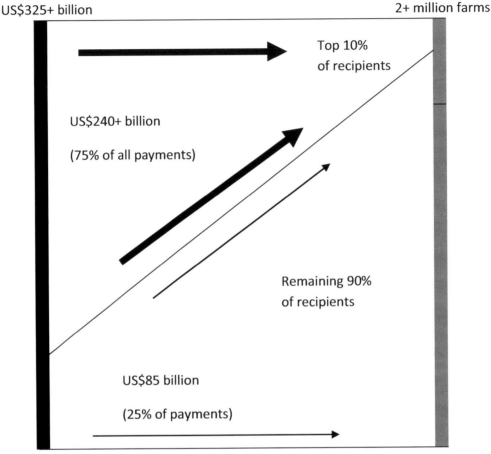

US$325+ billion

2+ million farms

Top 10%
of recipients

US$240+ billion

(75% of all payments)

Remaining 90%
of recipients

US$85 billion

(25% of payments)

Note
Compiled utilizing databank maintained by Environmental Working Group at http://farm.ewg.org/
progdetail.php?fips=00000&progcode=total&page=conc.

et al. 2019; Schattman et al. 2018). One review of this literature "found that farmers'
agreement with the statement 'climate change is occurring' ranged between 54 and 80
percent" (Chatrchyan et al. 2017, 7). The authors then created a weighted average based
on the sample size in the studies reviewed, concluding "that 65 percent of the U.S.
farmers surveyed in various regions of the United States believe that climate change is
happening" (Ibid.), which is not far from the roughly 70 percent reported in studies
posing the same question to the general public (e.g., Leiserowitz et al. 2018; Morning
Consult/Politico 2018). Curiously, however, that same review found farmers and ranch-
ers agreeing that climate change is at least partially due to human activity only 40
percent of the time—a figure well below surveys of the general public, which place the
figure at 60 percent (e.g., Morning Consult/Politico 2018) or greater (e.g., Leiserowitz
et al. 2018).

Implications

At the risk of overgeneralizing, the impacts discussed in this section refer to those associated with what we might call the global **food system**, which can be defined as the entire array of activities—from input production and distribution to on-farm activities, marketing, processing, wholesale, and retail—that connect seed (and gene) to the mouths of consumers. To speak of a "system" is to refer not just to certain agricultural practices but also (and equally) to regulatory, economic, social, and legal structures that reinforce the use of those practices (and even the ecological base that makes it all possible). Food production affects more than our stomachs, touching our lives in a variety of ways.

Environmental Impacts

Where to begin? Let's start with water. As I have already discussed agriculture's link to water in Chapter 5, this discussion will be brief.

Let's begin with the concept of **irrigation efficiency**. Irrigation efficiency refers to the ratio of water that evaporates to what saturates the soil. The efficiency of traditional gravity irrigation, a method still widely used throughout the developing world, is about 40 percent—meaning that 60 percent of the water applied is lost to evaporation. Sprinkler systems, conversely, have an efficiency range of between 60 and 70 percent, whereas drip irrigation systems are between 80 and 90 percent efficient (Seckler 1996). Conventional understandings of irrigation efficiency refer to the minimal amount of water that can be applied to achieve maximum yield. Yet there are other ways to understand this concept. It could be defined as the maximization of crop production per unit of applied water. This admittedly means we stop striving for maximum yields, as the relationship between yields and applied water is linear only up to roughly 50 percent of **full irrigation** (which refers to the amount of water needed to achieve maximum yield). After this point, the yield curve takes on a curvilinear shape from increased surface evaporation, runoff, and deep percolation, until turning downward from anaerobic root-zone conditions, disease, and the leaching of nutrients (English et al. 2002; see Figure 8.2). Conventional wisdom has farmers irrigating for maximum yield—the moment on the figure just prior to the curve turning downward. Yet if freshwater were to become additionally scarce, it might make more sense to strive for, say, 80 percent yields, especially if that could be achieved with half the water that would otherwise be needed to obtain the remaining 20 percent (and thus maximum) yield.

Another highly visible subject is agriculture-related **hypoxia**. Hypoxia refers to a state where oxygen concentrations in a body of water fall below the level necessary to sustain most animal life. The Gulf of Mexico is home to one of the Western Hemisphere's largest **dead zones**—the name given to bodies of water with low levels of dissolved oxygen. There are more than 400 dead zones in the world today, 94 percent of which are in regions that will experience at least a 2° Celsius temperature increase by the end of the century thanks to climate change; in other words, those areas are only going to get more "dead" (Altieri and Gedan 2015). The one found in the Gulf of Mexico is the product of excess nitrogen coming down through the Mississippi River. The majority of this excess nitrogen (roughly two-thirds) comes from agriculture and, to a lesser extent, lawns. Nitrogen levels in the Raccoon River, for example, which is part of the watershed of the Mississippi River,

FIGURE 8.2 General Relationships between Yields and Total Amount of Water Applied

Source: Author.

forced Des Moines Water Works in Iowa to build the world's largest nitrate removal plant treatment facility in 1991. Nitrate concentrations in this river have increased more than threefold since the 1950s (Eller 2015). Between 2015 and 2016, nitrogen pollution from the state spiked at 46 percent (Eller 2018). After making its way into the Gulf, the nitrogen fuels the rapid growth of algae and plankton. When those organisms die and sink to the bottom, they decay and in doing so rob the water of oxygen (see Case Study 8.1). In 2014, the Gulf's dead zone measured 13,080 square kilometers (5,052 square miles), or more than twice the size of the state of Delaware (EPA 2015a).

According to the FAO (2019), the livestock sector generates an estimated 8.1 giga-tonnes of CO_2 equivalents a year, representing about 16 percent of all human-generated greenhouse gas emissions. Cattle (beef and milk cows) are the main contributor to the sector's emissions, releasing about five gigatonnes CO_2 equivalents annually, which represents about 62 percent of the entire sector's emissions. Pigs, poultry, buffaloes and small ruminants have much lower emissions, representing between 7 and 11 percent of the sector's emissions (FAO 2019; see ECOnnection 8.1). The FAO also compares the performance of different animals by expressing emissions on a per protein basis. In doing so, buffalo meat has the highest emission intensity, with an average of 404 kg CO_2 equiv-alents per kg of protein, followed by beef meat, with an average of 295 kg CO_2 equiva-lents per kg of protein. Meat and milk from small ruminants (e.g., sheep and goat) and milk from buffalo represent the third, fourth, and fifth highest emission intensities among commodities with averages of 201, 148, and 140 kg CO_2 equivalents per kg of protein. Cattle milk, chicken meat, and eggs and pork have lower emission intensities still, all below 100 kg CO_2 equivalents per kg of protein (FAO 2019).

Last, it is important that I say a few words about agriculture's links to soil erosion. A third of the Earth's land is severely degraded and fertile soil is being lost at the rate of 24 billion tonnes a year, according to a United Nations-backed study (Watts 2017). Deep tilling, multi-annual harvests, and the extensive use of agrochemicals have increased yields

CASE STUDY 8.1
Mobile Bay Jubilee

Jubilee is the name given to an event on the shores of Mobile Bay on Alabama's Gulf Coast when hordes of crab, shrimp, flounder, and eels leave deeper waters for shallower areas in the bay. The event often occurs more than once a year. The jubilee attracts many people, most of whom come looking to load up on free, abundant, and easy-to-catch seafood. It was not until the 1960s that a cause for the event was determined: hypoxia. During jubilees, sea life becomes trapped between the shore and an advancing water mass low in dissolved oxygen (May 1973). Low levels of dissolved oxygen in the water can also cause marine life to become lethargic and slow, which further simplifies the task of catching these animals.

ECOnnection 8.1
Fish In Fish Out
(FIFO) Ratio

Aquaculture has undergone many of the same structural changes as agriculture. These producers also find themselves trying to stay on the aquacultural treadmill, which is to say they are under tremendous pressure to raise as many fish as they can with as little feed as possible. This becomes especially challenging with larger predators such as salmon, which require comparatively large amounts of feed to produce body mass. The FIFO (Fish In Fish Out) ratio is the measurement of the amount they need. It indicates how much wild fish must be used as animal feed in order to produce an equivalent weight unit of farmed fish. So: if 1 kilogram of wild fish is used to produce the feed of 1 kilogram of farmed fish, the FIFO ratio is 1. Any value more than 1 means that more than 1 kilogram of wild fish is required to produce 1 kilogram of farmed fish. In the mid-1990s the FIFO ratio for salmon was 7.5 (that's right, it took 7.5 kilograms of wild fish to produce 1 kilogram of farmed fish), while today the figure is between 3 and 0.5 (that's right, on some farms the ratio is *still* above one). Food for thought: If the current global consumption rate of fish of 17 kilograms per capita per year is to be maintained by 2050 (in light of a growing global population), aquaculture would have to reduce its average FIFO ratio from approximately 0.6 in 2008 to 0.3 units of marine fish to produce a unit of farmed fish. One way to do this would be to eat more of those fish with lower FIFO ratios, like catfish (at 0.5:1), tilapia (0.4:1), and milkfish (0.2:1), an already popular fish in Asia.

at the expense of long-term sustainability. Yet over time this intensification diminishes fertility and can lead to abandonment of land and, without care to properly amend/restore the soil, ultimately desertification. Reductions in productivity due to these processes have been observed on 20 percent of the world's cropland, 16 percent of its forest land, 19 percent of grassland, and 27 percent of rangeland (Watts 2017).

Community Impacts

There is a large, rich body of literature looking at the impact of industrial agriculture on communities. The most famous of these studies, and one of the first, was conducted almost three-quarters of a century ago. Overseen by Walter Goldschmidt, a United States Department of Agriculture (USDA) anthropologist, and funded by the USDA, the study looks at two California communities in the early 1940s: Arvin, where large, absentee-owned, non-family-operated farms were more numerous, and Dinuba, where locally owned, family-operated farms were the norm (the names of both towns are pseudonyms). The researchers concluded that industrial agriculture had, overall, a negative impact on a variety of community quality-of-life indicators (Goldschmidt 1978). For example, relative to Dinuba, Arvin's population had a smaller middle class, a higher proportion of hired workers, lower mean family incomes, higher rates of poverty, poorer-quality schools, and fewer churches, civic organizations, and retail establishments. Residents of Arvin also had less local control over public decisions because of disproportional political influence by outside agri-business interests. Goldschmidt's research was rediscovered in the 1970s, perhaps in response to rapid changes in agriculture during this time. Research since the 1970s has overwhelmingly supported the Goldschmidt thesis (Lobao and Stofferahn 2008; Parkins 2015; see ECOnnection 8.2).

It is important to clarify that *industrial agriculture* in this tradition often goes beyond the size of an operation by also incorporating indicators of farm organization. According to this literature, features like absenteeism (when land is leased and the owners live outside the community), contract farming, dependency on hired labor, and operation by farm managers (as opposed to owner-operator situations) place a greater burden on communities than when surrounding farms—even large ones—lack these characteristics. Large-scale, family-owned farms, for example, still tend to purchase their inputs, farm equipment, and services locally; volunteer their time at local organizations, such as church groups, school fund-raisers, and the like; and regularly interact with their neighbors.

Research has also looked at the impact of large-scale livestock-feeding operations—aka CAFOs—on community well-being and public health. Neighbors of CAFOs have been found to have higher levels of respiratory and digestive disturbances (Radon et al. 2007). They also have abnormally high rates of psychological disorders, such as anxiety, depression, and sleep disturbances (Bokowa 2010). Children living on or near hog farms have abnormally high rates of asthma (Guidry et al. 2015). These rates are known to increase proportionally with the size of the operation (Donham et al. 2016). North Carolina school administrators report rates of asthma among the student population at levels well above the state average in schools within three miles of one or more large hog-feeding facilities (Mirabelli et al. 2006). Post-traumatic stress disorder has also been reported among residents living near CAFOs (Donham et al. 2007, 2016). This can result from things such as a reduction in one's quality of life or property values. For example, one study looking at a community in rural Kentucky found price reductions of 23 to 32 percent for residential properties sold within 1.25 miles of the facility, and much larger losses northeast (downwind) of the facility (Simons et al. 2014). Researchers have also documented that a significant level of social tension—specifically between producers and their neighbors—can emerge when CAFOs are sighted within a community (Doane 2014).

ECOnnection 8.2
Negative Impacts of Industrialized Farms

Social scientists report the following negative impacts that industrialized farms have on community well-being:

SOCIOECONOMIC WELL-BEING
- greater income inequality, higher rates of poverty, or both
- higher rates of unemployment
- reduced employment opportunities.

SOCIAL FABRIC
- decline in local population
- social class structure becomes poorer (as a result of, for instance, increases in hired labor).

SOCIAL DISRUPTION
- increases in crime rates and civil suits
- general increase in social conflict
- greater childbearing among teenagers
- increased stress and social-psychological problems
- swine CAFOs located in census blocks with high poverty and minority populations
- deterioration of relationships between farming neighbors
- more stressful neighborly relations

- deterioration in community organizations; less involvement in social life
- decrease in local-level political decision making (as outside interests gain influence)
- reduction in the quality of public services
- decreased retail trade and fewer, less diverse retail companies
- reduced enjoyment of outdoor experience (especially when living near CAFO)
- neighbors of hog CAFOs report upper-respiratory and digestive-tract disorders and eye problems
- residences closest to hog CAFOs experience declining values relative to those more distant.

Social scientists report the following negative impacts that industrialized farms have on the health of the environment:

- depletion of water and other energy resources
- increase in Safe Drinking Water Act violations
- air quality problems
- increased risks of nutrient overload in soils.

Source: Based on a review of literature by Lobao and Stofferahn (2008) and Parkins (2015).

Malnutrition and the Green Revolution

The **green revolution** refers to a series of strategies developed during the mid- to late twentieth century to combat starvation by expanding the global production of staple food crops through crop breeding. Was the green revolution a success? It depends. For example, we unequivocally grow more calories globally today than we did a half century ago. So as a food calorie revolution, the green revolution *was* an unqualified success. But calories do not make a nutritious diet, as evidenced by the green revolution's links to

micronutrient malnutrition—a condition that results from a diet lacking in sufficient quantities of micronutrients.

Micronutrient malnutrition plagues more than a billion around the world because of widespread deficiencies in key vitamins and minerals, particularly vitamin A, iodine, iron, and zinc. Most of these individuals live in low-income countries and are more often than not deficient in more than one micronutrient (CDC 2015). Children are particularly sensitive to micronutrient malnutrition because they have higher nutritional requirements per kilogram of body weight. Micronutrient deficiencies cause an estimated 1.1 million of the 3.1 million child deaths globally—in other words, more than one-third—that occur each year as a result of undernutrition (IFPRI 2014). A consensus is emerging that growth lost in early years from malnutrition is, at best, only partially regained during childhood and adolescence with dietary improvements. One study, examining children aged 12–24 months at the peak of the drought in rural Zimbabwe in 1994–1995 had average heights well below those of comparable children not affected by this event when measured at ages 60–72 months (Hoddinott and Kinsey 2001). Another study notes that among children in rural Zimbabwe who were exposed to the 1982–1984 droughts, average heights at late adolescence were reduced by 2.3 centimeters compared to children not exposed to this nutritional shock (Alderman et al. 2006). Some studies have attempted to calculate the costs of malnutrition. A recent study looking at the lifetime social costs of iodine deficiency, iron-deficiency anaemia, and vitamin A deficiency in children aged 6–23 months in Pakistan calculated losses to their national economy at US$209 million and 175,000 disability-adjusted life-years (DALYs). The authors therefore point out that there are potentially huge cost savings that can be had if the government spent money on subsidizing the cost of foods rich in micronutrients—a case where government expenditures would actually *save* taxpayers' money over the long run (Wieser et al. 2018).

Though just to be clear: micronutrient deficiencies do not just affect residents of poorer countries. Those in affluent countries suffer plenty too, just in different ways. A study recently published in the prestigious journal *JAHA* (*Journal of the American Heart Association*) found that high levels of micronutrient deficiency—noted specifically are deficiencies in calcium, folate, magnesium, zinc, and vitamins C, D, E, and K—was a strong independent predictor of hospitalization for one year or death in a sample of patients residing in the United States (Lennie et al. 2018).

There is no disputing that the green revolution has occurred at the expense of dietary diversity. For evidence of this I point to a study published in the *Proceedings of the National Academy of Sciences* that reveals an emerging standard global food supply consisting increasingly of such energy-dense foods as soybeans, sunflower oil, and palm oil, along with more historically familiar staples like rice and wheat (Khoury et al. 2014). Wheat was found to be a major staple in 97.4 percent of all countries and rice in 90.8 percent, whereas soybean has become significant in 74.3 percent of countries. Meanwhile, many crops with long-held regional and cultural importance—cereals like sorghum, millet, and rye as well as root crops such as sweet potato, cassava, and yam—are disappearing from fields and diets. For example, a nutritious tuber crop known as oca, once grown throughout the Andean highlands, has declined significantly in this region both in cultivation and consumption.

Figure 8.3 illustrates these trends. As the figure details, soybean consumption has increased 282 percent in developing countries between 1969 and 2009, while the

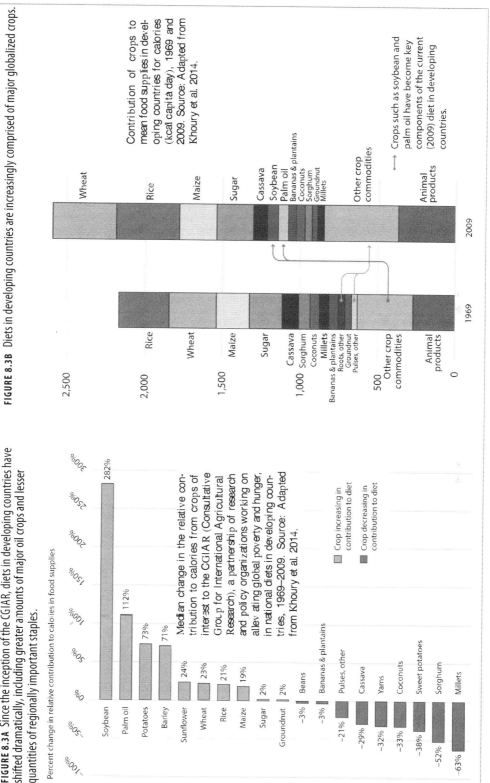

Shifting Dietary Trends Among Low-Income Countries, 1969–2009

FIGURE 8.3A Since the inception of the CGIAR, diets in developing countries have shifted dramatically, including greater amounts of major oil crops and lesser quantities of regionally important staples.

Percent change in relative contribution to calories in food supplies

Soybean 282%
Palm oil 112%
Potatoes 73%
Barley 71%
Sunflower 24%
Wheat 23%
Rice 21%
Maize 19%
Sugar 2%
Groundnut 2%
Beans –3%
Bananas & plantains –3%
Pulses, other –21%
Cassava –29%
Yams –32%
Coconuts –33%
Sweet potatoes –38%
Sorghum –52%
Millets –63%

Median change in the relative contribution to calories from crops of interest to the CGIAR (Consultative Group for International Agricultural Research), a partnership of research and policy organizations working on alleviating global poverty and hunger, in national diets in developing countries, 1969–2009. Source: Adapted from Khoury et al. 2014.

Crop increasing in contribution to diet
Crop decreasing in contribution to diet

FIGURE 8.3B Diets in developing countries are increasingly comprised of major globalized crops.

Contribution of crops to mean food supplies in developing countries for calories (kcal capita day), 1969 and 2009. Source: Adapted from Khoury et al. 2014.

Crops such as soybean and palm oil have become key components of the current (2009) diet in developing countries.

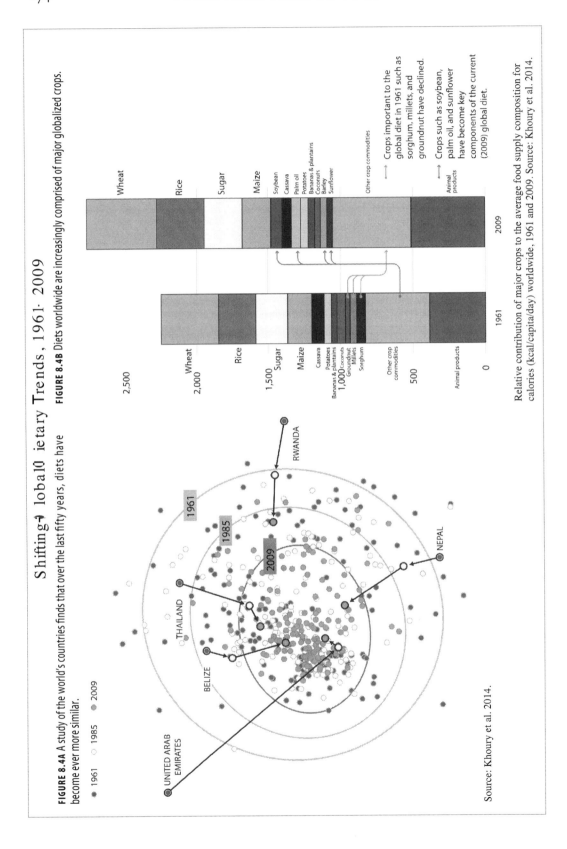

Shifting Global Dietary Trends, 1961- 2009

FIGURE 8.4A A study of the world's countries finds that over the last fifty years, diets have become ever more similar.

FIGURE 8.4B Diets worldwide are increasingly comprised of major globalized crops.

Relative contribution of major crops to the average food supply composition for calories (kcal/capita/day) worldwide, 1961 and 2009. Source: Khoury et al. 2014.

Source: Khoury et al. 2014.

consumption of millet and sorghum has decreased by more than half during that same time period. There is a stark nutritional disparity between foods at the top and at the bottom of the figure. Those being eaten at greater rates tend to be richer in macronutrients, while those disappearing are micronutrient rich. Not only that, many of the crops near the bottom of the figure are stress tolerant, which makes them particularly valuable when we talk about sustainably feeding future populations in the context of climate change.

Another way to visualize this move toward global diet homogeneity is through the diagram constructed, and graciously provided to me, by the lead author of the study cited above, Colin Khoury (see Figure 8.4). Notice the dietary "spread"—a dispersed set of light-colored dots—that existed a half century ago around the world. The global diet today is represented by a clear clumping of darker dots closer to the middle of the figure.

Fortunately, micronutrient malnutrition has received greater attention in recent years. As evidence of this, note the rise of what is known as **biofortification**—the breeding and, increasingly, genetic engineering of plants with the aim of bolstering their micronutrient content (e.g., Rehman et al. 2019). Biofortification strategies also do nothing to increase dietary diversity. They may, in fact, have just the opposite effect. Simply packing more nutrients in a handful of staple crops risks further shrinking the diets of those in the developing world, who have already seen their diets become dangerously narrow due to the green revolution with its **monocultures** (an agricultural practice of producing a single plant species over a wide area for a number of consecutive years). There is also the concern that fortification programs will draw attention away from the more important issue of food access, which in the end is a phenomenon with social, political, and economic roots. Lest we forget, biofortification schemes are premised on the idea that technology can solve the problem of malnutrition, thus absolving governments from responsibility and making it a problem that plant breeders and geneticists must fix, not politicians (Carolan 2018a).

The "Treadmills" of Agriculture

In the 1950s, agricultural economist Willard Cochrane (1958) introduced the concept of the "agricultural treadmill." According to Cochrane, farmers are under tremendous economic pressure to adopt new technologies and increase the size of their operations. The logic behind the argument is straightforward. Those first to adopt a technology (especially one that increases yields or a farm's efficiency) initially experience windfall profits from increased output—like in the case of hybrid corn, which immediately upon adoption doubled a farmer's yield. Soon other farmers, seeing the relative advantage of the technology and wanting to capture additional profits, choose also to adopt it. Yet the cumulative effect of the heightened output eventually exerts downward pressure on prices, as the market becomes flooded. It's important to realize that new agricultural technologies rarely do anything to directly increase consumer demand. At this point, those who have yet to adopt the technology now *must* adopt it if they wish to remain competitive in the market.

A consequence of being caught on the agricultural treadmill is the continual pressure to adopt the latest technologies and inputs while at the same time increasing the size of one's farming operation. This, however, raises one's operating costs, which in turn requires farmers to continually seek out ways to increase their output. Yet there are other input specific treadmills also at work here. The pesticide treadmill is perhaps the best known of these additional treadmills and was first discussed back in the 1970s (van den Bosch 1978). This is the phenomenon in which insects evolve to become resistant to pesticides, which leads to more applications, higher concentrations, and new chemicals, which leads to still further resistance, and so on. Studies going back as early as the 1970s note that despite large increases in pesticide use during the 1960s and 1970s, crop losses from insect pests were actually on the rise (Pimentel et al. 1978), a trend that continues to this day (Stará and Kocourek 2018). Whether we're discussing pesticides or fungicides (see ECOnnection 8.3), evolution has proven a formidable foe to agrichemical companies.

ECOnnection 8.3
Yes! We Have No Bananas

The banana that Americans first came to know was called the Gros Michel banana—also known as "Big Mike." If you went to the store between 1906 and 1960, Big Mike was the banana for sale. It was ubiquitous in grocery stores around the world. Big Mike met with a tragic end, however. Panama disease—a fungus resistant to fungicide—wiped it from the face of the global marketplace. A hurried search for a viable replacement led to the discovery of the Cavendish cultivar, which was resistant to the disease. (A *cultivar* refers to a race or variety of a plant created or selected intentionally and maintained through cultivation.) Now it seems that a new strain of Panama disease is attacking the Cavendish in Asia, and if it were to spread to other continents, it could cause the Cavendish to go the way of the Big Mike (Koeppel 2007).

Banana corporations have developed their industry entirely around not only a single product but a single cultivar—talk about specialization! The industry has been likened to a pipe from many countries to local supermarkets. But this pipe fits only one of the world's 1,000 banana varieties, which makes changing to a new variety very difficult and expensive.

The looming Panama disease threat has led to calls for the banana industry to move away from the monoculture (or, more accurately, monovarietal) model it has been using for more than 100 years (Prisco 2015). Growing multiple varieties will ensure that no single disease will be able to wipe out the entire industry, thus bringing resiliency to the industry. There are, however, hurdles to overcome. Many varieties, for example, cannot withstand the transportation and handling requirements of long-distance shipping. Other hurdles are more cultural. Take "baby bananas." These taste best when eaten in a far browner state than a traditional Cavendish. Yet most people are accustomed to the signature yellow color that the Cavendish (and Big Mike before it) has, which indicates ripeness before it goes brown. It will take some work to get people used to eating a banana that looks, through a Cavendish lens, noticeably overripe.

And before we shrug our shoulders thinking this will only impact affluent eaters looking for a quick, cheap source of potassium, more than 400 million people in Africa, Latin America, and Asia rely on bananas as staple foods. Moreover, raising them employs hundreds of thousands in these nations. To quote Silvia Campos, from Fairtrade International, the largest threat from Panama disease "is to the millions of people who rely on bananas and plantains as key components of their daily diets. They are also a key driver of the rural economies, providing jobs and incomes for workers and smallholders" (quoted in Fleming 2018).

Another input specific treadmill involves the use of synthetic fertilizers—also known as the fertilizer treadmill. Synthetic fertilizer can easily lead to a need for more fertilizer over time. This treadmill is particularly acute when tilth, which are levels of organic matter, and microorganism activity are diminished as a result of poor soil management practices and a general mining of one's land—problems that are all too common on farmland where synthetic fertilizers are used. Under such a scenario, the only option is to increase the applications of fertilizer in order to maintain one's yield.

Last, there is the seed treadmill. A number of protections, as discussed in Chapter 4, are used by the seed industry that either discourage or outright prevent farmers from saving their seeds and replanting them the following season. Moreover, as also discussed in Chapter 4, the knowledge about how to save and replant seeds is another resource that farmers lose when they cease practicing seed saving. This creates a dependency on seed companies. In the United States, for example, the rate of saving corn seed fell from approximately 100 percent at the turn of the twentieth century to less than 5 percent by 1960, while rates for soybean saving dropped from 63 percent in 1960 to 10 percent in 2001 (Howard 2009).

Solutions

In 2002, then Secretary-General of the United Nations (UN) Kofi Annan asked an appointed panel of experts how a green revolution could be achieved in Africa. After more than a year of study, the group had their answer. They questioned the one-size-fits-all approach to food security taken by the green revolution: "The diverse African situation implies that no single magic 'technological bullet' is available for radically improving African agriculture" (InterAcademy Council 2003). The panel's strategic recommendations explain that "African agriculture is more likely to experience numerous 'rainbow evolutions' that differ in nature and extent among the many systems, rather than one Green Revolution as in Asia" (InterAcademy Council 2003, xviii).

I've found the term *rainbow evolutions* useful when talking to students and the public about issues pertaining to food security. The term alters the scope of the discussion by, first, directing attention away from single magic-bullet thinking—hence the term *rainbow*. Second, it emphasizes how agricultural development cannot be divorced from the social, economic, and agroecological conditions of place—which is why the word *evolutions* is so apt. And as every place is different and unique, the term reminds us that solutions cannot be overgeneralized. The following are some potential colors of this ever-changing rainbow.

Agroecology

Small, diverse farms—also known as **polycultures**—that raise grains, fruits, vegetables, and livestock have been shown to outproduce, in terms of harvestable products per unit area, large, specialized (monoculture) operations. Yield advantages of small, diverse farms can range from 20 to 60 percent (Altieri and Nicholls 2008; Nicholls and Altieri 2018). A recent meta-analysis involving 26 studies and 301 observations examined whether polycultures can produce the following win-win relationship: increased yield *and* the internal control of crop pests. (Agroecology relies on internal versus external [pesticides] controls to keep problematic bugs—aka pests—in check. It's basic ecology: polycultures attract both "good" and "bad" bugs, and the former keep the latter under control. Agroecology therefore also refers to an **organic system**.) To quote the authors of the meta-analysis: "We found win-win relationships between per-plant yield of the primary crop and bio-control in polyculture systems" (Iverson et al. 2014, 1593; see ECOnnection 8.4).

The inverse relationship between farm size and productivity is the result of a more efficient use of land, water, biodiversity, and other agricultural resources by small farmers. Polycultures minimize losses from weeds, insects, and diseases by keeping ecological internal controls intact, and they use water, light, and nutrients more efficiently (Gliessman 2015). Small farms are also overwhelmingly owner operated, which, as discussed earlier, benefits rural communities and their economies.

Small, diverse operations are also more likely to be resilient to environmental events, pests, and disease. One reason is because polycultures tend to display more consistent yields than monocultures during extreme weather events (Gliessman 2015). In India, for

ECOnnection 8.4

Agroecology: Growing More Than Food and Fiber

When we think about agriculture, we tend to view it as being solely about food and fiber production. This is a terribly narrow—and perhaps even dangerous—view of all that is provided by this sector. Agriculture is important to us in such additional ways as:

DIET
- enhancement of nutritional quality and the cycling of trace elements
- food security.

PUBLIC HEALTH
- protection of the health of farmworkers and consumers
- suppression of vectors of human disease (e.g., mosquitoes, snails, ticks).

ENVIRONMENTAL SUSTAINABILITY
- preservation of biodiversity
- protection of wildlife
- preservation of our productive capacity against erosion, salinization, acidification, and compaction

- maintenance of an ecological community of natural enemies of pests and diseases of crops
- protection of the general environment against runoff, eutrophication, volatilization of nitrites, and dust in the atmosphere
- protection of water resources and quality.

RURAL DEVELOPMENT
- supporting employment, farm income, and rural life
- support for the economic independence of women.

NATIONAL DEVELOPMENT AND SOVEREIGNTY
- contributing to the international balance of payments
- defense of national sovereignty against possible dumping or political blackmail backed up by economic blockade
- food sovereignty.

Source: Based on Gliessman (2015).

example, the number of varieties a rice farmer grows increases with the variability of conditions (e.g., atmospheric, agronomic, pest ecology, and more). Thus, low terraces, which are wetter and prone to flooding, are planted with indigenous long-growing rice varieties. Upper terraces, in contrast, dry out more rapidly after the rains, so they are planted with drought-resistant, fast-growing varieties. In total, a small Indian rice farmer can plant up to ten different rice varieties (Dey et al. 2019).

Small-farm efficiency can also be attained with surprisingly little investment, especially when compared to the massive capital expenditures required of industrial farms. In Peru, for example, several NGOs and government agencies have created initiatives to restore abandoned terraces and build new ones by offering peasant communities low-interest loans or seeds and other inputs. Terraces reduce the losses associated with frost and drought, minimize soil erosion, improve water efficiency, and increase crop yields between 45 and 65 percent compared to crops raised on sloping land (e.g., Nicholls and Altieri 2018).

La Via Campesina and Other Peasant-Based Movements

La Via Campesina is viewed by many as the world's most important transnational social movement (Claeys 2015; Martínez-Torres and Rosset 2010; Val et al. 2019), a fact that surprises a great many in countries like the United States, where most have never heard of the organization. As its website explains:

> La Via Campesina is the international movement which brings together millions of peasants, small and medium-size farmers, landless people, women farmers, indigenous people, migrants and agricultural workers from around the world. It defends small-scale sustainable agriculture as a way to promote social justice and dignity. It strongly opposes corporate driven agriculture and transnational companies that are destroying people and nature.
>
> (www.viacampesina.org/en; see Image 8.1)

IMAGE 8.1 Representatives of La Via Campesina in Spain

Source: "2015 Mendillorriko Jaiak" by Mendillorri Bizitzen, September 4, 2015 under CC BY-SA 2.0.

CASE STUDY 8.2
Landless Workers' Movement (MST)

The Landless Workers' Movement in Brazil (also known as the MST, after its Portuguese title, Movimento dos Trabalhadores Rurais Sem Terra), which includes members throughout Latin America, is an estimated 1.5 million strong (MST 2015). The energy of the movement is due to the perceived unjust distribution of land throughout the region, especially in Brazil where 3 percent of the population own and control two-thirds of the country's arable land.

Under Brazilian law, a landowner risks losing title to his or her land by letting it lie idle, especially after someone else settles it and begins using it productively. Under such a scenario, the latter party could challenge the landholder's title to the land in court. The MST has sought to utilize this law to the advantage of landless peasants. To give their movement further legitimacy, MST leaders also point to a passage in Brazil's constitution that states that land should serve a "larger *social* function," which they interpret to mean that it should not be viewed solely through an economic lens.

Members of the MST thus seek to identify and occupy idle land and make it agriculturally productive, arguing that such actions meet the constitutional requirement of a "social function." While doing this, the MST is also pushing for broader land reform throughout the region.

The MST has recently encountered a new threat to its existence: the Brazilian government. The populist President—Jair Bolsonaro—and his administration have effectively designated the MST as a domestic *terrorist* group. To quote Nabhan Garcia, land issues secretary at the Agriculture Ministry:

> It is the challenge of this government to demonstrate to Congress that this [members of the MST squatting on land] is a thing very close to terrorism, or it could be said in some circumstances is terrorism, and to have a more severe application of the law.
>
> (quoted in Spring and Boadle 2019)

La Via Campesina is made up of 164 local and national organizations in 73 countries from Africa, Asia, Europe, and the Americas and collectively represents about 200 million peasant families. The movement is founded on the belief that for too long, rural and food policies have been developed in the absence of those most affected: namely, rural peoples, including women. The class profile of La Via Campesina is remarkably diverse: landless peasants, tenant farmers, sharecroppers, and rural workers largely in Latin America and Asia; small and part-time farmers in Europe, North America, Japan, and South Korea; peasant farmers and pastoralists in Africa; small family farms in Mexico and Brazil; middle-class (and some affluent) farmers in India; and poor urban (and urban-fringe) dwellers in countries like Brazil and South Africa.

A quick word about the term *peasant*, as it has historically signified a less than flattering identity. La Via Campesina, along with other peasant movements (see Case Study 8.2), seeks to recast the term *peasant* as an identity to be embraced. Delegates from the United Kingdom, when seeking to first name the movement, initially resisted the term La Via Campesina—which literally translates as "Peasant Way"—out of concern for the

MOVEMENT MATTERS 8.1
Food Sovereignty Movement Scores Victory in Ecuador, and Beyond

In 2008 the Ecuadorian Constitution declared food sovereignty a strategic goal and a government obligation, embracing many of the proposals put forward by Ecuadorian federations linked to La Via Campesina. (For a detailed analysis of this process see Giunta 2014.) For example, Article 13 of the Ecuadoran Constitution states: "Individuals and communities have the right to safe and permanent access to healthy, sufficient and nutritious food, preferably produced locally and in accordance with their different identities and cultural traditions." With regard to food sovereignty, Article 281 explains: "Food sovereignty is a strategic objective and an obligation of the State to guarantee that individuals, communities, towns and nationalities achieve permanent self-sufficiency with foods that are healthy and culturally appropriate."

More recently, the UN passed "Declaration on the Rights of Peasants and Other People Working in Rural Areas"—the first ever international law granting rights to peasants and landless workers, a group that encompasses roughly a third of the world's population. La Via Campesina was a major supporter of the declaration. This UN declaration looks to protect the rights of anyone who survives on artisanal or small-scale agriculture, including those from fishing communities, indigenous people, rural workers, and pastoralists (Brown 2019).

derogatory connotations attached to the term *peasant*. The delegates instead preferred the term *farmer*. Many outside the UK delegation, however, favored the term *peasant*, noting that *farmer* also had connotations that failed to capture the character of the movement and most of its participants (Desmarais 2008). A compromise was reached: keep the name La Via Campesina, but do not translate it into English. It has also been noted that the name La Via Campesina pays homage to Latin America's founding role in the movement.

La Via Campesina is responsible for elevating the term *food sovereignty* in the public consciousness (see Movement Matters 8.1). The term was first used publicly by the movement during the World Food Summit in 1996. As detailed in Table 8.2, food sovereignty speaks to a way of life that is in many ways diametrically opposed to the dominant view that presently dictates conventional food and agricultural policy.

The World Forum on Food Sovereignty was held in the village of Nyéléni in Mali, Africa, in February 2007. The meeting brought together 600 delegates from five continents to reaffirm the right to food sovereignty and to begin an international drive to reverse the worldwide decline in local community food production. The forum was organized through an alliance of diverse social movements: Friends of the Earth International, La Via Campesina, the World March of Women, the Network of Farmers' and Producers' Organizations of West Africa, the World Forum of Fish Harvesters and Fish Workers, and the World Forum of Fisher Peoples. The group wrote the Declaration of Nyéléni, in which you will find the following lengthy definition of food sovereignty. I quote the definition in full to give the reader an idea of just how expansive the concept is:

TABLE 8.2 View of Dominant and Food Sovereignty Models

ISSUE	DOMINANT MODEL VIEW	FOOD SOVEREIGNTY MODEL VIEW
Free trade	Everything ought to be governed by the market	Food should be exempt from trade agreements, as it is fundamentally different from, say, cars
Production priorities	Agro-exports	National and local markets
Subsidies	Claims to favor market logics yet relies heavily on government subsidies for the largest farms	Subsidies okay if they level the playing field and do not unduly harm small-scale farms in developing economies
Food	A commodity to be traded (fundamentally no different from any other commodity)	A unique commodity that everyone has a right to
Agriculture	Increasingly an occupation for those with access to significant amounts of credit, capital, land, and labor	A livelihood that should be available to all
Hunger	A technological/production problem	A problem of access (of food and of land to produce it)
Food security	Achieve through trade and by adopting Green Revolution principles	Improved by enabling the hungriest to produce food and by embracing Rainbow Evolution policies (see Chapter 12)
Seeds	Can be privatized (like land); a commodity with no cultural significance	A common heritage of humankind that everyone has a right to; an artifact that allows for the reproduction of culture
Overproduction	Is good (leads to cheap food)	Is bad (erodes food security around the world)
Peasantry	A holdover from feudalism (which no one wishes to return to); a pejorative term	"People of the land"; a proud identity for hundreds of millions around the world

Source: Adapted from Martínez-Torres and Rosset (2010) and Val et al. (2019).

Food sovereignty is the right of peoples to healthy and culturally appropriate food produced through ecologically sound and sustainable methods, and their right to define their own food and agriculture systems. It puts the aspirations and needs of those who produce, distribute and consume food at the heart of food systems and policies rather than the demands of markets and corporations. It defends the interests and inclusion of the next generation. It offers a strategy to resist and dismantle the current corporate trade and food regime, and directions for food, farming, pastoral and fisheries systems determined by local producers and users. Food sovereignty prioritizes local and national economies and markets and empowers peasant and family farmer-driven agriculture, artisanal-fishing, pastoralist-led grazing, and food production, distribution and consumption based on environmental, social and economic sustainability. Food sovereignty promotes transparent trade that guarantees just incomes to all peoples as well as the rights of consumers to control their food and nutrition. It ensures that the rights to use and manage lands, territories, waters, seeds, livestock and biodiversity are in the hands of those of us who produce food. Food sovereignty implies new social relations free of oppression and inequality between men and women, peoples, racial groups, social and economic classes and generations.

(IPC 2016)

Urban Gardens

As discussed in Chapter 6, more than half the world's population live in urban areas—a figure that is only going to increase in the decades ahead. The majority of those moving to cities in these rapidly urbanizing (low-income) nations are poor: those escaping hunger, conflict, and/or persecution from wherever they started out (Lundquist et al. 2015). Most urban poor in low-income nations spend the majority of their income on food. An estimated 60 percent of all household income generated by the poor in Asia goes toward purchasing food, compared to Canada and the United States, where the figure is closer to 10 percent (Carolan 2018a). Food insecurity among the urban poor is further exacerbated by diets composed heavily of tradable commodities (versus traditional foods) and a lack of space to grow their own food (Redwood 2010).

Although it is easy to brush urban agriculture aside as a nonviable strategy for developing food security, the role that urban agriculture currently plays in keeping millions from falling over the edge into abject hunger and poverty is quite surprising (see Image 8.2). One study examined urban centers in fifteen developing countries in Africa, Asia, Eastern Europe, and Latin America, looking specifically at the role played by urban agriculture in promoting food and economic security and diet diversity among the urban poor (Zezza and Tasciotti 2010). Participation in urban agriculture among poor households in the countries studied was as high as 81 percent. Urban agriculture was also shown to be of major economic significance, making up more than 50 percent of the income of poor households in certain countries. Two-thirds of the countries analyzed were shown to have a correlation between active participation in agricultural activities and greater household dietary diversity, even after controlling for economic welfare and other household characteristics. There was also a link—albeit not as robust as the others—between urban agriculture participation and the consumption of fruits and vegetables. Of course, urban farming schemes are only as healthy as the environments they take place within. Some well documented problems in deploying urban agriculture have to do with the high level of pollutants in urban areas that may cause health problems if the pollutants enter the food chain (see, e.g., Ferreira et al. 2018).

Before ending this chapter, I need to stress one important point (which I've given evidence for in previous chapters): do not think for a moment that our food problems lie only in production. This is *good* news, as the thought of having to further industrialize food

IMAGE 8.2 Community Garden in Downtown Denver, Colorado

Source: Author and James Hale.

production is not an attractive one, given the associated costs to the environment (e.g., climate change and soil erosion), community well-being (recall the Goldschmidt thesis), and public health (e.g., pesticide exposure). For one thing, hunger is ultimately a problem of access and distribution. The UN, for example, calculates that the world's average daily calorie availability is projected to rise from 2,789 kilocalories per person per day in 2000 to 3,130 kilocalories per person per day in 2050 (United Nations 2013). That's how many calories would be available if the food raised went to feeding people and not, say, cars (as biofuels) or landfills (as food waste). As detailed in Chapter 6, in the discussion of Amartya Sen's work on famines, producing more food does not do the world's hungry any good if they cannot afford or, more generally, do not have access to it. We also waste, as described in Chapter 3, an outrageous amount of food. Why continue pushing for higher yields and greater agricultural output if we are going to continue to throw a significant chunk of those productivity gains away? Some food for thought….

IMPORTANT CONCEPTS

- agroecology
- food sovereignty
- Goldschmidt thesis

- green revolution
- peasant-based movements
- rainbow evolutions
- the "treadmills" of agriculture

DISCUSSION QUESTIONS

1. It seems as though labor abuses and injustices take a backseat to issues of environmental sustainability when thinking and talking about food. Why do you think that is? How can we make all those involved in the growing and manufacturing and processing, transportation, preparing, and selling of food more visible?
2. What are some of the links between the green revolution and micronutrient malnutrition?
3. In many respects, people from lower-income countries are at the forefront of challenging the dominant global food system (like La Via Campesina and the Landless Workers' Movement). Why is that? What threats does this system pose to them?
4. Summarize the Goldschmidt thesis. Based on that literature, what policies would you recommend with the aim of enhancing rural community vitality and well-being?

SUGGESTED ADDITIONAL READINGS

Carolan, M. 2018. *The Real Cost of Cheap Food.* 2nd edn. New York: Earthscan/Routledge.

Howard, P. 2016. *Concentration and Power in the Food System: Who Controls What We Eat?* London: Bloomsbury Academic.

Mann, A. 2018. "Education for Food Sovereignty as Transformative Ethical Practice." *Policy Futures in Education*, 7(7): 862–877. https://doi.org/10.1177%2F1478210318816251.

Nogeire-McRae, T., E.P. Ryan, B.B. Jablonski, M. Carolan, H.S. Arathi, C.S. Brown, H.H. Saki, S. McKeen, E. Lapansky, and M.E. Schipanski. 2018. "The Role of Urban Agriculture in a Secure, Healthy, and Sustainable Food System." *BioScience*, 68(10): 748–759. https://doi.org/10.1093/biosci/biy071.

RELEVANT INTERNET LINKS

- www.fao.org/home/en. Food and Agriculture Organization of the United Nations (FAO).
- www.fcrn.org.uk. Food Climate Research Network. An excellent resource for those looking for cutting edge research dealing with the food system's impact on the environment, in addition to many other agrifood-related issues.
- www.foodmiles.com. Calculate the distance the food from your last meal has traveled (aka food miles).
- www.ruaf.org. Resource Centers on Urban Agriculture and Food Security.
- www.viacampesina.org/en. The website address for La Via Campesina.
- http://vimeo.com/27473286. Excellent short video about the La Via Campesina movement.

SUGGESTED VIDEOS

- *Big River* (2010). A sequel of sorts to *King Corn* (see below) that investigates the socioecological impacts of the main characters' acre of corn.
- *Edible City: Grow the Revolution* (2012). A journey through the Local Good Food movement that's taking root in the San Francisco Bay Area, across the nation, and around the world.
- *King Corn* (2008). Two friends learn about the food system by moving to Iowa and growing an acre of corn.
- *Lucent* (2014). An investigation of the practices of Australia's pig farms and slaughterhouses. Featuring a wealth of never seen before surveillance and handheld footage captured by a devoted team of animal rights activists.
- *Planeat* (2011). A look at the impacts of meat and dairy on the planet and our health.
- *Save the Farm* (2011). A popular organic farm in the middle of South Central Los Angeles is threatened by land developers, and community members take action.
- *Sustainable* (2016). Following the seasons on a farm owned by a seventh-generation Illinois farmer, the film shines a light on farming and the downsides of industrial agriculture.
- *The Harvest* (2011). A documentary about three of the close to half million migrant child farm laborers in the United States.
- *Turlock* (2013). In February 2012, the owners of A&L Poultry (a 50,000-hen egg farm) stopped feeding their hens, leaving the birds without food for more than two weeks. This documentary details what happened next.

Energy Production: Our Sun-ny Prospects

In 2009, China became the world's number one consumer of energy, overtaking the United States, which had previously been on top for close to a century. China consumed 2.252 billion tons of oil equivalent in 2009, which was about 4 percent more than the United States' 2.17 billion tons (the oil-equivalent metric represents all forms of energy consumed, including crude oil, nuclear power, coal, natural gas, and renewable sources like hydropower and biofuel) (Swartz and Oster 2010). And 2009 proved not to be a fluke, as China has managed to hold onto that top spot, increasing its energy consumption to 2.6 billion tons (or 23 percent of the world's total) in 2012 (Li 2014). By 2035, China's energy consumption is expected to reach 4.06 billion tons of oil equivalent, more than India, the United States, and the European Union combined (Reuters 2017). In 2017, the 4.06 figure replaced the previous estimated peak of 3.75 billion tons of oil equivalent, due in large part to an underestimation of transportation demand, which is now expected to increase through to 2050 (twenty years longer than previously estimated) (Ibid.). This is all to say: do not be surprised if that 4.06 billion tons of oil-equivalent estimate is at some point revised upward.

Many in the United States expressed a collective sigh of relief in 2009, not so much because they were happy that China is, quite literally, killing hundreds of thousands of its people annually through pollution (Li et al. 2019), but because they could finally point an indignant finger at someone other than themselves on the subject of energy consumption—how dare *they* do this? (I remember watching a couple of political pundits on television act precisely this way.) I still hear these expressions, even though they are dangerously misplaced. Although China might consume more energy in absolute terms, it comes nowhere close to out-consuming the United States on a per capita basis. So, in fairness, China's designation as "top energy-consuming nation" is just a consequence of demographics. It has more than four times the population of the United States, a fact that also helps put into some perspective why China is investing heavily in its energy sector (see Case Study 9.1). If the United States had China's population, it would easily hold the title, out-consuming China by a factor of four.

The cloud of energy, however, has a silver lining. (It's there; we just can't see it at the moment, thanks to the layer of coal dust and other fine particulates that presently cover

CASE STUDY 9.1

Three Gorges Dam

Three Gorges is the world's most notorious dam. The dam's body, completed in 2006, is located in China along the Yangtze River. The Three Gorges Dam generates significant quantities of electricity, roughly eight times that of the US Hoover Dam. But at what cost, beyond the roughly $24 billion spent to build it?

The massive project, with its 1,045 square kilometer (403 square miles) wide reservoir, broke the record books for numbers of people displaced (more than 1.2 million) and numbers of cities (13), towns (140), and villages (1,350) flooded. The reservoir also submerged roughly 100 archaeological sites, some dating back more than 12,000 years. People who were displaced were allocated plots of land and small stipends as compensation. The dam itself also creates an impassable barrier to one endangered mammal (the Yangtze finless porpoise) and two that are threatened (the Chinese river dolphin and the Chinese paddlefish). The Chinese government went so far as to admit that two foreseen consequences were actually worse than anticipated: deteriorating water quality and erosion. Toxic algal blooms regularly blight the river's many tributaries as a result of reduced water flow and nutrients from land-use changes. Landslides are also a frequent occurrence, some of which are due to tremors and small earthquakes caused by the tremendous weight of the reservoir itself (which lies on two major fault lines). To mitigate these problems, China has embarked on a ten-year effort that will cost $26.45 billion—more than the cost of the entire dam!

Source: Adapted from Hvistendahl (2008) and Stone (2011).

it.) While our thirst for energy is growing, as long as the sun exists we'll have plenty available to quench it, as electricity can be readily generated from solar, wind, geothermal, tidal, wave, and biomass. The sun, thanks to its energy and gravitational pull, is the source of all these renewables. At the moment, however, it's a case of where the "possible" and "probable" do not yet line up, though they could eventually, as I address in the Solutions section.

Fast Facts

- Roughly 7,200 million tons (Mt) of coal was produced globally in 2018. While the figure is up from 6,185 Mt in 2010, it is down from the 7,822 Mt produced in 2013. China increased its global share of coal production from 13.6 percent in the early 1970s to 45 percent in 2017. This percentage far exceeds the world's second largest coal producing nation, India, which accounted for less than 10 percent in 2017 (World Coal Association n.d.).
- Nuclear power plants supplied roughly 11 percent of the world's electricity in 2019, down from 13.5 percent in 2010. The United States generates the most nuclear energy, currently more than 800 Terawatt-hours (TWh), followed by France, with 380 TWh. Now for some North American statistics: Canada has 19 operable nuclear reactors, with a combined net

IMAGE 9.1

Source: "Coal Consuming China" by Han Jun Zeng (flickr.com/67661012@N04) is licensed copyright © 2014 under CC BY-SA 2.0.

Note: Coal remains a popular source of energy in China, even for some households, which use it for heating and cooking. This truck is making a coal delivery in Beijing.

capacity of 13.5 Gigawatt electrical (GWe), generating 15 percent of the country's electricity; Mexico has two operating nuclear reactors, with a combined net capacity of 1.6 GWe, generating 6 percent of the country's electricity; the United States has 98 operable nuclear reactors, with a combined capacity of 99.4 GWe, generating 20 percent of the country's electricity (World Nuclear Association 2019).

- The countries with the greatest share of world crude oil reserves (in barrels), as of 2019, are as follows: Venezuela (300.9 billion); Saudi Arabia (266.5 billion); Canada (169.7 billion); Iran (158.4 billion); Iraq (142.5 billion); Kuwait (101.5 billion); United Arab Emirates (97.8 billion); Russia (80.0 billion); Libya (48.4 billion); Nigeria (37.1 billion); United States (36.5 billion); Kazakhstan (30.0 billion); China (25.6 billion); Qatar (25.2 billion); and Brazil (12.7 billion) (CIA 2019).

Implications

The aforementioned vastness of global reserves makes coal deserving of closer scrutiny. It is the most carbon intensive of all fossil fuels, which is why it has been called "the real global warming culprit" (Perrow 2010, 66). Coal is about as far from green as you can get when all available energy sources are lined up. Yet I doubt we'll abandon it anytime soon, primarily because of its great abundance in countries like China and the United States—

numbers one and two, respectively, in terms of coal production *and* energy consumption, though at least twenty countries have pledged to phase out of coal by 2030 (see, e.g., ABC News 2017). Thank goodness for **clean coal**, right?

What *clean coal* means depends on whom you ask. When I was writing the first edition of *Society and the Environment* the industry-sponsored American Coalition for Clean Coal Electricity had this definition posted on its website: "Clean coal technology refers to technologies that improve the environmental performance of coal-based electricity plants. These technologies include equipment that increases the operational efficiency of power plants, as well as technologies that reduce emissions." Broadly speaking, then, clean coal, according to the coal industry and its wide net of proponents, refers to any coal-burning technology that is an improvement over what we used to have. That definition of *clean* might work for my four-year-old son who, after washing his dinner plate (which remains covered in food), tells me how dirty it used to be prior to dipping it in the sink. The first time he did that, I remember going to the sink and showing him "what clean really means." Perhaps someone ought to do that for the coal industry. If you search the American Coalition for Clean Coal Electricity's website today, you will no longer find a definition of clean coal. The assumption is that all coal is clean, thus making the term *clean coal* redundant. Instead you'll find a description of technologies that make coal clean, but no definition of clean coal itself.

Earlier chapters have covered many of the most significant socioecological implications of past and current energy use, with climate change chief among them. A substantial amount of time has also been spent describing the consequences of our collective addiction to oil and, in particular, the car. Yet the subject of energy *production* has yet to be given its due, particularly in regard to sources other than oil.

"Clean" Coal

Outside the coal-lobbying industry, *clean coal* typically means something more befitting the name. That something typically involves capturing and storing the CO_2 produced by coal-fired power plants, thereby preventing this greenhouse gas from being emitted into the atmosphere and contributing to climate change. Unfortunately, while carbon-capture technology has been shown to work on a small scale, it has yet to be successfully scaled up (see Case Study 9.2).

Besides the large expense, carbon capture of clean coal still comes with a significant ecological footprint. Lest we forget, that coal has to come from somewhere. Millions of acres of habitat across the United States have been radically altered over the past 150 years by **strip-mining** (a practice involving the removal of soil and rock overlaying the mineral deposit). There were fewer than 700 operational mines in the United States in 2017 (434 surface mines and 237 underground mines), down from 1,229 in 2012. More than half of the US coal mines operating in 2008 have since closed (EIA 2019a; see ECOnnection 9.1).

A single 500 megawatt coal-fired power plant emits three million tons of CO_2 and costs more than $500 billion a year when all the economic, health, and environmental impacts associated with each stage in the life cycle—extraction, transportation, processing, and combustion—are totaled (Epstein et al. 2011). To break this figure down a bit: $74.6 billion is "paid" by Appalachian communities—where much of the coal is

CASE STUDY 9.2
Incentivizing Carbon Capture

As of 2018, there were seventeen large-scale plants in the world, mostly in the United States, that were storing away about 40 million metric tons of CO_2—roughly 1 percent of global annual emissions. These figures will likely change, at least in the United States, in the years ahead. In early 2018, as part of a large omnibus budget bill signed by President Trump, incentives were introduced in the United States to practice carbon capture through 45Q tax credits (named after Section 45Q of the US tax code). With this legislation, those capturing and burying CO_2 would receive $50 per metric ton, while those that put the greenhouse gas to some use would receive $35 per metric ton. A study estimates that accelerated research, development, and deployment of the carbon capture technology could add $190 billion to US annual GDP by 2040, and add 780,000 jobs over the same period. One especially optimistic projection suggests that carbon capture could increase oil recovery by up to 900 million barrels per year. This could happen through a process of injecting CO_2 in aging oil fields, which would boost oil production while storing away the injected CO_2 in the process (Rathi 2018).

extracted—in terms of increased health care costs, injury, and death; costs linked to emissions total more than $187 billion; and the mercury set loose into the environment, with its negative effects on human health, comes with a price tag of almost $30 billion. And let us not forget about climate change. Each 500 megawatt coal-fired plant, in terms of climate change costs, passes onto the public, both present and future, an annual bill that can total more than $200 billion. Again, this is just *one* coal-fired power plant (see ECOnnection 9.2).

Hydraulic Fracturing (aka Fracking)

Natural gas production is expected to increase rapidly in the decades ahead in countries with rich natural gas reserves. President Obama called the United States the "Saudi Arabia of natural gas" in his 2012 State of the Union address, thanks in no small part to shale gas. (This is where **fracking** comes into play—see below for a definition.) Estimates suggest the shale gas reserves in the United States are sufficient to cover current production rates for nearly 100 years (EIA 2019b).

It is generally accepted that combustion of natural gas in power plants produces substantially less CO_2—35 to 70 percent lower, depending on the context—than that emitted by coal-fired power plants when equal amounts of energy are generated (US Department of Energy 2016). And yet, despite the fact that natural gas has lower greenhouse gas emissions than coal on a delivered power basis, we cannot ignore that the extraction and delivery of natural gas contributes meaningfully to climate change (see ECOnnection 9.3). The natural gas sector, from extraction to processing, transport to consumption, is responsible for 27 percent of US methane emissions and approximately 3 percent of the country's greenhouse gas emissions (US Department of Energy 2016).

ECOnnection 9.1
Mountaintop Removal Mining

Mountaintop removal mining involves clearing upper-elevation forests (typically at the summit of mountains), stripping the ground of topsoil, and using explosives to break up rocks to expose underlying yet relatively shallow coal seams. The practice is widespread throughout the central Appalachian region of the United States, particularly in eastern Kentucky, West Virginia, and southwestern Virginia. Studies have outlined the extensive environmental and public health consequences associated with this practice of coal extraction (e.g., Crosby et al. 2016; Hendryx et al. 2019). Those consequences include the following:

- ecological losses and downstream impacts: for example, burial of headwater streams leading to the permanent loss of ecosystems, declines in stream biodiversity, and elevated water concentrations of sulfate, calcium, and magnesium
- human health impacts: for example, contaminated groundwater and elevated levels of airborne and hazardous dust resulting in increased risk of lung and bronchus cancer
- mitigation problems: land reclaimed after

a mine is closed has lower organic content, low water-infiltration rates (which increases the risk of flash flooding), and low nutrient content.

Mountaintop mining is considerably more economical than traditional coal mining, as it is less labor intensive. Approximately 250 percent more coal can be extracted per worker using this technique than in traditional underground mines (Hendryx et al. 2019). It is no coincidence that the recent expansion of mountaintop mining has coincided with the loss of thousands of jobs over the past twenty years in the US coal industry. The industry claims the lost jobs are due to increasing government regulations when the data indicate *it* is the one to blame. Proponents of the practice often cast critics as looking to damage the economic livelihood of mining communities, perpetuating the false "jobs versus the environment" argument. This criticism ignores the fact that mountaintop mining is doing the damage by replacing labor with dynamite and heavy equipment, and in the end (as all mines eventually close) leaving communities with a devastated natural resource base and no alternative opportunities for employment (Poudyal et al. 2019).

Fracking works like this: a well is sunk several thousand feet into the shale formation, after which laterals are then drilled that fan out from the main vertical well. Fracking takes place when large amounts of water, sand, and a secret chemical mixture (it's considered proprietary knowledge) are injected into the well. The pressure from this mixture fractures the shale, which in turn releases the natural gas. Once the fracking process is done, the well goes into production, though some wells may require multiple frackings.

Fracking has come under increased scrutiny, as many homeowners in areas where the practice is common say it has tainted their drinking water, either with methane or with the wastewater produced by the process. And the research is beginning to back up those claims. A highly cited study published in the *Proceedings of the National Academy of Sciences* looked at sixty drinking-water wells in northeastern Pennsylvania and nearby areas in

ECOnnection 9.2

Floating on a Cloud ... of Fossil Fuel Emissions

"The cloud" is an apt term, but not for the reasons you might think. The name *cloud* in the context of the IT (information technology) sector does not have any single definition. The term is frequently used to refer to a wide range of internet-based platforms and services—from Facebook to Flickr, LinkedIn, and Google Maps—that store and deliver data from an online source to the gadget in front of you. The metaphor of a cloud certainly builds on the futurists' utopia of having finally overthrown matter. Cloud computing consumes nothing more than 1s and 0s. Right?

I do find the term apt, if the right metaphor is evoked. Cloud computing *clouds* our ability to see beyond the liquid crystal display in front of us. If "the cloud" were a country, it would have the fifth largest electricity demand in the world, at more than 700 billion kilowatt hours. Yet this demand is practically invisible. To give one example: the antivirus software company McAfee calculates that the electricity required to transmit the trillions of spam emails sent annually is equivalent to the amount required to power more than two million homes in the United States and produces

the same greenhouse gas emissions as over three million cars. Or another example: Facebook's first two data centers, in Oregon and North Carolina, while using a highly energy-efficient design and technology, were both located in areas where more than 60 percent of the electricity came from coal. So, while the US Environmental Protection Agency continues to work with the IT sector to expand its EnergyStar rating system to apply to data centers, the fact that these server farms continue to obtain a significant amount of their energy from coal largely cancels out any efficiency gains made in server technology. And my last example: the consulting business McKinsey & Company analyzed energy consumption by data centers used by pharmaceutical companies, military contractors, banks, and government agencies and found them to be using, on average, only 6–12 percent of the electricity powering their servers to perform computations. The remaining energy—roughly 90 percent of it—went to idling servers. In light of these figures, it should not come as a shock to learn that estimates indicate that the world's data centres will consume *one-fifth* of the Earth's power by 2025.

Source: Carolan (2014); Lima (2017).

New York State (Osborn et al. 2011). Dissolved methane concentrations in water from the thirty-four wells located more than one kilometer from fracking operations were tested to have, on average, about 1.1 milligrams of dissolved methane per liter. In water taken from twenty-six wells within one kilometer of at least one fracking site, methane concentrations averaged 19.2 milligrams. Isotopic analyses of the carbon in the methane showed it to have the same signature as that being recovered from nearby shale operations, thus implicating the fracking process. Other gases were also detected, which too were unique to the active gas-drilling areas. Ethane, another component of natural gas, and additional hydrocarbons were detected in 81 percent of water wells near fracking operations but in only 9 percent of water wells further away. Propane and butane were also more likely to be detected in wells closest to drilling areas.

A number of reviews of the literature (e.g., Hirsch et al. 2018; Saunders et al. 2018; Werner et al. 2015) list thousands of articles since the 1990s on the impact of fracking on public and environmental health. The authors of one review conclude that while the "methodological rigor" of the literature is mixed, the following is clear: "there is also no evidence to rule out such [negative] health impacts" (Werner et al. 2015, 1127). Social scientists are also starting to examine the location of these fracking wells in relation to the sociodemographics of a region. The findings are disconcerting (see Movement Matters 9.1). As one recent study concludes:

> This study applies Geographic Information Systems (GIS) and spatial analysis to determine whether certain vulnerable human populations are unequally exposed to pollution from unconventional gas wells in Pennsylvania, West Virginia, and Ohio.... Sociodemographic indicators include age (children and the elderly), poverty level, education level, and race at the census tract level.... The results demonstrate that the

ECOnnection 9.3

More Cheap Fracking Plastic

The vast majority of plastic manufactured in the United States is made from natural gas. Analysts have described shale gas as a "game changer," since it has allowed the United States to regain its position as a low-cost producer of all things plastic. These cheap disposable commodities are in turn being exported around the world, as evidenced by the fact that US exports of polyvinyl chloride—also known as PVC plastic—tripled between 2006 and 2011 (Carolan 2014). The price of ethane, a natural gas component that is converted to ethylene when exposed to heat and pressure—a process called *cracking*—has fallen dramatically in recent years in the United States. Ethylene is a key ingredient in the manufacture of polymers. In 2012 alone the cost of ethane dropped by 67 percent among Gulf Coast processors, driven in part by massive investments by chemical manufacturers in Texas (Kaskey 2012). Before the fracking boom, the most recent cracker (machinery used to convert ethane to ethylene) built in the United States was constructed in 2001. Now, crackers are in various

stages of planning or construction in dozens of communities in the United States. The plastic industry's interest in developing greener, bio-based plastics has been tempered thanks to fracking. Back when oil and gas prices were high, major petrochemical companies were busy exploring ways to make plastics from things like corn, sugar cane, sugar beets, and algae.

In 2016, with help from Texas Governor Greg Abbott, Exxon found a site for Project Yosemite on 1,400 acres north of Corpus Christi; the future site of a massive ethane cracker that will also include a monoethylene glycol unit and two polyethylene units. Before community members could take notice, county commissioners had already rezoned the farmland and Exxon was seeking $1 billion in tax breaks from the county and state. Exxon's cracker will consume 20 to 25 million gallons per day. The Port of Corpus Christi has plans to build a seawater desalination plant, though that comes with its own negative externalities. And let's not forget: the site is vulnerable to hurricanes (Carpenter 2019).

environmental injustice occurs in areas with unconventional wells in Pennsylvania with respect to the poor population. There are also localized clusters of vulnerable populations in exposed areas in all three states: Pennsylvania (for poverty and elderly population), West Virginia (for poverty, elderly population, and education level) and Ohio (for children).

(Ogneva-Himmelberger and Huang 2015, 165)

Nuclear Power

The Nuclear Energy Agency (2010) has proclaimed that nuclear power "could provide around 25 percent of global electricity with almost no CO_2 emissions." But it's not just industry types who are singing the praises of nuclear power; many environmentalists are too. Patrick Moore, the cofounder of Greenpeace who has famously become a nuclear power advocate, noted in a bulletin for the International Atomic Energy Agency that "nuclear energy is the only non-greenhouse-gas-emitting power source that can effectively replace fossil fuels while satisfying the world's increasing demand for energy" (Moore 2006, 56). These claims, while factually accurate, mask deeper, less green truths, which life-cycle analyses help make visible.

Some life-cycle analyses show nuclear power emitting many times more CO_2 emissions than wind energy once uranium refining and transportation, reactor construction, and waste disposal are considered. A typical nuclear plant uses roughly 900 miles of electrical cables, 170,000 tons of concrete, 32,000 tons of steel, 1,363 tons of copper, and 205,464 tons of other materials, many of which, like aluminium, are carbon intensive (Sovacool 2008). As for the other end of the life cycle, some estimates place the total energy required for decommissioning a nuclear plant to be as much as 50 percent more than the energy needed for its construction (Seier and Zimmermann 2014; see Image 9.2).

Figure 9.1 illustrates top-end and mean (signified by the X and the corresponding number) emissions from a review of life-cycle analyses on nuclear power (Sovacool 2008; see also Kadiyala et al. 2016; Serp et al. 2017). Proponents are correct when they say the operation phase has a relatively small CO_2 footprint. Yet nuclear plants and nuclear fuel do not just appear. Nor do they disappear at the end of their life cycle. After factoring in for the entire life cycle of nuclear power, a very different ecological footprint image emerges. Of the life-cycle studies reviewed, the mean total CO_2 estimate was 66.08 grams (g) of CO_2 equivalents (CO_2e) per kilowatt hour (kWh) (the highest was 288g CO_2e/kWh), which is consistent with more recent research on the subject (e.g., Sheldon et al. 2015; Zafrilla et al. 2014). It is also important to realize that nuclear plants are not all the same. Lower life cycle greenhouse gas emissions have been noted for those nuclear power generation systems that recycle plutonium in comparison to those nuclear power generation systems that do not. Similarly, the life cycle greenhouse gas emissions from nuclear power generation systems utilizing low quality uranium ore grades, which require greater levels of energy intensity, tend to be higher than those systems using high quality uranium ore grades (Kadiyala et al. 2016).

This is still far better than, say, coal's CO_2 life cycle, which has been estimated to range from 1,000g CO_2e/kWh (Gagnon et al. 2002) to as high as 1,426g CO_2e/kWh (Kiss and Rajovic 2015). Yet when compared to the CO_2 life-cycle footprint of wind and solar power, which according to a recent review of 153 life-cycle analyses places the means at

IMAGE 9.2 Underground Exploratory Studies Facility at Yucca Mountain

Source: Courtesy of the Department of Energy.

Note
The underground Exploratory Studies Facility at Yucca Mountain in Nevada built by the US Department of Energy to determine whether the location was suitable as a deep geological nuclear waste repository.

34.11 g CO_2e/kWh and 49.91 g CO_2e/kWh, respectively (Nugent and Sovacool 2014), nuclear comes up short.

Nuclear power is also expensive. Even with massive government subsidies, nuclear power remains uneconomical. One study calculates US subsidies to nuclear power to be 140 percent of the average wholesale price of power from this source (Koplow 2011). Nuclear power is struggling to survive as "alternative" energy sources (like wind and solar) move into the realm of "proven energy sources". As a result, the money being spent by the industry to lobby for increased government help is increasing. A recent report looking specifically at Pennsylvania shows that in 2018 Exelon Corporation—the owner of nuclear plants in the state—significantly increased its spending on lobbying compared to the previous five election cycles. Its spending in the state rose from an average of just over $646,000 per year between 2008 and 2016 to nearly $1.8 million in 2018 (Hullinger 2019). This lobbying appears to be working, as bills have emerged in numerous US states (e.g., Ohio, Pennsylvania) subsidizing zero-emissions energy. But here is the catch: nuclear power is being highlighted specifically (though not exclusively) for these zero-emission subsidies (Millsap

FIGURE 9.1 Range and Mean of CO$_2$ during the Life Cycle of Nuclear Power

A bar chart titled with y-axis "g CO$_2$e/kWh" ranging from 0 to 300. Bars and mean values (marked by X):
- Front end: bar to ~125, mean 25.09
- Construction: bar to ~35, mean (X)
- Operation: bar to ~45, mean 11.58
- Backend: bar to ~38, mean (X)
- Decommissioning: bar to ~57, mean 12.01
- Total: bar to ~277, mean 66.08

Source: Adapted principally from Sovacool (2008) with various data points corroborated by Kadiyala et al. (2016) and Serp et al. (2017).

Note
The mean is signified by the X and the corresponding number, in g CO$_2$e/kWh (grams of CO$_2$ equivalents per kilowatt hour).

 MOVEMENT MATTERS 9.1

The Fight over Local Control

In light of numerous instances where state governments outlawed local governments from controlling whether they allow fracking in their backyards (try Googling "Denton, Texas" and "fracking ban"), Colorado, as of summer 2019, is moving toward enacting a state law that expressly allows local governments to do precisely that. The bill also alters the authority of the Colorado Oil and Gas Conservation Commission (COGCC), changing the description of its duties from "fostering" the development of oil and gas to "regulating" it (Abbott 2019). Erin Martinez's husband and brother were killed in a 2017 home explosion in Firestone, Colorado, as the result of a leaky oil and gas flowline. She made a public appearance in Denver in the spring of 2019 to advocate for the bill's passage. In her words,

I'm here to support change that will hopefully keep this from ever happening again. No one should have to experience what my family has gone through the past two years.... I understand no one ever intended this to happen. I have no desire to destroy an industry. However, with great tragedy should also come great change.

(quoted in Abbott 2019)

CASE STUDY 9.3

Fukushima Nuclear Disaster as "Normal Accident"

A magnitude 9 earthquake struck Japan on March 11, 2011, quickly followed by a devastating tsunami that rose to a peak of 40 meters. Together, these events left 20,000 people dead or missing and 125,000 buildings destroyed (Watts 2011). They also triggered a third disaster: the multiple meltdowns of three reactors at the Fukushima Daiichi nuclear plant, which ultimately released more radiation than any accident since the meltdown at Chernobyl in 1986, though a growing number of scientists say that the total release at Fukushima is worse than even this event (McNeill 2011).

Charles Perrow's (1984) book *Normal Accidents* helps us think through events like the Fukushima nuclear disaster. Rather than ascribe the event to isolated equipment malfunction, operator error, or random acts of nature, Perrow makes the case that technological failures like what happened in Japan are the product of complex interacting systems. In this particular case, the root cause of failure lies in the tremendous complexity of nuclear plants. These "high-risk systems," as Perrow calls them, are inherently prone to failure regardless of how well they are managed or regulated. We therefore have two choices. One option is to radically redesign the systems to marginally reduce their complexity, by, say, moving the spent storage pools away from the site of power generation (Pidgeon 2011). The other option, which is also the surest way of avoiding these **normal accidents**, would be to abandon the technology entirely in favor of something less prone to catastrophic malfunction. A normal accident speaks of a failure that is inevitable, given the manner in which particular human and technological systems are organized. Extending this concept, might we call some of today's most pressing environmental problems—most notably global climate change—normal accidents?

2019). It's a pretty savvy move: a way to support a relatively unpopular energy generation platform (i.e., nuclear power) by creating a bill framed as subsidizing something that nearly everyone supports.

In a study examining the cost of nuclear power relative to electricity generated from coal, natural gas, and wind, nuclear power was found to be roughly 33 percent more expensive than coal, 20 percent more expensive than natural gas, and approximately the same price as electricity generated from wind (Boccard 2014). The technology also carries with it inherent—and to some degree incalculable—risks, not just of meltdown but of others related to weapons proliferation and the threat of terrorists targeting nuclear facilities. These realities further increase its costs, as expensive steps have to be taken to secure not only nuclear facilities but also the transportation of nuclear waste (see Case Study 9.3).

Solutions

Ten years ago I couldn't have been as optimistic as I am today about energy generation. We have known for a long time that, theoretically, there's more potential renewable energy on this planet than we know what to do with. A popular statistic along these lines is that every hour, the energy equivalent to what all of humankind uses in an entire year strikes the Earth's surface in the form of solar energy (Gilding 2011). Of course, we're a long way from capturing even a sizable fraction of this renewable energy. The point is that we can do it. It's now a matter of turning the technologically *possible* into the socially, economically, and politically *probable*.

Efficiency and Curtailment

For decades, the principal solution to the energy problem was conservation and sacrifice. In the late 1970s, President Jimmy Carter famously appeared on national television calling for energy conservation while wearing a sweater and sitting in front of a fireplace, a visual image that then presidential candidate Ronald Reagan later exploited when he argued that "energy conservation is being too cold in the winter and too warm in the summer" (quoted in Kempton et al. 1985, 131). And, to a significant degree, the mantra of sacrifice continues to be widely evoked among environmentalists. For example, of the seventy-seven "essential" skills touted to stop climate change in *The Life Earth Global Warming Survival Handbook* (Rothschild 2007), just three deal with efficiency-increasing actions. What's curious about these solutions is that comparisons of energy saved by curtailment versus those saved by increased efficiency show that the latter generally win out (Kastner and Stern 2015). While "turning out lights when leaving the room" continues to be parroted to our children, the evidence indicates that our focus might be better placed elsewhere.

I will be the first to admit that our energy problem will not be solved through efficiency gains alone (see Chapter 10, where the rebound effect and Jevons paradox are discussed). Yet as a pragmatic environmentalist, I think it is a mistake to ignore the low-hanging fruits that are socio-technological solutions, so long as they do not get in the way of deeper socioecological change. If you had a very high temperature from an infection, you would treat the fever as well as the infection, wouldn't you? For the moment, let's talk about ways we can tinker with our consumption of energy at the margins and save the discussion of systemic change for later chapters.

Take the compact fluorescent lightbulb (CFL). The average life of a CFL is between eight and fifteen times that of the traditional incandescent bulb but uses only 20 to 33 percent of the power of an equivalent incandescent—a truly remarkable gain in efficiency over the old lighting technology. Let's compare CFL and incandescent bulbs over a twelve-year period. During that time, you can either purchase fifteen incandescent bulbs and 1,500 kilowatt hours of electricity and spend roughly $225, or buy one CFL and 300 kilowatt hours of electricity at a cost of about $45. Yet the savings of CFLs pale when compared to the savings that could be had elsewhere through efficiency enhancements. The share of total world energy use (in 2017) by sector breaks down as follows: industrial, 55 percent; transportation, 18 percent; residential, 17 percent; and commercial, 11 percent (EIA 2017). I'm not saying we should leave lights on in empty rooms, just that we need to turn off those lights and still do more—so much more.

One problem is that the average person does not fully understand how their actions use or save energy. A variety of surveys have asked people to report their perceptions of energy consumption and savings for various household, transportation, and recycling activities (e.g., Attari et al. 2010; Wolske and Stern 2018; Zhang et al. 2018). The research is pretty clear: the majority of respondents ranked curtailment, like turning off lights and driving less, above efficiency improvements, such as installing more efficient appliances and windows. One especially ingenious study attempted to compare perceived energy used or saved with actual energy used/saved (Attari et al. 2010). The results of this research are illustrated in Figure 9.2. Although respondents' answers were close to accurate for less energy-intensive technologies and behavior, they *grossly underestimated* the energy consumption of appliances such as clothes washers, central air-conditioning systems, clothes dryers, and dishwashers. Take the case of lowering the hot water temperature in one's washing machine. Participants, on average, reported savings of less than 100 watt-hours. The actual savings is closer to 7,000 watt-hours.

Individuals also gave inaccurate answers when asked to compare consumption and savings related to transportation. For example, they significantly overestimated the savings attributable to reducing one's driving speed from seventy to sixty miles per hour for sixty miles. Conversely, they drastically underestimated—by almost a factor of ten—the energy savings derived from having their car tuned up twice a year. Pointing to these deficiencies in individuals' knowledge about energy consumption and savings, the study cited above concludes that "the serious deficiencies highlighted by these results suggest that well-designed efforts to improve the public's understanding of energy use and savings could pay large dividends" (Attari et al. 2010, 16054).

Studies indicate that public understanding of energy use could be enhanced by merely changing how we talk about certain phenomena. Take, for example, how we in the United States talk about energy use as it pertains to automobiles: as a ratio of volume of

FIGURE 9.2 Mean Perceptions of Energy Used or Saved versus Actual Energy Used or Saved

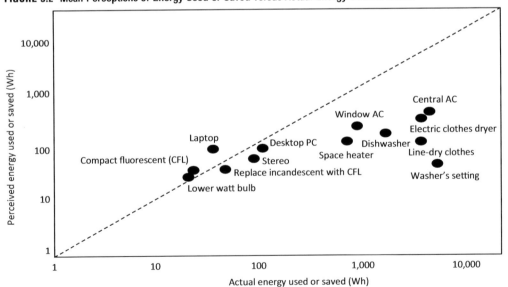

Source: Adapted from Attari et al. (2010).

Note
Wh: watt hours. The diagonal dashed line represents perfect accuracy.

consumption to a unit of distance—or specifically miles per gallon (mpg). Whereas people think that the amount of gas consumed by an automobile decreases as a linear function of a car's mpg, the actual relationship is curvilinear (see Figure 9.3). In one study, 171 participants from a national pool were given the following scenario:

> A town maintains a fleet of vehicles for town employee use. It has two types of vehicles. Type A gets 15 miles per gallon. Type B gets 34 miles per gallon. The town has 100 Type A vehicles and 100 Type B vehicles. Each car in the fleet is driven 10,000 miles per year.
>
> (Larrick and Soll 2008, 1594)

They were then asked to select a plan for replacing vehicles with the end goal of reducing overall gas consumption. Seventy-eight participants were given the following two options (framed in mpg terms): replace the 100 vehicles that get 15 mpg with vehicles that get 19 mpg, or replace the 100 vehicles that get 34 mpg with vehicles that get 44 mpg. Seventy-five percent chose the second option, which offers the largest gain in mpg *but not the greatest fuel savings*.

The remaining participants were given a policy choice framed in terms of gallons per 100 miles (gpm). This group was told that the town "translates miles per gallon into how many gallons are used per 100 miles. Type A vehicles use 6.67 gallons per 100 miles. Type B vehicles use 2.94 gallons per 100 miles" (Larrick and Soll 2008, 1594). Then they

FIGURE 9.3 Gallons of Gas Used per 10,000 Miles Driven

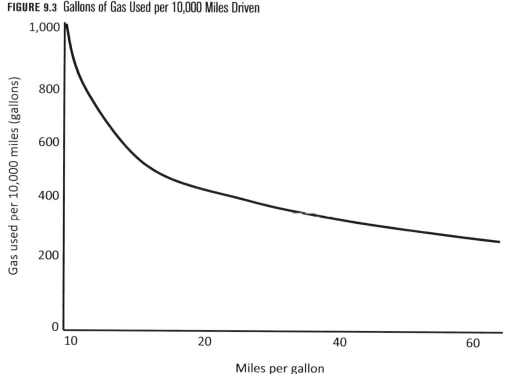

Source: Adapted from Larrick and Soll (2008).

were given the same choices as the other group, though these options were expressed in gpm, as opposed to mpg, terms. The percentage choosing the more fuel-efficient option increased from 25 percent in the mpg frame to 64 percent in the gpm frame. Based on this, the authors of the study conclude that whereas "mpg is useful for estimating the range of a car's gas tank, gpm allows consumers to understand exactly how much gas they are using on a given car trip or in a given year" (Larrick and Soll 2008, 1594; see ECOnnection 9.4).

Renewables

The current global power demand is about 18 terawatts (TW) (Marvel et al. 2013). If, however, the planet was powered by wind, solar, geothermal, tidal, and hydroelectric power, with no fossil-fuel or biomass combustion (that's right, *none*), something rather interesting would occur. Global power consumption would be considerably less, likely below 14 TW (Jacobson and Delucchi 2009). How can the power-generating *method* impact consumption levels? The decline is due to the fact that, in most cases, electrification is a more efficient way to use energy. To take just one example: whereas roughly 18 percent of the energy in gasoline is used to move a vehicle (the vast majority is lost as

ECOnnection 9.4

Social Sciences and Energy Transitions

Paul Stern (2017) wrote an influential paper a few years back titled, "How Can Social Science Research Become More Influential in Energy Transitions." Since then, a growing body of research has emerged identifying principles that could help change related human behavior related to energy consumption. Some of the findings related to that scholarship are summarized below.

- Even with strong financial incentives, marketing is often needed to convince target households to consider major actions. This includes informal marketing through social networks (e.g., peer-to-peer types of campaigns).
- To be effective, information about the choice and its benefits should be kept

simple, as well as valid and credible. Information should also include attributes of the choice that are important to consumers but absent from economic analyses (e.g., effects on comfort, well-being, home appearance, peer adoption rates).
- Make adoption easy: minimize paperwork; instant rebates are better than mail-order rebates; rebates are more convenient than tax credits; and tax credits are more convenient than loan-based programs.
- Programs are more effective when they provide credible quality assurance where adopters are given confidence that they will see the benefits that are promised, perhaps by offering contractual guarantees of performance for renewable energy systems.

Adapted from Stern (2017), Stern et al. (2018), and Wolske and Stern (2018).

heat), somewhere between 75 to 86 percent of the electricity delivered to an electric car is used to create motion.

Earlier I mentioned how every hour the energy equivalent of what humankind uses in an entire year strikes the Earth's surface as solar energy. Clearly, some of that solar radiation—such as that falling on open seas and atop remote mountains—cannot be captured in a cost-effective manner. Yet even when these and wind-deficient areas are subtracted, humanity is still left with plenty. For example, a team of scientists from the Lawrence Livermore National Laboratory calculated that wind turbines placed on the Earth's surface could extract at least 400 TW annually, whereas high-altitude wind power (suspending airborne kite-like turbines hundreds or even thousands of feet off the ground) could extract more than 1,800 TW (Marvel et al. 2013). As of 2018, wind contributes to slightly over 5 percent of the world's electricity portfolio (Global Energy Yearbook 2018).

Incentivizing Renewables and Household Efficiency

We can do so much more than we currently are doing to shift from a society based on fossil fuels to one based on renewable energy. Governments of affluent nations are spending tens of millions of dollars annually in renewable research and development (R&D). But relative to other expenditures, this is a remarkably small sum. According to the American Association for the Advancement of Science, the United States spent $4.36 billion on nondefense energy research in 2012. The good news is that this is more than twice the amount from a decade ago, adjusted for inflation—still considerably less, however, than what the government was spending in the late 1970s at the height of the energy crisis. The bad news: that's a fraction of the federal budget for health and space research and a really small fraction of what the Pentagon spent on defense and international security assistance (more than $700 billion). And the ugly news: funding for energy-related research has *dropped* globally since 2012 (IEA 2017).

A **carbon tax** is one widely discussed strategy to disincentivize the use of fossil fuels—especially coal—for electricity generation. The rationale behind such a tax is fairly simple. A carbon tax would make the market price of this fossil fuel more accurately reflect its true cost, for, as discussed earlier, electricity generated from this nonrenewable is currently incorrectly priced (to use standard economic parlance), as many of its real costs—such as to the environment and public health—are presently not accounted for. In other words, these costs are currently treated as an **externality** (a cost or benefit not transmitted through prices and incurred by a party who did not agree to the action causing the cost or benefit). It is also clear that coal-plant owners will only invest in technologies such as carbon capture and storage if they are convinced the price of carbon is going to remain high long enough to justify the additional expense associated with these facilities. A carbon tax would signal to investors that "cheap" (incorrectly priced) coal is a thing of the past and that investments in carbon capture make sense—and cents.

It is less clear, however, if a carbon tax would change consumer behavior (see ECOnnection 9.5). Households historically have not responded to rising energy prices by making sufficient energy-efficiency investments. Part of the reason for this is because, as stated earlier, people on average poorly estimate how their actions consume or save electricity. (I mentioned previously how individuals tend to overemphasize curtailment over efficiency improvements.) This is in part because efficiency improvements—such as installing new windows or buying new energy-efficient appliances—almost always require out-of-pocket costs, whereas curtailment (like turning lights off) costs nothing. A carbon tax, by making energy more expensive in the short term (before renewables catch up), could conceivably cause individuals to place even more emphasis on curtailment. As rising energy costs would no doubt be at the forefront of consumers' minds—the media love to remind people when these are increasing—this would likely cause people to become even more vigilant about turning things off. Conversely, efficiency improvements might be seen as an expense that cannot be afforded at the moment. I see it all the time. As more of their pay checks are redirected toward paying for rising energy costs, the last thing many consumers want to do is to spend even more money on, say, heating and cooling their homes by investing in a high-efficiency furnace or so-called high-performance windows, even though those short-term costs will eventually pay for themselves (many times over) in the long run.

There is an old saying that has been evoked in different forms over the centuries—from such diverse sources as Christianity, Eastern philosophy, and even Shakespeare—about how the depths of darkness also house the most brilliant light. There are clearly many ways that this can be interpreted. The one that interests me here is the environmental

ECOnnection 9.5
Social Norms and Behavior

The power of **social norms** tends to get properly emphasized in introductory sociology classes, but then, for some reason, it gets forgotten about in upper-level social science courses. The truth is social norms matter—a lot. Street musicians know this. So do baristas at coffee shops. That's why they put money into their guitar cases and tip jars: we know that when other people are doing something, the rest of us are more likely to follow. To be really effective, however, they should take it a step further and have a friend come by every few minutes and drop a dollar in. Why? The one predictor of giving money to a street musician is being near a person who gave money.

How many times have you been in a hotel and read the following message: "Please reuse your towel and help us save the environment"? If you're like me, you've come across it too many times to count. And yet we know from experimental evidence that this is a terribly ineffective message (see, e.g., Goldstein et al. 2008). So what works? Telling people that the average person actually does reuse their towels. For example, "More than 75 percent of the people in this hotel room reused their towels." We typically like to think of ourselves as normal, especially in relationship to our personally perceived reference groups. If we think our reference group is doing X, then we are more likely to start doing X too. One of the problems is that we're so caught up in changing people's attitudes—making them "think more ecologically"—that we're missing what really motivates us most of the time. Yes, we do some things because we feel deeply connected to X. But more often, the reasons for our behaviors are more mundane.

Source: Adapted from Cross (2014).

sociological interpretation. Namely, there is value in delving into the problems that plague us, for only through an understanding of their roots are lasting and real solutions proposed. Thus far, we've covered a lot of terrain that has encompassed both problems and solutions. But I dare say we have yet to roll up our sleeves and discuss what it is about how we organize society that makes environmental problems so prevalent. That changes in the proceeding chapters. The following section of the book goes to depths yet to be explored in the hope of uncovering that light of understanding that we'll need to organize a truly sustainable society.

IMPORTANT CONCEPTS

- clean coal
- energy curtailment versus efficiency
- hydraulic fracturing (aka fracking)
- normal accident
- nuclear power life cycle

DISCUSSION QUESTIONS

1. The process of shifting away from certain energy sources and toward others will create winners and losers as, for instance, jobs move out of one region and into another. What becomes of the "losers" (like rural coal-mining communities) in a so-called green economy?
2. I have had people tell me that even if fracking does negatively affect those living near wells, we shouldn't place their interests above those of society. Some contaminated wells are a small price to pay for cheap, domestically produced energy, they tell me. What's your response to such a position?
3. Why are governments not investing more in renewable R&D? Or should research into renewable energy be entirely left up to the private sector?
4. What are things either you or your parents have done to reduce your household's energy footprint? Why have you done what you did? Moreover, what has kept you (or your parents) from taking other steps?

SUGGESTED ADDITIONAL READINGS

Bugden, D., and R. Stedman. 2018. "Rural Landowners, Energy Leasing, and Patterns of Risk and Inequality in the Shale Gas Industry." *Rural Sociology*, 84(3): 459–488. https://doi.org/10.1111/ruso.12236.

Mayer, A., and S. Malin. 2019. "How Should Unconventional Oil and Gas Be Regulated? The Role of Natural Resource Dependence and Economic Insecurity." *Journal of Rural Studies*, 65: 79–89.

Stern, P.C. 2017. "How Can Social Science Research Become More Influential in Energy Transitions?" *Energy Research & Social Science*, 26: 91–95.

Williams, L., P. Macnaghten, R. Davies, and S. Curtis. 2015. "Framing 'Fracking': Exploring Public Perceptions of Hydraulic Fracturing in the United Kingdom." *Public Understanding of Science*, July 13.

RELEVANT INTERNET LINKS

- www.eia.gov/countries. US Energy Information Administration. This site offers a wealth of energy-related data for more than 200 countries.
- www.iaea.org. International Atomic Energy Agency. Information relating to nuclear power.
- www.thewindpower.net. An extensive global wind-turbine and wind-farm database.
- www.ucsusa.org. Union of Concerned Scientists' site on clean energy. Publications available for download and blogs.

SUGGESTED VIDEOS

- *Fracking in America* (2012). A critical look at the politics behind fracking in the United States.
- *Fractured Earth* (2015). A short but impassioned documentary about the impact of fracking in rural Pennsylvania.
- *GasHole* (2011). Film about the history of oil and existing viable alternatives to fossil fuels.
- *Gasland* (2010). An exposé of the widespread water pollution resulting from hydraulic fracturing.
- *Happening: A Clean Energy Revolution* (2017). The filmmaker embarks on a journey across the United States to meet pioneers of clean energy technology.
- *Inside Chernobyl* (2012). A film based on current conditions in Chernobyl and Pripyat, where the Soviet government tried to cover up a catastrophic nuclear accident.
- *Momenta* (2013). An environmental conservation film looking at communities in the Pacific Northwest and their fight against the coal export industry.
- *Reinventing Power: America's Renewable Energy Boom* (2018). Takes viewers across the United States to hear directly from the people making a clean energy future achievable.
- *The Cleantech Future* (2012). Explores what it takes to live in a clean world, a world where energy is 100 percent renewable, where water is no longer polluted, and where transportation is green.
- *The Ethics of Fracking* (2014). This documentary assesses all the costs that come with this form of energy extraction.
- *The Future of Energy* (2015). Set in Greensburg, Kansas, with a population of just under 1,000. In 2007, a tornado struck the town. The community decided to rebuild by harnessing the same power that was once the cause of its destruction: wind. Today, Greensburg is entirely powered by renewable wind energy.
- *The Last Drop* (2011). A story about the tar sands in the Canadian wilderness.
- *The Last Mountain* (2010). A remarkable exposé of the threats of coal mining and corporate greed on human, community, and environmental health.
- *The Next Wave* (2013). A look at some of the aftermaths of the disaster in Fukushima, Japan. Testing authorized by the government has detected a frightening spike in the occurrence of thyroid cancer in Fukushima children, and while doctors are unwilling to draw an authoritative link between the cancer and the nuclear radiation that spewed from the hazardous power plant, they're genuinely worried.
- *The Spill* (2010). www.pbs.org/wgbh/papges/frontline/the-spill. An investigation into the trail of problems—accidents, deaths, spills, and safety violations—that have long plagued the oil and energy company BP. Could the 2010 disaster in the Gulf of Mexico have been prevented?
- *Uranium: Is It a Country?* (2011). Highlights the opportunities and risks posed by nuclear energy, while paying particular attention to the costs of uranium mining.

Part III

ORGANIZING A SUSTAINABLE SOCIETY

Political Economy: Making Markets Fair and Sustainable

In his 1865 book, *The Coal Question*, in a chapter titled "Of the Economy of Fuel," William Stanley Jevons highlights the paradox of how the rising efficiency of coal used in production was associated with rising coal consumption. The Jevons paradox is based on a not-so-paradoxical principle: any time the cost of consuming a resource is reduced, people will respond by consuming more of it. Its implications, however, are profound. It suggests that in our rush to save the environment and natural resources through efficiency gains, we may be unintentionally hastening their demise. A related term is *the rebound effect*, which occurs when gains in efficiency fail to lead to proportional reductions in consumption—for example, when a 20 percent gain in efficiency leads to a reduction in consumption or waste of only 10 percent. When a rebound effect is more than 100 percent of the efficiency gain, it is called a Jevons paradox (see Case Study 10.1).

The line between where a rebound effect ends and a Jevons paradox begins, however, is quite murky. Take the efficiency gains of hybrid cars. By going further on each unit of gasoline, they are making travel by car cheaper, even with rising gas prices. And whenever something becomes cheaper, we respond by doing more of it. Let's say the efficiency gains accrued by your purchasing a new hybrid car still outweigh the losses incurred by your increases in driving—perhaps you now take more road trips on weekends after buying this vehicle. What precisely do you do with those savings? If you're like most people, you take those savings and spend them on something else—a vacation to Hawaii, a new iPhone, or perhaps another vehicle. The problem is that we tend to reinvest efficiency gains in additional consumption, which arguably nullifies the ecological gain of *any* gain in efficiency (Owen 2011).

The amount of energy required, for example, to produce each unit of the world's economic output—what is known as **energy intensity**—has fallen more or less steadily over the past half century. Energy intensity in the United States is more than half what it was in 1975 (Lovins 2014). Since 1980, world real GDP, based on United States Department of Agriculture (USDA) Economic Research Institute data, has also been growing faster

CASE STUDY 10.1
Macroeconomic Rebound Effect

If you search the peer-reviewed academic literature on the rebound effect you will find a lot of research arguing that it rarely offsets the entire efficiency gains made by energy efficiency innovations (e.g., Gillingham et al. 2016). So: while I might leave the lights on more at home now, such as when our family is traveling, because we have substituted those old incandescent bulbs for today's more efficient alternatives (e.g., halogen, LED), the extra use is not enough to offset the energy saved by getting rid of that ancient lighting technology. But that is a *micro*-level look at the rebound effect.

The peer-reviewed literature on what is known as the macroeconomic rebound effect is not so clear cut, principally because it is darn hard to

model all the variables—we're talking about either the entire national or the global economy, after all. The studies that have been done on the subject appear to indicate that energy savings in one sector of the economy usually translate into increased spending, and resource consumption, someplace else in the economy. A growing number of studies are looking at the macroeconomic rebound effect in China, as that country has made significant investments in improving its energy efficiency. To quote one such study: "Our results show that there is a statistically significant macroeconomic price rebound effect for China, for each province, and for the short run, intermediate run, and the long run" (Zhang and Lawell 2017, 202).

than global energy use (based on BP Statistical Data). That is to say, global energy intensity has been decreasing, on average, about 0.8 percent annually. Meanwhile, global **carbon intensity**—the amount of CO_2 emitted for each unit of economic output produced—fell by an average of roughly 1 percent a year from 2000 to 2014.

This is great—right? It would be, if subsequent increases in productivity were not occurring faster than the aforementioned efficiency gains. To put it simply, while we are producing each unit more efficiently, we are also producing so many more units that we've more than offset any gains in efficiency (see Figure 10.1). Thus, even with those aforementioned reductions in carbon and energy intensities, global CO_2 emissions are projected to increase, according to BP estimates—yes, *that* BP (not known for its climate change doom and gloom messaging)—by 25 percent between 2013 and 2035 (BP 2015). It seems we need to develop a language whereby we clearly differentiate between two distinct types of efficiencies. There is, on the one hand, *relative efficiency*, which refers to the well-documented decreasing (per unit) intensities. But there is also, on the other, and this is where real sustainability resides, *absolute efficiency*, which refers to a reduction in total throughput and emissions. From a long-term sustainability perspective, what good is the former if we continue to increase our overall impact on the environment?

Don't get me wrong: it is not that we should entirely discount relative efficiency gains. We must not confuse them, however, with absolute efficiency gains. Otherwise, we risk what I like to call **efficiency shifting**: namely, when money and resources saved through energy efficiency, such as from placing solar panels on the roof of a manufacturing plant, merely get shifted to and consumed by other goods and services, like increases in the use

FIGURE 10.1 Carbon Intensity and Meeting Climate Change Goals

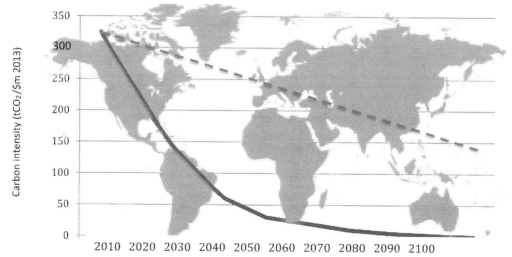

Source: Adapted from PWC (2019).

Note

At current rates of reducing carbon intensity—roughly 0.8 percent annually (signified by the dashed line)—we would be heading toward the IPCC's worst projected scenario, leading to a significant change (exceeding 4°C of warming). To meet the global carbon emission goal of limiting warming to 2°C the global economy needs to reduce carbon intensity by 6.2 percent a year *every year* between now and 2100 (signified by the solid line). Doing that will mean the global energy system will be essentially zero carbon by the end of this century.

of air travel for shipping or business-related travel. Another example: industry-level efficiencies gains in the United States or United Kingdom that occur merely because those countries, through regulations, pushed polluting companies and industrial practices into other countries. We see this shifting happen all the time. The money saved by homeowners through energy savings is used, for example, to buy more energy-using gadgets. Or note how the efficiency gains in the internal combustion engine made during the latter half of the twentieth century led to larger vehicles, ultimately giving birth to the sport utility vehicle (SUV) boom in the late 1990s.

Richard York and Shannon Bell (2019) make an important distinction, noting that there is a fundamental difference between developing the infrastructure for a new energy source (such as, say, wind and solar) and transitioning away from established energy sources. As they write,

> History shows us that although new energy sources have been successfully added to the global energy system and have grown to provide a large share of the overall energy supply, it is entirely *unprecedented* for these additions to cause a sustained decline in the use of established energy sources.
>
> (York and Bell 2019, 41; emphasis in original)

Figures 10.2 and 10.3 present the historical data backing up their claim. Figure 10.2 shows the various energy transitions (or more accurately, energy *additions*) over the last

FIGURE 10.2 Various Energy Transitions over the Last 200 Years

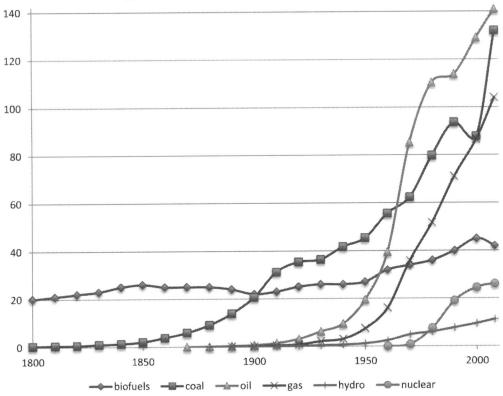

200 years. Figure 10.3 presents total global energy consumption in exajoules from numerous sources during that same time period. As we can see, no energy source has undergone a huge decline in consumption—e.g., we use twice as much biofuel now compared to when it was the principle energy source, while coal consumption has tripled since it was king back in the early part of the twentieth century. Hence, in York and Bell's (2019, 41) words, "There were not transitions away from established energy sources, but rather additions of new energy sources on top of established ones."

This chapter, like those that follow, goes deeper than the ones preceding it. It does not take a professional sociologist, ecologist, or economist to realize there is something profoundly amiss with the current system, that the path we are presently on is fundamentally unsustainable, and that real social change is needed. What that current system is and how it might be changed are the subjects of this chapter and the remaining ones. I begin by outlining the structures of the current system while also taking time in the "Solutions" section to reorient us toward more sustainable directions.

Fast Facts

- **Natural capital** is not like typical capital assets such as bridges, roads, buildings, and machinery. Like capital assets, ecosystems depreciate when misused or overused. But they also differ from reproducible capital assets in three important ways (Dasgupta 2006). First, depreciated natural capital is often either slow to recover, like a polluted lake, or irreparable,

FIGURE 10.3 Total Global Energy Consumption in Exajoules from Numerous Countries over Last 200 Years

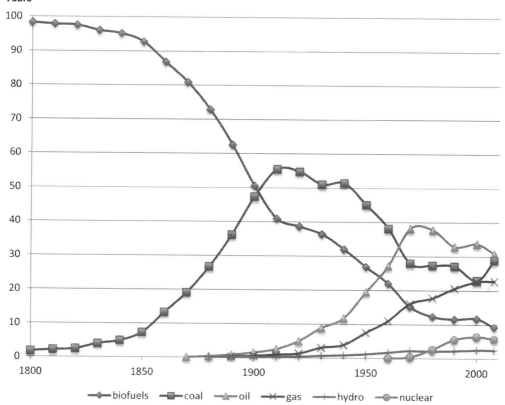

such as a species extinction. Second, it is often difficult to substitute one depleted or exhausted ecosystem or ecosystem service for another. It would be impossible, for example, to replace the pollination services provided by bees. And third, ecosystems can collapse abruptly, with little prior warning.

- While we tend to look to technology-based efficiency gains, let us not forget that economies waste resources when people distrust each other (e.g., distrust fosters hoarding, zero-sum thinking, and selfishness) (Jha 2019). Healthy social institutions, checks on government that limit corruption, and policy and norms that encourage social inclusion and creativity tend to attract investment, encourage innovation, and foster social and economic collaboration.

- The World Bank now measures the "true wealth" of nations, realizing that economies are built on economic and natural capital, as well as what they call "intangible" productive capital (e.g., human and social capital) (World Bank 2011; see also, e.g., Servaes and Tamayo, 2017). The World Bank calculates that this intangible capital may constitute as much as 80 percent of total wealth in most affluent nations.

Implications

Although environmental sociologists do not speak with one voice, they do share the belief that business as usual is not an option. Economic growth is not only portrayed as the ideal contraceptive, as discussed earlier when talking about population, but cast as *the* cure-all elixir to whatever social or environmental ill might be ailing us. Are progress, prosperity, and well-being positively correlated with—and thus essentially reducible to— economic growth? And can economic growth go on indefinitely? These are empirical questions. In the chapters that remain, I look to see what the data have to say about economic growth, as to whether it's the cure, disease, or something in between.

In this chapter, I address a significant body of environmental sociology's theoretical core, particularly that which offers an explicit critique of the present system's unsustainable growth imperative. In doing this, I avoid subscribing to any totalizing narratives. Many of my colleagues, for example, feel strongly about chalking up most of the environment's (and humanity's) ills to capitalism. Although I agree with many of their central points, I don't find it particularly helpful to place blame without also offering pragmatic alternatives. Without well thought out alternatives, I am not convinced any of our problems would be solved by merely doing away with capitalism, an admittedly problematic mode of production. Moreover, echoing a point I made in Chapter 1, I am not convinced that any one thing is responsible for the mess we're in—an argument I intend to bolster in the remaining chapters. But I don't wish to minimize these scholars' valuable contributions: they are correct in highlighting the inherent problems associated with how we presently organize society and allocate its resources.

The Growth Imperative

Capitalism, as currently practiced, makes growth an imperative rather than an option. Any business seeking to maintain its place in the market rather than grow will be hastily eliminated from the market by its competitors. Going without economic growth for any length of time causes the entire global macroeconomic edifice to shake. Under this scenario, debts go unpaid, credit subsequently dries up, unemployment skyrockets, and the previously mentioned circular engine of growth begins to stall. And (infinite) growth *needs* (infinite) resources. By every aggregate measure, even with the aforementioned relative efficiencies, our impact upon the environment (our net throughput) is increasing.

The hope—the *only* hope—for the status quo lies in something called **decoupling**, which refers to the ability of an economy to grow without corresponding increases in environmental pressures. Through decoupling, production processes are radically reconfigured and goods and services radically redesigned until economic output becomes entirely independent of material throughput. Right now, the two—economic output and material throughput—are tightly coupled: an increase in the former results in a more or less proportional increase in the latter. Only with decoupling can an economy grow indefinitely without risk of breaching ecological limits.

There is a small catch. Decoupling is looking more and more like a pipe dream. We cannot even achieve efficiency gains fast enough to offset global CO_2 increases in production and consumption. CO_2 is widely considered one of the easiest decoupling challenges for the simple reason that energy can be produced with no CO_2, as explained in Chapter 9. Compare this to, say, making a laptop with only renewable resources, which is at present an insurmountable challenge. The fact remains: energy production is tightly coupled to material resources and subsequently CO_2 emissions. So, when I come across a statistic like the fact that the average American today buys a new piece of clothing every five days, I get discouraged, as I know this growth in consumption comes with a growing ecological footprint. Global clothing production doubled in fifteen years, between the turn of the twenty-first century and 2015. During that time period, the average number of times clothing was worn before disposal declined by 36 percent—for China, the figure is 70 percent! Clothing manufacturing now contributes more greenhouse gas emissions than all global flights and maritime shipping combined. And as fast fashion is rarely recycled—it's designed to be cheap, not recyclable—its impacts extend well beyond climate change (Minter 2018).

The Treadmill of Production

The treadmill of production is one of the core theoretical frameworks in environmental sociology. Its roots extend back to Allan Schnaiberg's (1980) classic *The Environment: From Surplus to Scarcity*, where the concept is given its first thorough treatment. It is a macro-level framework, in that it places particular attention on institutions and social structures. It is also a quasi-Marxist framework. As John Bellamy Foster (2005, 7–8), a leading ecological Marxist, puts it, without directly naming "the system" at the heart of today's ecological crisis, this literature has developed the treadmill concept to the point that it has become the functional equivalent of capitalism.

According to treadmill of production scholars, modern capitalistic societies are driven by a never-ending commitment to growth, despite—and, equally, because of—its social and ecological costs. In pursuit of profit maximization, corporations are continually seeking ways to expand production. With the support of government and a complicit public, industrial production is allowed to expand, which in turn places still more demands on nature while creating growing amounts of waste. In other words, production begets more production, as all sectors of society depend on economic growth to solve the world's problems—e.g., unemployment, environmental degradation, and poverty and inequality—even though those very problems were caused, to various degrees, by growth itself. The following is a nonsequential breakdown of the treadmill logic from Schnaiberg and Gould (1994):

- Increasing accumulation and concentration of wealth as fewer businesses remain on the treadmill.
- Increasing movement of workers toward the private sector (as the public sector shrinks), thereby making it necessary to continually expand production in order to gain jobs and wages.
- Increasing allocations of wealth to businesses that replace labor with capital, which generates more profits for wealth holders and creates pressures for all wealth holders to adopt similar practices if they wish to remain competitive. This places smaller businesses, which do not have the capital to adopt these technologies, at a continual disadvantage. As smaller businesses then fall off the treadmill, wealth (first bullet point above) and market share become further concentrated.
- The net result of ever-increasing production is an ever-increasing need for greater ecological withdrawals (resource extraction and utilization) and additions (pollution).
- Societies become increasingly vulnerable to socioeconomic disorganization as their ecological resource base is undermined.

Internal Contradictions

Alongside capitalism's insatiable thirst for growth lie certain internal contradictions that threaten its very existence. Through the writings of Karl Marx, scholars have been able to identify some of these threats. Thus far, however, these contradictions have had just the opposite effect, speeding the treadmill up rather than slowing it down (or causing it to fall apart entirely). As highlighted in the previous section, capitalism has proven to be wily, using problems of its making to hasten the circular engine of growth and expand its reach, an invisible hand—to evoke Adam Smith's famous metaphor—that now extends not only around the globe but up into the heavens with the privatization of space and all the way down to the genetic level. The question remains: How long until these problems become so great, with climate change coming immediately to mind, that we can no longer turn to the market for our solutions?

Metabolic Rift

One such argument draws on some of Marx's more obscure comments on matters of economic growth and natural resource exploitation and the rift these processes create. These writings were rediscovered largely thanks to Foster (1999), who brought them to the attention of the environmental sociology community. And so was born (or reborn) the metabolic rift thesis, as it has come to be known.

Mid-nineteenth-century environmental crises—from declining agricultural soil fertility to rising levels of sewage in cities—and the equally deplorable living conditions of urban workers were linked, according to Marx, to a disruption, or rift, in a previously sustainable socioecological metabolism. This rift, for Marx, is tied to the expansion of capitalist modes of production and urbanization—the latter made possible because of the rise of the former and, in particular, the displacement of small-scale agriculture. This process created a rift in ecological systems, leading to environmental degradation at points of production and consumption as people and their waste became concentrated in cities.

Inspired by the work of German chemist Justus von Liebig and his (later in life) ecological critique of modern agricultural methods, Marx derided the problem of "soil exhaustion"—what we today would call soil depletion. At one point in Volume 1 of *Capital*, Marx ([1863] 1976, 638) writes that "all progress in capitalist agriculture is a progress in the art, not only of robbing the worker, but of robbing the soil." Concerns over soil exhaustion became rather acute in Britain in the early 1800s, arising as an important issue slightly later in North America and continental Europe in parallel with their emerging capitalist economies. Early on, the problem of diminished soil fertility was resolved by mixing into the soil guano (dung) imported from Peru, which was eventually replaced by artificial fertilizers.

During this period, soil exhaustion has been linked to the expansion of capitalism, which drew people into the cities to work in factories. As such, land had to be farmed utilizing more inputs to support a growing population and soon thereafter with machinery so a shrinking rural population could continue to farm all available arable land. Disconnecting people from the land caused major disruptions in the soil nutrient cycle in the form of too few nutrients in the countryside and far too many concentrated in cities, often in the form of sewage. The summer of 1858 in London was famously known as the summer of the Big Stink, as the smell of the River Thames was so foul that lawmakers were forced to flee Parliament for the countryside. These disruptions reeked both ecological and social havoc, a point Marx witnessed firsthand in London, where "they can do nothing better with the excrement produced by 4½ million people than pollute the Thames with it, at monstrous expense" (Marx [1863–1865] 1981, 195). And what was the solution to this problem? Was it to repair the rift by bringing agricultural practices in line with ecological limits? No. Instead, the solution was to exacerbate the rift through artificial fertilizers—a solution that also sped up the treadmill, as those inputs had to be manufactured and purchased. This move might have resolved the problem of soil exhaustion in the short term, but it did nothing to deal with the root of the rift, as evidenced by the fact that our food continues to be produced in a fundamentally unsustainable manner.

Take the case of Spain (Lassaletta et al. 2014). During the last five decades, the country has experienced a large expansion in the nutrient cycle of its agricultural sector, which has included a threefold increase in anthropogenic nitrogen (N) inputs. The principal driver of this increase is imported feed—soybean, corn, and soy cakes—from North America and Europe to supply a growing domestic livestock population, along with an increase in synthetic fertilizer use for the feed that is produced within the country. And driving that are changing consumption patterns, which have evolved from a Mediterranean diet to an animal-protein-rich diet. While the nitrogen load exported out of the country by its rivers is very low (6.5 percent of the total net N input), the authors conclude "the Spanish mainland is suffering from considerable pollution by local emissions of reactive nitrogen forms to air and water" (Lassaletta et al. 2014, 785). Figure 10.4

FIGURE 10.4 Nitrogen Traded from Spain to Other Countries and Vice Versa

Europe 75 $G_gN.yr^1$

North America 75 $G_gN.yr^1$

South America 517 $G_gN.yr^1$

Total import (2007): 813 GgN.yr^{-1}
Total Export : 171 GgN.yr^{-1}
Net Import-Export : 645 GgN. yr^{-1}

Net Export from Spain
> 100 GgN.yr^{-1}
10-100
5 - 10
1 - 5

Net Import to Spain
> 100 GgN.yr^{-1}
10-100
5 - 10
1 - 5

Note
$G_gN.yr$: Gigagram nitrogen per year.

illustrates the net N trades from Spain to other countries and vice versa. Note the large inflow of N (from feed imports to support livestock production) and the minuscule outflow of N, mostly to neighboring Portugal. This asymmetry reflects a Spanish agricultural system that has specialized in vegetal products with low N content (e.g., olive oil, wine, vegetables, and citrus fruit), which are largely exported.

The overarching critique of the metabolic-rift thesis is the notion that capitalism, by its nature, is slowly yet undeniably destroying the very thing it needs to survive: its material productive base (see ECOnnection 10.1). Clark and York put it as follows:

> "Metabolic rift" refers to an ecological rupture in the metabolism of a system. The natural processes and cycles (such as the soil nutrient cycle) are interrupted. The division between town and country is a particular geographical manifestation of the metabolic rift, in regards to the soil nutrient cycle. But the essence of a metabolic rift is *the rupture or interruption of a natural system.*
>
> (Clark and York 2005, 399; emphasis in the original)

Another Contradiction of Capitalism

Capitalism, as I've already described, has proven most resourceful. Population growth has no doubt aided its progress. There is also a geographical dimension to its success, most notably globalization. Yet, as Marx and Engels ([1848] 1978) noted so long ago, these tendencies produce contradictions, which must be resolved in some form so as not to derail the circulation of capital. And therein lies capitalism's transformational engine: these contradictions and tensions that it then "resolves." This has allowed capitalism to continue on the tracks without (yet?) a major derailing of its logics.

Marx and Engels predicted that eventually such tensions would become too much for capitalism: "The development of Modern Industry, therefore, cuts from under its feet the very foundation on which the bourgeoisie produces and appropriates productions. What the bourgeoisie, therefore, produces, above all, is its own grave-diggers" (Marx and Engels [1848] 1978, 483). The first contradiction of capitalism, as described by Marx and Engels, is overproduction—that eventually there will simply be too much stuff and not enough people able to buy it all. Logic would suggest that by continually substituting labor for capital, capitalism will eventually reach a point where low salaries and unemployment (and underemployment) will make it impossible for consumption rates to increase indefinitely. Before we reach this point, however, capitalism may hit a wall that stops it in its tracks. That's James O'Connor's thesis at least, which he calls the second contradiction of capital. Whereas the contradiction discussed by Marx and Engels centers on a crisis of demand, for O'Connor capitalism will, over time, witness a crisis of supply. This underproduction will occur as industry and the state—both of which are directed by the logics of capital—fail to protect the conditions of production, namely, the environment. "Put simply," in the words of O'Connor (1998, 245), "the second contradiction states that when individual capitals attempt to defend or restore profits by cutting or externalizing costs, the unintended effect is to reduce the 'productivity' of the conditions of production" (see ECOnnection 10.2). Or more simply still: no more resources, no more capitalism.

ECOnnection 10.1
Treadmill/Metabolic Rift: Declining Global Fish Stocks

Expansion of the capitalist enterprise into oceans has created another rift, signified by the depletion of fish stock (Longo et al. 2015; Neilson and São Marcos 2019). As natural limits are approached, new technology is required to improve productivity and (temporarily) resolve tensions. Initially, making boats faster (so they can cover more territory) and larger (so they can stay out longer) and equipping them with technology to fish deeper (so greater depths can be exploited) seemed to do the trick. For a while, these gains in efficiency helped to keep supply up and the retail price of fish down, even as global fish stocks shrunk.

These technological advances, however, did nothing to resolve the ecological tensions between capitalism and the aquatic ecosystems that are home to the world's ocean fish stock. In fact, they had precisely the opposite effect, as they sped up the treadmill. And so still more technological fixes were required. Enter capitalist aquaculture: a practice whereby fish are essentially treated like livestock. Yet the ecological limits still remain. As the most profitable farmed fish are carnivorous (e.g., Atlantic salmon), aquaculture continues to depend on wild fish, as they constitute the primary ingredient of fishmeal and fish oil. A farmed Atlantic salmon, for example, consumes four pounds of fishmeal for each one pound of live weight gain.

The treadmill of capital-intensive aquaculture is now running so fast that only a privileged few can compete in the market. A prawn farm in Queensland, Australia, for example, with all appropriate equipment, ponds, buildings, and processing facilities (*not* including land costs), is estimated to cost between AU$100,000 and AU$150,000 per hectare of pond. And the cost of an intensive pond-culture system that grows 50 tons of barramundi (also known as Asian sea bass) is AU$780,000. As the market becomes dominated by economically efficient (and ecologically inefficient) models of aquaculture, the small-scale fisher will find it increasingly difficult to remain economically viable. This is unfortunate, as the livelihoods of roughly fifty-five million people in less affluent nations are dependent on being able to sell the fish they catch.

Globalization of Environmental Goods and Bads

One myth that continues to be perpetuated is that economic growth is good for the environment. An example of a narrative supporting this myth comes from the Property and Environmental Research Center, the oldest pro-free market and private property institute in the United States. As one of the center's analysts writes, "Market forces also cause economic growth, which in turn leads to environmental improvements. Put simply, poor people are willing to sacrifice clean water and air, healthy forests, and wildlife habitat for economic growth" (Anderson 2004; see also Panayotou 2016). What this argument misses is that well-off people do this too. And when you factor in for scale of impact, the environmental footprint of the impoverished turns out to be minuscule compared to the ecological damage inflicted daily to maintain the standard of living the affluent have come to expect. This should already be perfectly clear, based on what has been discussed thus far in this book. But in case you still need a little more convincing, allow me to take on a cherished concept among growth enthusiasts: the Environmental Kuznets Curve.

Critiquing the Environmental Kuznets Curve

Simon Kuznets (1955), who won a Nobel Prize in economics in 1971, famously postulated that a country's transition from preindustrial to industrial to postindustrial initially leads to increasing income inequality, followed by greater income equality, and overall increases in per capita incomes. In the past two decades, the model was extended to environmental pollutants, as early analyses seemed to indicate that although air and water pollution levels frequently increased with initial economic growth, they eventually declined as countries reached a certain level of affluence (Dasgupta et al. 2002). This apparent pattern has come to be known as the Environmental Kuznets Curve (EKC). The EKC simply states that growth is (eventually) good for the environment. Although initially positively correlated with pollution, at some point economic growth becomes negatively associated with pollution and positively correlated with environmental quality (see Figure 10.5).

There was some early empirical support for the EKC. Grossman and Krueger (1994), for example, examined urban air pollution levels as well as water pollution for a number of countries. They found pollution indexes increased and then declined with economic affluence. In more recent years, however, the EKC has come under fire for mischaracterizing the extent of the environmental "efficiencies" that are said to be correlated with economic growth.

FIGURE 10.5 Environmental Kuznets Curve

Source: Author

ECOnnection 10.2
Capital Shaping Humans in Its Image: A Third Contradiction?

Some sociologists (e.g., Bates 2015; Dickens 2001, 2004; Namberger 2019) have applied Marx's writings in a unique way to speak about potential linkages between the biological and the social. According to one sociologist of this persuasion, Peter Dickens (2001, 106), "Capitalism, in conjunction with the various forms of biological predispositions ... may over the long term have been shaping human biology in its own image." For evidence of this phenomenon, Dickens points, among other things, to epidemiological work suggesting that the effects of the mother's environment are transmitted to her unborn child. The implication is that inadequate prenatal care—which can alter normal (in developmental terms) rates of metabolism, hormonal excretion, blood flow, and the like within the uterus—can potentially lead to individuals being born physiologically disadvantaged com-

pared to those with adequate resources and capital.

Or take a study published in the *Journal of Health and Social Behavior*, which found that the urban poor in the United States are experiencing accelerated aging at the cellular level and chronic stress, which is associated with a whole host of negative health outcomes (Geronimus et al. 2015). In short, the study demonstrates that these forms of physiological deterioration are linked to socioeconomic variables, namely income level and racial and ethnic identity. This research points to interesting questions concerning the interrelationship between society and biology. Can being socially underprivileged and disadvantaged produce physiological changes that amplify those aforementioned social conditions? Perhaps. It is a question worth exploring in greater detail.

One criticism centers on what has come to be known as the Pollution Haven Hypothesis (PHH). Following the logic of comparative advantage, it is reasonable to assume that developing economies with weaker environmental regulations (and lax government enforcement of whatever regulations do exist) would attract polluting industries. Thus, the PHH posits that what we are seeing with the EKC is actually the result of polluting industry moving from developed to developing countries in search of governments more likely to ignore its activities. Though a reasonable hypothesis, it does not stand up well to empirical scrutiny. Studies have found "little" (Kearsley and Riddel 2010, 905) to at best "some" (Eskelanda and Harrison 2003, 1) evidence in support of the PHH. One major reason is that environmental costs are, for most industries, a relatively small share of overall operating costs. In other words, the benefit of being able to pollute does not typically outweigh other costs that would be incurred as a result of relocating to a haven, such as a poor infrastructure or undertrained labor force.

It is important to point out that the PHH speaks only to *emissions* associated with production, ignoring, for example, the mountains of toxic e-waste that end up being shipped annually to less developed countries to be recycled. As mentioned in Chapter 3, the evidence is mixed as to what actually gets recycled and what is landfilled or incinerated. My point is that the ecological footprint of a nation is more—*much* more—than its emissions. There is ample anecdotal evidence indicating that affluent nations are exporting their "environmental impact" (to reference the *y* axis in Figure 10.4) to other nations. We just have to look beyond industrial air emissions to find it. E-waste is only one well-publicized example. We also must realize that residents of affluent nations might also pollute *differently* from their contemporaries in lower-income nations. An example of this is air travel. Some two million people daily—or 730 million annually—fly in the United States (Burns 2010). In Indonesia, by comparison, which has roughly 75 percent of the population found in the United States, approximately 50 million flights are taken annually (Baskoro 2011). The EKC's most fatal flaw, however, resides in its mistaking *relative* efficiency for *absolute* efficiency. Technically speaking, as I tell my students, the EKC and its inverted-U curve are both right and wrong. It all depends on how you define ecoefficiency (see ECOnnection 10.3). The data on this are clear: while the most affluent nations tend to be the most ecoefficient, as measured by ecological footprint per unit of GDP, they are also guilty of having, in absolute terms, the largest ecological footprints (see, e.g., Brizga et al. 2014; Toth and Szigeti 2016).

World-Systems Framework

Another body of literature highly critical of the EKC is the world-systems approach. This tradition in environmental sociology has produced a diverse array of sophisticated analyses to assess the relationship between world-system factors and environmental impacts. The relationship between affluent (aka "core") and less affluent (aka "periphery") nations, according to this literature, is an overwhelmingly exploitative one, as the former are able to extract far greater benefits from the present system than actors residing in the latter. Studies have shown, for example, that an EKC for CO_2 emissions may be fundamentally unattainable for many periphery nations, as their position in the global economy has effectively fixed them into a particular emissions trajectory. As a result, they are locked out of being able to adopt many of the greener technologies used in affluent nations, for reasons such as lack of credit, capital, expertise, and the like (see, e.g., Rosa et al. 2015). Other research in this tradition has extensively documented the gross asymmetry between core nations, which consume the vast majority of the world's resources and produce a sizable chunk of its pollution, and those that are more peripheral, which experience the vast majority of the environmental *impacts* (see, e.g., Clark et al. 2018).

Solutions

In light of the deeply embedded nature of the problems discussed throughout this book, I ask the reader for patience as solutions are rolled out over this chapter and the remaining ones that take aim at their roots. The problems we face are complex, which is why I am certain that no single proposed solution is sufficient. The problems are products of patterns of social organization, which though deeply flawed are not irreversible. I am not offering these solutions in an either/or spirit. Put them to work *collectively*—that's the source of my pragmatic optimism.

ECOnnection 10.3
Forest Transition Theory

In the early 1990s, Alexander Mather (1990, 1992) began writing about what became known as the Forest Transition Theory (FTT). Much like the EKC, the FTT speaks to a recurring pattern that countries seem to go through as they industrialize and urbanize. First, the theory posits, they go through a process of rapid deforestation while initially industrializing. At some point, however, after ascertaining a certain level of economic development, deforestation stops and reforestation begins.

Early formulations focused almost exclusively on Europe and North America. In the past ten years, greater focus has been placed on less affluent countries. The results have been mixed. A number of studies, for instance, illustrate how agricultural retreat and forest recovery in one area typically occur only at the expense of agricultural expansion and deforestation elsewhere (see, for example, Pfaff and Walker 2010). Evidence is also beginning to emerge suggesting that reforestation, in countries fortunate enough to undergo it, may only be a temporary phase, eventually giving way to still further drivers of deforestation (e.g., Iriarte-Goñi and Ayuda 2018). This appears to be happening in the eastern portion of the United States (Drummond and Loveland 2010). After a period of reforestation, recent prospects for additional forested land have diminished, as accelerated rates of forest cutting, low-density development in the countryside, and pressures placed on land from biofuels are, once again, causing a net loss of forests in this region (see Figure 10.6).

FIGURE 10.6 Forest Cover Changes in the Eastern United States

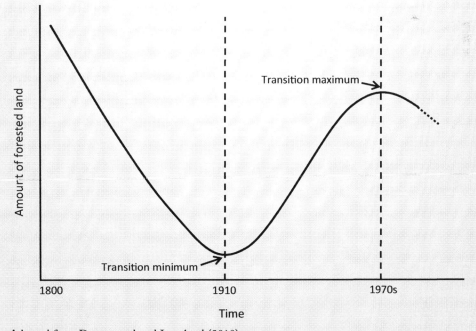

Source: Adapted from Drummond and Loveland (2010).

Total Cost Accounting

Many of the goods supplied by the environment are public in nature. A good is said to be public if it is nonrival and nonexcludable. Many ecological phenomena that we value, like biodiversity and clean air, exhibit these characteristics. Their nonrival character is evidenced by the fact that my use and enjoyment of these phenomena do not affect your use and enjoyment of them. For instance, my breathing as much clean air as I want does not affect your ability to stand next to me and enjoy the clean air too. They are also nonexcludable in the sense that it is usually rather difficult to prevent others from benefiting from their existence. Short of erecting domes around people or communities, how could you possibly make clean air excludable? Or take biodiversity, which is more problematic still from the standpoint of excludability. It benefits humanity in so many ways—from food security to the manufacturing of drugs, purifying of water, and enriching of spirit— that excludability means more than just keeping people out of a biologically diverse space.

As already discussed, the prevailing cost-price system is poorly equipped to account for damage to ecosystems and human communities. Climate change—the most significant market failure in history—is proof that current market mechanisms cannot be entrusted to protect long-term public and environmental health. Public goods tend to be underprovided—and underprotected—if left to the market, as costs are externalized and paid disproportionately by third parties, future generations, or society at large. This practice of socializing costs not only makes for a terribly unsustainable economic system but is also incredibly unfair—a point I'll elaborate on in a moment. What, then, are our options if total cost accounting (or at least more honest cost accounting) is the goal? (See Image 10.1.)

One strategy that has been around for a while is known as **Pigovian taxes**—taxes levied on companies that pollute or create excess social costs (called negative externalities). English economist Arthur Cecil Pigou (1912) argued a century ago that the existence of externalities justifies government action. He advocated for pollution-avoidance charges and welfare-damage costs (aka taxes), which would be applied to any and all offending businesses and activities. Such taxes would not only serve to disincentivize certain behaviors but also generate revenue to pay whatever costs were socialized (e.g., to clean up a polluted river), as well as any expenses associated with the administration and monitoring of businesses.

The largest problem associated with Pigovian taxes involves getting the tax rate just right. If too low, the taxes will not sufficiently disincentivize the behavior or provide sufficient revenue to pay for cleanup and enforcement; if too high, businesses will be unduly burdened for costs that are not their own. Relatedly, information in these matters is always imperfect. For instance, when dealing with nonpoint-source pollution—like greenhouse gases—how can we be sure we're not overcharging some and undercharging others?

A notable challenge to the logic of Pigovian taxes came from economist Ronald Coase (1960), who argued that well-defined property rights to resources would nullify the need for government intervention and save society the inevitable efficiencies associated with antipollution taxes, noting the difficulty of getting tax rates just right. Coase's argument— or what is known today as the **Coase theorem**—alleges that when property rights are involved, parties naturally gravitate toward the most efficient and mutually beneficial

IMAGE 10.1 Melbourne Solidarity Rally for Global #ClimateStrike #Fridays4Future Organised by #ExtinctionRebellion.

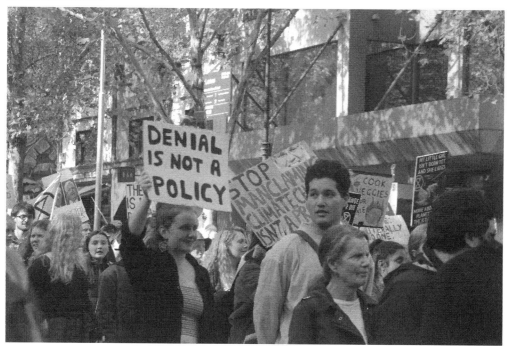

Source: "Melbourne Solidarity Rally for Global #ClimateStrike—Denial Is Not a Policy" by Takver (flickr.com/takver) is licensed copyright © 2019 under CC BY-SA 2.0.

Note
Several thousand people rallied outside the Victorian Parliament House before marching. This culminated in a mass die-in at the corner of Bourke and Swanston streets in the heart of Melbourne CBD. The march then proceeded up to Carlton Gardens.

outcome. Suppose a livestock producer holds the right to a stream (and thus the right—within limits—to pollute this stream) that a neighboring food processor draws its water from. Knowing precisely who owns what allows these individuals to negotiate an outcome that is suitable to both. The food processor has an incentive to pay the livestock producer to treat its wastewater, as long as that cost is less than the cost of treating its intake water. The livestock producer also has an incentive to accept payment, especially as it has an opportunity to profit from its waste. This is because the cost to the livestock producer of treating its concentrated manure will likely be less than the cost to the food processor of treating its more diluted intake water.

Unfortunately, real life is more complicated than idealized scenarios. What if there are thousands of competing businesses with interests in this outcome? What does the negotiating process look like, and how do we ensure all parties' interests are heard? Moreover, who decides what's sufficiently "clean" when talking about treating water? I promise you that a brewery's definition is astronomically stricter than a steel refinery's. There is also space to justify species extinction under such an arrangement. As long as the negotiating parties agree on a particular definition of *clean water*, what's to stop, say, an endangered bird that nests along the banks of the stream from going extinct if that definition does not suit the needs of wildlife? And what about future generations: Are they also to be left entirely out of this negotiating process?

Pricing tangible and visible costs is one thing, which is difficult enough. Yet there are no markets for many of the things we value that are associated with ecosystems and communities. The market price for a pickup load of logs, for example, says absolutely nothing about the value they played in a previous life for things like flood control, water purification, habitat, and carbon sinking. As William Rees (2009, 470), founding member and past president of the Canadian Society for Ecological Economics, correctly points out, "This is why the consumer purchasing a board foot of lumber—or just about anything else—doesn't come close to paying the full social cost of production." What, then, are we to do? Again, Rees (2009, 471) advises: "Such conclusions are not cause for despair but rather should liberate society from the dictates of oppressively wrong-headed economic models." Merely coming to the realization that the market can't solve all our problems is half the battle. Once we realize this, a world of possibilities opens up.

Fair versus Free Trade

If markets are insufficient, what, then, are our options? Let's take a step back and look more closely at the precise type of capitalism that's driving today's global economy. It typically goes by the name of *neoliberalism*. As David Harvey (2005, 2) explains in *A Brief History of Neoliberalism*,

> Neoliberalism is in the first instance a theory of political economic practices that proposes that human well-being can best be advanced by liberating individual entrepreneurial freedoms and skills within an institutional framework characterized by strong private property rights, free markets, and free trade.

As opposed to individual liberties (the holy grail in classic liberalism), neoliberalism sees salvation only through free enterprise—and a really no-holds-barred, dog-eat-dog approach to free enterprise at that (see ECOnnection 10.4).

What, then, is free enterprise? Or, better yet, taking another step back, what does *freedom* mean? The term *free* comes up a lot when talking about markets: free markets, free enterprise, free trade, and so on. Like a small but growing cadre of economists (see, for instance, Sen 1984; Jackson 2009), I have found twentieth-century English philosopher Isaiah Berlin's dual understanding of freedom useful in this context.

Conventional understandings of free markets remain dangerously fixated on only one side of this dual understanding, as evidenced by the fact that free markets are rarely ever fair (see ECOnnection 10.5). That is because most of this talk is heavily infused, to draw from Berlin, with "freedom *from*" rhetoric—freedom *from* other countries' production-oriented subsidies, freedom *from* government regulation, freedom *from* the state, and so forth. Freedom *from* talk is especially pervasive in neoliberal discourse. Isaiah Berlin ([1958] 1969, 127) describes this as "negative freedom," which refers to the "absence of interference." It seems as though when most people are asked about *freedom*, negative freedom is the type most have in mind—a freedom in which we are allowed to pursue actions unimpeded (see also Bell and Lowe 2000, 287–289).

ECOnnection 10.4
"Apolitical Ecologies" and Foucauldian Governance

The tendency to blame individuals for social and environmental problems is linked closely to the rise of neoliberalism and a shift toward neoliberal forms of what French philosopher Michel Foucault called "governance." Foucauldian governance, to admittedly oversimplify a highly nuanced concept, refers to the reduction of societal problems to an aggregate of individual ones. Doing this skillfully transfers responsibility for developing solutions from society as a whole onto individuals, making it up to individual consumers to do "the right thing." This move also supports the very system responsible for the problem in the first place. As good consumer-citizens, we are therefore taught to shop our way to safety, happiness, and sustainability by buying, in the case of environmental problems, ecofriendly products, high-efficiency gadgets, and carbon offsets.

Take the case of climate change. The most popular solutions are often individual ones, like buying hybrid cars, photovoltaic (PV) panels, and locally grown organic foods. Yet this disproportionately (and dangerously) places the focus on individual consumption choices rather than on creating policies that would enforce corporate accountability and lead to larger socioeconomic changes to the system responsible for the state we are in. In this sense, climate change can be seen as an **apolitical ecology**—a case in which explanations do not fully account for the asymmetries in power that first created it materially and then later define it as a problem to be solved by the same system that gave birth to it (Robbins 2012). This move effectively absolves that system of any blame.

IMAGE 10.2 Example of a Fair Trade Certified Label on a Familiar, Mass-Produced Chocolate Bar.

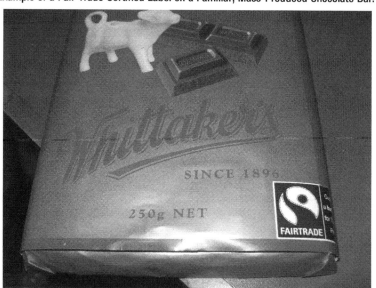

Source: "365/158—Fair Trade" by Jo Fothergill (flickr.com/photos/dragonsinger57) is licensed copyright © 2010 under CC BY-SA 2.0.

ECOnnection 10.5
Fair Trade

Fair trade represents a producer–consumer relationship through a supply chain that attempts to distribute economic benefits more fairly between all stakeholders (Raynolds and Bennett 2015; see Image 10.2). This is in contrast to the conventional supply-chain model, which primarily seeks the maximization of return somewhere in the middle of the food system. Fair trade makes trade fairer through a number of practices. Some of these practices include the following (taken from Nicholls and Opal 2005, 6–7):

- *Agreed-upon minimum prices that are often higher than those set by the market.* This is in recognition that agricultural commodity market prices, thanks to things like subsidies and monopoly conditions, are rarely fair. Farmers are therefore given a living wage for their work.
- *An additional social premium paid on top of the fair trade price.* This allows producers and farm laborers to collectively implement larger development projects (like the building of new schools). How the

money is spent is usually decided democratically, through cooperatives.

- *Purchasing directly from producers.* This reduces the number of profit-taking "middlemen" in the commodity chain and ensures that more of each dollar spent on the goods returns to producers.
- *Making credit available to producers.* As importers from affluent countries typically have greater access to credit than producers in developing countries, importers must prefinance a significant portion of the year's harvest.
- *Democratically organized farmers and workers.* This helps minimize labor abuses (e.g., child and slave labor) and ensures socially responsible production practices.

A decade ago few had heard of *fair trade.* Today, the label is almost as widely recognized globally as *organic.* The extra income earned by fair trade producers from US sales alone has increased from almost zero in 1998 to roughly $40 million in 2012 (Dragusanu et al. 2014).

In addition to its negative component, however, freedom also has a positive side. "Positive freedom"—or freedom *to*—refers to the ability "to lead one prescribed form of life ... that derives from the wish on the part of the individual to be his [or her] own master" (Berlin [1958] 1969, 127). Without the active pursuit of positive freedom, most people would not—indeed *could not*—feel free. To explain what I mean by this, I evoke an old English aphorism: "Freedom for the pike is death for the minnow." Without the pursuit of positive freedom for all—pikes and minnows alike—the pikes of the world would be clearly advantaged. And how do we actively pursue positive freedom for all? This is where the concept of *constraint*—which can only come from outside the market—comes into the picture. There must be some constraints if minnows are to prosper. Positive freedom, in other words, allows us to talk about constraint in the context of freedom without any sense of paradox (see Movement Matters 10.1).

Let's now apply this thinking to free markets, free enterprise, and the like. In order for me to be and feel free (and trade freely), I need some assurances that the pikes of the world will not freely have their way with me. This is why freedom—and, yes, free markets—*requires* some level of extramarket intervention. This intervention need not come solely in the form of government involvement. It can also exist as informal social norms, trust, and a shared sense of cooperation and responsibility. In a word, this constraint—where we seek to govern ourselves as well as our sustainable use of the ecological commons—can also emerge out of community (Ostrom 1999). (Community-based governance is discussed more fully in Chapter 11.)

There is nothing radical about this argument. We as citizens routinely support policies that tie our hands, whether through government-mandated retirement savings programs, restrictions on advertisements to children, or restrictions on commodities themselves. No one would support a society that allowed, say, unrestricted violence or the selling of poisoned food. Also remember that an argument *for* restrictions is not an argument *against* a market economy. We couldn't even have a market economy were it not for regulations. No business wishes to operate in a regulatory state of nature—too much uncertainty, instability, and chaos.

In the end, markets, even free ones, work only *because of* regulation. Business as we know it today could not exist without contracts, which are made possible by a web of

MOVEMENT MATTERS 10.1
Italy's Gruppi di Aquisto Soledale (GAS): Solidarity Purchasing Groups

From just one group in 1994, the movement Gruppi di Aquisto Soledale (GAS) now has more than 700 registered groups in Italy, though the actual number is estimated to be closer to 2,000, involving some 100,000 people (Maestripieri 2018). When a purchasing group puts people and environment before—or at least on a level equal to—profit, the group becomes a *solidarity* purchasing group. Such a network chooses the products and enrolls producers on the basis of respect for the environment and the solidarity between members of the group. Groups are typically set up by friends or neighbors who decide to pool their buying power and purchase collectively from local, organic, small-scale producers. Members of these groups believe that these guidelines lead to: the choice of local products (to minimize food miles); fair trade goods (to respect all producers by promoting their human rights, in particular those of women, children, and indigenous groups); reusable or compostable goods (to promote sustainable lifestyles); seasonal foods (to, for example, reduce energy and water footprints that come with growing out-of-season foods in greenhouses); and organic goods produced without the use of such inputs as pesticides or herbicides.

Some additional facts and figures relating to GAS:

- Size varies from 10 to 300 families in a group, with an average group size of 25 families.
- There are more groups in the affluent and social capital rich northern regions of the country.
- In addition to food, some GAS groups in cities like Milan are working together to coordinate larger bulk purchases of things like PV cells, electricity, and "ethical finance."

government-enforced rules and regulations. Regulation even helps businesses function by laying out clear rules about what they can and cannot do. As Harvard business professor Michael Porter argues, *stricter* environmental regulations are actually in the best interests of many businesses and countries, as they provide these actors with an important competitive advantage—what is known in the business community as the **Porter Hypothesis** (Frohwein and Hansjürgens 2005). The Porter Hypothesis notes that, among other things, regulation spurs innovation, as it creates incentives for businesses to adjust to social and environmental realities, like diminishing natural resources. Those nations and regions slow to commit to stricter environmental regulations are therefore doing themselves a grave disservice, a fact they will pay dearly for in the near future as their businesses struggle to compete against those better positioned to deal with the economic, social, and ecological realities of this century.

IMPORTANT CONCEPTS

- Environmental Kuznets Curve (EKC)
- fair versus free trade
- first and second contradictions of capitalism
- Forest Transition Theory (FTT)
- Foucauldian governance
- Isaiah Berlin's dual understanding of freedom
- metabolic rift
- neoliberalism
- Pollution Haven Hypothesis (PHH)
- rebound effect and the Jevons paradox
- relative versus absolute efficiency
- total cost accounting
- treadmill of production
- world-systems theory

DISCUSSION QUESTIONS

1. Have you ever invested in a more energy-efficient technology only to change your behavior and thus offset some (if not all) of those efficiency gains?
2. In order for capitalism to be sustainable over the long term, what is going to need to happen?
3. Is the treadmill of production an optimistic or pessimistic theoretical framework? Why?
4. What are your thoughts on the position taken about how free markets actually presuppose a degree of restraint and government intervention in order to be free?

SUGGESTED ADDITIONAL READINGS

Clark, T.P., S.B. Longo, B. Clark, and A.K. Jorgenson, 2018. "Socio-Structural Drivers, Fisheries Footprints, and Seafood Consumption: A Comparative International Study, 1961–2012." *Journal of Rural Studies*, 57: 140–146.

Gunderson, R., D. Stuart, B. Petersen, and S.J. Yun. 2018. "Social Conditions to Better Realize the Environmental Gains of Alternative Energy: Degrowth and Collective Ownership." *Futures*, 99: 36–44.

Lynch, M.J., P.B. Stretesky, and M.A. Long. 2018. "Green Criminology and Native Peoples: The Treadmill of Production and the Killing of Indigenous Environmental Activists." *Theoretical Criminology*, 22(3): 318–341.

York, R., and S.E. Bell. 2019. Energy Transitions or Additions?: Why a Transition from Fossil Fuels Requires More Than the Growth of Renewable Energy. *Energy Research & Social Science*, 51: 40–43.

RELEVANT INTERNET LINKS

- www.env-econ.net. An independently managed website on subjects related to environmental economics.
- www.fairtradeusa.org. Fair Trade USA.

SUGGESTED VIDEOS

- *Canada's Toxic Chemical Valley* (2013). The burial ground of the First Nation of Aamjiwnaang is located in Sarnia, Ontario. About seventy years ago it got some new neighbors. The first thing you notice when you visit Sarnia is the smell. Imagine a mixture of gasoline, melting asphalt, and a trace of rotten egg smacking you in the face and crawling up your nose every time you breathe.
- *Degrowth – from the Myth of Abundance to Voluntary Simplicity* (2016). The film tackles the big question of economic growth in a finite world from the point of view of a social and deeply ecological movement known as degrowth.
- *Dukale's Dream* (2015). A documentary about the inspiration behind Hugh Jackman's— yes, *that* Hugh Jackman—fair trade coffee company.
- *Green Death of the Forests* (2012). An unconventional film. It portrays the causes and consequences of deforestation in Indonesia as well as the tranquility and calm of wild nature. It contains no narrative or dialogue and yet helps us understand complex commodity chains.
- *The Dark Side of Chocolate* (2010). A team of journalists investigates how human trafficking and child labor in the Ivory Coast fuel the worldwide chocolate industry.
- *There's No Tomorrow* (2012). http://topdocumentaryfilms.com/theres-no-tomorrow. A half-hour animated documentary about resource depletion, energy, and the impossibility of infinite growth on a finite planet.

Governance: Biases and Blind Spots

Informational and governance challenges make ecological sustainability a daunting enough goal at the national level. With globalization, the barriers to sustainability—*real* sustainability—increase exponentially. If individual countries will not properly regulate what happens within their borders, no one can do it for them. Whereas today's most pressing environmental problems are global in scope, the regulatory arms available to monitor and enforce environmental law and policy weaken considerably when extended beyond their respective geopolitical borders. Meanwhile, the arms of our pollution reach around the globe. What are we to do? There are various ways to combat those gangly arms of pollution, which go beyond creating equally long arms of government.

This chapter, is interested, among other things, in detailing *why* current environmental regulations and policies look the way they do. Although there is an air of scientific objectivity to them, they ultimately rest on shifting sand, which is to say their logic is made possible only with the making of some questionable value judgments. In the "Solutions" section, alternative and arguably more just and sustainable methods of governance are suggested.

Fast Facts

- Trans-Pacific transportation of pollution from Asia to North America is well documented (Lafontaine et al. 2015). For example, a recent study focusing on US air quality shows that Chinese air pollution related to production for exports contributes, at a maximum and on a daily basis, 12–24 percent of sulfate pollution over the western US states (Lin et al. 2014). The authors thus point out that while eastern states are seeing improvements in air quality, partially as a result of importing goods from China—and thus not producing them and the associated emissions domestically—western states have not fared as well, because they're forced to breathe in this secondhand (for lack of a better word) pollution from Asia. US states are powerless to do anything about this transborder pollution. Consequently, they must include it in their planning, treating it essentially as if it were their own when seeking to meet federally mandated air quality standards (Parrish et al. 2011).

- What about future generations? If current trends continue, we will leave for our children a world radically different from the one we inhabit today. Global sea levels will rise by 0.8 to 2.0 meters by 2100, which places low-lying countries like Bangladesh and Pacific Island nations at severe risk of becoming submerged, in some cases entirely. Following current trends, the future will be less biologically and hence culturally diverse, drained of its resources and absorption capacities, and remarkably inequitable (United Nations 2015b).
- A recent study has investigated the discourses of climate change in corporate social responsibility reports produced by major oil companies from 2000 to 2013, looking specifically at the frequency of terms like "climate change" and "global warming" (Jaworska 2018). (Corporate social responsibility is a form of international private business self-regulation.) Initially, climate change was talked about as something that could be combated (via mitigation and adaptation). In recent years, however, corporate discourse has increasingly emphasized the risks and unpredictability associated with climate change. As the author explains, this discursive shift "positions the oil industry not as a contributor but as a *victim* of the phenomenon" (Jaworska 2018, 215; emphasis added).

Implications

Policy makers have tried being objective. They have tried ripping themselves out of their political communities when assessing and developing environmental policy, to be nowhere and no one while simultaneously everywhere and everyone. They have tried to be fair by stripping policy decisions of all ethical consequence and significance. Guided by the so-called comprehensive rationality of cost–benefit analysis, they have attempted being and doing all these things. Yet for reasons that I will now detail, these goals have neither lived up to their promise nor made the world more sustainable. In fact, they may well have made many things worse.

Welfare Economics and Cost–Benefit Analyses

At their core, cost–benefit analyses are guided by what is known as **welfare economics**. Welfare economics is a branch of microeconomics that seeks to evaluate well-being, with the assumption that human well-being is wholly reducible to *economic* well-being. Welfare economics thus subscribes to an extreme form of methodological reductionism, which involves reducing all choices and things to economic terms—usually a dollar amount. Whenever confronted with a choice, it is assumed humans, being the rational creatures we are, will always select the one that brings us the greatest benefit. Even proponents of this approach admit that this process inevitably involves making problematic value assignments. For instance, how does one assign value to biodiversity, a wetland, or a human life? Yet given the risk of regulatory agencies and politicians becoming captured by things like money and persuasive constituents, advocates of the cost–benefit analysis approach insist its objectivity preserves policy analyses' integrity by letting "the facts" decide things and not emotions, values, and subjective interests.

Insurmountable problems, however, remain with this approach. First, the framework is inherently incomplete. After all, it's naive to think all well-being can be reduced to economic well-being—a point I elaborate on in the next chapter. More problematic still, it is incapable of seeing its own flaws, as evidenced by the fact that the approach is based on an assumption of its own objectivity. Yet facts are incapable of speaking for themselves in matters of public health and environmental sustainability, given the tremendous amount of uncertainties involved (see Ethical Question 11.1). *People* have to speak for those facts. And *who* those people are can matter tremendously.

The **Pareto optimality standard** is a core economic principle driving, and justifying, cost–benefit analyses and welfare economics more generally. The Pareto standard deems a policy acceptable only if at least one individual is better off and no individuals are made worse off. Without passing that minimal bar, a policy will not even be considered. Yet does it matter *who* is made better off? Let's say Policy A makes Bill Gates, Warren Buffett, and Jeff Bezos (and only these three) *minimally* better off and no one worse off. Conversely, Policy B makes many destitute persons *considerably* better off but costs Gates, Buffett, and Bezos 20 bucks each—pocket change for either of them. I know what policy I would root for: Policy B. According to the Pareto optimality standard, however, because it explicitly doesn't care about issues of equity, *who* is being helped is irrelevant. So, anyone following the principle would have to choose Policy A, as it harms no one.

While claiming otherwise, this standard also makes normative assumptions by valuing only living human interests. But many other interests are worth valuing, like non-human life forms, future generations, and human communities, to name just a few. How are we ever going to make smart policy choices as long as we judge policies with a standard that is vastly prejudicial toward living human interests? Nobel Prize winning economist Amartya Sen makes plain the aimlessness—or "pointlessness," as Guido Calabresi (1991) famously called it—of this standard:

> An economy can be [Pareto] optimal … even when some people are rolling in luxury and others are near starvation as long as the starvers cannot be made better off without cutting into the pleasures of the rich. If preventing the burning of Rome would have made Emperor Nero feel worse off, then letting him burn Rome would have been Pareto-optimal. In short, a society or an economy can be Pareto-optimal and still be perfectly disgusting.
>
> (Sen 1970, 22)

The rush for welfare-economic policy analyses to make everything commensurate—that is to say, equal by way of reducing the world to monetary form—may make the approach appear objective, as technically all we are talking about are monetized costs and benefits. But this comes at great cost to society and the environment. An analysis of foreign aid policy calculates that the well-being of citizens in less affluent nations is one two-thousandth of the value of an American citizen (Kopczuk et al. 2005). With such a view of the citizens of poorer nations, is it any wonder why polluting industries and e-waste flow so readily to these parts of the world?

A widely circulated memo, dated December 12, 1991, leaked from the World Bank, articulated precisely such reasoning. Then chief economist for the World Bank Lawrence Summers (who was later appointed US Treasury secretary during the Clinton administration and subsequently served as president of Harvard University) penned the now infamous memo. It argued that the lower marginal cost of waste disposal in a poor country compared with the higher marginal cost of waste disposal in a waste-producing affluent country justifies the latter polluting the former. The memo further argued that the poorest

ETHICAL QUESTION 11.1
Unpacking "Science"

Funtowicz and Ravetz (1992) provide us with a well-known framework that allows us to move away from a singular view of science. When speaking of the highly ambiguous nature of today's environmental problems, they acknowledge that decisions can often only take place in a value-laden context. The practice of objective science, they contend, is ill-equipped to deal with any intermingling of facts and values and as such is grossly unprepared as a knowledge system for many of today's environmental problems. They develop their model around two variables, "systems uncertainty" and "decision stakes" (see Figure 11.1). When dealing with questions that involve low levels of each, they suggest the use of "applied science." When dealing with medium levels of both variables, "professional consultancy" is suggested. And when questions involve high levels of these two variables, "postnormal science" is called for.

According to Funtowicz and Ravetz, the way we practice science must change as we move from "applied" to "postnormal," as scientific questions require the making of additional value judgments. American nuclear physicist Alvin Weinberg (1972, 209) noted that there are questions "which can be asked of science and yet which cannot be answered by science." So what should we do? According to Funtowicz and Ravetz, as scientific questions increase in their complexity and systems uncertainty, so too should there be an increase in who is involved in finding answers to them.

Funtowicz and Ravetz's framework, however, also makes subtle value judgments. For instance, who decides if something falls within the realm of applied science or professional consultancy? Where precisely do we lay down the boundaries between these three types of science? And who decides what constitutes high decision stakes? Questions like these are not unique to Funtowicz and Ravetz's model. We confront them every time we make an environmental policy decision.

FIGURE 11.1 Postnormal Science Diagram

countries of Africa are vastly underpolluted, as they are underutilizing what affluent countries desperately need, namely, waste sinks.

In appearing to be non-ethical, the welfare-economic approach ends up being terribly *un*ethical. In an essay titled "The Rights of Statistical People," Lisa Heinzerling (2000, 189) puts the absurdity of this practice in plain sight:

> We do not, for example, believe that so long as it is worth $10 million to one person to see another person dead, and so long as current estimates of the value of human life are lower than $10 million, it is acceptable for the first person to shoot and kill the second.... Yet when it comes to regulatory programs that prevent deaths—deaths also due to the actions of other people—it has become commonplace to argue that the people doing the harm should be allowed to act so long as it would cost more for them to stop doing the harm than the harm is worth in monetary terms.

When we reduce human life to statistical terms, we deny those people the dignity of being thought of as humans. Similarly, by monetizing ecosystems and nonhuman life, we miss out on the opportunity to value things on their own terms. This can lead, for example, to the view that waste sinks in Africa ought to be filled with pollution from affluent nations just because sinks are substitutable.

It is entirely realistic to expect this approach to assign a lower value to those of lower socioeconomic status as well as to particular racial minorities, as certain ethnic groups are disproportionately overrepresented among lower-income strata. In having lower incomes and thus less buying power, welfare economics sees these people as having less value, literally, than those with higher incomes. Welfare economics therefore *justifies* certain types of environmental racism (Kysar 2010). Yet welfare economists are okay with this, as the outcome "would not be the result of a government decision to take racial characteristics into account; in fact it would not be a product of any group-level discrimination on the government's part" (Sunstein 2004, 391). So discrimination that can be justified with statistics is okay? And where's room for justice in all of this? How can we *ever* expect the economically disadvantaged to achieve upward mobility when our policy assessment tools view their lives as having less worth than those of the affluent?

Tyranny of the Present: Discounting

Welfare-economic policy analysis also has a distinct way of looking at the future. To its credit, it is consistent. It uses a technique to monetize future well-being, thus making it comparable with well-being today. Enter the practice of discounting.

Following this procedure, an increment of value today is worth more than that same increment in the future. Or, as noted by Cowen and Parfit (1992, 147), at a 5 percent discount rate, "one statistical death next year counts for more than a billion deaths in four hundred years." Seen through this lens, the foot-dragging we've been witnessing in regard to climate change policy starts making sense. Thanks to discounting, it is entirely possible to settle on a policy option that may knowingly result in human extinction hundreds of years from now, but because it also lowers the well-being of some today, it is deemed unacceptable. Douglas Kysar (2010, 148) has a wonderful term for this: "tyranny of the present" (see ECOnnection 11.1).

Let's review some of the logic that underlies discounting. Proponents of the practice argue that the procedure is necessary to ensure that current generations maximize their investment of financial *and* natural capital opportunities. This benefits, or so the argument goes, not only the living but also future generations by maximizing the option set bequeathed to them—a type of "trickle forward" reasoning (Kysar 2010, 162). But *what* precisely are these benefits we are leaving the future? Answer: monetized well-being. The exact stuff left for later generations is irrelevant, according to welfare-economic policy analysis. As articulated by two prominent welfare economists writing on the topic of sustainable development,

> There is no abstract reason to believe that preserving a particular environmental amenity (a forest, a lake) is always better for posterity than other investments that do not involve the environment in particular (expenditures on basic research, reductions in national debt).
>
> (Sunstein and Rowell 2007, 203)

Remember, at the core of this approach is the assumption of ultimate substitutability among different types of capital. Money is just as good as anything else—in fact *better* because it can be converted into a variety of things (as long as they are not extinct, depleted, or soiled beyond repair).

Eric Neumayer, a prominent welfare economist, has argued that future generations might actually prefer to face higher skin cancer rates if those risks come in exchange for some greater benefit. As Neumayer (1999, 40) explains, "Whether future generations will accept an increase in the rate of skin cancer or not depends on what they get in exchange for it." Even if he's right, how can we possibly know what future generations would accept in exchange for higher rates of skin cancer, and how can we be sure this Faustian bargain is agreeable to all and not just a privileged few? Welfare economists have even managed to justify the discounting of physical deformities, arguing that the cost to care for those

---

ECOnnection 11.1

Discounting and Forest Management

With harvesting cycles that are often longer than 20 years—and for some tree species they can extend well beyond 100 years—forestry management is premised on fairly long time horizons. The discount rate used therefore matters immensely. High discount rates greatly reduce the likelihood of sustainability, as they create little or no incentive to replant after one rotation, especially as long as there remains a substantial amount of unlogged forest to be exploited (Hultkrantz and Mantalos 2018). Lower discount rates, conversely, can make things like replanting incredibly attractive. This all matters enormously, as forestry provides us with so much more than just wood—from potential genetic materials to tourism, biodiversity, and carbon storage. Throughout much of the twentieth century, forestry discount rates were high and discouraged practices that would lead to truly sustainable yields.

deformities is likely to go down. In other words, we ought to value the avoidance of future deformities less than steps toward avoidance today (see, for example, Samida and Weisbach 2007). This argument, however, flatly misrepresents the ethical question at hand. "The nature of the ethical question on the table," remarks Kysar (2010, 170), "is not how to care for or cure a deformity that has already been suffered, but instead whether to inflict the pain in the first place." He continues:

> By presuming that there is no ethically relevant distinction between living as a non-deformed individual and living as a deformed individual who has received compensation, the economist's response violated the most fundamental ethical precept, that individuals should not be used without their consent as a means rather than as ends. Harm is inflicted—future individuals are used and indeed scarified without their consent—in order to promote well-being that they will not enjoy
>
> (Kysar 2010, 170; see Movement Matters 11.1)

The Self-Interested Straw Person

When weighing policy options, the welfare economist also assumes the worst of people. I am talking about the selfish, self-interested depiction of individual behavior assumed by most policy analysts today. Curiously, economists seem to best fit this model, which makes me wonder if this "truth" speaks less about human nature and more about the power of perception, a bit of a case of what we in the social sciences call a self-fulfilling prophecy. It has been shown, for example, that economics majors are more likely than non-economics students to free ride and less likely to work cooperatively, just as their discipline would predict (Carter and Irons 1991; Marwell and Ames 1981). One of the dangers of this assumption comes across in international relations. Because national governments are believed to be an aggregate of self-interested people, international policy not surprisingly assumes states to be equally selfish. This stance is of tremendous policy consequence as far as the environment is concerned.

For example, through this lens international relations are viewed as occurring in a space of self-interested competition, leaving no room for anything like cooperation. Yet given that so many of our problems are global in character, trust and collaboration are precisely what we need more of. As long as nation-states assume the worst of other nation-states, it is hard to see how global sustainability will ever be practically attained.

We see this continually in international negotiations over climate change. Countries such as the United States are unwilling to commit to any greenhouse gas reductions out of fear that other economies will selfishly free ride and do nothing. President Trump was making precisely this point when he said,

> Right now, we're at the cleanest we've ever been, and that's very important to me. But if we're clean but every other place on Earth is dirty, that's not so good. So I want clean air. I want clean water. Very important.
>
> (Quoted in Davenport and Friedman 2018)

Indeed, this same reasoning was at the heart of the US government's argument in *Massachusetts v. EPA*.

MOVEMENT MATTERS 11.1
Dams: Making Changes to How Things Are Counted

Perhaps you've heard the saying, "Not everything that counts can be counted." But remember also, just because we can count something doesn't mean *how* we count it can't change. Dams are an excellent example of this. Generations ago cost–benefit analyses were elementary by today's standards. I can imagine how the planners of the Hoover Dam ran the numbers: comparing things like capital costs (e.g., pounds of concrete and steel rebar) and labor costs (they didn't even have to worry about lawsuits back then) to the revenue generated from hydroelectric power and water storage and allocation. Today, we do a lot better at internalizing costs, which means those cost–benefit analyses look different, as evidenced by the fact that we're actually starting to tear dams down—an unthinkable act a few decades ago.

The Elwha River, which slices through northwest Washington's Olympic Peninsula, once hosted rich runs of chinook and red salmon. That all came to an end in 1913 with the completion of the Elwha River dam (see Image 11.1). While supplying electricity to the region, it cut off salmon coming from the Strait of Juan de Fuca, which connects with the Pacific Ocean. "There's nothing more painful than to see red salmon banging up against the dam, which is what you saw when you went there," remarked Interior Secretary Sally Jewell at the annual meeting of the Society of Environmental Journalists in New Orleans on September 5, 2014 (Main 2014). When the removal of the dam began in September 2011, it was the outcome of a long process, involving many stakeholders and a lot of hard work. The Lower Elwha Klallam Tribe had for years advocated for the removal of the Elwha dam.

The Federal Energy Regulatory Commission process requiring private hydropower dams to be licensed provided the tribe with an opportunity to intervene in an effort to restore the river and its salmon fisheries. In 1986, the tribe filed a motion to intervene. In 1992, thanks to the growing support of several environmental groups, and after a lengthy administrative process, Congress passed the Elwha River Ecosystems and Fisheries Restoration Act. This act directed the US Department of the Interior to study the feasibility of the river and fisheries restoration. In the 1995 Elwha Report, the secretary of the interior recommended removal of the dam, along with the Glines Canyon dam. The primary source of funding for the Elwha River Restoration Act came from the National Park Service Construction Budget. In 2009, the American Recovery and Reinvestment Act provided the remaining funding necessary to accomplish removal of both dams (Guarino 2013).

IMAGE 11.1

Source: "Lower Elwha River Dam" by brewbooks (flickr.com/brewbooks) is licensed copyright © 2007 under CC BY-SA 2.0.

Massachusetts v. EPA (549 US 497 [2007]) is a US Supreme Court case decided by a vote of five to four between twelve US states (and several US cities) and the Environmental Protection Agency (EPA). The former were seeking to force the latter to regulate CO_2 and other greenhouse gases as pollutants. The US government employed a couple of arguments in its defense. The first, building on this free-rider problem, went along the following lines: because it makes no difference at the global level whether the EPA does or does not regulate these emissions, as other countries (most notably China) will continue to pollute at ever greater levels, why bother with such regulations? The other argument was based on a welfare-economic approach to international relations: namely, forcing the US government to act unilaterally in regard to greenhouse gas emissions might hamper the President's ability to persuade key developing nations to reduce emissions. In other words, because states do not (and cannot) work together cooperatively and respond only to various sticks and carrots, the US government would rather wait to regulate its greenhouse gas emissions. This would give it a bargaining chip to play at some future negotiation to show other countries its willingness to reduce emissions.

Solutions

When I discuss with students the various social drivers that underlie today's environmental problems and equally create impediments to future solutions, many are initially frustrated. On the one hand, here is a case in which we literally just need to change how we think about things. On the other hand, the welfare-economic policy analysis is so entrenched in political, economic, and policy thinking that it will require a lot of work to move away from it. The approach is also remarkably efficient at getting the job done, even though its outputs are highly problematic and ultimately unsustainable. I will now detail some alternatives, though it will require a collective rolling up of our sleeves if we want to see the welfare-economic policy approach overturned.

From Tragedy to Drama

The assumption of a self-interested individual, which lies at the core of welfare-economic policy analysis, is not without some empirical grounding. This caricature is famously detailed in Garret Hardin's classic 1968 essay, "The Tragedy of the Commons," which includes relevant passages like this one:

> Picture a pasture open to all. It is to be expected that each herdsman will try to keep as many cattle as possible on the commons. Such an arrangement may work reasonably satisfactorily for centuries because tribal wars, poaching, and disease keep the numbers of both man and beast well below the carrying capacity of the land. Finally, however, comes the day of reckoning, that is, the day when the long-desired goal of social stability becomes a reality. At this point, the inherent logic of the commons remorselessly generates tragedy.
>
> (Hardin 1968, 1244)

Assuming that each herder wishes to maximize their gain, they begin to ponder the consequences of adding one more animal to their herd. It quickly dawns on them that

CASE STUDY 11.1
Grassland Management in Inner Mongolia

Pastoral communities living in Inner Mongolia have experienced their grasslands undergoing widespread degradation, threatening the livelihoods of local herders. One study has shown that this degradation is linked to changes in institutional contexts (Robinson et al. 2017). The authors note specifically the role that market integration and top-down policy interventions have played in decoupling formerly tight local social-ecological links (see the following discussion about common-property resource governance). This decoupling, along with weak land tenure security due to a complex and volatile policy landscape (e.g., herders have few assurances that any sustainable uses of the grassland today will benefit them in the future, which gives them little personal incentive to reduce stocking rates), suppresses local incentives for grassland conservation.

the costs and benefits of such an action are unevenly distributed. The herder receives all the proceeds from the sale of the additional animal. Yet the effects of overgrazing are shared by all. It is therefore perfectly rational for, and therefore expected that, herders in such a situation will continually add animals to their herd—*all* herders. And therein lies the tragedy: everyone acting in their own self-interests, when resources are shared and limited, will have catastrophic ends, leading Hardin to conclude, famously, "Freedom in a commons brings ruin to all" (Ibid.).

Yet as Dietz et al. (2002) highlight in their thorough review of the commons literature since Hardin's essay, prototypical scenarios—like Hardin's essay—always end up oversimplifying things. Some case studies tell a story similar to Hardin's. Many others have much happier endings.

One of the most relevant critiques leveled at Hardin is that he conflates common-property and open-access regimes. Common-property regimes are those in which

> the members of a clearly demarcated group have a legal right to exclude non-members of that group from using a resource. Open access regimes (*res nullius*)—including the classic cases of the open seas and the atmosphere—have long been considered in legal doctrine as involving no limits on who is authorized to use a resource.
>
> (Ostrom 2000, 335–336)

This is an important distinction, as common property should not be mistaken to mean everyone's property (Ciriacy-Wantrup and Bishop 1975). Under common-property regimes, users already have use rights that are maintained through thick webs of social relationships. What from the "outside" may look ungoverned, as there may be no formal laws and rules and state-sanctioned monitoring, could actually be well governed through local customs, trust, and informal social norms (see, for example, Goldman 1998; Longo et al. 2015).

It is of concern that resource privatization—one of Hardin's suggestions to avert the tragedy—may in fact be one of the reasons the tragedy is playing out in some parts of world (see Case Study 11.1). Late twentieth-century policy reforms are transforming common-property regimes into either state government owned or private-property regimes. When this happens, however, especially in developing nations, rarely are sufficient moneys and resources devoted to the monitoring of these now noncommon-property resources. "Thus, what had been de facto common property with some limitation on access and use patterns became de jure government [or individual] property—but due to the lack of enforcement, it frequently became de facto open access" (Dietz et al. 2002, 13).

The late Elinor Ostrom and her various collaborators extensively documented that common-property resource governance need not end tragically. As it turns out, we are not as self-centered as the welfare-economic approach makes us out to be. There are many examples of long enduring and sustainable common-property situations from around the world. Sustainable self-governance requires the development of rules and institutions that define such things as the physical boundaries of the property held in common, who has access to the resource, a sustainable rate of extraction and use, the methods for monitoring the resource, a system for resolving conflicts, and suitable sanctions and punishments for transgressions. In his classic study of a Swiss Alpine village, Robert Netting (1981) identifies five environmental variables that contribute to a resource being held as common rather than private property:

- the value of harvestable resource is low per unit of area
- what can be harvested varies considerably over time
- investment in improvements yields relatively small increases in the productivity of the resource
- overall costs can be reduced if activities (e.g., herding or processing dairy products) can be shared collectively
- infrastructure costs (e.g., fences and buildings) can be reduced if built on a larger scale.

Perhaps the largest omission in Hardin's essay, and precisely why we are not as self-centered as the welfare-economic caricature assumes, is the fact that people *talk to one another*. The role of face-to-face interaction in building social capital and establishing those aforementioned thick social relationships that can rein in otherwise selfish behavior is well documented in the social science literature (Borg et al. 2015; Flora 2008; Flora et al. 2009; social capital was introduced in Chapter 7). Some interesting laboratory experiments have been conducted to better understand the role that communication plays in averting tragedy-like outcomes. The verdict: the ability to communicate and coordinate drastically alters outcomes.

Group communication fosters the formation of group identity and therefore reduces the likelihood of selfish behaviors. Individuals, instead, are more willing to think in terms of what's best for the collective as opposed to what's exclusively best for them (Baumeister et al. 2015; Ostrom et al. 1994). When individuals are placed in a situation where they cannot communicate with others, they are more likely to act selfishly with regard to the use of shared resources (Ostrom et al. 1994).

More recently, research has gone beyond studying resources at a particular scalar level, looking instead at common-property resources that cut across many levels. One obvious difference between global and local resources is the extent of the former and inherent difficulties associated with monitoring and enforcing sustainable use patterns (Dietz et al. 2002). Building and maintaining social capital between groups from different continents with different backgrounds also complicates matters. Some common-property resources—like freshwater in an international basin or marine ecosystems—are best viewed in an international context. Their effective management therefore depends on the cooperation of appropriate international institutions and national, regional, and local institutions (Ostrom et al. 1999).

Ultimately, the evidence indicates that while complicating matters, the global character of some of today's environmental problems should not be viewed as a guaranteed ticket to a world of despair (Agrawal 2014; Bulkeley et al. 2014; see Case Study 11.2). Elinor Ostrom, who was awarded the 2009 Nobel Prize in Economic Sciences for her work on this very subject, and her collaborators explained the future potential of global governance as follows:

> The lessons from successful examples of CPR [common-property resource] management provide starting points for addressing future challenges. Some of these will be institutional, such as multilevel institutions that build on and complement local and regional institutions to focus on truly global problems. Others will build from improved technology. For example, more accurate long-range weather forecasts could facilitate improvements in irrigation management, or advances in fish tracking could allow more accurate population estimates and harvest management.... In the end, building from the lessons of past successes will require forms of communication, information, and trust that are broad and deep beyond precedent, but not beyond possibility.... There is much to learn from successful efforts as well as from failures.
>
> (Ostrom et al. 1999, 282)

Absolute Sustainability

Welfare-economic policy analyses have a very narrow understanding of "sustainability." According to proponents of this approach, it is necessary to ensure that current generations maximize their investment opportunities in the hope that benefits will trickle "forward" to later generations. Yet *what* are these benefits that we're leaving the future? The precise stuff, as I have mentioned, is irrelevant (see Sunstein and Rowell 2007, 203). Rather, what matters under this calculus is monetary value. This gives the approach the veneer of objectivity by removing from the decision-making process subjective values and emotions—after all, we're just talking about dollars and cents.

Clearly, however, *stuff* matters. To repeat a familiar adage: you can't eat GDP. Yet our welfare economist has a response to this: the perfect substitutability assumption. When resources become scarce, the higher market price will force innovation and lead, eventually, to suitable substitutes. Although the assumption might hold for some goods, like fuel (biofuels substituting for gasoline) and certain foods (high fructose corn syrup substituting for sugar), no one can seriously hold out similar hope for marine ecosystems, the ozone layer, clean air, and endangered species.

I return to my earlier call for absolute sustainability. Thomas Jefferson famously wrote in a letter to James Madison in 1789 that "the earth belongs in usufruct to the living"

Reducing Emissions from Deforestation and Forest Degradation

Reducing Emissions from Deforestation and Forest Degradation (REDD) is a collaborative international initiative under negotiation within the United Nations climate talks and other international forums that will help to compensate governments, communities, companies, and individuals in low-income countries for actions that protect forests (see Image 11.2). By placing a monetary value on the role forest ecosystems play in carbon capture and storage, REDD allows intact forests to compete with historically more lucrative land uses that have resulted in their destruction.

Forests absorb CO_2 from the atmosphere, but when they are destroyed or degraded, they release large amounts of this greenhouse gas, contributing significantly to global warming. A study published in *Science* estimates that the total CO_2 sink (absorption or uptake) capacity of the world's regrowth forests is equivalent to half the world's fossil fuel CO_2 emissions (Pan et al. 2011). More than global carbon sinks, forests are also people's homes. The number of forest-dependent indigenous people in the world total in the hundreds of millions—in India alone, the number has been estimated at anywhere from 275 to 400 million (Bhattacharya 2019). In short, forests directly support the livelihoods of millions of people who depend on these spaces for food, fuel, fodder for livestock, medicine, shelter, and religious/spiritual practices.

Initially, REDD was principally focused on reducing emissions from deforestation and forest degradation. By 2010, however, as set out in the Cancun Agreements, REDD became REDD+ to reflect new components. REDD+ includes:

- reducing emissions from deforestation
- reducing emissions from forest degradation
- conservation of forest carbon stocks
- sustainable management of forests
- enhancement of forest carbon stocks.

With this broader charge, REDD+ has the potential to simultaneously contribute to climate change mitigation and poverty alleviation while also conserving biodiversity and sustaining vital ecosystem services (REDD Desk 2015).

IMAGE 11.2

Source: "After the Rainforest, Uganda" by Rod Waddington (flickr.com/rod_waddington) is licensed copyright © 2014 under CC BY-SA 2.0.

(Sloan 1993, 281). (*Usufruct* means to have a legal right to enjoy and profit from something that belongs to another.) Given that the survival of future billions rides on our actions today, it seems we do indeed have something akin to a duty to leave a sufficient amount of stuff intact and minimally adulterated for the future. Monetary wealth will indeed protect some people in the future from climate change and provide some people with fish if the marine ecosystem were to collapse. Yet I am far less worried about the well-being of the world's future affluent; they will likely have the resources to protect and take care of themselves. It's the welfare of the other 99 percent of the world's population who will have considerably less that concerns me.

How, then, should we fold future generations into our thinking? Clearly, they cannot speak for themselves. Some economic theorists have begun to argue that the widely used constant discount rates are unjustified. When you set a fixed annual discount rate at, say, 5 percent, it is entirely possible to reject a policy option that may knowingly save the human race from extinction hundreds of years from now on the basis that it also lowers the well-being of some today. As opposed to the constant discount rate, some have suggested that the correct social discount rate should decrease with time, beginning, for example, for a short time at 3.5 percent and declining over the long run to 1 percent or less (Hepburn and Koundouri 2007).

Fleurbaey and Zuber (2013, 585–586) suggest the following twist when thinking about discount rates:

> Climate change policies [should] be evaluated with a negative discount rate ... when the present donor is richer than the future beneficiary. Thus, if we consider long-run policies, the discount rate should be negative when the poorest contributors to the policy are richer than the poorest beneficiaries.

Do not most climate change policies satisfy this condition? Mitigation efforts, for instance, should put the financial burden on the high emitters, who are typically among the members of the present generation living in affluent countries. Such policies will benefit members of future generations, especially those most at risk from the threats of climate change, many of whom are (and will be) low-income households living in low-income countries. Can we really expect that the poorest of future generations will be better off than the middle class of the present generation? If we cannot be absolutely sure of that, then perhaps the above suggestion has some ethical legs.

There are also some non-discounting options. Schelling (1995), for example, argues we should make investments explicitly for future peoples just as we do with foreign aid today; we could call these investments *future aid*. One benefit of this approach is that it brings the subject of future well-being into the sphere of public consciousness, as opposed to the standard practice, which is generally to never talk about future generations unless it is politically expedient to do so. Of course, this practice does not guarantee anything for future generations, as evidenced by the recent sharp decline in foreign aid by most affluent nations. And it could conceivably make matters worse for the future, as it could provide justification for even more egregiously unsustainable behavior under the guise of "aiding the future in other ways."

Others have suggested abandoning discounting altogether for something more democratic in character. Kopp and Portney (1999), for instance, propose mock referenda, in which a random sample of the population is presented with a detailed description of the likely effects—current and future—of various proposed policies. The participants would then vote for or against the policy (see also Dean et al. 2019.). As opposed to the disinterested rationality of the welfare-economic approach, this style of "rationality depends on the virtues of collective problem solving; it considers the reasonableness of ends in relation to the values they embody and the sacrifices we must make to achieve them" (Sagoff 1988, 70). Importantly, this approach is not necessarily antithetical to the welfare-economic framework. Things could still be monetized but only after the policy has been chosen. Thus, rather than *determining* the policy selected, "the value will simply be an ancillary effect of a policy choice that was premised on social values" (Kysar 2010, 114). This technique could stop the policy foot-dragging that currently exists around climate change. I try something similar to this with my students. They are presented with reports that calculate projected costs associated with the taking of major steps to mitigate humans' greenhouse gas emissions and adapting to changes already under way. They are then given other estimates as to the costs to society if nothing is done. This is followed by a conversation about the "value" of future generations and the impacts climate change could have on them. After these future costs are vaguely established (we never seem to settle on a fixed figure), I ask my students how they compare to the costs associated with implementing aggressive climate change policy today. Taking action today *always* proves the most cost-effective option.

The Precautionary Principle

There was a time in the United States when we talked more about environmental rights than optimal trade-offs, of steward obligations more than discounted welfare maximization, and of international cooperation more than global competitiveness (Kysar 2010). The Endangered Species Act of 1973, for instance, placed the value of species at "incalculable," thereby, for a time, excluding from consideration *any* economic calculus. Similarly, the UN Environment Programme Participation Act of 1973 declared that it "is the policy of the United States to participate in coordinated international efforts to solve environmental problems of global international concern" (*United States Code, 2000: Title 22, Foreign Relations and Intercourse* 2002, 159). As written in the National Environmental Policy Act of 1969 (Title I, § 101, [b], [1]), Congress recognized that it is the responsibility of the federal government to, among other things, "fulfill the responsibilities of each generation as trustee of the environment for succeeding generations." Finally, going back in time still further, we have the Delaney Clause. This 1958 amendment to the Food, Drugs, and Cosmetic Act of 1938 states that "the Secretary of the Food and Drug Administration shall not approve for use in food any chemical additive found to induce cancer in man, or, after tests, found to induce cancer in animals" (Merrill 1997, 313). Note the definitiveness of this language. There is no room for comparing an additive's health risks with its perceived economic benefits.

We currently assume the worst of people and the best of the technologies created by these self-centered, selfish people. When it comes to assessing the potential threats of novel technologies and setting up environmental, health, and safety regulations, the tendency, especially in the United States, is to take the position of "innocent until proven guilty." This represents, at its most basic level, the traditional risk assessment. Risk assessment, in effect, places the onus on regulatory agencies and the general public to prove that a given technology or industrial activity is not safe. Or, to put it another way, we have to falsify the statement "It's safe." This places us in a noticeably different regulatory environment from where we were when, say, the Delaney Clause was in full effect.

An alternative to the traditional risk assessment is the precautionary principle. The precautionary principle is generally recognized as having emerged in the 1970s, though its ethos dates back to the Hippocratic Oath, which states "First do no harm" (Steel 2014). Since then, the precautionary principle has flourished in a variety of settings. Arguably, its first international application came in 1984, at the First International Conference on Protection of the North Sea. From there, it has been integrated into numerous conventions and agreements, including, for example, the Maastricht Treaty on the European Union, the Barcelona Convention, the Global Climate Change Convention, and Principle 15 of the Rio Declaration. A popular definition comes from the 1998 Wingspread Statement on the Precautionary Principle:

> When an activity raises threats of harm to human health or the environment, precautionary measures should be taken even if some cause and effect relationships are not established scientifically. In this context the proponent of the activity, rather than the public, should bear the burden of proof.
>
> (Raffensperger and Tickner 1999, 8)

Admittedly, this statement leaves the concept ill-defined, vague, and difficult to translate into practical action. For instance, what constitutes a "threat"? What about those cases in which human well-being is enhanced while the health of the environment is threatened? What does the term *precautionary measures* mean? And who are the "proponents" that this statement refers to: those producing the technology in question, those who benefit from it, or those who may profit from it?

Proponents would argue that the function of such an "open" definition is to ensure that the principle remains variable and contingent, which is admirable given the indeterminate nature of the systems (ecological, social, and so on) that it seeks to protect. Yet in the face of such ambiguity, it then becomes left to interested parties—regulators, industry representatives, environmental advocacy organizations, and the like—to work out the details. What guarantee is there, then, that powerful actors will not shape those policy specifics to benefit their interests, while excluding the interests of the less powerful?

There are two applications of the precautionary principle: one "strong" and one "weak" (Carolan 2007). The precautionary principle has frequently been interpreted as calling for the absolute proof of safety before new technologies are adopted; this is a popular reading among its critics. This "strong" formulation, for example, can be seen in a statement by environmental writer Jeremy Leggett (1990, 459), when he argued that "the modus operandi we would like to see is: 'Do not emit a substance unless you have proof it will not do harm to the environment'." Thus, whereas traditional risk assessments presume things to be safe until proven guilty (harmful), under this variant of the precautionary principle, the assumption is that technologies are guilty (harmful) until proven safe. In this way, the responsibility of proof is placed on the shoulders of industry as opposed to the general public and regulatory agencies.

In principle, this position is commendable. It holds a certain degree of moral currency by providing what many would consider a fair and just way of regulating technology:

namely, those who stand to make millions from a given technology should likewise bear the burden of proof when demonstrating that such profits are not coming at the expense of humans, the environment, or both. Yet this approach has grave logical problems: namely, no product could ever meet the required threshold to be allowed onto the market. How does one prove that a given technology will do no harm to either humans or the environment? That is, how does one prove the statement "It's safe"?

Karl Popper ([1934] 1961) famously argued that theories often take the following form: all Xs are Ys. For example: "All snow is white" or "All bodies attract one another with a force proportional to the product of their masses and inversely proportional to the square of their distance apart." To refute such a theoretical form requires that one find a single X that is not also a Y. To prove such a theory, however, would require that one observe every single X to make sure that it is indeed also a Y. Yet this would mean that one must engage in an exhaustive search of not only the entire universe but of the universe from the beginning to the end of time. Logically, therefore, while refutations of theories appear to be at least possible, confirmations (as a basis for proof) are not.

One way to salvage the precautionary principle is to weaken our interpretation of *proof.* Ultimately, nothing in this world is *totally* safe. Water can be lethal when too much is ingested. The same can be said for tea, coffee, apples, oxygen, sunlight... Perhaps, then, a better way of putting it is seeking proof of being reasonably safe (Tickner 2003). With this move, we can now drink water and tea without the fear of regulatory agencies outlawing their use. Yet in doing this, the precautionary principle slips into something noticeably less novel. To speak of something being "reasonably safe" sounds an awful lot like risk assessment's claim to be about establishing "what's a reasonable risk."

Call it what you want: risk assessment, precautionary principle, or precautionary risk management—what we ultimately need are more open decision-making structures. And not just at the point of regulation. Regulation is something we do at the back end of the production process, *after* a product has been made. What about the decisions that are made at the front end of the production process, *before* a technology has been developed and mass-produced? As sociologist of science Brian Wynne (2002) points out, attempts to improve public participation in risk assessments, while admirable, have served to reinforce attention only on back-end science questions about consequences or risks instead of looking at why such widespread public dissatisfaction with modern technologies exists in the first place. In short, a democratic regulatory politics should not kick in only after a technology has been developed. It should inform the entire production process, from conceptual cradle to material grave. Doing this will encourage the production of technologies that are not only more just and less risky but also that are needed and will enhance social welfare. This is radically different from the current model, which involves producing goods and leaving it up to marketing departments to convince the public they are things they need.

IMPORTANT CONCEPTS

- corporate social responsibility
- discounting
- open-access versus common-property regimes
- postnormal science
- traditional risk assessment versus the precautionary principle
- tragedy of the commons
- welfare economics and cost–benefit analyses

DISCUSSION QUESTIONS

1. How should future generations be factored into our thinking when assessing policy options?
2. As many of today's problems are global, do we need something akin to a global governing body to deal with these threats? What are some of the potential benefits and costs of this scenario?
3. Should we be more cautious in our approach to novel technologies?
4. How does Elinor Ostrom's research, and that of others, in the governing-the-commons tradition give us hope?

SUGGESTED ADDITIONAL READINGS

Aven, T. 2018. "An Emerging New Risk Analysis Science: Foundations and Implications." *Risk Analysis*, 38(5): 876–888.

McCarthy, L. 2017. "Empowering Women through Corporate Social Responsibility: A Feminist Foucauldian Critique." *Business Ethics Quarterly*, 27(4): 603–631.

Morrison, T.H., W.N. Adger, K. Brown, M.C. Lemos, D. Huitema, J. Phelps, L. Evans, P. Cohen, A.M. Song, R. Turner, and T. Quinn. 2019. "The Black Box of Power in Polycentric Environmental Governance." *Global Environmental Change*, 57: 101934.

Myers, R., A.M. Larson, A. Ravikumar, L.F. Kowler, A. Yang, and T. Trench. 2018. "Messiness of Forest Governance: How Technical Approaches Suppress Politics in REDD+ and Conservation Projects." *Global Environmental Change*, 50: 314–324.

RELEVANT INTERNET LINKS

- www.iied.org/justice-forests-series-short-films. Two short films—*Tackling Forest Governance* and *Justice in the Forests*—about indigenous forest governance groups.
- www.youtube.com/watch?v=ByXM47Ri1Kc. Elinor Ostrom explains her pathbreaking research.
- www.youtube.com/watch?v=GgpEscvz168. An interview with a scholar who has studied REDD+ (see Case Study 11.2). Specifically, she explains the power and politics underlining this policy process, leading to its stalling in some cases.

SUGGESTED VIDEOS

- *Bikpela Bagarap (Big Damage)* (2011). www.bikpelabagarap.com. Filmed undercover, this documentary reveals the exploitation of forest communities in Papua New Guinea by Malaysian logging companies and corrupt politicians.
- *Canada's Toxic Chemical Valley* (2013). The burial ground of the First Nation of Aamjiwnaang is located in Sarnia, Ontario. About seventy years ago it got some new neighbors. The first thing you notice when you visit Sarnia is the smell. Imagine a mixture of gasoline, melting asphalt, and a trace of rotten egg smacking you in the face and crawling up your nose every time you breathe.
- *Green Gold* (2012). Documents large-scale ecosystem restoration projects in China, Africa, South America, and the Middle East, highlighting the enormous benefits to people and the planet of undertaking these efforts globally.
- *Rachel Carson's "Silent Spring"* (1993). Though twenty years old, this production from the PBS series *The American Experience* offers an excellent historical lesson for anyone not familiar with this landmark book and its pioneering author.
- *Seeing the Forest* (2015). A 30-minute film documenting a case in Oregon where rather than just designating a forest as a wilderness preserve (and thus off-limits to everyone) the Forest Service instigated a remarkable experiment in collaborative governance.
- *The Third Industrial Revolution: A Radical New Sharing Economy* (2018) (www.youtube.com/watch?v=QX3M8Ka9vUA). A 100-minute lecture (yes, it's rather long) by well-known futurist Jeremy Rifkin. According to Rifkin, a Third Industrial Revolution is unfolding giving rise to what he calls a new sharing economy.

12

Inequality and Growth: Prosperity for All

Since Rachel Carson's *Silent Spring*—a book said to have helped spark the modern environmental movement (Lytle 2007)—a widespread understanding has emerged concerning the costs of growth to the environment. A variety of social theories were detailed in Chapter 10 that attempt to paint a fairly thick causal arrow from growth to environmental degradation. Growth nevertheless remains a sacred cow of sorts. Its costs may be great, but the costs of forgoing it, so the thinking goes, are even greater. Environmental degradation remains, for many, an unfortunate but necessary condition for future prosperity. We've also had some luck at pushing the "limits" further and further out. Some forty-five-plus years ago, a handful of widely circulated books was published on the subject of rapidly approaching limits, such as *Limits to Growth* (Meadows et al. 1972) and *The Population Bomb* (Ehrlich 1968). These dire prophesies have yet to pan out. Their failure is relative rather than absolute. Their underlying premise about there being real limits is not wrong; we've just managed to delay hitting up against them. To which proponents of economic growth respond: What makes you so sure we will not delay hitting those limits indefinitely?

Critiquing economic growth on the grounds that it destroys the environment might resonate among the already converted. Yet experience has taught me that among the pro-growth diehards, another argumentative frame is required. What if I were to tell you that economic growth, beyond a certain point, contributes *nothing* to making us more prosperous, happy, or healthy? After a certain point, economic growth might even become regressive to society's overall well-being (Delhey and Dragolov 2016; Dietz et al. 2012; Easterlin 2015). This lack of correlation between happiness (or life satisfaction) and GDP growth over time can be explained by, among other things, the positional nature of consumer goods—once everyone else has a certain product, a new and better version is required to enhance one's status and to remain happy (Büchs and Koch 2019). It is called "positional" because our happiness is in part contingent on how we assess the *position* of our lifestyle and livelihood relative to those around us (and those we see on television, online, through social media, etc.). Ecological economist Herman Daly (1999) calls this **uneconomic growth:** growth that costs us more than it benefits us. In other words, it is growth that makes us *less* well off.

For a time, I too had thought that economic growth was synonymous with prosperity, which made the subject in my mind ethically thorny. On the one hand, I wanted to do right by the environment; on the other, I wanted to do right to humanity. Turns out, it's not a zero-sum game. The environment's gain is ours too, and vice versa. Allow me to explain.

Fast Facts

- Two hundred years ago, affluent, or what at the time were self-described as "civilized," countries had three times more wealth than so-called poor countries. By the end of colonialism, in the 1960s, the average inhabitant of the average affluent nation had become nine times wealthier relative to their contemporary in a low-income country. Today, they are roughly 100 times richer. The three richest people in the United States—Bill Gates, Jeff Bezos, and Warren Buffett—possess as much wealth (roughly, a $248.5 billion fortune) as the bottom half of the US population, or 160 million people. The richest 400 people in the United States, meanwhile, are worth a combined $2.68 trillion—the same wealth as the bottom 64 percent of the US population (that's 204 million people) (*Guardian* 2017). Meanwhile, the twenty-six richest people on Earth have the same net worth as the poorest half of the world's population (that's 3.8 billion people!) (Matthews 2019).
- According to the Millennium Ecosystem Assessment (2005), the total capital stock of the world—most notably natural capital—is degrading faster than wealth created in the formal economy. (Released in 2005, the *Millennium Ecosystem Assessment* involved more than 1,300 experts and provides one of the most thorough appraisals of the conditions and trends in the world's ecosystems and the services they provide.) To put it another way, more value is being destroyed than created—a classic case of uneconomic growth. Entities like the World Bank are thus starting to take greater notice of natural capital. In the Bank's own words,

> Gross Domestic Product (GDP) looks at only one part of economic performance—income—but says nothing about wealth and assets that underlie this income. For example, when a country exploits its minerals, it is actually depleting wealth. The same holds true for over-exploiting fisheries or degrading water resources.
>
> (World Bank 2015b)

- Some countries are able to accomplish plenty, in terms of outcomes we can all get behind, without overly costing the environment. Costa Ricans, for example, live slightly longer than the average citizen of the United States and report having much higher levels of life satisfaction. And they do all this with an ecological footprint that is less than one-quarter the size of the average person residing in the United States (Hickel 2019).

Implications

We are only a couple of pages into this chapter, and I have already made a number of bold statements. I do not make them casually. They are based on a remarkable array of research conducted over the past ten years. The last seventy years, since the end of World War II, has been a tremendous social experiment. By practically every empirical indicator, this experiment has not gone as planned. I am not arguing that economic growth is bad in itself, just that after a certain point there ceases to be any empirical justification for it as an end in itself.

Rethinking Growth

First, let's look at the relationship between planetary biophysical boundaries and a country's ability to achieve societal well-being for its citizens. Jason Hickel recently conducted the following insightful analysis. Using data on social and biophysical indicators (see Table 12.1) provided by O'Neill et al. (2018), Hickel makes the case that while it is theoretically possible for nations to achieve high levels of well-being while remaining *within* planetary boundaries, most nations must significantly rethink business as usual before our resources and sinks run out.

Hickel's (2019) argument is based on the data presented in Figure 12.1. The figure is a scatterplot of average biophysical impact for 151 nations with respect to planetary boundaries and social achievements: the former, x-axis, denotes planetary limits as "1" (anything over 1 represents ecological overshoot); the latter, y-axis, denotes "1" as a perfect score with respect to the social indicators in Table 12.1. Figure 12.1 shows that of nations that remain within all biophysical boundaries, Moldova does the best on social indicators, with an average social shortfall of 10 percent (with a score of 0.9). Of particular interest are countries like Cuba or Costa Rica. Take the case of Costa Rica. It is able to obtain a near perfect

FIGURE 12.1 Ecological Efficiency of Nations—Scatterplot of Average Biophysical Impact with Respect to Planetary Boundaries

Source: Jason Hickel.

Note

x-axis, with boundary—planetary limits—as 1 versus their achievement with respect to social thresholds; y-axis, with threshold—perfect score—as 1.

TABLE 12.1 Social and Biophysical Indicators Covered in the Dataset

Social Indicators	Societal well-being
Life Satisfaction	6.5 on 0–10 Cantril Scale (Gallup World Poll)
Healthy Life Expectancy	65 healthy life years
Nutrition	2,700 kcal per person per day
Sanitation	95% with access to improved sanitation facilities
Income	95% living on more than US$1.90 per day
Access to Energy	95% with access to electricity
Education	95% enrolment in secondary school
Social Support	90% say they have relatives or friends they can depend on
Democratic Quality	0.8 on −2.5–2.5 scale, average of Worldwide Governance Indicators on voice, accountability, and political stability
Equality	70 on 0–100 scale, based on Gini coefficient of household disposable income
Employment	94% of the labour force employed
Biophysical Indicators	**Boundary**
CO_2 Emissions	1.6 tonnes of CO_2 per person per year
Phosphorous	0.9 kilograms P per person per year
Nitrogen	8.9 kilograms N per person per year
Blue Water	574 cubic meters H_2O per person per year
eHANPP (an indicator of a county's land-use intensity)	2.6 tonnes per person per year
Ecological Footprint	1.7 global hectares (gha) per person per year
Material Footprint	7.2 tonnes per person per year

Source: Adapted from O'Neill et al. (2018).

social achievement score of 0.96 while overshooting planetary limits by 33 percent (a score of 1.33). Other countries, meanwhile, achieve similar levels of well-being at the expense of consuming many times over their planetary limits—those to the right of the figure.

Let's look now more exclusively at subjective measures of well-being and their relationship to economic growth. After a certain point, economic growth in itself does little to make people feel better off, as documented in Figure 12.2. (I gave a reason for this earlier in the chapter: the positional nature of consumer goods.) Yet shouldn't the ultimate goal of development be about making us happier and more satisfied with life as a whole? Once we have our basic material needs satisfied, more stuff is no guarantee of happiness. Again, any further happiness seems to be a product of how that additional wealth is used and distributed across society as a whole. There is remarkable variability across higher-income countries when it comes to how the average citizen feels about being satisfied with life as a whole. Studies show, for instance, that higher incomes are far more likely to be positively correlated to higher life evaluation and positive feelings in *more equal* nations (see, e.g., Ng and Diener 2019). We finally have empirical evidence to back up what we've been saying for generations: money doesn't buy happiness (see ECOnnection 12.1).

This stands in stark contrast to conventional macroeconomic theory. Yet even economic theory has a term that recognizes the absurdity of this premise. The **diminishing marginal utility** of stuff, and ultimately of money itself, speaks to the fact that having more of something eventually provides less additional satisfaction. (The so-called law of diminishing marginal utility, plainly stated, is that the more units of something we consume, the less added enjoyment we get from each additional unit.) Although I am

FIGURE 12.2 Relationship between Average per Capita Income and Percentage of Population Reporting Happiness and Satisfaction with Life as a Whole, Select Countries

Source: Adapted from Carolan (2018a) and Wilkinson and Pickett (2011).

Note

The solid line indicates the general relationship between *x* and *y* axes when all countries are tabulated.

getting a bit ahead of myself, this helps us understand why economic growth, after a certain point, might indeed be *negatively* correlated with happiness.

Clearly, all this stuff has done nothing to make the average American better off. This phenomenon of diminishing marginal utility also offers, as others have argued (Hall and Klitgaard 2018), justification for some level of redistribution. When you are starving, any food will bring an immediate bump in your feelings of satisfaction. At the opposite extreme, when a person in the United States is staring at a refrigerator and pantry overflowing with food, a little more will likely bring zero additional satisfaction. It might even be considered a burden, as they now have to find room for it. And for a growing number of people in high-income countries, the actual act of eating has become stressful, as they worry increasingly about obesity and obesity-related health risks. When talking about this in a class, I had a student thoughtfully ask, "Don't we at least need pro-growth policies to alleviate poverty? What will happen to them—the poor?"

The evidence just does not support the argument that current pro-growth policies do much for the poor. For every $100 of economic growth between 1990 and 2001, a mere *60 cents* went toward poverty reduction for those earning less than $1 a day (Gilding 2011). The poverty-alleviating logic of growth looks something like this: the rich get richer—remember what I said earlier about the three richest people in the United States—so the poor can be a little less poor (but still poor in the end). This is, in fact, the exact finding of a recent analysis in *Development Policy Review* (Akinci 2018). Looking at data for sixty-five countries during the period 1995–2011, the author lambasts the idea of so-called trickle-down economics:

> The experiences of the real world have shown that most of the populations in these countries have not benefited from income growth. In many countries, economic growth has been accompanied by rising inequality, which is associated with widening disparities, with the rich getting richer and the poor getting poorer. It can easily be observed using income distribution data sets that while inequality has tended to increase over intervals in developing countries, it has done so almost equally in developed countries.
>
> (Akinci 2018, 22)

If you dig a little deeper, the data get even more interesting. The problem with growth as currently practiced is not that it degrades the quality of life for some of the world's inhabitants. It is true that levels of global inequality have never been worse; after all, 2016 marked the first time in human history when the richest 1 percent had a combined wealth greater than the remaining 99 percent of the world's population (Oxfam 2015). Yet the rich suffer under this system too—though obviously their suffering is qualitatively different from that of someone in abject poverty. According to the data, economic growth makes life less satisfying for *all* of humanity, rich and poor alike.

Whereas absolute wealth is a poor indicator of a country's level of prosperity, inequality proves to be a strong indicator, as it is negatively correlated with a whole host of prosperity and well-being indicators. This holds even for a nation's affluent. The economically advantaged are better off if the country they live in is more equal. The data on this subject are compelling. More equal societies have fewer health and social problems (see Figure 12.4), treat women and children better, have a greater sense of collective responsibility to

ECOnnection 12.1

Freedom Isn't Free, and Apparently Best in Moderation

The United States based think tank the Heritage Center and the *Wall Street Journal* compile data resulting in the Index of Economic Freedom. There's a good chance you've heard it mentioned on CNN, MSNBC, or Fox, often in the context of praise for those countries with high index scores. This index is a series of ten economic measurements that have been grouped into four broad categories: rule of law (property rights, freedom from corruption); limited government (fiscal freedom, government spending); regulatory efficiency (business freedom, labor freedom, monetary freedom); and open markets (trade freedom, investment freedom, financial freedom). Countries that score 80 to 100 are considered "free," 79.9 to 70 "mostly free," 69.9 to 60 "moderately free," 59.9 to 50 "mostly un-free," and 49.9 to 40 "repressed."

Setting that index to the side for a moment, I also want to introduce what are known as **Happy Life Years** (HLYs). While life expectancy and self-reported satisfaction surveys are indicative of how well people thrive in a country, neither captures this matter completely. One could imagine, for example, a society where people live long but not happily, such as in cases where medical technologies stretch life out well after quality of life begins to diminish. Similarly, one could imagine that people live happily in a country but not for long,

perhaps as a result of overindulgence. Combining these measures resolves some of these limitations. It is common to measure the health of nations by the average number of years people live free from chronic illness: HLYs = life expectancy at birth x happiness score (on a scale of 0 to 1). For purposes of illustration, say life expectancy in Country X is 60 years. If everybody were perfectly happy (with a happiness score of 1), the average HLYs for this country would be 60. If, for example, the country's average happiness score was 0.5, the per capita HLYs lived would be 30.

Figure 12.3 examines the relationship between economic freedom (as captured in the Index of Economic Freedom) and HLYs. There are two rather striking features about this scatterplot. The first is that there is almost no correlation between the two variables. Economic freedom, in other words, appears to have little impact on a country's HLYs. More striking still is where the two variables do seem to have some relationship with each other. A relationship appears to materialize at the high end of the economic freedom score, and it is a negative one. Note how "mostly free" and "free" countries cannot seem to generate very high HLYs scores. Not a single country with an economic freedom score of 70 or greater averages 50 HLYs or more.

FIGURE 12.3 Relationship between Economic Freedom Score and Happy Life Years

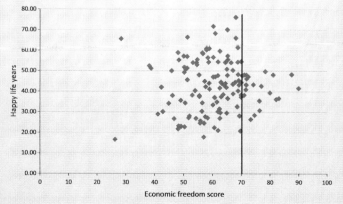

Source: Adapted from Carolan (2018a).

FIGURE 12.4 Relationship between Health and Social Problems and Income Inequality, Select High-Income Countries

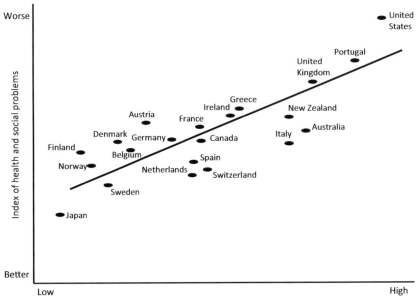

Source: Adapted from Wilkinson and Pickett (2011).

FIGURE 12.5 Relationship between Foreign Aid Spending and Income Inequality, Select High-Income Countries

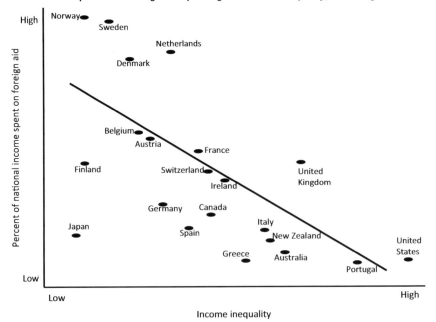

Source: Adapted from Wilkinson and Pickett (2011).

those in other countries (see Figure 12.5), lower rates of mental illnesses, are more willing to cooperate with international environmental agreements, and are more food secure (Bartels 2018; Wilkinson and Pickett 2011; Wilkinson et al. 2010).

Perhaps it is no coincidence that welfare economics, as detailed in the previous chapter, has found such favor in the United States. More equal countries tend to be more cooperative (Wilkinson and Pickett 2011). The high levels of inequality in the United States offer the perfect environment for a perspective that assumes people are self-interested and selfish. This also helps us make some sense of why most of the industrialized world chose to continue with the **Kyoto Protocol** despite the non-involvement of major greenhouse gas emitting countries like the United States and China. Perhaps this also explains why, in 2017, the United States withdrew from the Paris Agreement— I've already quoted President Trump in the previous chapter essentially saying that he does not trust other nations to reduce their greenhouse gas emissions so why should the US (he also doesn't believe climate change is real, which certainly played into his decision to withdraw)? The Paris Agreement, for those who don't know, is an agreement—signed in 2016—within the United Nations Framework Convention on Climate Change that deals with greenhouse gas emissions mitigation, adaptation, and finance. From a purely self-interested perspective, it makes no sense to comply with any part of these international agreements, given that any greenhouse gas reductions would easily be offset by nonsignatory countries. Perhaps the countries still in these agreements chose to do so out of a heightened sense of global responsibility; a sentiment, perhaps not coincidentally, more likely to be found among more equal societies—a characteristic that does not describe the United States.

Innovation also appears to be enhanced by equality, as more equal societies have higher levels of patents granted per capita. This may be due in part to their higher levels of social mobility and educational achievement: more equal societies are less likely to waste their potential human capital, since they provide greater opportunities for all of their members (Andersen 2018; Wilkinson et al. 2010). Think about this in the context of renewable energy. Those countries first to transition to renewable energy sources will have done so because they are highly adaptable and innovative. Are countries like the United States hindering their ability to make this transition due to their high levels of inequality? In sum, inequality is a tremendous source of inefficiency. The efficiency through which a society utilizes its resources to enhance its well-being increases at low to moderate levels of economic development but *declines* at high levels, particularly when combined with high levels of inequality (Andersen 2018; Dietz et al. 2012; Knight and Rosa 2011). A high level of inequality in a society is therefore not only morally problematic but bad policy, as it reduces everyone's welfare.

The Sociology of Consumption

Why do we consume so much stuff? The following five sociological mechanisms have been linked to escalating levels of consumption: social comparison, creation of self-identity, specialization, sociotechnical systems, and planned obsolescence. I briefly take each in turn, recognizing that this discussion represents the barest of overviews of a richly complex literature.

Social Comparison

More than a century ago Thorstein Veblen ([1899] 1967), in his analysis of Western European countries, introduced us to the now commonplace term **conspicuous consumption**: the idea that we consume, at least in part, to display to others our social power and status. In centuries past, the displaying of power and status was relatively straightforward, involving things like commanding large armies, possessing huge castles, and ruling over entire societies. Individuals today, however, no longer possess great armies or rule over a peasant class. According to Veblen, we therefore make social statements in other ways, such as by surrounding ourselves with nice things to signal to others our placement in the socioeconomic hierarchy. The mechanism of social comparison also has a ratcheting-up effect on consumption. Individuals attempt to display a social status above what their household income levels allow, as they constantly strive to outdo those around them—a phenomenon commonly known as "keeping up with the Joneses."

Creation of Self-Identity

Consumption is more than just the pursuit of status. It can also have a much deeper function. Our very sense of self is tied to it. The term *lifestyle* is important here, as attachment to groups, according to this argument, is an important source of personal identity. Thus, whether you have chosen, for example, a green lifestyle or that of someone who likes outdoor recreation (both popular among my students), consumption is tied to both. Association with the green lifestyle might require that you buy, say, organic food, a Toyota Prius, or solar panels for your house; at least these represent recent purchases by a friend of mine who embraces this lifestyle. If your identity is that of an outdoors person, you might, for example, walk around wearing clothes from Cabela's or Patagonia, depending on the type of outdoors persona you're trying to communicate to others.

Specialization

Henry Ford famously claimed that you could have the Model T automobile in any color as long as that color was black. That mentality reflects the logic of mass production. Today, more producers—perhaps to fit the aforementioned lifestyles and identities they support—are widening their range of what they produce to fit the specialized "needs" of consumers. An example of this is shoes. When my grandmother was growing up in rural Iowa in the 1920s, she had two pairs of shoes: one for work and one for dress. Fast-forward some ninety years to today. Now, two pairs of shoes would never do. We seem instead to "need" a specialized pair of shoes for almost every one of the day's activities: shoes for in the house, shoes for the garden, shoes for the gym (actually, there you'll need numerous different shoes depending on what you're doing), shoes for work, and so forth.

Sociotechnical Systems

This concept reminds us that there are broader sociological reasons that belie the concept of consumer choice. We should be careful not to look too exclusively at the individual, in other words, to understand why they choose to consume as they do. In some instances, that choice is made for them (as discussed earlier when talking about choosing to drive). Millions around the world, for example, did not choose to have their nondigital television sets become obsolete as analog television broadcasting was converted to and replaced by digital television. Similarly, if your grocery store does not carry organic food, you cannot choose to have an organic diet (nor can we say you're choosing a nonorganic diet). We can only choose what the sociotechnical system lets us choose.

Planned Obsolescence

After World War II, US automobile manufacturers were facing an uncertain future as more Americans became car owners. Once every household (or at least those that could afford one) owned a car, who would be left to buy new automobiles? The answer was to get people to purchase a new car every couple of years. But how? A well-maintained car would theoretically last decades, perhaps even a person's entire lifetime. How, then, could a car owner be cajoled into choosing to buy a new car even if the one currently owned was—from a functionality standpoint—perfectly fine? Enter planned obsolescence. The goal of planned obsolescence as it applies to automobiles is to make the one you currently have in your garage appear obsolete. This is accomplished with the occasional redesign of the car's interior and exterior so as to literally make your current model appear old (even if you just bought it last year). This process is also helped along by incrementally adding "upgrades"—like rear-view cameras, eleven-speaker surround sound, and satellite navigation—and convincing the buyer that they need these extra bells and whistles.

Planned obsolescence can take other forms too, like designing devices that cannot easily be taken apart and repaired (see Image 12.1). When things break down—and we

IMAGE 12.1 Phones Are Being Rendered Obsolete Even before You Buy Them!

Source: "New Phone Coming Soon" by Jason Tester Guerrilla Futures (flickr.com/streamishmc) is licensed copyright © 2012 under CC BY-ND 2.0.

know they will because there's no incentive to make products that last a lifetime—we're effectively required to buy new ones. I remember when the "on" button broke on my blender and how I was forced to get a new blender because there was no way to get it fixed—just because of a defective "on" button!

Environmental Justice

Closely related to the above discussion is the subject of environmental justice. As defined by the Environmental Protection Agency, environmental justice is about the

> fair treatment and meaningful involvement of all people regardless of race, color, national origin, or income with respect to the development, implementation, and enforcement of environmental laws, regulations, and policies. Fair treatment means that no population, due to policy or economic disempowerment, is forced to bear a disproportionate share of the negative human health or environmental impacts of pollution or environmental consequences resulting from industrial, municipal, and commercial operations or the execution of federal, state, local and tribal programs and policies.
>
> (EPA 2012; see Image 12.2)

Our understanding of environmental justice has grown as scholarship accumulates, showing the unequal distribution of environmental threats. These threats disparately affect

IMAGE 12.2 Dakota Access Pipeline Protest at the White House

Source: "Pipeline Protest," February 8, 2017 by Victoria Pickering (flickr.com/photos/vpickering/) is licensed copyright © 2017 under CC BY-SA 2.0.

not only those of lower socioeconomic status but also certain ethnic minorities. Pollution-based racial discrimination goes by the name of **environmental racism** (though the concept can be defined much more broadly to include racial discrimination in environmental policy making and enforcement of regulations and laws, in addition to the targeting of communities of color for toxic waste disposal and siting of polluting industries).

The birth of the term *environmental racism* has been traced back to 1982, when civil rights activists organized to stop the state of North Carolina from dumping 120 million pounds of soil laced with polychlorinated biphenyls in the predominantly African American county of Warren (Bullard 1990; Mohai et al. 2009). Out of this was born a new social movement whose aim has been to address concerns ignored by mainstream middle-class white environmentalists. The environmental justice movement has heavily (and rightly) criticized the conventional environmental movement for focusing too much on pristine ecological landscapes and not enough on people whose lives are threatened daily by ecological risk.

Some of the earliest research into this subject focused on the location of hazardous waste sites. The first was conducted by the US General Accounting Office in 1983 (GAO 1983). The study documented how African American communities in Southern US states hosted a disproportionate share of waste sites. This study was famously followed by a national study in 1987 by the United Church of Christ (UCC) Commission for Racial Justice (Chavis and Lee 1987): This pathbreaking study showed that toxic waste facilities across the United States were far more likely to end up in the backyards of people of color. According to the UCC study, race was the most important factor in predicting where these waste sites were located. In 1990, sociologist Robert Bullard (1990) published the now-classic book *Dumping in Dixie*. This work represents the first comprehensive examination of environmental racism by systematically linking hazardous facility siting with historical patterns of segregation in the Southern United States. Bullard documents in exquisite detail how communities of color have been deliberately targeted when locations were sought for society's waste (see ECOnnection 12.2).

Some twenty-five years after the UCC study, similar findings continue to be made. Some of the recent research utilizes GIS (geographic information system) technology and new methodological techniques to better control for proximity. Employing these new tools, environmental justice scholars in fact "find that the magnitude of racial disparities around hazardous waste facilities is *much greater* than what previous national studies have reported" (Mohai and Saha 2007, 343; emphasis added). Those who believe we live in a postracial society will be surprised to learn that the evidence suggests that environmental racism is more pronounced today than it was fifty years ago. A longitudinal study looking at Michigan from 1950 to 1990 concludes that "whereas significant racial, socioeconomic, and housing disparities at the time of siting were not in evidence for facilities sited prior to 1970, patterns of disparate siting were found for facilities sited after 1970" (Saha and Mohai 2005, 618).

Prior to the 1970s, we knew far less about the ecological risks associated with business as usual. The affluent therefore did not have as much reason to oppose living next to industrial facilities. Fortunately, we did not remain ignorant forever about ecological risk. The 1970s marked the beginning of unprecedented growth in public environmental concern and opposition to facilities that bring with them environmental harms. With this came growing opposition to the siting of facilities that threatened environmental and human health. People no longer wanted these operations sited in their backyards. Yet not everyone is in possession of sufficient resources to keep their backyards free of these facilities. Not surprisingly, then, the siting of hazardous waste facilities followed the path of least political resistance. And, as inequalities continue to grow in countries like the United States, the haves have many more resources to resist polluting industries being sited in their backyards than the have-nots. Hence the growing levels of environmental injustice.

Even when controlling for economic and sociopolitical variables, factors uniquely associated with race continue to correlate strongly with the location of the nation's hazardous waste facilities (Stretesky and McKie 2016). It's hard for me to believe that in each of those cases, there is overt racial discrimination going on. Perhaps some of this environmental racism is actually an artifact of environmental economism. **Economism**, for those unfamiliar with the term, refers to the act of reducing the world to economic dimensions, a practice, as discussed in Chapter 11, lying at the heart of welfare economics and a specific example of methodological reductionism. When assessing the costs and benefits of policy options, this approach assigns a lower value to those of lower socioeconomic status. As certain ethnic minorities make on average less than other groups, they will be disproportionately penalized by this approach. The welfare-economics approach, in other words, in some cases legitimizes environmental racism.

Whereas early environmental racism studies originated in the United States, the scope of research in recent years has spanned the world (see Case Study 12.1). Two types of environmental injustice are being increasingly cited: international and global (Martinez-Alier et al. 2016). On the one hand, in reference to the former and as discussed in previous chapters, polluting industries are moving around the world. In doing so, they too often follow the path of least political resistance, which places them squarely in the backyards of some of society's most marginalized. On the other hand, there are risks that are truly global in character, like climate change (Shue 2014). These threats exacerbate existing inequalities, as those best positioned in terms of resources to keep themselves safe are often those most responsible for the problems in the first place.

Solutions

The solution to the above problems, we know, does not lie in doing away entirely with inequality. People *are* different—in terms of their contributions, skills, and interests—and need to be treated (and rewarded) as such. Differential rewards motivate people to make the world a better place, though clearly people are not motivated *only* by reward. Moreover, there are diminishing marginal returns in those rewards. The opportunity to make another $10,000 means a whole lot more to someone currently making $10,000 a year than it does to someone whose annual salary is a couple of million dollars. At what point, then, is a society's innovative spirit maximized, and after which point does more inequality begin to be responsible for more harm than good? This is a question we need to be discussing (see Ethical Question 12.1).

A Postgrowth Society

It's curious why so many people continue to be enamoured with growth even in the face of mounting evidence that we shouldn't be, particularly after a certain point of affluence is

ECOnnection 12.2

The Plight of Native Americans

The term *ecocide* has been used to describe the US government's twentieth-century treatment of its Native peoples (Grinde and Johansen 1995), a fact that's not entirely denied by the US Department of Defense (DOD 2001, 3):

> In order to ensure that it meets its national security mission, DOD operates and trains on vast amounts of land, including American Indian and Alaska Native lands. Evidence of DOD's past use of these lands remains: hazardous materials, unexploded ordnance (UXO), abandoned equipment, unsafe buildings, and debris. This contamination degrades the natural environment and threatens tribal economic, social and cultural welfare.

Fifty years after the conclusion of the so-called Indian Wars, Native Americans were again uprooted from their land when the US government seized more than 300,000 acres of the Pine Ridge Reservation in South Dakota. (Families there were paid three cents an acre.) The government wanted this land as a practice bombing range for pilots before being sent off to fight for the Allies in World War II, an activity that laced the environment with contaminants (Bordewich et al. 2007).

The US government continues to unduly burden Native Americans with ecological risks up to this day. An analysis looking at closed military bases in the United States found that Native Americans are significantly more likely to be living next to these contaminated spaces than any other ethnic group (Hooks and Smith 2004). One particular risk highlighted by this study is unexploded ordnance, including mines and explosive shells, which have killed, maimed, and injured many. Native Americans continue to be threatened by their environment at levels that would be patently unacceptable to any less marginalized social group.

Then there is the case of Native Hawaiians seeking restitution for damage to the island of Kaho'olawe, degraded by close to fifty years of abuse from the US military through use as a target range for warplanes (Blackford 2004). Or take the case of the Mescalero Apache tribe of New Mexico, which has experienced decades of exploitation after uranium deposits were discovered on its land in the 1950s. Initially, uranium extraction was an involuntary activity imposed on tribes for purposes of nuclear power and out of the US military's desire for weapons-grade uranium. However, in recent decades the resource has developed into an economic necessity for the Mescalero Apache. For instance, when the tribe was approached with a proposal to build a monitored retrievable storage facility for nuclear waste on its land in the 1990s, the chief and tribal council welcomed the opportunity. The "need" for this facility arose from the tribe's socioeconomic vulnerability: the unemployment rate within the tribe was greater than 33 percent, and more than half of the tribe lived below the federal poverty line (Vickery and Hunter 2016).

This struggle is not unique to the United States. In South America, for instance, indigenous peoples in Brazil are once again fighting for their very existence after President Bolsonaro took office early in 2019. He has promised to "integrate" indigenous people into the rest of the population and has repeatedly questioned the legitimacy of their right to land and livelihood. President Bolsonaro wishes to revoke property claims so that timber, mining, and farming interests can overtake indigenous lands (see, e.g., Yin 2019).

CASE STUDY 12.1
Links between Commercial Shrimp Farms and Slavery

"Thai 'ghost ships' that enslave and even kill workers are linked to global shrimp supply chain," a *Guardian* investigation discovers (Hodal et al. 2014). The six-month investigation has established that:

> large numbers of men bought and sold like animals and held against their will on fishing boats off Thailand are integral to the production of prawns (commonly called shrimp in the US) sold in leading supermarkets around the world, including the top four global retailers: Walmart, Carrefour, Costco and Tesco.
>
> (Ibid.)

It is true that retailers and third-party certifying organizations are monitoring most of these shrimp farms. The slavery happens on some of the ships that catch fish that are then ground up into fishmeal and later fed to shrimp on those more visible shrimp farms.

attained. John Stuart Mill (1848, 317), one of the founding parents of economics, wrote clearly about the limitations of economic growth:

> It is scarcely necessary to remark that a stationary condition of capital and population implies no stationary state of human improvement. There would be as much scope as ever for all kinds of mental culture, and moral and social progress; as much room for improving the Art of Living and much more likelihood of its being improved, when minds cease to be engrossed by the art of getting on.

Economists Robert Ayres and Benjamin Warr (2009, xvi) argue that "the historic link between output (GDP) growth and employment has been weakened, if not broken." For the last two centuries, job losses in one sector were absorbed by another. This was particularly the case in higher-income countries, where, for example, workers displaced out of agriculture could often find employment in a thriving manufacturing sector. The problem, however, is that sectors that are expected to flourish this century employ very few people. Think data server farms. *CNBC* conducted a study in 2017 and discovered that half the states in the United States give special tax breaks for data server farms, where the cloud of computing data resides. They examined eleven incentive packages given to data centers of prominent internet companies—e.g., Microsoft, Google, Apple, Facebook, Amazon. After factoring in for the number of jobs these server farms generated, those incentives calculated to almost $2 million per job (LeRoy 2017).

Economies around the world are emerging out of the Great Recession of the late 2000s. And yet, that "recovery" is being experienced unevenly. Take the case of the United States. Jobs created in the last ten years are clustered in the cities and regions that were already well off. This has left one in every four new jobs for the bottom (economically speaking) 60 percent of zip codes. The most distressed communities and counties have seen *zero* net gains in employment and business establishment since 2000—most

ETHICAL QUESTION 12.1
Is There a Right Level of Inequality?

Although most people believe extreme poverty to be morally wrong, the morality of inequality is far from settled terrain. Most can agree that some inequality is not only fair but best for society, as differential reward (especially when that reward is equally available to all) encourages people to make the world a better place. Empirical evidence (and common sense) also indicates that too much inequality stifles innovation and drive. Where's the incentive when the haves have everything and the rest of society has little chance of ever having anything? Getting the level of differential reward right is therefore not only an ethical question but also one with profound practical consequences.

To help us think through this question, Herman Daly (1999) offers the following instructive observation. He proposes a factor of ten as an inequality ceiling. The US military and universities have managed to keep their ratios close to or even below this level while maintaining tremendous drive among individuals within these organizations. In the military, for instance, the highest paid generals make roughly ten times the wages of a private. In a university, the prized rank of distinguished professor brings with it a salary that is roughly three to four times that of a full-time non-tenure-track instructor. Mindy Grossman, the CEO of Weight Watchers International (WTW) made $33.4 million in 2018—5,908 times more than the company's median employee salary. Or take Mattel: Margaret Georgiadis, the company's CEO, made $31.3 million in 2018—4,987 times the company's median employee salary (Suneson 2018).

These CEOs make almost 200 times more than a top-ranking US general and distinguished professor. Is that an efficient and effective distribution of resources? Are these CEOs 200 times more motivated than US generals and distinguished professors? Do we believe the head of a company (*any* company) is delivering 200 times more value to society than a top military commander or, say, a Nobel Prize winning professor?

One way to frame this discussion is to talk about growing the middle class and expanding opportunities so people can have the freedom and liberty to pursue a life that is meaningful to them. Right now, far too many people lack these basic freedoms.

have in fact seen net losses on both accounts. Half of the adults living in these communities are trying to make a living with a high school education or less (Hart 2017a). Moreover, the US labour force is becoming increasingly dependent on large companies. To quote a report from 2017: "For the first time on record, U.S. companies are actually dying at a faster rate than they're being born, according to an analysis by the Economic Innovation Group, a non-profit research and advocacy organization" (Hart 2017b). Politicians might like to tout how the country's economy is "booming" and "benefiting all Americans"—to quote a recent White House press release (White House 2019). The truth isn't nearly this rosy.

The great twentieth-century economist John Maynard Keynes ([1930] 1963), writing some eighty years ago, believed that by the dawn of the twenty-first century, people would be working just a couple of days a week as a result of the remarkable productivity increases he (correctly) foresaw coming. He predicted (incorrectly) that rather than practicing overconsumption in order to keep everyone working *more* hours—to buy more stuff we would

ECOnnection 12.3

Consume Less, Yes ... But What About That Next Day Shipping?

Between 2017 and 2019, the time from purchase to delivery has declined from 5.2 days to 4.3 days. Amazon is even faster, at 3.2 days on average, though they now promise same day shipping in a number of markets. That's all great, for those who think they "need" stuff now. But it comes at great cost to the environment.

In 2017, UPS (United Postal Service) reported that the above trend has decreased the number of packages it drops off per mile, leading to more trucks on the road and higher greenhouse gas emissions. Not that Amazon with their same day delivery is the only player in all this we ought to be critical of. Given Amazon's scale, they are able to attain certain environmental efficiencies with their speedy delivery that smaller firms cannot achieve, though a few extra days on the road is almost always better from an environmental impact standpoint. As research has demonstrated, the trade-off between speed and carbon emissions gets larger with smaller retailers that make more customer deliveries, like meal kit services, florists, and grocery delivery services. Yet thanks to Amazon, companies of all sizes feel pressure to match their shipping, even though they lack Amazon's billion-dollar investment in the world's most sophisticated shipping logistics infrastructure.

Source: DePillis (2019).

need to work more—we would instead choose to take advantage of those increases in productivity to work less and increase our leisure time. Employment for everyone is possible when the average worker works, depending on the society, twenty hours a week (see Case Study 12.2). In such a scenario, overconsumption is neither possible, as a twenty-hour workweek doesn't allow for it, nor necessarily desired; with everyone in the same boat, the social pressures to overconsume are dramatically weakened (see ECOnnection 12.3). How could Keynes have predicted that we would instead decide to continue working longer hours that make us terribly unhappy so we can buy products that do nothing to enhance our well-being while depleting our natural resources and destroying the health of ourselves and our planet? Does that make any sense? Keynes didn't think so either.

There is an enormous difference between an economy purposefully designed to be indifferent to growth, where prosperity and well-being increase in the absence of economic growth, and a failing growth economy, where growth, prosperity, and well-being all decline while inequality increases. In a failing growth economy, out-of-control unemployment and crushing state, household, and personal debt seriously threaten that society's social and political stability. A failing economy, for instance, helped precipitate the 2011 Egyptian revolution. Conversely, an economy indifferent to growth—even one designed to hold steady and not grow—can avoid all this if intentionally constructed with these ends in mind.

CASE STUDY 12.2
Kellogg's Six-Hour Day

Breakfast cereal giant W.K. Kellogg implemented a policy back in 1930 that we could learn from today. In response to the Great Depression, Kellogg made his workforce of 1,500 move from a traditional eight-hour to a six-hour workday rather than lay off some 300 workers. The new arrangement meant everyone had to take a slight pay cut, but Kellogg also initiated production-based bonuses that could offset most of those losses. The policy was an unqualified success. The employees used their newly available time to pursue things of their choosing, which often involved activities that built family, community, and citizenship. In general, employees were happier under this new arrangement (Hunnicutt 1996). They also worked harder. The production, for example, of boxes of shredded whole wheat biscuits per hour increased from eighty-three to ninety-six once the workday was shortened (Botsman and Rogers 2010).

World War II changed everything. Franklin Roosevelt signed an executive order demanding, among other things, longer workdays so the production needs of a war economy could be met. The labor unions initially opposed the policy to return to an eight-hour workday but eventually acquiesced, as they fully expected a return to a six-hour workday after the war's conclusion (Hunnicutt 1996). Polls as late as 1946 found that 77 percent of men and 87 percent of women actually preferred a 30-hour workweek even if it meant lower wages (Fitz 2009). And the longer hours and larger paychecks did little to actually make the employees any better off. As one employee later reported,

> Everybody thought they were going to get rich when they got that eight-hour deal and it really didn't make a big difference…. Some went out and bought automobiles right quick and they didn't gain much on that because the car took the extra money they had.
>
> (Botsman and Rogers 2010, 46)

How do we do that? We can start by redirecting taxes away from things we generally want (like labor) to things we generally don't want (like pollution and waste). This encourages employment—a key difference from a failing growth economy—and discourages wasteful resource use and dependence, which can help buffer an economy from the shocks that come when access to those resources is disrupted (Gilding 2011). We can also institute policies that encourage a shorter workweek. The government already regulates how much children can work. Why can't it do the same for everyone? By working less, we will also spend less. And as growth is no longer an imperative, we can tighten access to credit, thereby reducing or eliminating personal debt entirely. What would you choose, if given the choice: being caught on what Juliet Schor (1992) has termed the **work–spend cycle** (where we work to spend, which in turn requires us to work more) or having an extra month (or more) of vacation time a year to spend with family and friends? If you are anything like the people I have asked, you will very likely prefer the latter.

As noted earlier, once we're well fed, clothed, adequately sheltered, educated, and feel generally secure, happiness comes from something other than just more stuff and additional wealth. By working less, we will have time to finally engage in those activities that truly make us happy. We will have time to engage in "mental culture" and "social progress" and improve overall the "Art of Living," to borrow terms used by John Stuart Mill. Decades of social capital research point to the benefits that accrue to individuals and society as a whole when people have the opportunity to engage with one another on a personal level (see Bartolini et al. 2016). Moving away from our current obsession with growth will also address the aforementioned problems associated with rabid inequality. As the late Henry Wallich (1972), former governor of the US Federal Reserve, famously put it, "Growth is a substitute for equality of income. So long as there is growth there is hope, and that makes large income differential tolerable."

We also shouldn't hold out hope for so-called service-based, postindustrial, or information-based economies. *Postindustrial* does not mean *postpollution*. These societies are built on an economy whereby manufacturing is reduced through trade, while consumption skyrockets, with the help of an expanding financial sector, so we can buy all this stuff. When all ecological impacts are actually accounted for, most service- or information-based economies are at least as resource hungry as industrial economies. We will also have to rethink how we do leisure and recreation in this new economy. With current practices, these sectors are extremely energy and resource intensive, and suggest that we need to rethink not only what we consume but also how we recreate and relax (Huang and Wang 2015). Recreation is also becoming expensive. Today many worry about whether they can afford the next big trip. I guess that's why I increasingly hear people comment when on vacation that they need a vacation from their vacation. In a postgrowth economy, leisure will once again be leisurely.

It is also worth asking why leisure today must involve going someplace. Or perhaps it is more accurate to characterize it as getting away—after all, that's often how we characterize vacations. Maybe, if we enhanced the attractiveness of communities, we could reduce the "need" to travel to distant places. This would not only be a tremendous ecological gain, recognizing the significant environmental footprint associated with air travel and everything else one does when touring a distant land, but would also help dampen the need we feel to (over) work, as we would no longer have this large expense looming on the horizon. And in the long term, this would have a virtuous effect. At present, contemporary communities are so lowly regarded that they offer few inducements to encourage people to stick around when they have free time. Making communities places we actually *want* to be will keep people within the community and thus further enhance the social and ecological dynamics of this space still further.

A modeling attempt by a Canadian economist illustrates how economic stabilization (growth of less than 0.1 percent annually) can successfully occur, though the entire transition will take a couple of decades (Victor 2019). Under the modeled Canadian scenario, unemployment and poverty were halved, the debt-to-GDP ratio was reduced by some 75 percent, and greenhouse gas emissions for the nation were cut by 20 percent. The model revealed a couple of important insights. Changes to investment and the structure of the labor market have to be handled carefully to make a postgrowth society work. While net business investment was reduced in the modeled scenario, there was also a significant shift in investment to public goods through changes in taxation and public spending. The model supports the point made earlier that it is not wealth per se that improves societal well-being and resilience but how that money is spent and distributed. Unemployment was avoided both by reducing the average number of working hours (while assuming that labor productivity continues to increase) and by sharing the work more equally across the available workforce. As certain European labor policies have already shown, reducing the working week is a relatively simple solution to the challenge of maintaining full employment with nonincreasing output (Jackson 2017).

Although it is difficult for some to conceive of how companies can flourish without growth, consider that this is precisely how small businesses—like so-called mom-and-pop establishments—have operated for centuries. Businesses under this model have costs and revenues. When profits are earned, some are reinvested back into the business to replace or upgrade worn-out equipment. The goal is not to "grow" but rather to reduce costs in the hope of increasing profits. As Juliet Schor (2010) notes, businesses can be quite successful in the market when they offer better quality for a given price, a strategy that can easily be hindered when owners become obsessed with growth. Continual expansion is neither necessary nor sufficient for profitability.

The point that prosperity comes not from wealth but from the efficient use of resources lies at the heart of alternative measures to GDP. Throughout much of the twentieth century, GDP was the gold standard of progress and prosperity; it was long assumed that growth could deliver unlimited happiness. Now that we know it does not, alternative measures of progress and prosperity are being developed. One of the most popular alternative measures is the Human Development Index (HDI). The HDI factors in a country's life expectancy as well as measures of literacy, education, and standards of living. The HDI was originally devised in 1990 by the Pakistani economist Mahbub ul Haq and the Indian economist Amartya Sen. Its goal, in the words of Haq (1995, 3), is to give "human capital"—*humanity* (versus money)—"the attention it deserves" when talking about and implementing policies directed at this nebulous thing we call development. (The HDI is now used widely in the international development community and by organizations like the United Nations.) In line with all that has already been discussed, beyond a certain level of affluence, wealth has no correlation to a country's HDI ranking.

In recent years, attempts have also been made to combine HDI with ecological indicators, as presently HDI ignores environmental variables. Figure 12.6 provides an example, plotting countries according to their HDI ranking and ecological footprint. Note the wide disparity between countries with high HDI scores and ecological footprints behind those corresponding levels of well-being. One country has managed to produce a high HDI score within the parameters of what ecological footprint scholars deem to be a truly sustainable economy (a footprint of 2.1 hectares per person or less): Cuba. It will be interesting to see if and how the new relationship between the United States and Cuba changes these scores in the future. Will the slow opening of Cuba to the US market make things better or worse for the average Cuban?

Another widely cited measure of progress, which considers a country's ecological condition, is the Happy Planet Index (HPI). The fundamental premise of the HPI is the acknowledgment that real prosperity can be said to have been reached only when the well-being of humankind does not come at the Earth's expense (New Economics Foundation 2017). HPI scores range from 0 to 100. High scores reflect a society with high life expectancy, high life satisfaction, and a low ecological footprint. This measure turns convention on its head. For example, the United States is unflatteringly ranked at one hundred and eighth (it held one hundred and fifth place in the prior, 2014, report), while Costa Rica comes out on top. Costa Ricans live slightly longer than Americans,

FIGURE 12.6 Human Development Index Plotted against Ecological Footprint

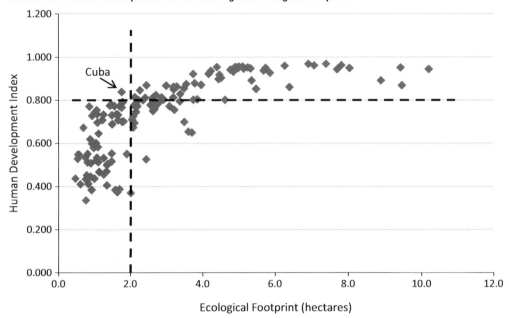

Source: Carolan (2018a).

Note
The Human Development Index (HDI) is calculated on a scale from 0 to 1, where 0 is the lowest and 1 is the highest.

report much higher levels of life satisfaction, and do all this with an ecological footprint that is less than one-third the size of the average US citizen. The HPI also supports the argument that it is not environmental throughput (aka growth) that makes a society great. Here is what the most recent Happy Planet Index report has to say about the top-ranking country:

> This year, Costa Rica has topped the Happy Planet Index rankings for the third time. Costa Ricans have higher wellbeing than the residents of many rich nations, including the USA and the UK, and live longer than people in the USA. This is achieved with a per capita Ecological Footprint that's just one third of the size of the USA's. Costa Rica is a world leader when it comes to environmental protection. 99% of electricity used in Costa Rica comes from renewable sources and the government is far ahead of many wealthier nations, having committed the country to becoming carbon neutral by 2021. Since abolishing its army in 1949, the country has reallocated its defense budget to funding education, health and pensions.
>
> (New Economics Foundation 2017, 2)

The Happy Planet Index report is careful not to paint Costa Rica as a perfect paradise. There remains important work to do, such as in regard to its unprogressive tax system, which "means that income inequality is particularly high." The report also reminds readers that the country "still has some way to go before it is completely sustainable" (New Economics Foundation 2017, 2).

Development as Freedom, Justice, and Empowerment

There is also good reason to believe readjustments to developmental policies and practices like those mentioned above would go a long way toward alleviating many of the environmental injustices described earlier. To work through this idea, I'll turn to Amartya Sen's thoughts on the subject and, in particular, his theory of justice where he speaks specifically about the pitfalls that come with making economic growth an end in itself. What makes Sen's approach to justice so interesting is his focus on capabilities, which are necessary for people to function fully in the lives they choose. It is Sen's contention that justice should not be about the distribution of goods and services but about how individuals are able to use those goods and services so they can flourish. In Sen's (1999, 74) words, the "focus has to be, in this analysis, on the freedoms generated by commodities, rather than on the commodities seen on their own." Our current focus on economic growth, conversely, cares nothing about what commodities do for people; all that matters is that commodities are produced and sold. In sum, Sen's focus on capabilities forces us to ask what is needed to transform mere economic growth into a truly prosperous life while also considering what might interrupt the process.

This discussion links up with something discussed back in Chapter 10, when I wrote about Berlin's dual understanding of freedom. Sen (1993) draws inspiration from Berlin in his writings on the subject. Prosperity requires positive rights, like the right to utilize goods and services in ways that allow people to flourish. But it also, and equally, requires negative rights, such as the right to live in an environment where that process is not interrupted by, say, toxic waste, environmental racism, patriarchy, or runaway inequality. Instead of offering a universal set of capabilities, Sen believes the communities in question are best positioned to decide what it is they value and the lives they wish to live:

> [The] problem is not with listing important capabilities, but with insisting on one pre-determined canonical list of capabilities, chosen by theorists without any general social discussion or public reasoning. To have such a fixed list, emanating entirely from pure theory, is to deny the possibility of fruitful public participation on what should be included and why.
>
> (Sen 2005, 158; see ECOnnection 12.4)

Environmental justice movements have much in common with Sen's theory of justice and his emphasis on capabilities. This is especially true for movements originating in low-income countries, where the development priorities of outsiders have threatened the functioning of local communities (Schlosberg 2013). A key component of almost any type of environmental justice activism is building community capacity and facilitating community empowerment (Roark 2015; see Movement Matters 12.1).

Evidence of capability building in the environmental justice movement is ubiquitous, especially at the local level. And I'm not just talking about strengthening social ties *within* communities. The reason why, for instance, a study looking at the location of waste incinerators in France discovered that "each additional 1 percent of a town's population that is foreign-born increased the odds that the town received an incinerator by 29 percent" (Laurian and Funderburg 2014, 424) is not solely because individuals within communities with incinerators fail to interact with each other. The communities

ECOnnection 12.4

Community Capitals Framework

There are a variety of ways to translate Sen's thinking about capabilities into a pragmatic developmental program. The HDI represents one attempt to put Sen's thoughts into practice. Yet arguably, any developmental approach that works to empower—rather than just enrich—squares well with Sen's writings.

Take the community capitals framework. According to this approach, sustainable development is the product of a triple bottom line, involving economic, social, and environmental accountability (Flora 2008). These three sustainability pillars come together when a variety of capitals are present in sufficient degree, including natural, built, financial, political, social, human, and cultural capitals. Although equally important in the achievement of the aforementioned triple

bottom line, investments in social and human capitals in particular, research shows, can produce a "spiraling up" effect that leads to the enhancement of all capitals over time (Emery and Flora 2006).

We can see in Table 12.2 the role of the various capitals at play in rural development and how they build on each other. A community capitals approach expands our understanding of return on investment, noting that it should be measured in terms of an increase in *all* capitals, rather than just in terms of economic growth (financial capital). Furthermore, community capitals research believes in involving people so they can direct change from within a community, a point that also fits with Sen's belief that only the communities—through debate and public reasoning—can determine what's best for them.

TABLE 12.2 Seven Capitals and Their Role in Creating Sustainable and Just Communities

CAPITAL	DEFINITION	ROLE IN CREATING SUSTAINABLE AND JUST COMMUNITIES
Natural	The natural biophysical assets of any given locale—can include natural resources (e.g., water, soil, air, minerals), amenities (e.g., trout streams and sandy beaches), and natural beauty.	These assets, when utilized in a manner cognizant of ecological limits, represent the ecological productive base for the long-term growth of other capitals.
Cultural	Institutionalized (widely shared) cultural symbols—attitudes, preferences, beliefs—that shape how we see the world, what we take for granted, and possible alternatives for social change.	By investing in cultural diversity (and including those who are traditionally excluded) biodiversity and different ways of approaching change can be utilized to the enhancement of all capitals.
Human	Includes the skills, knowledge, and abilities of the people within a community to enhance local as well as access outside resources.	Increasing the knowledge base of a community will help that community bolster its other capitals.
Social	The social glue of a community—includes levels of mutual trust, reciprocity, and a sense of shared identity and future.	A social lubricant in that it makes the enhancement of the other capitals considerably easier.
Political	Access to structures of power and power brokers as well as the ability to influence the rules and regulations that shape access to resources.	Political access greatly enhances a community's ability to bolster other capitals.
Financial	The financial resources available to invest in things like community capacity building and social entrepreneurship.	Financial resources can help pay for the maintenance and accumulation of other capitals.
Built	Infrastructure (also includes built "natural" areas, like reconstituted wetlands, ski runs, and artificial coral reefs).	Infrastructure supports other capitals.

Source: Carolan and Hale (2016)

MOVEMENT MATTERS 12.1
Fighting for Environmental Justice in China

Even with its authoritarian government, activists in China have managed successfully to collectively organize. An example of this involves citizen opposition to a waste-to-energy incinerator in the village of Panguanying in Hebei Province. Activists were successful because they were able to transcend the local arena and connect their plight with bigger environmental justice issues, such as the value of public input in siting decisions. For instance, villagers were able to demonstrate that there were no opportunities for public input even though incinerator proponents claimed otherwise. The message: if that could happen here it could happen anywhere in China. In recent years, Chinese NGOs have begun to actively work with local (rural) communities. This has been facilitated by, for example, the spread of the internet and social media and declining risks associated with protest as the state loosens some of its heavy-handed authoritarian policies. An informal network between villagers and urban environmental activists thus formed, which allowed local activists to have influence that extended all the way to Beijing.

Construction of the incinerator eventually came to a halt. Some have since suggested transforming the half-built facility into an environmental protection museum. More recent still (August 2017), it was revealed that a local activist is exploring the possibility of using the village as a site for a pilot project in waste reduction and sorting with residents; a project, I'm sure, that will be developed with close public involvement.

Adapted from Johnson et al. (2018).

themselves are marginalized, which is to say they are not well integrated with, say, community activists in other communities and broader structures of power (e.g., politicians). We must also not forget that one community's environmental justice movement victory is another's hazardous waste facility, as these "successes" typically just displace an unwanted land use onto another community (see, e.g., Bailey and Darkal 2018; Malin 2015).

The movement has also succeeded in making meaningful changes at the national level. Perhaps the most celebrated US example is President Clinton's Executive Order 12898, which mandates all federal agencies to ensure environmental justice in their operations. Another example is the Environmental Protection Agency's (EPA) National Environmental Justice Advisory Council, which is meant to provide advice and oversight of the EPA's environmental justice activities, though the effectiveness of this council has long been questioned by environmental justice scholars and activists.

IMPORTANT CONCEPTS

- Amartya Sen's theory of justice
- community capitals framework
- conspicuous consumption
- environmental justice
- five sociological mechanisms of consumption
- Happy Life Years (HLYs)
- Happy Planet Index (HPI)
- Human Development Index (HDI)
- limits to growth and postgrowth

DISCUSSION QUESTIONS

- What could you change about your own life that would both improve your well-being and reduce your ecological footprint? What's stopping you from making the change?
- As long as we create waste, we are going to have to put that waste somewhere. How do we keep that waste from finding its way into the backyards of *any* marginalized population?
- What do *progress* and *prosperity* mean to you?
- What conditions would have to be met for an economy to grow indefinitely? In such a scenario, would our happiness and well-being increase indefinitely too?

SUGGESTED ADDITIONAL READINGS

Büchs, M., and M. Koch. 2019. "Challenges for the Degrowth Transition: The Debate About Wellbeing." *Futures*, 105: 155–165.

Evans, D. 2019. "What is Consumption, Where Has It Been Going, and Does It Still Matter?" *The Sociological Review*, 67(3): 499–517.

New Economics Foundation. 2017. *The Happy Plant Index 2016: Briefing Paper*. http://happy planetindex.org/s/Briefing-paper-HPI-2016.pdf.

Wood, N., and K. Roelich. 2019. "Tensions, Capabilities, and Justice in Climate Change Mitigation of Fossil Fuels." *Energy Research & Social Science*, 52: 114–122.

RELEVANT INTERNET LINKS

- http://hdr.undp.org/en/statistics. Get the latest Human Development Index data and rankings here.
- https://neweconomics.org/campaigns/shorter-working-week. Short video from the New Economics Foundation on their Four-Day Workweek campaign.
- www.pvictor.com/models. Some of the models mentioned earlier from Victor (2019) can be found here.
- www.neweconomics.org. New Economics Foundation—home of the Happy Planet Index, among other interesting things.
- www.ted.com/talks/nic_marks_the_happy_planet_index.html. Nic Marks of the New Economics Foundation gives a TED talk titled "The Happy Planet Index."

- www.cnn.com/2019/07/15/business/fast-shipping-environmental-impact/index.html. Interesting video on the environmental costs of same-day shipping.

SUGGESTED VIDEOS

- *Four Indigenous Communities, One Goal: Environmental Justice* (2017). With financial backing from the United Nations Development Programme, the Equator Initiative supports the work of local and indigenous communities worldwide in creating sustainable development solutions. The Equator Prize recognizes those efforts. This short film (just over nine minutes) highlights the work of four of the recipients fighting for environmental justice. www.nationalgeographic.com/video/shorts/593071683609/.
- *Growthbusters: Hooked on Growth* (2011). A documentary that questions society's most fundamental beliefs about prosperity.
- *Last Call* (2014). The story of one of the most controversial and inspiring environmental books of all times, *The Limits to Growth* (1972). And yet, its message today is more relevant than ever, or so the film argues.
- *The Light Bulb Conspiracy* (2010). http://dotsub.com/view/aed3b8b2-1889-4df5-ae63-ad85f5572f27. Documents the strategic use of planned obsolescence over the past 100 years to increase the purchase frequency of consumer goods.
- *Tipping Point: The Age of the Oil Sands* (2011). For years, residents in a small community in northern Alberta, Canada, have been plagued by rare forms of cancer. This film chronicles their struggle as they attempt to get answers from the oil industry that is operating upstream from them.

Part IV

SHIFTING THE FOCUS TO RESULTS

From Our Beliefs to Our Behaviors: Pragmatic Environmentalism in Action

We come now to the final social driver that I address: us. Sometimes in sociology we get so caught up talking about structures, capital, organizations, and the like that we forget that people "mutually constitute"—to evoke a popular term among agency and structure theorists—those things that otherwise seem to have such power over us. In this chapter, I take a closer look at understandings, perceptions, and attitudes relevant to the problems and solutions discussed throughout this book, noting that these seemingly mental artifacts are fundamentally sociological, as they affect and are an effect of one's socioecological environment. Any positive change has ultimately to start with us. This point is important, as it takes us back to where this book began: talking about pragmatic environmentalism. The chapter concludes by revisiting this concept.

Fast Facts

- Based on fourteen dependent variables from two nationally representative data sets, a recent study found Evangelical Protestant affiliation, at statistically significant levels, to have a negative effect on future concerns about climate change and the exhaustion of natural resources (Smith et al. 2018). Moreover, in the authors' words, "each increasing unit of church attendance is predicted to cause a 1 percent decrease in the future concern about exhausting natural resources" (Smith et al. 2018, 311). Evangelicals also expressed a narrow understanding of social change. The authors argue this is due to the religious tradition's emphasis on individualism, which explains the population's interest in policies that achieve change incrementally, through individual transformation and responsibility, as opposed to collective action, structural change, and/or government intervention.
- A US national survey found that an individual's cultural worldviews not only shape the media outlets they observe but also influence how they cognitively process news/commentary about climate change (Newman et al. 2018). Specifically, individuals who score high in terms of "hierarchical values" prefer right-leaning media outlets, while individuals who

score high on "individualistic values" tend to avoid left-leaning and moderate news out-lets—if you hold one of these values you tend to hold the other (Druckman and McGrath 2019). Conversely, those holding "communitarian values" and "egalitarian values" tend to consume left-leaning and moderate news sources. In the authors' words, "we found that levels of climate change concern increase for both Hierarchical and Egalitarian individuals as exposure to left-leaning media increases"; they added that "increased exposure to right-leaning media lead to decreased levels of concern among individuals who score high in terms of Hierarchical and Individualistic values" (Newman et al. 2018, 986).

- There is a curious geographic pattern emerging in nations around the world, including the United States, the United Kingdom, Germany, and Switzerland: metropolitan areas—and associated lifestyle characteristics such as smaller housing units, proximity to cultural ameni-ties, and access to mass transit—have higher proportions of left-leaning voters than locations with lower population densities (e.g., Long et al. 2019; Martin and Webster 2018; Maxwell 2019). Research suggests that these divisions can run deep and involve more than some groups not getting their facts right. For, ultimately, what counts as a legitimate societal goal—something that facts alone cannot determine—is often in dispute (ECOnnection 13.1).

- Recent surveys indicate that among individuals concerned about the environment, the most common associated emotional feeling is one of helplessness (e.g., Landry et al. 2018; Leiserowitz et al., 2014). Studies indicate that this so-called learned helplessness—another reason for being fed-up with doom and gloom textbooks!—weaken an individual's willing-ness to turn those pro-environmental attitudes into pro-environmental behaviors (Hart-mann et al. 2014; Landry et al. 2018).

ECOnnection 13.1

Living Worlds Apart

Not too long ago, I interviewed farmers and agri-culture professionals in North Dakota and members of a very different agricultural com-munity: an urban farm cooperative. Individuals in each group were asked to "select three terms that describe what 'social justice' means to you" and "select three terms describing what 'autonomy' means to you." Before giving their answer, parti-cipants were shown a list of some fifty pre-defined terms. The terms respondents chose were then fed into software that generated word clouds. If a picture is worth 1,000 words, these particular images show more than thousands of sentences ever could—see Figures 13.1, 13.2, 13.3, and 13.4.

Perhaps the most immediate contrast with these social justice responses lies in how the rural North Dakotans' image (Figure 13.1) evokes a number of words associated with punishment, policing and due process. The terms chosen by the urban land cooperative (Figure 13.2), in con-trast, made no reference to punishment or polic-ing. Instead, they chose terms that overwhelmingly emphasized, to quote the most used term to come from this group, equity. There was also a divergence between groups in terms of whether social justice was something individuals achieve or whether it denotes a collective response, where a community (or even society) as a whole ensures justice for individuals. To explain this point requires that I introduce two additional word cloud images.

With regard to the autonomy word clouds, note the repeated emphasis the North Dakota group (Figure 13.3) placed on terms like "individualism," "self-determination," "self-rule," and "authority." In philosophical parlance, these terms align with the tradition of individualism, a position that emphasizes self-reliance and stresses human independence and liberty. These terms also tie in well with the North Dakota group's social justice word cloud, with its emphasis on words that stress individual responsibility and individual freedoms. This stands a world away from the urban farmer cooperative group (Figure 13.4), who associated autonomy with "interdependence," "cooperation," "solidarity" and "community." It might appear counterintuitive to link autonomy with concepts like interdependence

and solidarity, until you hear individuals from this group explain their position.

A single mother, for example, spoke directly to how independence arises for members of this group because of interdependence, rather than in spite of it. "We can accomplish a heck of a lot more together; I feel like I have more control over my life, more independence, when we can rely on each other." She added, "I certainly appreciate how sharing childcare opportunities as a community gives me the freedom to garden. But we can't forget that farming has always been a collective effort, of sharing seed and knowledge and work."

FIGURE 13.1 "Social Justice" Word Cloud, North Dakota Sample

FIGURE 13.3 "Autonomy" Word Cloud, North Dakota Sample

FIGURE 13.2 "Social Justice" Word Cloud, Urban Land Cooperative Sample

FIGURE 13.4 "Autonomy" Word Cloud, Urban Land Cooperative Sample

Source: Adapted from Carolan (2018b).

Implications

As detailed in this section, what and how we think are of tremendous sociological consequence. Unfortunately, there is not enough space to offer an exhaustive account of how and why attitudes and understandings are sociologically relevant to matters relating to the environment and pro-environmental behaviors. Instead, I concentrate on three quite different subjects, looking at how we think about nature, the roots of climate denial, and the values and attitudes that help drive consumerism.

Knowledge and Worldviews

A lot has been written about how Western philosophy, going all the way back to the ancient Greeks (Whitehead [1920] 1964), is responsible for bestowing on nature a type of secondary status (see, e.g., Carolan 2008a; Ingold 2000; Zwart 1997). According to this **worldview** (which refers to a fundamental cognitive orientation shared by individuals, within which is rooted the entirety of their knowledge), nature is inherently alien to us; while we perceive it, we dwell in a realm separate from it. This creates, in the words of the great twentieth-century philosopher Alfred North Whitehead ([1920] 1964, 30–31), "the nature apprehended in awareness and the nature [aka Nature] which is the cause of awareness." Western philosophy thus leaves us with an understanding of the universe as being filled with nothing more than dead, static matter—as exemplified, for instance, in the writings of Newton. The living and dynamic in this philosophical outlook reside only in human consciousness. This separation between thought (mind) and matter (body) has perplexed philosophers for centuries—and more recently even some environmental sociologists. How is it that these two realms interact if indeed they are truly independent of each other (see Ethical Question 13.1)? Such a division inevitably creates the need for a third thing that connects the two. Yet the slope this creates is a slippery one, for what then connects this third thing to the other two?

By making nature something separate from us—and the human condition more generally—we've objectified it. **Ecofeminism** offers a rich literature detailing the historical link between the objectification of women and the objectification of nature. *The Death of Nature* (Merchant 1980) argues that casting nature in the female gender (e.g., Mother Nature) strips it of activity and renders it passive, just as casting women as being closer to nature (as, for example, the "nurturing" sex) has had similar effects. As Merchant (1980, 169) argues, "As women's womb had symbolically yielded to the forceps, so nature's womb harbored secrets that through technology could be wrested from her grasp for use in the improvement of the human condition."

Metaphysics aside, I'm also convinced that our understandings of nature are in part a consequence of our relationship to this realm (Carolan 2008b, 2011). Knowledge, after all, is relational. Take, for example, the Batek, one of the indigenous ethnic minorities of peninsular Malaysia. These hunting and gathering "people of the forest"—a self-imposed identity (Tuck-Po 2004, 50)—have lived in the forest for centuries. For them, concepts like "nature" and "forest" are multivariate categories, depending largely on who is living within this environment. And there is always a *who* in their understandings of nature, as evidenced by the fact that they do not even have a word for *wilderness* (Tuck-Po 2004).

Or take research examining how understandings of nature differ between the Menominee—Wisconsin's oldest continuous residents—and their Anglo-European neighbors.

ETHICAL QUESTION 13.1
Is Pollution Natural?

Ecologically minded scholars like to talk about breaking free of the dichotomies of Western thought (e.g., mind–body, society–nature, human–animal, and so on). Yet where does that leave something like pollution? If humans are really part of nature, rather than separate from it, doesn't the same then hold for the *effects* of human activity? Pushing the question further: What about human-induced climate change? If humans and all their activities are natural, wouldn't anthropomorphically-driven climate change then hold the same status? Is that natural too?

The first (and obvious) response to these questions is that we make conceptual distinctions all the time—we need to if we want to talk about anything—though we should be careful how we create those distinctions and be willing to revisit them if they prove problematic or oppressive. (I am doing something a bit unusual here and weighing in on these questions because they can be and have been used to undermine the case for taking action toward climate change, and I want to make sure readers have some reasoned responses at their disposal when confronted by such arguments.)

A second, slightly more sophisticated, response would be to point out that the questions above evoke what is known as the "is–ought problem." First articulated by seventeenth-century philosopher David Hume, the problem goes something like this: just because something *is* doesn't automatically mean it *ought* to be. Or, to put it another way: statements of knowledge (e.g., "X is") are not statements of value (e.g., "X is how it ought to be"). For example, the *fact* that women have historically been subservient to men does not lead one logically to conclude that they *should* be treated this way. We can therefore say that the fact that life can and has changed the Earth's atmosphere for billions of years does not mean humans have a right to do so.

To conflate these statements of fact with statements of value is to commit a **naturalistic fallacy**. As a statement of value, the question "What impact *should* humans have on climate?" is entirely open for debate. This is why public participation is so crucial when developing environmental policy. Science alone is incapable of translating statements of "what is" (a scientific question) to statements of "what ought to be" (a policy question). Arguably, the best avenue for answering questions of value—questions of what ought to be—is through democratic means.

Whereas children of European descent demonstrated problems with recognizing that people are animals, the Menominee children grasped this idea fully (Longbottom and Slaughter 2016). As for the adults, Anglo-Europeans cited the importance of teaching their children that nature needs to be protected and if possible protected from humans (a viewpoint that places humans outside of nature), whereas Menominee adults stressed to their youth that people are part of nature (Bang et al. 2007). Perhaps not surprisingly, compared to their European neighbors, Menominee children and adults spend more of their time engaged in outdoor activities, where the natural world is foregrounded, and relatively less time engaged in practices where nature is backgrounded. Researchers point out how "the Menominee ecological orientation in reasoning strategies is paralleled in their framework orientation and practices" (Bang et al. 2007, 13871).

Tuck-Po (2004) explains how the Batek of peninsular Malaysia are able to identify native animals by their calls, a particularly important skill given the dense canopy of the forest which makes visual identification nearly impossible. Yet such local knowledge is being lost as embodiments and practices around the world change (recall the earlier discussion of memory banks in Chapter 4). Among the Seri, an indigenous community in the Mexican state of Sonora, the younger generation is losing their ability to identify native animals in photographs as a result of reduced interactions with these creatures (Nabhan 1997). Among the Salish people of Washington, young people are less successful than previous generations at identifying local plants according to their medicinal properties (Turner 2016). At one time, the language of the Rio Grande Pueblos allowed them to distinguish between many types of trees and plants. Today, children increasingly use their native term for *firewood* when speaking of trees and the word for *weed* when speaking of herbaceous plants because they've lost the local knowledge of their natural surroundings (Nabhan 1997). Yet it is more than just a problem of languages lost. We are losing the socioecological relationships that language is tethered to, for, as Abram explains (1996, 75), we "learn our native languages not mentally but bodily."

A survey of 1,927 Australians involving members of four religious groupings—Buddhists, Christian literalists and nonliteralists, and secularists—looked at their attitudes toward and their beliefs about: (1) whether climate change is human induced, (2) the level of consensus they think exists among scientists, (3) their own efficacy in being able to do anything about it, and (4) the need for policy responses (Morrison et al. 2015). The study shows that religion explains these differences even after taking into account sociodemographic factors. The atheist/agnostic/no religion group (43.8 percent) and Buddhists (45.7 percent) have a much higher percentage of people located in the "alarmed" and "concerned" segments than the sample overall (33.3 percent). Furthermore, atheist/agnostic/ no religion (16.3 percent) and Buddhists (2.9 percent) have a lower percentage of people located in the "doubtful" and "dismissive" segments than the sample overall (20.6 percent). The respondents who indicate affiliation with Christian denominations that have a literal interpretation of scripture have a smaller proportion of people located in the "alarmed" and "concerned" categories (19.6 percent). The Christian literalists also have a much higher percentage of people located in the "doubtful" and "dismissive" segments (30.2 percent) than the sample overall.

Denial and Countermovements

In her study of a small community in Norway, Norgaard (2011) finds evidence that a lack of action against climate change is often not the result of poor or incomplete knowledge. Those she interviewed knew climate change was happening. The area had experienced very late snowfall and warmer winter temperatures while she was conducting her research. October, November, and December 2000–2001 were 4° Celsius, 5° Celsius, and 1.5° Celsius, respectively, warmer than the 30-year average, and the winter as a whole was the second warmest in the previous 130 years. Consequently, the local ski area opened late, which had a noticeable negative recreational and economic impact on the community. Moreover, a popular lake used heavily for ice fishing did not freeze.

Literal denial describes a type of denial when people hold onto beliefs that are demonstrably false, as found among, say, climate change skeptics. *Implicatory denial* is when we fail to respond according to the moral and rational codes of the day; most citizens of Nazi Germany could be placed in this category. Norgaard's work describes another type of denial: how thinking about climate change raises disturbing emotions of fear about the future, guilt, and a sense of helplessness, which are resisted collectively through participation in such cultural practices as emotion management, norms of conversation, and the use of narratives to justify past and current actions. This type of denial, the ability to *collectively* ignore disturbing information, points, among other things, to the role of emotion in social movements and political action and highlights how global warming raises new threats to the workings of democracy. Norgaard explains how denial allowed citizens of this small community to acknowledge climate change while also pushing it from their conscious minds. One tactic was blame shifting. Many of her respondents were quick to blame, for example, "Amerika" and the Bush administration (the US president at the time). When asked about Norway's role in climate change, as the world's second largest exporter of oil, they were quick to dismiss this fact as insignificant, though the subject did make some uncomfortable.

Norgaard (2006, 336) reminds us that "citizens of wealthy nations who fail to respond to the issue of climate change benefit from their denial in short-run economic terms." She continues, "They also benefit by avoiding the emotional and psychological entanglement and identity conflicts that may arise from knowing that one is doing 'the wrong thing'" (Ibid.). Many who live in affluent nations can also afford to deny climate change. Although the subjects of Norgaard's study will not escape its consequences, their social positioning was such that climate change will profoundly affect people in less affluent nations long before it drastically alters their own lives.

Scholarship on the social construction of denial in the face of climate change has expanded greatly over the last decade, building on Norgaard's important insights. A recent study examining a coastal region in eastern Australia reminds us of the risks of overly praising place attachment and local awareness of environmental issues, which are often thought of as commensurate with a care for the natural environment (Bowden et al. 2019). This emphasis on experiences of place worked to abstract the community from the broader impacts of climate change. As the authors explain:

> Our case study also highlights elements of the ways in which these processes come together to produce a socially organised denial, which delays responding to climate change. By insisting that the indicators need to be seen (or felt), the community attempts to close itself off from the planetary system.
>
> (Bowden et al. 2019, 7)

The roots of climate denial have also been shown to be fed by political ideology and can span (and in turn be further reinforced by) countermovements. A **countermovement** is a social movement that arises to explicitly oppose an existing social movement. Meyer and Staggenborg (1996, 1635) point to three conditions that lead to openings for countermovements: the original movement shows signs of success; the interests of some populations are threatened by the original movement's goals; and political allies are available to aid oppositional mobilization. Jacques et al. (2008) look to these conditions to understand why the conservative movement in the United States launched a major countermovement against the environmental movement in the 1990s.

Environmentalism emerged as a global movement in the early 1990s with the aid of events such as the 1992 Earth Summit in Rio. This, combined with the fall of the Soviet Union, prompted the conservative movement to switch its talk of the "red scare" to a "green scare." The Republican takeover of Congress in 1994 also gave the countermovement access to political allies. Last, and perhaps most significantly, as environmentalists began calling for significant changes, the countermovement sought to brand environmentalism as a threat not only to economic progress but also the "American way of life." Jacques et al. (2008) point to the role that conservative think tanks (CTTs) have played in creating counterenvironmental knowledge and thereby espousing **environmental skepticism**—a position that attempts to undermine knowledge claims supporting the argument that environmental problems are real and that they are the result of human activity. Their search of English-language environmentally skeptical books published between 1972 (nothing prior to this could be found) and 2005 found 92.2 percent to have a clear link to one or more CTTs, either through author affiliation, or because the book was published by a CTT, or, the most common scenario, both (Jacques et al. 2008). Conducting a content analysis of 805 statements made by climate change countermovement organizations, McKie (2019) provides a useful typology of how denial is put to work for these groups. Specifically, she notes six denial (and related) techniques used by countermovements to neutralize climate change arguments: denial of responsibility; denial of inquiry; denial of victim; condemnation of the condemner; appeal to higher loyalties; and "other"—see Table 13.1.

Consumerism, Advertising, and Marketization

The following stunning admission is taken from an article by Rory Sutherland, vice chair of the marketing firm Ogilvy UK and then president of the Institute of Practitioners in Advertising:

> The truth is that marketing raises enormous ethical questions every day—at least it does if you're doing it right. If this were not the case, the only possible explanations are either that you believe marketers are too ineffectual to make any difference, or you believe that marketing activities only affect people at the level of conscious argument. Neither of these possibilities appeals to me. *I would rather be thought of as evil than useless.*

> (Sutherland 2010, 59; emphasis added)

Decades of studies note how advertising promotes rabid consumerism (see, e.g., Galbraith 1958). After all, economic growth relies on the unending creation of insatiable needs. As Ezra Mishan, longtime professor of economics at the London School of Economics, famously noted a half century ago, "Therefore to continue to regard the market, in an affluent and growing economy, as primarily a 'want-satisfying' mechanism is to close one's eyes to the more important fact, that it has become a want-*creating* mechanism" (Mishan 1967, 149; emphasis in the original). We also know that advertising further reinforces the values it reflects by normalizing them. On this point, talking specifically about smoking, Rory Sutherland (2010, 59) further confessed, "While I can accept that the purpose of tobacco advertising was not to encourage people to smoke, I find it

TABLE 13.1 Climate Change Counter Movement Neutralization Techniques

NAME	ORIGINAL DEFINITION	CLIMATE CHANGE DEFINITION
Denial of Responsibility (DOR)	Denial of responsibility is used to contend that the deviant or criminal act is accidental and/or fell victim to their social environment unable to control their actions.	Climate change is happening, but humans are not the cause.
Denial of Injury (DOI1 and DOI2)	Denial of harm or injury asserts (1) an act will not injure or significantly injure someone or something; and/or (2) there are likely positive impacts from this behavior.	(1) There is no significant harm caused by human action, and (2) there may even be some benefits.
Denial of Victim (DOV1 and DOV2)	Denial of Victim on one hand juxtaposes victim and offender as the deviant becomes the condemner and law enforcer.	(1) There are no climate change victims. (2) If climate change victims do exist, they deserve to be victimized.
Condemnation of the Condemner (COC)	Condemnation of the condemner shifts negative or criticisms of a deviant those condemning that person's actions, thereby rejecting the higher status of the condemners.	Climate change research is misrepresented by scientists, and manipulated by media, politicians, and environmentalists.
Appeal to Higher Loyalties (AHL)	Appeal to Higher Loyalties imitates a sacrifice to satisfy the requirements of an intimate social group.	Economic progress and development are more important than preventing climate change.
Other		Any argument that appears to be oppositional to climate change but not one of the above.

Adapted from McKie (2019).

astounding that anyone could barefacedly suggest that cigarette posters seen everywhere did not serve to normalise the habit."

A growing body of research is examining links between intrinsic and extrinsic values and consumption. *Intrinsic values* refer to aspects of life that we find inherently rewarding, whereas the reward of *extrinsic values* lies in the validation given to us by others. When you place greater importance on extrinsic values, you are more likely to express prejudice toward others, be less concerned about the environment and human rights, and express lower levels of personal well-being and happiness (Alexander et al. 2011; Goldsmith

2015). Adolescents who strongly endorse extrinsic values report being less likely to turn off lights in unused rooms, recycle, and engage in other pro-environmental behaviors (Kasser 2005). Other studies report a strong positive correlation between the ecological footprints of adults and their possession of extrinsic values (Kasser 2016). So which values do you suppose advertisers target? The vast majority of advertising is directed at appealing to extrinsic values, the very values associated with lower motivation to address social and environmental problems (Alexander et al. 2011). Advertisers have also learned that it is possible to advertise so-called green products through an appeal to extrinsic values, like using a famous celebrity to advertise the latest hybrid car. Such marketing campaigns promote extrinsic values by encouraging status competition and social comparison.

What are the cumulative effects of being endlessly seduced into becoming envious, status-seeking hyperconsumers looking for our next "happiness fix" with a swipe of the credit card or click of the mouse? Obviously, we do not rush to purchase everything we see advertised. But if almost every advertisement we see seeks to fuel our extrinsic values, it's reasonable to think this is going to have a measurable effect on people over the long term. Perhaps, to refer back to a point discussed in the previous chapter, this partially helps explain why so many people in the United States report such low levels of well-being and happiness: Americans are overexposed to advertisements directed at appeals to extrinsic values.

A study examined the impact of the use of Channel One—a daily 10-minute news bulletin with two minutes of advertisements—in US schools (Greenberg and Brand 1993). It compared the importance attached to extrinsic values in teenagers from two neighboring schools with very similar student and parent demographics: one had Channel One; the other did not. Teenagers enrolled at the school with Channel One had much higher levels of extrinsic values than the control group. This corroborates more recent research pointing to links between hours watching television, a lack of concern about environmental problems, and an increased prevalence of extrinsic values (Macias and Williams 2015).

A lot of television is watched in the United States. The country is also, as discussed in the previous chapter, a society with excessive levels of inequality. This is a powerful double whammy, as we know that inequality is perhaps the greatest driver of overconsumption (Aggarwal 2016). For one thing, status competition drives hyperconsumerism. Second, inequality—by heightening the distance between the haves and the have-nots and thus increasing the status of being a have—intensifies status competition. Throw endless hours of television watching into this mix, and you have the environment ripe for materialism that we see in affluent countries today (see ECOnnection 13.2.

Solutions

Changing how we think about things is no small feat. Fortunately, we have the benefit of decades of excellent social science research and illustrative examples from other countries to light our way. The task ahead may be daunting, but it's most definitely possible.

Advertisements, Freedom, and the Public Good

Although the majority of parents feel they are primarily responsible for their children, they do not feel they alone own this responsibility, especially when it comes to competing

ECOnnection 13.2
The "Money Makes You a Jerk" Thesis

Googling "money makes you a jerk" will yield over six million hits. The titles of articles from the first couple of pages describe similar content: e.g., "How having money makes you a jerk"; "If you were rich, you'd be a jerk too"; "Science closes in on the reason rich people are jerks"; "Why being rich makes you a jerk"; "It's not your imagination—rich people are jerks, say science"; and "Does money make you mean?". The articles reference a wealth of research that has been published, most since the early 2000s, on how money changes us, sometimes profoundly (see, e.g., Gąsiorowska and Hełka 2012; Kouchaki et al. 2013; Piff et al. 2012).

The thesis has been supported through dozens of novel natural and experimental observations. Participants in one study were primed by the presence of a large pile of Monopoly money. Those exposed to this play money were less willing to help someone who "accidentally" spilled a box of pencils (Vohs et al. 2006). In another design, participants filled out questionnaires while seated in front of a computer monitor. Some had screen savers that depicted money; others had fish swimming. Exposure to the former reduced participants' willingness to work in a team and increased their likelihood of viewing themselves as having less in common with the other participants (Ibid.). In another experiment, subjects unscrambled phrases that included words such as "salary" while a control group worked with nonmonetary terms. The group that worked with nonmonetary words spent an average of three minutes on a difficult puzzle before reaching out for help, while members of the money group resisted reaching out to others for assistance for more than five minutes. Moreover, those who unscrambled nonmonetary phrases spent, on average, approximately twice as much time assisting peers as those who had been primed with the money cues. These findings have been replicated through numerous other studies (Ibid.).

Numerous natural observations have also been made that support the thesis. Researchers in one study observed a busy four-way intersection and recorded that luxury car drivers were more likely to cut off other motorists instead of waiting to turn. The behavior was the same for both men and women upper-class drivers, regardless of the time of day or the amount of traffic (Piff et al. 2012). A different study reports that drivers of luxury vehicles were more likely to speed up to pass a pedestrian who was trying to use a crosswalk, rather than waiting for them to pass, even after making eye contact with that individual (Grewal 2012).

The tacit assumption of this social psychological research is that there is something about money per se that triggers this behavior. Is it *money* or *the system* within which most money circulates that makes us act this way?

with the deep pockets of multinational corporations and advertising companies that are trying to get into the minds and wallets of today's youth. The vast majority of the world's parents thus favor restrictions on advertising aimed at children (Oates and Tziortzi 2014). These sentiments have been found among parents in countries as diverse as, for example, the United States (Tripicchio et al. 2016), the Netherlands (van der Voort et al. 1992), China (Chan and McNeal 2003), and Chile (Correa et al. 2019).

Consumption is a thoroughly social activity. Once we accept this undeniable empirical truth, the argument against the regulation of advertisements falls apart. That argument goes something along the lines of the following: in the name of protecting individual freedom, one should be able to buy as much of whatever one likes; after all, the consumer knows best what they need. Establishing that those needs are products of social activity diminishes the argument that government intervention takes away from individual freedoms. For example, studies from around the world indicate that adolescents feel considerable pressure from peers and social media to buy stuff in order to fit in, whether we're talking about teens in Brazil (Gil et al. 2017), Australia (Francis and Davis 2015), Taiwan (Chang and Nguyen 2018), or the United States (Ordaz et al. 2018). In fact, it could easily be argued that government intervention *increases* personal freedoms by helping to shield individuals from the dictates of these particular sociological forces.

We could begin by regulating advertisements directed at children as this population, in the classical liberal tradition, is often seen as needing more protection than adults. We could also create advertising-free zones. Most places of religious worship are advertisement free. Why can't we do the same with schools and other public places where children are frequently present? Why not limit specific types of advertisement that are clearly meant for children? In Greece, for example, television advertisements for toys are banned between 7 a.m. and 9 p.m. In Norway and Quebec (a Canadian province), it is illegal to target through advertisements children under the age of twelve—Sweden had a similar ban, which started in 1991 but was repealed in 2010. Meanwhile, the European Union (EU) Audiovisual Media Services Directive provides EU-wide rules on advertising as it pertains to children. Namely, advertising shall not:

- directly exhort minors to buy a product or a service by exploiting their inexperience or credulity
- directly encourage minors to persuade their parents or others to purchase the goods or services being advertised
- exploit the special trust minors place in parents, teachers, or other persons
- unreasonably show minors in dangerous situations.

In addition:

- children's programs may only be interrupted if the scheduled duration is longer than thirty minutes
- product placement is not allowed in children's programs
- Member States and the European Commission should encourage audiovisual media service providers to develop codes of conduct regarding the advertising of certain foods in children's programs.

We also need to be aware of the dangers of putting all the responsibility on the shoulders of parents. As market-driven trends increasingly structure social interaction among children and teens, well-meaning parents who place restrictions on their kids' consumption patterns risk setting them up for social exclusion, which does not do their children any good. Finally, advertisements in countries such as the United States are a tax-deductible expense. By spending money on advertisements, which increases brand loyalty and the purchase frequency of the product advertised, businesses are also able to reduce their tax liability: a clear win–win scenario for companies. Yet this win comes at the

expense of individual and public health. The general public in the United States is subsidizing advertisements. Moreover, the hundreds of millions of dollars saved by businesses
annually through these deductions could help pay for public services that are currently
paid for by taxpayers.

Collaborative Consumption

Aristotle is said to have written that "on the whole, you find wealth much more in use
than in ownership" (Rifkin 2000, 76). Kevin Kelly (2012), founder of the influential
magazine *Wired*, has argued passionately that "access is better than ownership." We have
become so wrapped up in fighting for our right to own that we seem to have forgotten
why we wanted to own in the first place: for access and use. We are also guilty of over-
looking the fact that markets are not ends in themselves. Markets were developed to solve
problems of resource allocation; they were never meant to be the Holy Grail they have
become. What's important is efficient and fair resource allocation. Markets have long
been viewed as the best option to deliver those ends. But what if something better came
along?

Michael Spence, a 2001 Nobel laureate in economics and a senior fellow at Stanford's
Hoover Institution, wrote an article in *Forbes* titled "Markets Aren't Everything" (Spence
2009). In this piece, Spence celebrates the work of scholars like Elinor Ostrom who have
highlighted how common-property resources can quite effectively be managed without
the aid of formal markets. As Ostrom (1999) and others (e.g., Narain and Vij 2016) have
detailed, common-property resources (e.g., forests) have been effectively managed—in
some cases for centuries—thanks to things like informal social norms, trust, and social
capital. Yet what if, in this age of social media, Twitter, and the internet more generally,
something like a traditional commons is forming for consumers?

A generation ago, the thought of the nonmarket coordination of large groups of people
from around the world for purposes of resource allocation seemed absurd. The transaction
costs of such an endeavor were too great. If you had something and wanted to get rid of
it, your options were limited. You could put an ad in the paper or place fliers on community bulletin boards around your neighborhood. And even if someone got back to you,
the chances of a successful transaction were low (they might have wanted a different color,
model, and so on). That has all changed, which explains why the godfather of *Wired* is
proclaiming the virtues of access over ownership. For many consumer items, we no longer
need the market. Enter what has become known as "collaborative consumption" (ECOnnection 13.3).

One example of collaborative consumption is **peer-to-peer renting**: the process
whereby one private individual rents an underused item of theirs to another individual
(aka P2P renting). There are a number of peer-to-peer sites that create a low transaction
cost environment, allowing a type of commons to appear, like Zilok, Vrbo, Airbnb, and
Uber. These entities enable individuals to make use of those underused goods we all are
guilty of having by renting them to others, which in turn keeps those renters from purchasing the goods new.

Take the case of FoodCloud, a platform designed to recover food that would otherwise
go to waste. The non-profit company, which goes by the same name as its platform, is
based in Ireland. With its software, retailers upload details about food nearing its sell by

ECOnnection 13.3
Every Cloud Has a Silver Lining: From "Waste" to "Untapped Idling Capacity"

So much stuff—we're practically swimming in it! And apparently our homes and garages are not growing fast enough to contain it all. We increasingly feel the need to rent additional space for all that stuff we never or rarely use. (For those aged eighteen and older—as there is adult language— search "George Carlin talks about stuff" online for a witty sociological breakdown of our obsession over material things.) According to the Self-Storage Association (SSA), the following represent the self-storage sector in a snapshot: annual industry revenue, $38 billion; number of storage facilities, between 45,000 and 52,000; total rentable self-storage space, 1.7 billion square feet; self-storage per person, 5.4 square feet; percentage of households that rent self-storage units, 9.4 percent; average monthly cost of self-storage units, $88.85 (SSA 2019). Let me say that first point again: Americans are spending almost $40 billion dollars a year to store stuff that we hardly ever use. Let's be honest: if we used it would we be storing it at a distant location?

Rather than being wrenched by despair, I prefer taking a more optimistic slant on the above statistics, while also recognizing that we still need to change our ways. All that unused stuff has already extracted a significant toll on the environ-ment. Why not, then, put it to use so more stuff does not meet a similar fate, of consuming still more resources only to be born and lie idle in some rented storage space for years? All those unused goods represent an enormous idling capacity. The fact is, while the owners might not use that stuff, others could. So let's get it into the hands of those who would.

Just about every semester I survey my class of 100 undergraduate students and ask them about the things they own but never or rarely use. I had one class a couple of years back report collectively owning 101 power drills! Granted, two students owned ten between them, and eight did not own any. For something that was on average used for a couple of minutes annually, that is a tremendous amount of hole-making idling capacity. Even the cars the students owned spent more time parked than in use—a lot more. On average, my students report being in their cars about ten minutes a day. That leaves 1,430 minutes where the car is just sitting, yet still racking up costs in terms of depreciation, tax, title, license, insurance, and (in most cases) parking. How about you? Do you own things like a drill, a car, a snow blower, a power saw, or camping equipment? How often do *you* use them, honestly?

date or that is deemed too ugly to spend good money on. At the other end, local charities receive automatic alerts, asking if they wish to collect the food and distribute it to those in need. Tesco Ireland uses the platform in all of its 140 stores. In May 2016, Aldi announced its national partnership with FoodCloud. By November of that year, the retailer's seventy-nine participating stores reported donating over 500,000 meals (234 tonnes of food) thanks to this relationship (McHugh 2016).

Or take The Food Corridor. The company matches idle commercial kitchens with aspiring entrepreneurs through software, charging users a monthly membership fee. Think of all the kitchen space sitting out there not being used—school kitchens over the summer, church and synagogue kitchens, event spaces with kitchens…. Meanwhile, the cost of a commercial kitchen, as you might guess, is prohibitive. The Food Corridor brings together those with ideal kitchen space (there are plenty of these people) and those with aspirations to be food entrepreneurs who might lack the capital and/or credit (there are plenty of these people too). Yet this company does not just offer access to stuff. According to CEO Ashley Colpaart, "The long-term goal is to be a (decentralized) incubator, for startups, for communities, even. More than providing access to space we want to create resilient food systems" (Carolan 2018b, 15). The Food Corridor launched the Network for Incubator and Commissary Kitchens in July 2018 as a Facebook group that hosts approximately 1,400 members. This network of food activists, entrepreneurs, and practitioners shares data, best practices, and technical assistance to build vibrant communities through successful shared-use kitchen businesses. These exchanges include support for what, in the business world, is called ecosystem services, like food liability insurance, label printing, and food safety tools. Which is exactly what must take place if we want to dislodge old ways of thinking. If you have questions about, say, shared-use kitchen businesses, but the people with "answers" know only the status quo, why would we expect anything to change?

Before we start uncritically celebrating the sharing economy, let's turn our attention to a platform that everyone has at least heard of: Uber. Launched in 2010, Uber reached its first billion rides in 2015, a total it saw doubled just six months later. In the summer of 2017, another milestone was announced: five billion trips worldwide. One study found that the average Uber driver makes $364 a month, which was among the highest incomes of the sharing platforms surveyed (Earnest 2017). Another study tried to calculate the average per hour wage for Uber drivers. They arrived at $15.68 per hour, before factoring in for expenses like gas, maintenance, and depreciation (Campbell 2017). Other analyses, meanwhile, paint a far less optimistic financial picture, after calculating for "hidden costs", like taxes that your employer would otherwise pay for you, namely Social Security and Medicare that you owe under the Self-Employment Contributions Act, or SECA (Weiner 2015).

For many Uber drivers surveyed, their Uber income is supplemental (Ravenelle 2017; Schor 2017). There's nothing wrong with that per se, except that they are crowding out workers who depend on the income of service jobs. These are tasks traditionally performed by people who have not gone to college and who come from lower socioeconomic households. Generally, people with PhDs who make more than $100,000 a year do not drive taxis on the side. But some of them may drive for Uber. In some cases, sharing platforms might be pushing out those whom the sole ownership economy has already placed in a precarious position.

Yet our analysis should not end here. As this chapter tries to make clear, we need to think bigger—*systemically*, if you will. How does Uber impact larger labor and transportation markets? Uber has proven to be as aggressive and shrewd as any monopolistic corporation. It has been reported, for example, that Uber has assigned its Internet Protocol (IP) to the tax haven of Bermuda, leaving less than 2 percent of its net revenue taxable by the US government (Kocieniewski 2016). Thus, one hand takes jobs away from the already vulnerable while the other hides its money overseas robbing government programs of their tax base. What happens when Uber crushes its competition, local taxi companies, Lyft, Grab (in Southeast Asia), Ola (in India), all of them, the world over? Über Uber.

With its drivers not having anywhere else to go, Uber would be well positioned to start taking an even bigger commission. (In the last few years, its original 20 percent commission rate has crept up, in some markets, to 30 percent.) And just wait until there are self-driving cars, when today's well-paid drivers become tomorrow's latest Uber roadkill.

One way to unpack these platforms, acknowledging that, for example, Uber and The Food Corridor are arguably enacting different visions of a sharing economy, is to understand that the idea of collaboration consumption can and does take different forms. Some practices involve creating *access* to material things. Perhaps that is why Uber has been so successful, because it really hasn't changed much, other than who we get car rides from. Others focus on creating and exchanging *knowledge*. Still others are centered on building *community*. And some do all of these things to various degrees, which is perhaps where I'd locate The Food Corridor—or at least its aspirations (Carolan 2018b).

Let's also not forget about the *social* value added through at least some forms of collaborative consumption. When you consume collaboratively, you build social networks, nurture trust, and generate social capital. As a sociologist, I cannot deny the social nature of shopping. Yet when we shop, we do not really establish any new social networks. We might build trust and a sense of camaraderie among the family and friends we are shopping with, though equally, shopping has been shown to create animosity and jealousy among even loved ones who shop together (Kasser 2016; see ECOnnection 13.4). The tentative early evidence suggests that collaborative consumption not only strengthens already existing (aka strong) ties but also builds new (aka weak) ones between people with different backgrounds (Carolan 2018b; Ozanne and Ozanne 2016). Perhaps these ties could even be used to further push for social change by way of consumer activism, such as through traditional boycotts or more recently through "buycotts" (see Case Study 13.1).

Globalization of Environmental Concern

Here's some good news: there appears to be a global diffusion of views and values concerning environmental protection (Helm et al. 2018; Mohai et al. 2010; Pampel 2014). Environmental concern has been defined by Dunlap and Jones (2002, 485) as "the degree to which people are aware of problems regarding the environment and support efforts to solve them and/or indicate a willingness to contribute personally to their solution." As environmental attitudes are often taken to be synonymous with environmental concern (Dunlap and Jones 2002; Ester 1981), I will use the two concepts interchangeably (see ECOnnection 13.5).

Until recently, there was much debate between scholars about the globalization of environmental concern. Conventional wisdom had long assumed that widespread citizen concern for environmental quality was confined to wealthy nations. This presumption was grounded in the belief that residents of poor countries are too preoccupied with their material needs to support the postmaterialist value of environmental protection. The most famous champion of this view is Ronald Inglehart, who grounds his argument in two theories: Maslow's hierarchy of human needs and Mannheim's socialization hypothesis. Maslow argued that higher-order needs (e.g., concern for the environment) cannot be fully developed in people worried where their next meal is going to come from (a lower-order material need), whereas Mannheim's socialization hypothesis holds that "one's basic values reflect the conditions that prevailed during

ECOnnection 13.4

Not All Sharing is the Same: When "Collaborative Consumption" Harms Social Relations

Conceived by a Kansas City company that has been leasing combines for a couple of decades, MachineryLink Sharing advertises itself as a sharing platform—it's called MachineryLink Sharing, after all. The company promises to help farmers make money by renting, on a short-term basis, their equipment to those who cannot afford or who choose not to buy these machines outright. A single piece of farm equipment can cost hundreds of thousands of dollars, so peer-to-peer *renting* (let's call it what it is) of these items can run in the tens of thousands of dollars—I've personally seen the receipts from these "sharing" arrangements.

The following quotation is from my book *The Food Sharing Revolution* (Carolan 2018b). It describes an exchange I had with a Kansas farmer (Bart) who rents out his idle farm equipment through MachineryLink. Specifically, it is a story about how his relationship with his neighbor, Scott, has changed since using this sharing platform, prior to which Bart used to let his friend borrow his equipment.

Now that Bart was trucking his new pieces of equipment across the country, they were no longer available to be borrowed, or what some would call shared. This, in his words, "hasn't exactly been a plus as far as neighborly relations are concerned." This was neither the first nor the last time I heard stories in which formal sharing actually pushed people apart rather than bringing them together. As Bart described the rift with Scott, his explanation was telling. He seemed to be saying the platform encouraged the commodification of relationships: "I can make $20,000 or $30,000, or I can let my neighbour use it for free. You do the math. Unless I start charging the guy"—he was talking about Scott here—"a comparable rate, the tractor's going to the guy who's going to pay." Here, then, are more reasons to temper our sharing triumphalism with a critical eye, realizing that such exchanges are not without tradeoffs. As with this one: sharing more *this way* means sharing less *that way*.

(Carolan 2018b, 74)

one's pre-adult years" (Inglehart 1990, 68). With these two theories in tow, Inglehart argues that individuals residing in affluent countries will hold more postmaterialist values and that these values will grow as a result of generational cohort replacement (Inglehart 1990, 1997). Inglehart's argument was and still is attractive in some political circles, as it justifies the status quo and the belief—no matter how disconnected it is from empirical reality—that continued economic development will eventually lead all nations toward socially and politically tolerant, environmentally sustainable, and post-material futures (e.g., Henn et al. 2018).

CASE STUDY 13.1
Buycott

The term "buycott" has been around for a while. The idea of a buycott is to spend money in support of companies with which we agree, as opposed to focusing on *not* spending money on companies we dislike—a boycott. Recent research suggests that the buycott tactic is outpacing the more traditional boycott. A 2018 report based on 2,000 surveys of US and British consumers who were most activist-minded found 83 percent saying it was more important now to support companies they believe "do the right thing" and buy from them. Even among those who had taken part recently in a boycott, a greater share said supporting companies with purchases (79 percent) was what mattered most rather than boycotting (62 percent). Moreover, those who supported companies they liked were more likely to be women (56 percent, compared to 47 percent of boycotters), and were often younger

(41 percent were part of the millennial or Gen Z generations, compared to 33 percent of boycotters) (McGregor 2018).

Organisations like Hong Kong's Redress and the British-based The Wrap's Love Your Clothes campaign provide information on a more sustainable approach to fashion, to combat the trend toward fast fashion. They provide, for example, recommendations for designers who upcycle and instruct people on how to redesign and repair clothes. Apps have also emerged to help in this process, like Buycott and Good On You. Of course, other options—to keep on the topic of fashion—are not to buy but to *reuse*, which is where platforms like Rent the Runway come into the picture. Swap parties are coming back in vogue for this very reason—events that can also build social networks, which is an added plus.

ECOnnection 13.5
The New Environmental Paradigm (NEP)

The New Environmental Paradigm (NEP) has been called "the most widely used measure of EA [environmental attitudes] since its publication in 1978" (Hawcroft and Milfont 2010, 144). It continues to generate considerable intellectual insights and debates, with applications in countries across the world (e.g., Ntanos et al. 2019; Piasentin and Roberts 2018; Reyna et al. 2018). The original scale was first published in 1978 by Dunlap and Van Liere and consisted of twelve items—eight pro-NEP and four anti-NEP—on a four-point Likert scale, anchored by "strongly agree" and "strongly disagree." The higher the NEP score, the

greater an individual's level of environmental beliefs or ecological worldview (Dunlap 2008). In 2000, Dunlap and colleagues revised the NEP scale. The revised scale consists of fifteen items, eight pro-NEP and seven anti-NEP. Table 13.2 displays the twelve and fifteen items from the original and revised scales, respectively.

Economists have found the NEP scale to be an accurate predictor of willingness to pay in **contingent valuation** studies (see, e.g., Cooper et al. 2004; Kotchen and Reiling 2000). (Contingent valuation is a survey-based economic technique for placing a value on nonmarket resources.) The NEP scale has also been shown to predict both reported and observed behavior (see, e.g., Casey and Scott 2006). A growing body of evidence also indicates that environmental educational programs can lead to an increase in NEP scores among children (Atav et al. 2015; Piasentin and Roberts 2018) and among college students (Woodworth et al. 2011).

TABLE 13.2 New Environmental Paradigm (NEP), Original and Revised

ORIGINAL NEP (1978)	REVISED NEP (2000)
1 We are approaching the limit of the number of people the Earth can support.	1 We are approaching the limit of the number of people the Earth can support.
2 The balance of nature is very delicate and easily upset.	2 Humans have the right to modify the natural environment to suit their needs.
3 Humans have the right to modify the natural environment to suit their needs.	3 When humans interfere with nature it often produces disastrous consequences.
4 Mankind was created to rule over the rest of nature.	4 Human ingenuity will ensure that we do NOT make the earth unlivable.
5 When humans interfere with nature it often produces disastrous consequences.	5 Humans are severely abusing the environment.
6 Plants and animals exist primarily to be used by humans.	6 The Earth has plenty of natural resources if we just learn how to develop them.
7 To maintain a healthy economy we will have to develop a "steady-state" economy where industrial growth is controlled.	7 Plants and animals have as much right as humans to exist.
8 Humans must live in harmony with nature in order to survive.	8 The balance of nature is strong enough to cope with the impacts of modern industrial nations.
9 The Earth is like a spaceship with only limited room and resources.	9 Despite our special abilities humans are still subject to the laws of nature.
10 Humans need not adapt to the natural environment because they can remake it to suit their needs.	10 The so-called "ecological crisis" facing humankind has been greatly exaggerated.
11 There are limits to growth beyond which our industrialized society cannot expand.	11 The Earth is like a spaceship with very limited room and resources.
12 Mankind is severely abusing the environment.	12 Humans were meant to rule over the rest of nature.
	13 The balance of nature is very delicate and easily upset.
	14 Humans will eventually learn enough about how nature works to be able to control it.
	15 If things continue on their present course, we will soon experience a major catastrophe.

Source: Adapted from Dunlap and Van Liere (1978) and Dunlap et al. (2000).

Note: In the original NEP (1978), agreement with points 3, 4, 6, and 10 reflects an anti-NEP sentiment, while agreement with points 1, 2, 5, 7, 8, 9, 11, and 12 reflects a pro-NEP sentiment. In the revised NEP (2000), agreement with the even numbered points reflects anti-NEP opinions, while agreement with odd numbered points reflects pro-NEP opinions.

Yet not all research has been kind to Inglehart's postmaterialism thesis. Take, for example, the results of the twenty-four nation "Health of the Planet" survey (Dunlap and York 2008). Of the fourteen different measures of environmental concern employed, seven were found to be *negatively* related with national affluence. In other words, they indicated higher levels of environmental concern among residents of poor countries. As Dunlap and York (2008, 534) explain,

> citizens of poorer nations were significantly more likely to (1) express personal concern about environmental problems, (2) rate the quality of their national environments as poor, (3) rate the quality of their community environments as poor, (4) perceive environmental problems as health threats at present (5) and in the future, (6) rate six community-level environmental problems as serious, and (7) express support for six governmental environmental protection programs.

More recently, a twenty-five country analysis found that willingness to sacrifice to protect the environment is not unique to wealthy nations (Mostafa 2013). Even more devastating to the postmaterialism thesis, the study found that a country's ranking on a postmaterialism index was *negatively* correlated to pro-environmental intentions. Put another way, postmaterialist values were associated with *less* environmentalism. More recently still, Pampel (2014) found a high level of willingness to pay for environmental quality among all groups studied in a sample consisting of respondents from ninety-six nations. "These findings," in the words of the author, "support the global environmentalism theory, which points to burgeoning environmentalism across the world" (Pampel 2014, 57).

The big question is: What's driving this global diffusion of environmental concern? Some argue, like Inglehart, that whatever environmental concern resides in less affluent countries is the result of local, objective, environmental degradation. If your local environment is poisoned, so the argument goes, then of course you're going to express some concern about the environment. If this were true, then residents of poor nations should rate local environmental problems as more serious than their counterparts in affluent nations, where local environmental conditions are presumably better, whereas developed nations should rate global problems as more serious.

Another variable deserving mention is democracy. As democracy grows in a country, so does not only environmental concern but also environmental associations, which increase opportunities for activism and group formation (Longhofer and Schofer 2010; Sjöstedt and Jagers 2014). Information spreads more easily in a democracy than in an autocracy. Democracies also tend to be more responsive to the environmental needs of the public than nondemocracies (Quan and Reuveny 2006). After examining more than 100 countries, Quan and Reuveny (2006) conclude that, relative to less democratic countries, more democratic countries emit less CO_2 per capita, less NO_2 (nitrogen dioxide) per capita, and less organic pollution in water; experience lower deforestation rates and less land degradation; and have higher percentages of forested land.

I also wonder what effect inequality has on levels of environmental concern within a country, to draw on a variable discussed extensively in the previous chapter. We know, for example, that more equal societies have a greater sense of collective responsibility for those in other countries and that business leaders in more equal countries are more likely to agree that their governments should cooperate with international environmental agreements (Wilkinson and Pickett 2011). I would therefore not be surprised if more equal societies also have higher levels of environmental concern. That would explain why some studies find that citizens of wealthier countries are no more or no less concerned about environmental issues than those from poorer nations (Sulemana et al. 2016), while others find a negative correlation between national affluence and environmental concern (Gelissen 2007). Perhaps "level of societal inequality" ought to be looked at in future studies gauging levels of global environmental concern (Lo 2016).

Pro-Environmental Behavior

We know from decades of research that there is no magic bullet that triggers environmentally significant behavior. A classic study by Gardner and Stern (1996), for instance, examined four types of intervention: religious and moral appeals; education to change attitudes; efforts to change the incentive structure of behavior by providing various types of rewards and penalties; and community management (e.g., the establishment of norms, shared rules, and expectations). Each type was found to have some success at changing behavior, with moral and educational approaches performing least well. Without question, the most effective behavioral change strategy involved combinations of intervention types. In another study, incentives and education were found to be more effective when combined than the sum of the two interventions when carried out separately (Stern 1999).

An even more seminal study in environmental behavior from the 1980s found that even when electric utility companies subsidized 93 percent of the cost of home insulation, consumer response to the program varied dramatically across the regions studied, from 1 to almost 20 percent (Stern et al. 1986). Something other than the subsidy had to be accounting for the different insulation adoption rates. Researchers found that in addition to reducing financial barriers, utilities also needed to provide information about how insulation can improve household energy efficiency as well as help direct consumers to a reliable contractor.

Social norms are incredibly important in all of this too. What's especially remarkable about social norms is that they seem to have the capacity to elicit behavioral changes without any changes in values or attitudes. I would like to discuss briefly one example where behavioral change occurred in the *absence of attitudinal change*. This case study involves high schools from the school district where I live—Fort Collins, Colorado (Shelley et al. 2011, 2012).

Over a period of eight years, Rocky Mountain High School, which first opened in 1973, was able to reduce its electrical energy consumption to levels below that of the LEED-certified Fossil Ridge High School, built in 2005. (LEED stands for Leadership in Energy and Environmental Design and involves a rating system for the design, construction, and operation of green buildings, homes, and neighborhoods.) Although the LEED school was built for energy efficiency, in 2007 it consumed electricity at a higher rate (6.24 kilowatt hours per square foot) than the much older Rocky Mountain High School (4.79 kilowatt hours per square foot) because of the latter's highly successful energy conservation efforts. What did Rocky Mountain High School do to achieve these impressive results, where it was able to cut its electrical energy consumption in half over the span of a few years? As indicated by earlier research, no single thing led to the behavioral changes. The authors of this study (Shelley et al. 2011) cite a number of factors:

- Physical structures were added in the school that "communicated environmental values." Examples of this include the recycling center, the "Thanks a Watt" signs above electrical switches, and the clearly marked waste and recycling bins. Making these changes made it easy to be green, regardless of one's actual beliefs.
- Everyone was made a vested stakeholder. Giving staff and students a voice in the process enhanced their desire to see the project become a success and increased their willingness to work toward that end.
- Providing communication and feedback also proved important. Providing students and staff with regular reports on their energy consumption, as well as on how their consumption compared to other schools in the district, kept them vested in the project.

As mentioned, none of the respondents conveyed an actual change in their attitudes. Nevertheless, "even without a sense of environmental concern and without engaging in environmentally responsible behaviors at home, they participated in energy conservation and other efforts (such as recycling) within the organizational setting" (Shelley et al. 2011, 338).

Social Movements

It is impossible to cover the social movement literature in a few paragraphs, but that is no excuse not to cover it, however thinly, here. Social movements are a powerful mechanism—perhaps *the* most powerful—for change (see Image 13.1).

Picking up where we left off with our earlier discussion of the postmaterialist thesis: the framework is problematic in still another way—namely, with regard to its view of *politics*. Postmaterialism suggests that there is a simultaneous political shift happening in postmaterialist states, where the public, to quote Inglehart directly, is given "an increasingly important role in making specific decisions, not just a choice between two or more sets of decision-makers" (Inglehart 1977, 3). It is argued, in other words, that there is a link between a shift in individual and cultural values and subsequent (positive) political change. In other words, its argument goes something like this: as people attain a level of material well-being, develop postmaterialist values, and participate in politics in a way that reinforces these new values, the state will respond accordingly.

Wrong. "The reality," to quote Schlosberg (2019, 5), "is that the celebrated postmaterialist values and policies are regularly shut out by governments with strong vested interests and unresponsive political parties and processes." There is therefore a "governance gap" (Stolle and Micheletti 2013, 10) in these societies—a divergence between people's values and what the government makes possible. So, before you think social movements and collective action have no place in liberal democracies, think again. We need to act collectively—and not just shop collectively by way of buycotts and boycotts—to make sure the system is working for *us* and not for those entrenched interests.

Social movements can be analyzed in many different ways. One is through the lens of social networks, as a *movement* implies a level of coordination between actors that can only be achieved through sustained interaction, or networks. When movement activity is dense—high levels of interaction among members—there is a greater likelihood of solidarity, mutual support, and self-sacrifice (Crossley and Ibrahim 2012). Moreover, dense networks facilitate the establishment and transference of nonmainstream values and movement-specific subcultures, which further fuel intergroup cohesion and collective action (Krinsky and Crossley 2014).

These networks also engage in **framing** processes. Social movements construct collective action frames as their participants negotiate a shared understanding of the problem, how it should be handled, and the motivations behind their actions—the diagnostic, prognostic, and motivation frames, respectively (Snow and Benford 1988). Framing is also strategic, as it involves frame alignment processes. These processes include frame bridging (linking two or more frames), frame amplification (embellishment or clarification of existing values), frame extension (extending a frame beyond its initial scope), and frame transformation (changing old understandings or generating new ones) (Snow et al. 1986). With regard to frame transformation, Pellow and Brehm (2015; see also Pellow 2014) conducted an exhaustive study of "radical earth and animal liberation activists" (Pellow and Brehm 2015, 207) documenting how they build on deep ecology, ecofeminism, an environmental justice paradigm, and ecological movements, resulting in something entirely new, what activists call a "total liberation" frame. This frame reorganizes what it means to reduce harm to humans and the environment due to "a complete reordering of human/nonhuman relations" resulting in a desire for "equality for all beings" (Ibid.).

IMAGE 13.1 Rally against Kinder Morgan Oil Pipeline on Burnaby Mountain, British Columbia, Canada.

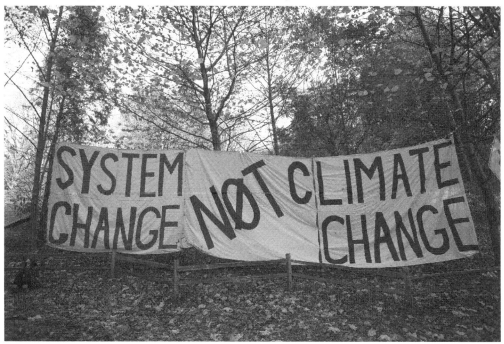

Source: "Rally against Kinder Morgan Oil Pipeline on Burnaby Mountain" by Mark Klotz (flickr.com/photos/markklotz/) is licensed copyright © 2014 under CC BY 2.0.

Why some movements succeed and others fail can also be thought about in terms of organizational resources. Discontent and a sense of injustice are common occurrences. And yet collective *grievances* do not always stimulate collective *action*. According to McCarthy and Zald (1977), movement actors must have access to resources—financial, social capital, leadership, effective organizers, and so forth—that allow them to turn grievances into action.

In addition to having resources, movement organizations' ability to effect change often depends on the broader sociopolitical environment. While a **resource mobilization framework** focuses heavily on internal organizational resources, a **political opportunity approach** considers external factors, such as the political context within which social movements are embedded (McAdam 1996). Take the marriage equality movement. The story of this movement is radically different today from the one told a decade ago. This is in part due to there being a different sociopolitical reality in place currently from that which existed even just a few years ago. This is not to suggest all hope is lost when political opportunities appear "closed," when, say, lawmakers are not only resistant but also potentially hostile to movement demands—a reality experienced by many environmental activists in a post-9/11 world (Deflem and McDonough 2015). Instead, such an environment may compel activists to approach the court system as a venue in which they perceive a better chance of generating social change (McCammon and McGrath 2015). The Endangered Species Act 1973, thanks specifically to its citizen suit provision, has a rich history of activists taking successful legal action when federal agencies appear to be dragging their feet in enforcing it (Baur and Irvin 2010). That said, citizen litigation tends to be concentrated in jurisdictions where support for environmental policies is strongest, which exacerbates state and regional disparities in the implementation and enforcement of federal regulatory programs (Adelman and Glicksman 2019).

Pragmatic Environmentalism

Pragmatic social theorists—as well as environmentalists—take actors' agency and creativity seriously. As a theoretical tradition, pragmatism offers an alternative to overt social structuralism (an approach giving priority to structures) and methodological individualism (an approach giving priority to individuals). Instead, it emphasizes the dynamic emergent interplay between the process of constructing and reconstructing meaning through action and routine, on the one hand, and structures and the environment, on the other. John Dewey, the great American philosopher and an early developer of pragmatism, worried about the interests, beliefs, and ideologies of elites becoming fixed, or static, and assuming a taken-for-granted status within the political and dominant social cultures. To combat this, he prescribed the technique of experimentalism, which essentially involves recruiting the broader public to constantly reflect on and question conventional habits and beliefs. Dewey believed this constituted an important first step in breaking up imposed rules of order and action, which is necessary if meaningful social change is to occur. The most likely time for established rules to be reformed, Dewey argued, is when existing institutions fail. During these moments, publics form that are commonly united through a shared threat or actual harm. (Think of the possible "publics" that could be organized as a response to climate change.) Thus, social and environmental problems are inherently *hopeful*, in the sense that they create openings for creativity, change, and an enlivened democracy.

And what of those who choose not to be initially enrolled in this collective activity? Fortunately, there are many ways to engage people in selecting pro-environmental behaviors without having to make them into so-called environmentalists. For example, let's say we are able to get people to choose to leave their car in the garage, or perhaps not even buy one. As long as they are doing this, does it really matter—at least initially—what their attitudes toward the environment or even automobiles are? Anna Peterson (2009) reminds us that attitudes and values have the potential to change in radical ways in response to behavioral changes. She gives the example of the 1954 US Supreme Court decision *Brown v. Board of Education of Topeka*, the landmark court ruling that struck down the infamous "separate but equal" rule made famous in the *Plessy v. Ferguson* US Supreme Court ruling from 1899. Peterson (2009, 132) points out that "while school desegregation certainly did not end racism, it has had a significant effect on the lives and values of both white and black southerners," and ultimately concludes, "Brown generated major shifts in values that probably would not have occurred had institutions and practices not changed first" (Ibid.). She goes on to suggest that an "environmental *Brown v. Board of Education*" could, over time, help generate "environmental values as well as positive practical results" (Ibid.).

Something else we've learned over the past couple of decades is that getting people *talking and working together* is an immensely powerful force. The late Elinor Ostrom, as mentioned in an earlier chapter, won a Nobel Prize in economics in 2009 for her tireless research on precisely this point, though the idea that thick social networks can overwhelm desires to act selfishly has been articulated by social and political theorists for quite some time (see, e.g., Dryzek 1990; Eckersley 1992; Habermas 1962). Sometimes the formation of these collectivities is abrupt and immediate: think of the speed at which a shared global public formed in the wake of 9/11. More often, however, their formation is a slow grind, even for threats that are global and significant in scope, like climate change. In the end, *people* are going to have to do the work; structures are not going to change themselves. What are you going to do?

IMPORTANT CONCEPTS

- climate change denial
- collaborative consumption
- consumerism
- framing
- globalization of environmental concern
- Inglehart's postmaterialism thesis
- intrinsic and extrinsic values
- New Environmental Paradigm (NEP)
- political opportunity approach
- postmaterialism thesis
- pragmatic environmentalism
- resource mobilization framework

DISCUSSION QUESTIONS

1. We have long practiced a type of collaborative consumption with public libraries. Why do we not collaboratively consume more stuff, beyond books, movies, and music?
2. In what ways do some of your own pro-environmental attitudes not match up with certain behaviors? Why do you think this gap exists?
3. What are your thoughts on *Wired* founder Kevin Kelly's argument that "access is better than ownership"?
4. To revisit a question first posed at the end of Chapter 2: Why do some people continue to deny the existence of anthropogenic climate change? What are your thoughts on some of the explanations given above to this question?
5. Have you used a so-called sharing economy platform? How would you categorize the type of "sharing" it facilitated—e.g., did it provide access to stuff, build knowledge, engender community…?

SUGGESTED ADDITIONAL READINGS

Arcidiacono, D., A. Gandini, and I. Pais. 2018. "Sharing What? The 'Sharing Economy' in the Sociological Debate". *The Sociological Review*, 66(2): 275–288. https://doi.org/10.1177%2F0038026118758529.

Bernstein, J., and B.W. Szuster. 2019. "The New Environmental Paradigm Scale: Reassessing the Operationalization of Contemporary Environmentalism." *Journal of Environmental Education*, 50(2): 73–83.

Ives, C.D., and J. Kidwell. 2019. "Religion and Social Values for Sustainability." *Sustainability Science*, 14: 1355–1362. https://doi.org/10.1007/s11625-019-00657-0.

Schlosberg, D., 2019. "From Postmaterialism to Sustainable Materialism: The Environmental Politics of Practice-Based Movements." *Environmental Politics*. DOI: 10.1080/09644016.2019.1587215.

Temper, L., F. Demaria, A. Scheidel, D. Del Bene, and J. Martinez-Alier. 2018. "The Global Environmental Justice Atlas (EJAtlas): Ecological Distribution Conflicts as Forces for Sustainability." *Sustainability Science*, 13(3): 573–584.

RELEVANT INTERNET LINKS

- www.democracynow.org/2018/9/14/climate_capitalism_is_killing_our_communities. Video titled "'Climate Capitalism Is Killing Our Communities': Protesters Disrupt Gov. Brown's SF Climate Summit" September 14, 2018.
- www.scorai.org. Sustainable Consumption Research and Action Initiative (SCORAI) is a network of academics and practitioners interested in better understanding the interface of material consumption, human fulfillment, lifestyle satisfaction, and macroeconomic and technological change.
- www.youtube.com/watch?v=DNBY8yNXGoA. "What's Next for the Sharing Economy?"

SUGGESTED VIDEOS

- *END: CIV Resist or Die* (2011). If your homeland were invaded by aliens who cut down the forests, poisoned the water and air, and contaminated the food supply, would you resist?
- *Fierce Green Fire* (2014). www.democracynow.org/2014/4/22/earth_day_special_fierce_green_fire. Explores the environmental movement's global rise.
- *Meet the Climate Sceptics* (2011). A journey into the heart of climate skepticism to examine the key arguments against human-generated global warming and try to understand the people who are making it.
- *Shareconomy (Sharing Economy)* (2014). Ten-minute video on the sharing economy. Available, among other places, on YouTube.
- *The Evolution of Ecological Consciousness* (2013). It wasn't until the 1930s that we started to agree that there were such things as ice ages. It wasn't until the 1970s that plate tectonics was understood in geology. Our understanding of this planet is constantly developing and evolving.
- *The Third Industrial Revolution: A Radical New Sharing Economy* (2018). www.youtube.com/watch?v=QX3M8Ka9vUA. A 100-minute lecture (yes, it's rather long) by well-known futurist Jeremy Rifkin. According to Rifkin, a Third Industrial Revolution is unfolding giving rise to what he calls a new sharing economy.
- *We the Tiny House People* (2012). This is a journey into the tiny homes of people searching for simplicity, self-sufficiency, minimalism, and happiness by creating shelter in caves, converted garages, trailers, tool sheds, river boats, and former pigeon coops.
- *Words from the Edge* (2013). For many years the environmental movement has assumed that if you want to get people to do something, what you have to do is to make a sufficiently depressing film or write a sufficiently horrific and miserable leaflet and get that into their hands and they will simply act: "Oh my God, that's terrible, I'll go and plant some carrots." Actually it doesn't work that way.

Glossary

Abject poverty: Most severe state of poverty. Those living in this state cannot meet basic needs for food, water, shelter, sanitation, and health care.

Adaptation (climate change): Actions taken to adjust socioecological systems in response to existing or predicted climatic effects in order to reduce harmful effects.

Agrobiodiversity: All forms of life directly relevant to agriculture, including crops and livestock but also many other organisms, such as soil, fauna, weeds, pests, and predators.

Anaerobic decomposition: The breaking down of biodegradable material by microorganisms in an environment lacking oxygen.

Apolitical ecology: When conventional explanations do not fully account for the asymmetries in power that first created a problem materially and then later define it as a problem to be solved by the same system that gave birth to it.

Arable land: Land that can be cultivated to grow crops.

Biochar: Charcoal derived from the thermochemical decomposition of organic material at heightened temperatures in the absence of oxygen. Biochar is used to improve soil fertility and sequester carbon. Biochar oil and gas by-products can also be used as biofuels.

Biocultural diversity: Recognizes that cultural diversity does not merely parallel biological diversity but is profoundly interrelated with it.

Biodiversity hotspots: A biogeographic region with a significant reservoir of biodiversity that is under threat from humans.

Biofortification: The breeding and, increasingly, genetic engineering of plants with the aim of higher micronutrient content.

Biohazards: Environmental threats resulting from biological agents or conditions.

Biopiracy: The loss of biocultural diversity through legal and sometimes illegal means.

Birth rate: The ratio of live births to total population of a specified community, usually expressed per 1,000 people per year.

"Bonding" social capital: Social ties that link people together who are primarily alike according to established characteristics.

"Bridging" social capital: Social ties that link people together across social cleavages.

Buyer power: An effect that results when a market has numerous sellers but only one or a few buyers.

Cap and trade: A scheme that involves the trading of a limited number of emission allowances. A regulatory authority establishes this limit, which is typically lower than the historical level of emissions.

Carbon credits: Units of carbon emissions that can be purchased or sold to meet compliance with carbon emission caps.

Carbon intensity: The amount of CO_2 emitted for each unit of economic output produced.

Carbon offsets: Reduction in emissions of CO_2 (or greenhouse gases more generally) in order to compensate for (offset) an emission released elsewhere.

Carbon tax: Tax on fossil fuels that seeks to reduce the emissions of CO_2.

Clean coal: Defined by the coal industry as any technologies that improve the environmental performance of coal-based electricity plants, which include equipment that increases the operational efficiency of power plants as well as technologies that reduce emissions. Elsewhere, it refers to the CO_2 capture and (long-term) storage of emissions.

Climate change: A change in climate patterns that results from human activity such as burning fossil fuels.

Climate change refugees: Populations that have been displaced as a result of climate change.

Coase theorem: When property rights are involved, parties naturally gravitate toward the most efficient and mutually beneficial outcome.

Collective coverage: Proportion of an area serviced by the municipal waste stream.

Commodity chain: The collective networks that encompass the beginning and end of a product's life cycle.

Community severance: The physical or social separation of an individual from the rest of the community.

Conspicuous consumption: The idea that we consume, at least in part, to display to others our social power and status.

Contingent valuation: A survey-based economic technique for placing a value on nonmarket resources.

Convention on Biological Diversity: An international, legally binding treaty that entered into force in 1993. The convention has three main goals: conservation of biological diversity; sustainable use of biological resources; and fair and equitable sharing of benefits arising from genetic resources.

Cornucopian: Someone who believes unending progress, economic growth, and material abundance can be had with advancements in technology.

Corporate Social Responsibility: A form of international private business self-regulation.

Countermovement: A social movement that arises to explicitly oppose an existing social movement.

Cultural hotspots: A biogeographic region with a significant reservoir of cultural diversity that is under threat of extinction.

Daylighting: The practice of uncovering previously concealed natural amenities.

Dead zones: The name given to bodies of water with low levels of dissolved oxygen.

Decoupling: The ability for an economy to grow without corresponding increases in environmental pressures.

Demographic inertia: A well-documented demographic phenomenon relating to how a time lag is to be expected before the full effects of changes to a fertility rate are seen.

Demographic transition model: A model detailing the historical changes in birth rates and death rates for explaining rapid population growth. A country is said to have passed through the demographic transition when it moves from a condition of high birth rates and death rates (and a relatively small population) to low birth rates and death rates (and a relatively large population).

Desalinization: The removal of salt and other minerals from saline water.

Diminishing marginal utility: The more units of something we consume, the less added enjoyment we get from each additional unit.

Disability-adjusted life-years (DALYs): The sum of years of potential life lost from premature mortality and the years of productive life lost from disability.

Disease vectors: An organism, such as a mosquito or tick, that carries disease-causing microorganisms from one host to another.

Diversionary reframing: Diverting attention away from real problems by trying to reframe the debate as being about something else.

Down-cycling: The process of converting waste into new materials or products of lesser quality and decreased functionality.

Ecofeminism: An area of study that examines the historical (and present) links between the objectification of women and the objectification of nature.

Economism: The act of reducing the world to economic dimensions.

Ecosystem services: The processes by which the environment produces resources that we often take for granted but need for our survival, such as clean air and water, timber, habitat for fisheries, and pollination of native and agricultural plants.

Efficiency shifting: When money and resources saved through energy efficiency merely get shifted to and consumed by other goods and services.

Embodied energy: The sum total of the energy utilized throughout an entire product life cycle.

Energy intensity: The amount of energy required to produce each unit of the world's economic output.

Environmental racism: Racial discrimination in environmental policy making and enforcement of regulations and laws, in addition to the targeting of communities of color for toxic waste disposal and siting of polluting industries.

Environmental skepticism: A position that attempts to undermine knowledge claims supporting the argument that environmental problems are real and that they are the result of human activity.

Exponential growth: Constant growth in a system where the amount added is proportional to the amount present.

Ex situ: Sampling, transferring, and storage of a species in a place other than the original location in which it was found, such as a zoo or seed bank.

Extended producer responsibility: Holding the manufacturer responsible for a product beyond the time of sale, thereby relieving consumers, governments, future generations, and the environment from the costs associated with landfilling and recycling hazardous materials.

Externality: Cost or benefit not transmitted through prices and incurred by a party that did not agree to the action causing the cost or benefit.

Family planning: Educational, social, and medical services that empower individuals to make choices around reproduction.

Food sovereignty: A movement and way of life that is diametrically opposed to the dominant view that presently dictates conventional food and agricultural policy.

Food system: The entire array of activities—from input production and distribution to on-farm activities, marketing, processing, wholesale, and retail—that connect seed (and gene) to the mouths of consumers.

Footprint shifting (life cycle): Making efficiency gains at one point in a commodity's life cycle while creating a larger environmental load at another point.

Fracking: A method of extracting natural gas from deep wells; also known as hydraulic fracturing.

Framing: Involves the social construction of social phenomena—by mass media, political or social movements, political leaders, or other actors and organizations—whereby symbols, words, or phrases are given distinct meanings with the aim of organizing people into social groups, e.g., social movements.

Full irrigation: The amount of water needed to achieve maximum yield.

Global land grab: International land deals whereby corporations, investment firms, and/or state-owned enterprises lease or purchase large tracts of land in other countries for the production of food that is then exported to the country that is "home" to said investment.

Greenhouse effect: When a portion of the sun's radiation that enters the atmosphere is absorbed by the planet's atmosphere due to greenhouse gases like CO_2 rather than being reradiated back into space.

Greenhouse gases: Any gases in the atmosphere that absorb and emit radiation within the thermal infrared range.

Green revolution: A series of strategies developed during the mid- to late twentieth century to combat starvation by expanding the global production of staple food crops through crop breeding.

Habitat fragmentation: The emergence of discontinuities (or fragmentation) in an organism's preferred environment (or habitat).

Happy Life Years (HLYs): A measurement of the health of a nation found through multiplying life expectancy at birth by happiness score (on a scale of 0 to 1).

Heat island effect: Because concrete, tarmac, and other common construction materials absorb heat readily, built-up areas tend to be warmer than nearby rural areas.

Hypoxia: A state when oxygen concentrations in a body of water fall below the level necessary to sustain most animal life.

Indigenous knowledge: Knowledge unique to a given community, culture, or society.

Informal settlements: Unplanned housing constructed on land illegally or not in compliance with current building regulations, or both.

In situ: The management of a species at the location of discovery.

Intergovernmental Panel on Climate Change (IPCC): Established in 1988 by two UN organizations, the United Nations Environment Programme and the World Meteorological Organization, to provide scientific assessments on issues relating to climate change. As the IPCC is the internationally accepted authority on the subject, the world's governments look to it as the official advisory body on climate change.

Irrigation efficiency: The ratio of water that evaporates to that which saturates the soil.

Islandization (habitat): The breaking up of habitats without wildlife corridors to connect them.

Kyoto Protocol: An international treaty brokered by the UN, signed in 1997, that binds signatory nations to reduce their emissions of greenhouse gases. At Kyoto (where the agreement was first signed), nations agreed to cut their emissions of six greenhouse gases by an average of 5 percent overall, compared with 1990 levels, in what was termed the first commitment period, which was to end in 2012.

Landfill: A method of solid waste disposal where refuse is buried between layers of dirt.

Low-elevation coastal zones: Areas within 10 meters of mean sea level.

Market concentration: The dominance of a particular market by a few large firms as a result of acquisition, mergers, and other processes.

Market environmentalism: A theory that emphasizes markets as a solution to environmental problems.

Maternal mortality ratio: The number of women who die from pregnancy-related causes while pregnant or within 42 days of pregnancy termination per 100,000 live births.

Mechanical revolution: The gradual substitution of capital for labor in agriculture.

Megacities: Cities with more than ten million residents.

Memory banks: Spaces that preserve not only genetic material but the skills to grow and save seeds and prepare the fruits of those labors.

Micronutrient malnutrition: A condition that results from a diet lacking in sufficient quantities of micronutrients.

Mitigation: Making reductions in the concentration of greenhouse gases by reducing their sources, increasing sink capacity, or both.

Monocultures: An agricultural practice of producing a single plant species over a wide area for a number of consecutive years.

Mountaintop removal mining: Clearing upper-elevation forests (typically at the summit of mountains), stripping the ground of topsoil, and using explosives to break up rocks to expose underlying yet relatively shallow coal seams.

Municipal solid waste: All solid waste originating from homes, industries, businesses, demolition, land clearing, and construction.

Natural capital: Assets indispensable for human survival and economic activity provided by the ecosystem.

Naturalistic fallacy: When statements of fact are conflated with statements of value.

Neoliberalism: A set of economic practices grounded in the belief that human well-being is best advanced by limiting (if not eliminating) government and liberating individual entrepreneurial freedoms within legal and institutional frameworks that support strong private property rights, free markets, and free trade.

Neo-Malthusians: Those who advocate for the control of population growth.

Nongovernmental organization (NGO): Any legally constituted organization that operates independently from any government.

Nonpoint-source pollution: Pollution that is more diffuse, making the source harder to pinpoint.

Normal accidents: A failure that is inevitable, given the manner in which particular human and technological systems are organized.

One-child policy: First introduced in 1978, this policy restricts married urban couples in China to one child, though exceptions are allowed, such as for rural couples and certain ethnic minorities.

Open source seeds: Seeds that cannot be patented, licensed, or commodified in any way, even in those instances where they have been bred or genetically modified into something new.

Organic system (agriculture): A farm management system that seeks to enhance biodiversity while minimizing the use of off-farm inputs.

Pareto optimality standard: Deems a policy acceptable only if at least one individual is better off and no individuals are made worse off.

Pay-as-you-drive auto insurance: Insurance whose rate (but not coverage) is contingent on, among other things, the number of miles driven.

Peasant-based movements: Social movements that began in the Global South and that centrally involve peasants. In this context "peasant" is not a pejorative term but one of empowerment.

Peer-to-peer renting: The practice of one private individual renting an underused item to another individual.

Pigovian taxes: Taxes levied on companies that pollute or create excess social costs (called negative externalities).

Point-source pollution: Pollution with an identifiable source.

Political opportunity approach: Argues that the success or failure of social movements is primarily affected by political opportunities.

Polycultures: Small, diverse farms that raise grains, fruits, vegetables, and livestock.

Popular epidemiology: A type of citizen science in which laypeople are involved and which requires a lower level of statistical confidence when claiming the existence of causal links.

Porter Hypothesis: Regulation spurs innovation, as it creates incentives for businesses to adjust to social and environmental realities.

Precision agriculture: A suite of techniques that are said to make farming more efficient, and controlled through the use of information technology and a wide array of items such as GPS guidance, control systems, sensors, robotics, drones, autonomous vehicles, GPS-based soil sampling, automated hardware, and big data.

Pronatal social norms: Individual attitudes and societal expectations that promote high fertility rates.

Resource mobilization framework: Emphasizes the ability of a movement's members to acquire resources and to mobilize people toward accomplishing the movement's goals.

Role strain: Tensions that emerge when expectations from holding multiple roles clash.

Salinization: The buildup of salt in soil and groundwater.

Sequestering CO$_2$: The act of removing CO$_2$ from the atmosphere and holding it in a sink.

Sink (greenhouse gases): A natural or artificial reservoir—like a forest—that holds and stores greenhouses gases for an indefinite period, thus preventing their accumulation in the atmosphere.

Social constructivism: An approach that focuses entirely on the sociologically dependent knowledge of a phenomenon rather than on any inherent qualities that the thing possesses itself.

Social norms: Standards of behavior shared by a social group.

Sociological drivers: Real phenomena, which can only be fully grasped with the help of social theory, that underlie today's environmental problems.

Sociological imagination: A way of thinking that involves making connections between the particular and the general over time and across scales.

Species problem: The inherent ambiguity surrounding the use and definition of the species concept.

Street hierarchy: Eliminates connections between streets by funneling traffic up the hierarchy, from cul-de-sac streets to primary or secondary collector streets, arterial streets, and ultimately highways.

Strip-mining: The removal of soil and rock overlaying the mineral deposit.

Structure of agriculture: How farms, rural populations, and agribusiness firms are arranged to produce and distribute food and fiber.

Terminator technology: Genetically engineered seeds that produce sterile plants.

Tragedy of the commodity: Rather than being its savior, commodification of so-called natural capital contributes to the decline of biodiversity and ecosystem services.

Type I error: Concluding there is a causal link when there isn't one.

Type II error: Concluding there is not a causal link when there is one.

Uneconomic growth: Growth that costs us more than it benefits us.

Urban sprawl: The spreading of urban development into areas adjoining cities.

Vertical farming: The practice of farming "up," rather than "out."

Virtual water: Water used during the growing, making, or manufacturing of a given commodity.

Volatile organic compounds: Compounds that evaporate from housekeeping, maintenance, and building products made with organic chemicals.

Vulnerable road users: As defined by the World Health Organization, this population includes pedestrians, cyclists, and users of motorized two-wheel vehicles.

Waste regimes: The realization that institutions, regulations, policy initiatives, and social conventions determine not only what is waste but also how waste is valued.

Water footprint: An indicator of freshwater use that looks at both direct and indirect water use by a consumer or producer.

Water privatization: The treatment of water like any other commodity and leaving questions of access and sanitation to market mechanisms.

Welfare economics: A branch of microeconomics that seeks to evaluate well-being, with the assumption that human well-being is wholly reducible to economic well-being.

Wildlife corridors: Areas of habitat connecting wildlife populations and larger islands of habitat.

Work–spend cycle: Where we work to spend, which in turn requires us to work more.

Worldview: A fundamental cognitive orientation shared by individuals within which is rooted the entirety of their knowledge.

References

AAA (American Automobile Association). 2015. *Your Driving Costs*. Heathrow, FL. http://exchange.aaa.com/wp-content/uploads/2015/04/Your-Driving-Costs-2015.pdf.

Abbott, M. 2019. "Fracking Could Be Subject To Local Limits Under Proposed Bill". *Patch.com*, March 1. https://patch.com/colorado/boulder/fracking-could-be-subject-local-limits-under-proposed-bill.

ABC News. 2017. "Powering Past Coal Alliance: 20 Countries Sign Up to Phase Out Coal Power by 2030." *ABC News*, Nov 16. www.abc.net.au/news/2017-11-17/20-countries-have-signed-up-to-phase-out-coal-power-by-2030/9161056.

Abram, D. 1996. *The Spell of the Sensuous*. New York: Pantheon Books.

Adams, J., and M. White. 2015. "Characterisation of UK Diets According to Degree of Food Processing and Associations with Socio-Demographics and Obesity: Cross-Sectional Analysis of UK National Diet and Nutrition Survey (2008–12)," *International Journal of Behavioral Nutrition*, 12: 160–171. DOI: 10.1186/s12966–015-0317-y.

Adelman, D.E., and R.L. Glicksman. 2019. "The Limits of Citizen Environmental Litigation." *Natural Resources & Environment*, 33(4): 17–21.

Agapow, P., O. Bininda-Emonds, K. Crandall, J. Gittleman, G. Mace, J. Marshall, and A. Purvis. 2004. "The Impact of Species Concept on Biodiversity Studies." *Quarterly Review of Biology*, 79: 161–179.

Agence France-Presse. 2018. "A Tiny Michigan Town Is in a Water Fight with Nestle." *PRI*, February 4. www.pri.org/stories/2018-02-04/tiny-michigan-town-water-fight-nestle.

Aggarwal, R.M. 2016. "International Development and Sustainability." In *Sustainability Science*, edited by H. Heindricks, pp. 273–282. Dordrecht: Springer.

Agrawal, A. 2014. "Studying the Commons, Governing Common-Pool Resource Outcomes: Some Concluding Thoughts." *Environmental Science & Policy*, 36: 86–91.

Akinci, M. 2018. "Inequality and Economic Growth: Trickle-Down Effect Revisited." *Development Policy Review*, 36: O1–O24.

Alderman, H., J. Hoddinott, and B. Kinsey. 2006. "Long-Term Consequences of Early Childhood Malnutrition." *Oxford Economic Papers*, 58(3): 450–474.

Alexander, J., T. Crompton, and G. Shrubsole. 2011. *Think of Me as Evil: Opening the Ethical Debates in Advertising*. Public Interest Research Centre (PIRC) and WWF-UK. http://assets.wwf.org.uk/downloads/think_of_me_as_evil.pdf.

Alexandratos, N., and J. Bruinsma. 2012. *World Agriculture Towards 2030–50*. ESA Working Paper No. 12–03. Food and Agriculture Organization, United Nations, Rome. http://large.stanford.edu/courses/2014/ph240/yuan2/docs/ap106e.pdf.

Altieri, A., and K. Gedan. 2015. "Climate Change and Dead Zones." *Global Change Biology*, 21(4): 1395–1406.

Altieri, M., and C. Nicholls. 2008. "Scaling Up Agroecological Approaches for Food Sovereignty in Latin America." *Development*, 51(4): 472–480.

American Public Health Association. 2010. *The Hidden Health Costs of Transportation*. Washington, DC. www.apha.org/NR/rdonlyres/E71B4070-9B9D-4EE1-8F43-349D21414962/0/FINALHiddenHealthCostsShortNewBackCover.pdf.

Amuzu, D. 2018. "Environmental Injustice of Informal E-Waste Recycling in Agbogbloshie-Accra: Urban Political Ecology Perspective." *Local Environment*, 23(6): 603–618.

Anciaes, P.R., Jones, P., and Mindell, J.S. 2016. "Community Severance: Where Is It Found and at What Cost?" *Transport Reviews*, 36(3): 293–317.

Andersen, T.M., 2018. "Human Capital, Inequality, and Growth." In *The Welfare State Revisited*, edited by José Ocampo and Joseph E. Stiglitz, pp. 109–122. New York: Columbia University Press.

Anderson, T.L. 2004. "Why Economic Growth Is Good for the Environment." *Hoover Digest3*. www.perc.org/articles/why-economic-growth-good-environment.

Andrezejewski, A., and T. Smith. 2018. "Harvesting US Farm Subsidies." *OpenTheBooks.com*, August. https://issuu.com/openthebooks/docs/usfarmsubsidies_08072018?e=31597235/63670406.

Ansar, A., B. Flyvbjerg, A. Budzier, and D. Lunn. 2014. "Should We Build More Large Dams? The Actual Costs of Hydropower Megaproject Development." *Energy Policy*, 69: 43–56.

Ashworth, D., P. Elliott, and M. Toledano. 2014. "Waste Incineration and Adverse Birth and Neonatal Outcomes: A Systematic Review." *Environment International*, 69: 120–132.

Atav, E., B. Altunoğlu, and S. Sönmez. 2015. "The Determination of the Environmental Attitudes of Secondary Education Students." *Procedia-Social and Behavioral Sciences*, 174: 1391–1396.

Attari, S., M. DeKayb, C. Davidson, and W. Bruine de Bruin. 2010. "Public Perceptions of Energy Consumption and Savings." *Proceedings of the National Academy of Sciences*, 107(37): 16054–16059.

Ayres, R., and B. Warr. 2009. *The Economic Growth Engine: How Energy and Work Drive Material Prosperity*. Northampton, MA: Edward Elgar.

Bachram, H. 2004. "Climate Fraud and Carbon Colonialism: The New Trade in Greenhouse Gases." *Capitalism Nature Socialism*, 15(4): 5–20.

Badstuber, N. 2018. "London Congestion Charge Has Been a Huge Success. It's Time to Change It." *CityMetric*, March 12. www.citymetric.com/transport/london-congestion-charge-has-been-huge-success-it-s-time-change-it-3751.

Bailey, I., and Darkal, H. 2018. (Not) Talking about Justice: Justice Self-Recognition and the Integration of Energy and Environmental-Social Justice into Renewable Energy Siting. *Local Environment*, 23(3): 335–351.

Baldé, C.P., Forti V., Gray, V., Kuehr, R., Stegmann, P. 2017. *The Global E-waste Monitor 2017*. United Nations. https://drive.google.com/file/d/11DCXXZM-bflxHxk92gOXbweIceb40brP/view.

Balmford, A., R. Green, and J. Scharlemann. 2005. "Sparing Land for Nature: Exploring the Potential Impact of Changes in Agricultural Yield on the Area Needed for Crop Production." *Global Change Biology*, 11: 1594–1605.

Banerjee, A., and E. Duflo. 2011. "More Than 1 Billion People Are Hungry in the World: But What if the Experts Are Wrong?" *Foreign Policy* (May–June).

Bang, M., D. Medin, and S. Atran. 2007. "Cultural Mosaics and Mental Models of Nature." *Proceedings of the National Academy of Sciences*, 104(35): 13868–13874.

Barbier, E.B. 2015. "Climate Change Impacts on Rural Poverty in Low-Elevation Coastal Zones." *Estuarine, Coastal and Shelf Science*, 165: ii–iii.

Barnard, N. 2010. "Trends in Food Availability, 1909–2007." *American Journal of Clinical Nutrition*, 91: 1530S–1536S.

Bartels, L.M. 2018. *Unequal Democracy: The Political Economy of the New Gilded Age*. Princeton, NJ: Princeton University Press.

Bartolini, S., E. Bilancini, L. Bruni, and P. Porta, eds. 2016. *Policies for Happiness*. Oxford: Oxford University Press.

Baskoro, F.M. 2011. "Air Travel to Grow by 13% by Next Year, Industry Says." *Jakarta Globe*, December 8.

Bates, S. 2015. "The Emergent Body: Marxism, Critical Realism and the Corporeal in Contemporary Capitalist Society." *Global Society*, 29(1): 128–147.

Baumeister, R.F., S.E. Ainsworth, and K.D. Vohs. 2015. "Are Groups More or Less Than the Sum of Their Members? The Moderating Role of Individual Identification." *Behavioral and Brain Sciences*, May 4.

Baur, D., and W. Irvin. 2010. *Endangered Species Act: Law, Policy, and Perspectives*. New York: American Bar Association.

BBC. 2003. "Argentina Fights Flood Waters." *BBC News*, May 2. http://news.bbc.co.uk/2/hi/americas/2994301.stm.

Becker, M., M. Karpytchev, and F. Papa. 2019. "Hotspots of Relative Sea Level Rise in the Tropics." In *Tropical Extremes*, edited by V. Venugopal, pp. 203–262. Amsterdam: Elsevier.

Bell, M., and P. Lowe. 2000. "Regulated Freedoms: The Market and the State, Agriculture, and the Environment." *Journal of Rural Studies*, 16: 285–294.

Bellard, C., Leclerc, C., and Courchamp, F. 2014. "Impact of Sea Level Rise on the 10 Insular Biodiversity Hotspots." *Global Ecology and Biogeography*, 23(2): 203–212.

Berlin, I. (1958) 1969. *Four Essays on Liberty*. London: Oxford University Press.

Bershidsky, L. 2018. "Why We're Choking on Amazon Cardboard." *Bloomberg*, September 17. www.bloomberg.com/opinion/articles/2018-09-17/amazon-amzn-boxes-are-choking-the-rest-of-us (accessed March 18, 2019).

Bhattacharya, G. 2019. "Means of Livelihood and Forest Destruction in India: An Alarming Issue." *Research Journal of Social Sciences*, 10(1). www.aensi.in/assets/uploads/doc/037ee-44-54.14403.pdf.

Bicycle Dutch. 2018. "Dutch Bicycle Figures." January 2. https://bicycledutch.wordpress.com/2018/01/02/dutch-cycling-figures/.

Blackford, M. 2004. "Environmental Justice, Native Rights, Tourism, and Opposition to Military Control: The Case of Kaho'olawe." *Journal of American History*, 91(2): 1–43.

Blum, A.J., and P.J. Hotez. 2018. "Global 'Worming': Climate Change and Its Projected General Impact on Human Helminth Infections." *PLOS: Neglected Tropical Diseases*, 12(7). https://doi.org/10.1371/journal.pntd.0006370.

Boccard, N. 2014. "The Cost of Nuclear Electricity: France After Fukushima." *Energy Policy*, 66: 450–461.

Bokowa, A. 2010. "The Review of Odour Legislation." *Proceedings of the Water Environment Federation*, 20: 492–511.

Bolles, A. 1878. *Industrial History of the United States*. Norwich, CT: Henry Bill.

Bolsen, T., J.N. Druckman, and F.L. Cook. 2015. "Citizens', Scientists', and Policy Advisors' Beliefs about Global Warming." *The ANNALS of the American Academy of Political and Social Science*, 658(1): 271–295.

Booker, A., D. Johnston, and M. Heinrich. 2015. "Value Chains of Herbal Medicines—Ethnopharmacological and Analytical Challenges in a Globalizing World." In *Evidence-Based Validation of Herbal Medicine*, edited by P. Mukherjee, pp. 29–44. Amsterdam: Elsevier.

Bordewich, F., R. Klein, P. Smith, M. Buckingham, and E. Winograde. 2007. *No Reservations: Native American History and Culture in Contemporary Art*. Ridgefield, CT: Aldrich Contemporary Art Museum.

Bordoff, J., and P. Noel. 2008. "Pay-as-You-Drive Auto Insurance: A Simple Way to Reduce Driving-Related Harms and Increase Equity." Discussion paper 2008–2009, July. Brookings Institution, Washington, DC. www.brookings.edu/~/media/Files/rc/papers/2008/07paydbordoffnoel/07paydbordoffnoelpb.pdf.

Borg, R., A. Toikka, and E. Primmer. 2015. "Social Capital and Governance: A Social Network Analysis of Forest Biodiversity Collaboration in Central Finland." *Forest Policy and Economics*, 50: 90–97.

Boserup, E. 1965. *The Conditions of Agricultural Growth: The Economics of Agrarian Change Under Population Pressure*. Chicago, IL: Aldine.

Bosselman, A. 2019. "Denver's Buses and Trains Are Not Useful to Most People. A New Book Shows Why." *Street Blog Denver*, January 29. https://denver.streetsblog.org/2019/01/29/denvers-buses-and-trains-arent-useful-to-most-people-a-new-book-shows-why/.

Botsman, R., and R. Rogers. 2010. *What's Mine Is Yours: The Rise of Collaborative Consumption*. New York: Harper.

Bowden, V., D. Nyberg, and C. Wright. 2019. "Planning for the Past: Local Temporality and the Construction of Denial in Climate Change Adaptation. *Global Environmental Change*, 57. https://doi.org/10.1016/j.gloenvcha.2019.101939.

BP. 2015. *BP Energy Outlook, 2035*. www.bp.com/content/dam/bp/pdf/Energy-economics/energy-outlook-2015/Energy_Outlook_2035_booklet.pdf.

Bradshaw, S., and M. Fordham. 2015. "Double Disaster: Disaster Through a Gender Lens." In *Hazards, Risks and Disasters in Society*, edited by A. Collins, pp. 233–251. Amsterdam: Elsevier.

Bremner, B., and N. Lakshman. 2006. "Behind the Coke-Pepsi Pesticide Scare." *Business Week*, August 24. www.businessweek.com/globalbiz/content/aug2006/gb20060824_932216.htm.

Brizga, J., Z. Mishchuk, and A. Golubovska-Onisimova. 2014. "Sustainable Consumption and Production Governance in Countries in Transition." *Journal of Cleaner Production*, 63: 45–53.

Brogaard, L., A. Damgaard, M. Jensen, M. Barlaz, and T. Christensen. 2014. "Evaluation of Life Cycle Inventory Data for Recycling Systems." *Resources, Conservation and Recycling*, 87: 30–45.

Brown, K. 2019. "UN Passes First Ever Declaration for Peasant Rights." *Mongabay*, February 20. https://news.mongabay.com/2019/02/un-passes-first-ever-declaration-for-peasant-rights/.

Brown, K., and T. Kasser. 2005. "Are Psychological and Ecological Well-Being Compatible? The Role of Values, Mindfulness, and Lifestyle." *Social Indicators Research*, 74: 349–368.

Büchs, M., and M. Koch. 2019. "Challenges for the Degrowth Transition: The Debate about Wellbeing." *Futures*, 105: 155–165.

Bulkeley, H., L. Andonova, M. Betsill, D. Compagnon, T. Hale, M. Hoffmann, P. Newell, M. Paterson, S. VanDeveer, and C. Roger. 2014. *Transnational Climate Change Governance*. New York: Cambridge University Press.

Bullard, R. 1990. *Dumping in Dixie: Race, Class, and Environmental Quality*. Boulder, CO: Westview.

Bullard, R., ed. 2005. *The Quest for Environmental Justice: Human Rights and the Politics of Pollution*. San Francisco, CA: Sierra Club Books.

Burns, B. 2010. "TSA Myth or Fact: Leaked Images, Handcuffed Hosts, Religious Garb, and More!" *TSA Blog*, November 18. http://blog.tsa.gov/2010/11/tsa-myth-or-fact-leaked-images.html.

Cafruni, C.B., M.P. Pattussi, V. Backes, J.D. da Costa, M.T.A. Olinto, F.S. de Bairros, and R.L. Henn. 2019. "Neighbourhood Environment and Transport-Related and Leisure-Time Sedentary Behaviour Amongst Women in a City in Southern Brazil: A Multilevel Analysis." *International Journal of Public Health*, 64(4): 511–522.

Calabresi, G. 1991. "The Pointlessness of Pareto: Carrying Coase Further." *Yale Law Journal*, 100(5): 1211–1237.

Campbell, H. 2017. "RSG 2017 Survey Results: Driver Earnings, Satisfaction and Demographics." *The Ride Share Guy*. https://therideshareguy.com/rsg-2017-survey-results-driver-earnings-satisfaction-and-demographics/.

Cardinale, B. 2011. "Biodiversity Improves Water Quality Through Niche Partitioning." *Nature*, 472: 86–89.

Carnicer, J., J. Sardans, C. Stefanescu, A. Ubach, M. Bartrons, D. Asensio, and J. Peñuelas. 2015. "Global Biodiversity, Stoichiometry and Ecosystem Function Responses to Human-Induced C–N–P Imbalances." *Journal of Plant Physiology*, 172: 82–91.

Carolan, M. 2005a. "Realism Without Reductionism: Toward an Ecologically Embedded Sociology." *Human Ecology Review*, 12(1): 1–20.

Carolan, M. 2005b. "Society, Biology, and Ecology: Bringing Nature Back into Sociology's Disciplinary Narrative." *Organization and Environment*, 18: 393–421.

Carolan, M. 2007. "The Precautionary Principle and Traditional Risk Assessment: Rethinking How We Assess and Mitigate Environmental Threats." *Organization and Environment*, 20(1): 5–24.

Carolan, M. 2008a. "I Do Therefore There Is: Enlivening Socio-Environmental Theory." *Environmental Politics*, 18(1): 1–17.

Carolan, M. 2008b. "More-Than-Representational Knowledge/s of the Countryside: How We Think as Bodies." *Sociologia Ruralis*, 48(4): 408–422.

Carolan, M. 2008c. "When Good Smells Go Bad: A Socio-Historical Understanding of Agricultural Odor Pollution." *Environment and Planning A*, 40(5): 1235–1249.

Carolan, M.S. 2010. Decentering Biotechnology: Assemblages Built and Assemblages Masked. New York: Routledge.

Carolan, M. 2011. *Embodied Food Politics*. Burlington, VT: Ashgate.

Carolan, M. 2014. *Cheaponomics: The High Cost of Low Prices*. New York: Earthscan/Routledge.

Carolan, M. 2016. *The Sociology of Food and Agriculture*. New York: Earthscan/Routledge.

Carolan, M. 2017. *No One Eats Alone: Food as a Social Enterprise*. Washington, DC: Island Press.

Carolan, M. 2018a. *The Real Cost of Cheap Food*. New York: Earthscan.

Carolan, M. 2018b. *The Food Sharing Revolution: How Start-ups, Pop-ups, and Co-ops Are Changing the Way We Eat*. Washington, DC: Island Press.

Carolan, M. 2018c. "Justice Across Real and Imagined Food Worlds: Rural Corn Growers, Urban Agriculture Activists, and the Political Ontologies They Live By." *Rural Sociology*, 83(4): 823–856.

Carolan, M. 2019. "Urban Farming Is Going High Tech: Digital Urban Agriculture's Links to Gentrification and Land Use." *Journal of the American Planning Association*. DOI: 10.1080/01944363.2019.1660205.

Carolan, M., and J. Hale. 2016. "'Growing' Communities with Urban Agriculture: Generating Value Above and Below Ground." *Community Development*. DOI: 10.1080/15575330.2016.1158198.

Carolan, M., and D. Stuart. 2016. "Get Real: Climate Change and All That 'It' Entails." *Sociologia Ruralis*, 56(1): 74–95.

Carpenter, Z. 2019. "The Toxic Consequences of America's Plastics Boom." *The Nation*, March 14. www.thenation.com/article/plastics-pollution-crisis-fracking-petrochemicals/.

Carrington, D. 2018. "Global Food System is Broken, say World's Science Academies." *Guardian*, November 28. www.theguardian.com/environment/2018/nov/28/global-food-system-is-broken-say-worlds-science-academies.

Carruthers, D. 2008. "The Globalization of Environmental Justice: Lessons from the US–Mexico Border." *Society and Natural Resources*, 21: 556–568.

Carter, J., and M. Irons. 1991. "Are Economists Different, and if So, Why?" *Journal of Economic Perspectives*, 5(2): 171–177.

Casey, P., and K. Scott. 2006. "Environmental Concern and Behavior in an Australian Sample within an Ecocentric–Anthropocentric Framework." *Australian Journal of Psychology*, 58: 57–67.

Catton, W., and R. Dunlap. 1978. "Environmental Sociology: A New Paradigm." *American Sociologist*, 13: 41–49.

CDC (Centers for Disease Control and Prevention). 2015. "Micronutrient Facts." Atlanta, GA. www.cdc.gov/impact/micronutrients.

Central Bureau of Statistics. 2017. "More People Find the Environment Highly Polluted." September 19. www.cbs.nl/en-gb/news/2018/37/more-people-find-the-environment-highly-polluted.

Chan, K., and J. McNeal. 2003. "Parental Concern About Television Viewing and Children's Advertising in China." *International Journal of Public Opinion Research*, 15(2): 151–166.

Chandrasekhar, C., and J. Ghosh. 2019. "The Dynamics of India's Rice Export Boom." *The Hindu Business Line*, January 14. www.thehindubusinessline.com/opinion/columns/c-p-chandrasekhar/the-dynamics-of-indias-rice-export-boom/article25994349.ece.

Chang, S.C., and T.A. Nguyen. 2018. "Peer Pressure and Its Influence on Consumers in Taiwan." *African Journal of Business Management*, 12(8): 221–230.

Charles, D. 2014. "Plant Breeders Release First 'Open Source Seeds'." *NPR*, April 17. www.npr.org/sections/thesalt/2014/04/17/303772556/plant-breeders-release-first-open-source-seeds.

Chatrchyan, A.M., R.C. Erlebacher, N.T. Chaopricha, J. Chan, D. Tobin, and S.B. Allred. 2017. "United States

Agricultural Stakeholder Views and Decisions on Climate Change." *Wiley Interdisciplinary Reviews: Climate Change*, 8(5): e469. https://doi.org/10.1002/wcc.469.

Chavis, B., and C. Lee. 1987. *Toxic Wastes and Race in the United States: A National Report on the Racial and Socio-Economic Characteristics of Communities with Hazardous Waste Sites*. New York: Commission for Racial Justice, United Church of Christ.

Chazan, G. 2011. "Biofuels Industry Battles Past Bumps in the Road." *Wall Street Journal*, April 7.

Chen, C., J. Harries, H. Brindley, and M. Ringer. 2007. "Spectral Signatures of Climate Change in the Earth's Infrared Spectrum Between 1970 and 2006." Fifteenth American Meteorological Society Satellite Meteorology and Oceanography Conference, Amsterdam, September 10–13. www.eumetsat.eu/Home/Main/Publications/Conference_and_Workshop_Proceedings/groups/cps/documents/document/pdf_conf_p50_s9_01_harries_v.pdf.

Chen, W., and H.A. Klaiber. 2017. *Does Road Expansion Help Mitigate Congestion in China? An Evaluation of Vehicle-Kilometers Traveled*. Department of Agricultural, Environmental and Development Economics, Ohio State University. www.weichenecon.org/uploads/1/2/0/7/120708315/china_roads_-_manuscript.pdf.

Chensheng, L., K. Warchol, and R. Callahan. 2014. "Sub-Lethal Exposure to Neonicotinoids Impaired Honey Bees Winterization Before Proceeding to Colony Collapse Disorder." *Bulletin of Insectology*, 67(1): 125–130.

Chester, M., J. Sperling, E. Stokes, B. Allenby, K. Kockelman, C. Kennedy, L. Baker, J. Keirstead, and C. Hendrickson. 2014. "Positioning Infrastructure and Technologies for Low-Carbon Urbanization." *Earth's Future*, 2(1): 533–547.

Chesterton, A. 2018. "How Many Cars Are There in the World?" *Carsguide*, August 6. www.carsguide.com.au/car advice/how-many-cars-are-there-in-the-world-70629.

Chiu, M., B. Shah, L. Maclagan, M. Rezai, P. Austin, and J. Tu. 2015. "Walk Score and the Prevalence of Utilitarian Walking and Obesity among Ontario Adults: A Cross-Sectional Study." *Health Reports*, 26(7): 3–10.

Chrisafis, A. 2015. "France to Force Big Supermarkets to Give Unsold Food to Charities." *Guardian* (London), May 22.

CIA (Central Intelligence Agency). 2017. *CIA World Fact Book, 2017*. Washington, DC. www.cia.gov/library/publications/the-world-factbook/rankorder/2127rank.html.

CIA (Central Intelligence Agency). 2019. *CIA World Fact Book, 2019*. Washington, DC. www.cia.gov/library/publications/the-world-factbook/fields/264rank.html.

Ciriacy-Wantrup, S., and R. Bishop. 1975. "Common Property as a Concept in Natural Resource Policy." *National Resources Journal*, 15(4): 713–727.

Claeys, P. 2015. *Human Rights and the Food Sovereignty Movement: Reclaiming Control*. New York: Routledge.

Clark, B., and R. York. 2005. "Carbon Metabolism: Global Capitalism, Climate Change, and the Biospheric Rift." *Theory and Society*, 34: 391–428.

Clark, T.P., S.B. Longo, B. Clark, and A.K. Jorgenson. 2018. "Socio-Structural Drivers, Fisheries Footprints, and Seafood Consumption: A Comparative International Study, 1961–2012." *Journal of Rural Studies*, 57: 140–146.

Clausen, R., and S. Longo. 2012. "The Tragedy of the Commodity and the Face of AquAdvantage Salmon." *Development and Change*, 43(1): 229–251.

Clinton, N., M. Stuhlmacher, A. Miles, N. Uludere Aragon, M. Wagner, M. Georgescu, C. Herwig, and P. Gong. 2018. "A Global Geospatial Ecosystem Services Estimate of Urban Agriculture." *Earth's Future*, 6(1): 40–60.

Coase, R. 1960. "The Problem of Social Cost." *Journal of Law and Economics*, 3: 1–44.

Cochrane, W. 1958. *Farming Prices: Myth and Reality*. Minneapolis, MN: University of Minnesota Press.

Cohen, S. 2010. "Growing Public Support for Sustainability." *Huffington Post*, April 19. www.huffingtonpost.com/steven-cohen/growing-public-support-fo_b_542600.html.

Colbert, T. 2000. "Iowa Farmers and Mechanical Corn Pickers, 1900–1952." *Agricultural History*, 74(2): 530–544.

Cole, B.L., K.E. MacLeod, and R. Spriggs. 2019. "Health Impact Assessment of Transportation Projects and Policies: Living up to Aims of Advancing Population Health and Health Equity?" *Annual Review of Public Health*, 40: 305–318. https://doi.org/10.1146/annurev-publhealth-040617-013836.

Cole, R., P. Dunn, I. Hunter, N. Owen, and T. Sugiyama. 2015. "Walk Score and Australian Adults' Home-Based Walking for Transport." *Health & Place*, 35: 60–65.

Condon, P. 2010. *Seven Rules for Sustainable Communities*. Washington, DC: Island.

Conover, D., and S. Munch. 2002. "Sustaining Fisheries Yields over Evolutionary Time Scales." *Science*, 297: 94–96.

Conrad, S. 2011. "A Restorative Environmental Justice for Prison E-Waste Recycling." *Peace Review*, 23(3): 348–355.

Conrad, Z., M.T. Niles, D.A. Neher, E.D. Roy, N.E. Tichenor, and L. Jahns. 2018. "Relationship Between Food Waste, Diet Quality, and Environmental Sustainability." *PloS One*, 13(4): e0195405. https://doi.org/10.1371/journal.pone.0195405.

Conservation Measures Partnership. 2012. "Threats Taxonomy." www.conservationmeasures.org/initiatives/threats-actions-taxonomies/threats-taxonomy.

Cook, J., N. Oreskes, P.T. Doran, W.R. Anderegg, B. Verheggen, E.W. Maibach, J.S. Carlton, S. Lewandowsky, A.G. Skuce, S.A. Green, and D. Nuccitelli. 2016. "Consensus on Consensus: A Synthesis of Consensus Estimates on Human-Caused Global Warming." *Environmental Research Letters*, 11(4). https://iopscience.iop.org/article/10.1088/1748-9326/11/4/048002/meta.

Cooper, P., G. Poe, and I. Bateman. 2004. "The Structure of Motivation for Contingent Values: A Case Study of Lake Water Quality Improvement." *Ecological Economics*, 50: 69–82.

Corcelli, F., M. Ripa, and S. Ulgiati. 2018. "Efficiency and Sustainability Indicators for Papermaking from Virgin Pulp—An Energy-Based Case Study." *Resources, Conservation and Recycling*, 131: 313–328.

Correa, T., C. Fierro, M. Reyes, F.R.D. Carpentier, L.S. Taillie, and C. Corvalan. 2019. "Responses to the Chilean Law of Food Labeling and Advertising: Exploring Knowledge, Perceptions and Behaviors of Mothers of Young Children." *International Journal of Behavioral Nutrition and Physical Activity*, 16(1). https://doi.org/10.1186/s12966-019-0781-x.

Costanza, R., R. d'Arge, R. de Groot, S. Farber, M. Grasso, B. Hannon, S. Naeem, K. Limburg, J. Paruelo, R. O'Neill, R. Raskin, P. Sutton, and M. van den Belt. 1997. "The Value of the World's Ecosystem Services and Natural Capital." *Nature*, 387: 253–260.

Costanza, R., R. de Groot, P. Sutton, S. van der Ploeg, S. Anderson, I. Kubiszewski, S. Farber, and R. Turner. 2014. "Changes in the Global Value of Ecosystem Services." *Global Environmental Change*, 26: 152–158.

Cowen, T., and D. Parfit. 1992. "Against the Social Discount Rate." In *Philosophy, Politics, and Society*, edited by P. Laslett and J. Fishkin, pp. 144–161. New Haven, CT: Yale University Press.

Cox, D. 2019. "The Planet's Prodigious Poo Problem." *Guardian*, March 25. www.theguardian.com/news/2019/mar/25/animal-waste-excrement-four-billion-tonnes-dung-poo-faecebook.

Cox, J. 2009. "What Is Vertical Farming?" *OnEarth*, November 6. www.onearth.org/community-blog/what-is-vertical-farming.

Cox, J. 2014. "How Will the End of 'Buy One Get One Free' Affect Shoppers? Asks Extreme Couponer Jordon Cox." *The Mirror* (London), April 11.

Cox, J. 2019. "A Record Number of Americans Are 90 days Behind on Their Car Payments." *CNBC*, February 13. www.cnbc.com/2019/02/12/a-record-number-of-americans-are-90-days-behind-on-their-car-payments.html.

Crane, K. 2015. "Smog Solutions: A Fix to China's Pollution Problem Is Expensive but Worth It." *US News and World Report*, January 17.

Credit Suisse. 2018. *Global Wealth Report 2018*. www.credit-suisse.com/media/assets/corporate/docs/about-us/research/publications/global-wealth-report-2018-en.pdf.

Crosby, L., C. Tatu, and K. Charles. 2016. "Lung and Bronchus Cancer Deaths in Boone County, WV Before and After Mountaintop Removal Mining." *Journal of Rare Disorders: Diagnosis and Therapy*, 2(1): 1. http://raredisorders.imedpub.com/lung-and-bronchus-cancer-deaths-in-boone-county-wv-before-and-after-mountaintop-removal-mining.pdf.

Cross, J. 2014. "Three Myths of Behavioral Change." TEDx Colorado State University lecture, Fort Collins, CO, February 19. www.youtube.com/watch?v=l5d8GW6GdR0.

Crossley, N., and J. Ibrahim. 2012. "Critical Mass, Social Networks and Collective Action: The Case of Student Political Worlds." *Sociology*, 46: 596–612.

Crozet, Y. 2017. "Appraisal Methodologies and the Limits to Speed Gains." *Transportation Research Procedia*, 25: 2898–2912.

Crutzen, P. 2006. "Albedo Enhancement by Stratospheric Sulfur Injections: A Contribution to Resolve a Policy Dilemma?" *Climate Change*, 77(3–4): 211–220.

Csurhes, S. 2018. "Pushing 37 Weed Species Towards Extinction in Queensland." Paper presented at the 21st Australasian Weeds Conference. http://caws.org.nz/old-site/awc/2018/awc201811151.pdf.

Cunha, L. 2009. "Water: A Human Right or an Economic Resource?" In *Water Ethics*, edited by M. Ramón Llamas, L. Martínez-Cortina, and A. Mukherji, pp. 97–113. Boca Raton, FL: CRC.

Dahr, J. 2015. "Kisilu: The Climate Diaries." *Aljazeera*, December 2. www.aljazeera.com/programmes/witness/2015/12/kisilu-climate-diaries-151202130224609.html.

Daly, H. 1999. *Ecological Economics and the Ecology of Economics*. Northampton, MA: Edward Elgar.

Dankelman, I., K. Alam, W. B. Ahmed, Y. D. Gueye, N. Fatema, and R. Mensah-Kutin. 2008. *Gender, Climate Change, and Human Security: Lessons from Bangladesh, Ghana, and Senegal*. Women's Environment and Development Organization, New York. www.wedo.org/wp-content/uploads/hsn-study-final-may-20-2008.pdf.

Dasgupta, P. 2006. "Nature in Economics." *Environmental Resource Economics*, 39: 1–7.

Dasgupta, S., B. Laplante, H. Wang, and D. Wheeler. 2002. "Confronting the Environmental Kuznets Curve." *Journal of Economic Perspectives*, 16(1): 147–168.

Davenport, C., and L. Friedman. 2018. "How Trump Is Ensuring that Greenhouse Gas Emissions Will Rise." *New York Times*, November 26. www.nytimes.com/2018/11/26/climate/trump-greenhouse-gas-emissions.html.

Davis, A. 2015. "American Recycling Is Stalling, and the Big Blue Bin Is One Reason Why." *Washington Post*, June 20.

Dawson, T.P., A.H. Perryman, and T.M. Osborne. 2016. "Modelling Impacts of Climate Change on Global Food Security." *Climatic Change*, 134(3): 429–440.

Dean, M., R. Hickman, and C.L. Chen. 2019. "Testing the Application of Participatory MCA: The Case of the South Fylde Line." *Transport Policy*, 73: 62–70.

Deflem, M., and S. McDonough. 2015. "The Fear of Counterterrorism: Surveillance and Civil Liberties since 9/11." *Society*, 52(1): 70–79.

Defra (Department for Environment, Food, and Rural Affairs). 2011. "Waste Data Overview." London. www.defra. gov.uk/statistics/files/20110617-waste-data-overview.pdf.

Delhey, J., and G. Dragolov. 2016. "Happier Together: Social Cohesion and Subjective Well-Being in Europe." *International Journal of Psychology*, 51(3): 163–176.

Dell'Amore, C., 2013. "Last of The Last—20,000 Species Are Near Extinction: Is it Time to Rethink How We Decide Which to Save?" Zoo's Print, 28(12). https://zoosprint.zooreach.org/index.php/zp/article/download/1328/1226.

Delucchi, M. 2004. *Summary of Theory, Data, Methods, and Results: Report #1 in the Series: The Annualized Social Cost of Motor-Vehicle Use in the United States, Based on 1990–91 Data.*" Research Report UCD-ITS-RR-96–03(01)_rev1, Institute of Transportation Studies, University of California, Davis, CA.

Demographia 2019. *15th Annual Demographia International Housing Affordability Survey: 2019.* www.demographia. com/dhi.pdf.

DePillis, L. 2019. "America's Addiction to Absurdly Fast Shipping Has a Hidden Cost." *CNN*, July 15. www.cnn. com/2019/07/15/business/fast-shipping-environmental-impact/index.html.

Desmarais, A. 2008. "The Power of Peasants: Reflections on the Meanings of La Via Campesina." *Journal of Rural Studies*, 24:138–149.

Despommier, D. 2010. *The Vertical Farm: Feeding the World in the 21st Century.* New York: Thomas Dunne Books.

Dey, A., K. Sarma, U. Kumar, S. Mohanty, T. Kumar, and B.P. Bhatt. 2019. "Prospects of Rice-Fish Farming System for Low Lying Areas in Bihar, India." *Organic Agriculture*, 9(1): 99–106.

Dickens, P. 2001. "Linking the Social and Natural Sciences: Is Capital Modifying Human Biology in Its Own Image?" *Sociology*, 35: 93–110.

Dickens, P. 2004. *Society and Nature: Changing Our Environment, Changing Ourselves.* Malden, MA: Polity.

Dickens, P., and J. Ormrod. 2007. *Cosmic Society: Towards a Sociology of the Universe.* New York: Routledge.

Dietz, T., and E. Rosa. 1994. "Rethinking the Environmental Impacts of Population, Affluence, and Technology." *Human Ecology Review*, 1: 277–300.

Dietz, T., N. Dolsak, E. Ostrom, and P. Stern. 2002. *The Drama of the Commons.* Washington, DC: National Academies Press.

Dietz, T., G. Gardner, J. Gilligan, P. Stern, and M. Vandenbergh. 2009. "Household Actions Can Provide a Behavioral Wedge to Rapidly Reduce US Carbon Emissions." *Proceedings of the National Academy of Sciences*, 106(44): 18452–18456.

Dietz, T., F. Kenneth, C. Whitley, J. Kelly, and R. Kelly. 2015. "Political Influences on Greenhouse Gas Emissions from US States." *Proceedings of the National Academy of Sciences*, 112(27): 8254–8259.

Dietz, T., E. Rosa, and R. York. 2012. "Environmentally Efficient Well-Being: Is There a Kuznets Curve?" *Environmental Geography*, 32: 21–28.

Di Ruocco, A., P. Gasparini, and G. Weets. 2015. "Urbanisation and Climate Change in Africa: Setting the Scene." In *Urban Vulnerability and Climate Change in Africa: A Multidisciplinary Approach*, edited by S. Pauleit, A. Coly, S. Fohlmeister, P. Gasparini, G. Jørgensen, S. Kabisch, W.J. Kombe, S. Lindley, I. Simonis, and K. Yeshitela, pp. 1–35. Cham, Switzerland: Springer International.

D.M. 2014. "Japan's Demography: The Incredible Shrinking Country." Banyan [blog], *The Economist*, March 25. www.economist.com/blogs/banyan/2014/03/japans-demography.

Doane, M. 2014. "Politics and the Family Farm: When the Neighbors Poison the Well." *Anthropology Now*, 6(3): 45–52.

DOD (Department of Defense). 2001. "American Indian and Alaska Native Initiatives." In *Fiscal Year 2001 Defense Environmental Quality Program Annual Report to Congress.* www.denix.osd.mil/arc/EQFY2001.cfm.

Domingo, J., and M. Nadal. 2009. "Domestic Waste Composting Facilities: A Review of Human Health Risks." *Environment International*, 35: 382–389.

Domingo, J., J. Rovira, L. Vilavert, M. Nadal, M. Figueras, and M. Schuhmacher. 2015. "Health Risks for the Population Living in the Vicinity of an Integrated Waste Management Facility: Screening Environmental Pollutants." *Science of the Total Environment*, 518: 363–370.

Dong, H., and B. Qin. 2017. "Exploring the Link Between Neighborhood Environment and Mental Wellbeing: A Case Study in Beijing, China." *Landscape and Urban Planning*, 164: 71–80.

Donham, K., S. Wing, D. Osterberg, J. Flora, C. Hodne, K. Thu, and P. Thorne. 2007. "Community Health and Socioeconomic Issues Surrounding Concentrated Animal Feeding Operations." *Environmental Health Perspectives*, 115(2): 317–320.

Donham, K.J., A. Yoder, and L. Grafft. 2016. "Acute Injuries in Agriculture." In *Agricultural Medicine: Rural Occupational and Environmental Health, Safety, and Prevention*, edited by Kelley Donham and Anders Thelin, pp. 379–387. New York: Wiley.

Dooley, E. 2019. "California Touts Desalination, but Take It With a Grain of Salt." *Bloomburg News*, February 27. https://news.bloombergenvironment.com/environment-and-energy/california-touts-desalination-but-take-it-with-a-grain-of-salt.

Doublet, V., M. Labarussias, J. Miranda, R. Moritz, and R. Paxton. 2015. "Bees Under Stress: Sublethal Doses of a Neonicotinoid Pesticide and Pathogens Interact to Elevate Honey Bee Mortality Across the Life Cycle." *Environmental Microbiology*, 17(4): 969–983.

Dovey, K., and E. Pafka. 2016. "Urban Density Matters—but What Does It Mean?" *The Conversation*, May 20. https://theconversation.com/urban-density-matters-but-what-does-it-mean-58977.

Downs, A. 1962. "The Law of Peak-Hour Express-Way Congestion." *Traffic Quarterly*, 16(3): 393–409.

Dragusanu, R., D. Giovannucci, and N. Nunn. 2014. *The Economics of Fair Trade*. NBER Working Paper No. 20357. National Bureau of Economic Research, Cambridge, MA. www.nber.org/papers/w20357.pdf.

Druckman, J.N., and M.C. McGrath. 2019. "The Evidence for Motivated Reasoning in Climate Change Preference Formation." *Nature Climate Change*, 9: 111–119. DOI: 10.1038/s41558-018-0360-1.

Drummond, M., and T. Loveland. 2010. "Land-Use Pressure and a Transition to Forest-Cover Loss in the Eastern United States." *BioScience*, 60(4): 286–298.

Dryzek, J. 1990. *Discursive Democracy: Politics, Policy, and Political Science*. New York: Cambridge University Press.

Duncan, J., M. Carolan, and H. Wiskerke, eds. 2020. *Regenerative Sustainable Agriculture*. New York: Routledge.

Dunlap, R. 2008. "The New Environmental Paradigm Scale: From Marginality to Worldwide Use." *Journal of Environmental Education*, 40(1): 3–18.

Dunlap, R. 2010. "The Maturation and Diversification of Environmental Sociology: From Constructivism and Realism to Agnosticism and Pragmatism." In *The International Handbook of Environmental Sociology*, edited by M. Redclift and G. Woodgate, pp. 15–32. Northampton, MA: Edward Elgar.

Dunlap, R., and R. Jones. 2002. "Environmental Concern: Conceptual and Measurement Issues." In *Handbook of Environmental Sociology*, edited by R. Dunlap and W. Michelson, pp. 482–524. Westport, CT: Greenwood.

Dunlap, R., and K. Van Liere. 1978. "The New Environmental Paradigm." *Journal of Environmental Education*, 9: 10–19.

Dunlap, R., and R. York. 2008. "The Globalization of Environmental Concern and the Limits of the Postmaterialist Values Explanation." *Sociological Quarterly*, 49: 529–563.

Dunlap, R., K. Van Liere, A. Mertig, and R. Jones. 2000. "Measuring Endorsement of the New Ecological Paradigm: A Revised NEP Scale." *Journal of Social Issues*, 56: 425–442.

Duranton, G., and M. Turner. 2009. *The Fundamental Law of Road Congestion: Evidence from US Cities*. NBER Working Paper No. 15376. National Bureau of Economic Research, Cambridge, MA. www.nber.org/papers/w15376.pdf.

Earnest. 2017. "How Much Are People Making From the Sharing Economy?" *Earnest*, June 13. www.earnest.com/blog/sharing-economy-income-data/.

Earthman, G. 2014. "Research on Green Schools and Student Performance." In *Marketing the Green School: Form, Function, and the Future*, edited by T. Chan, pp. 38–52. Hershey, PA: IGI Global.

Easterlin, R. 2015. "Happiness and Economic Growth: The Evidence." In *Global Handbook of Quality of Life: Exploration of Well-Being of Nations and Continents*, edited by W. Glatzer, L. Camfield, V. Møller, and M. Rojas, pp. 283–300. Dordrecht, Netherlands: Springer.

E.B. 2015. "In the Bin: Recycling in America." Democracy in America [blog], *The Economist*, April 22. www.economist.com/blogs/democracyinamerica/2015/04/recycling-america.

Eccleston, C., and F. March. 2011. *Global Environment Policy: Concepts, Principles, and Practice*. Boca Raton, FL: CRC.

Eckersley, R. 1992. *Environmentalism and Political Theory: Towards an Ecocentric Approach*. London: University College London Press.

Eckhouse, B. 2018. "Solar Beats Coal on U.S. Jobs." *Bloomberg*, May 16. www.bloomberg.com/news/articles/2018-05-16/solar-beats-coal-on-u-s-jobs.

Eddy, M. 2016. "Germany Gleefully Leads List of World's Top Recyclers." *New York Times*, November 28. www.nytimes.com/2016/11/28/world/what-in-the-world/germany-gleefully-leads-list-of-worlds-top-recyclers.html.

Edmonds Institute. 2006. "Out of Brazil: A Peanut Worth Billions (to the US)." Edmonds, WA, March. www.edmonds-institute.org/outofbrazil.pdf.

Edney, M. 1997. *Mapping an Empire: The Geographical Construction of British India, 1765–1843*. Chicago, IL: University of Chicago Press.

EEA (European Environment Agency). 2013. *Managing Municipal Solid Waste: A Review of Achievements in 32 European Countries*. EEA Report No. 2/2013. www.eea.europa.eu/publications/managing-municipal-solid-waste/at_download/file.

Ehrhardt-Martinez, K., E. Crenshaw, and J. Jenkins. 2002. "Deforestation and the Environmental Kuznets Curve: A Cross-National Investigation of Intervening Mechanisms." *Social Science Quarterly*, 83(1): 226–243.

Ehrlich, P. 1968. *The Population Bomb*. San Francisco, CA: Sierra Club.

Ehrlich, P., and J. Holden. 1971. "Impact of Population Growth." *Science*, 171: 1212–1217.

EIA (Energy Information Administration). 2017. "International Energy Outlook 2017." www.eia.gov/outlooks/archive/ieo17/ieo_tables.php.

EIA (Energy Information Administration). 2018a. "What is U.S. Electricity Generation by Energy Source?" www.eia.gov/tools/faqs/faq.php?id=427&t=3.

EIA (Energy Information Administration). 2018b. "How much Energy is Consumed in U.S. Residential and Commercial Buildings?" www.eia.gov/tools/faqs/faq.php?id=86&t=1.

EIA (Energy Information Administration). 2019a. "More than Half of the U.S. Coal Mines Operating in 2008 Have Since Closed." www.eia.gov/todayinenergy/detail.php?id=38172.

EIA (Energy Information Administration). 2019b. "How Much Natural Gas Does the United States have, and How Long Will It Last?" www.eia.gov/tools/faqs/faq.php?id=58&t=8.

Eisler, M., M. Lee, J. Tarlton, G. Martin, J. Beddington, J. Dungait, H. Greathead, J. Liu, S. Mathew, H. Miller, T. Misselbrook, P. Murray, V. Vinod, R. Van Saun, and M. Winter. 2014. "Agriculture: Steps to Sustainable Livestock." *Nature*, 507: 32–34.

Ekelund, R., and R. Hébert. 1997. *A History of Economic Theory and Method*. 4th edn. New York: McGraw-Hill.

Eller, D. 2015. "The Real Story on Nitrate Levels in Iowa's Rivers." *Des Moines Register*, April 13.

Eller, D. 2018. "Iowa Nitrogen Pollution in the Water is Getting Worse, Despite Hundreds of Millions of Dollars in Spending, Study Shows." *Des Moines Register*, June 22.

Elliott, S., and I. Yusuf. 2014. "'Yes, We Can; but Together': Social Capital and Refugee Resettlement." *Kotuitui: New Zealand Journal of Social Sciences Online*, 9(2): 101–110.

Emery, M., and C. Flora. 2006. "Spiraling-Up: Mapping Community Transformation with Community Capitals Framework." *Community Development*, 37(1): 19–35.

Emperaire, L., and L. Eloy. 2015. "Amerindian Agriculture in an Urbanising Amazonia (Rio Negro, Brazil)." *Bulletin of Latin American Research*, 34(1): 70–84.

English, M., K. Solomon, and G. Hoffman. 2002. "A Paradigm Shift in Irrigation Management." *Journal of Irrigation and Drainage Engineering* (September–October): 267–277.

EPA (Environmental Protection Agency). n.d. "What If We Kept Our Cars Parked for Trips Less Than One Mile." Washington, DC. www.epa.gov/greenvehicles/what-if-we-kept-our-cars-parked-trips-less-one-mile.

EPA (Environmental Protection Agency). 2012. "Environmental Justice Key Terms." Washington, DC. www.epa.gov/region07/ej/definitions.htm.

EPA (Environmental Protection Agency). 2013. "Land Use Overview." Washington, DC. www.epa.gov/oecaagct/ag101/landuse.html.

EPA (Environmental Protection Agency). 2015a. "Northern Gulf of Mexico Hypoxic Zone." Washington, DC. www.water.epa.gov/type/watersheds/named/msbasin/zone.cfm.

EPA (Environmental Protection Agency). 2015b. "Sources of Greenhouse Gas Emissions." Washington, DC. www.epa.gov/climatechange/ghgemissions/sources/transportation.html.

EPA (Environmental Protection Agency). 2016. "Fast Facts on Transportation Greenhouse Gas Emissions." Washington, DC. www.epa.gov/greenvehicles/fast-facts-transportation-greenhouse-gas-emissions.

EPA (Environmental Protection Agency). 2019. *Inventory of US Greenhouse Gas Emission and Sinks, 1990–2017*. EPA 430-9-19-0051. Office of Atmospheric Programs, EPA, Washington, DC. www.epa.gov/sites/production/files/2019-02/documents/us-ghg-inventory-2019-main-text.pdf.

Epstein, P., J. Buonocore, K. Eckerle, M. Hendryx, B. Stout, R. Heinberg, R. Clapp, B. May, N. Reinhart, M. Ahern, S. Doshi, and L. Glustrom. 2011. "Full Cost Account for the Life Cycle of Coal." *Annals of the New York Academy of Sciences*, 1219: 73–98

Eric, G., K. Sarica, and W. Tyner. 2015. "Analysis of Impacts of Alternative Policies Aimed at Increasing US Energy Independence and Reducing GHG Emissions." *Transport Policy*, 37: 121–133.

Eriksson, C., T. Bodin, and J. Selander. 2017. "Burden of Disease from Road Traffic and Railway Noise—A Quantification of Healthy Life Years Lost in Sweden." *Scandinavian Journal of Work, Environment & Health*, 43(6): 519–525. DOI: 10.5271/sjweh.3653.

Eskelanda, G., and A. Harrison. 2003. "Moving to Greener Pastures? Multinationals and the Pollution Haven Hypothesis." *Journal of Development Economics*, 70: 1–23.

Ester, P. 1981. "Environmental Concern in the Netherlands." In *Progress in Resource Management and Environment Planning*, edited by T. O'Riordan and R. Turner, pp. 81–108. New York: Wiley.

Ewing, R., R. Brownson, and D. Berrigan. 2006. "Relationship Between Urban Sprawl and Weight of United States Youth." *American Journal of Preventative Medicine*, 31(6): 464–474.

Ewing, R., G. Meakins, S. Hamidi, and A.C. Nelson. 2014. "Relationship Between Urban Sprawl and Physical Activity, Obesity, and Morbidity—Update and Refinement." *Health and Place*, 26: 118–126.

Ewing, R., T. Schmid, R. Killingsworth, A. Zlot, and S. Raudenbush. 2003. "Relationship Between Urban Sprawl and Physical Activity, Obesity, and Morbidity." *American Journal of Health Promotion*, 18(1): 47–57.

Fan, L. 2018. "China Founds Pesticide Office to Combat Pollution Overuse." *China Dialogue*, October 16. www. chinadialogue.net/article/show/single/en/10148-China-founds-pesticide-office-to-combat-pollution-overuse.

Fan, X., X. Li, J. Yin, and J. Liang. 2019. "Temporal Characteristics and Spatial Homogeneity of Virtual Water Trade: A Complex Network Analysis." Water Resources Management, 33(4): 1467–1480.

FAO (Food and Agriculture Organization). 2002. *Reducing Poverty and Hunger: The Critical Role of Financing for Food, Agriculture, and Rural Development*. International Fund for Agricultural Development, World Food Program, United Nations, Rome. www.fao.org/docrep/003/Y6265e/y6265e00.htm.

FAO (Food and Agriculture Organization). 2013. *Tackling Climate Change through Livestock*. United Nations, Rome. www.fao.org/docrep/018/i3437e/i3437e.pdf.

FAO (Food and Agriculture Organization). 2015. *Climate Change and Food Systems*. United Nations, Rome. www. fao.org/3/a-i4332e.pdf.

FAO (Food and Agriculture Organization). 2017. *The Future of Food and Agriculture Trend and Challenges*. United Nations, Rome. www.fao.org/3/a-i6583e.pdf.

FAO (Food and Agriculture Organization). 2019. *Global Livestock Environmental Assessment Model*. United Nations, Rome. www.fao.org/gleam/results/en/.

Feinberg, M., and Willer, R. 2013. "The Moral Roots of Environmental Attitudes." *Psychological Science*, 24(1): 56–62.

Feldt, T., T. Fobil, J. Wittsiepe, M. Wilhelm, H. Till, A. Zoufaly, G. Burchard, and T. Göen. 2014. "High Levels of PAH-Metabolites in Urine of E-Waste Recycling Workers from Agbogbloshie, Ghana." *Science of the Total Environment*, 466–467: 369–376.

Ferreira, A.J.D., R.I.M.M. Guilherme, C.S.S. Ferreira, and M.F.L. Oliveira,. 2018. "Urban Agriculture, a Tool towards More Resilient Urban Communities?" *Current Opinion in Environmental Science & Health*, 5: 93–97.

Fischetti, M. 2012. "How Much Water Do Nations Consume?" *Scientific American*, May 21. www.scientificamerican. com/article/graphic-science-how-much-water-nations-consume.

Fisher, W. 1943. "The Bengal Famine: 50,000 Indians Weekly Succumb to Disease and Starvation in Spreading Catastrophe." *Life*, 15(21): 16–20.

Fishman, E. 2015. "Bikeshare: A Review of Recent Literature." *Transport Reviews*, 36(1): 92–113.

Fitz, D. 2009. "What's Wrong with a 30-Hour Work Week?" *Z Magazine*, July. www.zcommunications.org/whats-wrong-with-a-30-hour-work-week-by-don-fitz.

Flatø, M., R. Muttarak, and A. Pelser. 2017. "Women, Weather, and Woes: The Triangular Dynamics of Female-Headed Households, Economic Vulnerability, and Climate Variability in South Africa." *World Development*, 90: 41–62.

Fleming, I. 2018. "Science's Search for a Super Banana." *Guardian*, August 5. www.theguardian.com/science/2018/ aug/05/science-search-for-a-super-banana-panama-disease-gm-gene-editing.

Fleurbaey, M., and S. Zuber. 2013. "Climate Policies Deserve a Negative Discount Rate." *Chicago Journal of International Law*, 13(2): 565–595.

Flora, C. 2008. "Social Capital and Community Problem Solving Combining Local and Scientific Knowledge to Fight Invasive Species." *Learning Communities*, 2: 30–39.

Flora, C., M. Livingston, I. Honyestewa, and H. Koiyaquaptewa. 2009. "Understanding Access to and Use of Traditional Foods by Hopi Women." *Journal of Hunger and Environmental Nutrition*, 4: 158–171.

Forbes. 2017. "Green Buildings Power Savings & Returns." *Forbes*, June 22. www.forbes.com/sites/morgan-stanley/2017/06/22/green-buildings-power-savings-returns/#2d5ba1d64a9b.

Forgie, V., P. Horsley, and J. Johnston. 2001. *Facilitating Community-Based Conservation Initiatives*. Science for Conservation Report No. 169. Department of Conservation, Wellington, New Zealand. www.doc.govt.nz/ upload/documents/science-and-technical/Sfc169.pdf.

Foster, J.B. 1999. "Marx's Theory of Metabolic Rift: Classical Foundations for Environmental Sociology." *American Journal of Sociology*, 105(2): 366–405.

Foster, J.B. 2005. "The Treadmill of Accumulation: Schnaiberg's Environment and Marxian Political Economy." *Organization and Environment*, 18(1): 7–18.

Foster, J., B. Clark, and R. York. 2010. *The Ecological Rift: Capitalism's War on the Earth*. New York: Monthly Review Press.

Fox, T. 2013. *Global Food: Waste Not Want Not*. Institution of Mechanical Engineers, United Kingdom. www.imeche. org/docs/default-source/reports/Global_Food_Report.pdf.

Francis, J.E., and T. Davis. 2015. "Adolescents' Sustainability Concerns and Reasons for Not Consuming Sustainably." *International Journal of Consumer Studies*, 39(1): 43–50.

Fraser, C. 2009. *Rewilding the World*. New York: Henry Holt.

Frederick, C., W. Riggs, and J. Gilderbloom. 2018. "Commute Mode Diversity and Public Health: A Multivariate Analysis of 148 US cities." *International Journal of Sustainable Transportation*, 12(1): 1–11.

Freeman, L. 2001. "The Effects of Sprawl on Neighborhood Social Ties: An Explanatory Analysis." *Journal of the American Planning Association*, 67(1): 69–77.

Frohwein, T., and B. Hansjürgens. 2005. "Chemicals Regulation and the Porter Hypothesis: A Critical Review of the New European Chemicals Regulation." *Journal of Business Chemistry*, 2(1): 19–36.

Fukuda-Parr, S. 2003. "The Human Development Paradigm." *Feminist Economics*, 9(2–3): 301–317.

Funtowicz, S., and J. Ravetz. 1992. "Three Types of Risk Assessment and the Emergence of Post Normal Science." In *Social Theories of Risk*, edited by S. Krimsky and D. Golding, pp. 230–251. New York: Praeger.

Gagnon, L., C. Belanger, and Y. Uchiyama. 2002. "Lifecycle Assessment of Electricity Generation Options: The Status of Research in Year 2001." *Energy Policy*, 30: 1267–1278.

Galbraith, K. 1958. *The Affluent Society*. New York: Penguin.

Galvin, K., T. Beeton, and M. Luizza. 2018. "African Community-Based Conservation: A Systematic Review of Social and Ecological Outcomes." *Ecology and Society*, 23(3): 39. https://doi.org/10.5751/ES-10217-230339.

GAO (General Accounting Office). 1983. *Siting of Hazardous Waste Landfills and Their Correlation with Racial and Economic Status of Surrounding Communities*. Washington, DC: US Government Printing Office.

Gardner, G., and P. Stern. 1996. *Environmental Problems and Human Behavior*. Boston, MA: Allyn and Bacon.

Gardner, G., and P. Stern. 2008. "The Short List." *Environment Magazine*, 50(5): 12–25.

Garming, H., and H. Waibel. 2009. "Pesticides and Farmer Health in Nicaragua: A Willingness-to-Pay Approach to Evaluation." *European Journal of Health Economics*, 10(2): 125–133.

Gąsiorowska, A., and A. Hełka. 2012. "Psychological Consequences of Money and Money Attitudes in Dictator Game." *Polish Psychological Bulletin*, 43(1): 20–26.

Gelissen, J. 2007. "Explaining Popular Support for Environmental Protection: A Multi-Level Analysis of 50 Nations." *Environment and Behavior*, 39: 392–415.

Gemenne, F., J. Barnett, N. Adger, and G. Dabelko. 2014. "Climate and Security: Evidence, Emerging Risks, and a New Agenda." *Climatic Change*, 123(1): 1–9.

Geronimus, A., J. Pearson, E. Linnenbringer, A. Schulz, A. Reyes, E. Epel, J. Lin, and E. Blackburn. 2015. "Race-Ethnicity, Poverty, Urban Stressors, and Telomere Length in a Detroit Community-Based Sample." *Journal of Health and Social Behavior*, 56(2): 199–224.

Gil, L.A., A. Dwivedi, and L.W. Johnson. 2017. "Effect of Popularity and Peer Pressure on Attitudes toward Luxury among Teens." *Young Consumers*, 18(1): 84–93.

Gilding, P. 2011. *The Great Disruption*. New York: Bloomsbury.

Gille, Z. 2007. *From the Cult of Waste to the Trash Heap of History: The Politics of Waste in Socialist and Postsocialist Hungary*. Bloomington, IN: University of Indiana Press.

Gillingham, K., D. Rapson, and G. Wagner. 2016. "The Rebound Effect and Energy Efficiency Policy." *Review of Environmental Economics and Policy*, 10(1): 68–88.

Giunta, I. 2014. "Food Sovereignty in Ecuador: Peasant Struggles and the Challenge of Institutionalization." *Journal of Peasant Studies*, 41(6): 1201–1224.

Gliessman, S. 2015. *Agroecology: The Ecology of Sustainable Food Systems*. 3rd edn. Boca Raton, FL: CRC.

Global Energy Yearbook. 2018. "Share of Wind and Solar Electricity Production." https://yearbook.enerdata.net/renewables/wind-solar-share-electricity-production.html.

Goldman, M., ed. 1998. *Privatizing Nature: Political Struggles for the Global Commons*. New Brunswick, NJ: Rutgers University Press.

Goldschmidt, W. 1978. *As You Sow: Three Studies in the Social Consequences of Agribusiness*. Montclair, NJ: Allanheld, Osmun.

Goldsmith, E. 2015. *Social Influence and Sustainable Consumption*. London: Springer.

Goldstein, N., R. Cialdini, and V. Griskevicius. 2008. "A Room with a Viewpoint: Using Social Norms to Motivate Environmental Conservation in Hotels." *Journal of Consumer Research*, 35(3): 472–482.

Gooch, M., A. Felfel, and N. Marenick. 2010. *Food Waste in Canada*. George Morris Center, University of Guelph, Ontario. www.vcmtools.ca/pdf/Food%20Waste%20in%20Canada%20120910.pdf.

Goswami, P., and S. Nishad. 2015. "Virtual Water Trade and Time Scales for Loss of Water Sustainability: A Comparative Regional Analysis." *Scientific Reports*, 5: 9306. www.nature.com/articles/srep09306.

Grand View Research. 2018. *Bottled Water Market Size, Share & Trends Analysis Report By Product (Purified Water, Mineral Water, Spring Water, Sparkling Water), By Region (Asia Pacific, North America, Europe), And Segment Forecasts, 2018–2025*. www.grandviewresearch.com/industry-analysis/bottled-water-market.

Grant, K., F. Goldizen, P. Sly, M. Brune, M. Neira, M. van den Berg, and R. Norman. 2013. "Health Consequences of Exposure to E-Waste: A Systematic Review." *Lancet Global Health*, 1(6): e350–e361.

Greenberg, B.S., and J.E. Brand. 1993. "Television News and Advertising in Schools: The 'Channel One' Controversy." *Journal of Communication*, 43(1): 143–151.

Grewal, D. 2012. "How Wealth Reduces Compassion: As Riches Grow, Empathy for Others Seems to Decline." *Scientific American*, April 10. www.scientificamerican.com/article/how-wealth-reduces-compassion/.

Grimberg, B., S. Ahmed, C. Ellis, Z. Miller, and F. Menalled. 2018. "Climate Change Perceptions and Observations of Agricultural Stakeholders in the Northern Great Plains." *Sustainability*, 10(5): 1687. https://doi.org/10.3390/su10051687.

Grinde, D., and B. Johansen. 1995. *Ecocide of Native America: Environmental Destruction of Indian Lands and Peoples.* Santa Fe, NM: Clear Lights.

Grossman, G., and A. Krueger. 1994. *Economic Growth and the Environment.* NBER Working Paper No. W4364. National Bureau of Economic Research, Cambridge, MA.

Grunwald, M. 2008. "The Clean Energy Scam." *Time*, March 27.

Grunwald, M. 2015. "Inside the War on Coal." *Politico*, May 26. www.politico.com/agenda/story/2015/05/inside-war-on-coal-000002.

Guardian. 2017. "The Three Richest People in the US Own as Much Wealth as the Bottom Half of the Nation's Population." November 9. www.scmp.com/news/world/united-states-canada/article/2119052/three-richest-people-us-own-much-wealth-bottom-half.

Guarino, J. 2013. "Tribal Advocacy and the Art of Dam Removal: The Lower Elwha Klallam and the Elwha Dams." *American Indian Law Journal*, 2(1): 114–145.

Guidry, V., C. Gray, A. Lowman, D. Hall, and S. Wing. 2015. "Data Quality from a Longitudinal Study of Adolescent Health at Schools Near Industrial Livestock Facilities." *Annals of Epidemiology*, 25(7): 532–538.

Gustavsson, J., R. Otterdijk, and A. Meybeck. 2011. *Global Food Losses and Food Waste.*" Food and Agriculture Organization of the United Nations, Rome. www.fao.org/docrep/014/mb060e/mb060e00.pdf.

Habermas, J. 1962. *The Structural Transformation of the Public Sphere.* Darmstadt, Germany: Hermann Luchterhand.

Hall, C., and K. Klitgaard. 2018. *Energy and the Wealth of Nations: An Introduction to Biophysical Economics.* Dordrecht: Springer.

Hamidi, S., R. Ewing, Z. Tatalovich, J. Grace, and D. Berrigan. 2018. "Associations between Urban Sprawl and Life Expectancy in the United States." *International Journal of Environmental Research and Public Health*, 15(5): 861. https://doi.org/10.3390/ijerph15050861.

Hamilton, C. 2015. "The Risks of Climate Engineering." *New York Times*, February 12.

Han, M., and G. Chen. 2018. "Global Arable Land Transfers Embodied in Mainland China's Foreign Trade." *Land Use Policy*, 70: 521–534.

Han, M.Y., G.Q. Chen, and M. Dunford. 2019. "Land Use Balance for Urban Economy: A Multi-Scale and Multi-Type Perspective." *Land Use Policy*, 83: 323–333.

Haq, M. ul. 1995. *Reflections on Human Development.* New York: Oxford University Press.

Hardin, G. 1968. "The Tragedy of the Commons." *Science*, 162: 1243–1248.

Harley, B. 1989. "Deconstructing the Map." *Cartographica*, 26: 1–20.

Harries, J., H. Brindley, P. Sagoo, and R. Bantges. 2001. "Increases in Greenhouse Forcing Inferred from the Outgoing Longwave Radiation Spectra of the Earth in 1970 and 1997." *Nature*, 410: 355–357.

Harris, L., and H. Hazen. 2006. "Power of Maps: (Counter) Mapping for Conservation." *ACME: An International E-Journal for Critical Geographies*, 4: 99–130.

Hart, K. 2017a. "The Large Parts of America Left Behind by Today's Economy." *Axios*, Sept 25. www.axios.com/the-large-parts-of-america-left-behind-by-todays-economy-1513305693-70d3114b-c79c-403d-902c-ec5b128f793f.html.

Hart, K. 2017b. "The Disappearing Start-up." *Axios*, July 11. www.axios.com/the-disappearing-startup-1513304013-037c4674-fc79-4eda-b68a-0779d3e3e5c1.html.

Hartmann, P., V. Apaolaza, C. D'souza, J.M. Barrutia, and C. Echebarria. 2014. "Environmental Threat Appeals in Green Advertising: The Role of Fear Arousal and Coping Efficacy." *International Journal of Advertising*, 33(4): 741–765.

Harvey, D. 2005. *A Brief History of Neoliberalism.* New York: Oxford University Press.

Hasan, A. 2014. "A Tale of Two Cities: Density Regulations vs Reality." International Institute for Environment and Development. www.iied.org/tale-two-cities-density-regulations-vs-reality.

Hassan, A., S.S. Ismail, A. Elmoustafa, and S. Khalaf. 2017. "Evaluating Evaporation Rate from High Aswan Dam Reservoir Using RS and GIS Techniques." *The Egyptian Journal of Remote Sensing and Space Science*, 21(3): 285–293.

Hauck, J., C. Görg, R. Varjopuro, O. Ratamäki, J. Maes, H. Wittmer, and K. Jax. 2013. "'Maps Have an Air of Authority': Potential Benefits and Challenges of Ecosystem Service Maps at Different Levels of Decision Making." *Ecosystem Services*, 4: 25–32.

Hawcroft, L., and T. Milfont. 2010. "The Use (and Abuse) of the New Environmental Paradigm Scale over the Last 30 Years: A Meta-Analysis." *Journal of Environmental Psychology*, 30: 143–158.

Hazen, H., and P. Anthamatten. 2004. "Representation of Ecoregions by Protected Areas at the Global Scale." *Physical Geography*, 25: 499–512.

Heinke, J., C. Müller, M. Lannerstad, D. Gerten, and W. Lucht. 2019. "Freshwater Resources under Success and Failure of the Paris Climate Agreement." *Earth System Dynamics*, 10(2): 205–217.

Heinzerling, L. 2000. "The Rights of Statistical People." *Harvard Environmental Law Review*, 24: 189–207.

Heller, M., and G. Keoleian. 2015. "Greenhouse Gas Emission Estimates of US Dietary Choices and Food Loss." *Journal of Industrial Ecology*, 19(3): 391–401.

Helm, S.V., A. Pollitt, M.A. Barnett, M.A. Curran, and Z.R. Craig. 2018. "Differentiating Environmental Concern in the Context of Psychological Adaption to Climate Change." *Global Environmental Change*, 48: 158–167.

Hendryx, M., S.D. Yonts, Y. Li, and J. Luo. 2019. "Mountaintop Removal Mining and Multiple Illness Symptoms: A Latent Class Analysis." *Science of The Total Environment*, 657: 764–769.

Henn, M., B. Oldfield, and J. Hart. 2018. "Postmaterialism and Young People's Political Participation in a Time of Austerity." *British Journal of Sociology*, 69(3): 712–737.

Hepburn, C., and P. Koundouri. 2007. "Recent Advances in Discounting: Implications for Forest Economics." *Journal of Forest Economics*, 13(2–3): 169–189.

Hertsgaard, M. 2010. "The Grapes of Wrath: Climate Change and the Wine Industry." *PBS*, April 30. www.pbs.org/wnet/need-to-know/economy/the-grapes-of-wrath-climate-change-and-the-wine-industry/263.

Hickel, J. 2019. "Is It Possible to Achieve a Good Life for All Within Planetary Boundaries?" *Third World Quarterly*, 40(1): 18–35.

Hibbard, P., S. Teirney, P. Darling, S. Cullman. 2018. *The Economic Impacts of the Regional Greenhouse Gas Initiative on Nine Northeast and Mid-Atlantic States*. RGGI Project Series, Analysis Group. www.analysisgroup.com/globalassets/uploadedfiles/content/insights/publishing/analysis_group_rggi_report_april_2018.pdf.

Hirsch, J., A.V. Diez Roux, K.A. Moore, K.R. Evenson, and D.A. Rodriguez. 2014. "Change in Walking and Body Mass Index following Residential Relocation: The Multi-Ethnic Study of Atherosclerosis." *American Journal of Public Health*, 104: e49–e56.

Hirsch, J., K.A. Moore, K.R. Evenson, D.A. Rodriguez, and A.V.D. Roux. 2013 "Walk Score® and Transit Score® and Walking in the Multi-Ethnic Study of Atherosclerosis." *American Journal of Preventive Medicine*, 45: 158–166.

Hirsch, J.K., K.B. Smalley, E.M. Selby-Nelson, J.M. Hamel-Lambert, M.R. Rosmann, T.A. Barnes, D. Abrahamson, S.S. Meit, I. GreyWolf, S. Beckmann, and T. LaFromboise. 2018. "Psychosocial Impact of Fracking: A Review of the Literature on the Mental Health Consequences of Hydraulic Fracturing." *International Journal of Mental Health and Addiction*, 16(1): 1–15.

Hodal, K., C. Kelly, and F. Lawrence. 2014. "Revealed: Asian Slave Labour Producing Prawns for Supermarkets in US, UK." *Guardian*, June 10. www.theguardian.com/global-development/2014/jun/10/supermarket-prawns-thailand-producedslave-labour.

Hoddinott, J., and B. Kinsey. 2001. "Child Growth in the Time of Drought." *Oxford Bulletin of Economics and Statistics*, 63(4): 409–436.

Hoekstra, A. 2015. "The Water Footprint: The Relation Between Human Consumption and Water Use." In *The Water We Eat: Combining Virtual Water and Water Footprints*, edited by M. Antonelli and F. Greco, pp. 35–50. Cham, Switzerland: Springer.

Hoekstra, A., and M. Mekonnen. 2012. "The Water Footprint of Humanity." *Proceedings of the National Academy of Sciences*, 109(9): 3232–3237.

Hollis, A. 2019. "African Americans Are Disproportionately Exposed to Extreme Heat." *Ecowatch*, July 23. www.ecowatch.com/african-americans-extreme-heat-exposure-2639313007.html.

Holt, W., ed. 2012. *Urban Areas and Global Climate Change*. Bingley, UK: Emerald.

Hooks, G., and C. Smith. 2004. "The Treadmill of Destruction: National Sacrifice Areas and Native Americans." *American Sociological Review*, 69(4): 558–575.

House of Commons. 2010. *The Regulation of Geoengineering: Fifth Report of Session 2009–10*. Science and Technology Committee, House of Commons, Parliament of Great Britain.

House of Lords. 2014. *Counting the Cost of Food Waste: EU Food Waste Prevention*, HL Paper 154. House of Lords, Parliament of Great Britain. www.parliament.uk/documents/lords-committees/eu-sub-com-d/food-waste-prevention/154.pdf.

Howard, P. 2009. "Visualizing Consolidation in the Global Seed Industry, 1996–2008." *Sustainability*, 1: 1266–1287.

Howe, P.D. 2018. "Perceptions of Seasonal Weather are Linked to Beliefs about Global Climate Change: Evidence from Norway." *Climatic Change*, 148(4): 467–480.

Huang, K., and J. Wang. 2015. "Greenhouse Gas Emissions of Tourism-Based Leisure Farms in Taiwan." *Sustainability*, 7(8): 11032–11049.

Hughes, T. 1969. "Technological Momentum in History: Hydrogenation in Germany, 1898–1933." *Past and Present*, 44(1): 106–132.

Hullinger, L. 2019. "Exelon Spent Millions in Lobbying after Announcing TMI Closure." *York Dispatch*, April 9. www.yorkdispatch.com/story/news/local/2019/04/02/exelon-corp-nearly-tripled-its-lobbying-expenditures-between-2016-and-2018-and-soon-see-if-paid-off/3325424002/.

Hultkrantz, L., and P. Mantalos. 2018. "Hedging with Trees: Tail-Hedge Discounting of Long-Term Forestry Returns." *Journal of Forest Economics*, 30: 52–57.

Hunnicutt, B. 1996. *Kellogg's Six-Hour Day*. Philadelphia, PA: Temple University Press.

Hunter, M., and J. Gibbs. 2007. *Fundamentals of Conservation Biology*. 3rd edn. Malden, MA: Blackwell.

Hurst, D. 2010. "Growers Go Bananas over Waste." *Brisbane Times*, January 7.

Hvistendahl, M. 2008. "China's Three Gorges Dam: An Environmental Catastrophe." *Scientific American*, March 25.

Hymel, K. 2019. "If You Build It, They Will Drive: Measuring Induced Demand for Vehicle Travel in Urban Areas." *Transport Policy*, 76: 57–66.

ICTSD (International Center for Trade and Sustainable Development). 2010. "Food Giant Nestlé Accused of Biopiracy." *Bridges Trade BioRes*, 10(10): 3. http://ictsd.org/downloads/biores/biores10-10.pdf.

IEA (International Energy Agency). 2017. "Commentary: Declining Energy Research Budgets Are a Cause for Concern." www.iea.org/newsroom/news/2017/october/commentary-declining-energy-research-budgets-are-a-cause-for-concern.html.

IEA (International Energy Agency). 2019. "Energy Efficiency: Buildings." www.iea.org/topics/energyefficiency/buildings/.

IFPRI (International Food Policy Research Institute). 2014. *2014 Global Hunger Index: The Challenge of Hidden Hunger*. Bonn.

Ingber, S. 2018. "Japan's Population Is in Rapid Decline." *NPR*, December 21. www.npr.org/2018/12/21/679103541/japans-population-is-in-rapid-decline.

Inglehart, R. 1977. *The Silent Revolution*. Princeton, NJ: Princeton University Press.

Inglehart, R. 1990. *Culture Shift in Advanced Industrial Society*. Princeton, NJ: Princeton University Press.

Inglehart, R. 1997. *Modernization and Postmodernization: Cultural, Economic, and Political Change in 43 Societies*. Princeton, NJ: Princeton University Press.

Ingold, T. 2000. *The Perception of the Environment: Essays on Livelihood, Dwelling, and Skill*. New York: Routledge.

Institute for Lifecycle Energy Analysis. 2002. "Reusable Versus Disposable Cups." http://sustainability.tufts.edu/downloads/Comparativelifecyclecosts.pdf.

InterAcademy Council. 2003. *Realising the Promise and Potential of African Agriculture: Science and Technology Strategies for Improving Agricultural Productivity and Food Security in Africa*. Amsterdam. www.cgiar.org/pdf/agm04/agm04_iacpanel_execsumm.pdf.

International Energy Agency. 2019. "Biofuels for transport." www.iea.org/tcep/transport/biofuels/.

IPC (International Planning Committee for Food Sovereignty). 2016. "What Is IPC?" www.foodsovereignty.org/about-us (accessed March 3, 2016).

IPCC. 2014. *Climate Change 2014: Mitigation of Climate Change*. Cambridge: Cambridge University Press.

IPCC. 2018. *Global Warming of 1.5°C*. IPCC Special Report. https://report.ipcc.ch/sr15/pdf/sr15_spm_final.pdf.

Ipsos. 2018. "Global Views on the Environment." May 24. www.ipsos.com/sites/default/files/ct/news/documents/2018-05/node-425546-425741.zip.

Iriarte-Goñi, I., and M.I. Ayuda. 2018. "Should Forest Transition Theory Include Effects on Forest Fires? The Case of Spain in the Second Half of the Twentieth Century." *Land Use Policy*, 76: 789–797.

Islam, M., and M. Hasan. 2016. "Climate-Induced Human Displacement: A Case Study of Cyclone Aila in the South-West Coastal Region of Bangladesh." *Natural Hazards*, 81(2): 1051–1071.

Iverson, A., L. Marín, K. Ennis, D. Gonthier, B. Connor-Barrie, J. Remfert, B. Cardinale, and I. Perfecto. 2014. "Do Polycultures Promote Win-Wins or Trade-Offs in Agricultural Ecosystem Services? A Meta-Analysis." *Journal of Applied Ecology*, 51(6): 1593–1602.

Jackson, T. 2009. *Prosperity Without Growth*. London: Earthscan.

Jackson, T. 2017. *Prosperity Without Growth*. 2nd edn. London: Earthscan.

Jacobson, M., and M. Delucchi. 2009. "A Plan to Power 100 Percent of the Planet with Renewables." *Scientific American*, October 26.

Jacques, P., R. Dunlap, and M. Freeman. 2008. "The Organisation of Denial: Conservative Think Tanks and Environmental Skepticism." *Environmental Politics* 17(3): 349–385.

Japan Times. 2019. "Addressing the Nation's Food Waste Problem." *Japan Times*, May 26. www.japantimes.co.jp/opinion/2019/05/26/editorials/addressing-nations-food-waste-problem/#.XThUS5NKh24.

Jaworska, S. 2018. "Change but No Climate Change: Discourses of Climate Change in Corporate Social Responsibility Reporting in the Oil Industry." *International Journal of Business Communication*, 55(2): 194–219.

Jebaraj, P. 2011. "Development of Bt Brinjal: A Case of Bio-Piracy." *Hindu*, August 10.

Jevons, W. 1865. *The Coal Question*. London: Macmillan.

Jha, A. 2019. "Financial Reports and Social Capital." *Journal of Business Ethics*, 155(2): 567–596.

Johnson, T., A. Lora-Wainwright, and J. Lu. 2018. "The Quest for Environmental Justice in China: Citizen Participation and the Rural–Urban Network against Panguanying's Waste Incinerator." *Sustainability Science*, 13(3): 733–746.

Jones, C., and D. Kammen. 2014. "Spatial Distribution of US Household Carbon Footprints Reveals Suburbanization Undermines Greenhouse Gas Benefits of Urban Population Density." *Environmental Science & Technology*, 48(2): 895–902.

Jorgenson, A. 2006. "Unequal Ecological Exchange and Environmental Degradation: A Theoretical Proposition and Cross-National Study of Deforestation, 1990–2000." *Rural Sociology*, 71(4): 681–712.

Kadiyala, A., R. Kommalapati, and Z. Huque. 2016. "Quantification of the Lifecycle Greenhouse Gas Emissions from Nuclear Power Generation Systems." *Energies*, 9(11): 863. https://doi.org/10.3390/en9110863.

Kahl, V.F.S., D. Simon, M. Salvador, C.D.S. Branco, J.F. Dias, F.R. da Silva, C.T. de Souza, and J. da Silva. 2016. "Telomere Measurement in Individuals Occupationally Exposed to Pesticide Mixtures in Tobacco Fields." *Environmental and Molecular Mutagenesis*, 57(1): 74–84.

Kashem, S., A. Irawan, and B. Wilson. 2014. "Evaluating the Dynamic Impacts of Urban Form on Transportation and Environmental Outcomes in US Cities." *International Journal of Environmental Science and Technology*, 11(8): 2233–2244.

Kaskey, J. 2012. "Cheap Gas from Fracking Fuels Profits at LyondellBasell." *Bloomberg News*, October 16. www.bloomberg.com/news/2012-10-15/cheap-gas-from-fracking-fuels-profits-at-lyondellbasell-energy.html.

Kassam, A., R. Scammell, K. Connolly, R. Orange, K. Willsher, and R. Ratcliffe. 2015. "Europe Needs Many More Babies to Avert a Population Disaster." *Guardian* (London), August 22.

Kasser, T. 2005. "Frugality, Generosity, and Materialism in Children and Adolescents." In *What Do Children Need to Flourish? Conceptualizing and Measuring Indicators of Positive Development*, edited by K. Moore and L. Lippman, pp. 357–373. New York: Springer Science.

Kasser, T. 2016. "Materialistic Values and Goals." *Annual Review of Psychology*, 67: 489–514.

Kastner, I., and P. Stern. 2015. "Examining the Decision-Making Processes behind Household Energy Investments: A Review." *Energy Research & Social Science*, 10: 72–89.

Katz, J. 2008. "Poor Haitians Resort to Eating Mud." *National Geographic*, January 30. http://news.nationalgeographic.com/news/2008/01/080130-AP-haiti-eatin.html.

Kauman, L. 2010. "'Toxic Metals' Ties to Work in Prisons." *New York Times*, October 26.

Kaye, L. 2015. "Unilever, P&G Join Closed Loop Fund to Boost Municipal Recycling." *Triple Pundit: People, Planet, Profit*, February 9. www.triplepundit.com/2015/02/unilever-pg-join-closed-loop-fund-boost-municipal-recycling.

Kearsley, A., and M. Riddel. 2010. "A Further Inquiry into the Pollution Haven Hypothesis and the Environmental Kuznets Curve." *Ecological Economics*, 69: 905–919.

Keegan, P. 2009. "Zipcar: The Best New Idea in Business." *CNNMoney*, August 27. http://money.cnn.com/2009/08/26/news/companies/zipcar_car_rentals.fortune.

Kellstedt, P., S. Zahran, and A. Vedlitz. 2008. "Personal Efficacy, the Information Environment, and Attitudes Toward Global Warming and Climate Change in the United States." *Risk Analysis*, 28(1): 113–126.

Kelly, B., J. Halford, E. Boyland, K. Chapman, I. Bautista-Castaño, C. Berg, M. Caroli, B. Cook, J. Coutinho, T. Effertz, E. Grammatikaki, K. Keller, R. Leung, Y. Manios, R. Monteiro, C. Pedley, H. Prell, K. Raine, E. Recine, L. Serra-Majem, S. Singh, and C. Summerbell. 2010. "Television Food Advertising to Children: A Global Perspective." *American Journal of Public Health*, 100(9): 1730–1736.

Kelly, K. 2012. "Access Is Better Than Ownership." *Exponential Times*. www.exponentialtimes.net/videos/access-better-ownership-0 (accessed July 3, 2012).

Kempton, W., C. Harris, J. Keith, and J. Weihl. 1985. "Do Consumers Know What Works in Energy Conservation?" In *Families and the Energy Transition*, edited by J. Byrne, D. Schulz, and M. Sussman, pp. 115–132. New York: Haworth.

Kennedy, D. 2012. *Rooftop Revolution: How Solar Power Can Save Our Economy—and Our Planet—from Dirty Energy*. San Francisco, CA: Berrett-Koehler.

Kerr, J. 2013. "Deal Allowing Nestlé to Draw Ontario Water During Droughts Under Review." *Globe and Mail* (Toronto), August 19.

Keynes, J.M. (1930) 1963. "Economic Possibilities of Our Grandchildren." In *John Maynard Keynes: Essays in Persuasion*, pp. 358–373. New York: Norton.

Khoury, C., A. Bjorkman, H. Dempewolf, J. Ramirez-Villegas, L. Guarino, A. Jarvis, L. Rieseberg, and P. Stuik. 2014. "Increasing Homogeneity in Global Food Supplies and the Implications for Food Security." *Proceedings of the National Academy of Sciences*, 111(11): 4001–4006.

Kiss, F., and V. Rajovic. 2015. "Life Cycle Inventory Analysis of Lignite-Based Electricity Generation: Case Study of Serbia." *Journal of Production Engineering*, 18(1): 61–64.

Kjellstrom, T., D. Briggs, C. Freyberg, B. Lemke, M. Otto, and O. Hyatt. 2016. "Heat, Human Performance, and Occupational Health: A Key Issue for the Assessment of Global Climate Change Impacts." *Annual Review of Public Health*, 37: 97–112.

Kloppenburg, J. 2014. "The Unexpected Outcome of the Open Source Seed Initiative's Licensing Debate." *Opensource.com*, June 3. http://opensource.com/law/14/5/legal-issues-open-source-seed-initiative.

Kneebone, E., and N. Holmes. 2015. *The Growing Distance Between People and Jobs in Metropolitan America*. Brookings Institute, Washington, DC. www.brookings.edu/~/media/research/files/reports/2015/03/24-job-proximity/srvy_jobsproximity.pdf.

Knight, K., and E. Rosa. 2011. "The Environmental Efficiency of Well-Being: A Cross-National Analysis." *Social Science Research*, 40: 931–949.

Kocieniewski, D. 2016. "The Sharing Economy Doesn't Share Wealth." *Bloomberg Business Week*, April 6. www.bloomberg.com/news/articles/2016-04-06/the-sharing-economy-doesn-t-share-the-wealth.

Koeppel, D. 2007. *Banana: The Fate of the Fruit That Changed the World*. New York: Hudson Street.

Konur, O. 2018. *Bioenergy and Biofuels*. Boca Raton, FL: CRC Press.

Koohsari, M.J., T. Sugiyama, A. Shibata, K. Ishii, T. Hanibuchi, Y. Liao, N. Owen, and K. Oka. 2018. "Walk Score® and Japanese Adults' Physically-Active and Sedentary Behaviors." *Cities*, 74: 151–155.

Kopczuk, W., J. Slemrod, and S. Yitzhaki. 2005. "The Limitations of Decentralized World Redistribution: An Optimal Taxation Approach." *European Economic Review*, 49(4): 1051–1079.

Koplow, D. 2011. *Nuclear Power: Still Not Viable Without Subsidies*. Union of Concerned Scientists, Cambridge, MA. www.ucsusa.org/sites/default/files/legacy/assets/documents/nuclear_power/nuclear_subsidies_report.pdf.

Kopp, R., and P. Portney. 1999. "Mock Referenda for Intergenerational Decisionmaking." In *Discounting and Intergenerational Equity*, edited by P. Portney and J. Weyant, pp. 87–98. Washington, DC: Resources for the Future.

Kotchen, M., and S. Reiling. 2000. "Environmental Attitudes, Motivations, and Contingent Valuation of Nonuse Values." *Ecological Economics*, 32: 93–107.

Kouchaki, M., K. Smith-Crowe, A.P. Brief, and C. Sousa. 2013. "Seeing Green: Mere Exposure to Money Triggers a Business Decision Frame and Unethical Outcomes." *Organizational Behavior and Human Decision Processes*, 121(1): 53–61.

Koutroulis, A.G., L.V. Papadimitriou, M.G., Grillakis, I.K. Tsanis, K. Wyser, and R.A. Betts. 2018. "Freshwater Vulnerability under High End Climate Change. A Pan-European Assessment." *Science of the Total Environment*, 613: 271–286.

Kozloff, N. 2010. *No Rain in the Amazon: How South America's Climate Change Affects the Entire Planet*. New York: Palgrave.

Krinsky, J., and N. Crossley. 2014. "Social Movements and Social Networks: Introduction." *Social Movement Studies*, 13(1): 1–21.

Kuznets, S. 1955. "Economic Growth and Income Inequality." *American Economic Review*, 45(1): 1–28.

Kysar, D. 2010. *Regulating from Nowhere: Environmental Law and the Search for Objectivity*. New Haven, CT: Yale University Press.

Lafontaine, S., J. Schrlau, J. Butler, Y. Jia, B. Harper, S. Harris, L. Bramer, K. Waters, A. Harding, and S. Simonich. 2015. "Relative Influence of Trans-Pacific and Regional Atmospheric Transport of PAHs in the Pacific Northwest, US." *Environmental Science & Technology*, 49(23): 13807–13816.

Landry, N., R. Gifford, T.L. Milfont, A. Weeks, and S. Arnocky. 2018. "Learned Helplessness Moderates the Relationship between Environmental Concern and Behavior." *Journal of Environmental Psychology*, 55: 18–22.

Lappé, A. 2014. "World Bank Wants Water Privatized, Despite Risks." *American Aljazeera*, April 17. http://america.aljazeera.com/opinions/2014/4/water-managementprivatizationworldbankgroupifc.html.

Larrick, R., and J. Soll. 2008. "The MPG Illusion." *Science*, 320: 1593–1594.

Larsen, B.B., E.C. Miller, M.K. Rhodes, and J.J. Wiens. 2017. "Inordinate Fondness Multiplied and Redistributed: The Number of Species on Earth and the New Pie of Life." *The Quarterly Review of Biology*, 92(3): 229–265.

Lassaletta, L., G. Billen, E. Romero, J. Garnier, and E. Aguilera. 2014. "How Changes in Diet and Trade Patterns Have Shaped the N Cycle at the National Scale: Spain (1961–2009)." *Regional Environmental Change*, 14(2): 785–797.

Laurian, L., and R. Funderburg. 2014. "Environmental Justice in France? A Spatio–Temporal Analysis of Incinerator Location." *Journal of Environmental Planning and Management*, 57(3): 424–446.

La Viña, A., and L. Ang. 2011. "Implementing the REDD-Plus Safeguards: The Role of Social Accountability." Working Paper, 1 September. Affiliated Network on Social Accountability, East Asia and the Pacific, Philippines. www.theredddesk.org/sites/default/files/resources/pdf/2011/implementing_the_redd_safeguards_the_role_of_social_accountability.pdf.

Leach, M., and I. Scoones. 2015. *Carbon Conflicts and Forest Landscapes in Africa*. London and New York: Routledge.

Leahy, S. 2019. "One Million Species at Risk of Extinction, UN Report Warns." *National Geographic*, May 6. www.nationalgeographic.com/environment/2019/05/ipbes-un-biodiversity-report-warns-one-million-species-at-risk/.

Leder, S., G.R. Newsham, J.A. Veitch, S. Mancini, and K.E. Charles. 2016. "Effects of Office Environment on Employee Satisfaction: A New Analysis. *Building Research & Information*, 44(1): 34–50.

Leggett, J. 1990. "Global Warming: A Greenpeace View." In *Global Warming: A Greenpeace Report*, edited by J. Leggett, pp. 457–480. Oxford: Oxford University Press.

Leiserowitz, A., E. Maibach, C. Roser-Renouf, G. Feinberg, S. Rosenthal, and J. Marlon. 2014. *Climate Change in the American Mind: Americans' Global Warming Beliefs and Attitudes in November, 2013*. Yale Project on Climate Change Communication, Yale University and George Mason University, New Haven, CT.

Leiserowitz, A., E. Maibach, and S. Rosenthal. 2018. *Politics and Global Warming*, Yale University and Center for Climate Change Communication, George Mason University. http://climatecommunication.yale.edu/wp-content/uploads/2019/01/Climate-Change-American-Mind-December-2018.pdf.

Leiserowitz, A., N. Smith, and J. Marlon. 2010. *Americans' Knowledge of Climate Change*. Yale Project on Climate Change Communication, Yale University. http://environment.yale.edu/climate/files/ClimateChangeKnowledge2010.pdf.

Lennie, T.A., C. Andreae, M.K. Rayens, E.K. Song, S.B. Dunbar, S.J. Pressler, S. Heo, J. Kim, and D.K. Moser. 2018. "Micronutrient Deficiency Independently Predicts Time to Event in Patients with Heart Failure." *Journal of the American Heart Association*, 7(17): e007251. https://doi.org/10.1161/JAHA.117.007251.

LeRoy, G. 2017. "Tens of Billions in 'Corporate Welfare' Tax Deals about to Be Exposed Like Never Before." *CNBC*, July 11. www.cnbc.com/2017/07/11/states-pay-as-much-as-2-million-per-job-to-attract-tech-companies.html.

Levasseur, M., M. Généreux, J. Bruneau, A. Vanasse, E. Chabot, C. Beaulac, and M. Bédard. 2015. "Importance of Proximity to Resources, Social Support, Transportation and Neighborhood Security for Mobility and Social Participation in Older Adults: Results from a Scoping Study." *BMC Public Health*, 15(1): 503.

Levin, E.L., and H. Murakami. 2019. "Impact of Anthropogenic Climate Change on United States Major Hurricane Landfall Frequency." Journal of Marine Science and Engineering, 7(5): 135. https://doi.org/10.3390/jmse7050135.

Li, M. 2014. *Peak Oil, Climate Change, and the Limits to China's Economic Growth*. New York: Routledge.

Li, W., L. Pei, A. Li. K. Luo, Y. Cao, R. Li, and Q. Xu. 2019. "Spatial Variation in the Effects of Air Pollution on Cardiovascular Mortality in Beijing, China." *Environmental Science and Pollution Research*, 26(3): 2501–2511.

Lieskovský, J., and M. Bürgi. 2018. "Persistence in Cultural Landscapes: A Pan-European Analysis. *Regional Environmental Change*, 18(1): 175–187.

Lima, J. 2017. "Data Centres of the World Will Consume 1/5 of Earth's Power by 2025." *Data-Economy*, Dec 12. https://data-economy.com/data-centres-world-will-consume-1-5-earths-power-2025/.

Lin, J., D. Pan, S. Davis, Q. Zhang, K. He, C. Wang, D. Streets, D. Wuebbles, and D. Guan. 2014. "China's International Trade and Air Pollution in the United States." *Proceedings of the National Academy of Sciences*, 111(5): 1736–1741.

Lindhqvist, T., and K. Lidgren. 1990. "Modeller för Förlängt Producentansvar [Model for Extended Producer Responsibility]." In *Från vaggan till Graven: Sex Studier av Varors Miljöpåverkan* [*From the Cradle to the Grave: Six Studies of the Environmental Impacts of Products*] (DS1991: 9), pp. 7–44. Stockholm: Ministry of the Environment.

Litman, T. 2011. *Transportation Cost and Benefit Analysis Techniques, Estimates and Implications*. Victoria Transport Policy Institute, Victoria, Canada. www.vtpi.org/tca/tca00.pdf (accessed August 21, 2015).

Litman, T. 2016. *Parking Management*. Victoria Transport Policy Institute, Victoria, Canada. www.vtpi.org/park_man.pdf.

Liu, J., G. Daily, P. Ehrlich, and G. Luck. 2003. "Effects of Household Dynamics on Resource Consumption and Biodiversity." *Nature*, 421: 530–533.

Lo, A.Y. 2016. "National Income and Environmental Concern: Observations from 35 countries." *Public Understanding of Science*, 25(7): 873–890. DOI: 10.1177/0963662515581302.

Lobao, L., and C. Stofferahn. 2008. "The Community Effect of Industrial Farming: Social Science Research and Challenges to Corporate Farming Laws." *Agriculture and Human Values*, 25: 219–240.

Lockwood, C. 2019. "Building Retro." *Urban Land*, November/December. www.esbnyc.com/sites/default/files/uli_building_retro_fits.pdf.

Lomax, T., D. Schrank, S. Turner, L. Geng, Y. Li, and N. Koncz. 2011. *Real-Timing the 2010 Urban Mobility Report*. University Transportation Center for Mobility, Texas Transportation Institute, Texas A&M University, College Station, TX. http://utcm.tamu.edu/publications/final_reports/Lomax_10-65-55.pdf.

Long, J.A., W.P. Eveland Jr., and M.D. Slater. 2019. "Partisan Media Selectivity and Partisan Identity Threat: The Role of Social and Geographic Context." *Mass Communication and Society*, 22(2): 145–170.

Longbottom, S.E., and V. Slaughter. 2016. "Direct Experience With Nature and the Development of Biological Knowledge." *Early Education and Development*, 27(8): 1145–1158. DOI: 10.1080/10409289.2016.1169822.

Longhofer, W., and E. Schofer. 2010. "National and Global Origins of Environmental Association." *American Sociological Review*, 75(4): 505–533.

Longo, S.B., and B. Clark. 2016. "An Ocean of Troubles: Advancing Marine Sociology." *Social Problems*, 63(4): 463–479.

Longo, S., R. Clausen, and B. Clark. 2015. *The Tragedy of the Commodity: Oceans, Fisheries, and Aquaculture*. New Brunswick, NJ: Rutgers University Press.

Lonsdorf, K. 2011. "From Freeways to Waterways: What Los Angeles Can Learn from Seoul." *KCET*, August 9. www.kcet.org/socal/departures/landofsunshine/la-river/from-freeways-to-waterways-what-los-angeles-can-learn-from-seoul.html.

Lovejoy, T. 1980. "A Projection of Species Extinctions." In *The Global 2000 Report to the President*, Vol. 2, edited by G. Barney, pp. 328–373. Washington, DC: US Government Printing Office.

Lovins, E. 2014. "Energy Intensity: The Secret Revolution." *Forbes*, July 18. www.forbes.com/sites/amory-lovins/2014/07/18/energy-intensity-the-secret-revolution.

Lovins, L.H., and B. Cohen. 2011. Climate Capitalism: Capitalism in the Age of Climate Change. New York: Hill and Wang.

Lundquist, J., D. Anderton, and D. Yaukey. 2015. *Demography: The Study of Human Population*. 4th edn. Long Grove, IL: Waveland.

Lupala, Z., L. Lusambo, Y. Ngaga, and A. Makatta. 2015. "The Land Use and Cover Change in Miombo Woodlands Under Community Based Forest Management and Its Implication to Climate Change Mitigation: A Case of Southern Highlands of Tanzania." *International Journal of Forestry Research*, 2015: 459102. www.hindawi.com/journals/ijfr/2015/459102/abs.

Lytle, M. 2007. *The Gentle Subversive: Rachel Carlson and the Rise of the Environmental Movement*. New York: Oxford University Press.

Macias, T., and K. Williams. 2015. "Know Your Neighbors, Save the Planet: Social Capital and the Widening Wedge of Pro-Environmental Outcomes." *Environment and Behavior*, 48(3): 391–420.

MacKenzie, D., and G. Spinardi. 1995. "Tacit Knowledge, Weapons Design, and the Uninvention of Nuclear Weapons." *American Journal of Sociology*, 101(1): 44–99.

Maestripieri, L. 2018. "Are Solidarity Purchasing Groups a Social Innovation? A Study Inspired by Social Forces." *Partecipazione e Conflitto*, 10(3): 955–982.

Magni, G. 2017. "Indigenous Knowledge and Implications for the Sustainable Development Agenda." *European Journal of Education*, 52(4): 437–447.

Main, D. 2014. "As World's Largest Dam Removal Is Completed, Fish Already Returning." *Newsweek*, September 9.

Malin, S. 2015. *The Price of Nuclear Power: Uranium Communities and Environmental Justice*. New Brunswick, NJ: Rutgers University Press.

Marcotullio, P., S. Hughes, A. Sarzynski, S. Pincetl, L. Sanchez Peña, P. Romero-Lankao, D. Runfola, and K. Seto. 2014. "Urbanization and the Carbon Cycle: Contributions from Social Science." *Earth's Future*, 2(1): 496–514.

Marinelli, J. 2011. *Landscape for Life*. US Botanic Garden and the Lady Bird Johnson Wildflower Center, University of Texas, Austin. www.landscapeforlife.org/publications/LFL_Workbooks_Print_downloadable.pdf.

Martin, D. 2014. *Edible: An Adventure into the World of Eating Insects and the Last Great Hope to Save the Planet*. New York: Houghton Mifflin.

Martin, G.J., and S.W. Webster. 2018. "Does Residential Sorting Explain Geographic Polarization?" *Political Science Research and Methods*, 1–17. https://doi.org/10.1017/psrm.2018.44.

Martin-Ortega, J., R. Ferrier, I. Gordon, and S. Khan. 2015. *Water Ecosystem Services: A Global Perspective*. New York: Oxford University Press.

Martinez-Alier, J., L. Temper, D. Del Bene, and A. Scheidel. 2016. "Is There a Global Environmental Justice Movement?" *Journal of Peasant Studies*, 43(3): 731–755.

Martínez-Torres, M., and P. Rosset. 2010. "La Vía Campesina: The Birth and Evolution of a Transnational Social Movement." *Journal of Peasant Studies*, 37: 149–175.

Marvel, K., B. Kravitz, and K. Caldeira. 2013. "Geophysical Limits to Global Wind Power." *Nature Climate Change*, 3(2): 118–121.

Marwell, G., and R. Ames. 1981. "Economists Free Ride, Does Anyone Else?" *Journal of Public Economics*, 15: 295–310.

Marx, K. (1863) 1976. *Capital*. Vol. 1. New York: Vintage.

Marx, K. (1863–1865) 1981. *Capital*. Vol. 3. New York: Vintage.

Marx, K., and F. Engels. (1848) 1978. "Manifesto of the Communist Party." In *The Marx–Engels Reader*, edited by Robert C. Tucker, pp. 469–500. New York: Norton.

Mason, S., V. Welch, and J. Neratko. 2018. *Synthetic Polymer Contamination in Global Drinking Water*. Department of Geology & Environmental Sciences, State University of New York at Fredonia. https://orbmedia.org/sites/default/files/FinalBottledWaterReport.pdf.

Mather, A. 1990. *Global Forest Resources*. London: Bellhaven.

Mather, A. 1992. "The Forest Transition." *Area*, 24: 367–379.

Matthews, D. 2019. "Are 26 Billionaires Worth More Than Half the Planet? The Debate, Explained." *Vox*, January 22. www.vox.com/future-perfect/2019/1/22/18192774/oxfam-inequality-report-2019-davos-wealth.

Mattisson, K., C. Håkansson, and K. Jakobsson. 2015. "Relationships between Commuting and Social Capital among Men and Women in Southern Sweden." *Environment and Behavior*, 47(7): 734–753.

Maxwell, R. 2019. "Cosmopolitan Immigration Attitudes in Large European Cities: Contextual or Compositional Effects?" *American Political Science Review*, 113(2): 456–474.

May, E. 1973. "Extensive Oxygen Depletion in Mobile Bay, Alabama." *Limnology and Oceanography*, 18: 353–366.

Mayden, R. 1997. "A Hierarchy of Species Concepts: The Denouement in the Saga of the Species Problem." In

Species: The Units of Biodiversity, edited by M. Claridge, H. Dawah, and M. Wilson, pp. 381–424. New York: Chapman and Hall.

Mazumdar, S., V. Learnihan, T. Cochrane, and R. Davey. 2018. "The Built Environment and Social Capital: A Systematic Review." *Environment and Behavior*, 50(2): 119–158.

Mbuvi, M., J. Musyoki, W. Ayiemba, and J. Gichuki. 2015. "Determining the Potential for Introducing and Sustaining Participatory Forest Management: A Case Study of South Nandi Forest of Western Kenya." *International Journal of Biodiversity and Conservation*, 7(3): 190–201.

McAdam, D. 1996. "Conceptual Origins, Current Problems, Future Directions." In *Comparative Perspectives on Social Movements*, edited by D. McAdam, J. McCarthy, and M. Zald, pp. 23–40. New York: Cambridge University Press.

McCammon, H., and A. McGrath. 2015. "Litigating Change? Social Movements and the Court System." *Sociology Compass*, 9(2): 128–139.

McCarthy, J., and M. Zald. 1977. "Resource Mobilization and Social Movements: A Partial Theory." *American Journal of Sociology*, 82: 1212–1241.

McGregor, J. 2018. "Why 'Buycotts' Could Overtake Boycotts among Consumer Activists." *Washington Post*, February 28. www.washingtonpost.com/news/on-leadership/wp/2018/02/28/why-buycotts-could-overtake-boycotts-among-consumer-activists/?utm_term=.ea6c46457afe.

McHugh, R. 2016. "Aldi Ireland Donates 500,000 Meals to Charity through FoodCloud." *Business World*, November 14. www.businessworld.ie/agricultural-news/Aldi-Ireland-donates-500-000-meals-to-charity-through-FoodCloud-566538.html.

McKie, R.E. 2019. "Climate Change Counter Movement Neutralization Techniques: A Typology to Examine the Climate Change Counter Movement." *Sociological Inquiry*, 89(2): 288–316.

McMichael, P. 2009. "Banking on Agriculture: A Review of the World Development Report, 2008." *Journal of Agrarian Change*, 9(2): 235–246.

McNeill, D. 2011. "Why the Fukushima Disaster Is Worse Than Chernobyl." *The Independent* (London), August 29.

Meadows, D., D. Meadows, J. Randers, and W. Behrens. 1972. *The Limits to Growth*. New York: Universe Books.

Meijaard, E., and V. Nijman. 2003. "Primate Hotspots on Borneo: Predictive Value for General Biodiversity and the Effects of Taxonomy." *Conservation Biology*, 17: 725–732.

Mekonnen, M., and Y. Hoekstra. 2011. "The Green, Blue and Grey Water Footprint of Crops and Derived Crop Products." *Hydrology and Earth System Sciences*, 15(5): 1577–1600.

Menon, G. 1991. "Ecological Transition and the Changing Context of Women's Work in Tribal India." *Purusartha*, 14: 291–314.

Merchant, C. 1980. *The Death of Nature: Women, Ecology, and the Scientific Revolution*. San Francisco, CA: Harper-Collins.

Merchant, E. 2018. "Trump Can't Save Coal: More Capacity Closed in 2018 Than First Three Years of Obama Administration." *GreenTechMedia*, February 19. www.greentechmedia.com/articles/read/trump-cant-save-coal#gs.M7nHlzda.

Merrill, R. 1997. "Food Safety Regulation: Reforming the Delaney Clause." *Annual Review of Public Health*, 18: 313–340.

Meyer, D.S., and S. Staggenborg. 1996. "Movements, Countermovements, and the Structure of Political Opportunity." *American Journal of Sociology*, 101: 1628–1660.

Mill, J.S. 1848. *Principles of Political Economy*. Boston, MA: Charles C. Little and James Brown.

Millennium Ecosystem Assessment. 2005. *Ecosystems and Human Well-Being: Synthesis*. Washington, DC: Island.

Millsap, A. 2019. "State Nuclear Subsidies Not Needed." *Forbes*, April 19. www.forbes.com/sites/adammillsap/2019/04/19/state-nuclear-subsidies-not-needed/#33e0f0ff111d.

Ministry of Home Affairs. 2018. *Annual Report 2017–18*. Government of Australia. www.homeaffairs.gov.au/reports-and-pubs/Annualreports/2017-18/01-annual-report-2017-18.pdf.

Minter, A. 2018. "No One Wants Your Used Clothes Anymore." *Bloomberg*, January 15. www.bloomberg.com/opinion/articles/2018-01-15/no-one-wants-your-used-clothes-anymore.

Mirabelli M., S. Wing, S. Marshall, and T. Wilcosky. 2006. "Asthma Symptoms among Adolescents Who Attend Public Schools That Are Located Near Confined Swine Feeding Operations." *Pediatrics*, 118: e66–e75.

Mishan, E. 1967. *The Costs of Economic Growth*. Middlesex, MA: Penguin.

Modern Agriculture. 2018. "The Beeconomy: Economics and Insect Pollination." *Modern Agriculture*, April 27. https://modernag.org/biodiversity/beeconomy-economic-value-pollination/.

Mohai, P., and R. Saha. 2007. "Racial Inequality in the Distribution of Hazardous Waste: A National-Level Reassessment." *Social Problems*, 54(3): 343–370.

Mohai, P., D. Pellow, and J.T. Roberts. 2009. "Environmental Justice." *Annual Review of Environment & Resources*, 34: 405–430.

Mohai, P., S. Simões, and S. Brechin. 2010. "Environmental Concerns, Values, and Meanings in the Beijing and Detroit Metropolitan Areas." *International Sociology*, 25(6): 778–817.

Møllegaard, S., and M. Jæger. 2015. "The Effect of Grandparents' Economic, Cultural, and Social Capital on Grand-Children's Educational Success." *Research in Social Stratification and Mobility*, 42: 11–19.

Moore, P. 2006. "Nuclear Re-Think." *International Atomic Energy Agency Bulletin*, 48(1): 56–58.

Morgan Stanley. 2016. "Bricks, Mortar, and Carbon." www.morganstanley.com/content/dam/msdotcom/en/assets/p dfs/8497233GSFBricksMortarResSheetm4.pdf?v=11.

Morning Consult/Politico. 2018. *National Tracking Poll #181159 December 04-04.* https://morningconsult.com/wp-content/uploads/2018/12/181159_crosstabs_POLITICO_RV_v1_AP.pdf.

Morrison, M., R. Duncan, and K. Parton. 2015. "Religion Does Matter for Climate Change Attitudes and Behavior." *PLOS One*, 10(8): e0134868.

Mostafa, M. 2013. "Wealth, Post-Materialism and Consumers' Pro-Environmental Intentions: A Multilevel Analysis Across 25 Nations." *Sustainable Development*, 21(6): 385–399.

Mozell, R., and L. Thach. 2014. "The Impact of Climate Change on the Global Wine Industry: Challenges and Solutions." *Wine Economics and Policy*, 3(2): 81–89.

MST (Movimento dos Trabalhadores Rurais Sem Terra). 2015. "What Is the MST?" *Friends of the MST*. www.mst brazil.org (accessed August 7, 2015).

Mubako, S.T. 2018. "Blue, Green, and Grey Water Quantification Approaches: A Bibliometric and Literature Review." *Journal of Contemporary Water Research & Education*, 165(1): 4–19.

Mufson, S. 2014. "Here's the Grassroots Political Story behind the New York Fracking Ban." *Washington Post*, December 18.

Myrskyla, M., H.-P. Kohler, and F. Billari. 2009. "Advances in Development Reverse Fertility Declines." *Nature*, 460: 741–743.

Nabhan, G. 1997. *Cultures of Habitat*. Washington, DC: Counterpoint.

Namberger, V. 2019. *The Reproductive Body at Work: The South African Bioeconomy of Egg Donation*. Abingdon, UK: Routledge.

Narain, V., and S. Vij. 2016. "Where Have All the Commons Gone?" *Geoforum*, 68: 21–24.

Nash, M.P., dir. 2010. *Climate Refugees: The Human Face of Climate Change* [video]. Los Angeles, CA: LA Think Tank.

National Footprint Accounts. 2019. "National Footprints Accounts." *Global Footprint Network*. https://data.foot-printnetwork.org/#/?/.

National Research Council. 2015. *Climate Intervention: Reflecting Sunlight to Cool Earth*. Washington, DC: National Academies Press.

Naughton, K., and D. Welsh. 2019. "This is What Peak Car Looks Like." *Bloomberg*, February 28. www.bloomberg.com/news/features/2019-02-28/this-is-what-peak-car-looks-like.

Nazarea, V. 2005. *Heirloom Seeds and Their Keepers: Marginality and Memory in the Conservation of Biological Diversity*. Tucson, AZ: University of Arizona Press.

NEI (Nuclear Energy Institute). 2012. "World Statistics." Washington, DC. www.nei.org/resourcesandstats/nuclear_statistics/worldstatistics (accessed June 7, 2012).

Neilson, A.L., and R. São Marcos. 2019. "Reframing Marine Resource Management with Relational Ontologies and Hybrid Entanglements: Fishing for Empathy between Azorean Fishers and Scientists." *Marine Policy*, 105: 30–37.

Netting, R. 1981. *Balancing on an Alp: Ecological Change and Continuity in a Swiss Mountain Community*. New York: Cambridge University Press.

Neumayer, E. 1999. "Global Warming: Discounting Is Not the Issue, but Substitutability Is." *Energy Policy*, 27: 33–34.

New Economics Foundation. 2017. *The Happy Planet Index 2016*. London. http://happyplanetindex.org/s/Briefing-paper-HPI-2016.pdf.

Newman, A. 2011. "N.J. to Leave Regional Cap-and-Trade Scheme." *New American*, May 31. www.thenewamerican.com/tech-mainmenu-30/environment/7689-nj-to-leave-regional-cap-and-trade-scheme.

Newman, T.P., E.C. Nisbet, and M.C. Nisbet. 2018. "Climate Change, Cultural Cognition, and Media Effects: Worldviews Drive News Selectivity, Biased Processing, and Polarized Attitudes." *Public Understanding of Science*, 27(8): 985–1002.

Ng, W., and E. Diener. 2019. "Affluence and Subjective Well-Being: Does Income Inequality Moderate their Associations?" *Applied Research in Quality of Life*, 14(1): 155–170.

Nguyen, T.P.L., G. Seddaiu, and P.P. Roggero. 2019. "Declarative or Procedural Knowledge? Knowledge for Enhancing Farmers' Mitigation and Adaptation Behaviour to Climate Change." *Journal of Rural Studies*, 67: 46–56.

NHDES (New Hampshire Department of Environmental Services). 2012. "Time It Takes for Garbage to Decompose in the Environment." Concord, NH. http://des.nh.gov/organization/divisions/water/wmb/coastal/trash/documents/marine_debris.pdf (accessed March 28, 2012).

Nicholls, A., and C. Opal. 2005. *Fair Trade: Market-Driven Ethical Consumption*. Thousand Oaks, CA: Sage.

Nichols, B., and K. Kockelman. 2014. "Pay-as-You-Drive Insurance: Its Impacts on Household Driving and Welfare." *Transportation Research Record: Journal of the Transportation Research Board*, 2450: 76–82.

Nicholls, C.I., and M.A. Altieri. 2018. "Pathways for the Amplification of Agroecology." *Agroecology and Sustainable Food Systems*, 42(10): 1170–1193.

N.L. 2010. "What's Up Pussycat? Saving the Tiger." Babbage [blog], *The Economist*, November 24. www.economist.com/blogs/babbage/2010/11/saving_tiger.

Norgaard, K. 2006. "'We Don't Really Want to Know': Environmental Justice and Socially Organized Denial of Global Warming in Norway." *Organization and Environment*, 19(3): 347–370.

Norgaard, K. 2011. *Living in Denial: Climate Change, Emotions, and Everyday Life*. Cambridge, MA: MIT Press.

Norman, E., C. Cook, and A. Cohen, eds. 2015. *Negotiating Water Governance: Why the Politics of Scale Matter*. Burlington, VT: Ashgate.

Ntanos, S., G. Kyriakopoulos, M. Skordoulis, M. Chalikias, and G. Arabatzis. 2019. "An Application of the New Environmental Paradigm (NEP) Scale in a Greek Context." *Energies*, 12(2): 239.

Nuclear Energy Agency. 2010. "Nuclear Energy and Addressing Climate Change." November. www.oecd-nea.org/press/in-perspective/2010-addressing-climate-change.pdf.

Nugent, D., and B. Sovacool. 2014. "Assessing the Lifecycle Greenhouse Gas Emissions from Solar PV and Wind Energy: A Critical Meta-Survey." *Energy Policy*, 65: 229–244.

Oakland Institute. 2017. *Carbon Colonialism*. www.oaklandinstitute.org/sites/oaklandinstitute.org/files/uganda_carbon_colonialism.pdf.

Oates, C., and N. Tziortzi. 2014. "Parents' Beliefs about, and Attitudes towards, Marketing to Children." In *Advertising to Children: New Directions, New Media*, edited by M. Blades, C. Oates, F. Blumberg, and B. Gunte, pp. 115–136. New York: Palgrave.

O'Connor, J. 1998. *Natural Causes: Essays in Ecological Marxism*. New York: Guildford.

OECD (Organization for Economic Cooperation and Development). 2015a. *Aligning Policies for a Low-Carbon Economy*. Paris: OECD.

OECD (Organization for Economic Cooperation and Development). 2015b. *OECD Studies on Water Stakeholder Engagement for Inclusive Water Governance*. Paris: OECD.

Ogneva-Himmelberger, Y., and L. Huang. 2015. "Spatial Distribution of Unconventional Gas Wells and Human Populations in the Marcellus Shale in the United States: Vulnerability Analysis." *Applied Geography*, 60: 165–174.

Ohring, G., P. Romanov, R. Ferraro, A. Heidinger, I. Laszlo, C.-Z. Zou, and M. Foster. 2014. "Satellite Observations of North American Climate Change." In *Climate Change in North America*, edited by G. Ohring, pp. 95–165. Cham, Switzerland: Springer.

O'Lenick, C.R., O.V. Wilhelmi, R. Michael, M.H. Hayden, A. Baniassadi, C. Wiedinmyer, A.J. Monaghan, P.J. Crank, and D.J. Sailor. 2019. "Urban Heat and Air Pollution: A Framework for Integrating Population Vulnerability and Indoor Exposure in Health Risk Analyses." *Science of the Total Environment*, 660: 715–723.

Oliver, M., H. Badland, and K. Villanueva. 2017 "How Does the Neighbourhood Built Environment Influence Child Development?" In *Children's Health and Wellbeing in Urban Environments*, edited by Christina R. Ergler, Robin Kearns, and Karen Witten, pp. 45–58. Abingdon, UK: Routledge.

Olivier, J., G. Janssens-Maenhout, M. Muntean, and J. Peters. 2014. *Trends in Global CO$_2$ Emissions: 2014 Report*. PBL Netherlands Environmental Assessment Agency and Institute for Environment and Sustainability of the European Commission's Joint Research Centre. http://edgar.jrc.ec.europa.eu/news_docs/jrc-2014-trends-in-global-co2-emissions-2014-report-93171.pdf.

O'Neill, D.W., A.L. Fanning, W.F. Lamb, and J.K. Steinberger. 2018. "A Good Life for All within Planetary Boundaries." *Nature Sustainability*, 1(2): 88–95. www.nature.com/articles/s41893-018-0021-4.

OPEC (Organization of the Petroleum Exporting Countries). 2014. "OPEC Share of World Crude Oil Reserves, 2014." www.opec.org/opec_web/en/data_graphs/330.htm.

Ordaz, D.L., L.M. Schaefer, E. Choquette, J. Schueler, L. Wallace, and J.K. Thompson. 2018. "Thinness Pressures in Ethnically Diverse College Women in the United States." *Body image*, 24: 1–4.

Orsini, F., M. Dubbeling, H. Zeeuw, and G. Gianquinto, eds. 2017. *Rooftop Urban Agriculture*. Cham, Switzerland: Springer.

Osborn, S.G., A. Vengosh, N.R. Warner, and R.B. Jackson. 2011. "Methane Contamination of Drinking Water Accompanying Gas-Well Drilling and Hydraulic Fracturing." *Proceedings of the National Academy of Sciences*, 108(20): 8172–8176.

Ostrom, E. 1999. *Governing the Commons: The Evolution of Institutions for Collective Action*. New York: Cambridge University Press.

Ostrom, E. 2000. "Private and Common Property Rights." In *Encyclopedia of Law and Economics*, Vol. 3, edited by B. Bouckaert and G. De Geest, pp. 332–379. London: Edward Elgar.

Ostrom, E., J. Burger, C. Field, R. Norgaard, and D. Policansky. 1999. "Revisiting the Commons: Local Lessons, Global Challenges." *Science*, 284(5412): 278–282.

Ostrom, E., R. Gardner, and J. Walker. 1994. *Rules, Games, and Common-Pool Resources*. Ann Arbor, MI: University of Michigan Press.

Owen, D. 2011. *The Conundrum*. New York: Riverhead Books.

Oxfam. 2015. "Richest 1% Will Own More Than All the Rest by 2016." www.oxfam.org/en/pressroom/pressre-leases/2015-01-19/richest-1-will-own-more-all-rest-2016.

Ozanne, L., and J.L. Ozanne. 2016. "How Alternative Consumer Markets Can Build Community Resiliency." *European Journal of Marketing*, 50(3/4): 1–17.

Pacala, S., and R. Socolow. 2004. "Stabilization Wedges: Solving the Climate Problem for the Next 50 Years with Current Technologies." *Science*, 305: 968–972.

Pampel, F. 2014. "The Varied Influence of SES on Environmental Concern." *Social Science Quarterly*,95(1): 57–75.

Pan, Y., R. Birdsey, J. Fang, R. Houghton, P. Kauppi, W. Kurz, and O. Phillips. 2011. "A Large and Persistent Carbon Sink in the World's Forests." *Science*, 333(6045): 988–993.

Panayotou, T. 2016. "Economic Growth and the Environment." In *The Environment in Anthropology*, edited by Nora Haenn, Allison Harnish, and Richard Wilk, pp. 140–148. New York: New York University Press.

Pariatamby, A., and M. Tanaka, eds. 2014. *Municipal Solid Waste Management in Asia and the Pacific Islands*. Singapore: Springer.

Parker, L. 2015. "Ocean Trash: 5.25 Trillion Pieces and Counting, but Big Questions Remain." *National Geographic*, January 11. http://news.nationalgeographic.com/news/2015/01/150109-oceans-plastic-sea-trash-science-marine-debris.

Parkins, J. 2015. "Industrial Agriculture and Community Outcomes: A Preliminary Study of Goldschmidt's Hypothesis in Rural Canada." Working paper, University of Alberta, Canada. https://ageconsearch.umn.edu/record/206563/.

Parrish, D., H. Singh, L. Molina, and S. Madronich. 2011. "Air Quality Progress in North American Megacities: A Review." *Atmospheric Environment*, 45: 7015–7025.

Parsons, L. 2018. "Structuring the Emotional Landscape of Climate Change Migration: Towards Climate Mobilities in Geography." *Progress in Human Geography*, 43(4): 670–690. https://doi.org/10.1177/0309132518781011.

Pellow, D. 2014. *Total Liberation: The Power and Promise of Animal Rights and the Radical Earth Movement*. Minneapolis, MN: University of Minnesota Press.

Pellow, D. 2017. "Environmental Inequalities and the U.S. Prison System: An Urgent Research Agenda." *International Journal of Earth and Environmental Sciences* 2: 140–141.

Pellow, D., and H. Brehm. 2015. "From the New Ecological Paradigm to Total Liberation: The Emergence of a Social Movement Frame." *Sociological Quarterly*, 56: 185–212.

Perrow, C. 1984. *Normal Accidents: Living with High Risk Technologies*. Princeton, NJ: Princeton University Press.

Perrow, C. 2010. "Organizations and Global Warming." In *Routledge Handbook of Climate Change and Society*, edited by C. Lever-Tracy, pp. 59–77. New York: Routledge.

Peterson, A. 2009. *Everyday Ethics and Social Change: The Education of Desire*. New York: Columbia University Press.

Peterson, A., and A. Navarro-Siguenza. 1999. "Alternative Species Concepts as Bases for Determining Priority Conservation Areas." *Conservation Biology*, 13: 427–431.

Peterson, E. 2009. *A Billion Dollars a Day: The Economics and Politics of Agricultural Subsidies*. Malden, MA: Wiley-Blackwell.

Pew Research Center. 2017. "After Seismic Political Shift, Modest Changes in Public's Policy Agenda." Washington, DC, January 24. www.people-press.org/2017/01/24/after-seismic-political-shift-modest-changes-in-publics-policy-agenda/.

Pfaff, A., and R. Walker. 2010. "Regional Interdependence and Forest 'Transitions': Substitute Deforestation Limits the Relevance of Local Reversals." *Land Use Policy*, 27: 119–127.

Pfeffer, M. 1983. "Social Origins of Three Systems of Farm Production in the United States." *Rural Sociology*, 48(4): 540–562.

Piasentin, F.B., and L. Roberts. 2018. "What Elements in a Sustainability Course Contribute to Paradigm Change and Action Competence? A Study at Lincoln University, New Zealand." *Environmental Education Research*, 24(5): 694–715.

Pickering, A. 1999. *Constructing Quarks: A Sociological History of Particle Physics*. Chicago, IL: University of Chicago Press.

Pidgeon, N. 2011. "In Retrospect: Normal Accidents." *Nature*, 477(7365): 404–405.

Piff, P., D. Stancato, S. Côté, R. Mendoza-Denton, and D. Keltner 2012. "Higher Social Class Predicts Increased Unethical Behavior," *Proceedings of the National Academy of Sciences*, 109(11): 4086–4091.

Pigou, A.C. 1912. *Wealth and Welfare*. London: Macmillan.

Pimentel, D., and M. Burgess. 2014. "Environmental and Economic Costs of the Application of Pesticides Primarily in the United States." In *Integrated Pest Management*, Vol. 3, edited by D. Pimentel and R. Peshin, pp. 47–72. New York: Springer.

Pimentel, D., J. Krummel, D. Gallahan, J. Hough, A. Merrill, I. Schreiner, P. Vittum, F. Koziol, E. Back, D. Yen, and S. Fiance. 1978. "Benefits and Costs of Pesticide Use in United States Food Production." *BioScience*, 28(772): 778–784.

Pimm, S., C. Jenkins, R. Abell, T. Brooks, J. Gittleman, L. Joppa, P. Raven, C. Roberts, and J. Sexton. 2014. "The Biodiversity of Species and Their Rates of Extinction, Distribution, and Protection." *Science*, 344(6187): 1246752.

Pitrelli, S. 2018. "Italy's Wine Industry Is Being Tested by the Effects of Climate Change in Its Vineyards." *Washington Post*, October 28. www.washingtonpost.com/world/europe/how-climate-change-is-upending-the-patterns-and-predictability-of-italys-wine-industry/2018/10/28/3ae7a9a0-c71e-11e8-9c0f-2ffaf6d422aa_story.html?utm_term=.0849942a9887.

Popper, K. (1934) 1961. *The Logic of Scientific Discovery*. New York: Science Editions.

Potter, D. 2015. "Why Isn't Desalination the Answer to All California's Water Problems?" *KQED*, December 18. http://ww2.kqed.org/science/2015/12/18/why-isnt-desalination-the-answer-to-all-californias-water-problems.

Pouchard, A. 2014. "San Francisco Is Rapidly Becoming the Recycling Capital of the World." *Business Insider*, June 17. www.businessinsider.com/san-francisco-is-rapidly-becoming-the-recycling-capital-of-the-world-2014-6.

Poudyal, N.C., B.R. Gyawali, and M. Simon. 2019. "Local Residents' Views of Surface Mining: Perceived Impacts, Subjective Well-Being, and Support for Regulations in Southern Appalachia." *Journal of Cleaner Production*, 217: 530–540.

Prisco, J. 2015. "Why Bananas as We Know Them Might Go Extinct (and What to Do About It)." *CNN*, July 22. www.cnn.com/2015/07/22/africa/banana-panama-disease.

Putnam, R. 2001. *Bowling Alone: The Collapse and Revival of American Community*. New York: Simon and Schuster.

PWC (PricewaterhouseCoopers). 2019. *The Low Carbon Economy Index 2018*. London. www.pwc.co.uk/services/sustainability-climate-change/insights/low-carbon-economy-index.html.

Quan, L., and R. Reuveny. 2006. "Democracy and Environmental Deregulation." *International Studies Quarterly*, 50: 935–956.

Rabobank Group. 2010. *Sustainability and Security of the Global Food Supply Chain*. Utrecht, Netherlands. www.rabobank.nl/images/rabobanksustainability_29286998.pdf.

Radon, K., A. Schulze, V. Ehrenstein, R. van Strien, G. Praml, and D. Nowak. 2007. "Environmental Exposure to Confined Animal Feeding Operations and Respiratory Health of Neighboring Residents." *Epidemiology*, 18: 300–308.

Raffensperger, C., and J. Tickner, eds. 1999. *Protecting Public Health and the Environment: Implementing the Precautionary Principle*. Washington, DC: Island.

Ramon, K. 2011. "Debates on Protecting Traditional Knowledge in an Age of Globalization." In *Interdisciplinary Perspectives in Political Theory*, edited by M. Kulkarni, pp. 189–215. Thousand Oaks, CA: Sage.

Rathi, A. 2018. "Once on the Sidelines, Carbon Capture Is Now Being Touted As an Economic Win". *Quartz*, July 25. https://qz.com/1335075/once-on-the-sidelines-carbon-capture-is-now-being-touted-as-an-economic-win/.

Ravallion, M., S. Chen, and P. Sangraula. 2007. *New Evidence on the Urbanization of Global Poverty*. Policy Research Working Paper 4199. World Bank. http://siteresources.worldbank.org/INTWDR2008/Resources/2795087-1191427986785/RavallionMEtAl_UrbanizationOfGlobalPoverty.pdf.

Ravenelle, A.J. 2017. "Sharing Economy Workers: Selling, Not Sharing." *Cambridge Journal of Regions, Economy and Society*, 10(2): 281–295.

Ray, D., N. Mueller, P. West, and J. Foley. 2013. "Yield Trends Are Insufficient to Double Global Crop Production by 2050." *PLOS One*, 8(6): e66428.

Raynolds, L., and E. Bennett, eds. 2015. *Handbook of Research on Fair Trade*. Cheltenham, UK: Elgar.

REDD Desk. 2015. "Forests: Why Are They Important?" July 10. http://thereddesk.org/what-redd#toc-1.

Redwood, M. 2010. "Commentary: Food Price and Volatility and the Urban Poor." In *Urban Agriculture: Diverse Activities and Benefits for City Society*, edited by C. Pearson, pp. 5–6. London: Earthscan.

Rehman, H.M., J.W. Cooper, H.M. Lam, and S.H. Yang. 2019. "Legume Biofortification Is an Underexploited Strategy for Combatting Hidden Hunger." *Plant, Cell & Environment*, 42(1): 52–70.

Rees, W. 2009. "True Cost Economics." In *Berkshire Encyclopedia of Sustainability*, edited by C. Laszlo, pp. 468–471. Great Barrington, MA: Berkshire Publishing.

Reiss, A. 2019. "New York's Shadow Transit." *The New Yorker*. https://projects.newyorker.com/story/nyc-dollar-vans/.

REN21 Secretariat. 2010. *Renewables 2010: Status Report, Renewable Action Policy Network for the 21st Century (REN21)*. Paris.

Reuters. 2017. "China's Energy Demand to Peak in 2040 As Transportation Demand Grows: CNPC." *Reuters*, August 16. https://uk.reuters.com/article/us-china-cnpc-outlook/chinas-energy-demand-to-peak-in-2040-as-transportation-demand-grows-cnpc-idUKKCN1AW0DF.

Revi, A. 2008. "Climate Change Risk: An Adaptation and Mitigation Agenda for Indian Cities." *Environment and Urbanization*, 20(1): 207–229.

Revkin, A. 2009. "Peeling Back Pavement to Expose Watery Havens." *New York Times*, July 17.

Reyna, C., E. Bressán, D. Mola, A. Belaus, and M.V. Ortiz. 2018. "Validating the Structure of the New Ecological Paradigm Scale among Argentine Citizens through Different Approaches." *Pensamiento Psicológico*, 16(1): 107–118.

Rideout, B. 2005. "The Effect of a Brief Environmental Problems Module on Endorsement of the New Ecological Paradigm in College Students." *Journal of Environmental Education*, 37(1): 3–11.

Rifkin, J. 2000. *The Age of Access: The New Culture of Hypercapitalism, Where All of Life Is a Paid-For Experience*. New York: Tarcher.

Ríos-Touma, B., and A. Ramírez. 2019. "Multiple Stressors in the Neotropical Region: Environmental Impacts in Biodiversity Hotspots." In *Multiple Stressors in River Ecosystems*, edited by Sergi Sabater, Arturo Elosegi, and Ralf Ludwig, pp. 205–220. Amsterdam: Elsevier.

Roark, P. 2015. *Social Justice and Deep Participation: Theory and Practice for the 21st Century*. New York: Palgrave.

Robbins, P. 2012. *Political Ecology*. 2nd edn. Malden, MA: Wiley.

Robinson, B.E., P. Li, and X. Hou. 2017. "Institutional Change in Social-Ecological Systems: The Evolution of Grassland Management in Inner Mongolia." *Global Environmental Change*, 47: 64–75.

Roe, A. 2015. "Free the Buses: Riders Say Transit Is a Human Right." *Equal Voice for Families*, April 14. www.equal-voiceforfamilies.org/free-the-buses-riders-say-transit-is-a-human-right.

Roe, J., and M. Knöll. 2018. "Adolescent Health and Wellbeing: Advocating a Role for Urban Design." *The Lancet Child & Adolescent Health*, 2(10): 697–699.

Rosa, E., and T. Dietz. 1998. "Climate Change and Society: Speculation, Construction, and Scientific Investigations." *International Sociology*, 13: 421–455.

Rosa, E., T. Rudel, R. York, A. Jorgenson, and T. Dietz. 2015. "The Human (Anthropogenic) Driving Forces of Global Climate Change." In *Climate Change and Society: Sociological Perspectives*, edited by R. Dunlap and R. Brulle, pp. 32–60. New York: Oxford University Press.

Roser, M. 2015. "Child Mortality." *Our World in Data*. http://ourworldindata.org/data/population-growth-vital-statistics/child-mortality.

Rothschild, D. 2007. *The Live Earth Global Warming Survival Handbook*. New York: Rodale Books.

Sagoff, M. 1988. *The Economy of the Earth*. New York: Cambridge University Press.

Saha, R., and P. Mohai. 2005. "Historical Context and Hazardous Waste Facility Siting: Understanding Temporal Patterns in Michigan." *Social Problems*, 52(4): 618–648.

Sallis, J.F., T.L. Conway, K.L. Cain, J.A. Carlson, L.D. Frank, J. Kerr, K. Glanz, J.E. Chapman, and B.E. Saelens. 2018. "Neighborhood Built Environment and Socioeconomic Status in Relation to Physical Activity, Sedentary Behavior, and Weight Status of Adolescents. *Preventive Medicine*, 110: 47–54.

Samida, D., and D. Weisbach. 2007. "Paretian Intergenerational Discounting." *University of Chicago Law Review*, 74(1): 145–170.

Sapkota, P., R.J. Keenan, J.A. Paschen, and H.R. Ojha. 2016. "Social Production of Vulnerability to Climate Change in the Rural Middle Hills of Nepal." *Journal of Rural Studies*, 48: 53–64.

Sarthi, P., A. Agrawal, and A. Rana. 2015. "Possible Future Changes in Cyclonic Storms in the Bay of Bengal, India, Under Warmer Climate." *International Journal of Climatology*, 35(7): 1267–1277.

Saunders, P.J., D. McCoy, R. Goldstein, A.T. Saunders, and A. Munroe. 2018. "A Review of the Public Health Impacts of Unconventional Natural Gas Development." *Environmental Geochemistry and Health*, 40(1): 1–57.

Schade, C., and D. Pimentel. 2010. "Population Crash: Prospects for Famine in the Twenty-First Century." *Environment, Development and Sustainability*, 12(2): 245–262.

Schattman, R., V. Méndez, S. Merrill, and A. Zia. 2018. "Mixed Methods Approach to Understanding Farmer and Agricultural Advisor Perceptions of Climate Change and Adaptation in Vermont, United States." *Agroecology and Sustainable Food Systems*, 42(2): 121–148.

Schelling, T. 1995. "Intergenerational Discounting." *Energy Policy*, 23: 395–401.

Schiller, P., and J. Kenworthy. 2017. *An Introduction to Sustainable Transportation: Policy, Planning, and Implementation*. 2nd edn. London: Routledge.

Schlesinger, J., E. Munishi, and A. Drescher. 2015. "Ethnicity as a Determinant of Agriculture in an Urban Setting: Evidence from Tanzania." *Geoforum*, 64: 138–145.

Schlosberg, D. 2013. "Political Challenges of the Climate-Changed Society." *PS: Political Science & Politics*, 46(1): 13–17.

Schlosberg, D., 2019. "From Postmaterialism to Sustainable Materialism: The Environmental Politics of Practice-Based Movements." *Environmental Politics*. https://doi.org/10.1080/09644016.2019.1587215.

Schnaiberg, A. 1980. *The Environment: From Surplus to Scarcity*. New York: Oxford University Press.

Schnaiberg, A., and K. Gould. 1994. *Environment and Society: The Enduring Conflict*. New York: St. Martin's.

Schor, J. 1992. *The Overworked American*. New York: Basic Books.

Schor, J. 2010. *Plenitude: The New Economics of True Wealth*. New York: Penguin.

Schor, J.B. 2017. "Does the Sharing Economy Increase Inequality within the Eighty Percent?: Findings from a Qualitative Study of Platform Providers." *Cambridge Journal of Regions, Economy and Society*, 10(2): 263–279.

Seales, R. 2017. "The Country Where 70% of Millennials Are Homeowners." *BBC*, April 6. www.bbc.com/news/world-39512599.

Seckler, D. 1996. *The New Era of Water Resources Management: From "Dry" to "Wet" Water Savings*. International Irrigation Management Institute, Colombo, Sri Lanka. www.iwmi.cgiar.org/Publications/IWMI_Research_Reports/PDF/pub001/REPORT01.pdf.

Seier, M., and T. Zimmermann. 2014. "Environmental Impacts of Decommissioning Nuclear Power Plants: Methodical Challenges, Case Study, and Implications." *International Journal of Life Cycle Assessment*, 19(12): 1919–1932.

Sen, A. 1970. *Collective Choice and Social Welfare*. San Francisco, CA: Holden-Day.

Sen, A. 1981. *Poverty and Famines: An Essay on Entitlement and Deprivation*. New York: Oxford University Press.

Sen, A. 1984. "The Living Standard." *Oxford Economic Papers*, 36: 74–90.

Sen, A. 1993. "Markets and Freedom." *Oxford Economic Papers*, 45: 519–541.

Sen, A. 1994. *Population and Reasoning*. Working Paper Series No. 94.06. Harvard Center for Population and Development Studies, Harvard School of Public Health, Harvard University.

Sen, A. 1999. *Development as Freedom*. New York: Anchor.

Sen, A. 2005. "Human Rights and Capabilities." *Journal of Human Development*, 6(2): 151–166.

Seo, B., and R. Chiu. 2014. "Social Cohesiveness of Disadvantaged Communities in Urban South Korea: The Impact of the Physical Environment." *Housing Studies*, 29(3): 407–437.

Serp, J., C. Poinssot, and S. Bourg. 2017. "Assessment of the Anticipated Environmental Footprint of Future Nuclear Energy Systems. Evidence of the Beneficial Effect of Extensive Recycling." *Energies*, 10(9): 1445. https://doi.org/10.3390/en10091445.

Servaes, H., and A. Tamayo. 2017. "The Role of Social Capital in Corporations: A Review." *Oxford Review of Economic Policy*, 33(2): 201–220.

Seshadri, S. 2001. "Prevalence of Micronutrient Deficiency Particularly of Iron, Zinc, and Folic Acid in Pregnant Women in South East Asia." *British Journal of Nutrition*, 85: S87–S92.

Seto, K., B. Guneralp, and L. Hutyra. 2012. "Global Forecasts of Urban Expansion to 2030 and Direct Impacts on Biodiversity and Carbon Pools." *Proceedings of the National Academy of Sciences*, 109(40): 16083–16088.

Shapiro, S., and A. Hinde. 2017. "On the Pace of Fertility Decline in Sub-Sahara Africa." *Demographic Research* 37(40): 1327–1338.

Sheldon, S., S. Hadian, and O. Zik. 2015. "Beyond Carbon: Quantifying Environmental Externalities as Energy for Hydroelectric and Nuclear Power." *Energy*, 84(1): 36–44.

Shelley, C., J. Cross, W. Franzen, P. Hall, and S. Reeve. 2011. "Reducing Energy Consumption and Creating a Conservation Culture in Organizations: A Case Study of One Public School District." *Environment and Behavior*, 4(3): 316–343.

Shelley, C., J. Cross, W. Franzen, P. Hall, and S. Reeve. 2012. "How to Go Green: Creating a Conservation Culture in a Public High School through Education, Modeling, and Communication." *Journal of Environmental Education*, 43(3): 143–161.

Shemkus, S. 2014. "Fighting the Seed Monopoly." *Guardian* (London), May 2.

Shove, E., F. Trentmann, and R. Wilk. 2009. *Time, Consumption, and Everyday Life: Practice, Materiality, and Culture*. New York: Berg.

Shu, C. 2018. "Amazon Puts $10M in Closed Loop Fund to Make Recycling Easier in More American Cities." *TechCrunch*, October 10. https://techcrunch.com/2018/10/16/amazon-puts-10m-in-closed-loop-fund-to-make-recycling-easier-in-more-american-cities (accessed March 18, 2019).

Shue, H. 2014. *Climate Justice: Vulnerability and Protection*. New York: Oxford.

Simon, J. 1981. *The Ultimate Resource*. Princeton, NJ: Princeton University Press.

Simon, M. 2018. "Carbon Capture Is Messy and Fraught—But It Might Be Essential." *Wired*, October 29. www.wired.com/story/carbon-capture-is-messy-and-fraught-but-might-be-essential/.

Simons, R., Y. Seo, and S. Robinson. 2014. "The Effect of a Large Hog Barn Operation on Residential Sales Prices in Marshall County, KY." *Journal of Sustainable Real Estate*, 6(2): 93–111.

Sisson, P. 2017. "How a Return to Multigenerational Living Is Shifting the Housing Market." *Curbed*, November 21. www.curbed.com/2017/11/21/16682850/multigenerational-homes-millennials-immigration-family.

Sjöstedt, M., and S. Jagers. 2014. "Democracy and the Environment Revisited: The Case of African Fisheries." *Marine Policy*, 43: 143–148.

Skousen, M. 2011. *Econopower: How a New Generation of Economists Is Transforming the World*. New York: Wiley.

Sloan, H. 1993. "The Earth Belongs in Usufruct to the Living." In *Jeffersonian Legacies*, edited by P. Onuf, pp. 281–315. Charlottesville, VA: University Press of Virginia.

Smart, M., K. Ralph, B. Taylor, C. Turley, and A. Brown. 2014. *Honey, Can You Pick-Up Groceries on Your Way Home? Analyzing Activities and Travel among Students and in Non-Traditional Households*. University of California Transportation Center, UCLA, Los Angeles. www.uctc.net/research/papers/UCTC-FR-2014-07.pdf.

Smil, V. 2004. *China's Past, China's Future: Energy, Food, Environment*. New York: Routledge.

Smith, E. 2001. "On the Coevolution of Cultural, Linguistic, and Biological Diversity." In *Biocultural Diversity: Linking Language, Knowledge, and the Environment*, edited by L. Maffi, pp. 95–117. Washington, DC: Smithsonian Institution Press.

Smith, K., L. Hempel, and K. MacIlroy. 2018. "What's 'Evangelical' Got to Do with It? Disentangling the Impact of Evangelical Protestantism on Environmental Outcomes." *Environmental Politics*, 27(2): 292–319. DOI: 10.1080/09644016.2017.1384185.

Snow, D., and R. Benford. 1988. "Ideology, Frame Resonance, and Participant Mobilization." *International Social Movement Research*, 1: 197–218.

Snow, D., E. Rochford, S. Worden, and R. Benford. 1986. "Frame Alignment Processes, Micro-Mobilization, and Movement Participation." *American Sociological Review*, 51: 464–481.

Sobo, E. 2017. *Dynamics of Human Biocultural Diversity: A Unified Approach*. New York: Routledge.

Society of the Plastics Industry. 1988. "Plastic Packaging Resins." American Chemistry Council. http://plastics.americanchemistry.com/Plastic-Resin-Codes-PDF.

Socolow, R. 2011. "Wedges Reaffirmed." *Bulletin of the Atomic Scientists*, September 27. www.thebulletin.org/web-edition/features/wedges-reaffirmed.

Song, X.P. 2018. "Global Estimates of Ecosystem Service Value and Change: Taking into Account Uncertainties in Satellite-Based Land Cover Data. *Ecological Economics*, 143: 227–235.

Sovacool, B. 2008. "Valuing the Greenhouse Gas Emissions from Nuclear Power: A Critical Survey." *Energy Policy*, 36: 2950–2963.

Spence, M. 2009. "Markets Aren't Everything." *Forbes*, October 12. www.forbes.com/2009/10/12/economics-nobel-elinor-ostrom-oliver-williamson-opinions-contributors-michael-spence.html.

Spieler, C. 2018. Trains, Buses, People: An Opinionated Atlas of US Transit. Washington, DC: Island Press.

Spring, J., and A. Boadle. 2019. "Brazil to Fight Invasions by Landless Workers: Official." *Rutgers*, January 14. www.reuters.com/article/us-brazil-landrights/brazil-to-fight-invasions-by-landless-workers-official-idUSKCN1P82AV.

SSA (Self Storage Association). 2019. "Self-Storage Sector Snapshot." March 11. www.sparefoot.com/self-storage/news/1432-self-storage-industry-statistics/.

Staddon, C. 2016. *Managing Europe's Water Resources: Twenty-First Century Challenges*. Abingdon, UK: Routledge.

Stará, J., and F. Kocourek. 2018. "Seven-Year Monitoring of Pyrethroid Resistance in the Pollen Beetle (Brassicogethes aeneus F.) during Implementation of Insect Resistance Management. *Pest Management Science*, 74(1): 200–209.

Statista. 2015. "Per Capita Consumption of Bottled Water Worldwide in 2009 and 2014, by Leading Countries (in Gallons)." www.statista.com/statistics/183388/per-capita-consumption-of-bottled-water-worldwide-in-2009.

Statista. 2019. "Bottled Water." www.statista.com/outlook/20010000/100/bottled-water/worldwide.

Steel, D. 2014. *Philosophy and the Precautionary Principle*. New York: Cambridge University Press.

Stein, P. 2015. "Bike-Share Programs Are Expanding Worldwide; Are They Successful?" *Washington Post*, May 22.

Stephenson, J., F. Berkes, N. Turner, and J. Dick. 2014. "Biocultural Conservation of Marine Ecosystems: Examples from New Zealand and Canada." *Indian Journal of Traditional Knowledge*, 13(2): 257–265.

Stepp J., S. Cervone, H. Castaneda, A. Lasseter, G. Stocks, and Y. Gichon. 2004. "Development of a GIS for Global Biocultural Diversity." *Policy Matters*, 13: 267–270.

Sterling, E., and E. Vintinner. 2012. "How Much Is Left? An Overview of the Crisis." In *A Pivotal Moment: Population, Justice, and the Environmental Challenge*, edited by L. Mazur, pp. 193–204. Washington, DC: Island.

Stern, P. 1999. "Information, Incentives, and Pro-Environmental Consumer Behavior." *Journal of Consumer Policy*, 22: 461–478.

Stern, P.C. 2017. "How Can Social Science Research Become More Influential in Energy Transitions?" *Energy Research & Social Science*, 26: 91–95.

Stern, P., E. Aronson, J. Darley, D. Hill, E. Hirst, W. Kempton, and T. Wilbanks. 1986. "The Effectiveness of Incentives for Residential Energy Conservation." *Evaluation Review*, 10(2): 147–176.

Stern, P.C., I. Wittenberg, K.S. Wolske, and I. Kastner. 2018. "Household Production of Photovoltaic Energy: Issues in Economic Behavior." In *Cambridge Handbook of Psychology and Economic Behaviour*, edited by A. Lewis, pp. 541–566. 2nd edn. New York: Cambridge University Press.

Stolle, D., and M. Micheletti. 2013. *Political Consumerism: Global Responsibility in Action*. Cambridge: Cambridge University Press.

Stone, R. 2011. "The Legacy of the Three Gorges Dam." *Science*, 333(6044): 817.

Stretesky, P.B., and R. McKie. 2016. "A Perspective on the Historical Analysis of Race and Treatment Storage and Disposal Facilities in the United States." *Environmental Research Letters*, 11(3): 031001.

Stuart, D., R. Gunderson, and B. Petersen. 2019. "Climate Change and the Polanyian Counter-Movement: Carbon Markets or Degrowth?" *New Political Economy*, 24(1): 89–102.

Stuart, T. 2009. *Waste: Uncovering the Global Food Scandal*. New York: Norton.

Stutt, J., P. Shattuck, V. Kumar, and D. Sosland. 2017. *Outpacing the Nation: RGGI's environmental and economic success.* Acadia Center. https://acadiacenter.org/wp-content/uploads/2017/09/Acadia-Center_RGGI-Report_Outpacing-the-Nation.pdf.

Swift, P., D. Painter, and M. Goldstein. 2006. "Residential Street Typology and Injury Accident Frequency." VMT Congress of New Urbanism. https://massengale.typepad.com/venustas/files/SwiftSafetyStudy.pdf.

Subbaraman, R., and S. Murthy. 2015. "The Right to Water in the Slums of Mumbai, India." *Bulletin of the World Health Organization*, 93: 815–816. DOI: 10.2471/BLT.15.155473.

Subramaniam, M. 2014. "Neoliberalism and Water Rights: The Case of India." *Current Sociology*, 62(3): 393–411.

Sulemana, I., H.S. James, and C.B. Valdivia. 2016. "Perceived Socioeconomic Status as a Predictor of Environmental Concern in African and Developed Countries." *Journal of Environmental Psychology*, 46: 83–95. DOI: 10.1016/j.jenvp.2016.04.002.

Suneson, G. 2018. "From AMC Networks's Josh Sapan to Broadcom's Hock Tan: These Are the Highest Paid CEOs of 2018." *USA Today*, December 21. www.usatoday.com/story/money/2018/12/21/highest-paid-ceos-2018/38756663/.

Sunstein, C. 2004. "Valuing Life: A Plea for Disaggregation." *Duke Law Journal*, 54: 384–445.

Sunstein, C., and A. Rowell. 2007. "On Discounting Regulatory Benefits: Risk, Money, and Intergenerational Equity." *University of Chicago Law Review*, 74(1): 171–208.

Sutherland, R. 2010. "We Can't Run Away from the Ethical Debates in Marketing." *Market Leader*, January. www.marketing-society.org.uk/SiteCollectionDocuments/knowledge-zone/market-leader/january-2010.pdf.

Swartz, S., and S. Oster. 2010. "China Tops US in Energy Use." *Wall Street Journal*, July 18.

Szasz, A. 2007. *Shopping Our Way to Safety: How We Changed from Protecting the Environment to Protecting Ourselves.* Minneapolis, MN: University of Minnesota Press.

Tanny, N., and M. Rahman. 2016. "Climate Change Vulnerabilities of Women in Bangladesh." *The Agriculturists*, 14(2): 113–123.

Tanzi, A., and W. Lu. 2018. "Tokyo's Reign as World's Largest City Fades." *Bloomberg*, July 13. www.bloomberg.com/news/articles/2018-07-13/tokyo-s-reign-as-world-s-largest-city-fades-demographic-trends.

Taylor, D., C. Taylor, and J. Taylor. 2012. *Empowerment on an Unsustainable Planet*. New York: Oxford University Press.

Taylor, J., and S. Lovell. 2015. "Urban Home Gardens in the Global North: A Mixed Methods Study of Ethnic and Migrant Home Gardens in Chicago, IL." *Renewable Agriculture and Food Systems*, 30(1): 22–32.

Taylor, P., and C. Streck. 2018. "Ending Tropical Deforestation: The Elusive Impact of the Deforestation-Free Supply Chain Movement." *World Resources Institute*, June. https://wriorg.s3.amazonaws.com/s3fs-public/ending-tropical-deforestation-supply-chain-movement.pdf?_ga=2.262785420.1409479234.1553176423-1113961780.1553176423.

Texas A&M Transportation Institute. 2013. "As Traffic Jams Worsen, Commuters Allowing Extra Time for Urgent Trips." College Station, TX, February 5. http://tti.tamu.edu/2013/02/05/as-traffic-jams-worsen-commuters-allowing-extra-time-for-urgent-trips.

The Economist. 2015. "Spring Tide: Pollution Fears Are Driving the Chinese towards Expensive Branded Waters." February 26. www.economist.com/business/2015/02/26/spring-tide.

Thompson, M. 1979. *Rubbish Theory*. New York: Oxford University Press.

Thyberg, K.L., D.J. Tonjes, and J. Gurevitch. 2015. "Quantification of Food Waste Disposal in the United States: A Meta-Analysis." *Environmental Science & Technology*, 49(24): 13946–13953.

Tickner, J. 2003. "The Role of Environmental Science in Precautionary Decision Making." In *Precaution: Environmental Science and Preventive Public Policy*, edited by J. Tickner, pp. 3–20. Washington, DC: Island.

Torres, A., O. Sarmiento, C. Stauber, and R. Zarama. 2013. "The Ciclovia and Cicloruta Programs: Promising Interventions to Promote Physical Activity and Social Capital in Bogotá, Colombia." *American Journal of Public Health*, 103(2): e23–e30.

Toth, G., and C. Szigeti. 2016. "The Historical Ecological Footprint: From Over-Population to Over-Consumption." *Ecological Indicators*, 60: 283–291.

Tranter, P. 2012. "Effective Speed: Cycling Because It's 'Faster.'" In *City Cycling*, edited by J. Pucher and R. Buehler, pp. 57–74. Cambridge, MA: MIT Press.

Tripicchio, G., M. Heo, L. Diewald, S.M. Noar, R. Dooley, A. Pietrobelli, K.S. Burger, and M.S. Faith. 2016. "Restricting Advertisements for High-Fat, High-Sugar Foods during Children's Television Programs: Attitudes in a US Population-Based Sample." *Childhood Obesity*, 12(2): 113–118.

Trzupek, R. 2011. "Natural Gas Will Repower America." *Real Clear Energy*, October 18. www.realclearenergy.org/articles/2011/10/18/natural_gas_will_repower_america_106319.html.

Tuck, S., C. Winqvist, F. Mota, J. Ahnström, L. Turnbull, and J. Bengtsson. 2014. "Land-Use Intensity and the Effects of Organic Farming on Biodiversity: A Hierarchical Meta-Analysis." *Journal of Applied Ecology*, 51: 746–755.

Tuck-Po, L. 2004. *Changing Pathways*. Lanham, MD: Lexington Books.

Tudge, C. 2010. "How to Raise Livestock—and How Not to." In *The Meat Crisis*, edited by J. D'Silva and J. Webster, pp. 9–21. London: Earthscan.

Turner, N.J. 2016. "'We Give Them Seaweed': Social Economic Exchange and Resilience in Northwestern North America." *Indian Journal of Traditional Knowledge*, 15(1): 5–15.

Twidell, J., and T. Weir. 2015. *Renewable Energy Resources*. New York: Routledge.

UNDP (United Nations Development Programme). 1990. *Human Development Report, 1990*. New York: Oxford University Press.

UNEP (United Nations Environmental Programme). 2007. *Declaration of the Rights of Indigenous People*. Sixty-first Session, UN General Assembly, New York.

UNICEF 2018. "Maternal and Newborn Health Disparities, Ethiopia." https://data.unicef.org/wp-content/uploads/country_profiles/Ethiopia/country%20profile_ETH.pdf.

United Nations. 2002. "General Comment No. 15." Economic and Social Council, United Nations, New York. www.citizen.org/documents/ACF2B4B.pdf.

United Nations. 2004. "World Population to 2020." Economic and Social Affairs, United Nations, New York. www.un.org/esa/population/publications/longrange2/WorldPop2300final.pdf.

United Nations. 2005. "Fact Sheet 7: Mega Cities." Working Paper No. ESA/P/WP/200. Economic and Social Affairs, Population Division, United Nations, New York. www.jkgeography.com/uploads/1/0/8/4/108433405/un_mega_cities_fact_sheet.pdf.

United Nations. 2010. *Solid Waste Management in the World's Cities*. London: Earthscan.

United Nations. 2013. *Global Food and Nutrition Scenarios: Final Report*. Millennium Institute, United Nations, Washington, DC. www.un.org/en/development/desa/policy/wess/wess_bg_papers/bp_wess2013_millennium_inst.pdf.

United Nations. 2014. "Should International Refugee Law Accommodate Climate Change?" *United Nations News*, July 3. www.un.org/apps/news/story.asp?NewsID=48201#.VYqUa2CI1UQ.

United Nations. 2015a. "Energy." United Nations Habitat. http://unhabitat.org/urban-themes/energy.

United Nations. 2015b. *The Millennium Development Goals Report 2015*. www.un.org/millenniumgoals/2015_MDG_Report/pdf/MDG%202015%20rev%20(July%201).pdf.

United Nations. 2018. "68% of the World Population Projected to Live in Urban Areas by 2050, says UN." www.un.org/development/desa/en/news/population/2018-revision-of-world-urbanization-prospects.html.

United Nations. 2019. "World Population Prospects." https://population.un.org/wpp/Graphs/.

United States Code, 2000: Title 22, Foreign Relations and Intercourse. 2002. Washington, DC: US Government Printing Office.

US Bureau of Reclamation. 2015. "Lower Colorado River Operations Schedule." www.usbr.gov/lc/region/g4000/hourly/rivops.html.

US Department of Energy. 2016. "Life Cycle Analysis of Natural Gas Extraction and Power Generation." www.osti.gov/biblio/1480993-life-cycle-analysis-natural-gas-extraction-power-generation.

US Department of Energy. 2018. "Global Ethanol Production." https://afdc.energy.gov/files/u/data/data_source/10331/10331_world_ethanol_production.xlsx.

US Federal Highway Administration. 2018. "Explore Vehicle Trips Data." https://nhts.ornl.gov/vehicle-trips.

Val, V., P.M. Rosset, C. Zamora Lomelí, O.F. Giraldo, and D. Rocheleau. 2019. "Agroecology and La Via Campesina I. The Symbolic and Material Construction of Agroecology through the Dispositive of 'Peasant-to-Peasant' processes." *Agroecology and Sustainable Food Systems*, 43(7–8): 872–894. DOI: 10.1080/21683565.2019.1600099.

van den Bosch, R. 1978. *The Pesticide Conspiracy*. Garden City, NY: Doubleday.

Vandergeest, P. 1996. "Mapping Nature: Territorialization of Forest Rights in Thailand." *Society and Natural Resources*, 9: 159–175.

van der Hoek, W., F. Konradsen, K. Athukorala, and T. Wanigadewa. 1998. "Pesticide Poisoning: A Major Health Problem in Sri Lanka." *Social Science and Medicine*, 46(4): 495–504.

van der Voort, T., P. Nikken, and J. van Lil. 1992. "Determinants of Parental Guidance of Children's Television Viewing: A Dutch Replication Study." *Journal of Broadcasting and Electronic Media*, 36(1): 61–74.

Veblen, T. (1899) 1967. *The Theory of the Leisure Class: An Economic Study of Institutions*. New York: Funk and Wagnalls.

Verheijen, F., S. Jeffery, M. van der Velde, V. Penížek, M. Beland, A. Bastos, and J. Keizer. 2013. "Reductions in Soil Surface Albedo as a Function of Biochar Application Rate: Implications for Global Radiative Forcing." *Environmental Research Letters*, 8(4): 044008.

Vervoort, W. 2014. "Dams Are Not the Smart Way to Secure Water for Agriculture." *Conversation*, October 21. http://theconversation.com/dams-are-not-the-smart-way-to-secure-water-for-agriculture-33193.

Vickery, J., and L.M. Hunter. 2016. "Native Americans: Where in Environmental Justice Theory and Research?" *Society & Natural Resources*, 29(1): 36–52.

Vickrey, W. 1968. "Automobile Accidents, Tort Law, Externalities, and Insurance: An Economist's Critique." *Law and Contemporary Problems*, 33: 464–487.

Victor, P. 2019. *Managing without Growth: Slower by Design, Not Disaster*. 2nd edition. Northampton, MA: Edward Elgar.

Vidal, J. 2015. "Water Privatisation: A Worldwide Failure?" *Guardian*, January 30. www.theguardian.com/global-development/2015/jan/30/water-privatisation-worldwide-failure-lagos-world-bank.

Vijayan, V. 1987. *Keoladeo National Park Ecology Study*. Bombay: Bombay Natural History Society.

Vijayan, V. 1991. *Keoladeo National Park Ecology Study, 1980–1990*. Bombay: Bombay Natural History Society.

Voelcker, J. 2014. "1.2 Billion Vehicles on World's Roads Now, 2 Billion by 2035: Report." *Green Car Reports*, July 29. www.greencarreports.com/news/1093560_1-2-billion-vehicles-on-worlds-roads-now-2-billion-by-2035-report.

Vohs, K.D., N.L. Mead, and M.R. Goode. 2006. "The Psychological Consequences of Money." *Science*, 314(5802): 1154–1156.

Wallich, H. 1972. "Zero Growth." *Newsweek*, January 24, p. 62.

Wang, X., C. Shao, C. Yin, and C. Zhuge. 2018. "Exploring the Influence of Built Environment on Car Ownership and Use with a Spatial Multilevel Model: A Case Study of Changchun, China." *International Journal of Environmental Research and Public Health*, 15(9): 1868. https://doi.org/10.3390/ijerph15091868.

Watson, I. 2013. "China: The Electronic Wastebasket of the World." *CNN*, May 30. www.cnn.com/2013/05/30/world/asia/china-electronic-waste-e-waste.

Watts, J. 2011. "Fukushima Disaster: It's Not Over Yet." *Guardian* (London), September 9.

Watts, J. 2017. "Third of Earth's Soil Is Acutely Degraded Due to Agriculture." *Guardian* September 12. www.theguardian.com/environment/2017/sep/12/third-of-earths-soil-acutely-degraded-due-to-agriculture-study.

Watts, N., W.N. Adger, S. Ayeb-Karlsson, Y. Bai, P. Byass, D. Campbell-Lendrum, T. Colbourn, P. Cox, M. Davies, M. Depledge, and A. Depoux. 2017. "The Lancet Countdown: Tracking Progress on Health and Climate Change." *The Lancet*, 389(10074): 1151–1164.

Weinberg, A. 1972. "Science and Trans-Science." *Minerva*, 10: 209–222.

Weiner, J. 2015. "The Hidden Costs of Being an Uber Driver." *Washington Post*, February 20. www.washingtonpost.com/news/get-there/wp/2015/02/20/the-hidden-costs-of-being-an-uber-driver/?utm_term=.5540ab991241.

Welling, R. 2019. "The Tacaná Watersheds: Implementing Transboundary Water Governance through Local Community Ecosystem Based Action." International Union for Conservation of Nature, March 22. https://panorama.solutions/en/solution/tacana-watersheds-implementing-transboundary-water-governance-through-local-community.

Werner, A., S. Vink, K. Watt, and P. Jagals. 2015. "Environmental Health Impacts of Unconventional Natural Gas Development: A Review of the Current Strength of Evidence." *Science of the Total Environment*, 505: 1127–1141.

Wesseling, C., L. Castillo, and C. Elinder. 1993. "Pesticide Poisonings in Costa Rica." *Scandinavian Journal of Work, Environment and Health*, 19(4): 227–235.

Wheeler, D. 2011. *Quantifying Vulnerability to Climate Change: Implications for Adaptation Assistance*. Working Paper 240 (January). Center for Global Development, Washington, DC. http://re.indiaenvironmentportal.org.in/files/file_Wheeler_Quantifying_Vulnerability_FINAL.pdf.

White, L. 1967. "The Historical Roots of Our Ecologic Crisis." *Science*, 155: 1203–1207.

Whitehead, A.N. (1920) 1964. *Concept of Nature*. Cambridge: Cambridge University Press.

White House. 2014. "Fact Sheet: The Economic Challenge Posed by Declining Pollinator Populations." Office of the Press Secretary, Washington, DC, June 20. www.whitehouse.gov/the-press-office/2014/06/20/fact-sheet-economic-challenge-posed-declining-pollinator-populations.

White House. 2019. "The Trump Economic Boom is Benefiting All Americans." White House News Clips, May 6. www.whitehouse.gov/briefings-statements/trump-economic-boom-benefiting-americans/.

WHO (World Health Organization). n.d. "DALYs/YLDs Definition." www.who.int/mental_health/management/depression/daly/en/.

WHO (World Health Organization). 2011. *Burden of Disease from Environmental Noise: Quantification of Healthy Life Years Lost in Europe*. Geneva. www.euro.who.int/__data/assets/pdf_file/0008/136466/e94888.pdf.

WHO (World Health Organization). 2012. "WHO Definition of Health." Geneva. www.who.int/about/definition/en/print.html (accessed May 19, 2012).

WHO (World Health Organization). 2018a. *Global Status Report on Road Safety 2018*. Geneva. www.who.int/violence_injury_prevention/road_safety_status/2018/en/.

WHO (World Health Organization). 2018b. "Road Traffic Injuries." Geneva. www.who.int/news-room/fact-sheets/detail/road-traffic-injuries.

Wichelns, D. 2010. *Agricultural Water Pricing: United States*. Organisation for Economic Co-operation and Development. www.oecd.org/unitedstates/45016437.pdf.

Wiedmann, T., and M. Lenzen. 2018. "Environmental and Social Footprints of International Trade." *Nature Geoscience*, 11(5): 314–321.

Wiener-Bronner, D. 2019. "Forget Plastic Straws: Starbucks Has a Cup Problem." *CNN.com*, February 27. www.cnn.com/interactive/2019/02/business/starbucks-cup-problem/index.html (accessed March 18, 2019).

Wieser, S., B. Brunner, C. Tzogiou, R. Plessow, M.B. Zimmermann, J. Farebrother, S. Soofi, Z. Bhatti, I. Ahmed, and Z.A. Bhutta. 2018. "Reducing Micronutrient Deficiencies in Pakistani Children: Are Subsidies on Fortified Complementary Foods Cost-Effective?" *Public Health Nutrition*, 21(15): 2893–2906.

Wilkinson, R., and K. Pickett. 2011. *The Spirit Level: Why More Equal Societies Are Almost Always Better*. New York: Penguin Books.

Wilkinson, R., K. Pickett, and R. De Vogli. 2010. "Equality, Sustainability, and Quality of Life." *BMJ*, 341: c5816.

Willett, W., J. Rockström, B. Loken, M. Springmann, T. Lang, S. Vermeulen, T. Garnett, D. Tilman, F. DeClerck, A. Wood, and M. Jonell. 2019. "Food in the Anthropocene: The EAT–Lancet Commission on Healthy Diets from Sustainable Food Systems." *The Lancet*, 393(10170): 447–492.

Williams, D.S., M. Máñez Costa, C. Sutherland, L. Celliers, and J. Scheffran. 2019. "Vulnerability of Informal Settlements in the Context of Rapid Urbanization and Climate Change. *Environment and Urbanization*, 31(1): 157–176. https://doi.org/10.1177/0956247818819694.

Williamson, T. 2002. "Sprawl, Politics, and Participation: A Preliminary Analysis." *National Civic Review*, 91(3): 235–244.

Wilson, E.O. (1992) 1999. *The Diversity of Life*. New York: Norton.

Wily, L. 1999. "Moving Forward in African Community Forestry: Trading Power, Not Use Rights." *Society & Natural Resources*, 12(1): 49–61.

WNA (World Nuclear Association). 2015. "World Nuclear Power Reactors and Uranium Requirements." London. www.world-nuclear.org/info/Facts-and-Figures/World-Nuclear-Power-Reactors-and-Uranium-Requirements.

Wolske, K.S., and P.C. Stern. 2018. "Contributions of Psychology to Limiting Climate Change: Opportunities through Consumer Behavior." *Psychology and Climate Change: Human Perceptions, Impacts, and Responses*, edited by Susan Clayton and Christie Manning, pp. 127–160. London: Academic Press.

Wolsko, C., H. Ariceaga, and J. Seiden. 2016. "Red, White, and Blue Enough to Be Green: Effects of Moral Framing on Climate Change Attitudes and Conservation Behaviors." *Journal of Experimental Social Psychology*, 65: 7–19.

Wood, D. 1993. "The Power of Maps." *Scientific American*, 268(5): 88–94.

Woodworth, B., M. Steen-Adams, and P. Mittal. 2011. "Role of an Environmental Studies Course on the Formation of Environmental Worldviews: A Case Study of a Core Curriculum Requirement Using the NEP Scale." *Journal of Environmental Studies and Sciences*, 1(2): 126–137.

World Bank. 2011. *The Changing Wealth of Nations: Measuring Sustainable Development in the New Millennium. Environment and Development*. Washington, DC. http://hdl.handle.net/10986/2252.

World Bank. 2012. *What a Waste: A Global Review of Solid Waste Management*. Washington, DC. http://siteresources.worldbank.org/INTURBANDEVELOPMENT/Resources/336387-1334852610766/What_a_Waste2012_Final.pdf.

World Bank. 2015a. "Data: Indicators." http://data.worldbank.org/indicator.

World Bank. 2015b. "Natural Capital Accounting." www.worldbank.org/en/topic/environment/brief/environmental-economics-natural-capital-accounting.

World Bank. 2015c. "Renewable Internal Freshwater Resources per Capita." http://data.worldbank.org/indicator/ER.H2O.INTR.PC.

World Bank. 2017. "Chart: Globally, 70% of Freshwater Is Used for Agriculture." https://blogs.worldbank.org/opendata/chart-globally-70-freshwater-used-agriculture.

World Bank. 2018. "Groundswell: Preparing for Internal Climate Migration." World Bank, Washington, DC. http://hdl.handle.net/10986/29461.

World Bank Group. 2018. *What a Waste 2.0: A Global Snapshot of Solid Waste Management to 2050*. World Bank, Washington, DC. https://openknowledge.worldbank.org/bitstream/handle/10986/30317/9781464813290.pdf.

World Coal Association. n.d. "Resources" www.worldcoal.org/resources/statistics.

World Nuclear Association. 2019. "Nuclear power in the world today." www.world-nuclear.org/information-library/current-and-future-generation/nuclear-power-in-the-world-today.aspx.

Wu, W., X. Yize, L. Guangchun, Z. Weilin, L. Hualiang, R. Shannon, and X. Yanjun. 2013. "Temperature–Mortality Relationship in Four Subtropical Chinese Cities: A Time-Series Study Using a Distributed Lag Non-Linear Model." *Science of the Total Environment*, 449: 355–362.

Wynne, B. 2002. "Risk and Environment as Legitimatory Discourses of Technology: Reflectivity Inside and Out?" *Current Sociology*, 50: 459–477.

Xichuan, H. 2014. "A Canal Too Far." *The Economist*, September 27.

Xing, Y., Z. Li, Y. Fan, and H. Hou. 2010. "Biohydrogen Production from Dairy Manures with Acidification Pretreatment by Anaerobic Fermentation." *Environmental Science and Pollution Research*, 17(2): 392–399.

Yin, X. 2019. "New Gold Rush in Protected Yanomami Indigenous Area in Brazil." *The Rio Times*, July 8. https://riotimesonline.com/brazil-news/brazil/new-gold-rush-in-indigenous-protected-areas-in-brazil-threatens-yanomami/.

York, R. 2006. "Review of *Cultures of Environmentalism* by Steve Yearly." *Organization and Environment*, 19: 142–144.

York, R. 2010. "The Paradox at the Heart of Modernity: The Carbon Efficiency of the Global Economy." *International Journal of Sociology*, 40(2): 6–22.

York, R., and S.E. Bell. 2019. "Energy Transitions or Additions?: Why a Transition from Fossil Fuels Requires More Than the Growth of Renewable Energy." *Energy Research & Social Science*, 51: 40–43.

York, R., E. Rosa, and T. Dietz. 2003. "Footprints on the Earth: The Environmental Consequences of Modernity." *American Sociological Review*, 68(2): 279–300.

Yu, K. 2018. "Thousands of Dirty Water Bottles Bring to Light China's Water Woes." *SBS News*, July 9. www.sbs.com.au/news/thousands-of-dirty-water-bottles-bring-to-light-china-s-water-woes.

Yuwono, A.S., and N.S. Ersa. 2018. "Evaluation of Medical Solid Waste Management: A Case Study of Two Hospitals in Bogor, Indonesia." *International Journal of Applied Environmental Sciences*, 13(3): 323–337.

Zafrilla, J., A. Cadarso, F. Monsalve, and C. de la Rúa. 2014. "How Carbon-Friendly Is Nuclear Energy? A Hybrid MRIO-LCA Model of a Spanish Facility." *Environmental Science & Technology*, 48(24): 14103–14111.

Zarfl, C., A. Lumsdon, J. Berlekamp, L. Tydecks, and K. Tockner. 2015. "A Global Boom in Hydropower Dam Construction." *Aquatic Sciences*, 77(1): 161–170.

Zezza, A., and L. Tasciotti. 2010. "Urban Agriculture, Poverty, and Food Security: Empirical Evidence from a Sample of Developing Countries." *Food Policy*, 35: 265–273.

Zhang, J., and C.Y.C.L. Lawell. 2017. "The Macroeconomic Rebound Effect in China." *Energy Economics*, 67: 202–212.

Zhang, W. 2018. "Global Pesticide Use: Profile, Trend, Cost/Benefit and More." *Proceedings of the International Academy of Ecology and Environmental Sciences*, 8(1): 1–27.

Zhang W.J., and G.H. Liu. 2017. "Situation and Development of Worldwide Agri-environment: Agricultural Land Uses, Fertilizers Consumption and Carbon Dioxide Equivalent Emissions." *Environmental Skeptics and Critics*, 6(1): 1–8.

Zhang, Y., X. Bai, F.P. Mills, and J.C. Pezzey. 2018. "Rethinking the Role of Occupant Behavior in Building Energy Performance: A Review." *Energy and Buildings*, 172: 279–294.

Zhou, Y., N. Li, W. Wenxiang, W. Jidong, and S. Peijun. 2014. "Local Spatial and Temporal Factors Influencing Population and Societal Vulnerability to Natural Disasters." *Risk Analysis*, 34(4): 614–639.

Zwart, H. 1997. "What Is an Animal? A Philosophical Reflection on the Possibility of a Moral Relationship with Animals." *Environmental Values*, 6: 377–392.

Index

Page numbers in **bold** denote tables, those in *italics* denote figures.

abject poverty 25, 256
Abram, D. 286
absolute efficiency 210
absolute sustainability 243–6
adaptation 29, 38
advertisements 290–3
advertising 288–90
African Americans: heat index and 22
agriculture 75–6, 183; diet 178; environmental
    sustainability 178; industrial 170; mechanization of
    163; national development and sovereignty 178;
    public health 178; rural development 178; structure
    of 162; "treadmills" of 175–7; water 99–103
agrobiodiversity: conservation 84–7
agroecology 177–9
air pollution 155, 158, 220
Amazon 268
Amazon Effect 66
American Automobile Association 140
American Buffalo Skulls pile *69*
American Coalition for Clean Coal Electricity 190
anaerobic decomposition 47
annual global vehicle sales 158
apolitical ecologies 227
apolitical ecology 227
arable land 122, 123
Asda 58
Athens, cityscape *119*
atmospheric regulation 77
attitudes: behaviors, relationship 10–12
auto insurance 157
automobile, transportation 10
automobile reliance 148
avian endemism 74
Ayres, Robert 266

baby bananas 176

Back to the Future, Part III (1990) 7
Bahamas 24
Barcelona Convention 247
behavioral realism 35
behaviors: attitudes, relationship 10–12; change 130
Bekoff, Marc 73
Bell, Shannon 211, 212
Berlin, Isaiah 226, 273
Beyond Coal and Gas Jamboree 2018; Australia *32*
Beyond Coal campaign 32
Bharatpur Bird Sanctuary 74
bicycle parking 152
"Big Mike" 176
bikes 8
bike-share programs 151
biochar 41
biocultural diversity 77–8
biodiversity 68–87; agrobiodiversity conservation 84–7;
    biocultural diversity 77–8; biopiracy 78–80;
    changing definitions of 70–4; community
    conservation 80–4; fuel driving ecosystem services
    75–7; habitat and 145–8; hotspots 24, 74;
    implications 70–80; solutions 80–7; threats to **71**
biodiversity-dependent services 68
biofortification 175
biohazards 52
biopiracy 78–80
bioprospecting 78
birth control methods 130
birth rates 115
blue water footprint 90
Bombay Natural History Society 74
"bonding" social capital 147
Boserup, Ester 133, 134
Boserup effect 134
bottled water: top global consumers of **95**
Bowling Alone 147

Brazil 70
"bridging" social capital 147
A Brief History of Neoliberalism 226
Brisbane city council wildlife corridor *146*
Brown v. *Board of Education of Topeka* 305
Bullard, Robert 263
butane 193
buycott 298
buyer power 59
buy-one-get-one (BOGO) free promotion 59

Calabresi, Guido 234
Campos, Silvia 176
cap and trade programs 39
capitalism 214, 216; contradiction of 216, 218
capitals, rural development 274
capital shaping humans, contradiction 221
carbon capture, incentivizing 191
"Carbon Colonialism" 41
carbon credits 39
carbon dioxide (CO_2) 18; equivalent 21; fertilizer effect
    24; removal 38
Carbon Disclosure Project (CDP) 37
carbon emission reductions **36**
carbon emissions 33
carbon markets 39–41
carbon offsets 39–41
carbon tax 38, 203
Caribbean Sea islands 24
carshare vehicles 152
Carson, Rachel 1, 251
Carter, Jimmy 199
ceramic cup, uses *50*
Cheonggyecheon stream, daylighting: in South Korea
    155
China's water woes 94
choice riders *versus* dependent rides 156
Christian theology 9
cities with ten million inhabitants **120**
Clark, B. 218
clean coal 190
clean water 225
climate change 6, 17, 90, 158, 224, 233; behavioral
    change 35; carbon markets and offsets 39–41;
    children, women, and elderly 25–7; competition 30;
    conflict 30; discourses of 233; environmental
    movements 31–3; ethnic tension 30; fault lines 30;
    food-related vulnerabilities, populations 26; food
    security 24–5; green building 35–7; implications
    19–30; population displacement 30; refugees 28–30;
    solutions 31–41; stabilization triangle and wedges
    33–4; urban and health impacts of **23**; urban areas
    20–4; US public's knowledge of 19; water 103; weak
    states 30; wine industry and 25; women and
    vulnerability *27*
climate change counter movement neutralization
    techniques **289**
climate engineering *see* geoengineering
climate refugees: Indonesia and Bangladesh 29

Closed Loop Fund 66
close loop fund 53
cloud 193
Club of Rome 115
CO_2 emissions 33; countries, fair share 122
coal 32, 188
The Coal Question 209
Coase, Ronald 224
Coase theorem 224
Cochrane, Willard 175
collaborative consumption 293–7
collective coverage 59, **60**
collective mobilization 3
Colorado Oil and Gas Conservation Commission
    (COGCC) 197
Colpaart, Ashley 295
commercial shrimp farms and slavery 266
commodification 73
commodities for sale **164–5**
commodity chain 49
common-property regimes 242
common-property resource 242, 243
communitarian values 282
community capitals framework 274
community conservation 80–4
community garden, Denver *184*
community severance 148
Concentrated Animal Feeding Operations (CAFOs)
    163, 170, 171
conservation decision making **82**
conservation maps power 75
conservative think tanks (CTTs) 288
conspicuous consumption 260
consumerism 288–90
contingent valuation studies 298
controlled landfills 45
Convention of Biological Diversity (CBD) 39, 79, 80
cornucopian 134
corporate social responsibility 233
Costanza, R. 72
cost–benefit analyses 233–6
countermovements 286–8
Cowen, T. 236
crude oil reserves 189
cultural hotspots 77

Dahr, Julia 28
Daly, Herman 251, 267
Dams 239
Dawson, T.P. 24
daylighting 155
dead zones 167
death causes, age **144**
decision stakes 235
decoupling 214
Delaney Clause 246, 247
Delucchi, Mark 152
democracy 123
demographic inertia 128, 131

demographic transition model 125, 126
denial 286–8
desalinization 104; in California 105
Despommier, D. 135
Dewey, John 304
Dickens, Peter 221
Dietz, T. 33, 118, 241
diminishing marginal utility 255
disability-adjusted life-years (DALYs) 145, 172
discounting 236–8; and forest management 237
disease vectors 68
dishwashers 49
dollar vans 159
down-cycling 65
Dumping in Dixie 263
Dunlap, Riley 11, 296, 300
Duru-Haitemba woodlands 82

ecocide 265
ecofeminism 284
ecological footprint per capita 116
ecological solutions 2
economic growth 213, 256
economic sustainability 81
economic well-being 233
economism 264
ecosystem 74; services 68, 72
effective speed 143
efficiency shifting 210
egalitarian values 282
Ehrlich, Paul 116
electronic databases 62
Elwha River Ecosystems and Fisheries Restoration Act
    239
embodied energy 46
Endangered Species Act of 1973 246, 304
energy curtailment 199
energy efficiency, passenger modes **150**
energy intensity 209
energy production 187–205; clean coal 190–1; efficiency
    and curtailment 199–202; hydraulic fracturing (aka
    fracking) 191–5; implications 189–98; incentivizing
    renewables and household efficiency 203–5; nuclear
    power 195–8; renewables 202–3; solutions 198–202
energy transitions *212*; and social sciences 202
energy waste: and life-cycle analysis 49–50
Engels, F. 218
environmental and social costs, pesticides **101**
environmental anxiety 1
environmental concern globalization 296
environmental degradation 251
environmental education 3
environmentalism 31, 288
environmental justice 262–4; in China 275; movements
    273
Environmental Kuznets Curve 220–2
environmental movements 31–3
environmental problems 1
Environmental Protection Agency (EPA) 240

environmental racism 263
environmental skepticism 288
environmental sociologist 4
environmental sociology 11
environmental solutions 1
environmental sustainability 81
The Environment: From Surplus to Scarcity 215
Essay on Population 123
ethane 193
Ethiopia: family planning 130
evangelical protestant affiliation 281
everyone needs water *107*
e-waste 61–2; and public health 62
Exelon Corporation 196
exponential growth 115
ex situ conservation 77
extended producer responsibility (EPR) 64–6
externality 203
extrinsic values 289, 290

fair trade 228
fair *versus* free trade 226–30
family-friendly labor policies 8
family planning, Ethiopia 130
family planning programs 127
famine-related suffering 123
Federal Energy Regulatory Commission 239
feeding: automobile population 124; nonhuman animal
    population 123–4
fermentation 18
fermenting bacteria 18
fertility rates 117
fight against packaging 64
Filmmaker's Diary notes 28
fisheries 76
fish in fish out (FIFO) ratio 169
fishing communities 26
Fishman, Elliot 151
flash flooding 109
flavors, community conservation 81
Fleurbaey, M. 245
food 162–84; agroecology 177–9; community impacts
    170; environmental impacts 167–9; implications
    167–77; La Via Campesina and peasant-based
    movements 179–83; malnutrition and green
    revolution 171–5; population 121–3; solutions
    177–84; "treadmills" of agriculture 175–7; urban
    gardens 183–4
Food and Agriculture Organization (FAO) 24, 26, 53,
    124, 163, 168
food loss flows *46*
food security 24–5
The Food Sharing Revolution 297
food sovereignty movement: dominant model **182**; in
    Ecuador 181; World Forum on 181
food waste 53–9
footprint shifting 49
forest management: and discounting 237
forests 75, 76

Forest Transition Theory (FTT) 223
fossil fuels 41; emissions 193
Foster, John Bellamy 215, 216
Foucauldian governance 227
fracking 191–5
fracking plastic 194
framing processes 303
freedom 290–3
free parking 152, 158
fuel 8
fuel driving ecosystem services 75–7; agriculture 75–6;
    atmospheric regulation 77; fisheries 76; forests 76;
    water 77
fuel-saving technologies 157
Fukushima nuclear disaster 198
full irrigation 167
Funtowicz, S. 235
future aid 245

garbage burning, New York City *44*
Gardner, G. 301
gendered norms 27
genetically engineered (GE) food 38
Geneva Convention of 1949 106
geoengineering 38–9
Geographic Information Systems (GIS) 194
ghost ships 266
Gille, Zsuzsa 56
global average water footprint **102**
global carbon intensity 210
Global Climate Change Convention 247
global energy consumption *213*
global fish stocks 219
global food system 167
global land grab 122
global mean caloric consumption 24
global warming 17, 19
Goldschmidt, Walter 170
Goldschmidt thesis 170, 184
Gould, K. 215
governance 232–48; absolute sustainability 243–6;
    implications 233–40; precautionary principle 246–8;
    self-interested straw person 238–40; solutions
    240–8; tragedy to drama 240–3; tyranny of present,
    discounting 236–8; welfare economics and cost–
    benefit analyses 233–6
grand narratives 2
grassland management, Inner Mongolia 241
grassroots organizations 108
Great Pacific garbage patch 48
Great Recession 159
green building 35–7
greenhouse effect 18, 31
greenhouse gases 17–41; emissions 138, 141; population
    117
green revolution 171–5, 177
green water footprint 90
grey water footprint 90
Gros Michel banana 176

gross domestic product (GDP) 127, 252, 271
Grossman, G. 220
groundwater 103
Gruppi di Aquisto Soledale (GAS) 229

habitat fragmentation 145, 146
Happy Life Years (HLYs) 257
Happy Planet Index (HPI) 271, 272
Hardin, Garret 240–2
Harris, L. 75
Harvey, David 96, 226
Hawaii, Hurricanes *30*
Hazen, H. 75
heat index 22
heat island effect 20, *22*
Heinzerling, Lisa 236
Hickel, Jason 253
high density polyethylene (HDPE) 54
higher quality diets 46
high-occupancy vehicle (HOV) lanes 153
highway congestion, fundamental law 152
Hippocratic Oath 247
"The Historical Roots of Our Ecologic Crisis" 9
household income 140; annual miles per driver by **140**
House of Lords 54, 59
Hughes, Thomas 7
Human Development Index (HDI) 271, *272*, 274
human health 68
human-induced climate change 17
human-power mobility, Netherlands 10
Hume, David 285
hydraulic fracturing (aka fracking) 191–5
hydrologic extremes 104
hypoxia 167

implicatory denial 286
indigenous knowledge 79
individual freedoms 283
individualism 2–4
individualist thinking 3
individual responsibility 283
industrial agriculture 170
industrial-grade dishwashers 49
industrialized farms, negative impacts 171
industrial livestock farms 163
inequality and growth 3, 251–75; consumption sociology
    259–64; environmental justice 262–4; freedom,
    justice, and empowerment, development 273–5;
    implications 252–9; level of 267; planned
    obsolescence 261–2; postgrowth society 264–72;
    rethinking growth 253–9; self-identity creation 260;
    social comparison 260; sociotechnical systems
    260–1; solutions 264–75; specialization 260
infectious disease, limits 68
informal settlements 20
Inglehart, Ronald 296
INRIX 2018 Global Traffic Scorecard 143
in situ conservation 77
interconnected street model 154

Intergovernmental Panel on Climate Change (IPCC) 24
International Monetary Fund (IMF) 97
intrinsic values 289
inverted quarantine 96
IPAT model 118
Ipsos poll 2018 1
irreplaceable bee 76
irrigation efficiency 167
islandization 146

Jacques, P. 287, 288
Japan: rapidly shrinking country 126
Jefferson, Thomas 243
Jevons, William Stanley 209
Jevons paradox 209
Jewell, Sally 239
Jones, R. 296

Kellogg's six-hour day 269
Kelly, Kevin 293
Keynes, John Maynard 267
Khoury, Colin 175
King Coal 32
Kisilu: The Climate Diaries 28
knowledge 284
Kopp, R. 245
Krueger, A. 220
Kuznets, Simon 220
Kyoto Protocol 40, 259
Kysar, Douglas 236, 238

landfills 45
Landless Workers' Movement (MST) 180
large taxpayer-funded roads 152
La Via Campesina: representatives of *179*
La Via Campesina (Peasant Way) 179–83
laws of ecology 6
learned helplessness 282
least-developed countries (LDCs) 127, 128
Leggett, Jeremy 247
Liebig, Justus von 216
life-cycle analysis (LCA) 49–51
The Life Earth Global Warming Survival Handbook 199
lifestyle 260
light-emitting diodes (LEDs) 135
literal denial 286
Litman, Todd 152
London congestion charge 160
low density polyethylene (LDPE) 54
low-elevation coastal zones (LECZ) 23, 24
Lower Elwha Klallam Tribe 239

MacKenzie, D. 78
macroeconomic rebound effect 210
Madison, James 243
Mahbub ul Haq 271
malnutrition 171–5
Malthus, Thomas 123
market concentration 59

market environmentalism 96
marketization 288–90
Marx, Karl 216–18
Massachusetts v. *EPA* (549 US 497 [2007]) 238, 240
material things, momentum 7–10
maternal mortality ratio 130
Mather, Alexander 223
McCarthy, J. 304
McFly, Marty 7
McKie, R.E. 288
mechanical revolution 162
megacities 103, 135
memory banks 86
memory making 86
Merchant, C. 284
metabolic rift 9, 216–19
methane 18
Meyer, D.S. 287
micronutrient deficiencies 172
micronutrient malnutrition 172
micro transit movement 159
micro-watershed councils: in Mexico and Guatemala 109
Mill, John Stuart 266, 270
Millennium Ecosystem Assessment 252
Miombo woodlands 82
Mishan, Ezra 288
mitigation 38; strategies 31
mixed recycling program 11
Mobile Bay jubilee 169
mobility services 158
monetary wealth 245
"money makes you a jerk" thesis 291
monocultures 175
Moore, Patrick 195
moral framing, conservation behaviors 87
mountaintop removal mining 192
multimodality 151
municipal solid waste (MSW) 45, 51, 52, 61; management 63–4
Municipal Transportation Association (MUNI) 159
Myungbak, Lee 155

National Biodiversity Authority (NBA) 80
National Environmental Policy Act of 1969 246
national fertility rates 117
National Water Policy 100
Native Americans: plight of 265
natural capital 212–13
natural ecological processes 6
naturalistic fallacy 285
Nature 69
Nazarea, Virginia 78
negative externalities 224
negative freedom 226
neoliberalism 96, 100, 226
neo-Malthusians 123
Nestlé 80, 108
Netherlands 1

Netting, Robert 242
Neumayer, Eric 237
New Environmental Paradigm (NEP) 298–9
nitrous oxide 18
noise pollution 158
nongovernmental organizations (NGOs) 110
nonpoint-source pollution 109
Norgaard, K. 286–7
normal accidents 198
Normal Accidents 198
North Pacific Gyre 48
Nuclear Energy Agency 195
nuclear power: life cycle of 195, *197*; plants 188

objective facts 4
ocean fertilization 38
O'Connor, James 218
"Of the Economy of Fuel" 209
one-child policy, China 115, *128*
O'Neill, D.W. 253
Open Source Seed Initiative (OSSI) 85
open source seeds 85
organic system 178
Ostrom, Elinor 242, 305

Pampel, F. 300
Pareto optimality standard 234
Parfit, D. 236
Paris Agreement 259
participatory forest management: in Kenya 84
patent law 79
patriarchal norms 26
pay-as-you-drive auto insurance 157
peak car 158
peasant-based movements 179–83
peer-to-peer renting 293
per capita food lost/wasted *57*
per capita freshwater supply 89
per capita greenhouse gas emissions 132
Perrow, Charles 198
Peterson, Anna 305
Pigou, Arthur Cecil 224
Pigovian taxes 224
planned obsolescence 261–2
plastic packaging resins **55–6**
plastic waste 52
Plessy v. *Ferguson* US 305
point-source pollution 109
political economy 13, 209–30; contradiction of
    capitalism 218; environmental goods and bads
    globalization 219–20; Environmental Kuznets
    Curve 220–2; fair *versus* free trade 226–30; growth
    imperative 214–15; implications 213–22; internal
    contradictions 216; metabolic rift 216–18; solutions
    222–30; total cost accounting 224–6; treadmill of
    production 215; world-systems framework 222
political opportunity approach 304
pollution 48, 285; and public health 141–5; trans-pacific
    transportation of 232–48

Pollution Haven Hypothesis (PHH) 221
polycultures 177
polyethylene terephthalate (PET) 54
polypropylene (PP) 54
polystyrene (PS) 54
polyvinyl chloride (PVC) 54
Popper, Karl 248
popular epidemiology 61
population 115–35; cities, future role 131–3; CO_2
    emissions growth **118**; Ethiopia 130; feeding,
    automobile population 124; feeding, nonhuman
    animal population 123–4; food 121–3; greenhouse
    gases 117; implications 117–24; Japan 126; in
    Kerala, India 129; population explosion, case 133–4;
    share of **118**; socioeconomic development 127–31;
    solutions 125–35; urban sprawl 117–21
The Population Bomb (1968) 116
population mobility 127
Porter, Michael 230
Porter Hypothesis 230
Portney, P. 245
positive freedom 228
postnormal science 235
potential emissions reduction (PER) 35
poverty 3
pragmatic environmentalism 304–5
pragmatic environmentalist 2
pragmatism 2
precautionary principle 246–8
precision agriculture 25
pro-environmental behavior 301–2
pronatal social norms 125
propane 193
public good 290–3
public health 59–61; and e-waste 62; and pollution
    141–5; and value judgments 61
public transit movement 159
public transportation systems 8
Putnam, Robert 147, 148

quality of life 68
Quan, L. 300

rainbow evolutions 177
Ravetz, J. 235
Reagan, Ronald 199
reasonably achievable emissions reduction (RAER) 35
rebound effect 209
recycling 10, 51–3; trends 53
recycling loophole 54
Reducing Emissions from Deforestation and Forest
    Degradation (REDD) 244
Rees, William 226
Regional Greenhouse Gas Initiative (RGGI) 40
regional per capita greenhouse gas emissions *21*
relative efficiency 210
relative efficiency *versus absolute* efficiency 230
renewable water resources (RWR) **91**
resource mobilization framework 304

return on investment 73
Reuveny, R. 300
"The Rights of Statistical People" 236
Rio Declaration, Principle 15, 247
rooftop revolution 4
Rosa, E. 118
Rubbish Theory 47
runoff *versus* soil infiltration **93**

sacrifice 11
salinization 103
Schelling, T. 245
Schnaiberg, Allan 215
Schor, Juliet 269, 271
Seed Savers Exchange (SSE) 86
Self-Employment Contributions Act 295
self-interested straw person 238–40
Self-Storage Association (SSA) 294
Sen, Amartya 115, 123, 234, 271, 273
sequestering CO_2 41
shale gas 194
Shopping Our Way to Safety (2007) 96
Silent Spring 1, 251
Simon, Julian 134
sinks 34
small-farm efficiency 179
small-particle air pollution 155
Smith, Adam 216
social action 5
social and biophysical indicators **254**
social behavior 204
social capital 147; "bonding" 147; "bridging" 147
social constructivism 4
social Darwinism 4–5
social disruption 171
social fabric 171
social justice 282
social movements 302–4
social norms 204
social relations 297
social sciences: contribution 4–7; and energy transitions 202; operational space for 5, 6; socioecological operational space for 7
social sustainability 81
social theories 6
socioecological benefits 83
socioeconomic development: in Kerala, India 129
socioeconomic well-being 171
sociological drivers 9
sociological imagination 5
sociological mechanisms, consumption 259–64
sociological momentum 7
sociological structures 8
sociology 4; of environmental issues 6
sociotechnical systems 260–1
Socolow, Robert 34
solar radiation management 38
solidarity purchasing groups 229
solid waste generation **47**

species problem 70
Spence, Michael 293
Spieler, C. 156
Spinardi, G. 78
stabilization triangle and wedges 33–4
Staggenborg, S. 287
Stern, Paul 202, 301
STIRPAT 118
street hierarchy 154–6
strip-mining 190
Stuart, Diana 6
Stuart, Tristram 58
Subramaniam, M. 100
surface water 103
sustainability 81
Sutherland, Rory 288
synthetic fertilizer 177
systems uncertainty 235
Szasz, Andrew 96

talus tunnels 145
technological bullet 177
technological innovation 24
technologically possible *versus sociologically probable* 4
technological momentum 7
temperature–mortality relationship 27
terminator technology 86
Texas Transportation Institute at Texas A&M University 141
theory of justice 273
therapeutic applications 68
Thompson, M. 47
Three Gorges Dam 188
three Rs (reduce, reuse, and recycle), environmentalism 53
tomato spotted wilt virus (TSWV) 79
total cost accounting 224–6
traditional, commuter, and automobile cities, diagrams *139*
Traditional Knowledge Data Libraries (TKDLs) 79
traditional risk assessments 246, 247
tragedy of commodity 73
"The Tragedy of the Commons" 240
Trains, Buses, People: An Opinionated Atlas of US Transit (Spieler) 156
trans-pacific transportation: of pollution 232–48
transportation 138–60; community 147–8; dense, livable, intermodal cities 149–54; disincentivizing, car 156–8; habitat and biodiversity 145–8; implications 141–8; mode of 138; pollution and public health 141–5; solutions 148–59; street hierarchy to interconnectivity 154–6
transportation model 8
transportation policy: value judgments in 153
transportation-related health outcomes cost: United States **142**
transport-related energy consumption *149*
trash can 44
treadmill, capital-intensive aquaculture 219

treadmill, production 9
treadmill of production 215
trickle-down economics 256
"trickle forward" reasoning 237
Trump 1, 238, 259
Tuck-Po, L. 286
Type I error 61
Type II errors 61

Uber 295, 296
The Ultimate Resource 134
unbundle parking 152
uncollected waste 60
UN Convention on the Elimination of All Forms of
    Discrimination Against Women of 1979 104
UN Convention on the Rights of the Child of 1989 104
uneconomic growth 251
UN Environment Programme Participation Act of 1973
    246
United Nations 29, 68, 73, 119, 121, 131; global
    population growth, median projection 116
United Nations Framework Convention on Climate
    Change 259
United Postal Service (UPS) 268
United States of America and the Klamath Indian Tribe v.
    Ben Adair (1983) 94
urban areas 20–4
urban density 134, *149*
urban density, contextualizing 133
urban development policies 152
urban farm cooperative 282
urban gardens 183–4
urban land cooperative 282
urban sprawl 117–21
US Bureau of Reclamation 99
USDA farm payments, asymmetries *166*
US Food Administration *58*

value judgments 13, 61; in transportation policy 153
Veblen, Thorstein 260
The Vertical Farm 135
vertical farming 135
Vickrey, William 157
virtual water 90, 100
virtual water content: global per unit average **93**
volatile organic compounds 121
vulnerable populations 195
vulnerable road users 145

walking facilities 152
Walk Score® 141
Wallich, Henry 270
Warr, Benjamin 266
waste 44–66; energy waste and life-cycle analysis 49–50;
    e-waste 61–2; extended producer responsibility
    (EPR) 64–6; food waste 53–9; implications 47–62;
    MSW management 63–4; and public health 59–61;
    recycling 51–3; solutions 63–6
waste regimes 56
water 77, 89–110; agriculture 99–103; bottled water
    95–6; climate change 103; demand 104; governance
    109–10; groundwater 103; human right at right
    value 104–8; hydrologic extremes 104; implications
    94–104; privatizing 96–8; quality 104; solutions
    104–10; surface water 103
water cycle 89
water footprint 89
water footprint (WF) composition **92**
water privatization 97; India and 100
water scarcity 89
water subsidies 99
weather-related hazards 24
Weight Watchers International (WTW) 267
welfare economics 233–6
welfare-economics approach 264
well-being indicators **129**
well-organized social movement 3
Western Christianity 9
White, Lynn Jr. 9
Whitehead, Alfred North 284
WHO 95
wildlife corridors 146
Wilson, Edward O. 69
work–spend cycle 269
World Bank 97, 98, 213, 234
World Health Organization (WHO) 68, 90, 145
world population estimates *131*
world-systems framework 222
worldview 284
worldview, privileging 9
Wynne, Brian 248

Yale Project 19
York, Richard 6, 211, 212, 218, 300

Zald, M. 304
Zuber, S. 245